Knowledge and Inquiry
Readings in Epistemology

Knowledge and Inquiry
Readings in Epistemology

edited by
K. Brad Wray

broadview press

NATIONAL LIBRARY OF CANADA CATALOGUING IN PUBLICATION DATA

Knowledge and inquiry: readings in epistemology / K. Brad Wray, editor.

Includes bibliographical references.
ISBN 1-55111-413-5

1. Knowledge, Theory of. I. Wray, K. Brad, 1963–

BD161.K56 2002   121   C2002-901659-2

BROADVIEW PRESS, LTD.
is an independent, international publishing house, incorporated in 1985.

North America	*United Kingdom and Europe*
Post Office Box 1243,	(Plymbridge North) Thomas Lyster, Ltd.
Peterborough, Ontario,	Units 3 & 4a, Ormskirk Industrial Park
Canada K9J 7H5	Old Boundary Way, Burscough Rd.
	Ormskirk, Lancashire L39 2YW
3576 California Road,	Tel: (01695) 575112
Orchard Park, New York	Fax: (01695) 570120
USA 14127	*books@tlyster.co.uk*
Tel: (705) 743-8990	Australia
Fax: (705) 743-8353	St. Clair Press
	P.O. Box 287, Rozelle, NSW 2039
customerservice@broadviewpress.com	Tel: (612) 818-1942
www.broadviewpress.com	Fax: (612) 418-1923

Broadview Press gratefully acknowledges the financial support of the Ministry of Canadian Heritage through the Book Publishing Industry Development Program.

Cover design by Alvin Choong.

Printed in Canada

for Lori

Table of Contents

Acknowledgements

I wish to acknowledge the generosity and cooperation of the following authors, publishers and copyright holders for making available the following pieces:

"The Myth of the Given" by Roderick Chisholm appeared in *The Foundations of Knowing*, p. 126–147, and 204–205, 1982 (Minneapolis: University of Minnesota Press, copyright by Prentice-Hall).

"The Coherence Theory of Empirical Knowledge" by Laurence BonJour appeared in *Philosophical Studies*, 29, p. 281–312, 1976 (copyright by Kluwer Academic Publishers, Dordrecht, Netherlands). Reprinted by permission of Kluwer Academic Publishers.

"The Foundationalism-Coherentism Controversy: Hardening Stereotypes and Overlapping Theories" by Robert Audi appeared in *The Structure of Justification*, 1993 edited by Robert Audi (copyright by Cambridge University Press, New York, NY). Reprinted by permission of Cambridge University Press.

"Can Empirical Knowledge Have a Foundation" by Laurence BonJour appeared in *American Philosophical Quarterly*, 15: 1, p. 1–13, 1978 (copyright by North American Philosophical Publications, Inc.). Reprinted by permission of North American Philosophical Publications, Inc.

"What is Justified Belief" by Alvin I. Goldman appeared in *Justification and Knowledge*, p. 1–23, 1979 edited by George S. Pappas (copyright by Kluwer Academic Publishers, Dordrecht, Netherlands). Reprinted by permission of Kluwer Academic Publishers.

"The Internalism/Externalism Controversy" by Richard Fumerton appeared in *Philosophical Perspectives, 2 Epistemology*, 1988 edited by Jame E. Tomberlin (copyright by Ridgeview Publishing Co., Atascadero, CA). Reprinted by permission of Ridgeview Publishing Company.

"Is Justified True Belief Knowledge?" by Edmund Gettier appeared in *Analysis*, 23: 6, p. 121–123, 1963 (copyright by Edmund Gettier). Reprinted by permission of Edmund Gettier.

"An Alleged Defect in Gettier Counter-examples" by Richard Feldman appeared in *Australasian Journal of Philosophy*, 52: 1, p. 68–69, 1974 (copyright by Oxford University Press, Oxford, UK). Reprinted by permission of Oxford University Press, and Richard Feldman.

"Why Solve the Gettier Problem?" by Earl Conee appeared in *Philosophical Analysis: A Defense by Example*, p. 55–58, 1988 edited by David A. Austin (copyright by Kluwer Academic Publishers, Dordrecht, Netherlands). Reprinted by permission of Kluwer Academic Publishers.

"Brains in Vats" by Hilary Putnam appeared as Chapter 1 of *Reason, Truth and History*, p. 1–21, 1981 by Hilary Putnam (copyright by Cambridge University Press). Reprinted with the permission of Cambridge University Press.

"Knowledge" by Thomas Nagel from *The View From Nowhere* by Thomas Nagel, copyright 1986 by Thomas Nagel. Used by permission of Oxford University Press, Inc.

"Skepticism and the Possibility of Knowledge" by Barry Stroud appeared in *The Journal of Philosophy*, LXXXI: 10, p. 545–551, 1984 (copyright by The Journal of Philosophy, Inc.). Reprinted by permission of The Journal of Philosophy Inc., and Barry Stroud.

"Epistemology Naturalized" by W.V. Quine from *Ontological Relativity and Other Essays* by W.V. Quine. Copyright 1969 Columbia University Press. Reprinted by permission of the publishers.

"On Naturalizing Epistemology" by Robert Almeder appeared in *American Philosophical Quarterly*, 27: 4, p. 263–279, 1990 (copyright by North American Philosophical Publications, Inc.). Reprinted by permission of North American Philosophical Publications, Inc.

"Why Reason Can't Be Naturalized" by Hilary Putnam appeared in *Realism and Reason: Philosophical Papers, Volume 3*, p. 229–247, 1983 by Hilary Putnam (copyright by Cambridge University Press). Reprinted with the permission of Cambridge University Press.

"Feminist Epistemology: An Interpretation and Defense" by Elizabeth Anderson appeared in *Hypatia*, 10: 3, p. 50–84, 1995 (copyright by Indiana University Press). Reprinted by permission of Indiana University Press.

"Rethinking Standpoint Epistemology: What is 'Strong Objectivity'?" by Sandra Harding appeared in *Feminist Epistemologies*, p. 49–82, 1993 edited by Linda Alcoff and Elizabeth Potter (copyright by Routledge. Inc.). Reprinted by permission of Routledge, Inc., and Sandra Harding.

I also wish to thank the students in my epistemology classes at both the University of Calgary and the University of British Columbia. This reader evolved from these courses. I thank Julia Gaunce, Kathryn Brownsey, Tammy Roberts, and Don LePan, at Broadview, for their help in seeing this book into print. I also thank the referees whose advice Broadview sought for their insightful feedback on my proposal. Further, I thank Andrew Irvine for encouragement and advice as I worked on the book. Finally, I thank my partner, Lori, for her continuous support and encouragement, and all the fun times we've had together. It is to her that this book is dedicated.

PREFACE

This anthology deals with four themes in the theory of knowledge: (1) epistemic justification; (2) the analysis of knowledge and Gettier problems; (3) scepticism; and (4) recent developments in epistemology. All the readings are unedited and contemporary, with Edmund Gettier's 1963 paper being the oldest, making the text a great way to introduce students to contemporary analytic philosophy.

The readings are divided into three sections. Each section includes a brief introduction to the readings, a series of study questions, and a list of suggested readings. These are designed to aid students in learning the material, and writing essays. The questions are intended to make salient to students the most pressing and contentious issues in contemporary debates. Section 1 deals with foundationalism, coherentism, and reliabilism, and includes articles by Roderick Chisholm, Laurence BonJour, Robert Audi, Alvin Goldman and Richard Fumerton. Because the debate between foundationalists and coherentists has played such a central role in contemporary epistemology, I have included quite lengthy articles on these topics by BonJour and Audi. Section 2 deals with two topics, the analysis of knowledge and Gettier problems, and a variety of forms of and responses to scepticism. Included are articles by Edmund Gettier, Earl Conee, Richard Feldman, Hilary Putnam, Thomas Nagel, and Barry Stroud. Section 3 introduces students to recent developments in naturalized, feminist and social epistemology. Included are articles by W.V. Quine, Robert Almeder, Hilary Putnam, Elizabeth Anderson, Sandra Harding, Helen Longino, John Hardwig, Richard Rorty, and Philip Kitcher.

It is this last longer section that distinguishes this text most from other epistemology texts, emphasizing current less traditional developments in epistemology. The readings in this final section are all concerned with the relationship between epistemology and science. Some address the issue of the relevance of scientific knowledge to epistemology, others address the issue of developing an epistemology of scientific knowledge. By focussing on science and scientific knowledge, the readings in this section provide students with an opportunity to reflect on and apply what they are learning in epistemology to what they are learning in their other classes, in particular, their classes in the natural and social sciences. In this way, the abstract problems addressed in traditional epistemology are rendered more concrete and pressing. The text is designed to help students develop an appreciation of the complexity of knowledge and inquiry.

SECTION I
EPISTEMIC JUSTIFICATION

SECTION 1: EPISTEMIC JUSTIFICATION

The readings in this first section deal with the issue of epistemic justification. Many philosophers believe that in order for one to know something, one must be justified in believing it. But, philosophers are divided on what is required in order to have a justified belief. The various readings present a number of competing theories of epistemic justification.

In the first reading, Roderick Chisholm presents a foundationalist theory of epistemic justification. He argues that all justified beliefs gain some degree of justification from beliefs that are "given." Such beliefs, unlike other beliefs, can only be justified by reiterating the belief. So, for example, the belief "I seem to see a car" is self-justifying, whereas the belief "I see a car" is not. If asked to justify the latter belief, one could cite the former. But, if asked to justify the former, one can only restate the belief.

In the second reading, Laurence BonJour presents an argument against foundationalist theories of justification. He argues that the sorts of beliefs that the foundationalist claims are justified independently of other beliefs, in fact, derive their warrant from other beliefs. In particular, the alleged foundational beliefs must have some quality that enables one to identify them as foundational. Moreover, your beliefs that (a) beliefs with this quality (whatever it is) are apt to be true, and (b) the particular belief in question has this quality, justify you in accepting a particular belief. Consequently, BonJour concludes, no belief is self-justifying, contrary to what the foundationalist claims.

In the third reading, BonJour develops and defends a coherence theory of justification. Unlike foundationalists, coherence theorists argue that no beliefs are self-justifying. Rather, according to the coherence theorist, beliefs are justified provided they cohere with your other beliefs. The fact that a particular belief coheres with the rest of your beliefs is thought to provide good grounds for believing that that belief is apt to be true. Significantly, the coherence theorist believes that the only thing that can provide justification for a belief is another belief.

In the fourth reading, Robert Audi develops and defends a foundationalist theory of epistemic justification, one that differs from Chisholm's version. Like Chisholm, Audi maintains that some beliefs are justified independently of other beliefs, and that all other beliefs, that is, non-foundational beliefs, ultimately trace their justification to these foundational beliefs. Further, Audi even grants that coherence plays some role in justification. But, he argues that coherence theorists have exaggerated the significance of the relationship between coherence and epistemic justification. Whereas coherence theorists maintain that coherence is sufficient for justification, Audi argues that justification is only negatively dependent on coherence. As he expresses the point, incoherence undermines justification, but coherence does not constitute justification. Audi believes that psychologically direct beliefs, beliefs we cannot resist accepting, are foundational. Such beliefs, though, need not be self-justifying. Hence, whereas Chisholm would claim that your belief that "that is a car" is not foundational, Audi would say it is foundational.

In the fifth reading, Alvin Goldman develops and defends a different sort of theory of justification, a reliabilist theory of justification. Reliabilists argue that beliefs are justified in virtue of the processes by which they are acquired or sustained. That is, if you were to acquire a particular belief through relying on the process of sight, and your visual perceptual processes generally yield true beliefs, then your belief is justified. Alternatively, if you were to acquire a belief through some process that frequently leads to false belief, then you would be unjustified, even if that particular belief happens to be true. Significantly, supporting reasons play a far less significant role in reliabilist theories than in the other types of theories.

In the sixth and final reading, Richard Fumerton presents an argument against externalist theories of justification, theories like Goldman's reliabilism. Fumerton believes that externalists have redefined key epistemic concepts, like "knowledge" and "justification," in such a way that the concepts are no longer of interest to philosophers. That is, the sorts of puzzles and problems that have traditionally engaged epistemologists are rendered uninteresting and obsolete by the way in which externalists understand these key epistemic concepts. Fumerton also argues that foundationalism is the correct theory of epistemic justification.

1.1

THE MYTH OF THE GIVEN: THEORY OF KNOWLEDGE IN AMERICA

Roderick Chisholm

1

The doctrine of "the given" involved two theses about our knowledge. We may introduce them by means of a traditional metaphor:

   (I)   The knowledge that a person has at any time is a structure or edifice, many parts and stages of which help to support each other, but which as a whole is supported by its own foundation.

The second thesis is a specification of the first:

   (II)   The foundation of one's knowledge consists (at least in part) of the apprehension of what have been called, variously, "sensations," "sense-impressions," "appearances," "sensa," "sense-qualia," and "phenomena."

These phenomenal entities, said to be at the base of the structure of knowledge, are what was called "the given." A third thesis is sometimes associated with the doctrine of the given, but the first two theses do not imply it. We may formulate it in terms of the same metaphor.

   (III)   The *only* apprehension that is thus basic to the structure of knowledge is our apprehension of "appearances" (etc.)—our apprehension of the given.

Theses (A) and (B) constitute the "doctrine of the given"; thesis (C), if a label were necessary, might be called "the phenomenalistic version" of the doctrine.

The first two theses are essential to the empirical tradition in Western philosophy. The third is problematic for traditional empiricism and depends in part, but only in part, on the way in which the metaphor of the edifice and its foundation is defined and elaborated.

I believe it is accurate to say that, at the time at which our study begins, most American epistemologists accepted the first two theses and thus accepted the doctrine of the given. The expression "the given" became a term of contemporary philosophical vocabulary partly because of its use by C.I. Lewis in his *Mind and the World-Order* (Scribner, 1929). Many of the philosophers who accepted the doctrine avoided the expression because of its association with other more controversial parts of Lewis's book—a book that might be taken (though mistakenly, I think) also to endorse thesis (C), the "phenomenalistic version" of the doctrine. The doctrine itself—theses (A) and (B)—became a matter of general controversy during the period of our survey.

Thesis (A) was criticized as being "absolute" and thesis (B) as being overly "subjective." Both criticisms may be found in some of the "instrumentalistic" writings of John Dewey and philosophers associated with him. They may also be found in the writings of those philosophers of science ("logical empiricists") writing in the tradition of the Vienna Circle. (At an early stage of this tradition, however, some of these same philosophers seem to have accepted all three theses.) Discussion became entangled in verbal confusions—especially in connection with the uses of such terms as "doubt," "certainty," "appearance," and "immediate experience." Philosophers, influenced by the work that Ludwig Wittgenstein had been doing in the 1930s, noted such confusions in detail, and some of them seem to have taken the existence of such confusions to indicate that (A) and (B) are false.[1] Many have rejected both theses as being inconsistent with a certain theory of thought and reference; among them, in addition to some of the critics just referred to, we find philosophers in the tradition of nineteenth century "idealism."

Philosophers of widely diverging schools now believe that "the myth of the given" has finally been dispelled.[2] I suggest, however, that, although thesis (C), "the phenomenalistic version," is false, the two theses, (A) and (B), that constitute the doctrine of the given are true.

The doctrine is not merely the consequence of a metaphor. We are led to it when we attempt to answer certain questions about *justification*—our justification for supposing, in connection with any one of the things that we know to be true, that it is something that we know to be true.

2

To the question "What justification do I have for thinking I know that *a* is true?" one may reply: "I know that *b* is true, and if I know that *b* is true then I also know that *a* is true." And to the question "What justification do I have for thinking I know that *b* is true?" one may reply: "I know that *c* is true, and if I know that *c* is true then I also know that *b* is true." Are we thus led, sooner or later, to something *n* of which one may say: "What justifies me in thinking I know that *n* is true is simply that *n* is true." If there is such an *n*, then the belief or statement that *n* is true may be thought of either as a belief or statement that "justifies itself" or as a belief or statement that is itself "neither justified nor unjustified." The distinction—unlike that between a Prime Mover that moves itself and a Prime Mover that is neither in motion nor at rest—is largely a verbal one; the essential thing, if there is such an *n*, is that it provides a stopping place in the process, or dialectic, of justification.

We may now reexpress, somewhat less metaphorically, the two theses I have called the "doctrine of the given." The first thesis, that our knowledge is an edifice or structure having its own foundation, becomes (A) "every statement, which we are justified in thinking that we know, is justified in part by some statement that justifies itself." The second thesis, that there are appearances ("the given") at the foundation of our knowledge, becomes (B) "there are statements about appearances that thus justify themselves." (The third thesis—the "phenomenalistic version" of the doctrine of the given—becomes (C) "there are no self-justifying statements that are not statements about appearances.")

Let us now turn to the first of the two theses constituting the doctrine of the given.

3

"Every justified statement is justified in part by some statement that justifies itself." Could it be that the question this thesis is supposed to answer is a question that arises only because of some mistaken assumption? If not, what are the alternative ways of answering it? And did any of the philosophers with whom we are concerned actually accept any of these alternatives? The first two questions are less difficult to answer than the third.

There are the following points of view to be considered, each of which *seems* to have been taken by some of the philosophers in the period of our survey.

1) One may believe that the questions about justification that give rise to our problem are based on false assumptions and hence that they *should not be asked* at all.

2) One may believe that no statement or claim is justified unless it is justified, at least in part, by some other justified statement or claim that it does not justify; this belief may suggest that one should continue the process of justifying *ad indefinitum*, justifying each claim by reference to some additional claim.

3) One may believe that no statement or claim *a* is justified unless it is justified by some other justified statement or claim *b*, and that *b* is not justified unless it in turn is justified by *a*; this would suggest that the process of justifying is, or should be, *circular*.

4) One may believe that at some particular claims *n* the process of justifying should stop, and one may then hold of any such claim *n* either: (a) *n* is justified by something—viz., *experience or observation*—that is not itself a claim and that therefore cannot be said itself either to be justified or unjustified; (b) *n* is itself *unjustified*; (c) *n justifies itself*; or (d) *n* is *neither justified nor unjustified*.

These possibilities, I think, exhaust the significant points of view; let us now consider them in turn.

4

"The questions about justification that give rise to the problem are based on false assumptions and therefore should not be asked at all."

The questions are *not* based on false assumptions; but most of the philosophers who discussed the questions put them in such a misleading way that one is very easily misled into supposing that they *are* based upon false assumptions.

Many philosophers, following Descartes, Russell, and Husserl, formulated the questions about justification by means of such terms as "doubt," "certainty," and "incorrigibility," and they used, or misused, these terms in such a way that, when their questions were taken in the way in which one would ordinarily take them, they could be shown to be based on false assumptions. One may note, for example, that the statement, "There is a clock on the mantelpiece" is not self-justifying—for to the question "what is your justification for thinking you know that there is a clock on the mantelpiece?" the proper reply would be to make some other statement (e.g., "I saw it there this morning and no one would have taken it away"—and one may then go on to ask "But are there any statements that can be said to justify themselves?" If we express these facts, as many philosophers did, by saying that the statement "There is a clock on the mantelpiece" is one that is not "certain," or one that may be "doubted," and if we then go on to ask "Does this doubtful statement rest on other statements that are certain and incorrigible?" then we are using terms in an extraordinarily misleading way. The question "Does this doubtful statement rest on statements that are certain and incorrigible?"—if taken as one would ordinarily take it—does rest on a false assumption, for (we may assume) the statement that a clock is on the mantelpiece is one that is not doubtful at all.

John Dewey, and some of the philosophers whose views were very similar to his, tended to suppose, mistakenly, that the philosophers who asked themselves "What justification do I have for thinking I know this?" were asking the quite different question "What more can I do to verify or confirm that this is so?" and they rejected answers to the first question on the ground that they were unsatisfactory answers to the second.[3] Philosophers influenced by Wittgenstein tended to suppose, also mistakenly, but quite understandably, that the question "What justification do I have for thinking I know this?" contains an implicit challenge and presupposes that one does not have the knowledge concerned. They then pointed out, correctly, that in most of the cases where the question was raised (e.g., "What justifies me in thinking I know that this is a table?") there is no ground for challenging the claim to knowledge and that questions presupposing that the claim is false should not arise. But the question "What justifies me in thinking I know that this is a table?" does not challenge the claim to know that this is a table, much less presuppose that the claim is false.

The "critique of cogency," as Lewis described this concern of epistemology, presupposes that we *are* justified in thinking we know most of the things that we do think we know, and what it seeks to elicit is the nature of this justification. The enterprise is like that of ethics, logic, and aesthetics:

> The nature of the good can be learned from experience only if the content of experience be first classified into good and bad, or grades of better and worse. Such classification or grading already involves the legislative application of the same principle which is sought. In logic, principles can be elicited by

generalization from examples only if cases of valid reasoning have first been segregated by some criterion. In esthetics, the laws of the beautiful may be derived from experience only if the criteria of beauty have first been correctly applied.[4]

When Aristotle considered an invalid mood of the syllogism and asked himself "What is wrong with this?" he was not suggesting to himself that perhaps nothing was wrong; he presupposed that the mood *was* invalid, just as he presupposed that others were not, and he attempted, successfully, to formulate criteria that would enable us to distinguish the two types of mood.

When we have answered the question, "What justification do I have for thinking I know this?" what we learn, as Socrates taught, is something about ourselves. We learn, of course, what the justification happens to be for the particular claim with which the question is concerned. But we also learn, more generally, what the criteria are, if any, in terms of which we believe ourselves justified in counting one thing as an instance of knowing and another thing not. The truth that the philosopher seeks, when he asks about justification, is "already implicit in the mind which seeks it, and needs only to be elicited and brought to clear expression."[5]

Let us turn, then to the other approaches to the problem of "the given."

5

"No statement or claim would be justified unless it were justified, at least in part, by some other justified claim or statement that it does not justify."

This regressive principle might be suggested by the figure of the building and its supports: no stage supports another unless it is itself supported by some other stage beneath it—a truth that holds not only of the upper portions of the building but also of what we call its foundation. And the principle follows if, as some of the philosophers in the tradition of logical empiricism seemed to believe, we should combine a frequency theory of probability with a probability theory of justification.

In *Experience and Prediction* (U. of Chicago, 1938) and in other writings, Hans Reichenbach defended a "probability theory of knowledge" that seemed to involve the following contentions:

1) To justify accepting a statement, it is necessary to show that the statement is probable.

2) To say of a statement that it is probable is to say something about statistical frequencies. Somewhat more accurately, a statement of the form "It

is *probable* that any particular *a* is *b*" may be explicated as saying "Most *a*s are *b*s." Or, still more accurately, to say "The probability is *n* that a particular *a* is a *b*" is to say "The limit of the relative frequency with the property of being a *b* occurs in the class of things having the property *a* is *n*."

3) Hence, by (2), to show that a proposition is probable it is necessary to show that a certain statistical frequency obtains; and, by (1), to show that a certain statistical frequency obtains it is necessary to show that it is probable that the statistical frequency obtains; and therefore, by (2), to show that it is probable that a certain statistical frequency obtains, it is necessary to show that a certain frequency of frequencies obtains....

4) And therefore "there is no Archimedean point of absolute certainty left to which to attach our knowledge of the world; all we have is an elastic net of probability connections floating in open space" (p. 192).

This reasoning suggests that an infinite number of steps must be taken to justify acceptance of any statement. For, according to the reasoning, we cannot determine the probability of one statement until we have determined that of a second, and we can not determine that of the second until we have determined that of a third, and so on. Reichenbach does not leave the matter here, however. He suggests that there is a way of "descending" from this "open space" of probability connections, but, if I am not mistaken, we can make the descent only by letting go of the concept of justification.

He says that, if we are to avoid the regress of probabilities of probabilities of probabilities..., we must be willing at some point merely to make a guess; "there will always be some blind posits on which the whole concatenation is based" (p. 367). The view that knowledge is to be identified with certainty and that probable knowledge must be "imbedded in a framework of certainty" is "a remnant of rationalism. An empiricist theory of probability can be constructed only if we are willing to regard knowledge as a system of posits."[6]

But if we begin by assuming, as we do, that there is a distinction between knowledge, on the one hand, and a lucky guess, on the other, then we must reject at least one of the premises of any argument purporting to demonstrate that knowledge is a system of "blind posits." The unacceptable conclusion of Reichenbach's argument may be so construed as to follow from premises (1) and (2); and premise (2) may be accepted as a kind of definition (though there are many who believe that this definition is not adequate to all of the uses of the term "probable" in science and everyday life.) Premise (1), therefore is the one we should reject, and there are good reasons, I think, for rejecting (1), the thesis that "to justify accepting a proposition it is necessary to show that the proposition is probable." In fairness to Reichenbach, it should be added that he never explicitly affirms premise (1); but some such premise is essential to his argument.

6

"No statement or claim *a* would be justified unless it were justified by some other justified statement or claim *b* that would not be justified unless it were justified in turn by *a*."

The "coherence theory of truth," to which some philosophers committed themselves, is something taken to imply that justification may thus be circular; I believe, however, that the theory does not have this implication. It does define "truth" as a kind of systematic consistency of beliefs or propositions. The truth of a proposition is said to consist, not in the fact that the proposition "corresponds" with something that is not itself a proposition, but in the fact that it fits consistently into a certain more general system of propositions. This view may even be suggested by the figure of the building and its foundations. There is no difference in principle between the way in which the upper stories are supported by the lower, and that in which the cellar is supported by the earth just below it, or the way in which the stratum of earth is supported by various substrata farther below; a good building appears to be a part of the terrain on which it stands and a good system of propositions is a part of the wider system that gives it its truth. But these metaphors do not solve philosophical problems.

The coherence theory did in fact appeal to something other than logical consistency; its proponents conceded that a system of false propositions may be internally consistent and hence that logical consistency alone is no guarantee of truth. Brand Blanshard, who defended the coherence theory in *The Nature of Thought,* said that a proposition is true provided it is a member of an internally consistent system of propositions and *provided further* this system is "the system in which everything real and possible is coherently included."[7] In one phase of the development of "logical empiricism" its proponents seem to have held a similar view: a proposition—or, in this case, a statement—is true provided it is a member of an internally consistent system of statements and *provided further* this system is "the system which is actually adopted by mankind, and especially by the scientists in our culture circle."[8]

A theory of truth is not, as such, a theory of justification. To say that a proposition is true is not to say that we are justified in accepting it as true, and to say that we are justified in accepting it as true is not to say that it is true. (I shall return to this point in the final section.) Whatever merits the coherence theory may have as an answer to certain questions about truth, it throws no light upon our present epistemological question. If we accept the coherence theory, we may still ask, concerning any proposition *a* that we think we know to be true, "What is my justification for thinking I know that *a* is a member of the system of propositions in which everything real and possible is coherently included, or that *a* is a member of the system of propositions that is actually adopted by mankind and by the scientists of our culture circle?" And when we ask such a question, we are confronted, once again, with our original alternatives.

7

If our questions about justification do have a proper stopping place, then, as I have said, there are still four significant possibilities to consider. We may stop with some particular claim and say of it that either:

a) It is justified by something—by experience, or by observation—that is not itself a claim and that, therefore, cannot be said either to be justified or to be unjustified;

b) It is justified by some claim that refers to our experience or observation, and the claim referring to our experience or observation has *no* justification;

c) It justifies itself; or

d) It is itself neither justified nor unjustified.

The first of these alternatives leads readily to the second, and the second to the third or to the fourth. The third and the fourth—which differ only verbally, I think—involve the doctrine of "the given."

Carnap wrote, in 1936, that the procedure of scientific testing involves two operations: the "confrontation of a statement with observation" and the "confrontation of a statement with previously accepted statements." He suggested that those logical empiricists who were attracted to the coherence theory of truth tended to lose sight of the first of these operations—the confrontation of a statement with observation. He proposed a way of formulating simple "acceptance rules" for such confrontation and he seemed to believe that, merely by applying such rules, we could avoid the epistemological questions with which the adherents of "the given" had become involved.

Carnap said this about his acceptance rules: "If no foreign language or introduction of new terms is involved, the rules are trivial. For example: 'If one is hungry, the statement "I am hungry" may be accepted'; or: 'If one sees a key one may accept the statement "there lies a key."'"[9] As we shall note later, the first of these rules differs in an important way from the second. Confining ourselves for the moment to rules of the second sort—"If one sees a key one may accept the statement 'there lies a key'"—let us ask ourselves whether the appeal to such rules enables us to solve our problem of the stopping place.

When we have made the statement "There lies a key," we can, of course, raise the question "What is my justification for thinking I know, or for believing, that there lies a key?" The answer would be "I see the key." We cannot ask "What is my justification for seeing a key?" But we *can* ask "What is my justification for thinking that it is a *key* that I see?" and, if we *do* see that the thing is a key, the question will have an answer. The answer might be "I see that it's shaped like a key and that it's in the lock, and I remember that a key is usually here." The possibility of this question, and its answer, indicates that we cannot stop our questions about justification merely by appealing to observation or experience. For, of the statement "I observe that that is an A," we can ask, and answer, the question "What is my justification for thinking that I observe that there is an A?"

It is relevant to note, moreover, that conditions may exist under which seeing a key does *not* justify one in accepting the statement "There is a key" or in believing that one sees a key. If the key were so disguised or concealed that the man who saw it did not recognize it to be a key, then he might not be justified in accepting the statement "There is a key." If Mr. Jones unknown to anyone but himself is a thief, then the people who see him may be said to see a thief—but none of those who thus sees a thief is justified in accepting the statement "There is a thief."[10]

Some of the writings of logical empiricists suggest that, although some statements may be justified by reference to other statements, those statements [which] involve "confrontation with observation" are not justified at all. C.G. Hempel, for example, wrote that "the acknowledgement of an experiential statement as true is psychologically motivated by certain experiences; but within the system of statements which express scientific knowledge or one's beliefs at a given time, they function in the manner of postulates for which no grounds are offered."[11] Hempel conceded, however, that this use of the term "postulate" is misleading and he added the following note of clarification: "When an experiential sentence is accepted 'on the basis of direct experiential evidence,' it is indeed not asserted arbitrarily; but to describe the evidence in question would simply mean to repeat the experiential statement itself. Hence, in the context of cognitive justification, the statement functions in the manner of a primitive sentence."[12]

When we reach a statement having the property just referred to—an experiential statement such that to describe its evidence "would simply mean to repeat the experiential statement itself"—we have reached a proper stopping place in the process of justification.

8

We are thus led to the concept of a belief, statement, claim, proposition, or hypothesis, that justifies itself. To be clear about the concept, let us note the way in which we would justify the statement that we have a certain belief. It is essential, of course, that we distinguish justifying the statement *that* we have a certain belief from justifying the belief itself.

Suppose, then, a man is led to say "I believe that Socrates is mortal" and we ask him "What is your justification for thinking that you believe, or for thinking that you know that you believe, that Socrates is mortal?" To this strange question, the only appropriate reply would be "My justification for thinking I believe, or for thinking that I know that I believe, that Socrates is mortal is simply that I *do* believe that Socrates is mortal." One justifies the statement simply by reiterating it; the statement's justification is what the statement says. Here, then, we have a case that satisfies Hempel's remark quoted above; we describe the evidence for a statement merely by repeating the statement. We could say, as C.J. Ducasse did, that "the occurrence of belief is its own evidence."[13]

Normally, as I have suggested, one cannot justify a statement merely by reiterating it. To the question "What justification do you have for thinking you know that there can be no life on the moon?" it would be inappropriate, and impertinent, to reply by saying simply "There *can* be no life on the moon," thus reiterating the fact at issue. An appropriate answer would be one referring to certain *other* facts—for example, that we know there is insufficient oxygen on the moon to support any kind of life. But to the question "What is your justification for thinking you know that you believe so and so?" there is nothing to say other than "I *do* believe so and so."

We may say, then, that some statements are self-justifying, or justify themselves. And we may say, analogously, that certain beliefs, claims, propositions, or hypotheses are self-justifying, or justify themselves. A statement, belief, claim, proposition, or hypothesis may be said to be self-justifying for a person, if the person's justification for thinking he knows it to be true is simply the fact that it *is* true.

Paradoxically, these things I have described by saying that they "justify themselves" may *also* be described by saying that they are "neither justified nor unjustified." The two modes of description are two different ways of saying the same thing.

If we are sensitive to ordinary usage, we may note that the expression "I believe that I believe" is ordinarily used, not to refer to a second-order belief about the speaker's own beliefs, but to indicate that the speaker has not yet made up his mind. "I *believe that I believe* that Johnson is a good president" might properly be taken to indicate that, if the speaker *does* believe that Johnson is a good president, he is not yet firm in that belief. Hence there is a temptation to infer that, if we say of a man who is firm in his belief that Socrates is mortal, that he is "justified in believing that he believes that Socrates is mortal," our statement "makes no sense." A temptation also arises to go on and say that it "makes no sense" even to say of such a man, that his *statement* "I believe that Socrates is mortal" is one which is "justified" for him.[14] After all, what would it mean to say of a man's statement about his own belief, that he is *not* justified in accepting it?[15]

The questions about what does or does not "make any sense" need not, however, be argued. We *may* say, if we prefer, that the statements about the beliefs in question are "neither justified nor unjustified." Whatever mode of description we use, the essential points are two. First, we may appeal to such statements in the process of justifying some *other* statement or belief. If they *have* no justification they may yet *be* a justification—for something other than themselves. ("What justifies me in thinking that he and I are not likely to agree? The fact that I believe that Socrates is mortal and he does not.") Second, the making of such a statement does provide what I have been called a "stopping place" in the dialectic of justification; but now, instead of signaling the stopping place by reiterating the questioned statement, we do it by saying that the question of its justification is one that "should not arise."

It does not matter, then, whether we speak of certain statements that "justify themselves" or of certain statements that are "neither justified nor unjustified," for in either case we will be referring to the same set of statements. I shall continue to use the former phrase.

There are, then, statements about one's own beliefs ("I believe that Socrates is mortal")—and statements about many other psychological attitudes—that are self-justifying. "What justifies me in believing, or in thinking I know, that I *hope* to come tomorrow? Simply that I *do* hope to come tomorrow." Thinking, desiring, wondering, loving, hating, and other such attitudes are similar. Some, but by no means all, of the statements we can make about such attitudes, when the attitudes are our own, are self-justifying—as are statements containing such phrases as "I think I remember" or "I seem to remember" (as distinguished from "I remember"), and "I think that I see" and "I think that I perceive" (as distinguished from "I see" and "I perceive"). Thus, of the two examples Carnap introduced in connection with his "acceptance rules" discussed above viz., "I am hungry" and "I see a key," we may say that the first is self-justifying and the second is not.

The "doctrine of the given," it will be recalled, tells us (A) that every justified statement, about what we think we know, is justified in part by some statement that justifies itself and (B) that there are statements about appearances that thus justify themselves. The "phenomenalistic version" of the theory adds (C) that statements about appearances are the *only* statements that justify themselves. What we have been saying is that the first thesis, (A), of the doctrine of the given is true and that the "phenomenalistic version," (C), is false; let us turn now to thesis (B).

9

In addition to the self-justifying statements about psychological attitudes, are there self-justifying statements about "appearances"? Now we encounter difficulties involving the word "appearance" and its cognates.

Sometimes such words as "appears," "looks," and "seems" are used to convey what one might also convey by such terms as "believe." For example, if I say "It appears to me that General de Gaulle was successful," or "General de Gaulle seems to have been successful," I am likely to mean only that I believe, or incline to believe, that he has been successful; the words "appears" and "seems" serve as useful hedges, giving me an out, should I find out later that de Gaulle was not successful. When "appear"-words are used in this way, the statements in which they occur add nothing significant to the class of "self-justifying" statements we have just provided. Philosophers have traditionally assumed, however, that such terms as "appear" may also be used in a quite different way. If this assumption is correct, as I believe it is, then this additional use does lead us to another type of self-justifying statement.

In the final chapter we shall have occasion to note some of the confusions to which the substantival expression "appearance" gave rise. The philosophers who exposed these confusions were sometimes inclined to forget, I think, that things do appear to us in various ways.[16] We can alter the appearance of anything we like merely by doing something that will affect our sense organs or the conditions of observation. One of the important epistemological questions about appearance is "Are there self-justifying statements about the ways in which things appear?"

Augustine, refuting the skeptics of the late Platonic Academy, wrote: "I do not see how the Academician can refute him who says: "I know that this appears white to me, I know that my hearing is delighted with this, I know this has an agreeable odor, I know this tastes sweet to me, I know that this feels cold to me." …When a person tastes something, he can honestly swear that he knows it is sweet to his palate or the contrary, and that no trickery of the Greeks can dispossess him of that knowledge."[17] Suppose, now, one were to ask "What justification do you have for believing, or thinking you know, that this appears white to you, or that that tastes bitter to you?" Here, too, we can only reiterate the statement: "What justifies me in believing, or in thinking I know, that this appears white to me and that that tastes bitter to me is that this *does* appear white to me and that *does* taste bitter."

An advantage of the misleading substantive "appearance," as distinguished from the verb "appears," is that the former may be applied to those sensuous experiences which, though capable of being appearances of things, are actually not appearances of anything. Feelings, imagery, and the sensuous content of dreams and hallucination are very much like the appearances of things and they are such that, under some circumstances, they could be appearances of things. But if we do not wish to say that they are experiences wherein some external physical things *appears* to us, we must use some expression other than "appear." For "appear," in its active voice, requires a grammatical subject and thus requires a term that refers, not merely to a way of appearing, but also to *something that appears*.

But we may avoid *both* the objective "*Something* appears blue to me," and the substantival "I sense a blue *appearance*." We may use another verb, say "sense," in a technical way, as many philosophers did, and equate it in meaning with the passive voice of "appear," thus saying simply "I *sense* blue," or the like. Or better still, it seems to me, and at the expense only of a little awkwardness, we can use "appear" in its passive voice and say "I am *appeared to* blue."

Summing up, in our new vocabulary, we may say that the philosophers who talked of the "empirically given" were referring, not to "self-justifying" statements and beliefs generally, but only to those pertaining to certain "ways of being appeared to." And the philosophers who objected to the doctrine of the given, or some of them, argued that no statement about "a way of being appeared to" can be "self-justifying."

10

Why would one suppose that "This appears white" (or, more exactly, "I am now appeared white to") is not self-justifying? The most convincing argument was this: If I say "This appears white," then, as Reichenbach put it, I am making a "comparison between a present object and a formerly seen object."[18] What I am saying *could* have been expressed by "The present way of appearing is the way in which white objects, or objects that I believe to be white, ordinarily appear." And this new statement, clearly, is not self-justifying; to justify it, as Reichenbach intimated, I must go on and say something further—something about the way in which I remember white objects to have appeared.

"Appears white" *may* thus be used to abbreviate "appears the way in which white things normally appear." Or "white thing," on the other hand, *may* be used to abbreviate "thing having the color of things that ordinarily appear white." The phrase "appear white" as it is used in the second quoted expression cannot be spelled out in the manner of the first; for the point of the second can hardly be put by saying that "white thing" may be used to abbreviate "thing having the color of things that ordinarily appear the way in which *white things* normally appear." In the second expression, the point of "appears white" is not to *compare* a way of appearing with something else; the point is to say something about the way of appearing itself. It is in terms of this second sense of "appears white"— that in which one may say significantly and without redundancy "Things that are white may normally be expected to appear white"—that we are to interpret the quotation from Augustine above. And, more generally, when it was said that "appear"-statements constitute the foundation of the edifice of knowledge, it was not intended that the "appear"-statements be interpreted as statements asserting a comparison between a present object and any other object or set of objects.

The question now becomes "Can we formulate any significant 'appear'-statements *without* thus comparing the way in which some object appears with the way in which some other object appears, or with the way in which the object in question has appeared at some other time? Can we interpret 'This appears white' in such a way that it may be understood to refer to a present way of appearing *without* relating that way of appearing to any other object?" In *Experience and Prediction,* Reichenbach defended his own view (and that of a good many others) in this way:

> The objection may be raised that a comparison with formerly seen physical objects should be avoided, and that a basic statement is to concern the present fact only, as it is. But such a reduction would make the basic statement empty. Its content is just that there is a similarity between the present object and one formerly seen; it is by means of this relation that the present object is described. Otherwise the basic statement would consist in attaching an individual symbol, say a number, to the present object; but the introduction of such a symbol would help us in no way, since we could not make use of it to construct a comparison with other things. Only in attaching the same symbols to different objects, do we arrive at the possibility of constructing relations between the objects [pp. 176–77].

It is true that, if an "appear"-statement is to be used successfully in communication, it must assert some comparison of objects. Clearly, if I wish *you* to know the way things are now appearing to me, I must relate these ways of appearing to something that is familiar to you. But our present question is not "Can you understand me if I predicate something of the way in which something now appears to me without relating that way of appearing to something that is familiar to you?" The question is, more simply, "Can I predicate anything of the way in which something now appears to me without thereby comparing that way of appearing with something else?" From the fact that the first of these two questions must be answered in the negative it does not follow that the second must also be answered in the negative.[19]

The issue is not one about communication, nor is it, strictly speaking, an issue about language; it concerns, rather, the nature of thought itself. Common to both "pragmatism" and "idealism," as traditions in American philosophy, is the view that to *think* about a thing, or to *interpret* or *conceptualize* it, and hence to have a *belief* about it, is essentially to relate the thing to *other* things, actual or possible, and therefore to "refer beyond it." It is this view—and not any view about language or communication—that we must oppose if we are to say of some statements about appearing, or of any other statements, that they "justify themselves."

To think about the way in which something is now appearing, according to the view in question, is to relate that way of appearing to something else, possibly to certain future experiences, possibly to the way in which things of a certain sort may be commonly expected to appear. According to the "conceptualistic pragmatism" of C.I. Lewis's *Mind and the World-Order* (1929), we grasp the present experience, any present way of appearing, only to the extent to which we relate it to some future experience.[20] According to one interpretation of John Dewey's "instrumentalistic" version of pragmatism, the present experience may be used to present or disclose something else but it does not present or disclose itself. And according to the idealistic view defended in Brand Blanshard's *The Nature of Thought,* we grasp our present experience only to the extent that we are able to include it in the one "intelligible system of universals" (vol. 1, p. 632).

This theory of reference, it should be noted, applies not only to statements and beliefs about "ways of being appeared to" but also to those other statements and beliefs I have called "self-justifying." If "This appears white," or "I am appeared white to," compares the present experience with something else, and thus depends for its justification on what we are justified in believing about the something else, then so, too, does "I believe that Socrates is mortal" and "I hope that the peace will continue." This general conception of thought, therefore, would seem to imply that no belief or statement can be said to justify itself. But according to what we have been saying, if there is no belief or statement that justifies itself, then it is problematic whether any belief or statement is justified at all. And therefore, as we might expect, this conception of thought and reference has been associated with skepticism.

Blanshard conceded that his theory of thought "does involve a degree of scepticism regarding our present knowledge and probably all future knowledge. In all likelihood there will never be a proposition of which we can say, "This that I am asserting, with precisely the meaning I now attach to it, is absolutely true."[21] On Dewey's theory, or on one common interpretation of Dewey's theory, it is problematic whether anyone can now be said to *know* that Mr. Jones is working in his garden. A.O. Lovejoy is reported to have said that, for Dewey, "I am about to have known" is as close as we ever get to "I know."[22] C.I. Lewis, in his *An Analysis of Knowledge and Valuation* (Open Court, 1946) conceded in effect that the conception of thought suggested by his earlier *Mind and the World-Order* does lead to a kind of skepticism;

according to the later work there *are* "apprehensions of the given" (cf. pp. 182–83)—and thus beliefs that justify themselves.

What is the plausibility of a theory of thought and reference that seems to imply that no one knows anything?

Perhaps it is correct to say that when we think about a thing we think about it as having certain properties. But why should one go on to say that to think about a thing must always involve thinking about some *other* thing as well? Does thinking about the other thing then involve thinking about some third thing? Or can we think about one thing in relation to a second thing without thereby thinking of a third thing? And if we can, then why can we not think of one thing—of one thing as having certain properties—without thereby relating it to another thing?

The linguistic analogue of this view of thought is similar. Why should one suppose—as Reichenbach supposed in the passage cited above and as many others have also supposed—that to *refer* to a thing, in this instance to refer to a way of appearing, is necessarily to relate the thing to some *other* thing?

Some philosophers seem to have been led to such a view of reference as a result of such considerations as the following: We have imagined a man saying, in agreement with Augustine, "It just does appear white—and that is the end of the matter." Let us consider now the possible reply that "It is not the end of the matter. You are making certain assumptions about the language you are using; you are assuming, for example, that you are using the word 'white' or the phrase 'appears white,' in a way in which you have formerly used it, or in the way in which it is ordinarily used, or in the way in which it would ordinarily be understood. And if you state your justification for this assumption, you *will* refer to certain other things—to yourself and to other people, to the word 'white,' or to the phrase 'appears white,' and to what the word or phrase has referred to or might refer to on other occasions. And therefore, when you say 'This appears white' you are saying something, not only about your present experience, but also about all of these other things as well."

The conclusion of this argument—the part that follows the "therefore"—does not follow from the premises. In supposing that the argument is valid, one fails to distinguish between (1) *what* it is that a man means to say when he uses certain words and (2) his assumptions concerning the adequacy of these words for *expressing* what it is that he means to say; one supposes, mistakenly, that what justifies (2) must be included in what justifies (1). A Frenchwoman not yet sure of her English, may utter the words "There are apples in the basket," intending thereby to express her belief that there are potatoes in the basket. If we show her that she has used the word "apples" incorrectly, and hence that she is mistaken in her assumption about the ways in which English speaking people use and understand the word "apples," we have not shown her anything relevant to her *belief* that there are apples in the basket.

Logicians now take care to distinguish between the *use* and *mention* of language (e.g., the English word "Socrates" is mentioned in the sentence "'Socrates' has eight letters" and is used but not mentioned in "Socrates is a Greek.")[23] As we shall have occasion to note further in the next chapter, the distinction has not always been observed in writings on epistemology.

11

If we decide, then, that there is a class of beliefs or statements that are "self-justifying," and that this class is limited to certain beliefs or statement about our own psychological states and about the ways in which we are "appeared to," we may be tempted to return to the figure of the edifice: our knowledge of the world is a structure supported entirely by a foundation of such self-justifying statements or beliefs. We should recall, however, that the answers to our original Socratic questions had *two* parts. When asked "What is your justification for thinking that you know *a*?" one may reply "I am justified in thinking I know *a*, because (1) I know *b* and (2) if I know *b* then I know *a*." We considered our justification for the *first* part of this answer, saying "I am justified in thinking I know *b*, because (1) I know *c* and (2) if I know *c* then I know *b*." And then we considered our justification for the first part of the second answer, and continued in this fashion until we reach the point of self-justification. In thus moving toward "the given," we accumulated, step by step, a backlog of claims that we did not attempt to justify—those claims constituting the *second* part of each of our answers. Hence our original claim—"I know that *a* is true"—does not rest on "the given" alone; it also rests upon all of those other claims that we made en route. And it is not justified unless these other claims are justified.

A consideration of these other claims will lead us, I think, to at least three additional types of "stopping place," which we are concerned, respectively, with memory, perception, and what Kant called the a priori. I shall comment briefly on the first two here.

It is difficult to think of any claim to empirical knowledge, other than the self-justifying statements we have just considered, that does not to some extent rest on an appeal to memory. But the appeal to memory—"I remember that A occurred"—is not self-justifying. One may ask "And what is your justification for thinking that you remember that A occurred?" and the question will have an answer—even if the answer is only the self-justifying "I think that I remember that A occurred." The statement "I remember that A occurred" does, of course, imply "A occurred"; but "I think that I remember that A occurred" does not imply "A occurred" and hence does not imply "I remember that A occurred." For we can remember occasions—at least we think we can remember them—when we learned, concerning some event we had thought we remembered, that the event had not occurred at all, and consequently that we had not really remembered it. When we thus find that one memory conflicts with another, or, more accurately, when we thus find that one thing that we think we remember conflicts with another thing that we think we remember, we may correct one or the other by making further inquiry; but the results of any such inquiry will always be justified in part by other memories, or by other things that we think that we remember. How then are we to choose between what seem to be conflicting memories? Under what conditions does "I think that I remember that A occurred" serve to justify "I remember that A occurred"?

The problem is one of formulating a rule of evidence—a rule specifying the conditions under which statements about what we think we remember can justify statements about what we do remember. A possible solution, in very general terms, is "When we think that we remember, then we are justified in believing that we do remember, provided that what we think we remember does not conflict with anything else that we think we remember; when what we think we remember does conflict with something else we think we remember, then, of the two conflicting memories (more accurately, ostensible memories) the one that is justified is the one that fits in better with the other things that we think we remember." Ledger Wood made the latter point by saying that the justified memory is the one that "coheres with the system of related memories"; C.I. Lewis used "congruence" instead of "coherence." [24] But we cannot say precisely what is meant by "fitting in," "coherence," or "congruence" until certain controversial questions of confirmation theory and the logic of probability have been answered. And it may be that the rule of evidence is too liberal; perhaps we should say, for example, that when two ostensible memories conflict neither one of them is justified. But these are questions that have not yet been satisfactorily answered.

If we substitute "perceive" for "remember" in the foregoing, we can formulate a similar set of problems about perception; these problems, too, must await solution.[25]

The problems involved in formulating such rules of evidence, and in determining the validity of these rules, do not differ in any significant way from those that arise in connection with the formulation, and validity, of the rules of logic. Nor do they differ from the problems posed by moral and religious "cognitivists" (the "nonintuitionistic cognitivists").... The status of ostensible memories and perceptions, with respect to that experience which is their "source," is essentially like that which such "cognitivists" claim for judgments having an ethical or theological subject matter. Unfortunately, it is also like that which other "enthusiasts" claim for still other types of subject matter.

12

What, then, is the status of the doctrine of "the given"—of the "myth of the given"? In my opinion, the doctrine is correct in saying that there are some beliefs or statements that are "self-justifying" and that among such beliefs and statements are some that concern appearances or "ways of being appeared to"; but the "phenomenalistic version" of the doctrine is mistaken in implying that our knowledge may be thought of as an edifice that is supported by appearances alone.[26] The cognitive significance of "the empirically given" was correctly described—in a vocabulary rather different from that which I have been using—by John Dewey:

> The alleged primacy of sensory meanings is mythical. They are primary only in logical status; they are primary as tests and confirmation of inferences concerning matters of fact, not as historic originals. For, while it is not usually needful to carry the check or test of theoretical calculations to the point of irreducible sensa, colors, sounds, etc., these sensa form a limit approached in careful analytic certifications, and upon critical occasions it is necessary to touch the limit....Sensa are the class of irreducible meanings which are employed in verifying and correcting other meanings. We actually set out with much coarser and more inclusive meanings and not till we have met with failure from their use do we ever set out to discover those ultimate and harder meanings which are sensory in character.[27]

The Socratic questions leading to the concept of "the given" also lead to the concept of "rules of evidence." Unfortunately some of the philosophers who stressed the importance of the former concept tended to overlook that of the latter.

NOTES

[1]   Philosophers in other traditions also noted these confusions. See, for example, John Wild, "The Concept of the Given in Contemporary Philosophy," *Philosophy and Phenomenological Research,* 1 (1940), 70–82.

[2]   The expression "myth of the given" was used by Wilfrid Sellars in "Empiricism and the Philosophy of Mind," in Herbert Feigl and Michael Scriven, eds., *Foundations of Science and the Concepts of Psychology and Psychoanalysis,* Minnesota Studies in the Philosophy of Science, vol. 1 (U. of Minn., 1956), pp. 253–329.

[3]   Dewey also said that, instead of trying to provide "Foundations for Knowledge," the philosopher should apply "what is known to intelligent conduct of the affairs of human life" to "the problems of men." John Dewey, *Problems of Men* (Philosophical, 1946), pp. 6–7.

[4]   C.I. Lewis, *Mind and the World-Order* (Scribner, 1929), p. 29.

[5]   *Ibid.,* p. 19. Cf. Hans Reichenbach, *Experience and Prediction* (U. of Chicago, 1938), p. 6; C.J. Ducasse, "Some Observations Concerning the Nature of Probability, *Journal of Philosophy,* 38 (1941), esp. 400–401.

[6]   Hans Reichenbach, "Are Phenomenal Reports Absolutely Certain?" *Philosophical Review,* (1952), 147–59; the quotation is from p. 150.

[7]   Brand Blanshard, *The Nature of Thought,* vol. 2 (Macmillan, 1940), p. 276.

[8]   C.G. Hempel, "On the Logical Positivists' Theory of Truth," *Analysis,* 2 (1935), 49–59; the quotation is from p. 57.

[9]   Rudolf Carnap, "Truth and Confirmation," in Herbert Feigl and W.S. Sellars, eds., *Readings in Philosophical Analysis* (Appleton, 1949), p. 123. The portions of the article quoted above first appeared in "Wahrheit und Bewährung," *Actes du congrès internationale de philosophie scientifique,* 4 (Paris; 1936), 18–23.

[10]   Cf. Nelson Goodman, *The Structure of Appearance* (Harvard, 1951), p. 104. If Goodman's book, incidentally, is not discussed in his collection of essays, the fault is with our conventional classification of philosophical disciplines. The book, which is concerned with an area falling between logic and metaphysics, is one of the most important philosophical works written by an American during the period being surveyed.

[11]   C.G. Hempel, "Some Theses on Empirical Certainty," *Review of Metaphysics,* (1952), 621–29; the quotation is from p. 621.

[12]   *Ibid.*, p. 628. Hempel's remarks were made in an "Exploration" in which he set forth several theses about "empirical certainty" and then replied to objections by Paul Weiss, Roderick Firth, Wilfrid Sellars, and myself.

[13]   C.J. Ducasse, "Propositions, Truth, and the Ultimate Criterion of Truth, "*Philosophy and Phenomenological Research*, 4 (1939), 317–40; the quotation is from p. 339.

[14]   Cf. Normal Malcolm, "Knowing of Other Minds," *Journal of Philosophy*, 55 (1958), 969–78. Reprinted in Malcolm, *Knowledge and Certainty: Essays and Lectures* (Prentice-Hall, 1963).

[15]   The principle behind this way of looking at the matter is defended in detail by Max Black in *Language and Philosophy*, p. 116 ff.

[16]   One of the best criticisms of the "appearance" (or "sense-datum") terminology was O.K. Bouwsma's "Moore's Theory of Sense-Data," in *The Philosophy of G.E. Moore*, pp. 201–221. In *Perceiving: A Philosophical Study* (Cornell, 1957), I tried to call attention to certain facts about appearing which, I believe, Bouwsma may have overlooked.

[17]   Augustine, *Contra academicos*, xi, 26; translated by Sister Mary Patricia Garvey as *Saint Augustine Against the Academicians* (Marquette, 1942); the quotations are from pp. 68–69.

[18]   *Experience and Prediction*, p. 176.

[19]   It may follow, however, that "the vaunted incorrigibility of the sense-datum language can be achieved only at the cost of its perfect utility as a means of communication" (Max Black, *Problems of Analysis* p. 66), and doubtless, as Black added, it would be "misleading to say the least" to speak of a "language that cannot be communicated"—cf. Wilfrid Sellers, "Empiricism and the Philosophy of Mind"—but these points do affect the epistemological question at issue.

[20]   This doctrine was modified in Lewis's later *An Analysis of Knowledge and Valuation* (Open Court, 1946) in a way that enabled him to preserve the theory of the given.

[21]   *The Nature of Thought*, vol. 2, pp. 269–70. Blanshard added, however, that "for all the ordinary purposes of life" we *can* justify some beliefs by showing that they cohere "with the system of present knowledge"; and therefore, he said, his theory should not be described as being "simply sceptical" (vol. 2, p. 271). Cf. W.H. Werkmeister, *The Basis and Structure of Knowledge* (Harper, 1946), part II.

[22]   Quoted by A.E. Murphy in "Dewey's Epistemology and Metaphysics," in P.A. Schlipp, ed., *The Philosophy of John Dewey* (Northwestern, 1939), p. 203. Dewey's theory of inquiry, however, was not intended to be an epistemology and he did not directly address himself to the questions with which we are here concerned.

[23]   Cf. W.V. Quine, *Mathematical Logic* (Norton, 1940; rev. ed., Harvard, 1951), sec. 4.

[24]   Ledger Wood, *The Analysis of Knowledge* (Princeton, 1941), p. 81; C.I. Lewis, *An Analysis of Knowledge and Valuation*, p. 334.

[25]   Important steps toward solving them were taken by Nelson Goodman in "Sense and Certainty," *Philosophical Review*, 61 (1952), 160–67, and by Israel Scheffler in "On Justification and Commitment," *Journal of Philosophy*, 51 (1954), 180–90. The former paper is reprinted in Roland Houde and J.P. Mullally, eds., *Philosophy of Knowledge*, (Lippincott, 1960), pp.

97–103.

[26]   Alternatives to the general metaphor of the edifice are proposed by W.V. Quine in the introduction to *Methods of Logic* (Holt, 1950; rev. ed., 1959), in *From a Logical Point of View* (Harvard, 1953), and in *Word and Object* (Wiley, 1960).

[27]   John Dewey, *Experience and Nature*, 2nd ed. (Norton, 1929), p. 327.

1.2

CAN EMPIRICAL KNOWLEDGE HAVE A FOUNDATION?

Laurence BonJour

The idea that empirical knowledge has, and must have, a *foundation* has been a common tenet of most major epistemologists, both past and present. There have been, as we shall see further below, many importantly different variants of this idea. But the common denominator among them, the central thesis of epistemological foundationism as I shall understand it here, is the claim that certain empirical beliefs possess a degree of epistemic justification or warrant which does not depend, inferentially or otherwise, on the justification of other empirical beliefs, but is instead somehow immediate or intrinsic. It is these non-inferentially justified beliefs, the unmoved (or self-moved) movers of the epistemic realm as Chisholm has called them,[1] that constitute the foundation upon which the rest of empirical knowledge is alleged to rest.

In recent years, the most familiar foundationist views have been subjected to severe and continuous attack. But this attack has rarely been aimed directly at the central foundationist thesis itself, and new versions of foundationism have been quick to emerge, often propounded by the erstwhile critics themselves. Thus foundationism has become a philosophical hydra, difficult to come to grips with and seemingly impossible to kill. The purposes of this paper are, first, to distinguish and clarify the main dialectical variants of foundationism, by viewing them as responses to one fundamental problem which is both the main motivation and the primary obstacle for foundationism; and second, as a result of this discussion to offer schematic reasons for doubting whether any version of foundationism is finally acceptable.

The main reason for the impressive durability of foundationism is not any overwhelming plausibility attaching to the main foundationist thesis in itself, but rather the existence of one apparently decisive argument which seems to rule out all non-skeptical alternatives to foundationism, thereby showing that *some* version of foundationism must be true (on the assumption that skepticism is false). In a recent statement by Quinton, this argument runs as follows:

> If any beliefs are to be justified at all,…there must be some terminal beliefs that do not owe their…credibility to others. For a belief to be justified it is not enough for it to be accepted, let alone merely entertained: there must also be good reason for accepting it. Furthermore, for an inferential belief to be justified the beliefs that support it must be justified themselves. There must, therefore, be a kind of belief that does not owe its justification to the support provided by others. Unless this were so no belief would be justified at all, for to justify any belief would require the antecedent justification of an infinite series of beliefs. The terminal…beliefs that are needed to bring the regress of justification to a stop need not be strictly self-evident in the sense that they somehow justify themselves. All that is required is that they should not owe their justification to any other beliefs.[2]

I shall call this argument the *epistemic regress argument,* and the problem which generates it, *the epistemic regress problem.* Since it is this argument which provides the primary rationale and argumentative support for foundationism, a careful examination of it will also constitute an exploration of the foundationist position itself. The main dialectical variants of foundationism can best be understood as differing attempts to solve the regress problem, and the most basic objection to the foundationist approach is that it is doubtful that any of these attempts can succeed. (In this paper, I shall be concerned with the epistemic regress argument and the epistemic regress problem only as they apply to empirical knowledge. It is obvious that an analogous problem arises also for *a priori* knowledge, but there it seems likely that the argument would take a different course. In particular, a foundationist approach might be inescapable in an account of *a priori* knowledge.)

I

The epistemic regress problem arises directly out of the traditional conception of knowledge as *adequately justified true belief*[3]—whether this be taken as a fully adequate definition of knowledge or, in light of the apparent counter-examples discovered by Gettier,[4] as merely a necessary but not sufficient condition. (I shall assume throughout that the elements of the traditional conception are at least necessary for knowledge.) Now the most natural way to justify a belief is by producing a justificatory argument: belief *A* is justified by citing some other (perhaps conjunctive) belief *B*, from which *A* is inferable in some acceptable way and which is thus offered as a reason for accepting *A*.[5] Call this *inferential justification*. It is clear, as Quinton points out in the passage quoted above, that for *A* to be genuinely justified by virtue of such a justificatory argument, *B* must itself be justified in some fashion; merely being inferable from an unsupported guess or hunch, e.g., would confer no genuine justification upon *A*.

Two further points about inferential justification, as understood here, must be briefly noted. First, the belief in question need not have been *arrived at* as the result of an inference in order to be inferentially justified. This is obvious, since a belief arrived at in some other way (e.g., as a result of wishful thinking) may later come to be maintained solely because it is now seen to be inferentially justifiable. Second, less obviously, a person for whom a belief is inferentially justified need not have explicitly rehearsed the justificatory argument in question to others or even to himself. It is enough that the inference be available to him if the belief is called into question by others or by himself (where such availability may itself be less than fully explicit) and that the availability of the inference be, in the final analysis, his reason for holding the belief.[6] It seems clear that many beliefs which are quite sufficiently justified to satisfy the justification criterion for knowledge depend for their justification on inferences which have not been explicitly formulated and indeed which could not be explicitly formulated without considerable reflective effort (e.g., my current belief that this is the same piece of paper upon which I was typing yesterday).[7]

Suppose then that belief *A* is (putatively) justified via inference, thus raising the question of how the justifying premise-belief *B* is justified. Here again the answer may be in inferential terms: *B* may be (putatively) justified in virtue of being inferable from some further belief *C*. But then the same question arises about the justification of *C*, and so on, threatening an infinite and apparently vicious regress of epistemic justification. Each belief is justified only if an epistemically prior belief is justified, and that epistemically prior belief is justified only if a still prior belief is justified, etc., with the apparent result that justification can never get started—and hence that there is no justification and no knowledge. The foundationist claim is that only through the adoption of some version of foundationism can this skeptical consequence be avoided.

Prima facie, there seem to be only four basic possibilities with regard to the eventual outcome of this potential regress of epistemic justification: (i) the regress might terminate with beliefs for which no justification of any kind is available, even though they were earlier offered as justifying premises; (ii) the regress might proceed infinitely backwards with ever more new premise beliefs being introduced and then themselves requiring justification; (iii) the regress might circle back upon itself, so that at some point beliefs which appeared earlier in the sequence of justifying arguments are appealed to again as premises; (iv) the regress might terminate because beliefs are reached which are justified—unlike those in alternative (i)—but whose justification does not depend inferentially on other empirical beliefs and thus does not raise any further issue of justification with respect to such beliefs.[8] The foundationist opts for the last alternative. His argument is that the other three lead inexorably to the skeptical result, and that the second and third have additional fatal defects as well, so that some version of the fourth, foundationist alternative must be correct (assuming that skepticism is false).

With respect to alternative (i), it seems apparent that the foundationist is correct. If this alternative were correct, empirical knowledge would rest ultimately on beliefs which were, from an epistemic standpoint at least, entirely arbitrary and hence incapable of conferring any genuine justification. What about the other two alternatives?

The argument that alternative (ii) leads to a skeptical outcome has in effect already been sketched in the original formulation of the problem. One who opted for this alternative could hope to avoid skepticism only by claiming that the regress, though infinite, is not vicious; but there seems to be no plausible way to defend such a claim. Moreover, a defense of an infinite regress view as an account of how empirical knowledge is actually justified—as opposed to how it might in principle be justified—would have to involve the seemingly dubious thesis that an ordinary knower holds a literally infinite number of distinct beliefs. Thus it is not surprising that no important philosopher, with the rather uncertain exception of Peirce,[9] seems to have advocated such a position.

Alternative (iii), the view that justification ultimately moves in a closed curve, has been historically more prominent, albeit often only as a dialectical foil for foundationism. At first glance, this alternative might seem even less attractive than the second. Although the problem of the knower having to have an infinite number of beliefs is no longer present, the regress itself, still infinite, now seems undeniably vicious. For the justification of each of the beliefs which figure in the circle seems now to presuppose *its own* epistemically prior justification: such a belief must, paradoxically, be justified before it can be justified. Advocates of views resembling alternative (iii) have generally tended to respond to this sort of objection by adopting a holistic conception of justification in which the justification of individual beliefs is subordinated to that of the closed systems of beliefs which such a view implies; the property of such systems usually appealed to as a basis for justification is internal *coherence*. Such coherence theories attempt to evade the regress problem by abandoning the view of justification as essentially involving a linear order of dependence (though a non-linear view of justification has never been worked out in detail).[10] Moreover, such a coherence theory of empirical knowledge is subject to a number of other familiar and seemingly decisive objections.[11] Thus alternative (iii) seems unacceptable, leaving only alternative (iv), the foundationist alternative, as apparently viable.

As thus formulated, the epistemic regress argument makes an undeniably persuasive case for foundationism. Like any argument by elimination, however, it cannot be conclusive until the surviving alternative has itself been carefully examined. The foundationist position may turn out to be subject to equally serious objections, thus forcing a re-examination of the other alternatives, a search for a further non-skeptical alternative, or conceivably the reluctant acceptance of the skeptical conclusion.[12] In particular, it is not clear on the basis of the argument thus far whether and how foundationism can itself solve the regress problem; and thus the possibility exists that the epistemic regress argument will prove to be a two-edged sword, as lethal to the foundationist as it is to his opponents.

II

The most straightforward interpretation of alternative (iv) leads directly to a view which I will here call *strong foundationism*. According to strong foundationism, the foundational beliefs which terminate the regress of justification possess sufficient epistemic warrant, independently of any appeal to inference from (or coherence with) other empirical beliefs, to satisfy the justification condition of knowledge and qualify as acceptable justifying premises for further beliefs. Since the justification of these *basic beliefs*, as they have come to be called, is thus allegedly not dependent on that of any other empirical belief, they are uniquely able to provide secure starting-points for the justification of empirical knowledge and stopping-points for the regress of justification.

The position just outlined is in fact a fairly modest version of strong foundationism. Strong foundationists have typically made considerably stronger claims on behalf of basic beliefs. Basic beliefs have been claimed not only to have sufficient non-inferential justification to qualify as knowledge, but also to be *certain, infallible, indubitable,* or *incorrigible* (terms which are usually not very carefully distinguished).[13] And most of the major attacks on foundationism have focused on these stronger claims. Thus it is important to point out that nothing about the basic strong foundationist response to the regress problem demands that basic beliefs be more than adequately justified. There might of course be other reasons for requiring that basic beliefs have some more exalted epistemic status or for thinking that in fact they do. There might even be some sort of indirect argument to show that such a status is a consequence of the sorts of epistemic properties which are directly required to solve the regress problem. But until such an argument is given (and it is doubtful that it can be), the question of whether basic beliefs are or can be certain, infallible, etc., will remain a relatively unimportant side-issue.

Indeed, many recent foundationists have felt that even the relatively modest version of strong foundationism outlined above is still too strong. Their alternative, still within the general aegis of the foundationist position, is a view which may be called *weak foundationism.* Weak foundationism accepts the central idea of foundationism—viz. that certain empirical beliefs possess a degree of independent epistemic justification or warrant which does not derive from inference or coherence relations. But the weak foundationist holds that these foundational beliefs have only a quite low degree of warrant, much lower than that attributed to them by even modest strong foundationism and insufficient by itself to satisfy the justification condition for knowledge or to qualify them as acceptable justifying premises for other beliefs. Thus this independent warrant must somehow be augmented if knowledge is to be achieved, and the usual appeal here is to coherence with other such minimally warranted beliefs. By combining such beliefs into larger and larger coherent systems, it is held, their initial, minimal degree of warrant can gradually be enhanced until knowledge is finally achieved. Thus weak foundationism, like the pure coherence theories mentioned above, abandons the linear conception of justification.[14]

Weak foundationism thus represents a kind of hybrid between strong foundationism and the coherence views discussed earlier, and it is often thought to embody the virtues of both and the vices of neither. Whether or not this is so in other respects, however, relative to the regress problem weak foundationism is finally open to the very same basic objection as strong foundationism, with essentially the same options available for meeting it. As we shall see, the key problem for any version of foundationism is whether it can itself solve the regress problem which motivates its very existence, without resorting to essentially *ad hoc* stipulation. The distinction between the two main ways of meeting this challenge both cuts across and is more basic than that between strong and weak foundationism. This being so, it will suffice to concentrate here on strong foundationism, leaving the application of the discussion to weak foundationism largely implicit.

The fundamental concept of strong foundationism is obviously the concept of a basic belief. It is by appeal to this concept that the threat of an infinite regress is to be avoided and empirical knowledge given a secure foundation. But how can there be any empirical beliefs which are thus basic? In fact, though this has not always been noticed, the very idea of an epistemically basic empirical belief is extremely paradoxical. For on what basis is such a belief to be justified, once appeal to further empirical beliefs is ruled out? Chisholm's theological analogy, cited earlier, is most appropriate: a basic belief is in effect an epistemological unmoved (or self-moved) mover. It is able to confer justification on other beliefs, but apparently has no need to have justification conferred on it. But is such a status any easier to understand in epistemology than it is in theology? How can a belief impart epistemic "motion" to other beliefs unless it is itself in "motion"? And, even more paradoxically, how can a belief epistemically "move" itself?

This intuitive difficulty with the concept of a basic empirical belief may be elaborated and clarified by reflecting a bit on the concept of epistemic justification. The idea of justification is a generic one, admitting in principle of many specific varieties. Thus the acceptance of an empirical belief might be morally justified, i.e. justified as morally obligatory by reference to moral principles and standards; or pragmatically justified, i.e. justified by reference to the desirable practical consequences which will result from such acceptance; or religiously justified, i.e. justified by reference to specified religious texts or theological dogmas; etc. But none of these other varieties of justification can satisfy the justification condition for knowledge. Knowledge requires *epistemic* justification, and the distinguishing characteristic of this particular species of justification is, I submit, its essential or internal relationship to the cognitive goal of truth. Cognitive doings are epistemically justified, on this conception, only if and to the extent that they are aimed at this goal—which means roughly that one accepts all and only beliefs which one has good reason to think are true.[15] To accept a belief in the absence of such a reason, however appealing or even mandatory such acceptance might be from other standpoints, is to neglect the pursuit of truth; such acceptance is, one might say, *epistemically irresponsible*. My contention is that the idea of being epistemically responsible is the core of the concept of epistemic justification.[16]

A corollary of this conception of epistemic justification is that a satisfactory defense of a particular standard of epistemic justification must consist in showing it to be truth-conducive, i.e. in showing that accepting beliefs in accordance with its dictates is likely to lead to truth (and more likely than any proposed alternative). Without such a meta-justification, a proposed standard of epistemic justification lacks any underlying rationale. Why after all should an epistemically responsible inquirer prefer justified beliefs to unjustified ones, if not that the former are more likely to be true? To insist that a certain belief is epistemically justified, while confessing in the same breath that this fact about it provides no good reason to think that it is true, would be to render nugatory the whole concept of epistemic justification.

These general remarks about epistemic justification apply in full measure to any strong foundationist position and to its constituent account of basic beliefs. If basic beliefs are to provide a secure foundation for empirical knowledge, if inference from them is to be the sole basis for the justification of other empirical beliefs, then that feature, whatever it may be, in virtue of which a belief qualifies as basic must also constitute a good reason for thinking that the belief is true. If we let "ϕ" represent this feature, then for a belief B to qualify as basic in an acceptable foundationist account, the premises of the following justificatory argument must themselves be at least justified:[17]

(i)   Belief B has feature ϕ.
(ii)   Beliefs having feature ϕ are highly likely to be true.

Therefore, B is highly likely to be true.

Notice further that while either premise taken separately might turn out to be justifiable on an *a priori* basis (depending on the particular choice of ϕ), it seems clear that they could not both be thus justifiable. For B is *ex hypothesi* an empirical belief, and it is hard to see how a particular empirical belief could be justified on a purely *a priori* basis.[18] And if we now assume, reasonably enough, that for B to be justified for a particular person (at a particular time) it is necessary, not merely that a justification for B exist in the abstract, but that the person in question be in cognitive possession of that justification, we get the result that B is not basic after all since its justification depends on that of at least one other empirical belief. If this is correct, strong foundationism is untenable as a solution to the regress problem (and an analogous argument will show weak foundationism to be similarly untenable).

The foregoing argument is, no doubt, exceedingly obvious. But how is the strong foundationist to answer it? *Prima facie*, there seem to be only two general sorts of answer which are even remotely plausible, so long as the strong foundationist remains within the confines of the traditional conception of knowledge, avoids tacitly embracing skepticism, and does not attempt the heroic task of arguing that an empirical belief could be justified on a purely *a priori* basis. First, he might argue that although it is indeed necessary for a belief to be justified and *a fortiori* for it to be basic that a justifying argument of the sort schematized above be in principle available in the situation, it is *not* always necessary that the person for whom the belief is basic (or anyone else) know or even justifiably believe that it is available; instead, in the case of basic beliefs at least, it is sufficient that the premises for an argument of that general sort (or for some favored particular variety of such argument) merely be *true*, whether or not that person (or anyone else) justifiably believes that they are true. Second, he might grant that it is necessary both that such justification exist and that the person for whom the belief is basic be in cognitive possession of it, but insist that his cognitive grasp of the premises required for that justification does not involve further empirical beliefs which would then require justification, but instead involves cognitive states of a more rudimentary sort which do not themselves require justification: *intuitions* or *immediate apprehensions*. I will consider each of these alternatives in turn.

III

The philosopher who has come the closest to an explicit advocacy of the view that basic beliefs may be justified even though the person for whom they are basic is not in any way in cognitive possession of the appropriate justifying argument is D. M. Armstrong. In his recent book, *Belief, Truth and Knowledge*,[19] Armstrong presents a version of the epistemic regress problem (though one couched in terms of knowledge rather than justification) and defends what he calls an "Externalist" solution:

> According to "Externalist" accounts of non-inferential knowledge, what makes a true non-inferential belief a case of *knowledge* is some natural relation which

holds between the belief-state...and the situation which makes the belief true. It is a matter of a certain relation holding between the believer and the world. [157].

Armstrong's own candidate for this "natural relation" is "that there must be a *law-like connection* between the state of affairs *Bap* [i.e. *a*'s believing that *p*] and the state of affairs that makes "*p*" true such that, given *Bap*, it must be the case that *p*." [166] A similar view seems to be implicit in Dretske's account of perceptual knowledge in *Seeing and Knowing*, with the variation that Dretske requires for knowledge not only that the relation in question obtain, but also that the putative knower *believe* that it obtains—though *not* that this belief be justified.[20] In addition, it seems likely that various views of an ordinary-language stripe which appeal to facts about how language is learned either to justify basic belief or to support the claim that no justification is required would, if pushed, turn out to be positions of this general sort. Here I shall mainly confine myself to Armstrong, who is the only one of these philosophers who is explicitly concerned with the regress problem.

There is, however, some uncertainty as to how views of this sort in general and Armstrong's view in particular are properly to be interpreted. On the one hand, Armstrong might be taken as offering an account of how basic beliefs (and perhaps others as well) satisfy the adequate-justification condition for knowledge; while on the other hand, he might be taken as simply repudiating the traditional conception of knowledge and the associated concept of epistemic justification, and offering a surrogate conception in its place—one which better accords with the "naturalistic" world-view which Armstrong prefers.[21] But it is only when understood in the former way that externalism (to adopt Armstrong's useful term) is of any immediate interest here, since it is only on that interpretation that it constitutes a version of foundationism and offers a direct response to the anti-foundationist argument set out above. Thus I shall mainly focus on this interpretation of externalism, remarking only briefly at the end of the present section on the alternative one.

Understood in this way, the externalist solution to the regress problem is quite simple: the person who has a basic belief need not be in possession of any justified reason for his belief and indeed, except in Dretske's version, need not even think that there is such a reason; the status of his belief as constituting knowledge (if true) depends solely on the external relation and not at all on his subjective view of the situation. Thus there are no further empirical beliefs in need of justification and no regress.

Now it is clear that such an externalist position succeeds in avoiding the regress problem and the anti-foundationist argument. What may well be doubted, however, is whether this avoidance deserves to be considered a *solution*, rather than an essentially *ad hoc* evasion, of the problem. Plainly the sort of "external" relation which Armstrong has in mind would, if known, provide a basis for a justifying argument along the lines sketched earlier, roughly as follows:

(i)   Belief *B* is an instance of kind *K*.

(ii)   Beliefs of kind *K* are connected in a law-like way with the sorts of states of affairs which would make them true, and therefore are highly likely to be true.

Therefore, *B* is highly likely to be true.

But precisely what generates the regress problem in the first place is the requirement that for a belief *B* to be epistemically justified for a given person *P*, it is necessary, not just that there be justifiable or even true premises available in the situation which could in principle provide a basis for a justification of *B*, but that *P* himself know or at least justifiably believe some such set of premises and thus be in a position to employ the corresponding argument. The externalist position seems to amount merely to waiving this general requirement in cases where the justification takes a certain form, and the question is why this should be acceptable in these cases when it is not acceptable generally: (If it were acceptable generally, then it would seem that any true belief would be justified for any person, and the distinction between knowledge and true belief would collapse.) Such a move seems rather analogous to solving a regress of causes by simply stipulating that although most events must have a cause, events of a certain kind need not.

Whatever plausibility attaches to externalism seems to derive from the fact that if the external relation in question genuinely obtains, then *P* will not go wrong in accepting the belief, and it is, in a sense, not an accident that this is so. But it remains unclear how these facts are supposed to justify *P*'s acceptance of *B*. It is clear, of course, that an external observer who knew both that *P* accepted *B* and that there was a law-like connection between such acceptance and the truth of *B* would be in a position to construct an argument to justify *his own* acceptance of *B*. *P* could thus serve as a useful epistemic instrument, a kind of cognitive thermometer, for such an external observer (and in fact the example of a thermometer is exactly the analogy which Armstrong employs to illustrate the relationship which is supposed to obtain between the person who has the belief and the external state of affairs [166ff.]). But *P* himself has no reason at all for thinking that *B* is likely to be true. From his perspective, it *is* an accident that the belief is true.[22] And thus his acceptance of *B* is no more rational or responsible from an epistemic standpoint than would be the acceptance of a subjectively similar belief for which the external relation in question failed to obtain.[23]

Nor does it seem to help matters to move from Armstrong's version of externalism, which requires only that the requisite relationship between the believer and the world obtain, to the superficially less radical version apparently held by Dretske, which requires that *P* also believe that the external relation obtains, but does not require that this latter belief be justified. This view may seem slightly less implausible, since it at least requires that the person have some idea, albeit unjustified, of why *B* is likely to be true. But this change is not enough to save externalism. One way to see this is to suppose that the person believes the requisite relation to obtain on some totally irrational and irrelevant basis, e.g. as a result of reading tea leaves or studying astrological charts. If *B* were an ordinary, non-basic belief, such a situation would surely preclude it being justified, and it is hard to see why the result should be any different for an allegedly basic belief.

Thus it finally seems possible to make sense of externalism only by construing the externalist as simply abandoning the traditional notion of epistemic justification and along with it anything resembling the traditional conception of knowledge. (As already remarked, this may be precisely what the proponents of externalism intend to be doing, though most of them are not very clear on this point.) Thus consider Armstrong's final summation of his conception of knowledge:

> *Knowledge of the truth of particular matters of fact* is a belief which must be true, where the "must" is a matter of law-like necessity. Such knowledge is a reliable representation or "mapping" of reality. [220]

Nothing is said here of reasons or justification or evidence or having the right to be sure. Indeed the whole idea, central to the western epistemological tradition, of knowledge as essentially the product of reflective, critical, and rational inquiry has seemingly vanished without a trace. It is possible of course that such an altered conception of knowledge may be inescapable or even in some way desirable, but it constitutes a solution to the regress problem or any problem arising out of the traditional conception of knowledge only in the radical and relatively uninteresting sense that to reject that conception is also to reject the problems arising out of it. In this paper, I shall confine myself to less radical solutions.

IV

The externalist solution just discussed represents a very recent approach to the justification of basic beliefs. The second view to be considered is, in contrast, so venerable that it deserves to be called the standard foundationist solution to the problem in question. I refer of course to the traditional doctrine of cognitive givenness, which has played a central role in epistemological discussions at least since Descartes. In recent years, however, the concept of the given, like foundationism itself, has come under serious attack. One upshot of the resulting discussion has been a realization that there are many different notions of givenness, related to each other in complicated ways, which almost certainly do not stand or fall together. Thus it will be well to begin by formulating the precise notion of givenness which is relevant in the present context and distinguishing it from some related conceptions.

In the context of the epistemic regress problem, givenness amounts to the idea that basic beliefs are justified by reference, not to further *beliefs*, but rather to states of affairs in the world which are "immediately apprehended" or "directly presented" or "intuited." This justification by reference to non-cognitive states of affairs thus allegedly avoids the need for any further justification and thereby stops the regress. In a way, the basic gambit of givenism (as I shall call positions of this sort) thus resembles that of the externalist positions considered above. In both cases the justificatory appeal to further beliefs which generates the regress problem is avoided for basic beliefs by an appeal directly to the non-cognitive world; the crucial difference is that for the givenist, unlike the externalist, the justifying state of affairs in the world is allegedly apprehended *in some way* by the believer.

The givenist position to be considered here is significantly weaker than more familiar versions of the doctrine of givenness in at least two different respects. In the first place, the present version does not claim that the given (or, better, the apprehension thereof) is certain or even incorrigible. As discussed above, these stronger claims are inessential to the strong foundationist solution to the regress problem. If they have any importance at all in this context it is only because, as we shall see, they might be thought to be entailed by the only very obvious intuitive picture of how the view is supposed to work. In the second place, givenism as understood here does not involve the usual stipulation that only one's private mental and sensory states can be given. There may or may not be other reasons for thinking that this is in fact the case, but such a restriction is not part of the position itself. Thus both positions like that of C. I. Lewis, for whom the given is restricted to private states apprehended with certainty, and positions like that of Quinton, for whom ordinary physical states of affairs are given with no claim of certainty or incorrigibility being involved, will count as versions of givenism.

As already noted, the idea of givenness has been roundly criticized in recent philosophical discussion and widely dismissed as a piece of philosophical mythology. But much at least of this criticism has to do with the claim of certainty on behalf of the given or with the restriction to private, subjective states. And some of it at least has been mainly concerned with issues in the philosophy of mind which are only distantly related to our present epistemological concerns. Thus even if the objections offered are cogent against other and stronger versions of givenness, it remains unclear whether and how they apply to the more modest version at issue here. The possibility suggests itself that modest givenness may not be a myth, even if more ambitious varieties are, a result which would give the epistemological foundationist all he really needs, even though he has usually, in a spirit of philosophical greed, sought considerably more. In what follows, however, I shall sketch a line of argument which, if correct, will show that even modest givenism is an untenable position.[24]

The argument to be developed depends on a problem within the givenist position which is surprisingly easy to overlook. I shall therefore proceed in the following way. I shall first state the problem in an initial way, then illustrate it by showing how it arises in one recent version of givenism, and finally consider whether any plausible solution is possible. (It will be useful for the purposes of this discussion to make two simplifying assumptions, without which the argument would be more complicated, but not essentially altered. First, I shall assume that the basic belief which is to justified by reference to the given or immediately apprehended state of affairs is just the belief that this same state of affairs obtains. Second, I shall assume that the given or immediately apprehended state of affairs is not itself a belief or other cognitive state.)

Consider then an allegedly basic belief that-p which is supposed to be justified by reference to a given or immediately apprehended state of affairs that-*p*. Clearly what justifies the belief is not the state of affairs simpliciter, for to say that would be to return to a form of externalism. For the givenist, what justifies the belief is the *immediate apprehension* or *intuition* of the state of affairs. Thus we seem to have three items present in the situation: the belief, the state of affairs which is the object of the belief, and the intuition or immediate apprehension of that state of affairs. The problem to be raised revolves around the nature of the last of these items, the intuition or immediate apprehension (hereafter I will use mainly the former term). It *seems* to be a cognitive state, perhaps somehow of a more rudimentary sort than a belief, which involves the thesis or assertion that-*p*. Now if this is correct, it is easy enough to understand in a rough sort of way how an intuition can serve to justify a belief with this same assertive content. The problem is to understand why the intuition, involving as it does the cognitive thesis that-*p*, does not *itself* require justification. And if the answer is offered that the intuition is justified by reference to the state of affairs that-*p*, then the question will be why this would not require a second intuition or other apprehension of the state of affairs to justify the original one. For otherwise one and the same cognitive state must somehow constitute both an apprehension of the state of affairs and a justification of that very apprehension, thus pulling itself up by its own cognitive bootstraps. One is reminded here of Chisholm's claim that certain cognitive states justify themselves,[25] but that extremely paradoxical remark hardly constitutes an explanation of how this is possible.

If, on the other hand, an intuition is not a cognitive state and thus involves no cognitive grasp of the state of affairs in question, then the need for a justification for the intuition is obviated, but at the serious cost of making it difficult to see how the intuition is supposed to justify the belief. If the person in question has no cognitive grasp of that state of affairs (or of any other) by virtue of having such an intuition, then how does the intuition give him a *reason* for thinking that his belief is true or likely to be true? We seem again to be back to an externalist position, which it was the whole point of the category of intuition or givenness to avoid.

As an illustration of this problem, consider Quinton's version of givenism, as outlined in his book *The Nature of Things*.[26] As noted above, basic beliefs may, according to Quinton, concern ordinary perceptible states of affairs and need not be certain or incorrigible. (Quinton uses the phrase "intuitive belief" as I have been using "basic belief" and calls the linguistic expression of an intuitive belief a "basic statement"; he also seems to pay very little attention to the difference between beliefs and statements, shifting freely back and forth between them, and I will generally follow him in this.) Thus "this book is red" might, in an appropriate context, be a basic statement expressing a basic or intuitive belief. But how are such basic statements (or the correlative beliefs) supposed to be justified? Here Quinton's account, beyond the insistence that they are not justified by reference to further beliefs, is seriously unclear. He says rather vaguely that the person is "aware" [129] or "directly aware" [139] of the appropriate state of affairs, or that he has "direct knowledge" [126] of it, but he gives no real account of the nature or epistemological status of this state of "direct awareness" or "direct knowledge," though it seems clear that it is supposed to be a cognitive state of some kind. (In particular, it is not clear what "direct" means, over and above "non-inferential.")[27]

The difficulty with Quinton's account comes out most clearly in his discussion of its relation to the correspondence theory of truth:

> The theory of basic statements is closely connected with the correspondence theory of truth. In its classical form that theory holds that to each true statement, whatever its form may be, a fact of the same form corresponds. The theory of basic statements indicates the point at which correspondence is established, at which the system of beliefs makes its justifying contact with the world. [139].

And further on he remarks that the truth of basic statements "is directly determined by their correspondence with fact" [143]. (It is clear that "determined" here means "epistemically determined.") Now it is a familiar but still forceful idealist objection to the correspondence theory of truth that if the theory were correct we could never know whether any of our beliefs were true, since we have no perspective outside our system of beliefs from which to see that they do or do not correspond. Quinton, however, seems to suppose rather blithely that intuition or direct awareness provides just such a perspective, from which we can in some cases apprehend both beliefs and world and judge whether or not they correspond. And he further supposes that the issue of justification somehow does not arise for apprehensions made from this perspective, though without giving any account of how or why this is so.

My suggestion here is that no such account can be given. As indicated above, the givenist is caught in a fundamental dilemma: if his intuitions or immediate apprehensions are construed as cognitive, then they will be both capable of giving justification and in need of it themselves; if they are non-cognitive, then they do not need justification but are also apparently incapable of providing it. This, at bottom, is why epistemological givenness is a myth.[28]

Once the problem is clearly realized, the only possible solution seems to be to split the difference by claiming that an intuition is a semi-cognitive or quasi-cognitive state,[29] which resembles a belief in its capacity to confer justification, while differing from a belief in not requiring justification itself. In fact, some such conception seems to be implicit in most if not all givenist positions. But when stated thus baldly, this "solution" to the problem seems hopelessly contrived and *ad hoc*. If such a move is acceptable, one is inclined to expostulate, then once again any sort of regress could be solved in similar fashion. Simply postulate a final term in the regress which is sufficiently similar to the previous terms to satisfy, with respect to the penultimate term, the sort of need or impetus which originally generated the regress; but which is different enough from previous terms so as not itself to require satisfaction by a further term. Thus we would have semi-events, which could cause but need not be caused; semi-explanatia, which could explain but need not be explained; and semi-beliefs, which could justify but need not be justified. The point is not that such a move is always incorrect (though I suspect that it is), but simply that the nature and possibility of such a convenient regress-stopper needs at the very least to be clearly and convincingly established and explained before it can constitute a satisfactory solution to any regress problem.

The main account which has usually been offered by givenists of such semi-cognitive states is well suggested by the terms in which immediate or intuitive apprehensions are described: "immediate," "direct," "presentation," etc. The underlying idea here is that of *confrontation*: in intuition, mind or consciousness is directly confronted with its object, without the intervention of any sort of intermediary. It is in this sense that the object is *given* to the mind. The root metaphor underlying this whole picture is vision: mind or consciousness is likened to an immaterial eye, and the object of intuitive awareness is that which is directly before the mental eye and open to its gaze. If this metaphor were to be taken seriously, it would become relatively simple to explain how there can be a cognitive state which can justify but does not require justification. (If the metaphor is to be taken seriously enough to do the foundationist any real good, it becomes plausible to hold that the intuitive cognitive states which result would after all have to be infallible. For if all need for justification is to be precluded, the envisaged relation of confrontation seemingly must be conceived as too intimate to allow any possibility of error. To the extent that this is so, the various arguments which have been offered against the notion of infallible cognitive states count also against this version of givenism.)

Unfortunately, however, it seems clear that the mental eye metaphor will not stand serious scrutiny. The mind, whatever else it may be, is not an eye or, so far as we know, anything like an eye. Ultimately the metaphor is just far too simple to be even minimally adequate to the complexity of mental phenomena and to the variety of conditions upon which such phenomena depend. This is not to deny that there is considerable intuitive appeal to the confrontational model, especially as applied to perceptual consciousness, but only to insist that this appeal is far too vague in its import to adequately support the very specific sorts of epistemological results which the strong foundationist needs. In particular, even if empirical knowledge at some point involves some sort of confrontation or seeming confrontation, this by itself provides no clear reason for attributing epistemic justification or reliability, let alone certainty, to the cognitive states, whatever they may be called, which result.

Moreover, quite apart from the vicissitudes of the mental eye metaphor, there are powerful independent reasons for thinking that the attempt to defend givenism by appeal to the idea of a semi-cognitive or quasi-cognitive state is fundamentally misguided. The basic idea, after all, is to distinguish two aspects of a cognitive state, its capacity to justify other states and its own need for justification, and then try to find a state which possesses only the former aspect and not the latter. But it seems clear on reflection that these two aspects cannot be separated, that it is one and the same feature of a cognitive state, viz. its assertive content, which both enables it to confer justification on other states and also requires that it be justified itself. If this is right, then it does no good to introduce semi-cognitive states in an attempt to justify basic beliefs, since to whatever extent such a state is capable of conferring justification, it will to that very same extent require justification. Thus even if such states do exist, they are of no help to the givenist in attempting to answer the objection at issue here.[30]

Hence the givenist response to the anti-foundationist argument seems to fail. There seems to be no way to explain how a basic cognitive state, whether called a belief or an intuition, can be directly justified by the world without lapsing back into externalism—and from there into skepticism. I shall conclude with three further comments aimed at warding off certain likely sorts of misunderstanding. First. It is natural in this connection to attempt to justify basic beliefs by appealing to *experience*. But there is a familiar ambiguity in the term "experience," which in fact glosses over the crucial distinction upon which the foregoing argument rests. Thus "experience" may mean either an *experiencing* (i.e., a cognitive state) or something *experienced* (i.e., an object of cognition). And once this ambiguity is resolved, the concept of experience seems to be of no particular help to the givenist. Second. I have concentrated, for the sake of simplicity, on Quinton's version of givenism in which ordinary physical states of affairs are among the things which are given. But the logic of the argument would be essentially the same if it were applied to a more traditional version like Lewis's in which it is private experiences which are given, and I cannot see that the end result would be different—though it might be harder to discern, especially in cases where the allegedly basic belief is a belief about another cognitive state. Third. Notice carefully that the problem raised here with respect to givenism is a logical problem (in a broad sense of "logical"). Thus it would be a mistake to think that it can be solved simply by indicating some sort of state which seems intuitively to have the appropriate sorts of characteristics; the problem is to understand how it is *possible* for any state to have those characteristics. (The mistake would be analogous to one occasionally made in connection with the free-will problem: the mistake of attempting to solve the logical problem of how an action can be not determined but also not merely random by indicating a subjective act of effort or similar state, which seems intuitively to satisfy such a description.)

Thus foundationism appears to be doomed by its own internal momentum. No account seems to be available of how an empirical belief can be genuinely justified in an epistemic sense, while avoiding all reference to further empirical beliefs or cognitions which themselves would require justification. How then is the epistemic regress problem to be solved? The natural direction to look for an answer is to the coherence theory of empirical knowledge and the associated non-linear conception of justification which were briefly mentioned above.[31] But arguments by elimination are dangerous at best: there may be further alternatives which have not yet been formulated; and the possibility still threatens that the epistemic regress problem may in the end be of aid and comfort only to the skeptic.[32]

NOTES

[1]   Roderick M. Chisholm, *Theory of Knowledge* (Englewood Cliffs, N.J., 1966), p. 30.

[2]   Anthony Quinton, *The Nature of Things* (London, 1973), p. 119. This is an extremely venerable argument, which has played a central role in epistemological discussion at least since Aristotle's statement of it in the *Posterior Analytics*, Book I, ch. 2–3. (Some have found an anticipation of the argument in the *Theaetetus* at 209E– 210B, but Plato's worry in that passage

appears to be that the proposed definition of knowledge is circular, not that it leads to an infinite regress of justification.)

[3]   "Adequately justified" because a belief could be justified to some degree without being sufficiently justified to qualify as knowledge (if true). But it is far from clear just how much justification is needed for adequacy. Virtually all recent epistemologists agree that certainty is not required. But the lottery paradox shows that adequacy cannot be understood merely in terms of some specified level of probability. (For a useful account of the lottery paradox, see Robert Ackermann, *Knowledge and Belief* (Garden City, N.Y., 1972), pp. 39–50.) Armstrong, in *Belief, Truth and Knowledge* (London, 1973), argues that what is required is that one's reasons for the belief be "conclusive," but the precise meaning of this is less than clear. Ultimately, it may be that the concept of knowledge is simply too crude for refined epistemological discussion, so that it may be necessary to speak instead of degrees of belief and corresponding degrees of justification. I shall assume (perhaps controversially) that the proper solution to this problem will not affect the issues to be discussed here, and speak merely of the reasons or justification making the belief *highly likely* to be true, without trying to say exactly what this means.

[4]   See Edmund Gettier, "Is Justified True Belief Knowledge?" *Analysis*, vol. 23 (1963), pp. 121–123. Also Ackermann, *op. cit.*, ch. V, and the corresponding references.

[5]   For simplicity, I will speak of inference relations as obtaining between beliefs rather than, more accurately, between the propositions which are believed. "Inference" is to be understood here in a very broad sense; any relation between two beliefs which allows one, if accepted, to serve as a good reason for accepting the other will count as inferential.

[6]   It is difficult to give precise criteria for when a given reason is *the* reason for a person's holding a belief. G. Harman, in *Thought* (Princeton, 1973), argues that for a person to believe for a given reason is for that reason to *explain* why he holds that belief. But this suggestion, though heuristically useful, hardly yields a usable criterion.

[7]   Thus it is a mistake to conceive the regress as a *temporal* regress, as it would be if each justifying argument had to be explicitly given before the belief in question was justified.

[8]   Obviously these views could be combined, with different instances of the regress being handled in different ways. I will not consider such combined views here. In general, they would simply inherit all of the objections pertaining to the simpler views.

[9]   Peirce seems to suggest a virtuous regress view in "Questions concerning Certain Faculties Claimed for Man," *Collected Papers* V, pp. 135–155. But the view is presented metaphorically and it is hard to be sure exactly what it comes to or to what extent it bears on the present issue.

[10]   The original statement of the non-linear view was by Bernard Bosanquet in *Implication and Linear Inference* (London, 1920). For more recent discussions, see Gilbert Harman, *Thought* (Princeton, 1973); and Nicholas Rescher, "Foundationalism, Coherentism, and the Idea of Cognitive Systematization," *The Journal of Philosophy*, vol. 71 (1974), pp. 695–708.

[11]   I have attempted to show how a coherence view might be defended against the most standard of these objections in "The Coherence Theory of Empirical Knowledge," *Philosophical Studies*, vol. 30 (1976), pp. 281–312.

[12]   The presumption against a skeptical outcome is strong, but I think it is a mistake to treat it as absolute. If no non-skeptical theory can be found which is at least reasonably plausible in its own right, skepticism might become the only rational alternative.

[13]   For some useful distinctions among these terms, see William Alston, "Varieties of Privileged Access," *American Philosophical Quarterly*, vol. 8 (1971), pp. 223–241.

[14]   For discussions of weak foundationism, see Bertrand Russell, *Human Knowledge* (New York, 1949), part II, ch. 11, and part V, chs. 6 and 7; Nelson Goodman, "Sense and Certainty," *Philosophical Review*, vol. 61 (1952), pp. 160-167; Israel Scheffler, *Science and Subjectivity* (New York, 1967), chapter V; and Roderick Firth, "Coherence, Certainty, and Epistemic Priority," *The Journal of Philosophy*, vol. 61 (1964), pp. 545– 557.

[15]   How good a reason must one have? Presumably some justification accrues from any reason which makes the belief even minimally more likely to be true than not, but considerably more than this would be required to make the justification adequate for knowledge. (See note 3, above.) (The James-Clifford controversy concerning the "will to believe" is also relevant here. I am agreeing with Clifford to the extent of saying that epistemic justification requires some positive reason in favor of the belief and not just the absence of any reason against.)

[16]   For a similar use of the notion of epistemic irresponsibility, see Ernest Sosa, "How Do You Know?" *American Philosophical Quarterly*, vol. 11 (1974), p. 117.

[17]   In fact, the premises would probably have to be true as well, in order to avoid Gettier-type counterexamples. But I shall ignore this refinement here.

[18]   On a Carnap-style *a priori* theory of probability it could, of course, be the case that very general empirical propositions were more likely to be true than not, i.e. that the possible state-descriptions in which they are true outnumber those in which they are false. But clearly this would not make them likely to be true in a sense which would allow the detached assertion of the proposition in question (on pain of contradiction), and this fact seems to preclude such justification from being adequate for knowledge.

[19]   Armstrong, *op. cit.*, chapters 11–13. Bracketed page references in this section are to this book.

[20]   Fred I. Dretske, *Seeing and Knowing* (London, 1969), chapter III, especially pp. 126-139. It is difficult to be quite sure of Dretske's view, however, since he is not concerned in this book to offer a general account of knowledge. Views which are in some ways similar to those of Armstrong and Dretske have been offered by Goldman and by Unger. See Alvin Goldman, "A Causal Theory of Knowing," *The Journal of Philosophy*, vol. 64 (1967), pp. 357–372; and Peter Unger, "An Analysis of Factual Knowledge," *The Journal of Philosophy*, vol. 65 (1968), pp. 157–170. But both Goldman and Unger are explicitly concerned with the Gettier problem and not at all with the regress problem, so it is hard to be sure how their views relate to the sort of externalist view which is at issue here.

[21]   On the one hand, Armstrong seems to argue that it is *not* a requirement for knowledge that the believer have "sufficient evidence" for his belief, which sounds like a rejection of the adequate-justification condition. On the other hand, he seems to want to say that the presence of the external relation makes it rational for a person to accept a belief, and he seems (though this is not clear) to have *epistemic* rationality in mind; and there appears to be no substantial

difference between saying that a belief is epistemically rational and saying that it is epistemically justified.

[22]   One way to put this point is to say that whether a belief is likely to be true or whether in contrast it is an accident that it is true depends significantly on how the belief is described. Thus it might be true of one and the same belief that it is "a belief connected in a law-like way with the state of affairs which it describes" and also that it is "a belief adopted on the basis of no apparent evidence"; and it might be likely to be true on the first description and unlikely to be true on the second. The claim here is that it is the believer's own conception which should be considered in deciding whether the belief is justified. (Something analogous seems to be true in ethics: the moral worth of a person's action is correctly to be judged only in terms of that person's subjective conception of what he is doing and not in light of what happens, willy-nilly, to result from it.)

[23]   Notice, however, that if beliefs standing in the proper external relation should happen to possess some subjectively distinctive feature (such as being spontaneous and highly compelling to the believer), and if the believer were to notice empirically, that beliefs having this feature were true a high proportion of the time, he would then be in a position to construct a justification for a new belief of that sort along the lines sketched at the end of section II. But of course a belief justified in that way would no longer be basic.

[24]   I suspect that something like the argument to be given here is lurking somewhere in Sellars' "Empiricism and the Philosophy of Mind" (reprinted in Sellars, *Science, Perception, and Reality* [London, 1963], pp. 127–196), but it is difficult to be sure. A more recent argument by Sellars which is considerably closer on the surface to the argument offered here is contained in "The Structure of Knowledge," his Machette Foundation Lectures given at the University of Texas in 1971, in Hector-Neri Castenada (ed.), *Action, Knowledge, and Reality: Critical Studies in Honor of Wilfrid Sellars* (Indianapolis, 1975), Lecture III, sections III–IV. A similar line of argument was also offered by Neurath and Hempel. See Otto Neurath, "Protocol Sentences," tr. in A. J. Ayer (ed.), *Logical Positivism* (New York, 1959), pp. 199–208; and Carl G. Hempel, "On the Logical Positivists' Theory of Truth," *Analysis*, vol. 2 (1934–5), pp. 49–59. The Hempel paper is in part a reply to a foundationist critique of Neurath by Schlick in "The Foundation of Knowledge," also translated in *Logical Positivism, op. cit.*, pp. 209–227. Schlick replied to Hempel in "Facts and Propositions," and Hempel responded in "Some Remarks on 'Facts' and Propositions," both in *Analysis*, vol. 2 (1934–5), pp. 65–70 and 93–96, respectively. Though the Neurath-Hempel argument conflates issues having to do with truth and issues having to do with justification in a confused and confusing way, it does bring out the basic objection to givenism.

[25]   Chisholm, "Theory of Knowledge," in Chisholm *et al.*, *Philosophy* (Englewood Cliffs, N.J., 1964), pp. 270ff.

[26]   *Op. cit.* Bracketed page references in this section will be to this book.

[27]   Quinton does offer one small bit of clarification here, by appealing to the notion of ostensive definition and claiming in effect that the sort of awareness involved in the intuitive justification of a basic belief is the same as that involved in a situation of ostensive definition. But such a comparison is of little help, for at least two reasons. First, as Wittgenstein, Sellars, and others have argued, the notion of ostensive definition is itself seriously problematic. Indeed, an

objection quite analogous to the present one against the notion of a basic belief could be raised against the notion of an ostensive definition; and this objection, if answerable at all, could only be answered by construing the awareness involved in ostension in such a way as to be of no help to the foundationist in the present discussion. Second, more straightforwardly, even if the notion of ostensive definition were entirely unobjectionable, there is no need for the sort of awareness involved to be *justified*. If all that is at issue is learning the meaning of a word (or acquiring a concept), then justification is irrelevant. Thus the existence of ostensive definitions would not show how there could be basic beliefs.

[28] Notice, however, that to reject an epistemological given does not necessarily rule out other varieties of givenness which may have importance for other philosophical issues. In particular, there may still be viable versions of givenness which pose an obstacle to materialist views in the philosophy of mind. For useful distinctions among various versions of givenness and a discussion of their relevance to the philosophy of mind, see James W. Cornman, "Materialism and Some Myths about Some Givens," *The Monist*, vol. 56 (1972), pp. 215–233.

[29] Compare the Husserlian notion of a "pre-predicative awareness."

[30] It is interesting to note that Quinton seems to offer an analogous critique of givenness in an earlier paper, "The Problem of Perception," reprinted in Robert J. Swartz (ed.), *Perceiving, Sensing, and Knowing* (Garden City, New York, 1965), pp. 497–526; cf. especially p. 503.

[31] For a discussion of such a coherence theory, see my paper cited in note 11, above.

[32] I am grateful to my friends Jean Blumenfeld, David Blumenfeld, Hardy Jones, Jeff Pelletier, and Martin Perlmutter for extremely helpful comments on an earlier version of this paper.

1.3

THE COHERENCE THEORY OF EMPIRICAL KNOWLEDGE

Laurence BonJour

In a paper written for a commemorative symposium on the philosophy of C.
I. Lewis, Roderick Firth remarks that Lewis liked to confront his Harvard
epistemology students with a fundamental choice between a foundation theory
of knowledge based on "the given," like that advocated so ably in Lewis's own
books, and "a coherence theory like that of Bosanquet."[1] As Firth notes, there
are many different philosophical views which have been called "coherence
theories," including theories of truth and meaning; but what Lewis seems to
have had primarily in mind is a coherence theory of *epistemic justification*: the
view that the epistemic warrant or authority of empirical statements derives
entirely from coherence and not at all from any sort of "foundation."[2] Since
Lewis's strong version of foundationism is by now everywhere in eclipse, it
seems appropriate to examine the Bosanquetian alternative.

The purpose of this paper is to explore, and tentatively defend, a view of
the Bosanquetian sort, which I shall call "the coherence theory of empirical
knowledge" (hereafter CTEK). As discussed here, the CTEK is not to be
identified with any specific historical view, though it has obvious affinities
with some. It is intended rather as an idealized reconstruction of a relatively
pure coherence theory, one which avoids all versions of foundationism.[3]

Views like the CTEK, though often employed as dialectical bogeymen,
have rarely been treated as serious epistemological alternatives, since they have
been thought to be subject to obvious and overwhelming objections. Thus the
essential first step in a defense of such a view is to provide a sketch of its
overall shape and rationale and show on this basis that these supposedly fatal
objections can be answered. Such a preliminary defense of the CTEK, aimed
at establishing its epistemological viability, is the goal of this paper.

|

The main watershed which divides the CTEK from opposing epistemological views is a familiar problem which I shall call "the regress problem." This problem arises directly out of the justification condition of the traditional explication of knowledge as adequately justified true belief.[4] The most obvious way in which beliefs are justified is *inferential justification*. In its most explicit form, inferential justification consists in providing an argument from one or more other beliefs as premises to the justificandum belief as conclusion.[5] But it is obviously a necessary condition for such inferential justification that the beliefs appealed to as premises be themselves *already* justified in some fashion; that a belief follows from unjustified premises lends it no justification. Now the premise-beliefs might also be justified inferentially, but such justification would only introduce further premise-beliefs which would have to be justified in some way, thus leading apparently to an infinite, vicious regress of epistemic justification. The justification of one belief would require the *logically antecedent* justification of one or more other beliefs, which in turn would require the logically antecedent justification of still further beliefs, etc. The result, seemingly inescapable so long as all justification is inferential in character, would be that justification could never even get started and hence that no belief would ever be genuinely justified.[6] Any adequate epistemological position must provide a solution to this problem, a way of avoiding the skeptical result—and the character of that solution will determine, more than anything else, the basic structure of the position.

One can find in the epistemological literature three main strategies for coping with the regress problem as it applies to empirical knowledge.[7]

(i) The historically most popular solution has been what may be called "strong foundationism," one version of the basic foundationist approach to epistemological issues. The basic thesis of foundationism in all of its forms is that certain empirical, contingent beliefs have a degree of epistemic warrant or justification which is non-inferential in character, i.e. which does not derive from other beliefs via inference in a way that would require those other beliefs to be antecedently justified. Strong foundationism is the view that the non-inferential warrant of these beliefs is sufficient *by itself* to satisfy the adequate-justification condition of knowledge and to qualify them as acceptable premises for the inferential justification of further beliefs. Thus these "basic beliefs" constitute the "foundation" upon which the rest of our empirical knowledge is based; the regress of justification terminates when such beliefs are reached.

Strong foundationism has many variants in recent philosophy which differ from each other in important ways, and many recent attacks on strong foundationism really apply to only some of these variants. One issue which divides these variants, is whether basic beliefs are, or need be, infallible, indubitable, and/or incorrigible, i.e. whether and to what extent they are subject to subsequent rejection in the way in which non-basic beliefs are.[8] A second issue is whether basic beliefs are always about subjective experience or whether they may sometimes be about ordinary physical objects. A third issue, perhaps the most important, is whether and how basic beliefs are themselves justified. The traditional view is Lewis's: they are justified by reference to "given" experience (so that their justification is derivative from other cognitive or at least quasi-cognitive states, but not from further *beliefs*). But other proponents of strong foundationist theories have appealed instead to facts about language-learning or about the causal antecedents of the belief (facts which need not be known to the person for whom the belief is justified—on pain of further regress); and some philosophers have seemed to hold, paradoxically, that basic beliefs need not be justified at all in order to constitute knowledge and provide suitable justifying premises for further beliefs, that the issue of their justification "does not arise."[9] What all such views have in common is the idea that basic beliefs, if justified at all, are not justified via any sort of inferential appeal to further beliefs that would require those further beliefs to be justified and would thus unleash the regress.

(ii) The main traditional alternative to strong foundationism is the CTEK. In first approximation, the CTEK involves two main theses. The first is that *all* epistemic justification for individual empirical beliefs is inferential in character and hence that there are no basic beliefs and no foundation for knowledge. The second is the twofold claim (a) that the regress of justification does not go on forever, which would involve an infinite number of distinct beliefs, but rather circles back upon itself, thus forming a closed system; and (b) that the primary unit of epistemic justification is such a system, which is justified in terms of its internal coherence. The main historical proponents of the CTEK were the absolute idealists, though they tended at times to conflate (or confuse) the CTEK with a coherence account of *truth*. A similar view was also held by certain of the logical positivists, especially Neurath and Hempel.[10] Among contemporary philosophers views resembling the CTEK to some extent have been held by Quine, Sellars, and others.[11] To most philosophers, however, the CTEK has seemed to be afflicted with insuperable difficulties.

(iii) The third view, a relative newcomer to the philosophical scene, amounts to an interesting hybrid of a foundation theory of knowledge with the CTEK; it may be called "weak foundationism." On this view, certain empirical beliefs ("initially credible beliefs") have a modicum of epistemic warrant which is non-inferential in character. But these beliefs are not basic beliefs, as that phrase was understood above, since their degree of non-inferential warrant is insufficient by itself to satisfy the adequate-justification condition of knowledge or to qualify them as acceptable justifying premises for other beliefs; this initial modicum of justification must be augmented by a further appeal to coherence before knowledge is achieved. Thus the solution to the regress problem is presumably (though this is seldom spelled out) that the regress moves ultimately in a circle, as in the CTEK, but that the warrant for the coherent system of beliefs which results derives *both* from coherence and from the non-inferential warrant of certain of its component beliefs. Versions of weak foundationism have been suggested by Russell and Goodman, and developed by Scheffler and, much more extensively, by Rescher.[12]

It is the regress problem which has provided the main motivation and much of the argumentative support for foundationist views. Most philosophers have thought that the CTEK was obviously incapable of providing an adequate solution to the problem and hence that some version of foundationism must be true. This argument by elimination has led them to overlook serious problems which pertain not only to particular versions of foundationism, but to the overall foundationist position itself.

II

The underlying motivation for the CTEK is the conviction that all foundationist accounts of empirical knowledge are untenable. The crucial problem is much the same for both versions of foundationism: what is the source or rationale of the non-inferential epistemic warrant which allegedly attaches to a basic belief (in strong foundationism) or to an initially credible belief (in weak foundationism)? If an empirical, contingent belief B, one which is not knowable *a priori*, is to have such warrant for a given person, it seems that he must have some *reason* for thinking that B is true or likely to be true (the degree of likelihood required depending on whether B is held to be basic or only initially credible). And it is hard to see what such a reason could consist in other than the justified beliefs both (a) that *B* has some property or feature Φ, and (b) that beliefs having the property or feature Φ are likely, to the appropriate degree, to be true. Such justified beliefs would provide the basis for a justifying argument for *B*, and reliance on them would of course mean that *B* was not basic or initially credible after all. But how can a person be justified in accepting a contingent belief if he does not believe, and *a fortiori* does not know, anything about it which makes it at all likely to be true? A standard of epistemic justification which yields this result would seem clearly to have severed the vital connection between epistemic justification and truth, thus leaving itself without any ultimate rationale. It is for reasons of this sort that the CTEK holds that the justification of particular empirical beliefs is always inferential in character, and that there can in principle be no basic (or initially credible) empirical beliefs and no foundation for empirical knowledge.[13]

This picture of the CTEK, however, though accurate as far as it goes, is seriously misleading because it neglects the systematic or holistic character of the view. The best way to see this is to return to the regress problem.

Having rejected foundationism, the CTEK must hold that the regress of justification moves in a circle (or at least a closed curve), since this is the only alternative to a genuinely infinite regress involving an infinite number of distinct beliefs. But this response to the regress problem will seem obviously inadequate to one who approaches the issue with foundationist preconceptions. For surely, it will be argued, such an appeal to circularity does not solve the regress problem. Each step in the regress is an argument whose premises must be justified *before* they can confer justification on the conclusion. To say that the regress moves in a circle is to say that at some point one (or more) of the beliefs which figured earlier as conclusions is now appealed to as a justifying premise. And this situation, far from solving the regress problem, yields the patently absurd result that the justification of such a belief (qua conclusion) depends on *its own* logically prior justification (qua premise): it cannot be justified unless it is *already* justified. And thus neither it nor anything which depends on it can be justified. Since justification is always finally circular in this way according to the CTEK, there can be on that view no genuine justification and no knowledge.

The tacit premise in this seemingly devastating line of argument is the idea that inferential justification is essentially *linear* in character, involving a linear sequence of beliefs along which warrant is transferred from the earlier beliefs in the sequence to the later beliefs via connections of inference. It is this linear conception of inferential justification that ultimately generates the regress problem. If it is accepted, the idea that justification moves in a circle will be obviously unacceptable, and only *strong* foundationism will be left as an alternative. (Even weak foundationism cannot accept a purely linear view of justification, since its initially credible beliefs are not sufficiently justified to serve as first premises for everything else.) Thus the basic response of the CTEK to the regress problem is not the appeal to circularity, which would be futile by itself, but rather the rejection of the linear conception of inferential justification.[14]

The alternative is a holistic or systematic conception of inferential justification (and hence of empirical justification in general, since all empirical justification is inferential for the CTEK): beliefs are justified by being inferentially related to other beliefs in the overall context of a coherent system. To make this view clear, it is necessary to distinguish two levels at which issues of justification can be raised. Thus the issue at hand may be merely the justification of a particular belief, or a small set of beliefs, in the context of a cognitive system whose overall justification is taken for granted; or it may be the global issue of the justification of the cognitive system itself. According to the CTEK it is the latter, global issue which is fundamental for the determination of epistemic justification. Confusion arises, however, because it is only issues of the former, more limited, sort which tend to be raised explicitly in actual cases.

At the level at which only the justification of a particular belief (or small set of such beliefs) is at issue, justification appears linear. A given justificandum belief is justified explicitly by citing other premise-beliefs from which it may be inferred. Such premise-beliefs can themselves be challenged, with justification being provided for them in the same fashion. But there is no serious danger of a regress at this level since the justification of the overall epistemic system (and thus of at least most of its component beliefs) is *ex hypothesi* not at issue. One thus quickly reaches premise-beliefs which are dialectically acceptable in that context.

If on the other hand no dialectically acceptable stopping point is reached, if the premise-beliefs which are offered by way of justification continue to be challenged, then the epistemic dialogue would, if ideally continued, eventually move in a circle, giving the appearance of a regress and in effect challenging the entire cognitive system. At this global level, however, the CTEK no longer conceives the relation between the various particular beliefs as one of linear dependence, but rather as one of mutual or reciprocal support. There is no ultimate relation of epistemic priority among the members of such a system and consequently no basis for a true regress. The component beliefs are so related that each can be justified in terms of the others; the direction in which the justifying argument actually moves depends on which belief is under scrutiny in a particular context. The apparent circle of justification is not vicious because the justification of particular beliefs depends finally not on other particular beliefs, as in the linear conception of justification, but on the overall system and its coherence.

Thus the fully explicit justification of a particular belief would involve four distinct steps of argument, as follows:

1. The inferability of that particular belief from other particular beliefs, and further inference relations among particular beliefs.
2. The coherence of the overall system of beliefs.
3. The justification of the overall system of beliefs.
4. The justification of the particular belief in question, by virtue of its membership in the system.

According to the CTEK, each of these steps depends on the ones which precede it. It is the neglecting of steps 2 and 3, the ones pertaining explicitly to the cognitive system, that is the primary source of the linear conception of justification and thus of the regress problem. This is a seductive mistake. Since the very same inferential connections between particular beliefs are involved in both step 1 and step 4, it is fatally easy to conflate these two, leaving out the two intermediary steps which involve explicit reference to the system.

Of the three transitions represented in this schematic argument, only the third, from step 3 to step 4, is reasonably unproblematic, depending as it does on the inferential relations that obtain between the justificandum belief and other beliefs of the system; in effect it is this transition that is made when an inferential justification is offered in an ordinary context. But the other two transitions are highly problematic, and the issues which they raise are crucial for understanding and assessing the CTEK.

The transition from step 1 to step 2, from the inference relations obtaining between particular beliefs to the coherence of the system as a whole, is rendered problematic by the serious vagueness and unclarity of the central conception of coherence. It is clear that coherence depends on the various sorts of inferential, evidential, and explanatory relations which exist among the members of a set of propositions, especially upon the more systematic of these.

Thus various detailed investigations by philosophers and logicians of such topics as explanation, confirmation, etc., may be taken to provide some of the essential ingredients of a general account of coherence. But the main job of giving such a general account, and in particular one which will provide a basis for *comparative* assessments of coherence, has scarcely been begun.[15] Neverthe-less, while the absence of such an account represents a definite lacuna in the CTEK, it cannot provide the basis for a decisive or even a very serious objection to the theory. This is so because coherence (or something very closely resembling it) is, and seemingly must be, a basic ingredient of rival epistemological theories as well. We have already seen that weak foundation-ism makes an explicit appeal to coherence. And it seems that even strong foundationism must appeal to coherence if it is to make sense of knowledge of the past, theoretical knowledge, etc. In fact, all of the leading proponents of alternatives to the CTEK employ the notion of coherence (sometimes by other names[16]) in their accounts.

Thus the problem of giving an adequate account of coherence is one which may safely be neglected by the sort of preliminary defense of the CTEK which is offered here. There are, however, some essential points concerning the concept which should be noted. First, coherence is not to be equated with consistency. A coherent system must be consistent, but a consistent system need not be very coherent. Coherence has to do with systematic connections between the components of a system, not just with their failure to conflict.[17] Second, coherence will obviously be a matter of degree. For a system of beliefs to be justified, according to the CTEK, it must not be merely coherent to some extent, but more coherent than any currently available alternative.[18] Third, coherence is closely connected with the concept of explanation. Exactly what the connection is I shall not try to say here. But it is clear that the coherence of a system is enhanced to the extent that observed facts (in a sense to be explicated below) can be explained within it and reduced to the extent that this is not the case. Since explanation and prediction are at the very least closely allied, much the same thing can be said about prediction as well.

The problems relating to the other problematic transition in the schematic argument, that from step 2 to step 3, are more immediately serious. What is at issue here is the fundamental question of the connection between coherence and justification: why, if a body of beliefs is coherent, is it thereby epistemical-ly justified? The force of this question is best brought out by formulating three related objections to the CTEK, centering on this point, which are usually thought to destroy all plausibility which it might otherwise have:

(I)   According to the CTEK, the system of beliefs which constitutes empirical knowledge is justified *solely* by reference to coherence. But coherence will never suffice to pick out one system of beliefs, since there will always be many other alternative, incompatible systems of belief which are equally coherent and hence equally justified according to the CTEK.

(II)   According to the CTEK, empirical beliefs are justified only in terms of relations to other beliefs and to the system of beliefs; at no point does any relation to the world come in. But this means that the alleged system of empirical knowledge is deprived of all *input* from the world. Surely such a self-enclosed system of beliefs cannot constitute empirical knowledge.

(III)   An adequate epistemological theory must establish a connection between its account of justification and its account of *truth*; i.e., it must be shown that justification, as viewed by that theory, is *truth-conductive*, that one who seeks justified beliefs is at least likely to find true ones. But the only way in which the CTEK can do this is by adopting a coherence theory of truth and the absurd idealistic metaphysics which goes along with it.

Of these three objections, (III) is the most basic and (I) is the most familiar. It is (II), however, which must be dealt with first, since the answer to it is essential for dealing with the other two objections. Fundamentally, the point made in (II) must simply be accepted: there must be some sort of input into the cognitive system from the world. Thus the answer to (II) must consist in showing how the CTEK can allow for such input. I shall attempt to lay the groundwork for this in the next section by offering a schematic account of how the crucial concept of *observation* fits into the CTEK, following which I shall return in the final section to the objections.

III

It may be thought that the suggestion that there is room in the CTEK for an appeal to observation involves an immediate contradiction in terms. For surely, the argument might go, it is essential to the very conception of observation that observational beliefs are *non-inferential* in character; and it is equally essential to the conception of the CTEK, as explained above, that *all* justified beliefs are *inferential*. Thus the CTEK can accord no significant epistemic role to observation (which surely constitutes an immediate *reductio ad absurdum* of the theory).

But this argument is mistaken. It rests on a confusion between two quite different ways in which a belief may be said to be inferential (or non-inferential). In the first place, there is the issue of how the belief was arrived at, of its *origin* in the thinking of the person in question: was it arrived at via an actual process of reasoning or inference from other beliefs or in some other way? In the second place, there is the issue of how the belief is *justified* or *warranted* (if at all): is it justified by virtue of inferential relations to other beliefs or in some other way? Thus there are two distinct senses in which a belief may be inferential (and corresponding senses in which it may be non-inferential). And the immediate force of the above objection rests on a failure to distinguish these senses, for it is in the *first* sense (inferential or non-inferential *origin*) that an observational belief is paradigmatically non-inferential; while it is in the *second* sense (inferential or non-inferential *warrant*) that the CTEK insists that all justified beliefs must be inferential. And there is nothing absurd about the idea that a belief might be arrived at in some non-inferential way (e.g., as a hunch) and only subsequently justified, via inference.

Proponents of the foundation theory will no doubt argue that this distinction at best only momentarily staves off the force of the objection, since observational beliefs are in fact non-inferential in both senses, even if somewhat more obviously so in the first sense, so that the contradiction remains. The CTEK, on the other hand, holds that observational beliefs are non-inferential in only the first sense, that their epistemic authority or warrant derives from inferential relations to other beliefs and thus ultimately from coherence, in the way outlined above. The immediate task here is to elaborate this latter view by showing in some detail how the justification of observational beliefs might be plausibly viewed as deriving from inference. In doing so I shall neglect, for the moment, the systematic dimension of coherence and concentrate more narrowly on the inferential relations which pertain immediately to observation, according to the CTEK.

It is best to begin by considering some examples before attempting a more general account. Consider, as a first example, the following simply case. As I look at my desk, I come to have the belief, among many others, that there is a red book on the desk. This belief is *cognitively spontaneous*: it is not arrived at via any sort of conscious ratiocinative process, but simply occurs to me, strikes me, in a coercive manner over which I have no control; thus it is clearly non-inferential in the first of the two senses distinguished above. Let us suppose, as would ordinarily be the case, that this belief is indeed an instance of knowledge. The question now becomes: how it is justified or warranted? The strong foundationist will claim either that the belief is itself a basic belief, or else that it is justified via inference from a further belief, presumably about my experience, which is basic. But what account can the CTEK offer as an alternative? What sort of inferential justification might be available for such a belief?

Once the question is put in this way, the main elements of the answer are, I think, readily discernible. First, the belief in question is a visual belief, i.e. it is produced by my sense of sight; and I am, or at least can be, introspectively aware of this fact. Second, the conditions of observation are of a specifiable sort: the lighting is good, my eyes are functioning normally, and there are no interfering circumstances; and again, I know or can know these facts about the conditions, via other observations and introspections. Finally, it is a true law about me (and indeed about a large class of relevantly similar observers) that my spontaneous visual beliefs in such conditions about that sort of subject matter (viz., medium-sized physical objects) are highly reliable, i.e. very likely to be true; and, once more, I know this law. Putting these elements together, I am in a position to offer the following justification for my belief:

(i)   I have a spontaneous visual belief that there is a red book on the desk.

(ii)   Spontaneous visual beliefs about the color and general classification of medium-sized physical objects are, in (specified) conditions, very likely to be true.

(iii)   The conditions are as specified in (ii).

Therefore, my belief that there is a red book on the desk is very likely to be true.

Therefore, (probably) there is a red book on the desk.[19]

There are two points which may be noted quickly about this justifying argument. First, all of the premises are empirical. Second, instead of assuming a listing of the conditions, I could have spoken instead in (ii) and (iii) of "standard conditions"; this would have had the effect of reducing the empirical content of (ii) and packing this content instead into (iii), but would have altered nothing of any real significance.

Consider now, more briefly, some contrasting examples. In all of the following cases I fail to have knowledge, despite the presence of a spontaneous visual belief. According to the account offered by the CTEK, the reason that I fail to know is that in each case one of the essential premises for an analogous justifying argument is unavailable to me. (a) Far on the other side of the campus a figure is coming toward me. I spontaneously believe that it is my friend George, and in fact it is; but the belief is not knowledge, because beliefs produced under those conditions (i.e. at very great distance) are not generally reliable, i.e. not likely enough to be true. (b) Watching the traffic, I spontaneously believe that the car going by is a Lotus, and in fact it is; but the belief is not knowledge, although the conditions of observation are excellent, because I am not very familiar with cars and my perceptual beliefs about them are not very reliable. (I am apt to think that almost any fancy sports car is a Lotus.) (c) Peering into the darkness, I spontaneously believe that there is a man in the bushes, and in fact there is; but the belief is not knowledge, both because the conditions are poor and because I am a bit paranoid and quite apt to imagine people in the bushes who are not there. (d) In a fun house (a house of mirrors), I spontaneously believe that there is a little fat man directly in front of me, across the room, and in fact there is; but the belief is not knowledge, because I do not know the conditions of perception (which are in fact quite normal) and hence am unable to supply the appropriate premise.

I submit that the contrast between these latter cases where I fail to have knowledge and the former one where I do have knowledge, and between analogous cases of the same sort, provides good evidence that arguments like the one sketched above are indeed involved in the justification of observational knowledge. It is an interesting exercise to attempt to give an account of the difference between such cases in strong foundationist terms.

There is one other sort of case which needs to be discussed. Looking at my desk, I come to know that there is no blue book on it. This knowledge clearly results from observation, but the sort of account sketched above is inapplicable, since I do not have a spontaneous visual belief that there is no blue book on the desk, I do not somehow see the absence of such a book; rather I simply fail to see its presence, i.e. I fail to have a spontaneous visual belief that there *is* a blue book on the desk, and my belief that there is not is an inference from my failure to spontaneously believe that there is. What this example illustrates is that spontaneous visual beliefs are reliable in two distinct senses: not only are they (in specifiable circumstances, about specifiable subject-matter) very likely to be true; but they are also very likely to be produced (in specifiable circumstances, about specifiable subject matter[20]), if they would be true if produced. It is this second sort of reliability that allows me to reason, in the case in point:

(i)   I have no spontaneous visual belief that there is a blue book on my desk.

(ii)   If there were a blue book on my desk, then, in (specified) conditions, it is highly likely that such a belief would be produced.

(iii) The conditions are as specified in (ii).

Therefore, (probably) there is not a blue book on my desk.

Clearly knowledge justified in this way is closely connected with observation, whether or not it should itself be called observational. (It is also an interesting question, which I shall not pause to discuss here, whether all negative observational or observation-related knowledge must be justified in this indirect fashion.)

The crucial point, for present purposes, is that all of the premises of this justifying argument (as of the earlier one) are empirical premises, including most especially the crucial general premise (ii) in each argument. It is not an *a priori* truth, but rather an empirical discovery, that certain sorts of cognitively spontaneous beliefs are epistemically reliable and others are not; that waking visual beliefs are reliable and that visual beliefs produced in dreams, though similar in other respects, are not reliable. There are possible worlds in which the positions of these two sorts of experience are exactly reversed, in which reliable visual beliefs occur during sleep and unreliable ones while awake. (In such worlds, of course, the causal genesis of dreams, and of waking visual beliefs as well, will no doubt be different in important ways, but this difference need not be reflected in the subjective character of the beliefs or in the known conditions.) Thus the reason that visual perceptual beliefs are epistemically justified or warranted is that we have empirical background knowledge which tells us that beliefs of that specific sort are epistemically reliable. This is the basic claim of the CTEK for *all* varieties of observation.

On the basis of these examples, I offer the following tentative sketch of a concept of observation compatible with the CTEK. According to this view, any mode of observation must involve three essential elements.

First, there must be a process of some sort which produces cognitively spontaneous beliefs about a certain range of subject matter. The process involved may be very complicated, involving such things as sense organs; the state of the mind and/or brain as a result of previous training or innate capacities; perhaps also the sorts of entities or events which philosophers have variously referred to by such terms as "immediate experience," "raw feels," and "sensa"; instruments of various kinds; perhaps even occult abilities of some sort (such as clairvoyance); etc.

Second, the beliefs thus produced must be *reliable* with respect to the subject matter in question in the two distinct ways discussed above (under specifiable conditions): on the one hand, it must be very likely that such beliefs, when produced, are true (if the requisite conditions are satisfied); and, on the other hand, if the person is in a situation in which a particular belief about that range of subject matter would be true (and if the requisite conditions are satisfied), then it must be very likely that such a belief will in fact be produced. This second sort of reliability is crucial; on it depends, in large part at least, the possibility of negative observational knowledge.

Third, and most importantly from the standpoint of the CTEK, the person must *know* all of these things, at least in a rough and ready way. He must be able to recognize beliefs which result from the process in question (though he need not know anything about the details of the process). He must know that such beliefs are reliable in the two senses specified. And he must know in a given case that any necessary conditions for reliability are satisfied. He will then be in a position, in a particular case, to offer the following justification for such a spontaneous belief:

(i)   I have a spontaneous belief that P (about subject-matter S) which is an instance of kind K.

(ii)   Spontaneous beliefs about S which are instances of K are very likely to be true, if conditions C are satisfied.

(iii) Conditions C are satisfied.

Therefore, my belief that P is (probably) true.

Therefore, (probably) P.

And he will also be in a position to argue for a negative conclusion on the basis of observation, in the following way:

(i)   I have no spontaneous belief that P (about subject-matter S) which is an instance of kind K.

(ii)   If P, then if conditions C are satisfied, it is very likely that I would have a spontaneous belief that P which was an instance of K.

(iii)   Conditions C are satisfied.

_____

Therefore, (probably) not-P.

These two schematic arguments are the basic schemata for the justification of observational knowledge, according to the CTEK.

The foregoing account of observation is obviously highly schematic and would require much more discussion to be complete. For present purposes, however, it will suffice to add five supplementary comments, by way of clarification, elaboration, and anticipation of possible objections, following which I shall return to a discussion of the main objection to the CTEK.

First. It needs to be asked what the exact status of the various inferences outlined above is supposed to be, relative to the actual cognitive state of a person who has observational knowledge. For it is only too obvious that such a person need not go explicitly through any such process of inference in order to have observational knowledge (on pain of making actual instances of observational knowledge vanishingly rare). But it is equally obvious that the inferences in question, in order to be a correct account of the observational knowledge of such a person, must be somehow relevant to his particular cognitive state and not merely an account which could be added, totally from the outside, by a philosopher. Thus the claim of the CTEK here (and indeed the analogous claim of foundation theories for the inferences which they typically postulate) must be that such inferences are in some way tacitly or implicitly involved in the cognitive state of a person who has observational knowledge, even though he does not rehearse them explicitly and indeed might well be unable to do so even if challenged. It is not necessary that the belief actually originate via inference, however tacit or even unconscious; but it must be the case that a tacit grasp of the *availability* of the inference is the basis for the continuing acceptance of the belief and for the conviction that it is warranted. It has to be claimed, in other words, that such inferences are indeed an adequate philosophical unpacking or explication of what is really involved in the observational knowledge of an ordinary person, even though he may never be explicitly conscious of them. Such a claim on the part of the CTEK, as also on the part of foundation theories, is obviously very difficult to establish. Ultimately, it must simply be asserted that careful reflection on actual cases of observational knowledge will reveal that something like this is tacitly involved, though ultimately it may have to be conceded that any philosophically adequate account of knowledge is an idealization which is only loosely approximated by ordinary cognition. (It is worth remarking, however, that the inferential apparatus postulated by the CTEK, on the above account, is surely more common-sensical and less esoteric than is the analogous apparatus typically postulated by the foundation theories.)

Second. It is obvious that the knowledge represented by the third premises of the illustrative and schematic justifying arguments set out above, viz. the knowledge of the conditions of observation, will itself normally be largely or wholly based on observation and must be justified in the same way. This means that the element of coherence enters in immediately—with many observational beliefs, which may be from the same sense or from different senses, serving (directly or indirectly) as premises for each other's justification.

Third. As was emphasized above, the second premises of the various arguments are empirical premises. More specifically, each such premise is an empirical *law* about certain classes of beliefs. But it is obvious that such laws cannot be viewed in general as having been arrived at inductively, since no inductive argument as ordinarily construed would be possible unless one was *already* in a position to make warranted observations. Confirming evidence *is* available from within the coherent system for such laws, and any such law can be empirically tested within the context of the others; but the cognitive system as a whole could not have been developed piecemeal from the ground up.[21]

Fourth. A more difficult problem is how the first premises of the various arguments are to be justified. It is obvious that such premises, for the most part at least, are to be regarded as the products of introspection, but how is introspective knowledge to be understood within the CTEK? It is tempting to treat introspection as just one more mode of observation, which would then be justified along the lines of the justification-schemata set forth above. Unfortunately, however, this will not quite do. Justifying an introspective belief along those lines would require as a first premise the claim that one had a spontaneous introspective belief of a certain sort. Thus, to return to the original example of my perceiving a red book on my desk, if premise (i) of the justifying argument for the claim is taken as the introspective belief to be justified, the first premise of the justifying argument would have to be:

(i)   I have a spontaneous introspective belief that I have a spontaneous visual belief that there is a red book on the desk.

This is all right by itself. But now if justification is demanded for this premise, and one attempts to give it along similar lines, the first premise required for the new justifying argument will be:

(i)   I have a spontaneous introspective belief that I have a spontaneous introspective belief that I have a spontaneous visual belief that there is a red book on the desk.

And since the challenge can be repeated again and again, we are seemingly off on a new regress, one which cannot be handled by the strategy set forth above, since the chain of arguments clearly does not move in a circle. I am not convinced that this regress is logically vicious, but it does not represent a plausible account of our actual introspective knowledge.[22]

How then is introspective knowledge to be handled by the CTEK—that is if it is to avoid collapsing back into the foundationist view that introspective beliefs are basic? The key to the answer is that although an introspective belief *could* be justified along the lines of the earlier justification-schema, only one of the three premises of such an argument is really indispensable for the work of justification. Thus premise (iii), concerning conditions of observation, can be dispensed with because introspection, unlike other modes of observation, is almost entirely impervious to conditions. And premise (i), the premise which produced our current difficulty, can also be dispensed with. It is a fact about human perceivers that their beliefs about introspective matters are in accord with and reflect their spontaneous introspective beliefs. This is a weak and unproblematic version of privileged access, which is traceable to the fact that in introspective matters we are always in the proper position to have spontaneous beliefs; and thus, unlike the situation with other modes of observation, there is no chance for a disparity between our potential spontaneous beliefs and our other beliefs about the same introspective subject matter to develop. Consequently the reliability which attaches to spontaneous introspective beliefs also attaches to beliefs about introspective subject-matter generally, whether spontaneous or not, and there is thus no need for premise (i) which stipulates that I have such a spontaneous belief.

Thus the only premise that is essential for a justification of introspective beliefs along the lines of the CTEK is the one corresponding to premise (ii) of the schematic argument, with the references to conditions of observation and to cognitive spontaneity excised:

(*) Introspective beliefs (or certain sorts) are very likely to be true.

Here the phrase "introspective beliefs" is to be taken to mean simply "beliefs about introspective subject matter"; such beliefs need not be cognitively spontaneous. It is premise (*) that underlies introspective knowledge, according to the CTEK.[23]

The appeal to premise (*) may perhaps give the appearance that the CTEK is only verbally distinct from foundationism, for it might be taken to be equivalent to treating introspective beliefs as basic or at least as initially credible. This would be a mistake. The basic difference is that premise (*), according to the CTEK, is an *empirical* premise, which must and does receive justification from within the rest of our cognitive system and which is subject to being reassessed and modified in light of that system. This fact about (*) is reflected in the parenthetical clause; all instances of introspection are not equally reliable, and the distinction among them must be made empirically. When an introspective belief is justified by appeal to premise (*), the appeal is still ultimately to coherence. Therefore, according to the CTEK, although introspective beliefs do play a unique and pivotal role in empirical knowledge, they do not constitute a foundation for that knowledge, as that notion has traditionally been understood; the basic thesis of foundationism can still be consistently rejected. (Indeed the CTEK does *not* insist that some premise like premise (*) must be maintained by any acceptable cognitive system. It is logically conceivable that no such premise might be true, that no variety of introspection might be consistently reliable, so that *any* premise of this sort would fail to yield coherent results in the long run. This point will be considered further below together with its bearing on the possibility of empirical knowledge.)

Fifth. It is worth noting explicitly that the conception of observation advanced here is implicitly much broader than the standard conceptions of sense-perception and introspection. On this view any process of empirical belief-production whose results are epistemically reliable counts as a mode of observation, whether or not it involves the traditional senses. Thus, for example, if there are people who have spontaneous clairvoyant or telepathic beliefs which are reliable, then for such people clairvoyance or telepathy is at least a potential mode of observation (though they must *know* that the beliefs in question are reliable if they are to have knowledge on this basis). Or, more interestingly, if (as often seems to be the case) a scientist who masters the use of an instrument such as a geiger counter or cloud chamber develops the capacity to have reliable spontaneous beliefs about theoretical entities and processes such as radioactivity or subatomic particles,[24] then these beliefs count as observational on the present account and can be justified directly, without reference to sense-experience, along the lines sketched above.

IV

This schematic account of the role of observation in the CTEK provides the essential ingredient for answering the three objections to that theory that were set out in Section II, above. The first two objections can be dealt with very simply and directly, while the third will require a more extended discussion and even then must be dealt with here in a less conclusive fashion.

I begin with objection (II), which alleges that a consequence of the CTEK is that empirical knowledge has no *input* from the world. In light of the discussion of observation, it should now be clear that the CTEK can allow for input into the cognitive system from the world, while insisting that this input must be understood in *causal* rather than epistemic terms. The world impinges upon the system of knowledge by causing cognitively spontaneous beliefs of various sorts, but these beliefs are epistemically justified or warranted only from within the system, along the lines set out above. And, in principle at least, any sort of causal impact of the world that is capable of producing such beliefs in a reliable way is capable of being justified as a species of observation.

Moreover, such observational beliefs need not merely augment the overall system, but may force the alteration or abandonment of parts of it—either because the observational belief is directly inconsistent with one or more other beliefs in the system or because such alteration will enhance the overall coherence of the system. (Of course the observational belief could itself be rejected for a similar reason, though if this is done very often the law which specifies the degree of reliability of that sort of observational belief will also have to be revised.) In this way, the CTEK provides an account of how a system of beliefs can be tested against the results of observation.[25]

Thus the CTEK clearly allows for the *possibility* of input from the world into the cognitive system, a possibility which is in fact realized in our cognitive system. But does it not also admit the possibility of empirical knowledge without such input? Suppose that a cognitive system either fails to attribute reliability to any observational beliefs at all, or else fails to attribute reliability to those introspective beliefs which are needed for the reliable recognition of other reliable observational beliefs. Such a state of affairs might be built into the system from the outset, or might result gradually from repeated revision of the system if conflicts between putative observations and other component beliefs were always adjudicated by rejecting the observation. Clearly such a system would fail to have any effective input from the world. And yet on the account of the CTEK given so far, it seems that such a system (or rather the contingent part thereof) might constitute empirical knowledge if only it were sufficiently coherent. And surely this is an absurd result.

This point is essentially sound. Any adequate account of empirical knowledge must *require*, not merely allow, input from the world into the cognitive system—for without such input any agreement between the system and the world would be purely fortuitous, and thus the beliefs of the system would not be knowledge. Thus the CTEK must require that for a cognitive system to be even a candidate for the status of empirical knowledge, it must include laws attributing a high degree of reliability to a reasonable variety of kinds of cognitively spontaneous beliefs, including those kinds of introspective beliefs which are required for the recognition of other sorts of reliable cognitively spontaneous beliefs. Call this "the observation requirement." It provides the basic answer to objection (II).[26]

It is important to understand clearly the status of this requirement within the CTEK. The need for the requirement is *a priori*: it is an *a priori* truth, according to the CTEK, that a cognitive system must attribute reliability to cognitively spontaneous beliefs to the degree indicated *if* it is to contain empirical knowledge. But it is *not* an *a priori* truth that the antecedent of this conditional is satisfied and hence also not an *a priori* truth that its consequent must be satisfied. Whether any cognitively spontaneous beliefs are in fact reliable is an empirical issue to be decided within the cognitive system purely on the basis of coherence. It is logically conceivable, according to the CTEK, that no variety of cognitively spontaneous belief is sufficiently reliable and hence that any system satisfying the observation requirement would become incoherent in the long run, so that coherence could be preserved only by denying reliability to enough cognitively spontaneous beliefs to violate the observation requirement. The observation requirement does *not* say that such a result must be incorrect, but only that if it were correct there would be no empirical knowledge.

Thus the observation requirement functions within the CTEK as a regulative meta-principle of epistemological assessment. It does not impinge directly on the operations of the coherence machinery, but rather provides a partial basis for categorizing the results of that process. This is the main difference between the CTEK and that very weak version of weak foundationism which would attribute initial credibility to all cognitively spontaneous beliefs and then require the preservation of a reasonably high proportion of them. For such a version of foundationism, it is true *prior* to the workings of coherence that cognitively spontaneous beliefs have this minimal degree of credibility—for which no empirical justification is thus ever offered. Whereas for the CTEK *all* epistemic warrant for empirical propositions is ultimately a matter of coherence.[27]

What then is the status of those contingent and seemingly empirical beliefs which appear within a cognitive system that violates the observation requirement? I would suggest that their status is quite analogous to, if not indeed identical with, that of imaginative or fictional accounts. It is a consequence of the holism advocated by the CTEK that the distinction between the category of empirical description and these other categories is not to be drawn with respect to particular beliefs but only with regard to systems of beliefs. And the empirical thrust of a cognitive system is precisely the implicit claim that its component beliefs will agree, in general at least, with those classes of cognitively spontaneous beliefs which it holds to be reliable. Thus the observation requirement might be viewed as a weak analogue of the old positivist verifiability criterion of empirical meaningfulness, now transposed so as to apply to systems rather than to individual statements.

The answer to objection (I), the alternative coherent systems objection, is already implicit in the foregoing discussion. For once it is clear that the CTEK involves the possibility that a system which is coherent at one time may be rendered incoherent by subsequent observational input, and once the requirement is accepted that any putative system of empirical knowledge must allow for this possibility, objection (I) in effect divides into two parts. Part one is the claim that *at a given moment* there may be many equally coherent empirical systems among which the CTEK provides no basis for decision. This claim is correct, but does not provide any basis for a serious objection, since the same thing will be true for any theory of knowledge imaginable. The important issue is whether these equally coherent systems will remain equally coherent and still distinct under the impact of observation in the long run.[28] Thus the second and crucial part of objection (I) will be the claim that even in the long run, and with the continuing impact of observation, there will be multiple, equally coherent empirical systems among which it will not be possible to decide. But, once the role of observation in the CTEK is appreciated, there seems little if any reason to accept this claim. The role of observation undercuts the idea that such alternatives can be simply constructed at will: such systems might be coherent at the beginning, but there is no reason to think that they would remain so as observations accumulate. This point is obvious enough if the observational components of the different systems involve the same concepts. But even if the observational components, or even the entire systems, involve different concepts so that they are not directly commensurable, there is no reason to think that one objective world will go on providing coherent input to incompatible systems in the long run.[29]

This brings us to objection (III), surely the most penetrating and significant of the three. Objection (III) contends that the CTEK will be unable to establish the vital connection between justification and truth, will be unable to show that its account of justification is truth-conducive, unless it also adopts the coherence theory of *truth*. It is certainly correct that a connection of this sort must be established by any adequate epistemology, even though this issue is rarely dealt with in a fully explicit fashion. Truth is after all the *raison d'etre* of the cognitive enterprise. The only possible ultimate warrant for an account of epistemic justification must therefore consist in showing that accepting such an account and seeking beliefs which are in accord with it is likely to yield the truth or at least more likely than would be the case on any alternative account. And the objection is also right that one who adopts a coherence theory of justification is in danger of being driven dialectically to espouse the coherence theory of truth as well. For the easiest and most straightforward way to establish a connection between a coherence account of justification and truth itself is to simply identify truth with justification-in-the-long-run, i.e. with coherence-in-the-long-run. Essentially this move was made by the absolute idealists and, in a different way, by Peirce. I assume here that such a coherence theory of truth is mistaken, that truth is to be understood at least roughly along the lines of the traditional correspondence theory. But if this is right, then the only way finally to justify the CTEK and answer objection (III) is to provide an argument to show that following the epistemic standards set by the CTEK is, in the long run, *likely* at least to lead to correspondence.[30]

I believe that it is possible to give such an argument, though I cannot undertake to provide a detailed account of it here. The main difficulty is an extrinsic one: no one has succeeded so far in giving an adequate account of the correspondence theory of truth,[31] and such an account is an indispensable ingredient of the envisaged argument. It is possible, however, to provide a rough sketch of the way in which the argument would go, given a very rough and intuitive conception of the correspondence theory: a proposition is true if it accords with an actual situation in the world, and otherwise false. (The argument is relative to the assumption that the observation requirement can be satisfied; if there were no possibility of reliable input from the world, then no set of epistemic standards would be likely to yield the truth.)

Suppose then that we have a hypothetical cognitive system which is coherent and satisfies the observation requirement as stipulated above, but fails to accord with reality. Our task is to show that such a system is unlikely to *remain* coherent (and continue to satisfy the observation requirement) unless it is revised in the direction of greater accord with reality. The way in which such revision *might* take place is obvious enough. If the lack of accord between the system and reality involves observable matters, then if the appropriate observations are actually made, they will produce inconsistency or incoherence within the system and force its revision. If the observations themselves are not rejected by such a revision, then the effect is to bring the system more into accord with reality. And this process *might* be repeated over and over until complete accord with reality is achieved in the very long run.

This, as I say, is what *might* happen. But is it *likely* to happen? The best way to show that it is likely to happen is to consider in turn each of the various seemingly plausible ways in which it might fail to happen, despite the lack of accord between system and reality stipulated above, and show that these are all *un*likely.

First. The process described above, whereby the system is revised in the direction of greater accord with the world, depends essentially on the occurrence of observational beliefs which conflict with other parts of the system and thus force the revision of the system. But any such revision involves a choice as to which of the conflicting beliefs to retain, and the system will come to accord more closely with reality only if this choice results in the retention of the observational beliefs and the exclusion of their competitors. Thus the most obvious way in which such revision in the direction of truth might fail to occur is that the choice be made consistently in favor of the non-observational beliefs in question, rejecting the observational beliefs. In the short run, it is quite likely that such a revision would produce a more justified result than would the alternative choice in favor of observation. But this could not happen in the long run. For if an inquirer or community of inquirers were to follow in the long run such a policy, deliberate or not, of resolving most such decisions in favor of the antecedent system and against the observational belief, this would inevitably have the effect of undermining the law that such observations are reliable and thus eventually violating the observation requirement. Thus this first possibility may be ruled out.

Second. Another way in which the envisaged revision in favor of truth might fail to take place is that, although the situations in the world which conflicted with the system were in fact observable, it might be the case that the inquirer or inquirers in question were simply never in the proper position to make the requisite observations, and so the conflict between the system and world would never be discovered. This possibility cannot be completely ruled out. But the longer the period of inquiry in question becomes, the more unlikely it is that this situation would continue, and this unlikelihood is increased as the supposed discrepancy between system and world is made larger.

Third. So far the assumption has been that the lack of accord between system and world involves aspects of the world which are observable. But suppose that this is not the case, that the aspects of the world in question are unobservable. There are various ways in which this might be so. First, and most basically, it might be the case that the aspects in question simply had no causal effects which were detectable by the sense organs or sensitive faculties of our community of inquirers, so that there would be no way that such inquirers could learn to observe those aspects. Second, it might be the case that, although the aspects in question did have causal impact on our inquirers, these inquirers simply had not learned to make observations of the appropriate sort. Third, it might be the case that although the aspects in question were in principle observable by our inquirers, there were barriers of some sort which prevented them from actually making the observations. Such barriers would include distance in space or time, impossibly hostile environments of various sorts, etc.

This sort of situation must be acknowledged as possible and even likely. The question is whether it could be overcome, given only the resources allowed by the CTEK, and if so, how likely it is that such an overcoming would occur.[32] The answer to the first part of the question is that it *could* be overcome, in either of two ways. In the first place, the unobservability of the aspects of the world in question might be overcome: the barriers might be transcended, the inquirers might learn to make the requisite observations, and/or new instruments might be developed which would create an appropriate causal linkage between these aspects and the sense organs of our observers. (See the remarks about instrumental observation at the end of Section III.) All of these things could happen, but there is no way to show that they are likely to happen in general. Thus the more important way in which the situation of unobservability might be overcome is by the development of *theories* concerning the unobservable aspects of the world. It is via theory construction that we come to know about the unobservable aspects of the world.

But is there any reason to think that such theory construction is likely to take place? The only possible answer on behalf of the CTEK, as indeed on behalf of any theory of knowledge, is that if enough aspects of the world are observable and if the unobservable aspects of the world have enough causal impact on the observable ones, then a fully coherent account of the observable aspects will in the long run lead to theories about the unobservable aspects. The main consideration here is that coherence essentially involves both prediction and explanation. An account of the observable world which was unable to predict and explain the observable effects of unobservable entities and processes would be to that extent incoherent. Thus to suppose that an ideally coherent account could be given of the observable aspects without any mention of the unobservable aspects would be in effect to suppose both that the world divides into two parts with no significant causal interaction between the two, and that this division coincides with that between the observable and the unobservable. And this is surely unlikely, even if one does not bring in the fact that the observable/unobservable line is not fixed once and for all.[33]

Fourth. There is one other apparently possible way to be considered in which there could be a lack of accord between one's cognitive system and reality without revision in the direction of truth being likely to take place. This alleged possibility is difficult to make fully clear, but it goes at least roughly as follows. Suppose that the conceptual picture which is given by the cognitive system, though failing to accord with the world, is isomorphic with it in the following way: for each kind of thing K, property of things P, etc., in the world there is a corresponding but distinct kind of think K^*, property of things P^*, etc., in the conceptual picture, and analogously for other kinds, properties, and whatever other categories of things are found in the world. The observational dispositions of the community of inquirers are such that they have observational beliefs about K^*'s when what they are actually observing is K's, etc. Under these conditions, the conceptual picture of the world would be fully coherent and would be in no danger of being rendered incoherent by observations, and yet *ex hypothesi* it would fail to accord with the world.[34]

Notice, however, that for this situation to occur, the laws, conceptual connections, etc., which pertain to the conceptually depicted kinds, properties, etc., must exactly mirror those which pertain to the actual kinds, properties, etc., of the world. If it is a true law in the world that instances of K_1 are always accompanied by instances of K_2, then it must be a law in the conceptual depiction that instances of K_1^* are always accompanied by instances of K_2^*, etc. For any discrepancy in such inferential patterns between the conceptual depiction and the world would be a basis for a potential conflicting observation. But despite this exact mirroring of all inferential patterns, it must still be the case that the kinds, properties, etc., of the world are not identical with those of the system. Thus one possible response by a proponent of the CTEK would be simply the denial that this sort of situation is indeed possible, on the grounds that the associated inferential patterns determine the kinds, properties, etc., completely, so that if these are the same there is no room left for a difference between the conceptually depicted world and the actual world. I think that there is merit in this claim, but a defense of it is impossible here.[35] In any case, it will suffice for present purposes merely to make the weaker claim that this sort of situation in which the inference patterns match but the kinds, etc., are still different is very unlikely, i.e. that the fact that one set of inference patterns mirror the other is a very good reason for supposing that the kinds, etc., are identical.

The foregoing considerations are an attempt to make plausible the following conclusion: it is highly unlikely, though not impossible, that a cognitive system which failed to accord with the world and which satisfied the observation requirement would be coherent and remain coherent under the impact of new observation, unless it was gradually revised in the direction of greater accord with the world. This is so because all of the apparent ways in which such revision could fail to take place represent highly unlikely situations.[36] This is obviously only a sketch of a line of argument which would have to be greatly elaborated in various ways to be really adequate. Here it is intended only to suggest the sort of answer which the CTEK can make to objection (III), how it can establish the truth-conduciveness of its view of justification, without resorting to the desperate expedient of the coherence theory of truth.

Thus the standard objections to views like the CTEK turn out to be in fact far less conclusive than has usually been thought, and it is reasonable to suppose that they can be successfully answered, once the role of observation in the theory is fully understood and appreciated. This in turn suggests that views like the CTEK are potentially viable accounts of empirical knowledge, worthy of far more serious attention than they have usually been given.[37]

NOTES

[1]   Roderick Firth, "Coherence, Certainty, and Epistemic Priority," *Journal of Philosophy* LXI (1964); reprinted in R. M. Chisholm and Robert Swartz (eds.), *Empirical Knowledge*, (Englewood Cliffs, N. J., Prentice-Hall, 1973), p. 459.

[2]   Firth, pp. 460, 463.

[3]   Whether or not the view presented here is an entirely *pure* coherence theory is mainly an issue of taxonomy. As will be seen, it does *not* hold that the only factor which determines the acceptability of a set of propositions as putative empirical knowledge is its internal coherence. It does claim, however, that the epistemic justification attaching to an empirical proposition always derives entirely from considerations of coherence—and thus is never immediate or intrinsic, as the foundationist claims. See pp. 194–195 and fn. 27.

[4]   That this cannot be a complete conception of knowledge is evident from the work of Gettier and those who have followed his lead. See Edmund Gettier, "Is Justified True Belief Knowledge?" *Analysis* XXIII (1963), pp. 121–123. But none of this literature has seriously challenged the view that the traditional conditions are at least *necessary* for knowledge, and that is enough to generate the problem to be discussed here.

[5]   The notion of an argument is to be taken very broadly here. Any sort of inferential relation between a belief (or set of beliefs) A and a further belief B which allows B to be justified relative to a justified acceptance of A will provide a basis for a justifying argument.

[6]   Notice that the important regress here is *logical* or *epistemic*, rather than *temporal*, in character. If it were a requirement for a belief to be justified that the justifying argument be explicitly given (perhaps only in thought) by the person in question, then clearly there would be a vicious temporal regress of justification in which no stopping place was ever reached (so long as all justification is inferential). But there is no reason to assume in this way that an explicit process of justification must actually take place before a belief is justified. It is enough, it would seem, that there be a justification which could be supplied if demanded and which in fact is the reason for the holding of the belief; but this need not be made explicit (to others or even to oneself) until and unless the issue is raised.

[7] The restriction to empirical knowledge is to be understood throughout the discussion of this paper, even where not made explicit. In particular, it is clear that a coherence theory of *a priori* knowledge would be hopeless, since at least some *a priori* inferential connections must be presupposed by any account of coherence.

[8] On the distinction between infallibility, indubitability, and incorrigibility, see William Alston, "Varieties of Privileged Access," *American Philosophical Quarterly* VIII (1971), 223–41.

[9] For Lewis's view, see his *Analysis of Knowledge and Valuation* (La Salle, Ill., Open Court, 1946), Chapters II, VII. An appeal to language-learning is made by Quinton in his paper "The Foundations of Knowledge," reprinted in Chisholm and Swartz. An example of the view that the issue of justification does not arise is J. L. Austin, *Sense and Sensibilia* (Oxford, Oxford University Press, 1962). These are only examples of two positions which are widely held.

[10] The clearest specimen of this idealist view is Brand Blanshard, *The Nature of Thought* (London, Allen & Unwin, 1939). See also F. H. Bradley, *Essays on Truth and Reality* (Oxford, Oxford University Press, 1914); and Bernard Bosanquet, *Implication and Linear Inference* (London, Macmillan, 1920). For the positivists, see Otto Neurath, "Protocol Sentences," translated in A. J. Ayer (ed.) *Logical Positivism* (New York, The Free Press, 1959), pp. 199–208; and Carl G. Hempel, "On the Logical Positivists' Theory of Truth," *Analysis* II (1934–35), 49–59. The Hempel paper is in part a reply to a foundationist critique of Neurath by Schlick in "The Foundation of Knowledge," also translated in *Logical Positivism*, pp. 209–227. Schlick replied to Hempel in "Facts and Propositions," and Hempel responded in "Some Remarks on 'Facts' and Propositions," both in *Analysis* II (1934–35), 65–70 and 93–96, respectively.

[11] See W. V. O. Quine, "Two Dogmas of Empiricism," in his *From a Logical Point of View* (Cambridge, Mass., Harvard University Press, 1953); also his *Word and Object* (New York, John Wiley & Sons, 1960), Chapter I; and Gilbert Harman, "Quine on Meaning and Existence II," *Review of Metaphysics* XXI (1967–68), 343–67. Sellars's writings on this subject are voluminous, but the most important are: "Empiricism and the Philosophy of Mind" (especially Section VIII) and "Some Reflections on Language Games," both reprinted in his *Science, Perception and Reality* (London, Routledge & Kegan Paul, 1963); "Givenness and Explanatory Coherence," *Journal of Philosophy* LXX (1973), 612–24; and "The Structure of Knowledge," his unpublished Machette Lectures, given at the University of Texas in the spring of 1971, especially Part 3, "Epistemic Principles." The view offered in this paper is closest to Sellars's and is, at certain points, strongly influenced by it, though I am very unsure how much of it Sellars would agree with. Others who have advocated somewhat similar views include Hall, Aune, Harman, and Lehrer. For Hall's view see his *Our Knowledge of Fact and Value* (Chapel Hill, University of North Carolina Press, 1961). Aune's views are to be found in his book *Knowledge, Mind, and Nature* (New York, Random House, 1967). For Harman, see his book *Thought* (Princeton, Princeton University Press, 1973). For Lehrer, see his *Knowledge* (Oxford, Oxford University Press, 1974).

[12] See Bertrand Russell, *Human Knowledge* (New York, Simon & Schuster, 1949), Part II, Chapter II, and Part V, Chapters 6 and 7; Nelson Goodman, "Sense and Certainty," *Philosophical Review* LXI (1952), 160–67; Israel Scheffler, *Science and Subjectivity* (New York, Bobbs-Merrill, 1967), Chapter 5; and Nicholas Rescher, *The Coherence Theory of Truth* (Oxford, Oxford University Press, 1973). Despite the title, Rescher's position in the book just

cited is not a version of the CTEK and still less of a coherence theory of truth. In a later book, *Methodological Pragmatism* (forthcoming from Basil Blackwell), Rescher seems to waver between a version of the CTEK and a version of weak foundationism. See my critical study, "Rescher's Idealistic Pragmatism," forthcoming from the *Review of Metaphysics*. Firth, in the paper cited in note 1, also opts, rather tentatively, for a version of weak foundationism.

[13]   Of course some of the justifying premises might be *a priori* in character. But the CTEK denies that this is ever the case for *all* of the premises which would be necessary to justify an empirical belief.

[14]   The original critique of the linear account of inference was by Bosanquet in *Implication and Linear Inference*. A more recent version is offered by Rescher in "Foundationalism, Coherentism, and the Idea of Cognitive Systematization," *Journal of Philosophy* LXXI (1974), 695–708. Harman's account of inference in *Thought* is in many ways a modernized version of Bosanquet.

[15]   A useful, though preliminary, account is contained in Hall, *op. cit.* See also Harman, *op. cit.*, and Lehrer, *op. cit.*, for further useful discussion.

[16]   Thus Lewis calls it "congruence" and Chisholm calls it "concurrence." See Lewis, *op. cit.*, Chapter 11, and Chisholm, *Theory of Knowledge* (Englewood Cliffs, N. J., Prentice-Hall, 1965), Chapter 3.

[17]   This point might seem too obvious to be worth making, but it has occasionally been overlooked, e.g. by Scheffler, *op. cit.*, Chapter 5. And Rescher's very idiosyncratic account of coherence in *The Coherence Theory of Truth* in effect is based only on consistency.

[18]   It is difficult to provide an exact gloss for the phrase "currently available alternative." The rough idea is that the currently available alternatives are those which would be considered by a reasonably careful and reflective inquirer. They do not include all of the theoretically possible alternative systems which might ideally be constructed; this would place justification as well as truth beyond our ken, since we could never in fact consider and certainly could never know that we had considered all such alternatives. On the other hand, the set of currently available alternatives may well include more than have actually occurred to a given inquirer or community of inquirers; there is an implicit epistemic obligation to seek out such alternatives.

[19]   I take this to be an instance of what Sellars calls "trans-level inference." See, e.g., *Science, Perception, and Reality*, p. 88.

[20]   The relevant conditions here need not be the same as for the other sort of reliability and indeed normally will not be.

[21]   Here I am expanding on some suggestive remarks of Sellars in "Givenness and Explanatory Coherence."

[22]   The reason for doubting that the regress is vicious is that in this special instance it seems possible to give the whole infinite series of arguments in a finite way. Thus premises (ii) and (iii) seem to be invariant for all the arguments in the series, and the various premises (i) can be recursively specified, since each is simply premise (i) of the previous argument with one more occurrence of the belief operator prefixed; thus the whole series of arguments can be recursively specified. Moreover, it might be argued on this basis that one who gives explicitly the first argument in the series thereby tacitly gives, or at least commits himself to, all the others: he has

asserted in the invariant premises (ii) and (iii), and by asserting the first premise (i), he commits himself to all the other premises (i) by the principle of epistemic logic whose violation yields "Moore's paradox." Thus the main objection to construing the justification of introspection as involving this infinite hierarchy of arguments is not simply that it is infinite, but rather that it is highly questionable that people do in fact believe, even dispositionally, the infinite set of first premises. And if this is so, then the series of arguments cannot be taken as an account of how introspective beliefs are in fact justified, even though it is possibly acceptable as an account of how they *could* be justified. If, on the other hand, one finds it plausible, as does e.g. Lehrer *(op. cit.*, p. 229), to hold that anyone who believes that *P* also believes that he believes that *P*, then it becomes plausible to hold that the infinite series of first premises is believed whenever the first one is. In this case the infinite series of arguments would represent a possible alternative to the account of the justification of introspection given in the text.

23   It might be thought that the justification of an introspective belief using premise (*) would still require the additional premise that the person indeed has the introspective belief in question—which would suffice to generate a regress. There is no doubt that the thesis that the person has the introspective belief in question figures in the justification. I would argue, however, that it does not figure as a *premise*, which would then require further justification, because the existence of that belief is *presupposed* by the very raising of the issue of justification in the first place.

24   Of course such beliefs will still, in the normal case, be *causally* dependent on normal sensory processes. My point is that the trained scientist, unlike the novice, need not *first* have an ordinary observational belief about the state of the instrument and *then* infer to the theoretical belief; instead the latter belief may itself be arrived at non-inferentially.

25   A complete account here would have to discuss intentional action and how it relates to one's cognitive system, since such action is obviously needed in most cases in order to put oneself in the correct position to make a relevant observation. I shall neglect this additional topic here. For some useful discussion see Sellars, "Some Reflections on Language Games."

26   The observation requirement, as stated, may seem too weak. It may be thought that at least two further requirements should be added: (a) that each of the kinds of cognitively spontaneous beliefs in question result from a unique causal process; and (b) that the various causal processes in question actually produce reliable beliefs. These additional requirements are indeed part of the notion of observation as set forth above. But they need not be made a part of this requirement, because failure to satisfy them will make it extremely unlikely that a cognitive system will both remain coherent and continue to satisfy the observation requirement as stated, in the long run. (A point worth adding is that the ability to have epistemically reliable cognitively spontaneous beliefs is presumably acquired via training, linguistic or otherwise, since it presupposes the grasp of a conceptual system. Such training, however, though presumably a causally necessary condition for the satisfaction of the observation requirement, is not a part of it.)

The observation requirement should also be understood to include the requirement, common to all adequate theories of knowledge, that a user of the system must make a reasonable attempt to seek out relevant observations if his results are to be justified.

[27]   It may still be questioned whether the CTEK, even if not a version of foundationism, is truly a *pure* coherence theory. Would it not be a purer coherence view to say simply that the most coherent system is justified, without adding the observation requirement? But although such a view would superficially involve a purer appeal to coherence at the empirical level, it would—if the claim that input from the world is an *a priori* requirement for empirical knowledge is correct—be *a priori* mistaken, and thus incoherent at the meta-epistemic level of epistemological reflection. Thus the CTEK seems to be as pure a coherence theory as is defensible.

[28]   I assume here, without discussion, that one can make sense of the notion of identity through change for cognitive systems.

[29]   This point is elaborated from a slightly different perspective in the discussion of truth and objection (III) which follows.

[30]   For an argument that this cannot be done, and hence that the CTEK cannot avoid a coherence theory of truth, see Blanshard, *op. cit.*, Chapters 25–26.

[31]   Sellars's writings on truth, if I read him right, are an attempt to provide such an account of truth from an epistemological perspective which is similar to that offered here. See "Truth and 'Correspondence'," reprinted in *Science, Perception and Reality*; and also his *Science and Metaphysics* (London, Routledge & Kegan Paul, 1968), Chapter V. See also my "Sellars on Truth and Picturing," *International Philosophical Quarterly* XIII (1973), 243–65.

[32]   Notice, however, that exactly the same problem will afflict any foundation theory whose basic (or initially credible) beliefs are limited to those which can count as observational for the CTEK. Since the category of basic beliefs is usually more, rather than less, restricted than this, this will mean virtually all foundation theories. And since foundation theories have no appeal at this point other than coherence, they will be able to solve this problem only if a solution is also available to the CTEK.

[33]   For a suggestive account of the rationale of theory construction in this spirit, see Sellars, "The Language of Theories," in *Science, Perception, and Reality*.

[34]   This argument was suggested to me by Richard Diaz.

[35]   Sellars's views on meaning would provide a basis for such an argument. See especially his "Inference and Meaning," *Mind* LXII (1953), 313–38. On Sellars's account the coherence account of justification thus rests on a coherence theory of meaning.

[36]   There are of course other logically possible ways in which a lack of accord could exist between a cognitive system and reality without observation operating to correct the system in the ways suggested. The assumption operative here and in the earlier discussion of objection (I) is that a mechanism for producing cognitively spontaneous beliefs is unlikely to yield coherent results in the long run unless it genuinely reflects objective reality. It is certainly not necessary that this be so: coherent results might conceivably be produced by hallucination, by a Cartesian demon, or even by pure chance. The claim here is only that all of these things are unlikely to happen, that each would represent an improbable coincidence relative to the envisaged situation.

[37]   Extremely helpful comments on an earlier version of this paper were offered by my colleagues Hardy Jones and Martin Perlmutter.

1.4

THE FOUNDATIONALISM-COHERENTISM CONTROVERSY: HARDENED STEREOTYPES AND OVERLAPPING THEORIES

Robert Audi

Foundationalism and coherentism each contain significant epistemological truths.[1] Both positions are, moreover, intellectually influential even outside epistemology. But most philosophers defending either position have been mainly concerned to argue for their view and to demolish the other, which they have often interpreted through just one leading proponent. It is not surprising, then, that philosophers in each tradition often feel misunderstood by those in the other. The lack of clarity—and unwarranted stereotyping—about both foundationalism and coherentism go beyond what one would expect from terminological and philosophical diversity: there are genuine obscurities and misconceptions. Because both positions, and especially foundationalism, are responses to the epistemic regress problem, I want to start with that. Once it is seen that this perennial conundrum can take two quite different forms, both foundationalism and coherentism can be better understood.

I. Two Conceptions of the Epistemic Regress Problem

It is widely agreed that the epistemic regress argument gives crucial support to foundationalism. Even coherentists, who reject the argument, grant that the regress problem which generates it is important in motivating their views.[2] There are at least two major contexts—often not distinguished—in which the regress problem arises. Central to one is pursuit of the question of how one knows or is justified in believing some particular thing, most typically a proposition about the external world, e.g. that one saw a bear in the woods.

This context is often colored by conceiving such questions as skeptical challenges, and this is the conception of them most important for our purposes. The challenges are often spearheaded by "How do you know?" Central to the other main context in which the regress problem arises are questions about what *grounds* knowledge or justification, or a belief taken to be justified or to constitute knowledge, where there is no skeptical purpose, or at least no philosophically skeptical one. Other terms may be used in framing these questions. People interested in such grounds may, for instance, want to know the source, basis, reasons, evidence, or rationale for a belief. We must consider the regress problem raised in both ways. I begin with the former.

Suppose I am asked how I know that p, say that there are books in my study. The skeptic, for instance, issues the question as a challenge. I might reply by citing a ground of the belief in question, say q: I have a clear recollection of books in my study. The skeptic then challenges the apparent presupposition that I know the ground to hold; after all, if I do have a ground, it seems natural to think that I should be able (at least on reflection) not just to produce it, but also to justify it: how else can I be entitled to take it as a ground? Thus, if "How do you know?" is motivated by a skeptical interest in knowledge, the question of how I know is likely to be reiterated, at least if my ground, q, is not self-evident; for unless q is self-evident, and in that sense a self-certifying basis for p, the questioner—particularly if skeptical—will accept my citing q as answering "How do you know that p?", only on the assumption that I *also* know that q. How far can this questioning reasonably go?

For epistemologists, the problem posed by "How do you know?" and "What justifies you?" is to answer such questions without making one or another apparently inevitable move that ultimately undermines the possibility of knowledge or even of justification. Initially, there seem to be three unpleasant options. The first is to rotate regressively in a vicious circle, say from p to q as a ground for p, then to r as a ground for q, and then back to p as a ground for r. The second option is to fall into a vicious regress: from p to q as a ground for p, then to r as a ground for q, then to s as a ground for r, and so on to infinity. The third option is to stop at a purported ground, say s, that does not constitute knowledge or even justified belief; but the trouble with this is that if one neither knows nor justifiedly believes s, it is at best difficult to see how citing s can answer the question of how one knows that p. The fourth option is to stop with something that is known or justifiedly believed, say r, but *not* known on the basis of any further knowledge or justified belief. Here the problem as many see it is that r, not being believed on any further ground, serves as just an arbitrary way of stopping the regress and is only capriciously taken to be known or justifiably believed. Thus, *citing r* as a final answer to the chain of queries seems dogmatic. I want to call this difficulty—how to answer, dialectically, questions about how one knows, or about what justifies one—the *dialectical form of the regress problem.*[3]

Imagine, by contrast, that we consider either the entire body of a person's apparent knowledge, as Aristotle seems to have done,[4] or a representative item of apparent knowledge, say my belief that there are books in my study, and ask on what this apparent knowledge is grounded (or based) and whether, if it is grounded on some further belief, *all* our knowledge or justified belief could be so grounded. We are now asking a structural question about knowledge, not requesting a verbal response in defense of a claim to it. No dialectic need even be imagined; we are considering a person's overall knowledge, or some presumably representative item of it, and asking how that body of knowledge is structured or how that item of knowledge is grounded. Again we get a regress problem: how to specify one's grounds without vicious circularity or regress or, on the other hand, stopping with a belief that does not constitute knowledge (or is not justified) or seems only capriciously regarded as knowledge. Call this search for appropriate grounds of knowledge the *structural form of the regress problem.*

To see how the two forms of the regress problem differ, we can think of them as arising from different ways of asking "How do you know?" It can be asked with *skeptical force*, as a challenge to people who either claim to know something or (more commonly) presuppose that some belief they confidently hold represents knowledge. Here the question is roughly equivalent to "Show me that you know." It can also be asked with *informational force*, as where someone simply wants to know by what route, such as observation or testimony, one came to know something. Here the question is roughly equivalent to "How is it that you know?" The skeptical form of the question does *not* presuppose that the person in question really has any knowledge, and, asked in this non-committal way, the question tends to generate the dialectical form of the regress. The informational form of the question typically *does* presuppose that the person knows the proposition in question. It is easy to assume that it does not matter in which way we formulate the problem. But it does matter, for at least four reasons.

Knowing versus showing that one knows. First, the dialectical form of the regress problem invites us to think that an adequate answer to "How do you know?" *shows* that we know. This is so particularly in the context of a concern to reply to skepticism. For the skeptic is not interested in the information most commonly sought when people ask how someone knows, say information about the origin of the belief, e.g. in first-hand observation as opposed to testimony. It is, however, far from clear that an adequate answer to the how-question must be an adequate answer to the show-question. If I tell you how I know there were injuries in the accident by citing the testimony of a credible witness who saw it, you may be satisfied; but I have not shown that I know (as I might by taking you to the scene), and the skeptic who, with the force of a challenge, asks how I know will not be satisfied. I have answered the informational form of the question, but not the skeptical form.

First-order versus second-order knowledge. Second, when the regress problem is dialectically formulated, any full non-skeptical answer to "How do you know that *p*?" will tend to imply an epistemic self-ascription, say "I know that *q*"; thus, my answer is admissible only if I both have the concept of knowledge—since I would otherwise not understand what I am attributing to myself—*and* am at least dialectically warranted in asserting that I do know that *q*. If you ask, informationally, how I know that there were injuries, I simply say (for instance) that I heard it from Janet, who saw them. But if you ask, skeptically, how I know it, I will realize that you will not accept evidence I merely *have*, but only evidence I *know*; and I will thus tend to say something to the effect that I *know* that Janet saw the injuries. Since this in effect claims knowledge of knowledge, it succeeds only if I meet the second-order standard for having knowledge that I know she saw this. If, however, the regress problem is structurally formulated, it is sufficient for its solution that there *be* propositions which, whether or not I believe them *prior* to being questioned, are both warranted for me (reasonable for me *to* believe) and together justify the proposition originally in question. For this to be true of me, I need only meet a first-order standard, e.g. by remembering the accident, and thereby be justified in believing that there were injuries.

Having, giving, and showing a solution. Third, and largely implicit in the first two points, the two formulations of the regress problem differ as to what must hold in order for there to *be*, and for *S* to *give*, an adequate answer to "How do you know?" or "What justifies you?" On the structural formulation, if there *are* warranted propositions of the kind just described, as where I am warranted in believing that there were injuries, the problem (as applied to *p*, the proposition in question) *has* a solution; and if I *cite* them in answering "How do you know that *p*?" I *give* a solution to the problem. The problem has a solution because of the mere existence of propositions warranted for me; and the solution is given, and the problem thus actually solved, by my simply affirming those propositions in answering "How do you know?" By contrast, when the problem is dialectically formulated, it is taken to have a solution only if there not only *are* such propositions, but I can show by *argument* that there are; and to give a solution I must not merely cite these propositions but also show that they are justified and that they in turn justify *p*. Thus, I cannot adequately say how I know there are books in my study by citing my recollection of them unless I can show by argument that it is both warranted and justifies concluding that there are indeed books there. Raising the structural form of the problem presupposes only that if I know that *p*, I have grounds of this knowledge that are expressible in propositions warranted for me; it does not presuppose that I can formulate the grounds or show that they imply knowledge. The structural form thus encourages us to conceive solutions as *propositional,* in the sense that they depend on the evidential propositions warranted for me; the dialectical form encourages conceiving solutions, as *argumental,* because they depend on what *arguments* about the evidence are accessible to me. I must be able to enter the dialectic with good arguments for *p*, not simply to be warranted in believing evidence propositions that justify *p*.

The process of justification versus the property of justification. Fourth, a dialectical formulation, at least as applied to justification (and so, often, to knowledge as at least commonly embodying justification), tends to focus our attention on the *process* of justification, i.e., of justifying a proposition, though the initial question concerns whether the relevant belief has the *property* of justification, i.e., of being justified. The skeptical forms of the questions "How do you know?" and "What justifies you?" tend to start a process of argument; "Show me that you know" demands a response, and what is expected is a process of justifying the belief that *p*. The informational form of those questions tends to direct one to cite a ground, such as clear recollection, and the knowledge or (property of) justification in question may be simply taken to be based on this ground. "By what route (or on what basis) do you know?" need not start a process (though it may). It implies that providing a good ground—one in virtue of which the belief that *p* has the property of being justified—will fully answer the question. Granted, the epistemologist pursuing the regress problem in either form must use second-order formulations (though in different ways); still, the criteria for knowledge and justified belief tend to differ depending on which approach is dominant in determining those criteria.

If I am correct in thinking that the dialectical and structural formulations of the regress problem are significantly different, which of them is preferable in appraising the foundationalism–coherentism controversy? One consideration is neutrality; we should try to avoid bias toward any particular epistemological theory. The dialectical formulation, however, favors coherentism, or at least non-foundationalism. Let me explain.

Foundationalists typically posit beliefs that are grounded in experience or reason and are direct—and so not grounded through other, mediating beliefs—in two senses. First, they are *psychologically direct*: non-inferential (in the most common sense of that term), and thus not held on the basis of (hence through) some further belief. Second, they are *epistemically direct*: they do not depend (inferentially) for their status as knowledge, or for any justification they have, on other beliefs, justification, or knowledge. The first kind of direct belief has no psychological intermediary of the relevant kind, such as belief. The second kind has no evidential intermediary, such as knowledge of a premise for the belief in question. Roughly, epistemically direct beliefs are not inferentially *based on* other beliefs or knowledge, and this point holds whether or not there is any actual *process* of inference. Now imagine that, in dealing with the dialectical form of the regress problem, say in answering the question of how I know I have reading material for tonight, I cite, as an appropriate ground, my knowing that there are books in my study. In choosing this as an example of knowledge, I express a belief that I do in fact know that there are books in the study. But am I warranted in this *second-order* belief, as I appear to be warranted simply in believing that there *are* books in the study (the former belief is construed as second-order on the assumption that knowing entails believing, and the belief that one knows is thus in some sense a belief about another belief)? Clearly it is far less plausible to claim that my second-order belief that I *know* there are books in my study is epistemically direct than to claim this status for my *perceptual* belief that there *are* books in it; for the latter seems non-inferentially based on my seeing them, whereas the former seems inferential, e.g. based on beliefs about epistemic status. Thus, foundationalists are less likely to seem able to answer the dialectical formulation of the problem, since doing that requires positing direct second-order knowledge (or at least direct, second-order justified belief).

In short, the dialectical form of the problem seems to require foundationalists to posit foundations of a higher order, and a greater degree of complexity, than they are generally prepared to posit. The same point emerges if we note that "How do you know?" can be repeated, and in some fashion answered, indefinitely. Indeed, because this question (or a similar one) is central to the dialectical formulation, that formulation tends to be inimical to foundationalism, which posits at least one kind of natural place to stop the regress: a place at which, even if a skeptical challenge *can* be adequately answered, having an answer to it is not necessary for having knowledge or justified belief.

It might seem, on the other hand, that the structural formulation, which stresses our actual cognitive makeup, is inimical toward coherentism, or at least non-foundationalism. For given our knowledge of cognitive psychology it is difficult to see how a normal person might *have* anything approaching an infinite chain of beliefs constituting knowings; hence, an infinite chain of answers to "How do you know?" seems out of the question. But this only cuts against an infinite regress approach in epistemology, not against any finitistic coherentism, which seems the only kind ever plausibly defended. Indeed, even assuming—as coherentists may grant—that much of our knowledge in fact arises, non-inferentially, from experiential states like seeing, the structural formulation of the problem allows *both* that, as foundationalists typically claim, there is non-inferential knowledge, and that, as coherentists typically claim, non-inferential beliefs are dialectically defensible indefinitely and (when true) capable of constituting knowledge only by virtue of coherence. The structural formulation may not demand that such defenses be available indefinitely; but it also does not preclude this nor even limit the mode of defense to circular reasoning.

I believe, then, that the structural formulation is not significantly biased against coherentism. Nor is it biased in favor of internalism over externalism about justification, where internalism is roughly the view that what justifies a belief, such as a visual impression, is internal in the sense that one can become (in some way) aware of it through reflection or introspection (internal processes), and externalism denies that what justifies a belief is always accessible to one in this sense. The dialectical formulation, by contrast, tends to favor internalism, since it invites us to see the regress problem as solved in terms of what propositions warranted for one are *also* accessible to one in answering "How do you know that *p*?" If the structural formulation is biased against internalism or coherentism, I am not aware of good reasons to think so, and I will work with it here.

II. The Epistemic Regress Argument

If we formulate the regress problem structurally, then a natural way to state the famous epistemic regress argument is along these lines. First, suppose I have knowledge, even if only of something so simple as there being a patter outside my window. Could all my knowledge be inferential? Imagine that this is possible by virtue of an infinite epistemic regress—roughly, an infinite series of knowings, each based (inferentially) on the next. Just assume that a belief constituting inferential knowledge is based on knowledge of some other proposition, or at least on a further belief of another proposition; the further knowledge or belief might be based on knowledge of, or belief about, something still further, and so on. Call this sequence an *epistemic chain*; it is simply a chain of beliefs, with at least the first constituting knowledge, and each belief linked to the previous one by being based on it. A standard view is that there are just four kinds: an epistemic chain might be infinite or circular, hence in either case unending and in that sense regressive; third, it might terminate with a belief that is not knowledge; and fourth, it might terminate with a belief constituting direct knowledge. The epistemic regress problem is above all to assess these chains as possible sources (or at least carriers) of knowledge or justification.

The foundationalist response to the regress problem is to offer a regress argument favoring the fourth possibility as the only genuine one. The argument can be best formulated along these lines:

1. If one has any knowledge, it occurs in an epistemic chain (possibly including the special case of a single link, such as a perceptual or a priori belief, which constitutes knowledge by virtue of being anchored directly in experience or reason);
2. the only possible kinds of epistemic chains are the four mutually exclusive kinds just sketched;
3. knowledge can occur only in the last kind of chain; hence,
4. if one has any knowledge, one has some direct knowledge.[5]

Some preliminary clarification is in order before we appraise this argument.

First, the conclusion, being conditional, does not presuppose that there *is* any knowledge. This preserves the argument's neutrality with respect to skepticism, as is appropriate since the issue concerns *conceptual* requirements for the possession of knowledge. The argument would have existential import, and so would not be purely conceptual, if it presupposed that there *is* knowledge and hence that at least one knower exists. Second, I take (1) to imply that inferential knowledge depends on at least one epistemic chain for its status *as* knowledge. I thus take the argument to imply the further conclusion that any inferential knowledge one has exhibits (inferential) *epistemic dependence* on some appropriate inferential connection, via some epistemic chain, to some non-inferential knowledge one has. Thus, the argument would show not only that if there is inferential knowledge, there *is* non-inferential knowledge, but also that if there is inferential knowledge, that very knowledge is *traceable* to some non-inferential knowledge as its foundation.

The second point suggests a third. If two epistemic chains should *intersect*, as where a belief that *p* is both foundationally grounded in experience and part of a circular chain, then if the belief is knowledge, that knowledge *occurs in* only the former chain, though the knowledge qua *belief* belongs to both chains. Knowledge, then, does not occur in a chain merely because the belief constituting it does. Fourth, the argument concerns the structure, not the content, of a body of knowledge and of its constituent epistemic chains. The argument may thus be used regardless of what purported items of knowledge one applies it to in any particular person. The argument does not presuppose that in order to have knowledge, there are specific things one must believe, or that a body of knowledge must have some particular content.

A similar argument applies to justification. We simply speak of *justificatory chains* and proceed in a parallel way, substituting justification for knowledge. The conclusion would be that if there are any justified beliefs, there are some non-inferentially justified beliefs, and that if one has any inferentially justified belief, it exhibits (inferential) *justificatory dependence* on an epistemic chain appropriately linking it to some non-inferentially justified belief one has, that is, to a foundational belief. In discussing foundationalism, I shall often focus on justification.

Full-scale assessment of the regress argument is impossible here. I shall simply comment on some important aspects of it to provide a better understanding of foundationalism and of some major objections to it.

Appeal to infinite epistemic chains has seldom seemed to philosophers to be promising. Let me suggest one reason to doubt that human beings are even capable of having infinite sets of beliefs. Consider the claim that we can have an infinite set of arithmetical beliefs, say that 2 is twice 1, that 4 is twice 2, etc. Surely for a finite mind there will be some point or other at which the relevant proposition cannot be grasped. The required formulation (or entertaining of the proposition) would, on the way "toward" infinity, become too lengthy to permit understanding it. Thus, even if we could read or entertain it part by part, when we got to the end we would be unable to remember enough of the first part to grasp and thereby believe what the formulation expresses. Granted, we could believe that the formulation just read expresses *a* truth; but this is not sufficient for believing *the truth* that it expresses. That truth is a specific mathematical statement; believing, of a formulation we cannot even get before our minds, or remember, in toto, that it expresses *some* mathematical truth is not sufficient for believing, or even grasping, the true statement in question. Since we cannot understand the formulation as a whole, we cannot grasp that truth; and what we cannot grasp, we cannot believe. I doubt that any other lines of argument show that we can have infinite sets of beliefs; nor, if we can, is it clear how infinite epistemic chains could account for any of our knowledge. I thus propose to consider only the other kinds of chain.

The possibility of a circular epistemic chain as a basis of knowledge has been taken much more seriously. The standard objection has been that such circularity is vicious, because one would ultimately have to know something on the basis of itself—say *p* on the basis of *q*, *q* on the basis of *r*, and *r* on the basis of *p*. A standard reply has been that if the circle is wide enough and its content sufficiently rich and coherent, the circularity is innocuous. I bypass this difficult matter, since I believe that coherentism as most plausibly formulated does not depend on circular chains.

The third alternative, namely that an epistemic chain terminates in a belief which is not knowledge, has been at best rarely affirmed; and there is little plausibility in the hypothesis that knowledge can originate through a belief of a proposition *S* does not know. If there are exceptions, it is where, although I do not know that *p*, I am justified, to *some* extent, in believing that *p*, as in making a reasonable estimate that there are at least thirty books on a certain shelf. Here is a different case. Suppose it vaguely seems to me that I hear strains of music. If, on the basis of the resulting, somewhat justified belief that there is music playing, I believe that my daughter has come home, as she has, do I know this? The answer is not clear. But this apparent indeterminacy would not help anyone who claims that knowledge can arise from belief which does not constitute knowledge. For it is equally unclear, and for the same sort of reason, whether my belief that there is music playing is *sufficiently* reasonable—say, in terms of how good my perceptual grounds are—to give me knowledge that music is playing. The stronger our tendency to say that I know she is home, the stronger our inclination to say that I do after all know that there are strains of music in the air. Notice something else. In the only cases where the third kind of chain seems likely to ground knowledge (or justification), there is a degree—apparently a substantial degree—of justification. If there can be an epistemic chain which ends with belief that is not knowledge only because it ends, in this way, with justification, then we are apparently in the general vicinity of knowledge. We seem to be at most a few degrees of justification away. Knowledge is not emerging from nothing, as it were—the picture originally evoked by the third kind of epistemic chain—but from something characteristically much like it: justified true belief. There would thus be a foundation after all: not bedrock, but perhaps ground that is nonetheless firm enough to yield a foundation we can build upon.

The fourth possibility is that epistemic chains which originate with knowledge end in non-inferential knowledge: knowledge not inferentially based on further knowledge (or further justified belief). That knowledge, in turn, is apparently grounded in experience, say in my auditory impression of music or in my intuitive sense that if A is one mile from B, then B is one mile from A. This non-inferential grounding of my knowledge can explain how that knowledge is (epistemically) direct. It arises, non-inferentially—and so without any intermediary premise that must be known along the way—from (I shall assume) one of the four classical kinds of foundational material, namely, perception, memory, introspection, and reason.

Such direct grounding in experience also seems to explain why a belief so grounded may be expected to be *true*; for experience seems to connect the beliefs it grounds to the reality they are apparently about, in such a way that what is believed concerning that reality tends to be the case. For empirical beliefs at least, this point seems to explain best why we have those beliefs. Let me illustrate all this. Normally, when I know that there is music playing, it is just because I hear it, and not on the basis of some further belief of mine; hence, the chain grounding my knowledge that my daughter has come home is anchored in my auditory perception, which in turn reflects the musical reality represented by my knowledge that there is music playing. This reality explains both my perception and, by explaining that, indirectly explains my believing the proposition I know on the basis of this perception—that my daughter is home.

The non-inferentially grounded epistemic chains in question may differ in many ways. They differ *compositionally*, in the sorts of beliefs constituting them, and *causally*, in the kind of causal relation holding between one belief and its successor. This relation, for instance, may or may not involve the predecessor belief's being necessary or sufficient for its successor: perhaps, on grounds other than the music, I would have believed my daughter was home; and perhaps not, depending on how many indications of her presence are accessible to me. Such chains also differ *structurally*, in the kind of *epistemic transmission* they exhibit; it may be deductive, as where I infer a theorem from an axiom by rigorous rules of deductive inference, or inductive, as where I infer from the good performance of a knife that others of that kind will also cut well; or the transmission of knowledge or justification may combine deductive and inductive elements. Epistemic chains also differ *foundationally*, in their ultimate grounds, the anchors of the chains; the grounds may, as illustrated, be perceptual or rational, and they may vary in justificational strength.

Different proponents of the fourth possibility have held various views about the character of the *foundational knowledge*, i.e., the beliefs constituting the knowledge that makes up the final link and anchors the chain in experience or reason. Some, including Descartes, have thought that the appropriate beliefs must be infallible, or at least indefeasibly justified.[6] But in fact all that the fourth possibility requires is *non-inferential knowledge*, knowledge not (inferentially) based on other knowledge (or other justified belief). Non-inferential knowledge need not be of self-evident propositions, nor constituted by indefeasibly justified belief, the kind whose justification cannot be defeated. The case of introspective beliefs, which are paradigms of those that are non-inferentially justified, supports this view, and we shall see other reasons to hold it.

III. Fallibilist Foundationalism

The foundationalism with which the regress argument concludes is quite generic and leaves much to be determined, such as how *well* justified foundational beliefs must be if they are to justify a superstructure belief based on them. In assessing the foundationalist–coherentist controversy, then, we need a more detailed formulation. The task of this section is to develop one. I start with a concrete example.

As I sit reading on a quiet summer evening, I sometimes hear a distinctive patter outside my open window. I immediately believe that it is raining. It may then occur to me that if I do not bring in the lawn chairs, the cushions will be soaked. But this I do not believe immediately, even if the thought strikes me in an instant; I believe it on the basis of my prior belief that it is raining. The first belief is perceptual, being grounded directly in what I hear. The second is inferential, being grounded not in what I perceive but in what I believe. My belief that it is raining expresses a premise for my belief that the cushions will be soaked. There are many beliefs of both kinds. Perception is a major source of beliefs; and, from beliefs we have through perception, many others arise inferentially. The latter, inferential beliefs are then based on the former, perceptual beliefs. When I see a headlight beam cross my window and immediately believe, perceptually, that a car's light is moving out there, I may, on the basis of that belief, come to believe, inferentially, that someone has entered my driveway. From this proposition in turn I might infer that my doorbell is about to ring; and from that I might infer still further propositions. Assuming that knowledge implies belief, the same point holds for knowledge: much of it is perceptually grounded, and much of it is inferential.[7] There is no definite limit on how many inferences one may draw in such a chain, and people differ in how many they tend to draw. Could it be, however, that despite the apparent obviousness of these points, there really *is* no non-inferential knowledge or belief, even in perceptual cases? If inference can take us forward indefinitely beyond perceptual beliefs, why may it not take us backward indefinitely from them? To see how this might be thought to occur, we must consider more systematically how beliefs arise, what justifies them, and when they are sufficiently well grounded to constitute knowledge.

Imagine that when the rain began I had not trusted my ears. I might then have believed just the weaker proposition that there was a pattering sound and only on that basis, and after considering the situation, come to believe that it was raining. We need not stop here, however. For suppose I do not trust my sense of hearing. I might then believe merely that it *seems* to me that there is a patter, and only on that basis believe that there is such a sound. But surely this cannot go much further, and in fact there is no need to go even this far. Still, what theoretical reason is there to stop? It is not as if we had to articulate all our beliefs. Little of what we believe is at any one time before our minds being inwardly voiced. Indeed, perhaps we can have infinitely many beliefs, as some think we do.[8] But, as I have already suggested, it is simply not clear that a person's cognitive system can sustain an infinite set of beliefs, and much the same can be said regarding a circular cognitive chain.

Even if there could be infinite or circular belief chains, foundationalists hold that they cannot be sources of knowledge or justification. The underlying idea is in part this. If knowledge or justified belief arises through inference, it requires belief of at least one premise; and that belief could produce knowledge or justified belief of a proposition inferred from the premise only if the premise belief is itself an instance of knowledge or is at least justified. But if the premise belief is justified, it must be so by virtue of *something*—otherwise it would be self-justified, and hence one kind of foundational belief after all. If, however, experience cannot do the justificatory work, then the belief must derive its justification from yet another set of premises, and the problem arises all over again: what justifies that set? In the light of such points, the foundationalist concludes that if any of our beliefs are justified or constitute knowledge, then some of our beliefs are justified, or constitute knowledge, simply because they arise (in a certain way) from experience or reflection (including intuition as a special case of reflection). Indeed, if we construe experience broadly enough to include logical reflection and rational intuition, then experience may be described as the one overall source. In either case, there appear to be at least four basic sources of knowledge and justified belief: perception; consciousness, which grounds, e.g., my knowledge that I am thinking about the structure of justification; reflection, which is, for instance, the basis of my justified belief that if A is older than B and B is older than C, then A is older than C; and memory: I can be justified in believing that, say, I left a light on simply by virtue of the sense of recalling my having done so.[9]

Particularly in the perceptual cases, some foundationalists tend to see experience as a mirror of nature.[10] This seems to some foundationalists a good, if limited, metaphor because it suggests at least two important points: first, that some experiences are *produced* by external states of the world, somewhat as light produces mirror images; and second, that (normally) the experiences in some way *match* their causes, for instance in the color and shape one senses in one's visual field.[11] If one wants to focus on individual perceptual beliefs, one might think of a thermometer model; it suggests both the causal connections just sketched, but also, perhaps even more than the mirror metaphor, *reliable* responses to the external world.[12] From this causal–responsiveness perspective, it is at best unnatural to regard perceptual beliefs as inferential. They are not formed by inference from anything else believed but directly reflect the objects and events that cause them.

The most plausible kind of foundationalism will be fallibilist (moderate) in at least the following respects—and I shall concentrate on foundationalism about justification, though much that is said will also hold for foundationalism about knowledge. First, as a purely philosophical thesis about the *structure* of justification, foundationalism should be neutral with respect to skepticism and should not entail that there *are* justified beliefs. Second, if it is fallibilistic, it must allow that a justified belief, even a foundational one, be false. To require here justification of a kind that entails truth is to require that justified foundational beliefs be infallible. Third, superstructure beliefs may be only inductively, hence fallibly, justified by foundational ones and thus (unless they are necessary truths) can be false even when the latter are true. Just as one's warranted beliefs may be fallible, one's inferences may be, also, leading from truth to falsity. If the proposition is sufficiently supported by evidence one justifiedly believes, one may justifiedly hold it on the basis of that evidence, even if one could turn out to be in error. Fourth, a fallibilist foundationalism must allow for *discovering* error or lack of justification, in foundational as well as in superstructure beliefs. Foundational beliefs may be discovered to conflict either with other such beliefs or with sufficiently well-supported superstructure beliefs.

These four points are quite appropriate to the inspiration of the theory as expressed in the regress argument: it requires epistemic unmoved movers, but not unmovable movers. Solid ground is enough, even if bedrock is better. There are also different kinds of bedrock, and not all of them have the invulnerability apparently belonging to beliefs of luminously self-evident truths of logic. Even foundationalism as applied to knowledge can be fallibilistic; for granting that false propositions cannot be known, foundationalism about knowledge does not entail that one's *grounds* for knowledge (at any level) are indefeasible. Perceptual grounds, e.g., may be overridden; and one can fail (or cease) to know a proposition not because it is (or is discovered to be) false, but because one ceases to be justified in believing it.

I take *fallibilist foundationalism*, as applied to justification, to be the inductivist thesis that

I. For any S and any t, (1) the structure of S's body of justified beliefs is, at t, foundational in the sense that any inferential (hence non-foundational) justified beliefs S has depend for their justification on one or more non-inferential (thus in a sense foundational) justified beliefs of S's; (2) the justification of S's foundational beliefs is at least typically defeasible; (3) the inferential transmission of justification need not be deductive; and (4) non-foundationally justified beliefs need not derive *all* of their justification from foundational ones, but only enough so that they would remain justified if (other things remaining equal) any other justification they have (say, from coherence) were eliminated.[13]

This is fallibilist in at least three ways. Foundational beliefs may turn out to be unjustified or false or both; superstructure beliefs may be only inductively, hence fallibly, justified by foundational ones and hence can be false even when the latter are true; and possibility of *discovering* error or lack of justification, even in foundational beliefs, is left open: they may be found to conflict either with other such beliefs or with sufficiently well-supported superstructure beliefs. Even foundationalism as applied to knowledge can forswear infallibility. For although false beliefs cannot be knowledge, what is known can be both contingent—and so might have been false—*and* based on defeasible grounds—and so might cease to be known. We can lose knowledge when our grounds for it are defeated by counterevidence. Even introspective grounds are overridable; hence, even self-knowledge is defeasible.

Since I am particularly concerned to clarify foundationalism in contrast to coherentism, I want to focus on the roles fallibilist foundationalism allows for coherence (conceived in any plausible way) in relation to justification. There are at least two important roles coherence may apparently play.

The first role fallibilist foundationalism allows for coherence—or at least for incoherence—is negative. Incoherence may defeat justification or knowledge, even the justification of a directly justified, hence foundational, belief (or one constituting knowledge), as where my justification for believing I am hallucinating books prevents me from knowing, or remaining justified in believing, certain propositions incoherent with it, say that the books in my study are before me. If this is not ultimately a role for coherence itself—which is the opposite and not merely the absence of incoherence—it *is* a role crucial for explaining points stressed by coherentism. Coherentists have not taken account of the point that incoherence is not merely the absence of coherence and cannot be explicated simply through analyzing coherence, nor accounted for as an epistemic standard only by a coherentist theory (a point to which I shall return); but they have rightly noted, for instance, such things as the defeasibility of the justification of a memorial belief owing to its incoherence with perceptual beliefs, as where one takes oneself to remember an oak tree in a certain spot, yet, standing near the very spot, can find no trace of one. Because fallibilist foundationalism does not require indefeasible justification on the part of the relevant memory belief, there is no anomaly in its defeat by perceptual evidence.

Second, fallibilist foundationalism can employ an *independence principle*, one of a family of principles commonly emphasized by coherentists, though foundationalists need not attribute its truth to coherence. This principle says that the larger the number of independent mutually coherent factors one believes to support the truth of a proposition, the better one's justification for believing it (other things being equal). The principle can explain, e.g., why my justification for believing, from what I hear, that my daughter has come home increases as I acquire new beliefs supporting that conclusion, say that there is a smell of popcorn. For I now have a confirmatory belief which comes through a different sense (smell) and does not depend for its justification on my other evidence beliefs.

Similar principles consistent with foundationalism can accommodate other cases in which coherence apparently enhances justification, for instance where a proposition's explaining, and thereby cohering with, something one justifiably believes, tends to confer some justification on that proposition. Suppose I check three suitcases at the ticket counter. Imagine that as I await them at the baggage terminal I glimpse two on the conveyor at a distance and tentatively believe that they are mine. The propositions that (a) the first is mine, (b) the second is, and (c) these two are side by side—which I am fully justified in believing because I can clearly see how close they are to each other—would be explained by the hypothesis that my three suitcases are now coming off together; and that hypothesis, in turn, derives some justification from its explaining what I already believe. When I believe the further proposition, independent of (a)–(c), that my third suitcase is coming just behind the second, the level of my justification for the hypothesis rises.

Fallibilist foundationalism thus allows for coherence to play a significant though restricted role in explicating justification, and it provides a major place for incoherence in this task. But there remains a strong contrast between the two accounts of justification, as we shall soon see.

IV. Holistic Coherentism

The notion of coherence is frequently appealed to in epistemological and other contexts, but it is infrequently explicated. Despite the efforts that have been made to clarify coherence, explaining what it is remains difficult.[14] It is not mere consistency, though *inconsistency* is the clearest case of incoherence. Whatever coherence is, it is a cognitively *internal* relation, in the sense that it is a matter of how one's beliefs (or other cognitive items) are related *to one another*, not to anything outside one's system of beliefs, such as one's perceptual experience. Coherence is sometimes connected with explanation; it is widely believed that propositions which stand in an explanatory relation cohere with one another and that this coherence counts toward that of a person's beliefs of the propositions in question. If the wilting of the leaves is explained by billowing smoke from a chemical fire, then presumably the proposition expressing the first event coheres with the proposition expressing the second (even if the coherence is not obvious and is relative to the context). Probability is also relevant: if the probability of one proposition you believe is raised by that of a second you believe, this at least counts toward the coherence of the first of the beliefs with the second. The relevant notions of explanation and probability are themselves philosophically problematic, but our intuitive grasp of them can still help us understand coherence.

In the light of these points, let us try to formulate a plausible version of coherentism as applied to justification. The central coherentist idea concerning justification is that a belief is justified by its coherence with other beliefs one holds. The unit of coherence may be as large as one's entire set of beliefs, though some may be more significant in producing the coherence than others, say because of differing degrees of their closeness in subject matter to the belief in question. This conception of coherentism would be accepted by a proponent of the circular view, but the thesis I want to explore differs from that view in not being *linear*: it does not take justification for believing that *p*, or knowledge that *p*, to emerge from an inferential line running from premises for *p* to that proposition as a conclusion from them, and from other premises to the first set of premises, and so on until we return to the original proposition as a premise. On the circular view, no matter how wide the circle or how rich its constituent beliefs, there is a line from any one belief in a circular epistemic chain to any other. In practice I may never trace the entire line, as by inferring one thing I know from a second, the second from a third, and so on until I reinfer the first. Still, on this view there is such a line for every belief constituting knowledge.

Coherentism need not, however, be linear, and I believe that the most plausible versions are instead holistic.[15] A moderate version of *holistic coherentism* might be expressed as follows:

II. For any *S* and any *t*, if *S* has any justified beliefs at *t*, then, at *t*, (1) they are each justified by virtue of their coherence with one or more others of *S*'s beliefs; and (2) they would remain justified even if (other things remaining equal) any justification they derive from sources other than coherence were eliminated.

The holism required is minimal, since the unit of coherence may be as small as one pair of beliefs—though it may also be as large as the entire system of S's beliefs (including the belief whose justification is in question, since we may take such partial "self-coherence" as a limiting case). But the formulation also applies to the more typical cases of holistic coherentism; in these cases a justified belief coheres with a substantial number of other beliefs, but not necessarily with all of one's beliefs. Some beliefs, like those expressing basic principles of one's thinking, can be justified only by coherence with a large and diverse group of related beliefs. Coherentist theories differ concerning the sense (if any) in which the set of beliefs whose coherence determines the justification of some belief belonging to it must be a "system."

To illustrate holistic coherentism, consider a question that evokes a justification. Ken wonders how, from my closed study, I know (or why I believe) that my daughter is home. I say that there is music playing in the house. He next wants to know how I can recognize my daughter's music from behind my closed doors. I reply that what I hear is the wrong sort of thing to come from any nearby house. He then asks how I know that it is not from a passing car. I say that the volume is too steady. He now wonders whether I can distinguish, with my door closed, my daughter's vocal music from the singing of a neighbor in her yard. I reply that I hear an accompaniment. In giving each justification I apparently go only one step along the inferential line: initially, for instance, just to my belief that there is music playing in the house. For my belief that my daughter is home *is* based on this belief about the music. After that, I do not even mention anything that this belief, in turn, is based on; rather, I defend my beliefs as appropriate, in terms of an entire pattern of interrelated beliefs I hold. And I may appeal to many different part of the pattern. For coherentism, then, beliefs representing knowledge do not lie at one end of a grounded chain; they fit a coherent pattern and are justified through their fitting it in an appropriate way.

Consider a variant of the case. Suppose I had seemed to hear music of neither the kind my daughter plays nor the kind the neighbors play nor the sort I expect from passing cars. The proposition that this is what I hear does not cohere well with my belief that the music is played by my daughter. Suddenly I recall that she was bringing a friend, and I remember that her friend likes such music. I might now be justified in believing that my daughter is home. When I finally hear her voice, I know that she is. The crucial thing here is how, initially, a kind of *incoherence* prevents justification of my belief that she is home, and how, as relevant pieces of the pattern develop, I become justified in believing, and (presumably) come to know, that she is. Arriving at a justified belief, on this view, is more like answering a question by looking up diverse information that suggests the answer than like deducing a theorem from axioms.

Examples like this show how a holistic coherentism can respond to the regress argument *without* embracing the possibility of an epistemic circle (though its proponents need not reject that either). It may deny that there are only the four kinds of possible epistemic chains I have specified. There is apparently another possibility, not generally noted: that the chain terminates with belief which is *psychologically direct* but *epistemically indirect* or, if we are talking of coherentism about justification, *justificationally indirect*. Hence, the last link is, as belief, direct, since it is non-inferential; yet, as knowledge, it is *indirect*, not in the usual sense that it is inferential but rather in the broad sense that the belief constitutes knowledge only by virtue of receiving support from other knowledge or belief. Thus, my belief that there is music playing is psychologically direct because it is simply grounded, causally, in my hearing and is not (inferentially) based on any other belief; yet my *knowledge* that there is music is not epistemically direct. It is epistemically, but not inferentially, based on the coherence of my belief that there is music with my other beliefs, presumably including many that constitute knowledge themselves. It is thus knowledge *through*, though not by inference from, other knowledge—or at least through justified beliefs; hence it is epistemically indirect and thus non-foundational.

There is another way to see how this attack on the regress argument is constructed. The coherentist grants that the belief element *in* my knowledge is non-inferentially grounded in perception and is in that sense direct; but the claim is that the belief constitutes knowledge only by virtue of coherence with my other beliefs. The strategy, then—call it the *wedge strategy*—is to sever the connection foundationalism usually posits between the psychological and the epistemic. In the common cases, foundationalists tend to hold, the basis of one's *knowledge* that p, say a perceptual experience, is also the basis of one's belief that p; similarly, for justified belief, the basis of its justification is usually also that of the belief itself. For the coherentist using the wedge strategy, the epistemic ground of a belief need not be a psychological ground. Knowledge and justification are a matter of how well the system of beliefs hangs together, not of how well grounded the beliefs are—and they may indeed hang: one could have a body of justified beliefs, at least some of them constituting knowledge, even if *none* of them is justified by a belief or experience in which it is psychologically grounded.

In a sense, of course, coherentism does posit a *kind* of foundation for justification and knowledge: namely, coherence. But so long as coherentists deny that justification and knowledge can be *non-inferentially* grounded in experience or reason, this point alone simply shows that they take justification and knowledge to be based on something (to be supervenient properties, as some would put it). Justification and knowledge are still grounded in the coherence of elements which themselves admit of justification and derive their justification (or status as knowledge) from coherence with other such items rather than from grounding in elements like sensory impressions (say of music), which, though not themselves justified or unjustified, confer justification on beliefs they ground.

Apparently, then, the circularity objection to coherentism can be met by construing the thesis holistically and countenancing psychologically direct beliefs. One could insist that if a non-inferential, thus psychologically direct, belief constitutes knowledge, it *must* be direct knowledge. But the coherentist would reply that in that case there will be two kinds of direct knowledge: the kind the foundationalist posits, which derives from grounding in a basic experiential or rational source, and the kind the coherentist posits, which derives from coherence with other beliefs and not from being based on those sources. This is surely a plausible response.

Is the holistic coherentist trying to have it both ways? Not necessarily. Holistic coherentism can grant that a variant of the regress argument holds for belief, since the only kind of inferential belief chain that it is psychologically realistic to attribute to us is the kind terminating in direct (non-inferential) belief. But even on the assumption that knowledge is constituted by (certain kinds of) beliefs, it does not follow that direct belief which constitutes knowledge is also direct *knowledge*. Epistemic dependence, on this view, does not imply inferential or psychological dependence; hence, a non-inferential belief can depend for its status as knowledge on other beliefs. Thus, the coherentist may grant a kind of *psychological foundationalism*—which says (in part) that if we have any beliefs at all, we have some direct (non-inferential) ones—yet deny epistemological foundationalism, which requires that there be knowledge which is epistemically (and normally also psychologically) direct, if there is any knowledge at all. Holistic coherentism may grant experience and reason the status of psychological foundations of our belief systems, but it denies that they are the basic sources of justification or knowledge.

V. Foundationalism, Coherentism, and Defeasibility

Drawing on our results above, this section considers how fallibilist foundationalism and holistic coherentism differ and, related to that, how the controversy is sometimes obscured by failure to take account of the differences.

There is one kind of case that seems both to favor foundationalism and to show something about justification that coherentism in any form misses. It might seem that coherence theories of justification are decisively refuted by the possibility of S's having, if just momentarily, only a single belief which is nonetheless justified, say that there is music playing. For this belief would be justified without cohering with any others S has. But could one have just a single belief? Could I, for instance, believe that there is music playing yet not believe, say, that there are (or could be) musical instruments, melodies, and chords? It is not clear that I could; and foundationalism does not assume this possibility, though the theory may easily be wrongly criticized for implying it. Foundationalism is in fact consistent with *one* kind of coherentism—*conceptual coherentism*. This is a coherence theory of the acquisition of concepts which says that a person acquires concepts, say of musical pieces, only in relation to one another and must acquire an entire family of related concepts in order to acquire any concept.

It remains questionable, however, whether my justification for believing that there is music playing ultimately *derives* from the coherence of the belief with others, i.e., whether coherence is even partly the basis of my justification in holding this belief.[16] Let us first note an important point. Suppose the belief turns out to be *in*coherent with a second, such as my belief that I am standing before the phonograph playing the music yet see no movement of its turntable; now the belief may *cease* to be justified, since if I really hear the phonograph, I should see its turntable moving. But this shows only that the belief's justification is *defeasible*—liable to being either overridden (roughly, outweighed) or undermined—should sufficiently serious incoherence arise. It does not show that the justification derives from coherence. In this case the justification of my belief grounded in hearing may be overridden. My better-justified beliefs, including the belief that a phonograph with a motionless turntable cannot play, may make it more reasonable for me to believe that there is *not* music playing in the house.

The example raises another question regarding the possibility that coherence is the source of my justification, as opposed to incoherence's constraining it. Could incoherence override the justification of my belief if I were not *independently* justified in believing that a proposition incoherent with certain other ones is, or probably is, false, e.g. in believing that if I do not see the turntable moving, then I do not hear music from the phonograph? For if I lacked such independent justification, should I not suspend judgment on, or even reject, the other propositions and retain my original belief? And aren't the relevant other beliefs or propositions—those that can override or defeat my justification—precisely the kind for which, directly or inferentially, we have some degree of justification through the experiential and rational sources, such as visual perception of a stockstill turntable? Note that the example shows that these beliefs or propositions need not be a priori; thus it is not open to coherentists to claim that only the a priori is an exception to the thesis that justification is determined by coherence.

A similar question arises regarding the crucial principles themselves. Could incoherence play the defeating role it does if we did not have a kind of foundational justification for principles to the effect that certain kinds of evidences or beliefs override certain other kinds? More generally, can we *use*, or even benefit from, considerations of coherence in acquiring justification, or in correcting mistaken presuppositions of justification, if we do not bring to the various coherent or incoherent patterns principles not derived from those very patterns? If, without such principles to serve as justified standards that guide belief formation and belief revision, we can become justified by coherence, then coherence would seem to be playing the kind of generative role that foundational sources are held to play in producing justification. One could become justified in believing that *p* by virtue of coherence even if one had no justified principles by which one could, for instance, inferentially connect the justified belief that *p* with others that cohere with it.

There is a second case, in which one's justification is simply undermined: one ceases to be justified in believing the proposition in question, though one does not become justified in believing it false. Suppose I seem to see a black cat, yet there no longer appears to be one there if I move five feet to my left. This experience could justify my believing, and lead me to believe, that I might be hallucinating. This belief in turn is to a degree incoherent with, and undermines the justification of, my visual belief that the cat is there, though it does not by itself justify my believing that there is *not* a cat there. Again, however, I am apparently justified, independently of coherence, in believing a proposition relevant to my overall justification for an apparently foundational perceptual belief: namely, the proposition that my seeing the cat there is incoherent with my merely hallucinating it there. The same seems to hold for the proposition that my seeing the cat there coheres with my feeling fur if I extend my hand to the feline focal point of my visual field. Considerations like these suggest that coherence has the role it does in justification only because *some* beliefs are justified independently of it.

Both examples illustrate an important distinction that is often missed.[17] It is between defeasibility and epistemic dependence or, alternatively, between *negative epistemic dependence*, which is a form of defeasibility, and *positive epistemic dependence*, the kind beliefs bear to the source(s) from which they *derive* any justification they have or, if they represent knowledge, their status as knowledge. The defeasibility of a belief's justification by incoherence does not imply that, as coherentists hold, its justification positively depends on coherence. If my garden is my source of food, I (positively) depend on it. The fact that people could poison the soil does not make their non-malevolence part of my food *source* or imply a (positive) dependence on them, such as I have on the sunshine. Moreover, it is the sunshine that (with rainfall and other conditions) explains both my having the food and the amount I have. The non-malevolence is necessary for, but does not explain, this; it alone, under the relevant conditions of potential for growth, does not even tend to produce food.

So it is with perceptual experience as a source of justification. Foundationalists need not deny that a belief's justification negatively depends on something else, for as we have seen they need not claim that justification must be indefeasible. It may arise, unaided by coherence, from a source like perception; yet it remains defeasible from various quarters—including conflicting perceptions. Negative dependence, however, does not imply positive dependence. The former is determined by the absence of something—defeaters; the latter is determined by the presence of something—justifiers. Justification can be defeasible by incoherence and thus overridden or undermined should incoherence arise, without owing its existence to coherence. Fallibilist foundationalism is not, then, a blend of coherentism, and it remains open just what positive role, if any, it must assign to coherence in explicating justification.

There is a further point that fallibilist foundationalism should stress, and in appraising the point we learn more about both coherentism and justification. If I set out to *show* that my belief is justified—as the dialectical formulation of the regress problem invites one to think stopping the regress of justification requires—I do have to cite propositions that cohere with the one to be shown to be justified for me, say that there is music in my house. In some cases, these are not even propositions one already believes. Often, in defending the original belief, one forms new beliefs, such as the belief one acquires, in moving one's head, that one can vividly see the changes in perspective that go with seeing a black cat. More important, these beliefs are highly appropriate to the *process* of self-consciously justifying one's belief; and the result of that process is twofold: forming the second-order belief that the original belief is justified and showing that the latter is justified. Thus, coherence is important in showing that a belief is justified. In *that* limited sense coherence is a pervasive element in justification: it is pervasive in the process of *justifying*, especially when that is construed as showing that one has justification.

Why, however, should the second-order beliefs appropriate to *showing* that a belief is justified be necessary for its *being* justified? They need not be. Indeed, why should one's simply having a justified belief imply even that one could be justified in holding the second-order beliefs appropriate to showing that it is justified? It would seem that just as a little child can be of good character even if unable to defend its character against attack, one can have a justified belief even if, in response to someone who doubts this, one could not show that one does. Supposing I have the sophistication to form a second-order belief that my belief that there is a cat before me is justified, the latter belief can be justified so long as the former is *true*; and it can be *true* that my belief about the cat is justified even if I am not justified in holding it or am unable to show that it is true. Justifying a second-order belief is a sophisticated process. The process is particularly sophisticated if the second-order belief concerns a special property like the justification of the original belief. Simply being justified in a belief about, say, the sounds around one is a much simpler matter. But confusion is easy here, particularly if the governing context is an imagined dialectic with a skeptic. Take, for instance, the question of how a simple perceptual belief "is justified." The very phrase is ambiguous. The question could be "By what process, say of reasoning, has the belief been (or might it be) justified?" or, on the other hand, "In virtue of what is the belief justified?" These are very different questions. The first invites us to conceive justification as a process of which the belief is a beneficiary, the second to conceive it as a property that a belief has, whether in virtue of its content, its genesis, or others of its characteristics or relations. Both aspects of the notion are important, but unfortunately much of our talk about justification makes it easy to run them together. A justified belief could be one that *has* justification or one that *has been* justified; and a request for someone's justification could be a request for a list of justifying factors or for a recounting of the process by which the person justified the belief.

Once we forswear the mistakes just pointed out, what argument is left to show the (positive) dependence of perceptual justification on coherence? I doubt that any plausible one remains, though given how hard it is to discern what coherence is, we cannot be confident that no plausible argument is forthcoming. Granted, one could point to the oddity of saying things like, "I am justified in believing that there is music playing, but I cannot justify this belief." Why is this odd if not because, when I have a justified belief, I can give a justification for it by appeal to beliefs that cohere with it? But consider this. Typically, in asserting something, say that there were lawsuits arising from an accident, I imply that, in some way or other, I *can* justify what I say, especially if the belief I express is, like this one, not plausibly thought to be grounded in a basic source such as perception. In the quoted sentence I deny that I can justify what I claim. The foundationalist must explain why that is odd, given that I can be justified in believing propositions even when I cannot show that I am (and may not even believe I am). The main point needed to explain this is that it is apparently my *asserting* that my belief is justified, rather than its being so, that gives the appearance that I must be able to give a justification of the belief. Compare "*She* is justified in believing that there is music playing, but (being an intuitive and unphilosophical kind of person) she cannot justify that proposition." This has no disturbing oddity, because the person said to have justification is not the one claiming it. Since she might be shocked to be asked to justify the proposition and might not know how to justify it, this statement might be true of her. We must not stop here, however. There are at least two further points.

First, there is quite a difference between *showing* that one is justified and simply *giving* a justification. I can give my justification for believing that there is music simply by indicating that I hear it. But this does not show that I am justified, at least in the sense of "show" usual in epistemology. That task requires not just exhibiting what justifies one but also indicating conditions for being justified *and* showing that one meets them. It is one thing to cite a justifier, such as a clear perception; it is quite another to show that it meets a sufficiently high standard to *be* a justifier of the belief it grounds. Certainly skeptics—and probably most coherentists as well—have in mind something more like the latter process when they ask for a justification. Similarly—and this is the second point—where a regress of justification is, for fallibilist foundationalism, stopped by giving a (genuine) justification for the proposition in question, and the regress problem can be considered soluble because such stopping is possible, the skeptic will not countenance any stopping place, and certainly not any solution, that is not dialectically defended by argument showing that one is justified.

To be sure, it may be that at least typically when we do have a justified belief we can give a justification for it. When I justifiedly believe that there is music playing, I surely can give a justification: that I hear it. But I need not *believe* that I hear it *before* the question of justification arises. That question leads me to focus on my circumstances, in which I first had a belief solely about the music. I also had a *disposition*, based on my auditory experience, to form the belief that I *hear* the music, and this is largely why, in the course of justifying that belief, I then *form* the further belief that I do hear it. But a disposition to believe something does not imply an actual belief of it, not even a dispositional one, as opposed to one manifesting itself in consciousness. If I am talking loudly and excitedly in a restaurant, I may be disposed to believe this—so much so that if I merely think of the proposition that I am talking loudly, I will form the belief that I am and lower my voice. But this disposition does not imply that I *already* believe that proposition—if I did, I would not be talking loudly in the first place. In the musical case, I tend to form the belief that I hear the music if, as I hear it, the question of whether I hear it arises; yet I need not have subliminally believed this already. The justification I offer, then, is not by appeal to coherence with other beliefs I already had—such as that I saw the turntable moving—but by reference to what has traditionally been considered a basic source of both justification and knowledge: perception. It is thus precisely the kind of justification that foundationalists are likely to consider appropriate for a non-inferential belief. Indeed, one consideration favoring foundationalism about both justification and knowledge, as least as an account of our everyday epistemic practices, including much scientific practice, is that typically we cease to offer justification or to defend a knowledge claim precisely when we reach a basic source.

VI. Coherence, Foundations, and Justification

There is far more to say in clarifying both foundationalism and coherentism. But if what I have said so far is correct, then we can at least understand their basic thrusts. We can also see how coherentism may respond to the regress argument—in part by distinguishing psychological from epistemic directness. And we can see how foundationalism may reply to the charge that, once made moderate enough to be plausible, it depends on coherence criteria rather than on grounding in experience and reason. The response is in part to distinguish negative from positive epistemic dependence and to argue that foundationalism does not make justification depend positively on coherence, but only negatively on (avoiding) incoherence.

One may still wonder, however, whether fallibilist foundationalism concedes enough to coherentism. Granted that it need not restrict the role of coherence any more than is required by the regress argument, it still denies that coherence is (independently) necessary for justification. As most plausibly developed, fallibilist foundationalism also denies that coherence is a *basic* (non-derivative) source of justification—or at least that if it is, it can produce *enough* justification to render a belief unqualifiedly justified or (given truth and certain other conditions) to make it knowledge. A single drop of even the purest water will not quench a thirst. The moderate holistic coherentism formulated above is parallel in this: while it may grant foundationalism its typical psychological picture of how belief systems are structured, it denies that foundational justification is (independently) necessary for justification and that it is a basic source of justification, except possibly of degrees of justification too slight for knowledge or unqualifiedly justified belief.

The issue here is the difference in the two conceptions of justification. Broadly, foundationalists tend to hold that justification belongs to a belief, whether inferentially or directly, by virtue of its grounding in experience or reason; coherentists tend to hold that justification belongs to a belief by virtue of its coherence with one or more other beliefs. This is apparently a difference concerning basic sources. To be sure, my formulation may make coherentism sound foundationalistic, because justification is grounded not in an inferential relation to premises but in coherence itself, which sounds parallel to experience or reason. But note three contrasts with foundationalism: (1) the source of coherence is *cognitive*, because the coherence is an internal property of the belief system, whereas foundationalism makes no such restriction; (2) coherence is an inferential or at least epistemic generator, in the sense that it arises, with or without one's having inferential beliefs, from relations among beliefs or their propositional objects, e.g. from entailment, inductive support, or explanation of one belief or proposition by another, whereas experiential sources and (for pure coherentists) even rational sources are a non-inferential generator of belief (these sources can produce and thereby explain belief, but they do not, according to coherentism, justify it); and (3) *S* has *inferential access* to the coherence-making relations: *S* can wield them in inferentially justifying the belief that *p*, whereas foundationalism does not require such access to its basic sources. Still, I want to pursue just how deep the difference between foundationalism and coherentism is; for once foundationalism is moderately expressed and grants the truth of conceptual coherentism, and once coherentism is (plausibly) construed as consistent with psychological foundationalism, it may appear that the views differ far less than the prevailing stereotypes would have us think.

It should help if we first contrast fallibilist foundationalism with *strong foundationalism* and compare their relation to coherentism. If we use Descartes' version as a model, strong foundationalism is deductivist, takes foundational beliefs as indefeasibly justified, and allows coherence at most a limited generative role. To meet these conditions, it may reduce the basic sources of justification to reason and some form of introspection. Moreover, being committed to the indefeasibility of foundational justification, it would not grant that incoherence can defeat such justification. It would also concede to coherentists, and hence to any independence principle they countenance, at most a minimal positive role, say by insisting that if a belief is supported by two or more independent cohering sources, its justification is increased at most "additively," that is, only by combining the justification transmitted separately from each relevant basic source.

By contrast, what fallibilist foundationalism denies regarding coherence is only that it is a basic (hence sufficient) source of justification. Thus, coherence by itself does not ground justification, and hence the independence principle does not apply to sources that have *no* justification; at most, the principle allows coherence to raise the level of justification originally drawn from other sources to a level higher than it would reach if those sources did not mutually cohere. Similarly, if inference is a basic source of coherence (as some coherentists seem to believe), it is not a basic source of justification. It may enhance justification, as where one strengthens one's justification for believing someone's testimony by inferring the same point from someone else's. But inference *alone* does not generate justification. Suppose I believe several propositions without a shred of evidence and merely through wishful thinking. I might infer any number of others; yet even if by good luck I arrive at a highly coherent set of beliefs, I do not automatically gain justification for believing any of them. If I am floating in mid-ocean, strengthening my boat with added nails and planks may make it hang together more tightly and thereby make me feel secure; but if nothing indicates my location, there is no reason to expect this work to get me any closer to shore. Coherence may, to be sure, enable me to draw a beautiful map; but if there are no experiences I may rely on to connect it with reality, I may follow it forever to no avail. Even to be justified in *believing* that it will correspond with reality, I must have some experiential source to work from.

A natural coherentist reply is that when we consider examples of justified belief, not only do we always find some coherence, we also apparently find the right sort to account for the justification. This reply is especially plausible if—as I suggest is reasonable—coherentism as usually formulated is modified to include, in the coherence base, *dispositions to believe*. Consider my belief that music is playing. It coheres both with my beliefs about what records are in the house, what music my daughter prefers, my auditory capacities, etc., *and* with many of my dispositions to believe, say to form the belief that no one else in the house would play that music. Since such dispositions can themselves be well grounded, say in perception, or poorly grounded, e.g. in prejudice, they admit of justification and, when they produce beliefs, can lead to reasonable inferences. These dispositions are thus appropriate for the coherence base, and including them among generators of coherence is particularly useful in freeing coherentism from implausibly positing all the beliefs needed for the justificational capacities it tends to take to underlie justified belief. We need not "store" beliefs of all the propositions needed for our own system of justified belief; the disposition to believe them is enough. Given this broad conception of coherence, it is surely plausible to take coherence as at least necessary for justified belief. And it might be argued that its justification is based on coherence, not on grounding in experience.

Let us grant both that the musical case does exhibit a high degree of coherence among my beliefs and dispositions to believe and even that the coherence is necessary for the justification of my belief. It does not follow that the justification is based on the coherence. Coherence could still be at best a *consequential necessary condition* for justification, one that holds as a result of the justification itself or what that is based on, as opposed to a *constitutive necessary condition*, one that either expresses part of what it *is* for a belief to be justified or constitutes a basic source of it. The relation of coherence to the properties producing it might be analogous to that of heat to friction: a necessary product of it, but not part of what constitutes it.

If coherence is a constitutive necessary condition for justification, and especially if it is a basic source of it, we might expect to find cases in which the experiential and rational sources are absent, yet there is sufficient coherence for justified belief. But this is precisely what we do not easily find, if we ever find it. If I discover a set of my beliefs that intuitively cohere very well yet receive no support from what I believe (or at least am disposed to believe) on the basis of experience or reason, I am not inclined to attribute justification to any of them. To be sure, if the unit of coherence is large enough to include my actual beliefs, then because I have so many that *are* grounded in experience or reason (indeed, few that are not), I will almost certainly not in fact have any beliefs that, intuitively, seem justified yet are not coherent with some of my beliefs so grounded. This complicates assessment of the role of coherence in justification. But we can certainly imagine beings (or ourselves) artificially endowed with coherent sets of beliefs *not* grounded in experience or reason; and when we do, it appears that coherence does not automatically confer justification.

One might conclude, then, that it is more nearly true that coherence is based on justification (or whatever confers justification) than that the latter is based on the former. Further, the data we have so far considered can be explained on the hypothesis that both coherence among beliefs and their justification rest on the beliefs' being grounded (in an appropriate way) in the basic sources. For particularly if a coherence theory of the acquisition of concepts is true, one perhaps cannot have a belief justified by a basic source without having beliefs—or at least dispositions to believe—related in an intimate (and intuitively coherence-generating) way to that belief. One certainly cannot have a justified belief unless no incoherence defeats its justification. Given these two points, it is to be expected that on a fallibilist foundationalism, justification will normally imply coherence, both in the positive sense involving mutual support and in the weak sense of the absence of potential incoherence. There is some reason to think, then, that coherence is not a basic source of justification and is at most a consequentially necessary condition for it.

There is at least one more possibility to be considered, however: that *given* justification from foundational sources, coherence can generate more justification than S would have from those sources alone. If so, we might call coherence a *conditionally basic* source, in that, where there is already some justification from other sources, it can produce new justification. This bears on interpreting the independence principle. It is widely agreed that our justification increases markedly when we take into account independent sources of evidence, as where I confirm that there is music playing by moving closer to enhance my auditory impression and by visually confirming that a phonograph is playing. Perhaps what explains the dramatic increase in my overall justification here is not just "additivity" of foundational justification but also coherence as a further source of justification.

There is plausibility in this reasoning, but it is not cogent. For one thing, there really are no such additive quantities of justification. Perhaps we simply combine degrees of justification, so far as we can, on analogy with combinations of independent probabilities. Thus, the probability of at least one heads on two fair coin tosses is not 1/2 + 1/2 (the two independent probabilities), which would give the event a probability of 1 and make it a certainty; the probability is 3/4, i.e., 1 minus the probability of two tails, which is 1/4. Insofar as degrees of justification are quantifiable, they combine similarly. Moreover, the relevant probability rules do not seem to depend on coherence; they seem to be justifiable by *a priori* reasoning in the way beliefs grounded in reason are commonly thought to be justifiable, and they appear to be among the principles one must *presuppose* if one is to give an account of how coherence contributes to justification. The (limited) analogy between probability and justification, then, does not favor coherentism and may well favor foundationalism.

There remains a contrast between, say, having six independent credible witnesses tell me that *p* on separate occasions which I do not connect with one another, and having them do so on a single occasion when I can note the coherence of their stories. In the first case, while my isolated beliefs cohere, I have no belief that they do, nor even a sense of their collective weight. This is not, to be sure, a case of six increments of isolated foundational justification versus a case of six cohering items of evidence. Both cases exhibit coherence; but in the second there is an additional belief (or justified disposition to believe): *that* six independent witnesses agree. Foundationalists as well as coherentists can plausibly explain how this additional belief increases the justification one has in the first case. It would be premature, then, to take cases like this to show that coherence is even a conditionally basic source of justification. It may only reflect other sources of justification, rather than contribute any.

VII. Epistemological Dogmatism and the Sources of Justification

Of the problems that remain for understanding the foundationalism–coherentism controversy, the one most readily clarified by the results of this paper, is the dogmatism objection. This might be expressed as follows. If one can have knowledge or justified belief without being able to show that one does, and even without a premise from which to derive it, then the way is open to claim just about anything one likes, defending it by cavalierly noting that one can be justified without being able to show that one is. Given the conception of the foundationalism–coherentism controversy developed here, we can perhaps throw some new light on how the charge of dogmatism is relevant to each position.

The notion of dogmatism is not easy to characterize, and there have apparently been few detailed discussions of it in recent epistemological literature.[18] My focus will be dogmatism as an epistemological attitude or stance, not as a trait of personality. I am mainly interested in what it is to hold a belief dogmatically. This is probably the basic notion in any case: a general dogmatic attitude, like the personality trait of dogmatism, is surely in some way a matter of having or tending to have dogmatically held beliefs.[19]

It will be useful to start with some contrasts. Dogmatism in relation to a belief is not equivalent to stubbornness in holding it; for even if a dogmatically held belief cannot be easily given up, one could be stubborn in holding a belief simply from attachment to it, and without the required disposition to defend it or regard it as better grounded than alternatives. For similar reasons, psychological certainty in holding a belief does not entail dogmatism. Indeed, even if one is both psychologically certain of a simple logical truth *and* disposed to reject denials of it with confidence and to suspect even well-developed arguments against it as sophistical, one does not qualify as dogmatic. The content of one's view is important: even moderate insistence on a reasonably disputed matter may bespeak dogmatism; stubborn adherence to the self-evident need not. An attitude that would be dogmatic in holding one belief may not be so in holding another.

Dogmatic people are often closed-minded, and dogmatically held beliefs are often closed-mindedly maintained; but a belief held closed-mindedly need not be held dogmatically: it may be maintained with a guilty realization that emotionally one simply cannot stand to listen to challenges of it, and with an awareness that it might be mistaken. Moreover, although people who hold beliefs dogmatically are often intellectually pugnacious in defending them, or even in trying to win converts, such pugnacity is not sufficient for dogmatism. Intellectual pugnacity is consistent with a keen awareness that one might be mistaken, and it may be accompanied by open-minded argumentation for one's view. Nor need a dogmatically held belief generate such pugnacity; I might be indisposed to argue, whether from confidence that I know or from temperament, and my dogmatism might surface only when I am challenged.

One thing all of these possible conceptions of dogmatism have in common is lack of a second-order component. But that component may well be necessary for a dogmatic attitude, at least of the full-blooded kind. Typically, a dogmatically held belief is maintained with a conviction (often unjustified) to the effect that one is right, e.g. that one knows, is amply justified, is properly certain, or can just see the truth of the proposition in question. Such a second-order belief is not, however, sufficient for a dogmatic attitude. This is shown by certain cases of believing simple logical truths. These can be held both with such a second-order belief and in the stubborn way typical of a dogmatic attitude yet not bespeak a dogmatic attitude. It might be held that in this case they would at least be held *dogmatically*; but if the imagined tenacity is toward, say, the principle that if a = b, and b = c, then a = c, one could not properly call the attitude dogmatic, and we might better speak of maintaining the belief steadfastly rather than dogmatically.

It might be argued, however, that even if the only examples of dogmatism so far illustrated are the second-order ones, there are still two kinds of dogmatism: first- and second-order. It may be enough, for instance, that one be *disposed* to have a certain belief, usually an unwarrantedly positive one, about the status of one's belief that *p*. Imagine that Tom thinks that Mozart is a far greater composer than Haydn, asserts it without giving any argument, and sloughs off arguments to the contrary. If he does not believe, but is disposed to believe on considering the matter, that his belief is, say, obviously correct, then he may qualify as dogmatically holding it. Here, then, there is no actual second-order attitude, but only a disposition to form one upon considering the status of one's belief. I want to grant that this kind of first-order pattern may qualify as dogmatism; but the account of it remains a second-order one, and it still seems that the other first-order cases we have considered, such as mere stubbornness in believing, are not cases of dogmatism. They may exhibit believing dogmatically, but that does not entail dogmatism as an epistemic attitude or trait of character, any more than doing something lovingly entails a loving attitude, or being a loving person. It appears, then, that at least the clear cases of dogmatically holding beliefs imply either second-order attitudes or certain dispositions to form them.

There may be no simple, illuminating way to characterize dogmatism with respect to a belief that p; but if there is, the following elements should be reflected at least as typical conditions and should provide the materials needed in appraising the foundationalism–coherentism controversy: (1) confidence that p, and significantly greater confidence than one's evidence or grounds warrant; (2) unjustified resistance to taking plausible objections seriously when they are intelligibly posed to one; (3) a willingness, or at least a tendency, to assert the proposition flat-out even in the presence of presumptive reasons to question it, including simply the conflicting views of one or more persons whom S sees or should see to be competent concerning the subject matter; and (4) a (second-order) belief, or disposition to believe, that one's belief is clearly true (or certainly true). Note, however, that (i) excessive confidence can come from mere foolhardiness and can be quite unstable; (ii) resistance to plausible objections may be due to intellectual laziness; (iii) a tendency to assert something flat-out can derive from mere bluntness; and (iv) a belief that one is right might arise not from dogmatism but merely from conceit, intellectual mistake (such as a facile anti-skepticism), or sheer error. Notice also that the notion of dogmatism is not just psychological, but also epistemic.

Of the four elements highly characteristic of dogmatism, the last may have the best claim to be an unqualifiedly necessary condition, and perhaps one or more of the others is necessary. The four are probably jointly sufficient; but this is not self-evident, and I certainly doubt that we can find any simple condition that is non-trivially sufficient, such as believing that one knows, or is justified in believing, that p (which one does believe), while also believing one has no reasons for believing that p.[20] This condition is not sufficient because it could stem from a certain view of knowledge and reasons, say a view on which one never has reasons (as opposed to a basis) for believing simple, self-evident propositions. The condition also seems insufficient because it could be satisfied by a person who lacks the first three of the typical conditions just specified.

Let us work with the full-blooded conception of a dogmatically held belief summarized by conditions (1)–(4). What, then, may we say about the standard charge that foundationalism is dogmatic, in a sense implying that it invites proponents to hold certain beliefs dogmatically? This charge has been leveled on a number of occasions,[21] and some plausible replies have been made.[22] Given the earlier sections of this chapter, it should be plain that the charge is more likely to seem cogent if foundationalism is conceived as answering the dialectical regress problem, as it has apparently been taken to do by, e.g., Chisholm.[23] For in this case a (doxastic) stopping place in the regress generated by "How do you know that *p*?" will coincide with the assertion of a second-order belief, such as that I know that *q*, e.g. that there is a window before me; and since knowledge claims are commonly justifiable by evidence, flatly stopping the regress in this way will seem dogmatic. Even if such a claim is justified by one's citing a non-doxastic state of affairs, such as a visual experience of a window, one is still asserting the existence of this state of affairs and hence apparently expressing knowledge: making what seems a tacit claim *to* it, though not actually claiming to *have* it.

We can formulate various second-order foundationalisms, for instance one which says that if *S* knows anything, then there is something that *S* directly knows *S* knows. But a foundationalist need not hold such a view, nor would one who does be committed to maintaining that many kinds of belief constitute such knowable foundations, i.e., are knowledge one can know one has, or that every epistemic chain terminates in them. In any event, moderate foundationalists will be disinclined to hold a second-order foundationalism, even if they think that we do in fact have some second-order knowledge. For one thing, if foundational beliefs are only defeasibly justified, it is likely to be quite difficult to know that they are justified, because this requires warrant for attributing certain grounds to the belief and may also require justification for believing that certain defeaters are absent. This is not to deny that there are kinds of knowledge which one may, without having evidence for this, warrantedly and non-dogmatically say one has, for instance where the first-order knowledge is of a simple self-evident proposition. My point is that foundationalism as such, at least in moderate versions, need not make such second-order knowledge (or justification) a condition for the existence of knowledge (or justification) in general.[24]

If we raise the regress problem in the structural form, there is much less temptation to consider foundationalism dogmatic. For there is no presumption that, with respect to anything I know, I non-inferentially know that I know it (and similarly for justification). Granted, on the assumption that by and large I am entitled, without offering evidence, to assert what I directly know, it may seem that even moderate foundationalism justifies me in holding—and expressing—beliefs dogmatically. But this is a mistake. There is considerable difference between what I know or justifiably believe and what I may warrantedly assert without evidence. It is, e.g., apparently consistent with knowing that *p*, say that there is music playing, that I have some reason to doubt that *p*; I might certainly have reason to think others doubt it and that they should not be spoken to as if their objections could not matter. Thus, I might know, through my own good hearing, that *p*, yet be unwarranted in saying that I know it, and warranted, with only moderate confidence, even in saying simply that it is true. Here "It is true" would *express*, but not *claim*, my knowledge; "I know it" explicitly claims knowledge and normally implies that I have justification for beliefs about my objective grounds, not just about my own cognitive and perceptual state.

Nothing said here implies that one *cannot* be justified in believing what one holds dogmatically. That one's attitude *in* holding that *p* is not justified does not imply that one's holding that *p* is itself not justified. It might be possible, for all I have said, that in certain cases one might even be justified, overall, in taking a dogmatic attitude toward certain propositions. This will depend on, among other things, the plausibility of the proposition in question and the level of justification one has for believing that one is right. But typically, dogmatic attitudes are not justified, and moderate foundationalism, far from implying otherwise, can readily explain this.

Furthermore, once the defeasibility of foundational beliefs is appreciated, then even if one does think that one may assert the propositions in question without offering evidence, one will not take the attitudes or other stances required for holding a belief dogmatically. As the example of my belief about the music illustrates, most of the time one is likely to be open to counterargument and may indeed tend to be no more confident than one's grounds warrant. To be sure, fallibilism alone, even when grounded in a proper appreciation of defeasibility, does not preclude dogmatism regarding many of one's beliefs. But it helps toward this end, and it is natural for moderate foundationalists to hold a fallibilistic outlook on their beliefs, especially their empirical beliefs, and to bear it in mind in framing an overall conception of human experience.

If foundationalism has been uncritically thought to encourage dogmatism, coherentism has often been taken to foster intellectual openness. But this second stereotypic conception may be no better warranted than the first. Much depends, of course, on the kind of coherentism and on the temperament of its proponent. Let us consider these points in turn.

What makes coherentism seem to foster tolerance is precisely what leads us to wonder how it can account for knowledge (at least without a coherence theory of truth). For as coherentists widely grant, there are indefinitely many coherent systems of beliefs people might in principle have; hence, to suppose that mine embodies knowledge and thus truth, or even justification and thus a presumption of truth, while yours does not, is prima facie unwarranted. But the moment the view is developed to yield a plausible account of knowledge of the world (an external notion), say by requiring a role for observation beliefs and other cognitively spontaneous beliefs, as some coherentists do, or by requiring beliefs accepted on the basis of a desire to believe truth and avoid error, as others do,[25] it becomes easy to think—and one can be warranted in thinking—that one's beliefs are more likely to constitute knowledge, or to be justified, than someone else's, especially if the other person(s) holds views incompatible with one's own. Indeed, while coherentism makes it easy to see how counterargument can be launched from a wide range of opposing viewpoints, it also provides less in the way of foundational appeals by which debates may be settled—and pretensions quashed. Is one likely to be less dogmatic where one thinks one can always encounter reasoned opposition from someone with a different coherent belief system, right or wrong, than where one believes one can be decisively shown to be mistaken by appeal to foundational sources of knowledge and justification? The answer is not clear; in any given case it will depend on a number of variables, including the temperament of the subject and the propositions in question. And could not my confidence that, using one or another coherent resource, I can always continue to argue for my view generate overconfidence just as much as my thinking that I (defeasibly) know something through experience or reason? Indeed, if coherence is as vague a notion as it seems, it seems quite possible both to exaggerate the extent of its support for one's own beliefs and underestimate the degree of coherence supporting an opposing belief. It turns out that coherentism can also produce dogmatism, even if its proponents have tended to be less inclined toward it than some foundationalists.

If there has been such a lesser inclination, it may be due to temperament, including perhaps a greater sympathy with skepticism, as much as to theoretical commitments. In any case, whether one dogmatically holds certain of one's beliefs surely does depend significantly on whether one is dogmatic in temperament or in certain segments of one's outlook. It may be that the tendency to seek justification in large patterns runs stronger in coherentists than in foundationalists, and that the latter tend more than the former to seek it instead in chains of argument or of inference. If so, this could explain a systematic difference in the degree of dogmatism found in the two traditions. But these tendencies are only contingently connected with the respective theories. Foundationalism can account for the justificatory importance of large patterns, and coherentists commonly conceive argument and inference as prime sources of coherence. One can also wax dogmatic in insisting that a pattern is decisive in justification, as one can dogmatically assert that a single perceptual belief is incontrovertibly veridical.

One source of the charge of dogmatism, at least as advanced by philosophers, is of course the sense that skepticism is being flatly denied. Moreover, the skeptic in us tends to think that any confident assertion of a non-self-evident, non-introspective proposition is dogmatic. On this score, foundationalism is again likely to seem dogmatic if it is conceived as an answer to the dialectical regress formulation. For it may then seem to beg the question against skepticism. But again, foundationalism is not committed to the existence of any knowledge or justified belief; and even a foundationalist who maintains that there is some need not hold that we directly know that there is. Granted, foundationalists are more likely to say, at some point or other, that skepticism is just wrong than are coherentists, who (theoretically) can always trace new justificatory paths through the fabric of their beliefs. But if this is true, it has limited force: perhaps in some such cases foundationalists would be warranted in a way that precludes being dogmatic, and perhaps coherentists are in effect repeating themselves in a way consistent with dogmatic reassertion of the point at issue.

It turns out, then, that fallibilist foundationalism is not damaged by the dogmatism objection and coherentism is not immune to it. Far from being dogmatic, fallibilist foundationalism implies that even where one has a justified belief one cannot show to be justified, one may (and at least normally can) *give* a justification for it. As to coherentism, it, too, may be a refuge for dogmatists, at least those clever enough to find a coherent pattern by which to rationalize the beliefs they dogmatically hold.

Conclusion

The foundationalism–coherentism controversy cannot be settled in a single essay. But we can now appreciate some often neglected dimensions of the issue. One dimension is the formulation of the regress problem itself; another is the distinction between defeasibility and epistemic dependence; still another is that between consequential and constitutive necessary conditions; and yet another is between an unqualifiedly and a conditionally basic source. Even if coherence is neither a constitutive necessary condition for justification nor even a conditionally basic source of it, there is still reason to consider it important for justification. It may even be a *mark* of justification, a common effect of the same causes as it were, or a virtue with the same foundations. Coherence is certainly significant as suggesting a negative constraint on justification; for incoherence is a paradigm of what defeats justification.

I have argued at length for the importance of the regress problem. It matters considerably whether we conceive the problem dialectically or structurally, at least insofar as we cast foundationalism and coherentism in terms of their capacity to solve it. Indeed, while both coherentism and foundationalism can be made plausible on either conception, coherentism is perhaps best understood as a response to the problem *in* some dialectical formulation, and foundationalism is perhaps best understood as a response to it in some structural form. Taking account of both formulations of the regress problem, I have suggested plausible versions of both foundationalism and coherentism. Neither has been established, though fallibilist foundationalism has emerged as the more plausible of the two. In clarifying them, I have stressed a number of distinctions: between the process and the property of justification, between dispositional beliefs and dispositions to believe, between epistemically and psychologically foundational beliefs, between defeasibility and epistemic dependence, between constitutive and consequential necessary conditions for justification, and between unqualified and conditionally basic sources of it. Against this background, we can see how fallibilist foundationalism avoids some of the objections commonly thought to refute foundationalism, including its alleged failure to account for the defeasibility of most and perhaps all of our justification, and for the role of coherence in justification. Indeed, fallibilist foundationalism can even account for coherence as a mark of justification; the chief tension between the two theories concerns not whether coherence is necessary for justification, but whether it is a basic source of it.

It is appropriate in closing to summarize some of the very general considerations supporting a fallibilist foundationalism, since that is a position which some have apparently neglected—or supposed to be a contradiction in terms—and others have not distinguished from coherentism. First, the theory provides a plausible and reasonably straightforward solution to the regress problem. It selects what seems the best option among the four and does not interpret that option in a way that makes knowledge or justification either impossible, as the skeptic would have it, or too easy to achieve, as they would be if they required no grounds at all or only grounds obtainable without the effort of observing, thinking, or otherwise taking account of experience. Second, in working from the experiential and rational sources it takes as epistemically basic, fallibilist foundationalism (in its most plausible versions) accords with reflective common sense: the sorts of beliefs it takes as non-inferentially justified, or as constituting non-inferential knowledge, are pretty much those that, on reflection, we think people are justified in holding, or in supposing to be knowledge, without any more than the evidence of the senses or of intuition. Third, fallibilist foundationalism is psychologically plausible, in two major ways: the account it suggests of the experiential and inferential genesis of many of our beliefs apparently fits what is known about their origins and development; and, far from positing infinite or circular belief chains, whose psychology is at least puzzling, it allows a fairly simple account of the structure of cognition. Beliefs arise both from experience and from inference; some serve to unify others, especially those based on them; and their relative strengths, their changes, and their mutual interactions are all explicable within the moderate foundationalist assumptions suggested. Fourth, the theory serves to integrate our epistemology with our psychology and even biology, particularly in the crucial case of perceptual beliefs. What causally explains why we hold them—sensory experience—is also what justifies them.

From an evolutionary point of view, moreover, many of the kinds of beliefs that the theory (in its most plausible versions) takes to be non-inferentially justified—introspective and memorial beliefs as well as perceptual ones—are plainly essential to survival. We may need a map, and not merely a mirror, of the world to navigate it; but if experience does not generally mirror reality, we are in no position to move to the abstract level on which we can draw a good map. If a mirror without a map is insufficiently discriminating, a map without a mirror is insufficiently reliable. Experience that does not produce beliefs cannot guide us; beliefs not grounded in experience cannot be expected to be true.

Finally, contrary to the dogmatism charge, the theory helps to explain cognitive pluralism. Given that different people have different experiences, and that anyone's experiences change over time, people should be expected to differ from one another in their non-inferentially justified beliefs and, in their own case, across time; and given that logic does not dictate what is to be inferred from one's premises, people should be expected to differ considerably in their inferential beliefs as well. Logic does, to be sure, tell us what *may* be inferred; but it neither forces inferences nor, when we draw them, selects which among the permissible ones we will make. Particularly in the case of inductive inference, say where we infer a hypothesis as the best explanation of some puzzling event, our imagination comes into play; and even if we were to build from the same foundations as our neighbors, we would often produce quite different superstructures.

A properly qualified foundationalism, then, has much to recommend it and exhibits many of the virtues that have been commonly thought to be characteristic only of coherentist theories. Fallibilist foundationalism can account for the main connections between coherence and justification, and it can provide principles of justification to explain how justification that can be plausibly attributed to coherence can also be traced—by sufficiently complex and sometimes inductive paths—to basic sources in experience and reason.[26]

NOTES

[1]   For recent statements of foundationalism see, e.g., R. M. Chisholm, *Theory of Knowledge* (Englewood Cliffs, N.J.: Prentice-Hall, 1977 and 1989), and, especially, "A Version of Foundationalism," *Midwest Studies in Philosophy* V (1980); William P. Alston, "Two Types of Foundationalism," *The Journal of Philosophy* LXXXIII, 7 (1976); Paul K. Moser, *Empirical Justification* (Dordrecht and Boston: D. Reidel, 1985); and Richard Foley, *The Theory of Epistemic Rationality* (Cambridge, Mass.: Harvard University Press, 1987). For detailed statements of coherentism, see, e.g., Wilfrid Sellars, "Givenness and Explanatory Coherence," *The Journal of Philosophy* LXX (1973); Keith Lehrer, *Knowledge* (Oxford: Oxford University Press, 1974); Gilbert Harman, *Thought* (Princeton, N.J.: Princeton University Press, 1975); and Laurence BonJour, *The Structure of Empirical Knowledge* (Cambridge, Mass.: Harvard University Press, 1985). For useful discussions of the controversy between foundationalism and coherentism, see C.F. Delaney, "Foundations of Empirical Knowledge—Again," *The New Scholasticism* L, 1 (1976), which defends a kind of foundationalism; and Brand Blanshard, "Coherence and Correspondence," in *Philosophical Interrogations*, edited by Sydney and Beatrice Rome (New York: Holt, Rinehart & Winston, 1964), which defends his earlier views against objections by critics quoted in the same chapter.

[2]   BonJour, e.g., says that the regress problem is "perhaps the most crucial in the entire theory of knowledge" (op. cit., p. 18); and he considers it the chief motivation for foundationalism (p. 17) and regards the failure of foundationalism as "the main motivation for a coherence theory" (p. 149).

[3]   Chisholm seems to raise the problem in this way when he says, "If we try Socratically to formulate our justification for any particular claim to know ('My justification for thinking that I know that *A* is the fact that *B*'), and if we are relentless in our inquiry ('and my justification for thinking that I know that *B* is the fact that *C*'), we will arrive, sooner or later, at a kind of stopping place ('but my justification for thinking that I know that *N* is simply the fact that *N*'). An example of *N* might be the fact that I seem to remember having been here before or that something now looks blue to me" (*Theory of Knowledge*, 1966, p. 2); cf. the 2nd ed., 1977, esp.

pp. 19–20. In these and other passages Chisholm seems to be thinking of the regress problem dialectically and taking a foundational belief to be second order. To be sure, he is talking about justification of any "claim to know"; but his and similar locutions—such as "knowledge claim"—have often been taken to apply to expressions of first-order knowledge, as where one says that it is raining, on the basis of perceptions which one would normally take to yield knowledge that it is.

[4]   See *Posterior Analytics*, Bk 3. Having opened Bk. 1 with the statement that "All instruction given or received by way of argument proceeds from pre-existent knowledge" (71a1–2), and thereby established a concern with the structure and presuppositions of knowledge, Aristotle formulated the regress argument as a response to the question of what is required for the existence of (what he called scientific) knowledge (72b4–24). (The translation is by W. D. Ross.)

[5]   The locus classicus of this argument is the *Posterior Analytics*, Bk. II. But while Aristotle's version agrees with the one given here insofar as his main conclusion is that "not all knowledge is demonstrative," he also says, "since the regress must end in immediate truths, those truths must be indemonstrable" (72b19–24), whereas I hold that direct knowledge does *not* require indemonstrability. There might be appropriate premises; *S*'s foundational belief is simply not based on them (I also question the validity of the inference in the second quotation, but I suspect that Aristotle had independent grounds for its conclusion).

[6]   In Meditation I, e.g., Descartes says that "reason already persuades me that I ought no less carefully to withhold my assent from matters which are not entirely certain and indubitable than from those which appear to me manifestly to be false" (from the Haldane and Ross translation).

[7]   That knowing a proposition implies believing it is not uncontroversial, but most epistemologists accept the implication. For defense of the implication see, e.g., Harman, op. cit, and my *Belief, Justification, and Knowledge* (Belmont, Calif.: Wadsworth, 1988).

[8]   See, e.g., Richard Foley, "Justified Inconsistent Beliefs," *American Philosophical Quarterly* 16 (1979). I have criticized the infinite-belief view in "Believing and Affirming," *Mind* XCI (1982).

[9]   It should be noted that memory is different from the other three in this: it is apparently not a *basic* source of knowledge, as it is of justification; i.e., one cannot know something from memory unless one has *come* to know it in some other mode, e.g. through perception. This is discussed in ch. 2 of my *Belief, Justification, and Knowledge*. Cf. Carl Ginet, *Knowledge, Perception, and Memory* (Dordrecht and Boston: D. Reidel, 1973).

[10]   The view that such experience is a mirror of nature is criticized at length by Richard Rorty in *Philosophy and the Mirror of Nature* (Princeton, N.J.: Princeton University Press, 1979). He has in mind, however, a Cartesian version of foundationalism, which is not the only kind and implies features of the "mirror" that are not entailed by the metaphor used here.

[11]   This does not entail that there are *objects* in the visual field which have their own phenomenal colors and shapes; the point is only that there is some sense in which experiences *characterized by* color and shape (however that is to be analyzed) represent the colors and shapes apparently instantiated in the external world.

[12]   This metaphor comes from D. M. Armstrong. See esp. *Belief, Truth, and Knowledge* (Cambridge: Cambridge University Press, 1973). His theory of justification and knowledge is reliabilist, in taking both to be analyzable in terms of their being produced or sustained by reliable processes (such as tactile belief-production), those that (normally) yield true beliefs more often than false. Foundationalism may, but need not, be reliabilist; and this chapter is intended to be neutral with respect to the choice between reliabilist and internalist views. For further discussion see Paul K. Moser, *Knowledge and Evidence* (Cambridge and New York: Cambridge University Press, 1989), and R. M. Chisholm, *Theory of Knowledge*, 3rd ed. (Englewood Cliffs, N.J.: Prentice-Hall, 1989).

[13]   Clause (4) requires "other-things-equal" because removal of justification from one source can affect justification from another even without being a basis of the latter justification; and the *level* of justification in question I take to be (as in the counterpart formulation of coherentism) approximately that appropriate to knowledge. The formulation should hold, however, for any given level.

[14]   For references to the main contemporary accounts, especially those by Lehrer and BonJour, see John B. Bender, *The Current Status of the Coherence Theory* (Dordrecht and Boston: Kluwer, 1989).

[15]   This applies to Sellars, Lehrer, and BonJour and is evident in the works cited in note 1. Their coherentist positions are not linear.

[16]   With this question in mind, it is interesting to read Donald Davidson, "A Coherence Theory of Truth and Knowledge," in Dieter Hendrich, ed., *Kant oder Hegel* (Stuttgart, 1976). Cf. Jaegwon Kim, "What is 'Naturalized Epistemology'?" *Philosophical Perspectives* 2 (1988).

[17]   This distinction seems to have been often missed, e.g. in Hilary Kornblith, "Beyond Foundationalism and the Coherence Theory," *Journal of Philosophy* LXXVII (1980).

[18]   One exception is David Shatz's "Foundationalism, Coherentism, and the Levels Gambit," *Synthese* 55, 1 (1983).

[19]   This suggestion may be controversial: an epistemic virtue theorist might argue that the trait is most basic and colors the attitude, and that these together are the basis for classifying beliefs as held dogmatically or otherwise. Most of my points will be neutral with respect to this priority issue.

[20]   Shatz, op. cit., p. 107, attributes a similar suggestion to me (from correspondence), and it is appropriate to suggest here why I do not mean to endorse it.

[21]   The dogmatism charge has been brought by, e.g., Bruce Aune in *Knowledge, Mind and Nature* (New York: Random House, 1967), pp. 41–3, and, by implication, by James Cornman and Keith Lehrer in *Philosophical Problems and Arguments*, 2nd ed. (New York: Macmillan, 1974), pp. 60–1. Alston goes so far as to say that "It is the aversion to dogmatism, to the apparent arbitrariness of putative foundations, that leads many philosophers to embrace some form of coherence or contextualist theory…" (op. cit., pp. 182–3).

[22]   See Alston, op. cit., for a reply (which supports mine) to the dogmatism charge.

[23] A formulation of the regress problem by Chisholm is cited in note 3. For a contrasting formulation see Anthony Quinton, *The Nature of Things* (London: Routledge & Kegan Paul, 1973), p. 119. Quinton, it is interesting to note, is sympathetic to the kind of moderate foundationalism that would serve as an answer to the problem in his formulation.

[24] It is natural to read Descartes as holding a second-order foundationalism; but if he did, he was at least not committed to it by even his strong foundationalism. That requires indefeasible foundations, but it is his commitment to vindicating knowledge in the face of skepticism that apparently commits him to our having second-order knowledge. Similar points hold for Aristotle, who indeed may have taken our second-order knowledge to be at least limited; he said, e.g., "It is hard to be sure whether one knows or not; for it is hard to be sure whether one's knowledge is based on the basic truths appropriate to each attribute—the differentia of true knowledge" (*Posterior Analytics* 76a26–28).

[25] I have in mind, for the observation requirement, BonJour, op. cit., and, for the motivational requirement, Keith Lehrer, e.g. in *Knowledge*.

[26] This chapter draws substantially on my "Foundationalism, Coherentism, and Epistemological Dogmatism," *Philosophical Perspectives* 2 (1988), 407–59 (edited by James E. Tomberlin). I thank Louis P. Pojman for many helpful comments on an earlier draft of much of the material and for permission to use selected passages from my two chapters in his book *The Theory of Knowledge: Contemporary Readings* (Belmont, Calif.: Wadsworth, 1992).

1.5

WHAT IS JUSTIFIED BELIEF?

Alvin Goldman

The aim of this paper is to sketch a theory of justified belief. What I have in mind is an explanatory theory, one that explains in a general way why certain beliefs are counted as justified and others as unjustified. Unlike some traditional approaches, I do not try to prescribe standards for justification that differ from, or improve upon, our ordinary standards. I merely try to explicate the ordinary standards, which are, I believe, quite different from those of many classical, e.g., "Cartesian," accounts.

Many epistemologists have been interested in justification because of its presumed close relationship to knowledge. This relationship is intended to be preserved in the conception of justified belief presented here. In previous papers on knowledge,[1] I have denied that justification is necessary for knowing, but there I had in mind "Cartesian" accounts of justification. On the account of justified belief suggested here, it *is* necessary for knowing, and closely related to it.

The term "justified", I presume, is an evaluative term, a term of appraisal. Any correct definition or synonym of it would also feature evaluative terms. I assume that such definitions or synonyms might be given, but I am not interested in them. I want a set of *substantive* conditions that specify when a belief is justified. Compare the moral term "right." This might be defined in other ethical terms or phrases, a task appropriate to meta-ethics. The task of normative ethics, by contrast, is to state substantive conditions for the rightness of actions. Normative ethics tries to specify non-ethical conditions that determine when an action is right. A familiar example is act-utilitarianism, which says an action is right if and only if it produces, or would produce, at least as much net happiness as any alternative open to the agent. These necessary and sufficient conditions clearly involve no ethical notions. Analogously, I want a theory of justified belief to specify in non-epistemic terms when a belief is justified. This is not the only kind of theory of justifiedness one might seek, but it is one important kind of theory and the kind sought here.

In order to avoid epistemic terms in our theory, we must know which terms are epistemic. Obviously, an exhaustive list cannot be given, but here are some examples: "justified", "warranted", "has (good) grounds", "has reason (to believe)", "knows that", "sees that", "apprehends that", "is probable" (in an epistemic or inductive sense), "shows that", "establishes that", and "ascertains that." By contrast, here are some sample nonepistemic expressions: "believes that", "is true", "causes", "it is necessary that", "implies", "is deducible from", and "is probable" (either in the frequency sense or the propensity sense). In general, (purely) doxastic, metaphysical, modal, semantic, or syntactic expressions are not epistemic.

There is another constraint I wish to place on a theory of justified belief, in addition to the constraint that it be couched in non-epistemic language. Since I seek an explanatory theory, i.e., one that clarifies the underlying source of justificational status, it is not enough for a theory to state "correct" necessary and sufficient conditions. Its conditions must also be appropriately deep or revelatory. Suppose, for example, that the following sufficient condition of justified belief is offered: "If S senses redly at t and S believes at t that he is sensing redly, then S's belief at t that he is sensing redly is justified." This is not the kind of principle I seek; for, even if it is correct, it leaves unexplained *why* a person who senses redly and believes that he does, believes this justifiably. Not every state is such that if one is in it and believes one is in it, this belief is justified. What is distinctive about the state of sensing redly, or "phenomenal" states in general? A theory of justified belief of the kind I seek must answer this question, and hence it must be couched at a suitably deep, general or abstract level.

A few introductory words about my *explicandum* are appropriate at this juncture. It is often assumed that whenever a person has a justified belief, he knows that it is justified and knows what the justification is. It is further assumed that the person can state or explain what his justification is. On this view, a justification is an argument, defense, or set of reasons that can be given in support of a belief. Thus, one studies the nature of justified belief by considering what a person might *say* if asked to defend, or justify, his belief. I make none of these sorts of assumptions here. I leave it an open question whether, when a belief *is* justified, the believer *knows* it is justified. I also leave it an open question whether, when a belief is justified, the believer can *state* or *give* a justification for it. I do not even assume that when a belief is justified

there is something "possessed" by the believer which can be called a "justification." I do assume that a justified belief gets its status of being justified from
some processes or properties that make it justified. In short, there must be
some justification-conferring processes or properties. But this does not imply
that there must be an argument, or reason, or anything else, "possessed" at the
time of belief by the believer.

*Justification has
nothing to do with the
knower.*

A theory of justified belief will be a set of principles that specify truth-
conditions for the schema S's belief in p at time t is justified, i.e., conditions
for the satisfaction of this schema in all possible cases. It will be convenient to
formulate candidate theories in a recursive or inductive format, which would
include (A) one or more base clauses, (B) a set of recursive clauses (possibly
null), and (C) a closure clause. In such a format, it is permissible for the
predicate "is a justified belief" to appear in recursive clauses. But neither this
predicate, nor any other epistemic predicate, may appear in (the antecedent of)
any base clause.[2]

Before turning to my own theory, I want to survey some other possible
approaches to justified belief. Identification of problems associated with other
attempts will provide some motivation for the theory I shall offer. Obviously,
I cannot examine all, or even very many, alternative attempts. But a few
sample attempts will be instructive.

Let us concentrate on the attempt to formulate one or more adequate base-
clause principles.[3] Here is a classical candidate:

(1)   If S believes p at t, and p is indubitable for S (at t), then S's belief in
       p at t is justified.   *indubitably*

To evaluate this principle, we need to know that "indubitable" means. It can
be understood in at least two ways. First, "p is indubitable for S" might mean:
"S has no *grounds* for doubting p." Since "ground" is an epistemic term,
however, principle (1) would be inadmissible on this reading, for epistemic
terms may not legitimately appear in the antecedent of a base-clause. A second
interpretation would avoid this difficulty. One might interpret "p is indubitable for S" psychologically, i.e., as meaning "S is psychologically incapable of
doubting p." This would make principle (1) admissible, but would it be
correct? Surely not. A religious fanatic may be psychologically incapable of
doubting the tenets of his faith, but that doesn't make his belief in them
justified. Similarly, during the Watergate affair, someone may have been so

blinded by the aura of the Presidency that even after the most damaging evidence against Nixon had emerged he was still incapable of doubting Nixon's veracity. It doesn't follow that his belief in Nixon's veracity was justified.

A second candidate base-clause principle is this:

(2)   If S believes p at t, and p is self-evident, then S's belief in p at t is justified.

To evaluate this principle, we again need an interpretation of its crucial term, in this case "self-evident." On one standard reading, "evident" is a synonym for "justified." "*Self*-evident" would therefore mean something like "directly justified", "intuitively justified", or "non-derivatively justified." On this reading "self-evident" is an epistemic phrase, and principle (2) would be disqualified as a base-clause principle.

However, there are other possible readings of "p is self-evident" on which it isn't an epistemic phrase. One such reading is: "It is impossible to understand p without believing it."[4] According to this interpretation, trivial analytic and logical truths might turn out to be self-evident. Hence, any belief in such a truth would be a justified belief, according to (2).

What does "it is *impossible* to understand p without believing it" mean? Does it mean "*humanly* impossible?" That reading would probably make (2) an unacceptable principle. There may well be propositions which humans have an innate and irrepressible disposition to believe, e.g., "Some events have causes." But it seems unlikely that people's inability to refrain from believing such a proposition makes every belief in it justified.

Should we then understand "impossible" to mean "impossible in principle", or "logically impossible"? If that is the reading given, I suspect that (2) is a vacuous principle. I doubt that even trivial logical or analytic truths will satisfy this definition of "self-evident." Any proposition, we may assume, has two or more components that are somehow organized or juxtaposed. To understand the proposition one must "grasp" the components and their juxtaposition. Now in the case of *complex* logical truths, there are (human) psychological operations that suffice to grasp the components and their juxtaposition but do not suffice to produce a belief that the proposition is true. But can't we at least *conceive* of an analogous set of psychological operations even for simple logical truths, operations which perhaps are not in the repertoire of human cognizers but which might be in the repertoire of some conceivable beings? That is, can't we conceive of psychological operations that would suffice to grasp the components and componential-juxtaposition of these simple propositions but do not suffice to produce *belief* in the propositions? I think we can conceive of such operations. Hence, for any proposition you choose, it will be possible for it to be understood without being believed.

Finally, even if we set these two objections aside, we must note that self-evidence can at best confer justificational status on relatively few beliefs, and the only plausible group are beliefs in necessary truths. Thus, other base-clause principles will be needed to explain the justificational status of beliefs in contingent propositions.

The notion of a base-clause principle is naturally associated with the idea of "direct" justifiedness, and in the realm of contingent propositions first-person-current-mental-state propositions have often been assigned this role. In Chisholm's terminology, this conception is expressed by the notion of a "*self-presenting*" state or proposition. The sentence "I am thinking", for example, expresses a self-presenting proposition. (At least I shall *call* this sort of content a "proposition", though it only has a truth value given some assignment of a subject who utters or entertains the content and a time of entertaining). When such a proposition is true for person S at time t, S is justified in believing it at t: in Chisholm's terminology, the proposition is "evident" for S at t. This suggests the following base-clause principle.

(3)   If p is a self-presenting proposition, and p is true for S at t, and S believes p at t, then S's belief in p at t is justified.

What, exactly, does "self-presenting" mean? In the second edition of *Theory of Knowledge*, Chisholm offers this definition. "h is self-presenting for S at t =df. h is true at t; and necessarily, if h is true at t, then h is evident for S at t."[5] Unfortunately, since "evident" is an epistemic term, "self-presenting" also becomes an epistemic term on this definition, thereby disqualifying (3) as a legitimate base-clause. Some other definition of self-presentingness must be offered if (3) is to be a suitable base-clause principle.

Another definition of self-presentation readily comes to mind. "Self-presentation" is an approximate synonym of "self-intimation", and a proposition may be said to be self-intimating if and only if whenever it is true of a person that person believes it. More precisely, we may give the following definition.

(SP)   Proposition p is self-presenting if and only if: necessarily, for any S and any t, if p is true for S at t, then S believes p at t.

On this definition, "self-presenting" is clearly not an epistemic predicate, so (3) would be an admissible principle. Moreover, there is initial plausibility in the suggestion that it is *this* feature of first-person-current-mental-state propositions—viz., their truth guarantees their being believed—that makes beliefs in them justified.

Employing this definition of self-presentation, is principle (3) correct? This cannot be decided until we define self-presentation more precisely. Since the operator "necessarily" can be read in different ways, there are different forms of self-presentation and correspondingly different versions of principle (3). Let us focus on two of these readings: a "*nomological*" reading and a "*logical*" reading. Consider first the nomological reading. On this definition a proposition is self-presenting just in case it is nomologically necessary that if *p* is true for *S* at *t*, then *S* believes *p* at *t*.[6]

Is the nomological version of principle (3)—call it "(3_N)"—correct? Not at all. We can imagine cases in which the antecedent of (3_N) is satisfied but we would not say that the belief is justified. Suppose, for example, that *p* is the proposition expressed by the sentence "I am in brain-state *B*", where "*B*" is shorthand for a certain highly specific neural state description. Further suppose it is a nomological truth that anyone in brain-state *B* will ipso facto *believe* he is in brain-state *B*. In other words, imagine that an occurrent belief with the content "I am in brain-state *B*" is realized whenever one is in brain-state *B*.[7] According to (3_N), any such belief is justified. But that is clearly false. We can readily imagine circumstances in which a person goes into brain-state *B* and therefore has the belief in question, though this belief is by no means justified. For example, we can imagine that a brain-surgeon operating on *S* artificially induces brain-state *B*. This results, phenomenologically, in *S*'s suddenly believing—out of the blue—that he is in brain-state *B*, without any relevant antecedent beliefs. We would hardly say, in such a case, that *S*'s belief that he is in brain-state *B* is justified.

Let us turn next to the logical version of (3)—call it "(3_L)"—in which a proposition is defined as self-presenting just in case it is logically necessary that if *p* is true for *S* at *t*, then *S* believes *p* at *t*. This stronger version of principle (3) might seem more promising. In fact, however, it is no more successful than (3_N). Let *p* be the proposition "I am awake" and assume that it is logically necessary that if this proposition is true for some person *S* and time *t*, then *S* believes *p* at *t*. This assumption is consistent with the further assumption that *S* frequently believes *p* when it is false, e.g., when he is dreaming. Under these circumstances, we would hardly accept the contention that *S*'s belief in this proposition is always justified. But nor should we accept the contention that the belief is justified when it is *true*. The truth of the proposition logically guarantees that the belief is *held*, but why should it guarantee that the belief is *justified*?

The foregoing criticism suggests that we have things backwards. The idea of self-presentation is that truth guarantees belief. This fails to confer justification because it is compatible with there being belief without truth. So what seems necessary—or at least sufficient—for justification is that belief should guarantee truth. Such a notion has usually gone under the label of "*infallibility*", or "*incorrigibility*." It may be defined as follows:

(INC)   Proposition p is incorrigible if and only if: necessarily, for any S and any t, if S believes p at t, then p is true for S at t.

Using the notion of incorrigibility, we may propose principle (4).

(4)   If p is an incorrigible proposition, and S believe p at t, then S's belief in p at t is justified.

As was true of self-presentation, there are different varieties of incorrigibility, corresponding to different interpretations of "necessarily." Accordingly, we have different versions of principle (4). Once again, let us concentrate on a nomological and a logical version, (4_N) and (4_L) respectively.

We can easily construct a counterexample to (4_N) along the lines of the belief-state/brain-state counterexample that refuted (3_N). Suppose it is nomologically necessary that if anyone believes he is in brain-state B then it is true that he is in brain-state B, for the only way this belief-state is realized is through brain-state B itself. It follows that "I am in brain-state B" is a nomolgically incorrigible proposition. Therefore, according to (4_N), whenever anyone believes this proposition at any time, that belief is justified. But we may again construct a brain-surgeon example in which someone comes to have such a belief but the belief isn't justified.

Apart from this counterexample, the general point is this. Why should the fact that S's believing p guarantees the truth of p imply that S's belief is justified? The nature of the guarantee might be wholly fortuitous, as the belief-state/brain-state example is intended to illustrate. To appreciate the point consider the following related possibility. A person's mental structure might be such that whenever he believes that p will be true (of him) a split second later, then p is true (of him) a split second later. This is because, we may suppose, his believing it brings it about. But surely we would not be compelled in such a circumstance to say that a belief of this sort is justified. So why should the fact that S's believing p guarantees the truth of p *precisely at the time of belief* imply that the belief is justified? There is no intuitive plausibility in this supposition.

The notion of *logical* incorrigibility has a more honored place in the history of conceptions of justification. But even principle (4_L), I believe, suffers from defects similar to those of (4_N). The mere fact that belief in p logically guarantees its truth does not confer justificational status on such a belief.

The first difficulty that (4_L) arises from logical or mathematical truths. Any true proposition of logic or mathematics is logically necessary. Hence, any such proposition p is logically incorrigible, since it is logically necessary that, for any S and any t, if S believes p at t then p is true (for S at t). Now assume that Nelson believes a certain very complex mathematical truth at time t. Since such a proposition is logically incorrigible, (4_L) implies that Nelson's belief in this truth at t is justified. But we may easily suppose that this belief of Nelson is not at all the result of proper mathematical reasoning, or even the result of appeal to trustworthy authority. Perhaps Nelson believes this complex truth because of utterly confused reasoning, or because of hasty and ill-founded conjecture. Then his belief is not justified, contrary to what (4_L) implies.

The case of logical or mathematical truths is admittedly peculiar, since the truth of these propositions is assured independently of any beliefs. It might seem, therefore, that we can better capture the idea of "belief logically guaranteeing truth" in cases where the propositions in question are *contingent*. With this in mind, we might restrict (4_L) to *contingent* incorrigible propositions. Even this amendment cannot save (4_L), however, since there are counterexamples to it involving purely contingent propositions.

Suppose that Humperdink has been studying logic—or, rather, pseudologic—from Elmer Fraud, whom Humperdink has no reason to trust as a logician. Fraud has enunciated the principle that any disjunctive proposition consisting of at least 40 distinct disjuncts is very probably true. Humperdink now encounters the proposition p, a contingent proposition with 40 disjuncts, the 7th disjunct being "I exist." Although Humperdink grasps the proposition fully, he doesn't notice that it is entailed by "I exist." Rather, he is struck by the fact that it falls under the disjunction rule Fraud has enunciated (a rule I assume Humperdink is not *justified* in believing). Bearing this rule in mind, Humperdink forms a belief in p. Now notice that p is logically incorrigible. It is logically necessary that if anyone believes p, then p is true (of him at that time). This simply follows from the fact that, first, a person's believing anything entails that he exists, and second, "I exist" entails p. Since p is logically incorrigible, principle (4_L) implies that Humperdink's belief in p is justified. But surely, given our example, that conclusion is false. Humperdink's belief in p is not at all justified.

One thing that goes wrong in this example is that while Humperdink's belief in p logically implies its truth, Humperdink doesn't *recognize* that his believing it implies its truth. This might move a theorist to revise (4_L) by adding the requirement that S "recognize" that p is logically incorrigible. But this, of course, won't do. The term "recognize" is obviously an epistemic term, so the suggested revision of (4_L) would result in an inadmissible base-clause.

II

Let us try to diagnose what has gone wrong with these attempts to produce an acceptable base-clause principle. Notice that each of the foregoing attempts confers the status of "justified" on a belief without restriction on *why* the belief is held, i.e., on what *causally initiates* the belief or *causally sustains* it. The logical versions of principles (3) and (4), for example, clearly place no restriction on causes of belief. The same is true of the nomological versions of (3) and (4), since nomological requirements can be satisfied by simultaneity or cross-sectional laws, as illustrated by our brain-state/belief-state examples. I suggest that the absence of causal requirements accounts for the failure of the foregoing principles. Many of our counterexamples are ones in which the belief is caused in some strange or unacceptable way, e.g., by the accidental movement of a brain-surgeon's hand, by reliance on an illicit, pseudo-logical principle, or by the blinding aura of the Presidency. In general, a strategy for defeating a noncausal principle of justifiedness is to find a case in which the principle's antecedent is satisfied but the belief is caused by some faulty belief-forming process. The faultiness of the belief-forming process will incline us, intuitively, to regard the belief as unjustified. Thus, correct principles of justified belief must be principles that make causal requirements, where "cause" is construed broadly to include sustainers as well as initiators of belief (i.e., processes that determine, or help to overdetermine, a belief's continuing to be held.)[8]

The need for causal requirements is not restricted to base-clause principles. Recursive principles will also need a causal component. One might initially suppose that the following is a good recursive principle: "If S justifiably believes q at t, and q entails p, and S believes p at t, then S's belief in p at t is justified." But this principle is unacceptable. S's belief in p doesn't receive justificational status simply from the fact that p is entailed by q and S justifiably believes q. If what causes S to believe p at t is entirely different, S's belief in p may well not be justified. Nor can the situation be remedied by adding to the antecedent the condition that S justifiably believes that q entails p. Even if he believes this, and believes q as well, he might not put these beliefs together. He might believe p as a result of some other wholly extraneous, considerations. So once again, conditions that fail to require appropriate causes of a belief don't guarantee justifiedness.

Granted that principles of justified belief must make reference to causes of belief, what kinds of causes confer justifiedness? We can gain insight into this problem by reviewing some faulty processes of belief-formation, i.e., processes whose belief-outputs would be classed as unjustified. Here are some examples: confused reasoning, wishful thinking, reliance on emotional attachment, mere hunch or guesswork, and hasty generalization. What do these faulty processes have in common? They share the feature of *unreliability*: they tend to produce *error* a large proportion of the time. By contrast, which species of belief-forming (or belief-sustaining) processes are intuitively justification-conferring? They include standard perceptual processes, remembering, good reasoning, and introspection. What these processes seem to have in common is *reliability*: the beliefs they produce are generally true. My positive proposal, then, is this. The justificational status of a belief is a function of the reliability of the process or processes that cause it, where (as a first approximation) reliability consists in the tendency of a process to produce beliefs that are true rather than false.

To test this thesis further, notice that justifiedness is not a purely categorical concept, although I treat it here as categorical in the interest of simplicity. We can and do regard certain beliefs as more justified than others. Furthermore, our intuitions of comparative justifiedness go along with our beliefs about the comparative reliability of the belief-causing processes.

Consider perceptual beliefs. Suppose Jones believes he has just seen a mountain-goat. Our assessment of the belief's justifiedness is determined by whether he caught a brief glimpse of the creature at a great distance, or whether he had a good look at the thing only 30 yards away. His belief in the latter sort of case is (*ceteris paribus*) more justified than in the former sort of case. And, if his belief is true, we are more prepared to say he *knows* in the latter case than in the former. The difference between the two cases seems to be this. Visual beliefs formed from brief and hasty scanning, or where the perceptual object is a long distance off, tend to be wrong more often than visual beliefs formed from detailed and leisurely scanning, or where the object is in reasonable proximity. In short, the visual processes in the former category are less reliable than those in the latter category. A similar point holds for memory beliefs. A belief that results from a hazy and indistinct memory impression is counted as less justified than a belief that arises from a distinct memory impression, and our inclination to classify those beliefs as *"knowledge"* varies in the same way. Again, the reason is associated with the comparative reliability of the processes. Hazy and indistinct memory impressions are generally less reliable indicators of what actually happened; so beliefs formed from such impressions are less likely to be true than beliefs formed from distinct impressions. Further, consider beliefs based on inference from observed samples. A belief about a population that is based on random sampling, or on instances that exhibit great variety, is intuitively more justified than a belief based on biased sampling, or on instances from a narrow sector of the population. Again, the degree of justifiedness seems to be a function of reliability. Inferences based on random or varied samples will tend to produce less error or inaccuracy than inferences based on non-random or non-varied samples.

Returning to a categorical concept of justifiedness, we might ask just *how* reliable a belief-forming process must be in order that its resultant beliefs be justified. A precise answer to this question should not be expected. Our conception of justification is *vague* in this respect. It does seem clear, however, that *perfect* reliability isn't required. Belief-forming processes that *sometimes* produce error still confer justification. It follows that there can be justified beliefs that are false.

I have characterized justification-conferring processes as ones that have a "tendency" to produce beliefs that are true rather than false. The term "tendency" could refer either to *actual* long-run frequency, or to a "propensity", i.e., outcomes that would occur in merely *possible* realizations of the process. Which of these is intended? Unfortunately, I think our ordinary conception of justifiedness is vague on this dimension too. For the most part, we simply assume that the "observed" frequency of truth versus error would be approximately replicated in the actual long-run, and also in relevant counterfactual situations, i.e., ones that are highly "realistic", or conform closely to the circumstances of the actual world. Since we ordinarily assume these frequencies to be roughly the same, we make no concerted effort to distinguish them. Since the purpose of my present theorizing is to capture our ordinary conception of justifiedness, and since our ordinary conception is vague on this matter, it is appropriate to leave the theory vague in the same respect.

We need to say more about the notion of a belief-forming *"process."* Let us mean by a "process" a *functional operation* or procedure, i.e., something that generates a *mapping* from certain states—"inputs"—into other states— "outputs." The outputs in the present case are states of believing this or that proposition at a given moment. On this interpretation, a process is a *type* as opposed to a *token*. This is fully appropriate, since it is only types that have statistical properties such as producing truth 80% of the time; and it is precisely such statistical properties that determine the reliability of a process. Of course, we also want to speak of a process as *causing* a belief, and it looks as if types are incapable of being causes. But when we say that a belief is caused by a given process, understood as a functional procedure, we may interpret this to mean that it is caused by the particular *inputs* to the process (and by the intervening events "through which" the functional procedure carries the inputs into the output) on the occasion in question.

What are some examples of belief-forming "processes" construed as functional operations? One example is reasoning processes, where the inputs include antecedent beliefs and entertained hypotheses. Another example is functional procedures whose inputs include desires, hopes, or emotional states of various sorts (together with antecedent beliefs). A third example is a memory process, which takes as input beliefs or experiences at an earlier time and generates as output beliefs at a later time. For example, a memory process might take as input a belief *at* t_1 that Lincoln was born in 1809 and generate as output a belief *at* t_n that Lincoln was born in 1809. A fourth example is perceptual processes. Here it isn't clear whether inputs should include states of the environment, such as the distance of the stimulus from the cognizer, or only events within or on the surface of the organism, e.g., receptor stimulations. I shall return to this point in a moment.

A critical problem concerning our analysis is the degree of generality of the process-types in question. Input-output relations can be specified very broadly or very narrowly, and the degree of generality will partly determine the degree of reliability. A process-type might be selected so narrowly that only one instance of it ever occurs, and hence the type is either completely reliable or completely unreliable. (This assumes that reliability is a function of *actual* frequency only.) If such narrow process-types were selected, beliefs that are intuitively unjustified might be said to result from perfectly reliable processes; and beliefs that are intuitively justified might be said result from perfectly unreliable processes.

It is clear that our ordinary thought about process-types slices them broadly, but I cannot at present give a precise explication of our intuitive principles. One plausible suggestion, though, is that the relevant processes are *content-neutral.* It might be argued, for example, that the process of *inferring p whenever the Pope asserts p* could pose problems for our theory. If the Pope is infallible, this process will be perfectly reliable; yet we would not regard the belief-outputs of this process as justified. The content-neutral restriction would avert this difficulty. If relevant processes are required to admit as input beliefs (or other states) with *any* content, the aforementioned process will not count, for its input beliefs have a restricted propositional content, viz., "*the Pope* asserts *p.*"

In addition to the problem of "generality" or "abstractness" there is the previously mentioned problem of the "*extent*" of belief-forming processes. Clearly, the causal ancestry of beliefs often includes events outside the organism. Are such events to be included among the "inputs" of belief-forming processes? Or should we restrict the extent of belief-forming processes to "*cognitive*" events, i.e., events within the organism's nervous system? I shall choose the latter course, though with some hesitation. My general grounds for this decision are roughly as follows. Justifiedness seems to be a function of how a cognizer deals with his environmental input, i.e., with the goodness or badness of the operations that register and transform the stimulation that reaches him. ("Deal with", of course, does not mean *purposeful* action; nor is it restricted to *conscious* activity.) A justified belief is, roughly speaking, one that results from cognitive operations that are, generally speaking, good or successful. But "*cognitive*" operations are most plausibly construed as operations of the cognitive faculties, i.e., "information-processing" equipment *internal* to the organism.

With these points in mind, we may now advance the following base-clause principle for justified belief.

(5)   If S's believing p at t results from a reliable cognitive belief-forming process (or set of processes), then S's belief in p at t is justified.

Since "reliable belief-forming process" has been defined in terms of such notions as belief, truth, statistical frequency, and the like, it is not an epistemic term. Hence, (5) is an admissible base-clause.

It might seem as if (5) promises to be not only a successful base clause, but the only principle needed whatever, apart from a closure clause. In other words, it might seem as if it is a necessary as well as a sufficient condition of justifiedness that a belief be produced by reliable cognitive belief-forming processes. But this is not quite correct, given our provisional definition of "reliability."

Our provisional definition implies that a reasoning process is reliable only if it generally produces beliefs that are true, and similarly, that a memory process is reliable only if it generally yields beliefs that are true. But these requirements are too strong. A reasoning procedure cannot be expected to produce true belief if it is applied to false premises. And memory cannot be expected to yield a true belief if the original belief it attempts to retain is false. What we need for reasoning and memory, then, is a notion of "*conditional reliability.*" A process is conditionally reliable when a sufficient proportion of its output-beliefs are true *given that its input-beliefs are true.*

With this point in mind, let us distinguish *belief-dependent* and *belief-independent* cognitive processes. The former are processes *some* of whose inputs are belief-states.[9] The latter are processes *none* of whose inputs are belief-states. We may then replace principle (5) with the following two principles, the first a base-clause principle and the second a recursive-clause principle.

(6$_A$)   If S's belief in p at t results ("immediately") from a belief-independent process that is (unconditionally) reliable, then S's belief in p at t is justified.

(6$_B$)   If S's belief in p at t results ("immediately") from a belief-dependent process that is (at least) conditionally reliable, and if the beliefs (if any) on which this process operates in producing S's belief in p at t are themselves justified, then S's belief in p at t is justified.[10]

If we add to (6$_A$) and (6$_B$) the standard closure clause, we have a complete theory of justified belief. The theory says, in effect, that a belief is justified if and only if it is "*well-formed*", i.e., it has an ancestry of reliable and/or conditionally reliable cognitive operations. (Since a dated belief may be over-determined, it may have a number of distinct ancestral trees. These need not all be full of reliable or conditionally reliable processes. But at least one ancestral tree must have reliable or conditionally reliable processes throughout).

The theory of justified belief proposed here, then, is an *Historical* or *Genetic* theory. It contrasts with the dominant approach to justified belief, an approach that generates what we may call (borrowing a phrase from Robert Nozick) "*Current Time-Slice*"theories. A Current Time-Slice theory makes the justificational status of a belief wholly a function of what is true of the cognizer *at the time* of belief. An Historical theory makes the justificational status of a belief depend on its prior history. Since my Historical theory emphasizes the reliability of the belief-generating processes, it may be called "*Historical Reliabilism.*"

The most obvious examples of current Time-Slice theories are "Cartesian Foundationalist theories, which trace all justificational status (at least of contingent propositions) to current mental states. The usual varieties of Coherence theories, however, are equally Current Time-Slice views, since they too make the justificational status of a belief wholly a function of *current* states of affairs. For Coherence theories, however, these current states include all other beliefs of the cognizer, which would not be considered relevant by Cartesian Foundationalism. Have there been other Historical theories of justified belief? Among contemporary writers, Quine and Popper have Historical epistemologies, though the notion of "justification" is not their avowed *explicandum*. Among historical writers, it might seem that Locke and Hume had Genetic theories of sorts. But I think that their Genetic theories were only theories of ideas, not of knowledge or justification. Plato's theory of recollection, however, is a good example of a Genetic theory of knowing.[11] And it might be argued that Hegel and Dewey had Genetic epistemologies (if Hegel can be said to have had a clear epistemology at all).

The theory articulated by (6_A) and (6_B) might be viewed as a kind of "Foundationalism," because of its recursive structure. I have no objection to this label, as long as one keeps in mind how different this "diachronic" form of foundationalism is from Cartesian, or other "synchronic" varieties of, Foundationalism.

Current Time-Slice theories characteristically assume that the justificational status of a belief is something which the cognizer is able to know or determine at the time of belief. This is made explicit, for example, by Chisholm.[12] The Historical theory I endorse makes no such assumption. There are many facts about a cognizer to which he lacks "privileged access," and I regard the justificational status of his beliefs as one of those things. This is not to say that a cognizer is necessarily ignorant, at any given moment, of the justificational status of his current beliefs. It is only to deny that he necessarily has, or can get, knowledge or true belief about this status. Just as a person can know without knowing that he knows, so he can have justified belief without knowing that it is justified (or believing justifiably that it is justified.)

A characteristic case in which a belief is justified though the cognizer doesn't know that it's justified is where the original evidence for the belief has long since been forgotten. If the original evidence was compelling, the cognizer's original belief may have been justified; and this justificational status may have been preserved through memory. But since the cognizer no longer remembers how or why he came to believe, he may not know that the belief is justified. If asked now to justify his belief, he may be at a loss. Still, the belief *is* justified, though the cognizer can't demonstrate or establish this.

The Historical theory of justified belief I advocate is connected in spirit with the causal theory of knowing I have presented elsewhere.[13] I had this in mind when I remarked near the outset of the paper that my theory of justified belief makes justifiedness come out closely related to knowledge. Justified beliefs, like pieces of knowledge, have appropriate histories; but they may fail to be knowledge either because they are false or because they founder on some other requirement for knowing of the kind discussed in the post-Gettier knowledge-trade.

There is a variant of the Historical conception of justified belief that is worth mentioning in this context. It may be introduced as follows. Suppose S has a set B of beliefs at time t_0, and some of these beliefs are *un*justified. Between t_0 and t_1 he reasons from the entire set B to the conclusion p, which he then accepts at t_1. The reasoning procedure he uses is a very sound one, i.e., one that is conditionally reliable. There is a sense or respect in which we are tempted to say that S's belief in p at t_1 is "justified." At any rate, it is tempting to say that the *person* is justified in believing p at t. Relative to his antecedent cognitive state, he did as well as could be expected: the *transition* from his cognitive state at t_0 to his cognitive state at t_1 was entirely sound. Although we may acknowledge this brand of justifiedness—it might be called "*Terminal-Phase Reliabilism*"—it is not a kind of justifiedness so closely related to knowing. For a person to know proposition p, it is not enough that the *final phase* of the process that leads to his belief in p be sound. It is also necessary that some entire history of the process be sound (i.e., reliable or conditionally reliable).

Let us return now to the Historical theory. In the next section of the paper, I shall adduce reasons for strengthening it a bit. Before looking at these reasons, however, I wish to review two quite different objections to the theory.

First, a critic might argue that *some* justified beliefs do not derive their justificational status from their causal ancestry. In particular, it might be argued that beliefs about one's current phenomenal states and intuitive beliefs about elementary logical or conceptual relationships do not derive their justificational status in this way. I am not persuaded by either of these examples. Introspection, I believe, should be regarded as a form of retrospection. Thus, a justified belief that I am "now" in pain gets its justificational status from a relevant, though brief, causal history.[14] The apprehension of logical or conceptual relationships is also a cognitive process that occupies time. The psychological process of "seeing" or "intuiting" a simple logical truth is very fast, and we cannot introspectively dissect it into constituent parts. Nonetheless, there are mental operations going on, just as there are mental operations that occur in *idiots savants,* who are unable to report the computational processes they in fact employ.

A second objection to Historical Reliabilism focuses on the reliability element rather than the causal or historical element. Since the theory is intended to cover all possible cases, it seems to imply that for any cognitive process C, if C is reliable in possible world W, then any belief in W that results from C is justified. But doesn't this permit easy counterexamples? Surely we can imagine a possible world in which wishful thinking is reliable. We can imagine a possible world where a benevolent demon so arranges things that beliefs formed by wishful thinking usually come true. This would make wishful thinking a reliable process in that possible world, but surely we don't want to regard beliefs that result from wishful thinking as justified.

There are several possible ways to respond to this case and I am unsure which response is best, partly because my own intuitions (and those of other people I have consulted) are not entirely clear. One possibility is to say that in the possible world imagined, beliefs that result from wishful thinking *are* justified. In other words we reject the claim that wishful thinking could never, intuitively, confer justifiedness.[15]

However, for those who feel that wishful thinking couldn't confer justifiedness, even in the world imagined, there are two ways out. First, it may be suggested that the proper criterion of justifiedness is the propensity of a process to generate beliefs that are true *in a non-manipulated environment,* i.e., an environment in which there is no purposeful arrangement of the world either to accord or conflict with the beliefs that are formed. In other words, the suitability of a belief-forming process is only a function of its success in "*natural*" situations, not situations of the sort involving benevolent or malevolent demons, or any other such manipulative creatures. If we reformulate the theory to include this qualification, the counterexample in question will be averted.

Alternatively, we may reformulate our theory, or reinterpret it, as follows. Instead of construing the theory as saying that a belief in possible world W is justified if and only if it results from a cognitive process that is reliable in W, we may construe it as saying that a belief in possible world W is justified if and only if it results from a cognitive process that is reliable *in our world.* In short, our conception of justifiedness is derived as follows. We note certain cognitive processes in the actual world, and form beliefs about which of these are reliable. The ones we believe to be reliable are then regarded as justification-conferring processes. In reflecting on hypothetical beliefs, we deem them justified if and only if they result from processes already picked out as justification-conferring, or processes very similar to those. Since wishful thinking is not among these processes, a belief formed in a possible world W by wishful thinking would not be deemed justified, even if wishful thinking is reliable in W. I am not sure that this is a correct reconstruction of our intuitive conceptual scheme, but it would accommodate the benevolent demon case, at least if the proper thing to say in that case is that the wishful-thinking-caused beliefs are unjustified.

Even if we adopt this strategy, however, a problem still remains. Suppose that wishful thinking turns out to be reliable *in the actual world*![16] This might be because, unbeknownst to us at present, there is a benevolent demon who, lazy until now, will shortly start arranging things so that our wishes come true. The long-run performance of wishful thinking will be very good, and hence even the new construal of the theory will imply that beliefs resulting from wishful thinking (in *our* world) are justified. Yet this surely contravenes our intuitive judgment on the matter.

Perhaps the moral of the case is that the standard format of a "conceptual analysis" has its shortcomings. Let me depart from that format and try to give a better rendering of our aim and the theory that tries to achieve that aim. What we really want is an *explanation* of why we count, or would count, certain beliefs as justified and others as unjustified. Such an explanation must refer to our *beliefs* about reliability, not to the actual *facts*. The reason we *count* beliefs as justified is that they are formed by what we *believe* to be reliable belief-forming processes. Our beliefs about which belief-forming processes are reliable may be erroneous, but that does not affect the adequacy of the explanation. Since we *believe* that wishful thinking is an unreliable belief-forming process, we regard beliefs formed by wishful thinking as unjustified. What matters, then, is what we *believe* about wishful thinking, not what is *true* (in the long run) about wishful thinking. I am not sure how to express this point in the standard format of conceptual analysis, but it identifies an important point in understanding our theory.

III

Let us return, however, to the standard format of conceptual analysis, and let us consider a new objection that will require some revisions in the theory advanced until now. According to our theory, a belief is justified in case it is caused by a process that is in fact reliable, or by one we generally believe to be reliable. But suppose that although one of S's beliefs satisfies this condition, S has no reason to believe that it does. Worse yet, suppose S has reason to believe that his belief is caused by an *un*reliable process (although *in fact* its causal ancestry is fully reliable). Wouldn't we deny in such circumstances that S's belief is justified? This seems to show that our analysis, as presently formulated, is mistaken.

Suppose that Jones is told on fully reliable authority that a certain class of his memory beliefs are almost all mistaken. His parents fabricate a wholly false story that Jones suffered from amnesia when he was seven but later developed *pseudo*-memories of that period. Though Jones listens to what his parents say and has excellent reason to trust them, he persists in believing the ostensible memories from his seven-year-old past. Are these memory beliefs justified? Intuitively, they are not justified. But since these beliefs result from genuine memory and original perceptions, which are adequately reliable processes, our theory says that these beliefs are justified.

Can the theory be revised to meet this difficulty? One natural suggestion is that the actual reliability of a belief's ancestry is not enough for justifiedness; in addition, the cognizer must be *justified in believing* that the ancestry of his belief is reliable. Thus one might think of replacing (6_A), for example, with (7). (For simplicity, I neglect some of the details of the earlier analysis.)

> (7)   If S's belief in p at t is caused by a reliable cognitive process, and S justifiably believes at t that his p-belief is so caused, then S's belief in p at t is justified.

It is evident, however, that (7) will not do as a base clause, for it contains the epistemic term "justifiably" in its antecedent.

A slightly weaker revision, without this problematic feature, might next be suggested, viz.,

> (8)   If S's belief in p at t is caused by a reliable cognitive process, and S believes at t that his p-belief is so caused, then S's belief in p at t is justified.

But this won't do the job. Suppose that Jones believes that his memory beliefs are reliably caused despite all the (trustworthy) contrary testimony of his parents. Principle (8) would be satisfied, yet we wouldn't say that these beliefs are justified.

Next, we might try (9), which is stronger than (8) and, unlike (7), formally admissible as a base clause.

(9)   If S's belief in p at t is caused by a reliable cognitive process, and S believes at t that his p-belief is so caused, and this meta-belief is caused by a reliable cognitive process, then S's belief in p at t is justified.

A first objection to (9) is that it wrongly precludes unreflective creatures—creatures like animals or young children, who have no beliefs about the genesis of their beliefs—from having justified beliefs. If one shares my view that justified belief is, at least roughly, *well-formed* belief, surely animals and young children can have justified beliefs.

A second problem with (9) concerns its underlying rationale. Since (9) is proposed as a substitute for (6_A), it is implied that the reliability of a belief's own cognitive ancestry does not make it justified. But, the suggestion seems to be, the reliability of a *meta-belief*'s ancestry confers justifiedness on the first-order belief. Why should that be so? Perhaps one is attracted by the idea of a "trickle-down" effect: if an n+1-level belief is justified, its justification trickles down to an n-level belief. But even if the trickle-down theory is correct, it doesn't help here. There is no assurance from the satisfaction (9)'s antecedent that the meta-belief itself is *justified*.

To obtain a better revision of our theory, let us re-examine the Jones case. Jones has strong evidence against certain propositions concerning his past. He doesn't *use* this evidence, but if he *were* to use it properly, he would stop believing these propositions. Now the proper use of evidence would be an instance of a (conditionally) reliable process. So what we can say about Jones is that he *fails* to use a certain (conditionally) reliable process that he could and should have used. Admittedly, had he used this process, he would have "worsened" his doxastic states: he would have replaced some true beliefs with suspension of judgment. Still, he couldn't have known this in the case in question. So, he failed to do something which, epistemically, he should have done. This diagnosis suggests a fundamental change in our theory. The justificational status of a belief is not only a function of the cognitive processes *actually* employed in producing it; it is also a function of processes that could and should be employed.

With these points in mind, we may tentatively propose the following revision of our theory, where we again focus on a base-clause principle but omit certain details in the interest of clarity.

(10)   If S's belief in p at t results from a reliable cognitive process, and there is no reliable or conditionally reliable process available to S which, had it been used by S in addition to the process actually used, would have resulted in S's not believing p at t then S's belief in p at t is justified.

There are several problems with this proposal. First, there is a technical problem. One cannot use an additional belief-forming (or doxastic-state-forming) process *as well as* the original process if the additional one would result in a different doxastic state. One wouldn't be using the original process at all. So we need a slightly different formulation of the relevant counterfactual. Since the basic idea is reasonably clear, however, I won't try to improve on the formulation here. A second problem concerns the notion of "*available*" belief-forming (or doxastic-state-forming) processes. What is it for a process to be "available" to a cognizer? Were scientific procedures "available" to people who lived in pre-scientific ages? Furthermore, it seems implausible to say that all "available" processes ought to be used, at least if we include such processes as gathering *new* evidence. Surely a belief can sometimes be justified even if additional evidence-gathering would yield a different doxastic attitude. What I think we should have in mind here are such additional processes as calling previously acquired evidence to mind, assessing the implications of that evidence, etc. This is admittedly somewhat vague, but here again our ordinary notion of justifiedness is vague, so it is appropriate for our analysans to display the same sort of vagueness.

This completes the sketch of my account of justified belief. Before concluding, however, it is essential to point out that there is an important use of "justified" which is not captured by this account but can be captured by a closely related one.

There is a use of "justified" in which it is not implied or presupposed that there is a *belief* that is justified. For example, if S is trying to decide whether to believe p and asks our advice, we may tell him that he is "justified" in believing it. We do not thereby imply that he *has* a justified *belief*, since we know he is still suspending judgement. What we mean, roughly, is that he *would* or *could* be justified if he were to believe p. The justificational status we ascribe here cannot be a function of the causes of S's believing p, for there is no belief by S in p. Thus, the account of justifiedness we have given thus far cannot explicate *this* use of "justified." (It doesn't follow that this use of "justified" has no connection with causal ancestries. Its proper use may depend on the causal ancestry of the cognizer's cognitive state, though not on the causal ancestry of his believing *p*.)

Let us distinguish two uses of "justified": an *ex post* use and an *ex ante* use. The *ex post* use occurs when there exists a belief, and we say *of that belief* that it is (or isn't) justified. The *ex ante* use occurs when no such belief exists, or when we wish to ignore the question of whether such a belief exists. Here we say of the *person*, independent of his doxastic state vis-à-vis *p*, that *p* is (or isn't) suitable for him to believe.[17]

Since we have given an account of *ex post* justifiedness, it will suffice if we can analyze *ex ante* justifiedness in terms of it. Such an analysis, I believe, is ready at hand. *S* is *ex ante* justified in believing *p* at *t* just in case his total cognitive state at *t* is such that from that state he could come to believe *p* in such a way that this belief would be *ex post* justified. More precisely, he is *ex ante* justified in believing *p* at *t* just in case a reliable belief-forming operation is available to him such that the application of that operation to his total cognitive state at *t* would result, more or less immediately, in his believing *p* and this belief would be *ex post* justified. Stated formally, we have the following:

(11)   Person *S* is *ex ante* justified in believing *p* at *t* if and only if there is a reliable belief-forming operation available to *S* which is such that if *S* applied that operation to his total cognitive state at *t*, *S* would believe *p* at *t*-plus-delta (for a suitably small delta) and that belief would be *ex post* justified.

For the analysans of (11) to be satisfied, the total cognitive state at *t* must have a suitable causal ancestry. Hence, (11) is implicitly an Historical account of *ex ante* justifiedness.

As indicated, the bulk of this paper was addressed to *ex post* justifiedness. This is the appropriate analysandum if one is interested in the connection between justifiedness and knowledge, since what is crucial to whether a person *knows* a proposition is whether he has an actual *belief* in the proposition that is justified. However, since many epistemologists are interested in *ex ante* justifiedness, it is proper for a general theory of justification to try to provide an account of that concept as well. Our theory does this quite naturally, for the account of *ex ante* justifiedness falls out directly from our account of *ex post* justifiedness.[18]

NOTES

[1]   "A Causal Theory of Knowing," *The Journal of Philosophy* 64, 12 (June 22, 1967): 357–372; "Innate Knowledge," in S.P. Stich, ed., *Innate Ideas* (Berkeley: University of California Press, 1975); and "Discrimination and Perceptual Knowledge," *The Journal of Philosophy* 73, 20 (November 18, 1976), 771–791.

[2]   Notice that the choice of a recursive format does not prejudice the case for or against any particular theory. A recursive format is perfectly general. Specifically, an explicit set of necessary and sufficient conditions is just a special case of a recursive format, i.e. one in which there is no recursive clause.

[3]   Many of the attempts I shall consider are suggested by material in William P. Alston, "Varieties of Privileged Access," *American Philosophical Quarterly* 8 (1971), 223–241.

[4]   Such a definition (though without the modal term) is given, for example, by W.V. Quine and J.S. Ullian in *The Web of Belief* (New York: Random House, 1970), p. 21. Statements are said to be self-evident just in case "to understand them is to believe them."

[5]   Englewood Cliffs, N.J.: Prentice-Hall, Inc., 1977, p. 22.

[6]   I assume, of course, that "nomologically necessary" is *de re* with respect to "S" and "t" in this construction. I shall not focus on problems that may arise in this regard, since my primary concerns are with different issues.

[7]   This assumption violates the thesis that Davidson calls "The Anomalism of the Mental." Cf. "Mental Events," in L. Foster and J.W. Swanson, eds., *Experience and Theory* (Amherst: University of Massachusetts Press, 1970). But it is unclear that this thesis is a necessary truth. Thus, it seems fair to assume its falsity in order to produce a counter-example. The example neither entails nor precludes the mental–physical identity theory.

[8]   Keith Lehrer's example of the gypsy lawyer is intended to show the inappropriateness of a causal requirement . (See *Knowledge,* Oxford: University Press, 1974, pp. 124–125.) But I find this example unconvincing. To the extent that I clearly imagine that the lawyer fixes his belief solely as a result of the cards, it seems intuitively wrong to say that he *knows*—or has a *justified belief*—that his client is innocent.

[9]   This definition is not exactly what we need for the purposes at hand. As Ernest Sosa points out, introspection will turn out to be a belief-dependent process since sometimes the input into the process will be a belief (when the introspected content is a belief). Intuitively, however, introspection is not the sort of process which may be merely conditionally reliable. I do not know how to refine the definition so as to avoid this difficulty, but it is a small and isolated point.

[10]   It may be objected that principles (6_A) and (6_B) are jointly open to analogues of the lottery paradox. A series of processes composed of reliable but less-than-perfectly-reliable processes may be extremely unreliable. Yet applications of (6_A) and (6_B) would confer justifiedness on a belief that is caused by such a series. In reply to this objection, we might simply indicate that the theory is intended to capture our ordinary notion of justifiedness, and this ordinary notion has been formed without recognition of this kind of problem. The theory is not wrong *as* a theory

of the ordinary (naive) conception of justifiedness. On the other hand, if we want a theory to do more than capture the ordinary conception of justifiedness, it might be possible to strengthen the principles to avoid lottery-paradox analogues.

[11] I am indebted to Mark Pastin for this point.

[12] Cf. *Theory of Knowledge,* Second Edition, pp. 17, 114–116.

[13] Cf. "A Causal Theory of Knowing," *op. cit.* The reliability aspect of my theory also has its precursors in earlier papers of mine on knowing: "Innate Knowledge," *op. cit.* and "Discrimination and Perceptual Knowledge," *op. cit.*

[14] The view that introspection is retrospection was taken by Ryle, and before him (as Charles Hartshorne points out to me) by Hobbes, Whitehead, and possibly Husserl.

[15] Of course, if people in world *W* learn *inductively* that wishful thinking is reliable, and regularly base their beliefs on this inductive inference, it is quite unproblematic and straightforward that their beliefs are justified. The only interesting case is where their beliefs are formed *purely* by wishful thinking, without using inductive inference. The suggestion contemplated in this paragraph of the text is that, in the world imagined, even pure wishful thinking would confer justifiedness.

[16] I am indebted here to Mark Kaplan.

[17] The distinction between *ex post* and *ex ante* justifiedness is similar to Roderick Firth's distinction between *doxastic* and *propositional* warrant. See his "Are Epistemic Concepts Reducible to Ethical Concepts?", in Alvin I. Goldman and Jaegwon Kim, eds., *Values and Morals, Essays in Honor of William Frankena, Charles Stevenson, and Richard Brandt* (Dordrecht: D. Reidel, 1978).

[18] Research on this paper was begun while the author was a fellow of the John Simon Guggenheim Memorial Foundation and of the Center for Advanced Study in the Behavioral Sciences. I am grateful for their support. I have received helpful comments and criticism from Holly S. Goldman, Mark Kaplan, Fred Schmitt, Stephen P. Stich, and many others at several universities where earlier drafts of the paper were read.

1.6

THE INTERNALISM/EXTERNALISM CONTROVERSY *

Richard Fumerton

Much of contemporary epistemology takes place in the shadow of the internalism/externalism debate. Its current place on the centre stage of epistemology seems appropriate given the dramatic revolution in our thought about historical and contemporary epistemological inquiry that would seem to be forced by certain paradigm externalist views. But although the controversy seems to strike deep at the heart of fundamental epistemological issues, I am not certain that it has been clearly defined. It seems to me that philosophers are choosing sides without a thorough understanding of what the respective views entail.

In this paper I want to explore a number of different ways of defining the technical distinction between internalist and externalist epistemologies. As is so often the case with technical philosophical distinctions, it is probably foolish to insist that there is only one "correct" way to define the distinction. I am interested in developing a way of understanding the controversy so that it leaves many philosophers already recognized as paradigm internalists and externalists in their respective categories, but this is not my main goal. Indeed, while my ultimate suggestion as to how to understand internalism will include as internalists many in the history of philosophy, it may be harder to find contemporary epistemologists who satisfy my internalist criteria. My primary concerns are to define the controversy in such a way that it a) involves a fundamentally important distinction, and b) articulates the source of the underlying dissatisfaction that internalists feel toward paradigm externalist analyses of epistemic concepts. At the very least, I want to articulate *this* internalist's view as to the critical mistake of externalism. As one who thinks that externalist analyses of epistemic concepts are somehow irrelevant to the traditional and appropriate philosophical interest in knowledge and justified belief, I am obviously interested in converting philosophers to my own brand of internalism, and the extreme version of foundationalism that it involves. My hope is that when philosophers realize the underlying source of their unhappiness with externalist epistemology, they will come home to a version of foundationalism that has been neglected too long. By way of achieving this last goal, I will also examine the object to one of the methodological assumptions underlying externalist epistemologies. But let us begin by trying to define the concepts of internalism and externalism.

Internalism and Internal States

The term "internalism" might suggest the view that S's knowing that P or having a justified belief that P, consists in S being in some *internal* state. We might, then, understand the externalist as one who is committed to the view that two individuals could be in identical "internal" states of mind while one knows, or has evidence, or has a justified belief, while the other does not. This is surely tempting, but everything hinges on how we understand "same internal state" and "same state of mind". If we include among the properties that define a state of mind *relational* properties, then it would seem obvious that an *externalist* can, and would, embrace the thesis that if my state of mind is identical to yours then I'll know what you know, I'll be justified in believing what you are justified in believing. Goldman, Nozick, Armstrong, and Dretske, to consider just a few externalists, are all willing to pick out a complex relational property that my belief has in virtue of which it constitutes knowledge or justified belief.[1] The relational property will typically be a complex nomological property, such as the property of being caused by a process which satisfies a certain description, or being such that it would not have occurred had not certain other conditions obtained. One gets all sorts of variations on externalism depending on how the relevant nomological relations are characterized. If we are trying to define a view that these externalists reject, then, we cannot simply define internalism as maintaining that one knows or has a justified belief in virtue of being in a certain kind of state of mind when we let the relevant kind be determined in part by its relational properties.

Shall we then say that an internalist identifies knowledge and justified belief with internal states of mind, meaning by internal states of mind, *nonrelational* properties of a mind? The externalist, correspondingly, would maintain only that two individuals could exemplify the same nonrelational properties while one knows or has a justified belief and the other does not. We could, but then we are going to be hardpressed to find very many internalists. Certainly, on this understanding of externalism, everyone who holds that a justified true belief can constitute knowledge even when the justification is logically compatible with the belief being false is committed to an externalist account of knowledge.[2] A non-redundant truth condition in the traditional analysis of knowledge clearly introduces a condition that goes beyond the nonrelational properties of the knower. But even if we restrict our attention to the concept of justified belief, there seem to be precious few philosophers who would identify the having of a justified belief with the exemplification of some nonrelational property (properties).

One of the classic foundationalist approaches to understanding noninferential knowledge identifies at least one condition for such knowledge as *direct acquaintance* with facts. I'll have more to say about this view later, but for now I would merely observe that at least some externalists take such positions to be paradigms of the sort of internalist epistemologies they are rejecting.[3] But clearly when someone like Russell talked about being acquainted with a fact, he intended to be referring to a *relation* that a subject bears to a fact. Having a noninferentially justified belief, on such a view, would *not* be identical with exemplifying nonrelational properties, and a Russellean would *not* argue that if two people were in the same nonrelational states they would have the same justified beliefs. It is not even clear that the externalists' favorite internalist, Descartes, would satisfy the above characterization of an internalist. If, for example, Descartes accepted a relational analysis of believing something to be the case, or having an idea of something, the states of mind that for him constitute knowledge and justified belief would not be nonrelational properties of a self. The only philosophers who could be internalists in the above sense are philosophers who embrace an adverbial theory of consciousness and identify some of the nonrelational properties, exemplification of which constitutes consciousness, with knowledge and justified belief. If one must believe all that in order to be an internalist, not very many philosophers, myself included, would want any part of the view.

Philosophers who have tried to ground knowledge and justified belief in acquaintance with facts have sometimes construed the facts with which one *can* be acquainted as themselves "modifications" of the mind. This might in turn suggest that one could usefully define the internalist as someone who is committed to the view that knowledge and justified belief must be identified either with nonrelational properties of the mind *or* with relational properties of the mind where the relata of the relations are the mind and its nonrelational properties. Such a definition would house more analyses of justified belief under the roof of internalism although any analysis of knowledge involving a nonredundant *truth* condition would still be externalist. But it is important to realize that such a definition of internalism would still leave philosophers who ground justified belief in acquaintance with nonmental facts (e.g.'s, the neutral monist's sense data, the epistemological direct realist's surfaces of physical objects, the Platonist's forms and their relations, the realist's universals and their relations) in the externalist's camp. And I don't think the paradigm externalist wants their company. More importantly, it looks as though we are defining the internalism/externalism debate in a *peculiar* way by putting into opposite camps *fundamentally* similar views. It seems to me that if I am trying to ground the concept of justified belief in acquaintance with nonrelational properties of the mind, and you are trying to ground the concept of justified belief in acquaintance with nonmental sense data, our views are fundamentally alike. The internalism/externalism controversy will not be getting at a *significant* issue if one of these views gets described as a form of internalism while the other is described as a form of externalism.

Internalism and Iteration

There is, of course, more than one natural way to understand the suggestion that conditions for knowledge or justification are internal to the cognizer, or are "in the mind" of the cognizer. When philosophers talked about sense data being "in the mind," for example, at least sometimes they seemed to be pointing to a feature of our *knowledge* of them.[4] Sense data are "in the mind" in the sense that one has a kind of privileged access to them. And this analogy suggests another way of trying to understand what is really at issue between the internalist and the externalist. At least some philosophers want to understand the internalist as someone who maintains that the necessary and sufficient conditions for satisfying epistemic concepts are conditions to which one has a privileged and direct access. "Access," of course, is itself an epistemic term. On this analysis of internalism, then, the internalist might be thought of as someone who is committed to the view that knowledge entails knowing (perhaps directly) that one knows; having a justified belief entails justifiably believing that one has a justified belief.

The above involves a very strong interpretation of having access to the conditions of knowledge and justified belief. A weaker conception of access could construe access as *potential* knowledge or justified belief. Thus a weaker version of internalism along these lines might insist that for a person to be justified in believing a proposition *P* that person must have "available" to him a method for discovering what the nature of that justification is. Let us consider both this strong and weak attempt to understand internalism as the view that having knowledge or justified belief entails having epistemic access to the conditions for knowledge and justified belief.

As someone who has always thought of himself as an internalist, one of my first concerns with the *strong* requirement of access is that it might saddle the internalist with a view that requires the *impossible* of knowledge and justified belief. As I shall make clear in my concluding remarks, I don't care if, on my analysis of epistemic terms, it turns our that dogs, computers, my Aunt Mary, or even the philosophically sophisticated, do not have *philosophically relevant* knowledge of, or justification for believing, what they think they know or are justified in believing. But I do not want to *define* knowledge and justified belief in such a way that having knowledge and justified belief involves a vicious regress. And the requirements that one must know that one knows P in order to know P; justifiably believe that one is justified in believing P in order to justifiably believe P, certainly seem to flirt with the prospect of a vicious regress.

In elaborating this point, one might, however, usefully distinguish inferential justification from noninferential justification. I *have* defended elsewhere the very strong principle that if one is to be justified in *inferring* one proposition P from another E one must be 1) justified in believing E *and* 2) justified in believing that E makes epistemically probable P. Foundationalists have traditionally maintained that if one accepts such a principle, the only way to avoid an infinite number of infinite regresses is to recognize the existence of noninferentially justified beliefs (including, of course, noninferentially justified beliefs in propositions of the form "E makes probable P"). My reservations with the strong requirement of access, then, have to do with the general thesis that *all* justification involves access to the conditions of justification. In his recent book [2], BonJour seems to defend a version of internalism defined in terms of a requirement of strong access and he argues, quite plausibly, that foundationalists are going to have an exceedingly difficult time ending the regress of justification within the context of this strong internalism.[5] If a belief that P has some feature X in virtue of which it is supposed to be noninferentially justified, BonJour's internalism requires us to justifiably believe that the feature X is present and that it makes probable the truth of P. The regress we were trying to end with noninferential justification is obviously about to begin again. If one accepts this incredibly strong version of internalism, it seems to me that one will not be able to escape BonJour's argument. Indeed it is all too evident that BonJour cannot escape his own argument as it might be applied to his coherentist alternative to foundationalism. To his credit, BonJour recognizes that his internalism requires that in order to have empirical justification, one must have *access* to what one believes and the relevant relations of coherence. Since the only kind of epistemic access to empirical propositions he recognizes is through coherence, one will have to find beliefs which cohere with beliefs about what one believes. But the problem rearises with respect to getting access to those beliefs and again we encounter a vicious regress. BonJour tries to save his view with his "doxastic presumption" (101–05) (you just take it for granted that your metabeliefs are by and large right), but it seems to me that if one reads the text closely, BonJour as much as admits that his view entails the most radical of skepticisms with respect to empirical justification (105).

The only way one can satisfy the requirement of strong access for justification is to allow the possibility of a mind having an infinite number of increasingly complex intentional states. If, for example, I hold (as I do) that my belief that P is noninferentially justified when I am acquainted with the fact that P, the thought that P, and the relation of correspondence between the thought that P and the fact that P (call these conditions X) I am not, on the above view, an internalist unless I am willing to assert that in order for X to constitute my noninferential justification for believing P, I must be acquainted with the fact that X, the thought that X, and the relation of correspondence between the thought that X and the fact that X (call *these* Y). And I must also hold that I am acquainted with the fact that Y, and so on. Now I am not saying that this view is obviously impossible to hold. One can suppose that people have an infinite number of thoughts (perhaps dispositional) and one can think of the "layers" of acquaintance as being like perfectly transparent sheets laid one on top of another. But do we, as internalists, want to let ourselves be painted into a corner this tight where the only escape is a view that might not even be intelligible?

While it is not precisely the same problem of a formal vicious regress, the possible limitations of the mind when it comes to considering facts of ever expanding complexity might also make a proponent of the acquaintance theory of noninferential justification reluctant to accept even the *weaker* requirement of access. Speaking for myself, I am not sure I can even keep things straight when I try to form the thought that my thought that my thought that my thought that P corresponds to my thinking that P corresponds to P. And this is still only a few levels away from the first order thought that P.

"Internalism" is, to be sure, a technical expression, but do we want to put a view like mine that refuses to accept either the strong or the weak requirement for access, but that defines noninferential justification in part by reference to the concept of direct acquaintance with facts, on the externalist side of the internalist/externalist controversy? My suspicion is that this is not how the issue is being understood. And to further reinforce the idea that we are not getting at the heart of the controversy by considering requirements of "access", we should reflect on how easily a mischievous externalist can "play along" with access requirements of internalism. For purposes of illustration let us take one of the paradigmatic externalist analyses of epistemic terms, the reliabilist analysis of justification offered by Goldman in [8].[6] In that article Goldman initially suggests the following recursive analysis of justification: A belief is justified if it results either from 1) a belief-independent process that is unconditionally reliable, or 2) a belief-dependent process that is conditionally reliable, where the "input" beliefs are themselves justified. Belief-independent processes do not have beliefs as their "input," and what makes them unconditionally reliable is that the "output" beliefs are usually true. Belief-dependent processes have as their "input" at least some beliefs, and what makes them conditionally reliable is that the "output" beliefs are usually true when the "input" beliefs are true. Qualifications having to do with the availability of alternative processes and the consequences of their hypothetical use are later suggested, but they need not concern us for the point I presently wish to discuss.

Now it is obviously a feature of Goldman's paradigmatic externalism that it does not require that a person whose belief is justified by being the result of some process have epistemic access to that process. My beliefs can be reliably produced even if I have no reason whatsoever for supposing that they are reliably produced. And this might seem to suggest that the important feature of externalism is its rejection of access requirements for justified belief. But suppose the externalist gets tired of hearing internalists complaining about allowing the possibility of having a justified belief with no justification for believing that it is justified.[7] It is useful to ask whether a reliabilist could remain within the spirit of reliabilism and at the same time allow that reliable processes yield justified beliefs only when one is justified in believing that the processes are reliable. Certainly, a reliabilist could accept our weak requirement of access—a reliabilist could allow that a reliable process $P1$ generates justified beliefs only if there is *available* a justification for believing that *P*1 is reliable. Interpreting this justification on the reliabilist's model would presumably require there being available a process *P*2 which could generate the belief that *P*1 is reliable. Of course, given the requirement of weak access, *P*2 would itself generate justified beliefs only if there were available a reliable process *P*3 which could generate the belief that *P*2 is reliable, and so on. But it is not obvious that all of these reliable processes or methods need be different (a reliabilist, as far as I can see, can allow, for example, the inductive justification of induction, perceptual justification of the reliability of perception, and so on) and in any event since they need only be available (as opposed to actually used) it is not clear that the regress is vicious.

Could a reliabilist accept even a strong requirement of access? Could a reliabilist even allow that a process P1 generates justified beliefs only if the believer actually justifiably believes that the process is reliable? This is clearly more problematic for there would actually have to be some reliable process *P*2 generating the belief that *P*1 is reliable, and some reliable process *P*3 generating the belief that *P*2 is reliable and so on. The coherence of such a view rests on considerations concerning the potential complexity of the mind that we have already discussed in the context of wondering whether classical foundationalism can cope with strong access requirements. But suppose, for the sake of argument, that our hypothetical reliabilist convinces us that the mind has a kind of infinite complexity that renders harmless even this regress. The important question to ask is whether this hypothetical reliabilist paying his externalist lip service to our requirements of access would make the dissatisfied internalist happy. And I think the answer is that he obviously would not. As long as the reliabilist/externalist keeps offering reliabilist/externalist accounts of knowing that one knows or being justified in believing that one has a justified belief, the internalist isn't going to feel that anything has been accomplished by getting this reliabilist to accept the view that knowing entails knowing that one knows; having a justified belief entails being justified in believing that one has a justified belief. The obvious moral to draw is that the fundamental disagreement between internalists and externalists is not really a disagreement over such questions as whether inferential justification entails actual or potential justified belief in the legitimacy of the inference, or more generally whether justification entails actual or potential access to the fact that the conditions of justification are satisfied.

Internalism and Normativity

One of the more nebulous criteria for distinguishing internalist and externalist analyses involves the suggestion that externalists ignore the *normativity* of epistemic judgments. And, certainly, many of the objections levelled at reliabilism, for example, make the claim that unreliability to which one has no actual or potential access cannot decide questions about the rationality or irrationality of beliefs because charges of irrationality are relevant to evaluations of epistemic *praise* and *blame*. If my beliefs are produced by unreliable processes when there is no possible way for me to find that out, in what sense am I to be blamed for having the belief? The inhabitants of demon worlds are no more blameworthy for their demon inducted false beliefs than are the inhabitants of non-demon worlds.[8]

Now in one sense I am perfectly prepared to admit, qua internalist, that when one characterizes a belief as irrational one is *criticizing* that belief, and since I think that externalist accounts are radically mistaken analyses of philosophically relevant epistemic concepts, I obviously think they have incorrectly analyzed the nature of this epistemic criticism. But being a kind of criticism is a very broad criterion for being normative. We criticize beliefs for being irrational, but we also criticize knives for being dull, cars for being too expensive, theories for being false. But does that make judgments about the dullness of knives, the cost of cars, and the falsehood of theories, normative judgments? Perhaps in a sense a judgment about the dullness of knives is *relevant* to a normative judgment about the goodness of that knife in that we usually consider dullness to be a property that makes the knife ineffective for achieving certain ends peculiar to the use of knives. But this is grist for the reliabilist's mill. We criticize the processes producing beliefs for being unreliable, the reliabilist might argue, because such processes typically fail to produce what we want from them—true beliefs.

Surely both internalists and externalists will agree that in some sense charges of irrationality can be construed as *criticisms*. But it is important to distinguish this virtual truism, a truism that isn't going to differentiate the two views, from so-called deontic analyses of epistemic terms, where a deontic analysis *defines* epistemic concepts using value terms. Deontic analyses of epistemic terms may well be incompatible with at least paradigm externalist views, but as an internalist I certainly don't want to be stuck with defending a deontic analysis of epistemic concepts. To *criticize* a person's *belief* is not to suggest that the person is morally reprehensible for having that belief. And this is so even if we successfully avoid the standard "conflicting duties" objections to deontic analyses that were raised against the view that Chisholm suggested in [3] (You've got the duty to believe you will get well—it might help—even though your evidence indicates you will probably die). Specifically, I would argue that a person's belief can be epistemically criticized even if we decide that the person is so far gone, is so irrational, that we do not think it even causally possible for him to figure out why his beliefs are irrational. Such a person is presumably not to be *blamed* for believing anything. He may be doing the very best he can with the potential he has, even though his best effort still results in the having of irrational beliefs. Put another way, we do not (should not) ethically criticize an irrational *person* for holding beliefs that we nevertheless *criticize* as irrational. Again, I do not think that the externalist has a plausible understanding of the conditions under which we philosophically criticize a belief as being irrational, but for the reasons I have tried to indicate, I do not think it is useful to try to understand the internalist/externalist debate as one over the normativity of epistemic judgments. In fact, I would argue that pure deontic analyses of epistemic terms involve a mistake very much like the mistake of externalism.

Externalism and What's Really Wrong With It

For someone whose primary interest is in defining the controversy, this section heading might seem unnecessarily contentious. But you will recall that my concern is to understand the internalist/externalist debate in such a way as to make clear what I take to be the source of the internalist's dissatisfaction with the view, and particularly this internalist's dissatisfaction with the view.

Old philosophical views have a way of resurfacing under new labels. And the roots of externalism go back further than the "naturalistic epistemology" encouraged by Quine. Rather, I think they lie with an old controversy concerning the correct analysis of epistemic probability. While the Russell of [15] clearly took epistemic probability to be a *sui generis* concept (see his discussion of the principle of induction) the Russell of [16] was bound and determined to reduce epistemic probability to a frequency conception of probability.[9] A crude attempt to define epistemic probability in terms of frequency might hold that one proposition E makes probable another proposition P when the pair is of a kind e/p such that usually when a proposition of the first kind is true, a proposition of the second kind is true. For our present purposes we can ignore the difficult questions involving the interpretation of the relevant frequencies, questions to which Russell devoted a great deal of attention. There is, it seems to me, an obvious connection between a frequency analysis of epistemic probability and the fundamental claims of such externalist epistemologies as reliabilism. Both are trying to understand fundamental epistemic concepts in terms of *nomological* concepts. The externalist/naturalist in epistemology (like his counterpart in ethics) is trying to define away the concepts fundamental to his discipline; he is trying to analyze fundamental epistemic concepts in terms of other non-epistemic concepts. Goldman's hard core reliabilism wants to explicate justified belief in terms of either a frequency or propensity (if that is any different) concept of probability. Nozick wants to define epistemic concepts in terms of nomological connections between facts and beliefs of the sort expressed by contingent subjunctive conditionals (in [14]). Armstrong appeals to this same concept of nomological necessity in trying to understand knowledge (in [1]). And if externalism involves a fundamental philosophical error, I would suggest that it is analogous to the alleged mistake of naturalism in ethics, or more accurately, the alleged mistake in ethics of trying to define the indefinable. I would urge you to consider the suggestion that it is a defining characteristic of an internalist epistemology that it takes fundamental epistemic concepts to be *sui generis*. No matter how much lip service our hypothetical reliabilist tries to pay to our insistence that justified belief entails being actually or potentially aware of the conditions of justification, he won't satisfy us as long as he continues to define the epistemic terms with which he pays us lip service in his naturalistic (nomological) way. It is the nomological analyses of epistemic concepts that leads us to keep moving up a level to ask the externalist how he knows that he knows, or knows that he knows that he knows. The externalist might be able to give correct answers within the framework of his view, but we, as internalists, will keep asking the questions until his answer invokes a concept of knowledge or justified belief not captured in terms of nomological connection. The real internalist/externalist controversy, I would suggest, concerns the extent to which sui generis epistemic concepts can be analyzed employing, or even be viewed as supervenient upon (where being supervenient upon involves a necessary connection stronger than causation), such nonepistemic nomological concepts as causation, universal and probabilistic law, and contingent subjunctive conditionals. Ironically, I never have been convinced that there is a naturalistic or definist fallacy in ethics. As an internalist, I am convinced that there is something analogous in epistemology and that it is at the heart of the internalism/externalism debate.

What are these sui generis epistemic concepts that defy reduction or analysis? This is obviously a question about which those who reject the externalists' views will themselves disagree. Perhaps the most famous contemporary philosopher associated with internalism today is Roderick Chisholm and despite periodic flirtations with deontic analyses of epistemic terms, I think one must ultimately take seriously his insistence that we take as primitive the concept of one proposition being more reasonable to believe than another (in, for example, [4]). I would myself locate the fundamental sui generis epistemic concepts elsewhere.

In rejecting externalism, I have tried to be clear that I reject it only as an analysis of philosophically relevant epistemic concepts. Knowing, or having a justified belief, in the externalist's sense doesn't satisfy our philosophical curiosity, doesn't answer our philosophical questions, because qua philosophers trying to be rational, we want more than to be automata responding to stimuli with beliefs. I would argue that we want *facts*, including facts about which propositions make probable others, before our consciousness. This notion of a fact being before consciousness is, of course, itself an epistemic concept, and my suggestion is that one of the fundamental sui generis concepts that defy further analysis or reduction is the concept of direct acquaintance with a fact that in part[10] defines the concept of noninferential knowledge. And in the case of inferential knowledge, what one really wants as an internalist is direct acquaintance with the fact that one's evidence makes epistemically probable one's conclusion. Acquaintance with evidential connections would clearly be impossible if evidential connections are to be understood in terms of frequencies or other nomological connections, and that indicates that the other epistemic concept which resists further analysis is the old Keynesean notion of making probable as a sui generis relation between propositions, analogous to, but obviously different from, entailment.[11] I haven't the space to develop this view here—I have done so elsewhere.[12] My only concern is to sketch the *kind* of view, with its reliance on sui generis epistemic concepts, that I would take to be paradigmatically internalist.

A Presupposition of Externalism

I would like to conclude by briefly commenting on what I take to be a primary motivation of externalist analyses of epistemic concepts. I have said that there are a number of different views as to what the sui generis epistemic concepts might be, and the ease with which one can avoid skepticism depends very much on the details of the view one accepts. But certainly if one accepts the extreme version of foundationalism I recommend, complete with its insistence that one must have noninferential justification for believing propositions asserting evidential connections, the externalist is going to think that the task of avoiding skepticism is impossible. The typical externalist is convinced that one simply cannot be acquainted with facts. And even the internalist will undoubtedly admit that the kinds of facts with which we can be directly acquainted constitute a tiny fraction of what we think we know. When it comes to inferential knowledge, one must take seriously Humean complaints about the phenomenological inaccessibility of the relevant probability connection even if one ultimately rejects those complaints. If one cannot find in thought sui generis probability relations holding between propositions, one may well despair of resolving skeptical problems within the framework of radical foundationalism. On the problem of justifying belief in propositions describing the external world, for example, one might begin to suspect that Hume was right when he suggested with respect to what man ends up believing that

> Nature has not left this to his choice, and has doubtless esteem'd it an affair of too great importance to be trusted to our uncertain reasonings and specula-tions. ([11], p. 187).

Hume's hypothesis, I suspect, is accepted by externalists, but they do not want its truth to cheat us out of knowledge and justified belief. One of the most attractive features of most versions of externalism is that it makes it easy for us to know what we think we know. As long as nature (we now prefer to talk about evolution) has ensured that we respond to certain stimuli with correct representations of the world, we will know and have justified belief. Indeed, given externalist epistemologies, there is no difficulty in any creature or machine capable of representing reality achieving knowledge and justified belief.

It seems to me, however, that contemporary epistemology has too long let its philosophical analyses of epistemic terms be *driven* by the desire to avoid skepticism, by the desire to accommodate "commonsense intuitions" about what we know or are justified in believing. It is true that we describe ourselves as knowing a great many things. We also say that the dog knows that its master is home, the rat knows that it will get water when it hears the bell, and the salmon knows that it must get upstream to lay its eggs. But it seems clear to me that one need not take seriously our love of anthropomorphizing when analyzing the concepts of knowledge and justified belief that concern philosophers. If Wittgenstein and his followers did nothing else they surely have successfully argued that terms like "know" are used in a wide variety of ways in a wide variety of contexts. As philosophers, however, we can and should try to focus on the philosophically relevant use of epistemic terms. And the philosophically relevant epistemic concepts are those, satisfaction of which, resolves philosophical curiosity and doubt. I remain convinced that the kind of knowledge a philosopher wants, the kind of knowledge that will resolve philosophical doubt, involves the kind of direct confrontation with reality captured by the concept of direct acquaintance. While this is not the place to argue the issue, Hume *may* have been right—it may not be possible to justify in a philosophically satisfying way much of what we unreflectively believe. If this should be true, we may still satisfy, of course, the externalist's criteria for knowledge and justified belief, and these criteria may even mark a perfectly clear and useful distinction between beliefs and kind of relations they bear to the world. Internalists will continue to feel, however, that the externalist has *redefined* fundamental epistemic questions so as to make them irrelevant to traditional philosophical concerns.

NOTES

* I would like to thank Richard Foley and Scott Macdonald for their helpful comments on a rough draft of this paper.

1 Goldman in [8], [9], and [10]; Nozick in [14]; Armstrong in [1]; and Dretske in (among others) [5].

2 This point is made by Luper-Foy in [13].

3 See Nozick in [14], p. 281.

4 Not always. Sometimes "in the mind" meant logically dependent on the mind—the mind was thought of as a necessary condition for their existence.

5 The argument is presented on p. 32 but is discussed in a number of places throughout the book.

6 I realize that Goldman has presented a more sophisticated view in his recent book [10]. But it is a view which strays rather far from his reliabilist intuitions. The idea that justification is a function of reliability in normal worlds where normal worlds are defined in terms of *beliefs* about this world is equivalent to abandoning the idea that justification involves beliefs which are (actually) reliably produced. Indeed the view seems to me to come closer to a version of coherentism than reliabilism. In any event, I gather from a paper he read at a conference in honor of Roderick Chisholm, [9], that he is now more inclined to go back to "hard core"

reliabilism for at least one fundamental concept of justification.

[7]   It is interesting to note that in [9] and [10] Goldman comes very close to accepting something at least analogous. He allows that the use of a method can generate a strongly justified belief only if the method has been acquired in a suitable fashion, acquired by other methods, or ultimately processes, that are either reliable or meta-reliable. He does *not* impose the requirement on *all* processes, however, and in any event his requirement seems to concern the reliable generation of methods, not *beliefs* about methods.

[8]   In [10], Goldman himself seems to be more concerned with hooking up *one* sense of justification, what he calls weak justification, to considerations of blameworthiness and praiseworthiness. The aforementioned retreat from pure reliabilism in [9] was presumably aimed at achieving this same end.

[9]   See particularly [16], Part V, Chapters V and V1.

[10]   Notice that I have nowhere argued that an internalist cannot make reference to concepts other than the *sui generis* epistemic concepts in analyses of epistemic terms.

[11]   See Keynes's discussion of this issue in [12], Chapter 1.

[12]   See particularly Chapter 2 of [6].

REFERENCES

[1]   D. M. Armstrong, *Belief, Truth, and Knowledge* (London: Routledge and Kegan Paul, 1968).

[2]   Laurence BonJour, *The Structure of Empirical Knowledge* (Cambridge: Harvard University Press, 1985).

[3]   R. M. Chisholm, *Perceiving* (Ithaca: Cornell University Press, 1957).

[4]   R. M. Chisholm, *Theory of Knowledge*, 2nd Edition, (Englewood Cliffs, N.J.: Prentice-Hall, 1977).

[5]   Fred Dretske, *Seeing and Knowing* (London: Routledge and Kegan Paul, 1969).

[6]   Richard Fumerton, *Metaphysical and Epistemological Problems of Perception* (Lincoln and London: University of Nebraska Press, 1985).

[7]   Richard Fumerton, "Inferential Justification and Empiricism," *Journal of Philosophy*, 73 (1976), 557–69.

[8]   Alvin Goldman, "What is Justified Belief," in Pappas, ed., *Justification and Knowledge* (Dordrecht: Reidel, 1979), 1–23.

[9]   Alvin Goldman, "Strong and Weak Justification," a paper read at Brown University, Fall, 1986, at a conference in honor of R. M. Chisholm.

[10]   Alvin Goldman, *Epistemology and Cognition* (Cambridge: Harvard University Press, 1986).

[11]   David Hume, *A Treatise of Human Nature*, ed. by L. A. Selby-Bigge (London: Oxford University Press, 1888).

[12]   John M. Keynes, *Treatise on Probability* (London: Macmillan, 1921).

[13]   Steven Luper-Foy, "The Reliabilist Theory of Rational Belief," *The Monist*, April, 1985, 203–25.

[14]   Robert Nozick, *Philosophical Explanations* (Cambridge: Harvard University Press, 1981).

[15]   Bertrand Russell, *The Problems of Philosophy* (Oxford: Oxford University Press, 1959).

[16]   Bertrand Russell, *Human Knowledge: Its Scope and Limits* (New York: Simon and Schuster, 1948).

Section 1: Study Questions

1. What is it that makes a belief self-justifying, according to Chisholm? Give five examples of foundational beliefs, and five examples of non-foundational beliefs.

2. Why does Chisholm claim that the phenomenalistic version of the doctrine of the given is mistaken? Give an example of a foundational belief that is not an "appearance."

3. Why does Chisholm think that it is a mistake to claim that all beliefs involve a comparison with other beliefs? What follows if Chisholm is wrong about this?

4. What is an argument by elimination? Why does BonJour call the epistemic regress argument an argument by elimination? What is BonJour's objection to this form of argument?

5. Why does BonJour think that the sorts of beliefs that foundationalists regard as basic are not self-justifying?

6. What is the regress problem? Why is it a problem of interest to epistemologists?

7. What does BonJour mean by "linear justification?" What is the alternative to it?

8. When a belief coheres with your belief system in the sense relevant to the coherence theory of justification what exactly does this involve? Be as specific as possible.

9. What does BonJour mean when he describes some beliefs as "cognitively spontaneous?" Give three examples of such beliefs. Give three examples of beliefs that are not cognitively spontaneous.

10. What does BonJour mean by the term "observation requirement?" What role does the observation requirement play in BonJour's theory?

11. What do you think is the most pressing problem confronting the coherence theory? How might the coherence theorist address this concern?

12. Audi draws a distinction between the structural form of the regress problem and the sceptical form. Explain the difference between the two.

13. Audi distinguishes between psychologically direct beliefs and epistemically direct beliefs. Explain the difference between the two.

14. Why does Audi refer to his position as *fallible* foundationalism? What other type of foundationalism is there? How does his foundationalist theory differ from Chisholm's?

15. What role does coherence play in a foundational theory of justification? What does Audi mean by "conceptual coherentism?" How does it differ from other forms of coherentism?

16. What is the wedge strategy to which Audi refers?

17. Audi distinguishes between positive and negative epistemic dependence. Explain the difference between these concepts.

18. How do externalist theories of justification differ from other theories of justification? Explain why BonJour objects to externalist theories of justification.

19. BonJour argues that the two aspects of a belief—its need for justification, and its capacity to provide justification—are inseparable. What would Audi say about this? Who is correct?

20. Why does Goldman claim that epistemic predicates should not appear in the antecedent of the base clause of an adequate theory of justification?

21. Goldman describes his theory of justification as an historical theory. How does such a theory differ from a current time-slice theory? Why does he believe that foundational theories and coherence theories are current time-slice theories?

22. Goldman notes that justification conferring processes can be construed either narrowly or very broadly. What relevance does the "generality" of justification conferring processes have for the issue of epistemic justification?

23. Goldman claims that a justified belief is a well-formed belief. What would Audi and BonJour say about Goldman's understanding of epistemic justification?

24. How would the reliabilist respond to the regress problem? Is this an adequate solution?

25. According to Fumerton, what is the key distinction between internalist and externalist accounts of justification?

26. What is Fumerton's key criticism of externalist accounts of justification? How might Goldman respond to this criticism?

27. Critically evaluate internalist accounts of justification. Are such accounts deficient in any respect?

Additional Readings

BonJour develops his coherence theory more fully in his *The Structure of Empirical Knowledge*.

Keith Lehrer develops an alternative coherence theory of justification in his *Self-Trust*.

A variety of criticisms of the coherence theory, complete with BonJour's and Lehrer's responses, are published in John Bender's (ed.) (1989) *The Current State of the Coherence Theory*.

Audi's foundationalist theory of justification is discussed in fuller detail in his *Belief, Justification, and Knowledge*.

Susan Haack attempts to develop a hybrid theory, which she calls "foundherentism," in her *Evidence and Inquiry*.

Goldman's reliabilist theory is discussed more fully in his *Epistemology and Cognition*.

Robert Nozick develops an alternative reliabilist theory in his *Philosophical Explanations*.

SECTION 2
KNOWLEDGE
AND SCEPTICISM

SECTION 2: KNOWLEDGE AND SCEPTICISM

The readings in this section address two issues. The first three readings are concerned with the issue of providing an analysis of propositional knowledge, knowledge expressible in sentences. The latter three readings deal with the issue of scepticism.

The first three readings are quite narrowly focussed on what has come to be called the Gettier problems. In the dialogue *Theaetetus*, Plato's character Socrates examines a number of different definitions of knowledge. The one he seems to settle on is that knowledge is justified true belief. Plato's definition went unchallenged until 1963, when Edmund Gettier presented two counterexamples of justified true beliefs that are not instances of knowledge. According to Gettier, these examples show that justified true belief is not sufficient for knowledge. That is, something besides justified true belief is required for knowledge. Although a very short paper, Gettier's paper generated much philosophical discussion and remains contentious.

Some philosophers are suspicious about the Gettier examples, arguing that they rely on a trick, or tacitly violate one of the conditions for knowledge. This criticism is addressed in the article by Richard Feldman. In fact, Feldman develops additional Gettier-type problems in an effort to show that the problems Gettier pointed to are not apt to be swept away easily or readily dismissed.

Other philosophers claim that the Gettier problems are not really important problems, and thus do not deserve the attention of philosophers. This issue is discussed by Earl Conee who argues that Gettier problems are worthy of philosophical attention. In fact, Conee believes that a solution to the Gettier problems would constitute something of great philosophical interest.

You should think about how to best deal with the Gettier problems. In particular, does a solution to the Gettier problems require a radical reworking of epistemology? Further, you should think back to the various theories of justification discussed in Section 1, and consider whether or not any of these theories have anything to offer by way of a solution to the Gettier problems.

The readings in the second half of this section address the issue of scepticism, a very old and persistent issue in philosophy. There are a variety of different sorts of challenges that the sceptic is thought to raise for epistemologists. Hilary Putnam deals with a contemporary version of Descartes' reflections on the possibility of an all-powerful evil demon that challenges whether or not we can really know if the world is as it appears to us. The sceptic, in Putnam's article, asks us to imagine the possibility that we are not really in touch with reality. Are we brains in vats, caused to have the experiences we have which lead us to believe that the world is as we believe it to be? The sceptic asks: how do you know you are not a brain in the vat? Putnam attempts to show that this particular form of scepticism is not viable.

Thomas Nagel has a different attitude toward scepticism. He believes that sceptical reflections are an integral part of our self perception, and that they are not to be as readily dismissed as Putnam suggests. He believes that scepticism and the notion of objectivity are intimately tied. Critical reflection on the latter will, inevitably, lead to critical reflection on the former. Further, he believes that resolving sceptical puzzles involves taking a perspective on ourselves that is not fully possible.

Barry Stroud, too, believes that scepticism is very important, and not to be easily dismissed. He tries to show that the sceptical challenge is an important one, and, in fact, important even if it cannot be addressed adequately. Further, Stroud is concerned that many people misunderstand what scepticism is about, and consequently fail to appreciate what we have to learn from scepticism.

You should aim to distinguish the various types of scepticism that each author deals with, and also try to articulate as clearly as possible the various sceptical hypotheses that these authors propose. Further, ask yourself: what is the appropriate response to sceptical hypotheses?

2.1

IS JUSTIFIED TRUE BELIEF KNOWLEDGE?

Edmund Gettier

Various attempts have been made in recent years to state necessary and sufficient conditions for someone's knowing a given proposition. The attempts have often been such that they can be stated in a form similar to the following:[1]

(a) S knows that P   *IFF*   (i)   P is true,
  (ii)   S believes that P, and
  (iii)   S is justified in believing that P.

For example, Chisholm has held that the following gives the necessary and sufficient conditions for knowledge:[2]

(b) S knows that P   *IFF*   (i)   S accepts P,
  (ii)   S has adequate evidence for P, and
  (iii)   P is true.

Ayer has stated the necessary and sufficient conditions for knowledge as follows:[3]

(c) S knows that P   *IFF*   (i)   P is true,
  (ii)   S is sure that P is true, and
  (iii)   S has the right to be sure that P is true.

I shall argue that (a) is false in that the conditions stated therein do not constitute a *sufficient* condition for the truth of the proposition that S knows that P. The same argument will show that (b) and (c) fail if "has adequate evidence for" or "has the right to be sure that" is substituted for "is justified in believing that" throughout.

I shall begin by noting two points. First, in that sense of 'justified' in which S's being justified in believing P is a necessary condition of S's knowing that

P, it is possible for a person to be justified in believing a proposition that is in fact false. Secondly, for any proposition P, if S is justified in believing P, and P entails Q, and S deduces Q from P and accepts Q as a result of this deduction, then S is justified in believing Q. Keeping these two points in mind, I shall now present two cases in which the conditions stated in (a) are true for some proposition, though it is at the same time false that the person in question knows that proposition.

Case I:

Suppose that Smith and Jones have applied for a certain job. And suppose that Smith has strong evidence for the following conjunctive proposition:

(d) Jones is the man who will get the job, and Jones has ten coins in his pocket.

Smith's evidence for (d) might be that the president of the company assured him that Jones would in the end be selected, and that he, Smith, had counted the coins in Jones's pocket ten minutes ago. Proposition (d) entails:

(e) The man who will get the job has ten coins in his pocket.

Let us suppose that Smith sees the entailment from (d) to (e), and accepts (e) on the grounds of (d), for which he has strong evidence. In this case, Smith is clearly justified in believing that (e) is true.

But imagine, further, that unknown to Smith, he himself, not Jones, will get the job. And, also, unknown to Smith, he himself has ten coins in his pocket. Proposition (e) is then true, though proposition (d), from which Smith inferred (e), is false. In our example, then, all of the following are true: (*i*) (e) is true, (*ii*) Smith believes that (e) is true, and (*iii*) Smith is justified in believing that (e) is true. But it is equally clear that Smith does not *know* that (e) is true; for (e) is true in virtue of the number of coins in Smith's pocket, while Smith does not know how many coins are in Smith's pocket, and bases his belief in (e) on a count of the coins in Jones's pocket, whom he falsely believes to be the man who will get the job.

Case II:

Let us suppose that Smith has strong evidence for the following proposition:

(f) Jones owns a Ford.

Smith's evidence might be that Jones has at all times in the past within Smith's memory owned a car, and always a Ford, and that Jones has just offered Smith a ride while driving a Ford. Let us imagine, now, that Smith has another friend, Brown, of whose whereabouts he is totally ignorant. Smith selects three place-names quite at random, and constructs the following three propositions:

(g) Either Jones owns a Ford, or Brown is in Boston;
(h) Either Jones owns a Ford, or Brown is in Barcelona;
(i) Either Jones owns a Ford, or Brown is in Brest-Litovsk.

Each of these propositions is entailed by (f). Imagine that Smith realizes the entailment of each of these propositions he has constructed by (f), and proceeds to accept (g), (h), and (i) on the basis of (f). Smith has correctly inferred (g), (h), and (i) from a proposition for which he has strong evidence. Smith is therefore completely justified in believing each of these three propositions. Smith, of course, has no idea where Brown is.

But imagine now that two further conditions hold. First, Jones does *not* own a Ford, but is at present driving a rented car. And secondly, by the sheerest coincidence, and entirely unknown to Smith, the place mentioned in proposition (h) happens really to be the place where Brown is. If these two conditions hold then Smith does *not* know that (h) is true, even though (*i*) (h) *is* true, (*ii*) Smith does believe that (h) is true, and (*iii*) Smith is justified in believing that (h) is true.

These two examples show that definition (a) does not state a *sufficient* condition for someone's knowing a given proposition. The same cases, with appropriate changes, will suffice to show that neither definition (b) nor definition (c) do so either.

NOTES

[1] Plato seems to be considering some such definition at *Theaetetus* 201, and perhaps accepting one at *Meno* 98.

[2] Roderick M. Chisholm, *Perceiving: a Philosophical Study,* Cornell University Press (Ithaca, New York, 1957), p. 16.

[3] A.J. Ayer, *The Problem of Knowledge,* Macmillan (London, 1956), p. 34.

2.2

Why Solve the Gettier Problem?

Earl Conee

The value of work on the Gettier Problem has been called into question. Michael Williams concludes a paper on this dark note: "That anything important turns on coming up with a solution to Gettier's problem remains to be shown."[1] Mark Kaplan argues for a gloomier view: "My message is that it is time to stop and face the unpleasant reality that we simply have no use for a definition of propositional knowledge."[2]

This is a fitting occasion[3] to offer a proof of the philosophical importance of the Gettier problem. Here is the proof:

1. Discovering an analysis of factual knowledge turns on solving the Gettier problem.
2. Discovering an analysis of factual knowledge is philosophically important.
3. Something philosophically important turns on solving the Gettier problem.

Neither Williams nor Kaplan addresses this sort of argument. They provide nothing that amounts to an objection to the first premise. Williams' paper contains no conspicuous objection to either premise. Williams does contend that the Gettier problem falls outside of a certain tradition in epistemology, and he may intend thereby to cast doubt on the problem's significance. In particular, Williams claims that traditional theories of knowledge are best construed as responses to radical skepticism, where radical skepticism is understood as the view that we can never have any reason to believe anything. Thus, the radical skeptic denies the possibility of justified belief. Those who accept Gettier's counterexamples assume that justified beliefs exist in the prosaic circumstances described in giving the examples. So, when such examples are simply taken as data for constructing an extensionally adequate analysis of factual knowledge, radical skepticism is assumed false. Thus, this project fails to respond to what Williams takes to be the traditional issue for a theory of knowledge—the threat of radical skepticism.[4]

It is surprising that Williams does not include as part of the traditional project the goal of explaining what knowledge really is. Williams does not argue for the merit of his extraordinary construal of the point of traditional theories of knowledge. The rest of his paper defends the further contention that solving the Gettier problem would also fail to contribute to a theory of reasoning, contrary to claims by Gilbert Harman.[5]

Neither of these negative points about work on the Gettier problem will be disputed here. It does no harm for present purposes simply to grant Williams' conclusions. It can be granted that an analysis of knowledge that solved the Gettier problem would not refute or support radical skepticism, and that would not contribute to a theory of reasoning. This is as far as Williams' paper goes toward establishing his conclusion about the lack of importance of the Gettier problem. It is sufficient for present purposes to note that Williams' paper does not make a decisive case against our premise 2 if, as is argued below, analyzing knowledge can be seen to have some other philosophical importance.[6]

Let us see whether Mark Kaplan's efforts add to a case against premise 2. First he argues that the sort of analysis against which Gettier's objections are effective is not a historically important sort of analysis. He contends that the Platonic accounts of knowledge in the *Theaetetus* and the *Meno* are in fact intended as accounts of knowledge of nonpropositional objects, and thus are not even on Gettier's topic of factual knowledge.[7] Kaplan observes that Descartes' account, though concerned with propositional knowledge, is immune to Gettier's objections. This is because on the Cartesian account justified yet false belief is impossible, while it must be possible for Gettier's counterexamples to succeed.[8]

This is Kaplan's argument against Gettier's having criticized a historically important account of knowledge. As in the case of Williams' conclusions, Kaplan's conclusion need not be disputed here. But it seems appropriate to mention that his argument for the conclusion is unfair to Gettier in one respect. The argument neglects that part of history which lies in the twentieth century. This is peculiar because Kaplan mentions that Gettier's objections are explicitly targeted against Ayer's account. The analyses of Russell, Ayer, and Chisholm provide a historically important view of factual knowledge against which Gettier's criticisms apply.

For present purposes it does no harm to waive this objection too. Let it be granted that the analyses that Gettier refutes do not have historical importance. Again, this is innocuous to the above argument for the importance of the Gettier problem, as long as analyzing factual knowledge is shown to be important for some other reason.

Kaplan also argues that a solution to the Gettier problem would neither advance nor clarify the proper conduct of rational inquiry. He indicates that once one has made best use of one's evidence and arrived at a justified belief, it follows that one has made a proper inquiry from the evidence. Gettier has established that knowledge requires something beyond justified true belief. But whatever that is, it is not something the inquirer can simultaneously make a separate check on. If one comes to have further evidence, it might show that one's justification relied on a falsehood, as in Gettier's examples. But at that further point either one lacks justification or one has new evidence that provides a new justification. The fact that justified belief is corrigible over time does not show that some justified true belief that is not known is a result of faulty inquiry. Kaplan contends that since the proprieties of rational inquiry concern only how to gain justification, solving the Gettier problem would not advance our understanding or practice of rational inquiry.[9]

One fault in this contention is noteworthy here, since it brings to light a philosophical contribution that a solution to the Gettier problem would make. The nature of proper inquiry depends on the goal of the inquiry. The ultimate goal of pure inquiry is not justified belief, nor is it justified true belief. The ultimate goal is knowledge. Thus, a rational inquirer who has merely done all that is required to gain a justified true belief may not have what he or she seeks. It is true that when a person's justified true belief is not knowledge because of the factors that Gettier's examples illustrate, the person does not realize this and may be unable to do anything that would result in knowledge. So any further inquiry will seem superfluous at the outset and may be futile. But success at attaining knowledge to replace mere justified true belief is sometimes available. When, as in Gettier's examples, a person has only a justified true belief in a certain existential generalization or a certain disjunction, further inquiry would sometimes result in the person's perceiving the fact that really does make the generalization or the disjunction true and thus yield knowledge. Additional inquiry may be crucial for achieving the goal of knowledge, though it is unnecessary for securing justification. Since a solution to the Gettier problem would informatively describe exactly what is sufficient for knowledge, it would illuminate what must be accomplished by further rational inquiry for the sake of genuinely knowing.

Once again, however, it is harmless for present purposes to set aside such objections. Let it be granted that solving the Gettier problem is useless for understanding or conducting rational inquiry. This point, together with his historical contention, constitutes Kaplan's case against the utility of analyzing knowledge.

The combined cases of Williams and Kaplan do not refute premise 2. Granting every point, they simply give us a list of four philosophically important things that would not be done by a solution to the Gettier problem: refuting or supporting radical skepticism, contributing to a theory of reasoning, improving some historically important account of knowledge, and improving our understanding or execution of rational inquiry.

An analysis of knowledge that solved the Gettier problem would accomplish something else that is philosophically important. It would provide us with independent conditions which are severally necessary and jointly sufficient for the existence of a case of factual knowledge. This is important because learning the elements of factual knowledge is itself a philosophical goal. The insightful and dedicated work on the Gettier problem by a diversity of philosophers attests to the philosophical interest in the topic. The philosophical goal of this research is an analysis of factual knowledge. There is no good reason to require that the research also have utility toward some other philosophical objective in order to justify this enterprise as worthwhile philosophy.[10] Learning which conditions constitute a solution to the Gettier problem would greatly enhance our understanding of factual knowledge. That makes solving the problem important.

University of Rochester

NOTES

[1] Michael Williams [1978], "Inference, Justification and the Analysis of Knowledge," *The Journal of Philosophy* LXXV (May) p. 263.

[2] Mark Kaplan [1985], "It's Not What You Know that Counts," *The Journal of Philosophy* LXXXII (July) p. 363.

[3] Editor's note: This paper was originally published in the book *Philosophical Analysis* (edited by David Austin), which was published by Kluwer in 1988 to honour Gettier's 60th birthday.

[4]   Williams [1978], pp. 249–250.

[5]   *Ibid.*, pp. 250–262. Harman responds in Harman [1978], "Using Intuitions about Reasoning to Study Reasoning: A Reply to Williams," *The Journal of Philosophy* LXXV (August) pp. 433–483.

[6]   In fairness to Williams, he may not have intended to make a conclusive case. He may have intended to establish no more than he asserts in the above citation—that the importance had not been shown.

[7]   Kaplan [1985], pp. 352–353.

[8]   *Ibid.*, p. 353.

[9]   *Ibid.*, pp. 354–356.

[10]   Sometimes the remark is made, as though in objection to such work, that conceptual analysis is a "sterile" or "fruitless" undertaking. But it is obvious that the search for an analysis of knowledge has spawned illuminating contributions on such topics as the defeat of evidence, causal and counterfactual conditions on knowledge and justification, and the epistemic role of external factors like social context and the reliability of belief-forming mechanisms. Anyway, suppose that the search for a solution to the Gettier problem had borne no fruit. Suppose that it had led quickly to an accurate by "sterile" analysis, useless in other philosophical undertakings. So what? How could this show that the analysis would be philosophically unimportant?

2.3

AN ALLEGED DEFECT IN GETTIER COUNTER-EXAMPLES

Richard Feldman

A number of philosophers have contended that Gettier counter-examples to the justified true belief analysis of knowledge all rely on a certain false principle. For example, in their recent paper "Knowledge Without Paradox,"[1] Robert G. Meyers and Kenneth Stern argue that "(c)ounter-examples of the Gettier sort all turn on the principle that someone can be justified in accepting a certain proposition h on evidence p even though p is false."[2] They contend that this principle is false, and hence that the counter-examples fail. Their view is that one proposition, p, can justify another, h, only if p is true. With this in mind, they accept the justified true belief analysis.

D. M. Armstrong defends a similar view in *Belief, Truth and Knowledge*.[3] He writes:

> This simple consideration seems to make redundant the ingenious argument of…Gettier's…article…Gettier produces counter-examples to the thesis that justified true belief is knowledge by producing true beliefs based on justifiably believed grounds,…but where these grounds are in fact *false*. But because possession of such grounds could not constitute possession of *knowledge*, I should have thought it obvious that they are too weak to serve as suitable grounds.[4]

Thus he concludes that Gettier's examples are defective because they rely on the false principle that false propositions can justify one's belief in other propositions. Armstrong's view seems to be that one proposition, p, can justify another, h, only if p is known to be true (unlike Meyers and Stern who demand only that p in fact be true).[5]

I think, though, that there are examples very much like Gettier's that do not rely on this allegedly false principle. To see this, let us first consider one example in the form in which Meyers and Stern discuss it, and then consider a slight modification of it.

> Suppose Mr. Nogot tells Smith that he owns a Ford and even shows him a certificate to that effect. Suppose, further, that up till now Nogot has always been reliable and honest in his dealings with Smith. Let us call the conjunction of all this evidence m. Smith is thus justified in believing that Mr. Nogot who is in his office owns a Ford (r) and, consequently, is justified in believing that someone in his office owns a Ford (h).[6]

As it turns out, though, m and h are true but r is false. So, the Gettier example runs, Smith has a justified true belief in h, but he clearly does not know h.

What is supposed to justify h in this example is r. But since r is false, the example runs afoul of the disputed principle. Since r is false, it justifies nothing. Hence, if the principle is false, the counter-example fails.

We can alter the example slightly, however, so that what justifies h for Smith is true and he knows that it is. Suppose he deduces from m its existential generalization:

(n)   There is someone in the office who told Smith that he owns a Ford and even showed him a certificate to that effect, and who up till now has always been reliable and honest in his dealings with Smith.

(n), we should note, is true and Smith knows that it is, since he has correctly deduced it from m, which he knows to be true. On the basis of n Smith believes h—someone in the office owns a Ford. Just as the Nogot evidence, m, justified r—Nogot owns a Ford—in the original example, n justifies h in this example. Thus Smith has a justified true belief in h, knows his evidence to be true, but still does not know h.

I conclude that even if a proposition can be justified for a person only if his evidence is true, or only if he knows it to be true, there are still counter-examples to the justified true belief analysis of knowledge of the Gettier sort. In the above example, Smith reasoned from the proposition m, which he knew to be true, to the proposition n, which he also knew, to the truth h; yet he still did not know h. So some examples, similar to Gettier's, do not "turn on the principle that someone can be justified in accepting a certain proposition...even though (his evidence)...is false."[7]

NOTES

[1] *The Journal of Philosophy* 70 (March 22, 1973): 147–60.

[2] Ibid., p. 147.

[3] (1973).

[4] Ibid., p. 152.

[5] Armstrong ultimately goes on to defend a rather different analysis.

[6] Meyers and Stern, *op. cit.*, p. 151.

[7] Ibid., p. 147.

2.4

Brains in a Vat

Hilary Putnam

An ant is crawling on a patch of sand. As it crawls, it traces a line in the sand. By pure chance the line that it traces curves and recrosses itself in such a way that it ends up looking like a recognizable caricature of Winston Churchill. Has the ant traced a picture of Winston Churchill, a picture that *depicts* Churchill?

Most people would say, on a little reflection, that it has not. The ant, after all, has never seen Churchill, or even a picture of Churchill, and it had no intention of depicting Churchill. It simply traced a line (and even *that* was unintentional), a line that *we* can "see as" a picture of Churchill.

We can express this by saying that the line is not "in itself" a representation[1] of anything rather than anything else. Similarity (of a certain very complicated sort) to the features of Winston Churchill is not sufficient to make something represent or refer to Churchill. Nor is it necessary: in our community the printed shape "Winston Churchill," the spoken words "Winston Churchill," and many other things are used to represent Churchill (though not pictorially), while not having the sort of similarity to Churchill that a picture—even a line drawing—has. If *similarity* is not necessary or sufficient to make something represent something else, how can *anything* be necessary or sufficient for this purpose? How on earth can one thing represent (or "stand for," etc.) a different thing?

The answer may seem easy. Suppose the ant had seen Winston Churchill, and suppose that it had the intelligence and skill to draw a picture of him. Suppose it produced the caricature *intentionally*. Then the line would have represented Churchill.

On the other hand, suppose the line had the shape WINSTON CHUR-CHILL. And suppose this was just accident (ignoring the improbability involved). Then the "printed shape" WINSTON CHURCHILL would *not* have represented Churchill, although that printed shape does represent Churchill when it occurs in almost any book today.

So it may seem that what is necessary for representation, or what is mainly necessary for representation, is *intention*.

But to have the intention that *anything*, even private language (even the words "Winston Churchill" spoken in my mind and not out loud), should *represent* Churchill, I must have been able to *think about* Churchill in the first place. If lines in the sand, noises, etc., cannot "in themselves" represent anything, then how is it that thought forms can "in themselves" represent anything? Or can they? How can thought reach out and "grasp" what is external?

Some philosophers have, in the past, leaped from this sort of consideration to what they take to be a proof that the mind is *essentially non-physical in nature*. The argument is simple; what we said about the ant's curve applies to any physical object. No physical object can, in itself, refer to one thing rather than to another; nevertheless, *thoughts in the mind* obviously do succeed in referring to one thing rather than another. So thoughts (and hence the mind) are of an essentially different nature than physical objects. Thoughts have the characteristic of *intentionality*—they can refer to something else; nothing physical has "intentionality," save as that intentionality is derivative from some employment of that physical thing by a mind. Or so it is claimed. This is too quick; just postulating mysterious powers of mind solves nothing. But the problem is very real. How is intentionality, reference, possible?

Magical theories of reference

We saw that the ant's "picture" has no necessary connection with Winston Churchill. The mere fact that the "picture" bears a "resemblance" to Churchill does not make it into a real picture, nor does it make it a representation of Churchill. Unless the ant is an intelligent ant (which it isn't) and knows about Churchill (which it doesn't), the curve it traced is not a picture or even a representation of anything. Some primitive people believe that some representations (in particular, *names*) have a necessary connection with their bearers; that to know the "true name" of someone or something gives one power over it. This power comes from the *magical connection* between the name and the bearer of the name; once one realizes that a name *only* has a contextual, contingent, conventional connection with its bearer, it is hard to see why knowledge of the name should have any mystical significance.

What is important to realize is that what goes for physical pictures also goes for mental images, and for mental representations in general; mental representations no more have a necessary connection with what they represent than physical representations do. The contrary supposition is a survival of magical thinking.

Perhaps the point is easiest to grasp in the case of mental *images*. (Perhaps the first philosopher to grasp the enormous significance of this point, even if he was not the first to actually make it, was Wittgenstein.) Suppose there is a planet somewhere on which human beings have evolved (or been deposited by alien spacemen, or what have you). Suppose these humans, although otherwise like us, have never seen *trees*. Suppose they have never imagined trees (perhaps vegetable life exists on their planet only in the form of molds). Suppose one day a picture of a tree is accidentally dropped on their planet by a spaceship which passes on without having other contact with them. Imagine them puzzling over the picture. What in the world is this? All sorts of speculations occur to them: a building, a canopy, even an animal of some kind. But suppose they never come close to the truth.

For *us* the picture is a representation of a tree. For these humans the picture only represents a strange object, nature and function unknown. Suppose one of them has a mental image which is exactly like one of my mental images of a tree as a result of having seen the picture. His mental image is not a *representation of a tree*. It is only a representation of the strange object (whatever it is) that the mysterious picture represents.

Still, someone might argue that the mental image is *in fact* a representation of a tree, if only because the picture which caused this mental image was itself a representation of a tree to begin with. There is a causal chain from actual trees to the mental image even if it is a very strange one.

But even this causal chain can be imagined absent. Suppose the "picture of a tree" that the spaceship dropped was not really a picture of a tree, but the accidental result of some spilled paints. Even if it looked exactly like a picture of a tree, it was, in truth, no more a picture of a tree than the ant's "caricature" of Churchill was a picture of Churchill. We can even imagine that the spaceship which dropped the "picture" came from a planet which knew nothing of trees. Then the humans would still have mental images qualitatively identical with my image of a tree, but they would not be images which represented a tree any more than anything else.

The same thing is true of *words*. A discourse on paper might seem to be a perfect description of trees, but if it was produced by monkeys randomly hitting keys on a typewriter for millions of years, then the words do not refer to anything. If there were a person who memorized those words and said them in his mind without understanding them, then they would not refer to anything when thought in the mind, either.

Imagine the person who is saying those words in his mind has been hypnotized. Suppose the words are in Japanese, and the person has been told that he understands Japanese. Suppose that as he thinks those words he has a "feeling of understanding." (Although if someone broke into his train of thought and asked him what the words he was thinking *meant*, he would discover he couldn't say.) Perhaps the illusion would be so perfect that the person could even fool a Japanese telepath! But if he couldn't use the words in the right contexts, answer questions about what he "thought," etc., then he didn't understand them.

By combining these science fiction stories I have been telling, we can contrive a case in which someone thinks words which are in fact a description of trees in some language *and* simultaneously has appropriate mental images, but *neither* understands the words *nor* knows what a tree is. We can even imagine that the mental images were caused by paint-spills (although the person has been hypnotized to think that they are images of something appropriate to his thought—only, if he were asked, he wouldn't be able to say of what). And we can imagine that the language the person is thinking in is one neither the hypnotist nor the person hypnotized has ever heard of—perhaps it is just coincidence that these "nonsense sentences," as the hypnotist supposes them to be, are a description of trees in Japanese. In short, everything passing before the person's mind might be qualitatively identical with what was passing through the mind of a Japanese speaker who was *really* thinking about trees—but none of it would refer to trees.

All of this is really impossible, of course, in the way that it is really impossible that monkeys should by chance type out a copy of *Hamlet*. That is to say that the probabilities against it are so high as to mean it will never really happen (we think). But it is not logically impossible, or even physically impossible. It *could* happen (compatibly with physical law and, perhaps, compatibly with actual conditions in the universe, if there are lots of intelligent beings on other planets). And if it did happen, it would be a striking demonstration of an important conceptual truth; that even a large and complex system of representations, both verbal and visual, still does not have an *intrinsic*, built-in, magical connection with what it represents—a connection independent of how it was caused and what the dispositions of the speaker or thinker are. And this is true whether the system of representations (words and images, in the case of the example) is physically realized—the words are written or spoken, and the pictures are physical pictures—or only realized in the mind. Thought words and mental pictures do not *intrinsically* represent what they are about.

The case of the brains in a vat

Here is a science fiction possibility discussed by philosophers: imagine that a human being (you can imagine this to be yourself) has been subjected to an operation by an evil scientist. The person's brain (your brain) has been removed from the body and placed in a vat of nutrients which keeps the brain alive. The nerve endings have been connected to a super-scientific computer which causes the person whose brain it is to have the illusion that everything is perfectly normal. There seem to be people, objects, the sky, etc; but really all the person (you) is experiencing is the result of electronic impulses travelling from the computer to the nerve endings. The computer is so clever that if the person tries to raise his hand, the feedback from the computer will cause him to "see" and "feel" the hand being raised. Moreover, by varying the program, the evil scientist can cause the victim to "experience" (or hallucinate) any situation or environment the evil scientist wishes. He can also obliterate the memory of the brain operation, so that the victim will seem to himself to have always been in this environment. It can even seem to the victim that he is sitting and reading these very words about the amusing but quite absurd supposition that there is an evil scientist who removes people's brains from their bodies and places them in a vat of nutrients which keep the brains alive. The nerve endings are supposed to be connected to a super-scientific computer which causes the person whose brain it is to have the illusion that...

When this sort of possibility is mentioned in a lecture on the Theory of Knowledge, the purpose, of course, is to raise the classical problem of scepticism with respect to the external world in a modern way. (*How do you know you aren't in this predicament?*) But this predicament is also a useful device for raising issues about the mind/world relationship.

Instead of having just one brain in a vat, we could imagine that all human beings (perhaps all sentient beings) are brains in a vat (or nervous systems in a vat in case some beings with just a minimal nervous system already count as "sentient"). Of course, the evil scientist would have to be outside—or would he? Perhaps there is no evil scientist, perhaps (though this is absurd) the universe just happens to consist of automatic machinery tending a vat full of brains and nervous systems.

This time let us suppose that the automatic machinery is programmed to give us all a *collective* hallucination, rather than a number of separate unrelated hallucinations. Thus, when I seem to myself to be talking to you, you seem to yourself to be hearing my words. Of course, it is not the case that my words actually reach your ears—for you don't have (real) ears, nor do I have a real mouth and tongue. Rather, when I produce my words, what happens is that the efferent impulses travel from my brain to the computer, which both causes me to "hear" my own voice uttering those words and "feel" my tongue moving, etc., and causes you to "hear" my words, "see" me speaking, etc. In this case, we are, in a sense, actually in communication. I am not mistaken about your real existence (only about the existence of your body and the "external world," apart from brains). From a certain point of view, it doesn't even matter that "the whole world" is a collective hallucination; for you do, after all, really hear my words when I speak to you, even if the mechanism isn't what we suppose it to be. (Of course, if we were two lovers making love, rather than just two people carrying on a conversation, then the suggestion that it was just two brains in a vat might be disturbing.)

I want now to ask a question which will seem very silly and obvious (at least to some people, including some very sophisticated philosophers), but which will take us to real philosophical depths rather quickly. Suppose this whole story were actually true. Could we, if we were brains in a vat in this way, *say* or *think* that we were?

I am going to argue that the answer is "No, we couldn't." In fact, I am going to argue that the supposition that we are actually brains in a vat, although it violates no physical law, and is perfectly consistent with everything we have experienced, cannot possibly be true. *It cannot possibly be true*, because it is, in a certain way, self-refuting.

The argument I am going to present is an unusual one, and it took me several years to convince myself that it is really right. But it is a correct argument. What makes it seem so strange is that it is connected with some of the very deepest issues in philosophy. (It first occurred to me when I was thinking about a theorem in modern logic, the "Skolem-Löwenheim Theorem," and I suddenly saw a connection between this theorem and some arguments in Wittgenstein's *Philosophical Investigations*.)

A "self-refuting supposition" is one whose truth implies its own falsity. For example, consider the thesis that *all general statements are false*. This is a general statement. So if it is true, then it must be false. Hence, it is false. Hence, it is false. Sometimes a thesis is called "self-refuting" if it is *the supposition that the thesis is entertained or enunciated* that implies its falsity. For example, "I do not exist" is self-refuting if thought by *me* (for any "*me*"). So one can be certain that one oneself exists, if one thinks about it (as Descartes argued).

What I shall show is that the supposition that we are brains in a vat has just this property. If we can consider whether it is true or false, then it is not true (I shall show). Hence it is not true.

Before I give the argument, let us consider why it seems so strange that such an argument can be given (at least to philosophers who subscribe to a "copy" conception of truth). We conceded that it is compatible with physical law that there should be a world in which all sentient beings are brains in a vat. As philosophers say, there is a "possible world" in which all sentient beings are brains in a vat. (This "possible world" talk makes it sound as if there is a *place* where any absurd supposition is true, which is why it can be very misleading in philosophy.) The humans in that possible world have exactly the same experiences that *we* do. They think the same thoughts we do (at least, the same words, images, thought-forms, etc., go through their minds). Yet, I am claiming that there is an argument we can give that shows we are not brains in a vat. How can there be? And why couldn't the people in the possible world who really *are* brains in a vat give it too?

The answer is going to be (basically) this: although the people in that possible world can think and "say" any words we can think and say, they cannot (I claim) *refer* to what we can refer to. In particular, they cannot think or say that they are brains in a vat (*even by thinking "we are brains in a vat"*).

Turing's test

Suppose someone succeeds in inventing a computer which can actually carry on an intelligent conversation with one (on as many subjects as an intelligent person might). How can one decide if the computer is "conscious?"

The British logician Alan Turing proposed the following test:[2] let someone carry on a conversation with the computer and a conversation with a person whom he does not know. If he cannot tell which is the computer and which is the human being, then (assume the test to be repeated a sufficient number of times with different interlocutors) the computer is conscious. In short, a computing machine is conscious if it can pass the "Turing Test." (The conversations are not to be carried on face to face, of course, since the interlocutor is not to know the visual appearance of either of his two conversational partners. Nor is voice to be used, since the mechanical voice might simply sound different from a human voice. Imagine, rather, that the conversations all carried on via electric typewriter. The interlocutor types in his statements, questions, etc., and the two partners—the machine and the person—respond via the electric keyboard. Also, the machine may *lie*—asked "Are you a machine," it might reply, "No, I'm an assistant in the lab here.")

The idea that this test is really a definitive test of consciousness has been criticized by a number of authors (who are by no means hostile in principle to the idea that a machine might be conscious). But this is not our topic at this time. I wish to use the general idea of the Turing test, the general idea of a *dialogic test of competence*, for a different purpose, the purpose of exploring the notion of *reference*.

Imagine a situation in which the problem is not to determine if the partner is really a person or a machine, but is rather to determine if the partner uses the words to refer as we do. The obvious test is, again, to carry on a conversation, and, if no problems arise, if the partner "passes" in the sense of being indistinguishable from someone who is certified in advance to be speaking the same language, referring to the usual sorts of objects, etc., to conclude that the partner does refer to objects as we do. When the purpose of the Turing test is as just described, that is, to determine the existence of (shared) reference, I shall refer to the test as the *Turing Test for Reference*. And, just as philosophers have discussed the question whether the original Turing test is a *definitive* test for consciousness, i.e. the question of whether a machine which "passes" the test not just once but regularly is *necessarily* conscious, so, in the same way, I wish to discuss the question of whether the Turing Test for Reference just suggested is a definitive test for shared reference.

The answer will turn out to be "No." The Turing Test for Reference is not definitive. It is certainly an excellent test in practice; but it is not logically impossible (though it is certainly highly improbable) that someone could pass the Turing Test for Reference and not be referring to anything. It follows from this, as we shall see, that we can extend our observation that words (and whole texts and discourses) do not have a necessary connection to their referents. Even if we consider not words by themselves but rules deciding what words may appropriately be produced in certain contexts—even if we consider, in computer jargon, *programs for using words*—unless those programs themselves *refer to something extra-linguistic* there is still no determinate reference that those words possess. This will be a crucial step in the process of reaching the conclusion that the Brain-in-a-Vat Worlders cannot refer to anything external at all (and hence cannot say *that* they are Brain-in-a-Vat Worlders).

Suppose, for example, that I am in the Turing situation (playing the "Imitation Game," in Turing's terminology) and my partner is actually a machine. Suppose this machine is able to win the game ("passes" the test). Imagine the machine to be programmed to produce beautiful responses in English to statements, questions, remarks, etc. in English, but that it has no sense organs (other than the hookup to my electric typewriter), and no motor organs (other than the electric typewriter). (As far as I can make out, Turing does not assume that the possession of either sense organs or motor organs is necessary for consciousness or intelligence.) Assume that not only does the machine lack electronic eyes and ears, etc., but that there are no provisions in the machine's program, the program for playing the Imitation Game, for incorporating inputs from such sense organs, or for controlling a body. What should we say about such a machine?

To me, it seems evident that we cannot and should not attribute reference to such a device. It is true that the machine can discourse beautifully about, say, the scenery in New England. But it could not recognize an apple tree or an apple, a mountain or a cow, a field or a steeple, if it were in front of one.

What we have is a device for producing sentences in response to sentences. But none of these sentences is at all connected to the real world. *If one coupled two of these machines and let them play the Imitation Game with each other, then they would go on "fooling" each other forever, even if the rest of the world disappeared!* There is no more reason to regard the machine's talk of apples as referring to real world apples than there is to regard the ant's "drawing" as referring to Winston Churchill.

What produces the illusion of reference, meaning, intelligence, etc., here is the fact that there is a convention of representation which *we* have under which the machine's discourse refers to apples, steeples, New England, etc. Similarly, there is the *illusion* that the ant has caricatured Churchill, for the same reason. But we are able to perceive, handle, deal with apples and fields. Our talk of apples and fields is intimately connected with our *non-verbal* transactions with apples and fields. There are "language entry rules" which take us from experiences of apples to such utterances as "I see an apple," and "language exit rules" which take us from decisions expressed in linguistic form ("I am going to buy some apples") to actions other than speaking. Lacking either language entry rules or language exit rules, there is no reason to regard the conversation of the machine (or of the two machines, in the case we envisaged of two machines playing the Imitation Game with each other) as more than syntactic play. Syntactic play that *resembles* intelligent discourse, to be sure; but only as (and no more than) the ant's curve resembles a biting caricature.

In the case of the ant, we could have argued that the ant would have drawn the same curve even if Winston Churchill had never existed. In the case of the machine, we cannot quite make the parallel argument; if apples, trees, steeples and fields had not existed, then, presumably, the programmers would not have produced that same program. Although the machine does not *perceive* apples, fields, or steeples, its creator–designers did. There is *some* causal connection between the machine and the real world apples, etc., via the perceptual experience and knowledge of the creator–designers. But such a weak connection can hardly suffice for reference. Not only is it logically possible, though fantastically improbable, that the same machine *could* have existed even if apples, fields, and steeples had not existed; more important, the machine is utterly insensitive to the *continued* existence of apples, fields, steeples, etc. Even if all these things *ceased* to exist, the machine would still discourse just as happily in the same way. That is why the machine cannot be regarded as referring at all.

The point that is relevant for our discussion is that there is nothing in Turing's Test to rule out a machine which is programmed to do nothing *but* play the Imitation Game, and that a machine which can do nothing *but* play the Imitation Game is *clearly* not referring any more than a record player is.

Brains in a vat (again)

Let us compare the hypothetical "brains in a vat" with the machines just described. There are obviously important differences. The brains in a vat do not have sense organs, but they do have *provision* for sense organs; that is, there are afferent nerve endings, there are inputs from these afferent nerve endings, and these inputs figure in the "program" of the brains in the vat just as they do in the program of our brains. The brains in a vat are *brains*; moreover, they are *functioning* brains, and they function by the same rules as brains do in the actual world. For these reasons, it would seem absurd to deny consciousness or intelligence to them. But the fact that they are conscious and intelligent does not mean that their words refer to what our words refer. The question we are interested in is this: do their verbalizations containing, say, the word "tree" actually refer to *trees*? More generally: can they refer to *external* objects at all?

(As opposed to, for example, objects in the image produced by the automatic machinery.)

To fix our ideas, let us specify that the automatic machinery is supposed to have come into existence by some kind of cosmic chance or coincidence (or, perhaps, to have always existed). In this hypothetical world, the automatic machinery itself is supposed to have no intelligent creator–designers. In fact, as we said at the beginning of this chapter, we may imagine that all sentient beings (however minimal their sentience) are inside the vat.

This assumption does not help. For there is no connection between the *word* "tree" as used by these brains and actual trees. They would still use the word "tree" just as they do, think just the thoughts they do, have just the images they have, even if there were no actual trees. Their images, words, etc., are qualitatively identical with images, words, etc., which do represent trees in *our* world; but we have already seen (the ant again!) that qualitative similarity to something which represents an object (Winston Churchill or a tree) does not make a thing a representation all by itself. In short, the brains in a vat are not thinking about real trees when they think "there is a tree in front of me" because there is nothing by virtue of which their thought "tree" represents actual trees.

If this seems hasty, reflect on the following: we have seen that the words do not necessarily refer to trees even if they are arranged in a sequence which is identical with a discourse which (were it to occur in one of our minds) would unquestionably *be about trees* in the actual world. Nor does the "program," in the sense of the rules, practices, dispositions of the brains to verbal behavior, necessarily refer to trees or bring about reference to trees through the connections it establishes between words and words, or *linguistic* cues and *linguistic* responses. If these brains think about, refer to, represent trees (real trees, outside the vat), then it must be because of the way the "program" connects the system of language to *non-verbal* input and outputs. There are indeed such non-verbal inputs and outputs in the Brain-in-a-Vat world (those efferent and afferent nerve endings again!), but we also saw that the "sense-data" produced by the automatic machinery do not represent trees (or anything external) even when they resemble our tree-images exactly. Just as a splash of paint might resemble a tree picture without *being* a tree picture, so, we saw, a "sense datum" might be qualitatively identical with an "image of a tree" without being an image of a tree. How can the fact that, in the case of the brains in a vat, the language is connected by the program with sensory inputs which do not intrinsically or extrinsically represent trees (or anything external) possibly bring it about that the whole system of representations, the language-in-use, *does* refer to or represent trees or anything external?

The answer is that it cannot. The whole system of sense-data, motor signals to the efferent endings, and verbally or conceptually mediated thought connected by "language entry rules" to the sense-data (or whatever) as inputs and by "language exit rules" to the motor signals as outputs, has no more connection to *trees* than the ant's curve has to Winston Churchill. Once we see that the *qualitative similarity* (amounting, if you like, to qualitative identity) between the thoughts of the brains in a vat and the thoughts of someone in the actual world by no means implies sameness of reference, it is not hard to see that there is no basis at all for regarding the brain in a vat as referring to external things.

The premisses of the argument

I have now given the argument promised to show that the brains in a vat cannot think or say that they are brains in a vat. It remains only to make it explicit and to examine its structure.

By what was just said, when the brain in a vat (in the world where every sentient being is and always was a brain in a vat) thinks "There is a tree in front of me," his thought does not refer to actual trees. On some theories that we shall discuss it might refer to trees in the image, or to the electronic impulses that cause tree experiences, or to the features of the program that are responsible for those electronic impulses. These theories are not ruled out by what was just said, for there is a close causal connection between the use of the word "tree" in vat-English and the presence of trees in the image, the presence of electronic impulses of a certain kind, and the presence of certain features in the machine's program. On these theories the brain is *right*, not *wrong* in thinking "There is a tree in front of me." Given what "tree" refers to in vat-English and what "in front of" refers to, assuming one of these theories is correct, then the truth-conditions for "There is a tree in front of me" when it occurs in vat-English are simply that a tree in the image be "in front of" the "me" in question—in the image—or, perhaps, that the kind of electronic impulse that normally produces this experience be coming from the automatic machinery, or, perhaps, that the feature of the machinery that is supposed to produce the "tree in front of one" experience be operating. And these truth-conditions are certainly fulfilled.

By the same argument, "vat" refers to vats in the image in vat-English, or something related (electronic impulses or program features), but certainly not to real vats, since the use of "vat" in vat-English has no causal connection to real vats (apart from the connection that the brains in a vat wouldn't be able to use the word "vat," if it were not for the presence of one particular vat—the vat they are in; but this connection obtains between the use of *every* word in vat-English and that one particular vat; it is not a special connection between the use of the *particular* word "vat" and vats). Similarly, "nutrient fluid" refers to a liquid in the image in vat-English, or something related (electronic impulses or program features). It follows that if their "possible world" is really the actual one, and we are really the brains in a vat, then what we now mean by "we are brains in a vat" is that *we are brains in a vat in the image* or something of that kind (if we mean anything at all). But part of the hypothesis that we are brains in a vat is that we aren't brains in a vat in the image (i.e. what we are "hallucinating" isn't that we are brains in a vat). So, if we are brains in a vat, then the sentence "We are brains in a vat" says something false (if it says anything). In short, if we are brains in a vat, then "We are brains in a vat" is false. So it is (necessarily) false.

The supposition that such a possibility makes sense arises from a combination of two errors: (1) taking *physical possibility* too seriously; and (2) unconsciously operating with a magical theory of reference, a theory on which certain mental representations necessarily refer to certain external things and kinds of things.

There is a "physically possible world" in which we are brains in a vat—what does this mean except that there is a *description* of such a state of affairs which is compatible with the laws of physics? Just as there is a tendency in our culture (and has been since the seventeenth century) to take *physics* as our metaphysics, that is, to view the exact sciences as the long-sought description of the "true and ultimate furniture of the universe," so there is, as an immediate consequence, a tendency to take "physical possibility" as the very touchstone of what might really actually be the case. Truth is physical truth; possibility physical possibility; and necessity physical necessity, on such a view. But we have just seen, if only in the case of a very contrived example so far, that this view is wrong. The existence of a "physically possible world" in which we are brains in a vat (and always were and will be) does not mean that we might really, actually, possibly *be* brains in a vat. What rules out this possibility is not physics but *philosophy*.

Some philosophers, eager both to assert and minimize the claims of their profession at the same time (the typical state of mind of Anglo-American philosophy in the twentieth century), would say: "Sure. You have shown that some things that seem to be physical possibilities are really *conceptual* impossibilities. What's so surprising about that?"

Well, to be sure, my argument can be described as a "conceptual" one. But to describe philosophical activity as the search for "conceptual" truths makes it all sound like *inquiry about the meaning of words*. And that is not at all what we have been engaging in.

What we have been doing is considering the *preconditions for thinking about, representing, referring to*, etc. We have investigated these preconditions *not* by investigating the meaning of these words and phrases (as a linguist might, for example) but by *reasoning a priori*. Not in the old "absolute" sense (since we don't claim that magical theories of reference are *a priori* wrong), but in the sense of inquiring into what is *reasonably* possible *assuming* certain general premises, or making certain very broad theoretical assumptions. Such a procedure is neither "empirical" nor quite "a priori," but has elements of both ways of investigating. In spite of the fallibility of my procedure, and its dependence upon assumptions which might be described as "empirical" (e.g. the assumption that the mind has no access to external things or properties apart from that provided by the senses), my procedure has a close relation to what Kant called a "transcendental" investigation; for it is an investigation, I repeat, of the *preconditions* of reference and hence of thought—preconditions built in to the nature of our minds themselves, though not (as Kant hoped) wholly independent of empirical assumptions.

One of the premises of the argument is obvious: that magical theories of reference are wrong, wrong for mental representations and not only for physical ones. The other premiss is that one cannot refer to certain kinds of things, e.g. *trees*, if one has no causal interaction at all with them,[3] or with things in terms of which they can be described. But why should we accept these premises? Since these constitute the broad framework within which I am arguing, it is time to examine them more closely.

The reasons for denying necessary connections between representations and their referents

I mentioned earlier that some philosophers (most famously, Brentano) have ascribed to the mind a power, "intentionality," which precisely enables it to *refer*. Evidently, I have rejected this as no solution. But what gives me this right? Have I, perhaps, been too hasty?

These philosophers did not claim that we can think about external things or properties without using representations at all. And the argument I gave above comparing visual sense data to the ant's "picture" (the argument via the science fiction story about the "picture" of a tree that came from a paint-splash and that gave rise to sense data qualitatively similar to our "visual images of trees," but unaccompanied by any *concept* of a tree) would be accepted as showing that *images* do not necessarily refer. If there are mental representations that necessarily refer (to external things) they must be of the nature of *concepts* and not of the nature of images. But what are *concepts*?

When we introspect we do not perceive "concepts" flowing through our minds as such. Stop the stream of thought when or where we will, what we catch are words, images, sensations, feelings. When I speak my thoughts out loud I do not think them twice. I hear my words as you do. To be sure it feels different to me when I utter words that I believe and when I utter words I do not believe (but sometimes, when I am nervous, or in front of a hostile audience, it feels as if I am lying when I know I am telling the truth); and it feels different when I utter words I understand and when I utter words I do not understand. But I can imagine without difficulty someone thinking just these words (in the sense of saying them in his mind) and having just the feeling of understanding, asserting, etc., that I do, and realizing a minute later (or on being awakened by a hypnotist) that he did not understand what had just passed through his mind at all, that he did not even understand the language these words are in. I don't claim that this is very likely; I simply mean that there is nothing at all unimaginable about this. And what this shows is not that concepts *are* words (or images, sensations, etc.), but that to attribute a "concept" or a "thought" to someone is quite different from attributing any mental "presentation," any introspectible entity or event, to him. Concepts are not mental presentations that intrinsically refer to external objects for the very decisive reason that they are not mental presentations at all. Concepts are signs used in a certain way; the signs may be public or private, mental entities or physical entities, but even when the signs are "mental" and "private," the sign itself apart from its use is not the concept. And signs do not themselves intrinsically refer.

We can see this by performing a very simple thought experiment. Suppose you are like me and cannot tell an elm tree from a beech tree. We still say that the reference of "elm" in my speech is the same as the reference of "elm" in anyone else's, viz. elm trees, and that the set of all beech trees is the extension of "beech" (i.e. the set of things the word "beech" is truly predicated of) both in your speech and my speech. Is it really credible that the difference between what "elm" refers to and what "beech" refers to is brought about by a difference in our *concepts*? My concept of an elm tree is exactly the same as my concept of a beech tree (I blush to confess). (This shows that the determination of reference is social and not individual, by the way; you and I both defer to experts who *can* tell elms from beeches.) If someone heroically attempts to maintain that the difference between the reference of "elm" and the reference of "beech" in *my* speech is explained by a difference in my psychological state, then let him imagine a Twin Earth where the words are switched. Twin Earth is very much like Earth; in fact, apart from the fact that "elm" and "beech" are interchanged, the reader can suppose Twin Earth is exactly like Earth. Suppose I have a *Doppelganger* on Twin Earth who is molecule for molecule identical with me (in the sense in which two neckties can be "identical"). If you are a dualist, then suppose my *Doppelganger* thinks the same verbalized thoughts I do, has the same sense data, the same dispositions, etc. It is absurd to think his psychological state is one bit different from mine: yet his word "elm" represents *beeches*, and my word "elm" represents elms. (Similarly, if the "water" on Twin Earth is a different liquid—say, XYZ and not H_2O—then "water" represents a different liquid when used on Twin Earth and when used on Earth, etc.) Contrary to a doctrine that has been with us since the seventeenth century, *meanings just aren't in the head*.

We have seen that possessing a concept is not a matter of possessing images (say, of trees—or even images, "visual" or "acoustic," of sentences, or whole discourses, for that matter) since one could possess any system of images you please and not possess the *ability* to use the sentences in situationally appropriate ways (considering both linguistic factors—what has been said before—and non-linguistic factors as determining "situational appropriateness"). A man may have all the images you please, and still be completely at a loss when one says to him "point to a tree," even if a lot of trees are present. He may even have the image of what he is supposed to do, and still not know what he is supposed to do. For the image, if not accompanied by the ability to act in a certain way, is just a *picture*, and acting in accordance with a picture is itself an ability that one may or may not have. (The man might picture himself pointing to a tree, but just for the sake of contemplating something logically possible; himself pointing to a tree after someone has produced the—to him meaningless—sequence of sounds "please point to a tree.") He would still not know that he was supposed to point to a tree, and he would still not *understand* "point to a tree."

I have considered the ability to use certain sentences to be the criterion for possessing a full-blown concept, but this could easily be liberalized. We could allow symbolism consisting of elements which are not words in a natural language, for example, and we could allow such mental phenomena as images and other types of internal events. What is essential is that these should have the same complexity, ability to be combined with each other, etc., as sentences in a natural language. For, although a particular presentation—say, a blue flash—might serve a particular mathematician as the inner expression of the whole proof of the Prime Number Theorem, still there would be no temptation to say this (and it would be false to say this) if that mathematician could not unpack his "blue flash" into separate steps and logical connections. But, no matter what sort of inner phenomena we allow as possible *expressions* of thought, arguments exactly similar to the foregoing will show that it is not the phenomena themselves that constitute understanding, but rather the ability of the thinker to employ these phenomena, to produce the right phenomena in the right circumstances.

The foregoing is a very abbreviated version of Wittgenstein's argument in *Philosophical Investigations*. If it is correct, then the attempt to understand thought by what is called "phenomenological" investigation is fundamentally misguided; for what the phenomenologists fail to see is that what they are describing is the inner *expression* of thought, but that the *understanding* of that expression—one's understanding of one's own thoughts—is not an *occurrence* but an *ability*. Our example of a man pretending to think in Japanese (and deceiving a Japanese telepath) already shows the futility of a phenomenological approach to the problem of *understanding*. For even if there is some introspectible quality which is present when and only when one *really* understands (this seems false on introspection, in fact), still that quality is only *correlated* with understanding, and it is still possible that the man fooling the Japanese telepath have that quality too and *still* not understand a word of Japanese.

On the other hand, consider the perfectly possible man who does not have any "interior monologue" at all. He speaks perfectly good English, and if asked what his opinions are on a given subject, he will give them at length. But he never thinks (in words, images, etc.) when he is not speaking out loud; nor does anything "go through his head," except that (of course) he hears his own voice speaking, and has the usual sense impressions from his surroundings, plus a general "feeling of understanding." (Perhaps he is in the habit of talking to himself.) When he types a letter or goes to the store, etc., he is not having an internal "stream of thought"; but his actions are intelligent and purposeful, and if anyone walks up and asks him "What are you doing?" he will give perfectly coherent replies.

This man seems perfectly imaginable. No one would hesitate to say that he was conscious, disliked rock and roll (if he frequently expressed a strong aversion to rock and roll), etc., just because he did not think conscious thoughts except when speaking out loud.

What follows from all this is that (a) no set of mental events—images or more "abstract" mental happenings and qualities—*constitutes* understanding; and (b) no set of mental events is *necessary* for understanding. In particular, *concepts cannot be identical with mental objects of any kind*. For, assuming that by a mental object we mean something introspectible, we have just seen that whatever it is, it may be absent in a man who does understand the appropriate word (and hence has the full blown concept), and present in a man who does not have the concept at all.

Coming back now to our criticism of magical theories of reference (a topic which also concerned Wittgenstein), we see that, on the one hand, those "mental objects" we *can* introspectively detect—words, images, feelings, etc.—do not intrinsically refer any more than the ant's picture does (and for the same reasons), while the attempts to postulate special mental objects, "concepts," which *do* have a necessary connection with their referents, and which only trained phenomenologists can detect, commit a *logical* blunder; for concepts are (at least in part) *abilities* and not occurrences. The doctrine that there are mental presentations which necessarily refer to external things is not only bad natural science, it is also bad phenomenology and conceptual confusion.

NOTES

[1] In this paper the terms "representation" and "reference" always refer to a relation between a word (or other sort of sign, symbol, or representation) and something that actually exists (i.e. not just an "object of thought"). There is a sense of "refer" in which I can "refer" to what does not exist; this is not the sense in which "refer" is used here. An older word for what I call "representation" or "reference" is *denotation*.

Secondly, I follow the custom of modern logicians and use "exist" to mean "exist in the past, present, or future." Thus Winston Churchill "exists," and we can "refer to" or "represent" Winston Churchill, even though he is no longer alive.

2   A. M. Turing, "Computing Machinery and Intelligence," *Mind* (1950), reprinted in A. R. Anderson (ed.), *Minds and Machines*.

3   If the Brains in a Vat will have causal connection with, say, trees *in the future*, then perhaps they can *now* refer to trees by description "the things I will refer to as 'trees' at such-and-such a future time." But we are to imagine a case in which the Brains in a Vat *never* get out of the vat, and hence *never* get into causal connection with trees, etc.

2.5

KNOWLEDGE

Thomas Nagel

1. Skepticism

The objective self is responsible both for the expansion of our understanding and for doubts about it that cannot be finally laid to rest. The extension of power and growth of insecurity go hand in hand, once we place ourselves inside the world and try to develop a view that accommodates this recognition fully.

The most familiar scene of conflict is the pursuit of objective knowledge, whose aim is naturally described in terms that, taken literally, are unintelligible: we must get outside of ourselves, and view the world from nowhere within it. Since it is impossible to leave one's own point of view behind entirely without ceasing to exist, the metaphor of getting outside ourselves must have another meaning. We are to rely less and less on certain individual aspects of our point of view, and more and more on something else, less individual, which is also part of us. But if initial appearances are not in themselves reliable guides to reality, why should the products of detached reflection be different? Why aren't they either equally doubtful or else valid only as higher-order impressions? This is an old problem. The same ideas that make the pursuit of objectivity seem necessary for knowledge make both objectivity and knowledge seem, on reflection, unattainable.

Objectivity and skepticism are closely related: both develop from the idea that there is a real world in which we are contained, and that appearances result from our interaction with the rest of it. We cannot accept those appearances uncritically, but must try to understand what our own constitution contributes to them. To do this we try to develop an idea of the world with ourselves in it, an account of both ourselves and the world that includes an explanation of why it initially appears to us as it does. But this idea, since it is we who develop it, is likewise the product of interaction between us and the world, though the interaction is more complicated and more self-conscious than the original one. If the initial appearances cannot be relied upon because they depend on our constitution in ways that we do not fully understand, this more complex idea should be open to the same doubts, for whatever we use to understand certain interactions between ourselves and the world is not itself the object of that understanding. However often we may try to step outside of ourselves, something will have to stay behind the lens, something in us will determine the resulting picture, and this will give grounds for doubt that we are really getting any closer to reality.

The idea of objectivity thus seems to undermine itself. The aim is to form a conception of reality which includes ourselves and our view of things among its objects, but it seems that whatever forms the conception will not be included by it. It seems to follow that the most objective view we can achieve will have to rest on an unexamined subjective base, and that since we can never abandon our own point of view, but can only alter it, the idea that we are coming closer to the reality outside it with each successive step has no foundation.

All theories of knowledge are responses to this problem. They may be divided into three types: *skeptical, reductive,* and *heroic.*

Skeptical theories take the contents of our ordinary or scientific beliefs about the world to go beyond their grounds in ways that make it impossible to defend them against doubt. There are ways we might be wrong that we can't rule out. Once we notice this unclosable gap we cannot, except with conscious irrationality, maintain our confidence in those beliefs.

Reductive theories grow out of skeptical arguments. Assuming that we do know certain things, and acknowledging that we could not know them if the gap between content and grounds were as great as the skeptic thinks it is, the reductionist reinterprets the content of our beliefs about the world so that they claim less. He may interpret them as claims about possible experience or the possible ultimate convergence of experience among rational beings, or as efforts to reduce tension and surprise or to increase order in the system of mental states of the knower, or he may even take some of them, in a Kantian vein, to describe the limits of all possible experience: an inside view of the bars of our mental cage. In any case on a reductive view our beliefs are not about the world as it is in itself—if indeed that means anything. They are about the world as it appears to us. Naturally not all reductive theories succeed in escaping skepticism, for it is difficult to construct a reductive analysis of claims about the world which has any plausibility at all, without leaving gaps between grounds and content—even if both are within the realm of experience.

Heroic theories acknowledge the great gap between the grounds of our beliefs about the world and the contents of those beliefs under a realist interpretation, and they try to leap across the gap without narrowing it. The chasm below is littered with epistemological corpses. Examples of heroic theories are Plato's theory of Forms together with the theory of recollection, and Descartes' defense of the general reliability of human knowledge through an a priori proof of the existence of a nondeceiving God.[1]

I believe, first of all, that the truth must lie with one or both of the two realist positions—skepticism and heroism. My terminology reflects a realistic tendency: from the standpoint of a reductionist, heroic epistemology would be better described as quixotic. But I believe that skeptical problems arise not from a misunderstanding of the meaning of standard knowledge claims, but from their actual content and the attempt to transcend ourselves that is involved in the formation of beliefs about the world. The ambitions of knowledge and some of its achievements are heroic, but a pervasive skepticism or at least provisionality of commitment is suitable in light of our evident limitations.

Though a great deal of effort has been expended on them recently, definitions of knowledge cannot help us here. The central problem of epistemology is the first-person problem of what to believe and how to justify one's beliefs—not the impersonal problem of whether, given my beliefs together with some assumptions about their relation to what is actually the case, I can be said to have knowledge. Answering the question of what knowledge is will not help me decide what to believe. We must decide what our relation to the world actually is and how it can be changed.

Since we can't literally escape ourselves, any improvement in our beliefs has to result from some kind of self-transformation. And the thing we can do which comes closest to getting outside of ourselves is to form a detached idea of the world that includes us, and includes our possession of that conception as part of what it enables us to understand about ourselves. We are then outside ourselves in the sense that we appear inside a conception of the world that we ourselves possess, but that is not tied to our particular point of view. The pursuit of this goal is the essential task of the objective self. I shall argue that it makes sense only in terms of an epistemology that is significantly rationalist.

The question is how limited beings like ourselves can alter their conception of the world so that it is no longer just the view from where they are but in a sense a view from nowhere, which includes and comprehends the fact that the world contains beings which possess it, explains why the world appears to them as it does prior to the formation of that conception, and explains how they can arrive at the conception itself. This idea of objective knowledge has something in common with the program of Descartes, for he attempted to form a conception of the world in which he was contained, which would account for the validity of that conception and for his capacity to arrive at it. But his method was supposed to depend only on propositions and steps that were absolutely certain, and the method of self-transcendence as I have described it does not necessarily have this feature. In fact, such a conception of the world need not be developed by proofs at all, though it must rely heavily on a priori conjecture.[2]

In discussing the nature of the process and its pitfalls, I want both to defend the possibility of objective ascent and to understand its limits. We should keep in mind how incredible it is that such a thing is possible at all. We are encouraged these days to think of ourselves as contingent organisms arbitrarily thrown up by evolution. There is no reason in advance to expect a finite creature like that to be able to do more than accumulate information at the perceptual and conceptual level it occupies by nature. But apparently that is not how things are. Not only can we form the pure idea of a world that contains us and of which our impressions are a part, but we can give this idea a content which takes us very far from our original impressions.

The pure idea of realism—the idea that there is a world in which we are contained—implies nothing specific about the relation between the appearances and reality, except that we and our inner lives are part of reality. The recognition that this is so creates pressure on the imagination to recast our picture of the world so that it is no longer the view from here. The two possible forms this can take, skepticism and objective knowledge, are products of one capacity: the capacity to fill out the pure idea of realism with more or less definite conceptions of the world in which we are placed. The two are intimately bound together. The search for objective knowledge, because of its commitment to a realistic picture, is inescapably subject to skepticism and cannot refute it but must proceed under its shadow. Skepticism, in turn, is a problem only because of the realist claims of objectivity.

Skeptical possibilities are those according to which the world is completely different from how it appears to us, and there is no way to detect this. The most familiar from the literature are those in which error is the product of deliberate deception by an evil demon working on the mind, or by a scientist stimulating our brain in vitro to produce hallucinations. Another is the possibility that we are dreaming. In the latter two examples the world is not totally different from what we think, for it contains brains and perhaps persons who sleep, dream, and hallucinate. But this is not essential: we can conceive of the possibility that the world is different from how we believe it to be in ways that we cannot imagine, that our thoughts and impressions are produced in ways that we cannot conceive, and that there is no way of moving from where we are to beliefs about the world that are substantially correct. This is the most abstract form of skeptical possibility, and it remains an option on a realist view no matter what other hypotheses we may construct and embrace.

2. Antiskepticism

Not everyone would concede this skepticism or the realism on which it depends. Recently there has been a revival of arguments against the possibility of skepticism, reminiscent of the ordinary language arguments of the fifties which claimed that the meanings of statements about the world are revealed by the circumstances in which they are typically used, so that it couldn't be the case that most of what we ordinarily take to be true about the world is in fact false.

In their current versions these arguments are put in terms of reference rather than meaning.[3] What we refer to by the terms in our statements about the external world, for example—what we are really talking about—is said to be whatever *actually* bears the appropriate relation to the generally accepted use of those terms in our language. (This relation is left undefined, but it is supposed to be exemplified in the ordinary world by the relation between my use of the word "tree" and actual trees, if there are such things.)

The argument against the possibility of skepticism is a *reductio*. Suppose that I am a brain in a vat being stimulated by a mischievous scientist to think I have seen trees, though I never have. Then my word "tree" refers not to what we now call trees but to whatever the scientist usually uses to produce the stimulus which causes me to think, "There's a tree." So when I think that, I am usually thinking something true. I cannot use the word "tree" to form the thought that the scientist would express by saying I have never seen a tree, or the words "material object" to form the thought that perhaps I have never seen a material object, or the word "vat" to form the thought that perhaps I am a brain in a vat. If I were a brain in a vat, then my word "vat" would not refer to vats, and my thought, "Perhaps I am a brain in a vat," would not be true. The original skeptical supposition is shown to be impossible by the fact that if it were true, it would be false. The conditions of reference permit us to think that there are no trees, or that we are brains in a vat, only if this is not true.

This argument is no better than its predecessors. First, I can use a term which fails to refer, provided I have a conception of the conditions under which it would refer—as when I say there are no ghosts. To show that I couldn't think there were no trees if there were none, it would have to be shown that this thought could not be accounted for in more basic terms which would be available to me even if all my impressions of trees had been artificially produced. (Such an analysis need not describe my *conscious* thoughts about trees.) The same goes for "physical object". The skeptic may not be able to produce on request an account of these terms which is independent of the existence of their referents, but he is not refuted unless reason has been given to believe such an account impossible. This has not been attempted and seems on the face of it a hopeless enterprise.

A skeptic does not hold that all his terms fail to refer; he assumes, like the rest of us, that those that do not refer can be explained at some level in terms of those that do. When he says, "Perhaps I have never seen a physical object," he doesn't mean (holding up his hand), "Perhaps *this*, whatever it is, doesn't exist!" He means, "Perhaps I have never seen anything with the spatiotemporal and mind-independent characteristics necessary to be a physical object—nothing of the kind that I take physical objects to be." It has to be shown that he couldn't have *that* thought if it were true. Clearly we will be pushed back to the conditions for the possession of very general concepts. Nothing here is obvious, but it seems clear at least that a few undeveloped assumptions about reference will not enable one to prove that a brain in a vat or a disembodied spirit couldn't have the concept of mind-independence, for example. The main issue simply hasn't been addressed.

Second, although the argument doesn't work it wouldn't refute skepticism if it did. If I accept the argument, I must conclude that a brain in a vat can't think truly that it is a brain in a vat, even though others can think this about it. What follows? Only that I can't express my skepticism by saying, "Perhaps I'm a brain in a vat." Instead I must say, "Perhaps I can't even *think* the truth about what I am, because I lack the necessary concepts and my circumstances make it impossible for me to acquire them!" If this doesn't qualify as skepticism, I don't know what does.

The possibility of skepticism is built into our ordinary thoughts, in virtue of the realism that they automatically assume and their pretensions to go beyond experience. Some of what we believe must be true in order for us to be able to think at all, but this does not mean we couldn't be wrong about vast tracts of it. Thought and language have to latch onto the world, but they don't have to latch onto it directly at every point, and a being in one of the skeptic's nightmare situations should be able to latch onto enough of it to meet the conditions for formulating his questions.[4]

Critics of skepticism bring against it various theories of how the language works—theories of verifiability, causal theories of reference, principles of charity. I believe the argument goes in the opposite direction.[5] Such theories are refuted by the evident possibility and intelligibility of skepticism, which reveals that by "tree" I don't mean just anything that is causally responsible for my impressions of trees, or anything that looks and feels like a tree, or even anything of the sort that I and others have traditionally called trees. Since those things could conceivably not be trees, any theory that says they have to be is wrong.

The traditional skeptical possibilities that we can imagine stand for limitless possibilities that we can't imagine. In recognizing them we recognize that our ideas of the world, however sophisticated, are the products of one piece of the world interacting with part of the rest of it in ways that we do not understand very well. So anything we come to believe must remain suspended in a great cavern of skeptical darkness.

Once the door is open, it can't be shut again. We can only try to make our conception of our place in the world more complete—essentially developing the objective standpoint. The limit to which such development must tend is presumably unreachable: a conception that closes over itself completely, by describing a world that contains a being that has precisely that conception, and explaining how the being was able to reach that conception from its starting point within the world. Even if we did arrive at such a self-transcendent idea, that wouldn't guarantee its correctness. It would recommend itself as a possibility, but the skeptical possibilities would also remain open. The best we can do is to construct a picture that might be correct. Skepticism is really a way of recognizing our situation, though it will not prevent us from continuing to pursue something like knowledge, for our natural realism makes it impossible for us to be content with a purely subjective view.

3. Self-transcendence

To provide an alternative to the imaginable and unimaginable skeptical possibilities, a self-transcendent conception should ideally explain the following four things: (1) what the world is like; (2) what we are like; (3) why the world appears to beings like us in certain respects as it is and in certain respects as it isn't; (4) how beings like us can arrive at such a conception. In practice, the last condition is rarely met. We tend to use our rational capacities to construct theories, without at the same time constructing epistemological accounts of how those capacities work. Nevertheless, this is an important part of objectivity. What we want is to reach a position as independent as possible of who we are and where we started, but a position that can also explain how we got there.

In a sense, these conditions could also be satisfied by a conception of the world and our place in it that was developed by other beings, different from us; but in that case the fourth element would not involve self-referential understanding, as it does in the understanding of ourselves. The closest we can come to an external understanding of our relation to the world is to develop the self-referential analogue of an external understanding. This leaves us in no worse position than an external observer, for any being who viewed us from outside would have to face the problem of self-understanding in its own case, to be reasonably secure in its pretensions to understand us or anything else. The aim of objectivity would be to reach a conception of the world, including oneself, which involved one's own point of view not essentially, but only instrumentally, so to speak: so that the form of our understanding would be specific to ourselves, but its content would not be.

The vast majority of additions to what we know do not require any advance in objectivity: they merely add further information at a level that already exists. When someone discovers a previously undetected planet, or the chemical composition of a hormone, or the cause of a disease, or the early influences on a historical figure, he is essentially filling in a framework of understanding that is already given. Even something as fruitful as the discovery of the structure of DNA is in this category. It merely extended the methods of chemistry into genetics. Discoveries like this may be difficult to make, but they do not involve fundamental alterations in the idea of our epistemic relation to the world. They add knowledge without objective advance.

An advance in objectivity requires that already existing forms of under-standing should themselves become the object of a new form of understanding, which also takes in the objects of the original forms. This is true of any objective step, even if it does not reach the more ambitious goal of explaining itself. All advances in objectivity subsume our former understanding under a new account of our mental relation to the world.

Consider for example the distinction between primary and secondary qualities, the precondition for the development of modern physics and chemistry. This is a particularly clear example of how we can place ourselves in a new world picture. We realize that our perceptions of external objects depend both on their properties and on ours, and that to explain both their effects on us and their interactions with each other we need to attribute to them fewer types of properties than they may initially appear to have.

Colin McGinn has argued convincingly that this is in the first instance an a priori philosophical discovery, not an empirical scientific one. Things have colors, tastes, and smells in virtue of the way they appear to us: to be red simply *is* to be the sort of thing that looks or would look red to normal human observers in the perceptual circumstances that normally obtain in the actual world. To be square, on the other hand, is an independent property which can be used to explain many things about an object, including how it looks and feels. (McGinn, ch. 7)

Once this is recognized and we consider how the various perceptible properties of objects are to be explained, it becomes clear that the best account of the appearance of colors will not involve the ascription to things of intrinsic color properties that play an ineliminable role in the explanation of the appearances: the way in which the appearances vary with both physical and psychological conditions makes this very implausible. Objective shape and size, on the other hand, enter naturally into an account of variable appearance of shape and size. So much is evident even if we have only a very rough idea of how as perceivers we are acted upon by the external world—an idea having to do primarily with the type of peripheral impact involved. It is then a short step to the conjecture that the appearances of secondary qualities are caused by other primary qualities of objects, which we can then try to discover.

The pressure to make an objective advance comes, here as elsewhere, from the incapacity of the earlier view of the world to include and explain itself—that is, to explain why things appear to us as they do. This makes us seek a new conception that can explain both the former appearances and the new impression that it itself is true. The hypothesis that objects have intrinsic colors in addition to their primary qualities would conspicuously fail this test, for it provides a poorer explanation of why they appear to have colors, and why those appearances change under internal and external circumstances, than the hypothesis that the primary qualities of objects and their effects on us are responsible for all the appearances.

Consider another example. Not all objective advances have been so widely internalized as this, and some, like general relativity and quantum mechanics, are advances beyond already advanced theories that are not generally accessible. But one huge step beyond common appearance was taken by Einstein with the special theory of relativity. He replaced the familiar idea of unqualified temporal and spatial relations between events, things, and processes by a relativistic conception according to which events are not without qualification simultaneous or successive, objects are not without qualification equal or unequal in size, but only with respect to a frame of reference. What formerly seemed to be an objective conception of absolute space and time was revealed to be a mere appearance, from the perspective of one frame of reference, of a world whose objective description from no frame of reference is not given in a four-dimensional coordinate system of independent spatial and temporal dimensions at all. Instead, events are objectively located in relativistic space-time, whose division into separate spatial and temporal dimensions depends on one's point of view. In this case it was reflection on electrodynamic phenomena rather than ordinary perception that revealed that the appearances had to be transcended. There was also, as with the primary-secondary quality distinction, and important philosophical element in the discovery that absolute simultaneity of spatially separated events was not a well-defined notion, in our ordinary system of concepts.

These examples illustrate the human capacity to escape the limits of the original human situation, not merely by travelling around and seeing the world from different perspectives, but by ascending to new levels from which we can understand and criticize the general forms of previous perspectives. The step to a new perspective is the product of epistemological insight in each case.

Of course it is also the product in some cases of new observations that can't be accommodated in the old picture. But the satisfactoriness of a new external perspective depends on whether it can place the internal perspective within the world in a way that enables one to occupy both of them simultaneously, with a sense that the external perspective gives access to an objective reality that one's subjective impressions are impressions of. Experience is not the sole foundation of our knowledge of the world, but a place must be found for it as part of the world, however different that world may be from the way it is depicted in experience.

Only objectivity can give meaning to the idea of intellectual progress. We can see this by considering any well-established objective advance, like the examples discussed already, and asking whether it could be reversed. Could a theory which ascribed intrinsic colors, tastes, smells, feels, and sounds to things account for the appearance that these are to be explained as the effects on our senses of primary qualities? Could a theory of absolute space and time explain the appearance that we occupy relativistic space-time? In both cases the answer is no. An objective advance may be superseded by a further objective advance, which reduces it in turn to an appearance. But it is not on the same level as its predecessors, and may well have been essential as a step on the route to its successors.

Still, the fact that objective reality is our goal does not guarantee that our pursuit of it succeeds in being anything more than an exploration and reorganization of the insides of our own minds. On a realist view this always remains a possibility, at least in the abstract, even if one isn't thinking of a specific way in which one might be deceived. A less radical point is that whatever we may have achieved we are only at a passing stage of intellectual development, and much of what we now believe will be overthrown by later discoveries and later theories.

A certain expectation of further advance and occasional retreat is rational: there have been enough cases in which what was once thought a maximally objective conception of reality has been included as appearance in a still more objective conception so that we would be foolish not to expect it to go on. Indeed we should want it to go on, for we are evidently just at the beginning of our trip outward, and what has so far been achieved in the way of self-understanding is minimal.

4. Evolutionary Epistemology

Because self-understanding is at the heart of objectivity, the enterprise faces serious obstacles. The pursuit of objective knowledge requires a much more developed conception of the mind in the world than we now possess: a conception which will explain the possibility of objectivity. It requires that we come to understand the operations of our minds from a point of view that is not just our own. This would not be the kind of self-understanding that Kant aimed for, that is, an understanding from within of the forms and limits of all our possible experience and thought (though that would be amazing enough, and there is no reason to suppose that it could be arrived at a priori). What is needed is something even stronger: an explanation of the possibility of objective knowledge of the real world which is itself an instance of objective knowledge of that world and our relation to it. Can there be creatures capable of this sort of self-transcendence? We at least seem to have taken some steps in this direction, though it is not clear how far we can go. But how is even this much possible? In fact, the objective capacity is a complete mystery. While it obviously exists and we can use it, there is no credible explanation of it in terms of anything more basic, and so long as we don't understand it, its results will remain under a cloud.

Some may be tempted to offer or at least to imagine an evolutionary explanation, as is customary these days for everything under the sun. Evolutionary hand waving is an example of the tendency to take a theory which has been successful in one domain and apply it to anything else you can't understand—not even to apply it, but vaguely to imagine such an application. It is also an example of the pervasive and reductive naturalism of our culture. "Survival value" is now invoked to account for everything from ethics to language. I realize that it is dangerous to enter into discussion of a topic on which one is not an expert, but since these speculations can't be ignored, and since even when they come from professional biologists they are in the nature of obiter dicta, let me try to say something about them.

The Darwinian theory of natural selection, assuming the truth of its historical claims about how organisms develop, is a very partial explanation of why we are as we are. It explains the selection among those organic possibilities that have been generated, but it does not explain the possibilities themselves. It is a diachronic theory which tries to account for the particular path evolution will take through a set of possibilities under given conditions. It may explain why creatures with vision or reason will survive, but it does not explain how vision or reasoning are possible.

These require not diachronic but timeless explanations. The range of biological options over which natural selection can operate is extraordinarily rich but also severely constrained. Even if randomness is a factor in determining which mutation will appear when (and the extent of the randomness is apparently in dispute), the range of genetic possibilities is not itself a random occurrence but a necessary consequence of the natural order. The possibility of minds capable of forming progressively more objective conceptions of reality is not something the theory of natural selection can attempt to explain, since it doesn't explain possibilities at all, but only selection among them.[6]

But even if we take as given the unexplained possibility of objective minds, natural selection doesn't offer a very plausible explanation of their actual existence. In themselves, the advanced intellectual capacities of human beings, unlike many of their anatomical, physiological, perceptual, and more basic cognitive features, are extremely poor candidates for evolutionary explanation, and would in fact be rendered highly suspect by such an explanation. I am not suggesting, as Kant once did (Kant, pp. 395-6), that reason has negative survival value and could from that point of view be replaced by instinct. But the capacity to form cosmological and subatomic theories takes us so far from the circumstances in which our ability to think would have had to pass its evolutionary tests that there would be no reason whatever, stemming from the theory of evolution, to rely on it in extension to those subjects. In fact if, per impossible, we came to believe that our capacity for objective theory were the product of natural selection, that would warrant serious skepticism about its results beyond a very limited and familiar range. An evolutionary explanation of our theorizing faculty would provide absolutely no confirmation of its capacity to get at the truth. Something else must be going on if the process is really taking us toward a truer and more detached understanding of the world.

There is a standard reply to skepticism about evolutionary explanation of the intellect, namely that Darwinian theory doesn't require every feature of an organism to be separately selected for its adaptive value. Some features may be the side effects of others, singly or in combination, that have been so selected, and if they are not harmful they will survive. In the case of the intellect, a common speculation is that rapid enlargement of the human brain occurred through natural selection after the development of an erect posture and the capacity to use tools made brain size an advantage. This permitted the acquisition of language and the capacity to reason, which in turn conferred survival value on still larger brains. Then, like an adaptable computer, this complex brain turned out to be able to do all kinds of things it wasn't specifically "selected" to do: study astronomy, compose poetry and music, invent the internal combustion engine and the long-playing record, and prove Gödel's theorem. The great rapidity of civilized cultural evolution requires that the brains which took part in it have been developed to full capacity from its beginning.

Since this is pure speculation, not much can be said about its consistency with the empirical evidence. We know nothing about how the brain performs the functions that permitted our hunter-gatherer ancestors to survive, nor do we know anything about how it performs the functions that have permitted the development and understanding of the mathematics and physics of the past few centuries. So we have no basis for evaluating the suggestion that the properties which were necessary to fit the brain for the first of these purposes turned out to be sufficient for the second as well, and for all the cultural developments that have led to it.

Spinoza gives this description of the process of intellectual evolution:

> As men at first made use of the instruments supplied by nature to accomplish very easy pieces of workmanship, laboriously and imperfectly, and then, when these were finished, wrought other things more difficult with less labour and greater perfection; and so gradually mounted from the simplest operations to the making of tools, and from the making of tools to the making of more complex tools, and fresh feats of workmanship, till they arrived at making, with small expenditure of labour, the vast number of complicated mechanisms which they now possess. So, in like manner, the intellect, by its native strength, makes for itself intellectual instruments, whereby it acquires strength for performing other intellectual operations, and from these operations gets again fresh instruments, or the power of pushing its investigations further, and thus gradually proceeds till it reaches the summit of wisdom. (Spinoza, p. 12)

The question is whether not only the physical but the mental capacity needed to make a stone axe automatically brings with it the capacity to take each of the steps that have led from there to the construction of the hydrogen bomb, or whether an enormous excess mental capacity, not explainable by natural selection, was responsible for the generation and spread of the sequence of intellectual instruments that has emerged over the last thirty thousand years. This question is unforgettably posed by the stunning transformation of bone into spaceship in Stanley Kubrick's *2001*.

I see absolutely no reason to believe that the truth lies with the first alternative. The only reason so many people do believe it is that advanced intellectual capacities clearly exist, and this is the only available candidate for a Darwinian explanation of their existence. So it all rests on the assumption that every noteworthy characteristic of human beings, or of any other organism, must have a Darwinian explanation. But what is the reason to believe that? Even if natural selection explains all adaptive evolution, there may be developments in the history of species that are not specifically adaptive and can't be explained in terms of natural selection.[7] Why not take the development of the human intellect as a probable counterexample to the law that natural selection explains everything, instead of forcing it under the law with improbable speculations unsupported by evidence? We have here one of those powerful reductionist dogmas which seem to be part of the intellectual atmosphere we breathe.

What, I will be asked, is my alternative? Creationism? The answer is that I don't have one, and I don't need one in order to reject all existing proposals as improbable. One should not assume that the truth about this matter has already been conceived of—or hold onto a view just because no one can come up with a better alternative. Belief isn't like action. One doesn't have to believe anything, and to believe nothing is not to believe something.

I don't know what an explanation might be like either of the possibility of objective theorizing or of the actual biological development of creatures capable of it. My sense is that it is antecedently so improbable that the only possible explanation must be that it is in some way necessary. It is not the kind of thing that could be either a brute fact or an accident, any more than the identity of inertial and gravitational mass could be; the universe must have fundamental properties that inevitably give rise through physical and biological evolution to complex organisms capable of generating theories about themselves and it. This is not itself an explanation; it merely expresses a view about one condition which an acceptable explanation should meet: it should show why this had to happen, given the relatively short time since the Big Bang, and not merely that it could have happened—as is attempted by Darwinian proposals. (I think an explanation of the original development of organic life should meet the same condition.) There is no reason to expect that we shall ever come up with such an explanation, but we are at such a primitive stage of biological understanding that there is no point in making any predictions.[8]

5. Rationalism

One image of self-reconstruction that has appealed to philosophers is Neurath's: that we are like sailors trying to rebuild our ship plank by plank on the high seas. This can be interpreted in more than one way. We might think of ourselves as simply rearranging and perhaps reshaping the planks, making small alterations one at a time, and using the materials we find ready to hand.[9] Such an image may fit the mundane case where knowledge is accumulated gradually and piecemeal, at a given objective level. But if we wish to depict the great objective advances on which real progress depends, we need a different image. Though we may incorporate parts of the original ship in the new one we are about to create, we call up out of ourselves most of the materials from which we will construct it. The place which we occupy for this purpose may be one we could not have reached except on the old ship, but it is really in a new world, and in some sense, I believe, what we find in it is already there. Each of us is a microcosm, and in detaching progressively from our point of view and forming a succession of higher views of ourselves in the world, we are occupying a territory that already exists: taking possession of a latent objective realm, so to speak.

I said earlier that the position to which I am drawn is a form of rationalism. This does not mean that we have innate knowledge of the truth about the world, but it does mean that we have the capacity, not based on experience, to generate hypotheses about what in general the world might possibly be like, and to reject those possibilities that we see could not include ourselves and our experiences. Just as important, we must be able to reject hypotheses which appear initially to be possibilities but are not. The conditions of objectivity that I have been defending lead to the conclusion that the basis of most real knowledge must be a priori and drawn from within ourselves. The role played by particular experience and by the action of the world on us through our individual perspectives can be only selective—though this is a very important factor, which makes the acquisition of such knowledge as we may have importantly subject to luck: the luck of the observations and data to which we are exposed and the age in which we live. Also important, for possession of the a priori component, are the possibilities and questions that are suggested to us and that we might not have formulated ourselves—like the boy in Plato's *Meno*.

If the possibilities, or at least some of them, are available a priori to any mind of sufficient complexity, and if the general properties of reality are fairly uniform throughout, then the pursuit of objective knowledge can be expected to lead to gradual convergence from different starting points. But this limit of convergence is not the definition of truth, as Peirce suggests: it is a consequence of the relation between reality and the mind, which in turn must be explained in terms of the kind of part of reality the mind is. Obviously the capacities of different minds, and of different species of mind, differ. But in our case the capacities go far beyond the merely adaptive. A reasonably intelligent human being is capable of grasping, even if it cannot generate on its own, an extraordinary and rich range of conceptual possibilities, as we know from what has been learned already. There is no reason to think our mental capacities mirror reality completely, but I assume we all carry potentially in our heads the possibilities that will be revealed by scientific and other developments over the next few thousand years at least: we just aren't going to be around for the trip—perhaps it should be called the awakening.

This conception of knowledge is in the rationalist tradition, though without the claim that reason provides an indubitable foundation for belief. Even empirical knowledge, or empirical belief, must rest on an a priori base, and if large conclusions are derived from limited empirical evidence a large burden must be carried by direct a priori formulation and selection of hypotheses if knowledge is to be possible at all.[10]

This accounts for the extremely high ratio of rational to empirical grounds for great theoretical advances like Newton's theory of gravitation or the special and general theories of relativity: even though the empirical predictions of those theories are enormous, they were arrived at on the basis of relatively limited observational data, from which they could not be deduced. And I would maintain that even induction, that staple of empiricism, makes sense only with a rationalist basis. Observed regularities provide reason to believe that they will be repeated only to the extent that they provide evidence of hidden *necessary* connections, which hold timelessly. It is not a matter of assuming that the contingent future will be like the contingent past.

The capacity to imagine new forms of hidden order, and to understand new conceptions created by others, seems to be innate. Just as matter can be arranged to embody a conscious, thinking organism, so some of these organisms can rearrange themselves to embody more and more thorough and objective mental representations of the world that contains them, and this possibility too must exist in advance. Although the procedures of thought by which we progress are not self-guaranteeing, they make sense only if we have a natural capacity for achieving harmony with the world far beyond the range of our particular experiences and surroundings. When we use our minds to think about reality, we are not, I assume, performing an impossible leap from inside ourselves to the world outside. We are developing a relation to the world that is implicit in our mental and physical makeup, and we can do this only if there are facts we do not know which account for the possibility. Our position is problematic so long as we have not even a candidate for such an account.

Descartes tried to provide one, together with grounds for certainty that it was true, by proving the existence of the right sort of God. While he was not successful, the problem remains. To go on unambivalently holding our beliefs once this has been recognized requires that we believe that something—we know not what—is true that plays the role in our relation to the world that Descartes thought was played by God. (Perhaps it would be more accurate to say that Descartes' God is a personification of the fit between ourselves and the world for which we have no explanation but which is necessary for thought to yield knowledge.)

I have no idea what unheard-of property of the natural order this might be. But without something fairly remarkable, human knowledge is unintelligible. My view is rationalist and antiempiricist, not because I believe a firm foundation for our beliefs can be discovered a priori, but because I believe that unless we suppose that they have a basis in something global (rather than just human) of which we are not aware, they make no sense—and they do make sense. A serious rationalist epistemology would have to complete this picture—but our beliefs may rest on such a basis even if we cannot discover it. There is no reason to assume that even if we are so organized as to be capable of partly understanding the world, we can also gain access to these facts about ourselves in a way that will fill the blanks in our understanding.[11]

A theory of reality with pretensions to completeness would have to include a theory of the mind. But this too would be a hypothesis generated by the mind, and would not be self-guaranteeing. The point is made by Stroud with reference to Quine's proposal of naturalized epistemology, which is essentially an empiricist psychological theory of the formation of empirical theories (Stroud, ch. 6). It applies equally to a possible rationalist theory of the mind's capacity for a priori theorizing. But of course we have neither of these theories: we don't even have a hypothesis about our capacity to transcend the phenomena. The idea of a full conception of reality that explains our ability to arrive at it is just a dream.

Nevertheless, it's what we aim toward: a gradual liberation of the dormant objective self, trapped initially behind an individual perspective of human existence. The hope is to develop a detached perspective that can coexist with and comprehend the individual one.

6. Double Vision

To summarize, what we can hope to accomplish along these lines is bound to be limited in several ways. First, we are finite beings, and even if each of us possesses a large dormant capacity for objective self-transcendence, our knowledge of the world will always be fragmentary, however much we extend it. Second, since the objective self, though it can escape the human perspective, is still as short-lived as we are, we must assume that its best efforts will soon be superseded. Third, the understanding of the world of which we are intrinsically capable—leaving aside limitations of time and technology—is also likely to be limited. As I shall argue in the next chapter, reality probably extends beyond what we can conceive of. Finally, the development of richer and more powerful objective hypotheses does nothing to rule out the known and unknown skeptical possibilities which are the other aspect of any realist view.

None of this will deter us from the effort to make objective progress so far as our minds, our culture, and our epoch may permit. But there are other dangers in the pursuit of that goal, dangers not of failure but of ambition. These dangers are of three kinds: excessive impersonality, false objectification, and insoluble conflict between subjective and objective conceptions of the same thing.

The first comes from taking too literally the image of the true self trapped in the individual human perspective. This is a compelling image, and many have succumbed to its attractions. If the real me views the world from nowhere, and includes the empirical perspective and particular concerns of TN as merely one of myriad sentient flickers in the world so viewed, then it may seem that I should take as little interest in TN's life and perspective as possible, and perhaps even try to insulate myself from it. But the discovery and awakening of the objective self with its universal character doesn't imply that one is not also a creature with an empirical perspective and individual life. Objective advance produces a split in the self, and as it gradually widens, the problems of integration between the two standpoints become severe, particularly in regard to ethics and personal life. One must arrange somehow to see the world both from nowhere and from here, and to live accordingly.

The second danger, that of false objectification, is one I have already discussed in connection with the philosophy of mind—though it arises also in other areas. The success of a particular form of objectivity in expanding our grasp of some aspects of reality may tempt us to apply the same methods in areas where they will not work, either because those areas require a new kind of objectivity or because they are in some respect irreducibly subjective. The failure to recognize these limits produces various kinds of objective obstinacy—most notably reductive analyses of one type of thing in terms that are taken from the objective understanding of another. But as I have said, reality is not just objective reality, and objectivity itself is not one thing. The kinds of objective concepts and theories that we have developed so far, mostly to understand the physical world, can be expected to yield only a fragment of the objective understanding that is possible. And the detachment that objectivity requires is bound to leave something behind.

The third problem, that of insoluble subjective-objective conflict, arises when we succeed in constructing an objective conception of something and then don't know what to do with it because it can't be harmoniously combined with the subjective conception we still have of the same thing. Sometimes an internal conception can't acknowledge its own subjectivity and survive, nor can it simply disappear.

Often an objective advance will involve the recognition that some aspects of our previous understanding belong to the realm of appearance. Instead of conceiving the world as full of colored objects, we conceive it as full of objects with primary qualities that affect human vision in certain subjectively understandable ways. The distinction between appearance and objective reality becomes the object of a new, mixed understanding that combines subjective and objective elements and that is based on recognition of the limits of objectivity. Here there is no conflict.[12]

But it may happen that the object of understanding cannot be so cleanly divided. It may happen that something appears to require subjective and objective conceptions that cover the same territory, and that cannot be combined into a single complex but consistent view. This is particularly likely with respect to our understanding of ourselves, and it is at the source of some of the most difficult problems of philosophy, including the problems of personal identity, free will, and the meaning of life. It is also present in the theory of knowledge, where it takes the form of an inability to hold in one's mind simultaneously and in a consistent form the possibility of skepticism and the ordinary beliefs that life is full of.

What should be the relation between the beliefs we form about the world, with their aspirations to objectivity, and the admission that the world might be completely different from the way we think it is, in unimaginable ways? I believe we have no satisfactory way of combining these outlooks. The objective standpoint here produces a split in the self which will not go away, and we either alternate between views or develop a form of double vision.

Double vision is the fate of creatures with a glimpse of the view *sub specie aeternitatis*. When we view ourselves from outside, a naturalistic picture of how we work seems unavoidable. It is clear that our beliefs arise from certain dispositions and experiences which, so far as we know, don't guarantee their truth and are compatible with radical error. The trouble is that we can't fully take on the skepticism that this entails, because we can't cure our appetite for belief, and we can't take on this attitude toward our own beliefs while we're having them. Beliefs are about how things probably are, not just about how they might possibly be, and there is no way of bracketing our ordinary beliefs about the world so that they dovetail neatly with the possibility of skepticism. The thought "I'm a professor at New York University, unless of course I'm a brain in a vat" is not one that can represent my general integrated state of mind.[13]

The problems of free will and personal identity yield similarly unharmonious conclusions. In some respects what we do and what happens to us fits very naturally into an objective picture of the world, on a footing with what other objects and organisms do. Our actions seem to be events with causes and conditions many of which are not our actions. We seem to persist and change through time much as other complex organisms do. But when we take these objective ideas seriously, they appear to threaten and undermine certain fundamental self-conceptions that we find it very difficult to give up.

Earlier I said it was impossible fully to internalize a conception of one's own personal identity that depended on the organic continuity of one's brain. Ordinarily, an objective view of something with a subjective aspect does not require us simply to give up the subjective view, for it can be reduced to the status of an appearance, and can then coexist with the objective view. But in these cases that option seems not to be available. We cannot come to regard our ideas of our own agency or of the purity of our self-identity through time as mere appearances or impressions. That would be equivalent to giving them up. Though our intuitive convictions about these things emerge very much from our own point of view, they have pretensions to describe not just how we appear to ourselves but how we are, in some as yet unspecified sense which appears to conflict with the objective picture of what we are. This problem arises even if the objective picture does not claim to take in everything—for what it willingly omits is only subjective appearance, and that is not good enough. The claims of both the objective and the subjective self seem to be too strong to allow them to live together in harmony.

This problem will reappear in later chapters, but let me mention one further example: Wittgenstein's unacknowledged skepticism about deduction. I believe his view is rightly regarded by Kripke as a form of skepticism because the external account it gives of what is really going on when we apply a formula or a concept to indefinitely many cases—what the apparently infinite reach of meaning really rests on—is not an account we can take on internally. For example we can't think of the correct application of "plus 2" as being determined by nothing more than the fact that a certain application is natural to those who share our language and form of life, or by anything else of the sort. In employing the concept we must think of it as determining a unique function over infinitely many cases, beyond all our applications and those of our community and independent of them, or else it would not be the concept it is. *Even if Wittgenstein is right*, we can't think of our thoughts this way while we have them. And even in the philosophical act of thinking naturalistically about how language and logic work, we can't take the Wittgensteinian stance toward *those* thoughts, but must think them straight.

I think a view deserves to be called skeptical if it offers an account of ordinary thoughts which cannot be incorporated into those thoughts without destroying them. One may be a skeptic about *x* no matter how sincerely one protests that one is not denying the existence of *x* but merely explaining what *x* really amounts to.[14]

NOTES

[1] A fourth reaction is to turn one's back on the abyss and announce that one is now on the other side. This was done by G. E. Moore.

[2] The idea is much closer to what Bernard Williams calls the absolute conception of reality, which is a more general description of Descartes' idea of knowledge. See Williams.

[3] See for example Putnam, ch. 1.

[4] There is perhaps one form of radical skepticism which could be ruled out as unthinkable, by an argument analogous to the *cogito*: skepticism about whether I am the kind of being who can have thoughts *at all*. If there were possible beings whose nature and relation to the world was such that nothing they did could constitute thinking, whatever went on inside them, then I could not wonder whether I was such a being, because if I were, I wouldn't be thinking, and even to consider the possibility that I may not be thinking is to think. But most forms of skepticism are not this extreme.

[5] This is a theme of Clarke's and Stroud's work on skepticism. See Stroud, pp. 205–6. Stroud's book is a highly illuminating discussion of skepticism and the inadequacy of most responses to it. He is nevertheless slightly more optimistic than I am about the possibility of finding something wrong with skepticism—and with the desire for an objective or external understanding of our position in the world that leads to it.

[6] Stephen Jay Gould reports that Francis Crick once said to him, "The trouble with you evolutionary biologists is that you are always asking 'why' before you understand 'how'" (Gould (2), p.10).

[7] See Gould (1) for details.

[8] It might be argued that the observation that the universe contains intelligent beings does not have to be explained in terms of fundamental principles which show it to be inevitable, because it has a much simpler explanation: if there were no such beings, there would be no observers and hence no observations. No general inferences can therefore be drawn from their existence. I am not persuaded by this argument. The fact that an observation can be predicted on this sort of ground does not mean that it needn't be explained by other, more fundamental principles as well.

It may be worth mentioning an analogy, the application of the anthropic principle in cosmology. The anthropic principle states that "what we can expect to observe must be restricted by the conditions necessary for our presence as observers" (Carter, p. 291). A special case of this is the strong anthropic principle: "the Universe (and hence the fundamental parameters on which it depends) must be such as to admit the creation of observers within it at some stage" (p. 294). About this Carter says that "even an entirely rigorous prediction based on the *strong* principle will not be completely satisfying from the physicist's point of view since the possibility will remain of finding a deeper underlying theory explaining the relationships that have been predicted" (p. 295). In other words, predictability does not always eliminate the need for explanation.

[9] As Neurath puts it, we are "never able to dismantle it in dry-dock and to reconstruct it there out of the best materials" (Neurath, p. 201).

[10] Both Chomsky and Popper have in very different ways rejected empiricist theories of knowledge and emphasized the incomprehensibility, at present, of our capacities to understand and think about the world. Chomsky in particular has argued that our innate capacity to learn languages is contrary to the empiricist conception of how the mind works. This is one aspect of his general attack on reductionism with respect to the mind. I believe that the scientific gaps between data and conclusions are of much greater importance to the theory of knowledge than the gap between the fragmentary linguistic data of early childhood and the grammar of the language that is learned from it, remarkable as that is. Somehow we call up whole worlds out of our heads, not just languages whose form has presumably evolved in part to suit our ability to learn them.

[11] It may be that those areas of knowledge that are entirely a priori permit greater access to their sources in us than do other types of knowledge—that we can develop a better understanding of how our thoughts can lead us to the truths of arithmetic than of how they can lead us to the truths of chemistry. It is possible to make discoveries about something a priori if our representation of the thing has so intimate a relation with the thing itself that the properties to be discovered are already buried in the representation. Thus we can think about mathematics because we are able to operate with a system of symbols whose formal properties make it capable of representing the numbers and all their relations. This system can itself be mathematically investigated. To what extent mathematics gives us a partial answer to the question of how the world that it describes can contain beings who will be able to arrive at some of its truths.

[12] This is McGinn's point; the scientific image doesn't on reflection conflict with the manifest image over secondary qualities.

[13] There is a further problem. In the course of arriving at a skeptical conclusion, we pass through thoughts to which we do not simultaneously take up a skeptical stance—thoughts about the relation of the brain to experience, for example. These appear in the skeptic's reasoning in unqualified form. In order to draw skeptical conclusions from the objective standpoint, we have to engage in the kind of direct thought about the world that skepticism undermines. This is like the Cartesian circle in reverse: Descartes tried to prove the existence of God by the use of reasoning on which we can rely only if God exists; the skeptic reaches skepticism through thoughts that skepticism makes unthinkable.

[14] See Kripke, p. 65.

BIBLIOGRAPHY

Carter, B. "Large Number Coincidences and the Anthropic Principle in Cosmology," in M. S. Longair (ed.), *Confrontation of Cosmological Theories with Observational Data*, Dordrecht: Reidel, 1974.

Clarke, T. "The Legacy of Skepticism", *Journal of Philosophy*, 1972.

Gould, S. J. (1) "Is a New and General Theory of Evolution Emerging?" *Paleobiology*, 1980.

(2) "Genes on the Brain," *New York Review of Books*, June 30, 1983.

Kant, I. *Foundations of the Metaphysics of Morals*, 1785; Prussian Academy ed., vol. IV.

Kripke, S. *Wittgenstein on Rules and Private Language*, Harvard University Press, 1982.

McGinn, C. *The Subjective View*, Oxford University Press, 1983.

Moore, G. E. "Proof of an External World," *Proceedings of the British Academy*, 1939.

Neurath, O. *"Protokollsätze"*, *Erkenntnis*, 1932–3; trans. F. Schick, in A. J. Ayer (ed.), *Logical Positivism*, New York: The Free Press, 1959.

Putnam, H. *Reason, Truth and History*, Cambridge University Press, 1981.

Spinoza, B. *On the Improvement of the Understanding*, tr. R. H. M. Elwes, in *The Chief Works of Benedict de Spinoza*, vol. II, New York: Dover, 1951.

Stroud, B. *The Significance of Philosophical Skepticism*, Oxford University Press, 1984.

Williams, B. *Descartes: The Project of Pure Inquiry*, Harmondsworth: Penguin, 1978.

2.6

SKEPTICISM AND THE POSSIBILITY OF KNOWLEDGE

Barry Stroud

Skepticism in recent and current philosophy represents a certain threat or challenge in the theory of knowledge. What is that threat? How serious is it? How, if at all, can it be met? What are the consequences if it cannot be met?

I obviously do not have time to go into all these questions, or into any of them thoroughly. I can only sketch a point of view in the hope of provoking some discussion.

The first question is clearly the place to start. I believe the true nature of the skeptical threat is still not properly understood, nor are the consequences of its not being met. That is one reason we have tended to give inadequate answers to the other questions. It is still widely felt that skepticism is not really worth taking seriously, so it hardly matters whether the challenge can be met or not. That kind of reaction seems to me to rest on a philosophical misconception.

Many would dismiss skepticism and defend not taking it seriously on the grounds that it is not a doctrine or theory any sensible person would contemplate adopting as the truth about our position in the world. It seems to them frivolous or perverse to concentrate on a view that is not even a conceivable candidate in the competition for the true or best theory as to how things are. I would grant—indeed insist—that philosophical skepticism is not something we should seriously consider adopting or accepting (whatever that means). But does that mean that it is silly to worry about skepticism? I think it does not. A line of thinking can be of deep significance and great importance in philosophy even if we never contemplate accepting a "theory" that claims to express it.

One reason that is so is that philosophy thrives on paradox, absurdity, dilemma, and difficulty. There are often what look like good arguments for surprising or outrageous conclusions. Taking the paradoxical reasonings seriously and re-examining the assumptions they rest on can be important and fruitful when there is no question at all of our ever contemplating adopting a "theory" or doctrine embodying the absurd conclusion.

The point is clearest in the case of antinomies—explicit contradictions. We know we cannot believe the conclusion; it couldn't possibly be true. To take The Liar, or Russell's paradox, seriously is not to hold open even the remote option of believing that someone who says he is lying speaks both truly and falsely, or that there is a set that both is and is not a member of itself. Such "theories" would be worse than outrageous as things to believe, but that in no way diminishes the need to take seriously the reasoning that leads to them.

The same is true even when the conclusion of the paradoxical or surprising reasoning falls short of explicit contradiction. The Eleatic doctrine that nothing moves, for example, need not be in any remote sense a live intellectual option for us in order for us to be rightly challenged, overwhelmed, perhaps even stumped, by Zeno's argument that Achilles can never overtake the Tortoise. The mere idea of something's being true at a time can seem to generate the absurd result that there is never any real alternative to what happens, that things are fated to happen as they do. We can be impelled to investigate that line of reasoning without thinking that otherwise we would have to adopt the "theory" that we have no control over what we do or what happens to us. Again, it seems undeniable that adding one more molecule to a table would not turn it into a non-table, any more than pulling one hair from a bushy head would make it bald. The discomfort I feel in the thought that an exactly similar step can be taken again, and again, does not show that I in any way consider accepting a "theory" according to which there could be a table the size and shape of the earth, or that a bushy head and a bald head are the same sort of thing.

Those modern philosophers most closely connected to the skeptical tradition and most impressed by skeptical reasoning—Descartes, Hume, and Russell, for example—do not hold that believing the conclusions of that reasoning is a real option for us. The ancient skeptics themselves seem not to have accepted, or to have contemplated accepting or declaring the truth of any "theory" either. They were highly anti-theoretical philosophers, and their strictures would have extended to any theoretical pronouncements put into their own mouths by their opponents as well. But none of that shows that skeptical ideas were not worth taking seriously or were not of great philosophical importance.

The importance of skepticism came always from the uses to which its ideas were put—different uses at different times. It is now widely understood to represent a certain threat or challenge in the theory of knowledge. That is not to say that everything in epistemology as we think of it today, or even in that challenge, can be traced back to the skeptical tradition alone. Exactly which skeptical ideas were important in defining the modern philosophical concern with human knowledge, how and to what extent they were used, and to what effect—all these are intriguing historical questions. Clearly, it is complicated. The role of sense-perception in our knowledge of the world became an important issue even for those apparently untouched by skepticism—by those in the atomist tradition, for example, from Galileo to Boyle and Locke, as well as by Descartes himself in his studies of optics and the physiology of perception. I want to concentrate for the moment on the problem or challenge itself. I think that, whatever its historical source, it has come to define, or perhaps even create, the philosophical concern with our knowledge of the world.

What do we want from a philosophical theory of knowledge? What is it supposed to do? It seems that we simply want to understand how we get the knowledge we have—to explain how it is possible. But I don't think that is enough to uniquely identify the philosophical problem.

Take what is usually called in philosophy "our knowledge of the world around us." Now it seems obvious, without any philosophical preconceptions, that there are countless ways of coming to know something about the world around us. I can find out that there is a bus-drivers' strike in Rome, for example, by waiting in vain for a bus or by reading a newspaper or by getting a letter from a friend. How many different ways of finding out is that? Is reading a newspaper only one way, or possibly many? Is reading it in the *New York Times* a different way of finding it out from reading it in the *New York Post*? It seems hopeless to try counting. Obviously we do not just want a list of sources. What we seek in philosophy is not just anything that is true about how we get knowledge of the world around us.

The philosophical interest in knowledge is general, and in at least two different ways. We are interested in all of our knowledge of the world taken all together, or in some domain characterized in general terms. To ask only how we come to know some things in the domain, given that we already know certain other things in it, is not to ask about all knowledge of that kind in general. And we don't just want a heterogeneous list of ways of coming to know. We want to find a single way, or a smaller number of very general "ways of knowing." To explain how they work will be to explain, in general, how knowledge of the kind in question is possible.

Is that enough, then, to identify what we are interested in in the philosophy of knowledge? I don't think so. Suppose we eventually establish contact with some beings elsewhere in space. We receive some regular signals, we send back similar messages, and eventually find ourselves communicating with something somewhere. We take the opportunity to find out about them. We ask them where they are, what it is like there, what they are like, how they send out their signals, how they receive ours, and so on. Suppose they do the same with us. One day there appears on our receiving screen the question "How do you come to know of the things around you?" We send back the answer "We see them with our eyes, we touch them with parts of our bodies, we hear the noises they make,…" That might be just what those beings want to know. Perhaps for them it's all a matter of sonar, or something we do not even understand. But even if that answer is just what the aliens want, is it what we want in philosophy?

I think we recognize that the philosophical question is not simply a request for information of this kind. What we want, rather, is some kind of *explanation* of our knowledge—some account of how it is possible. But what kind of explanation of its possibility? Our friends in space could send back a message pressing us for details. "Exactly how does seeing work?", they might ask. "What has to happen after light strikes your eye in order for you to know something about what is reflecting the light? How can you recognize the objects around you and pick them out from the background? Please send detailed explanation." We could send answers to some of their questions. We might even send them as much as we can of our science as it is and let them figure it out for themselves. Maybe they would send back better explanations than we've now got. That would be super naturalized epistemology, if not supernaturalized epistemology.

But would it be what we seek in philosophy? Sending them that information would be like sending them what we know about motion and acceleration, from which they could easily deduce that Achilles will have no trouble overtaking the Tortoise. Would that meet Zeno's challenge? What puzzles us in that case, if anything does, is how it is possible for Achilles to overtake the Tortoise *if* what Zeno relies on at each step of the argument is true. We want to know how overtaking is possible given those undeniable facts invoked by Zeno. That is how that challenge is to be met—not simply by reminding us of the obvious facts of motion and acceleration, or, worse still, by running off and overtaking a tortoise oneself.

The same is true in the case of our knowledge of the world. It is not enough simply to know something; and not just any explanation of how such knowledge is possible will do. It is true that we come to know of the things around us by seeing and touching them, but that is just the sort of information we could send to the aliens in space. Only they or others similarly removed from us would seek that kind of answer. The philosophical question has not yet been reached.

We want a general answer to the question. It should be expressed in terms of a general "way of knowing." And we find that general source in what we call "the senses" or "sense-perception." The problem then is to explain how we can get any knowledge at all of the world around us on the basis of sense-perception. But again, not just any explanations will do, any more than just any relevant information about motion and acceleration will answer Zeno's question. When our friends in space request such explanations we do not understand them to be asking a philosophical question about our knowledge. What *we* want is an explanation of how we could get any knowledge of things around us on the basis of sense-perception, given certain apparently undeniable facts about sense-perception.

The difficulty comes in philosophy when we try to see exactly how sense-perception works to give us knowledge of the world. We are led to think of seeing, or perceiving generally, in a certain way. What is in question is our knowledge of anything at all about the world, of any of the truths that are about things around us. The difficulty in understanding how sense-perception gives us knowledge of any such truths is that it seems at least possible to perceive what we do without thereby knowing something about the things around us. There have been many versions of that fundamental idea. But whether it is expressed in terms of "ideas" or "experiences" or "sense data" or "appearances" or "takings" or "sensory stimulations," or whatever it might be, the basic idea could be put by saying our knowledge of the world is "underdetermined" by whatever it is that we get through that source of knowledge known as "the senses" or "experience." Given the events or experiences or whatever they might be that serve as the sensory "basis" of our knowledge, it does not follow that something we believe about the world around us is true. The problem is then to explain how we nevertheless know that what we do believe about the world around us is in fact true. Given the apparent "obstacle," how is our knowledge possible?

It is an "obstacle" because it seems to make our knowledge impossible, just as the facts cited by Zeno seem to make overtaking impossible. If several different possibilities are all compatible with our perceiving what we do, the question is how we know that one of those possibilities involving the truth of our beliefs about the world does obtain and the others do not. That would seem to require an inference of some sort, some reasonable hypothesis or some form of reasoning that could take us from what we get in sense-perception to some proposition about the world around us. That hypothesis or principle of inference itself either will imply something about the world around us or it will not. If it does, it belongs among those propositions our knowledge of which has yet to be explained, so it cannot help explain that knowledge. If it does not, how can our acceptance of it lead to knowledge of the way things are around us? If it itself implies nothing about such things, and we could perceive what we do without knowing anything about such things, how is our knowledge to be explained? If we are in fact in that position, how is our knowledge of the world around us possible?

The problem is too familiar to need further elaboration here. I have wanted to stress only how very special a question it is about the possibility of knowledge, and what one must do to bring it before our minds in its proper philosophical form. That alone is thought to be enough to show that the question is frivolous or idle. The alleged "obstacle" to our knowledge is thought to be easily avoidable. Even if that quite special question cannot be answered satisfactorily, there is felt to be no good reason to ask it in the first place. The "assumptions" on which it is based are held to be wrong, misguided, and in any case not inevitable.

One familiar criticism is that the whole project is based on the mistaken assumption that there are or must be sensory "foundations" of our knowledge of the world which are in some way "epistemically prior" to the knowledge they serve to support. Abandon that assumption, it is suggested, and the whole problem, or the need to answer it as formulated, disappears. "Enlightened" epistemologists have accordingly moved beyond that quaint doctrine known as "foundationalism." They seek a "nonfoundational" theory of knowledge.

There is not time to go carefully into that complicated issue here. I think the suggestion does not penetrate very deeply into the sources of skepticism; it seems to me to get things almost exactly upside down. And regarding it as simply a matter of deciding to adopt or not adopt a certain "assumption" is just another way of not taking skepticism seriously. But if we ignore or reject out of hand the familiar traditional question I have tried to identify, what is left?

Suppose we abandon, or never reach, the idea or hope that our knowledge of the world around us is to be explained as being derived from some knowledge or experience that is not itself knowledge of the world around us—something that is "prior to" or "underdetermines" the knowledge we are interested in. What would we then need a philosophical "theory of knowledge" for? It might seem that we would simply have liberated ourselves from an unrealistic restriction, and we could then go ahead and simply explain how our knowledge is possible. But if we are free to explain it in terms of sense-perception that *does* amount to knowledge of the things around us, can we ever properly understand *all* our knowledge of the world—how any of it is possible at all?

The "liberated" question can easily be answered by saying that we know of the things around us by perceiving them. We see them, we touch them, we hear them, and so on. We even read about them in the newspaper. But that was just the sort of information we could send to the aliens in space. Is that the sort of thing we want to find out about our knowledge of the world when we wonder, as we do in philosophy, how any of it is possible? Obviously not. We already know all that. If it were the job of a "nonfoundational theory of knowledge" to give us answers like that, it would be even more tedious than skeptical "foundational" theories are now widely held to be.

I do not say that such "enlightened" "theories" or explanations could never tell us anything we do not already know. Obviously, when they got down to the physiological details, they could. But I think there is something we aspire to in the philosophical theory of knowledge that such explanations would not give us. We want an account of our knowledge of the world that would make all of it intelligible to us all at once. We want to see how knowledge of the world could come to be out of something that is not knowledge of the world. Without that, we will not have the kind of doubly general explanation we seek. I think skepticism in epistemology now represents, and perhaps always did represent, the possibility that such an explanation is impossible; that we cannot consider all our knowledge of the world all at once and still see it as knowledge. Given that project, the threat is that skepticism will be the only answer. That alone would not straightforwardly imply that we can know nothing of the world around us—that we can never know whether there is a bus drivers' strike in Rome, for example. But it would suggest that a certain kind of understanding of our position in the world might be beyond us. Taking that possibility seriously, trying to see whether it is so, and if so why, would then be what taking skepticism seriously would amount to. To dismiss it simply on the grounds that we do know many things and that it would be ridiculous to believe we do not would be like assuring us that Achilles will overtake the Tortoise, and that it would be ridiculous to believe that he will not. And we will be in a position to dismiss it on the ground that it is absurd even to seek the kind of understanding philosophers have sought of our knowledge only when we understand better what that goal is, why we seek it, why it is unattainable, and what a philosophical "theory of knowledge" that did not aspire to it would look like.

Section 2: Study Questions

1. Try to construct your own Gettier-type example.

2. Gettier claims to have presented two cases in which a person has a justified true belief, but the person in question does not know the belief in question. What is the basis of Gettier's claim that the person does not have knowledge? What is the conception of knowledge that Gettier presupposes when he raises this concern?

3. How might one alter the classic definition of knowledge in order to diffuse Gettier's criticism? Try to think of a fourth (perhaps even a fifth) condition you could add to the traditional definition of knowledge to diffuse the Gettier problems.

4. Critically evaluate Conee's argument.

5. Explain in your own words the philosophical significance of a solution to the Gettier problem.

6. Putnam argues that the claim "I am a brain in a vat" is self-refuting, and consequently one should not take seriously the possibility that one is a brain in a vat. Are there other forms of scepticism that are self-refuting? Can you think of sceptical hypotheses that are not self-refuting?

7. The aim of the sceptic is to show that we do not know what we think we know. Given that Putnam believes he has refuted a particular form of scepticism, what sort of knowledge has he secured for us?

8. Explain and critically evaluate Nagel's assessment of Putnam's response to the brain-in-the-vat hypothesis. Also, explain how Putnam might respond to Nagel's criticism.

9. Explain what Nagel believes the relationship is between objectivity and scepticism.

10. Nagel suggests that advances in objectivity lead us to see that things which we previously regarded as reality are in fact mere appearances. If Nagel is right about this, do we have any reason to think that our understanding of the world, including our understanding of objectivity, is correct? Provide a justification for your answer.

11. Why does Stroud object to construing the sceptical challenge as an alternative theory of knowledge?

12. According to Stroud, the sceptic argues that we could have the sorts of perceptions we have and the world be other than we believe it to be. Is there any way to meet this challenge and lay to rest the worries that the sceptic raises? Provide a justification for your answer.

13. Why does Stroud believe that reflecting on scepticism is a worthwhile philosophical enterprise even if the key sceptical challenge cannot adequately be addressed?

Additional Readings

There are many articles discussing Gettier problems and their implications. I list only a few recent articles that have been published in some of the most important philosophy journals.

These articles are concerned with either showing that the Gettier problems are themselves problematic or showing that criticisms of Gettier problems are misguided:

D.S.G. Schreiber's (1987) "The Illegitimacy of Gettier Examples," *Metaphilosophy*, Vol 18, pages 49–54.

Mark Kaplan's (1985) "It's Not What You Know That Counts," *Journal of Philosophy*, Vol. 82, pages 350–363.

Richard Kirkham's (1984), "Does The Gettier Problem Rest on a Mistake?," *Mind*, 93, pages 501–513.

Don Levi's (1995) "The Gettier Problem and the Parable of the Ten Coins," *Philosophy*, Vol. 70, pages 5–25.

Linda Zagzebski's (1994) "The Inescapability of Gettier Problems," *Philosophical Quarterly*, Vol. 44, pages 65–73.

These articles attempt to provide a solution to the Gettier problems:

Stephen Hetherington's (1999) "Knowing Failably," *The Journal of Philosophy*, Vol 96: 11, 565–587.

Stewart Cohen's (1998) "Contextualist Solutions to Epistemological Problems: Scepticism, Gettier, and the Lottery," *The Australasian Journal of Philosophy*, 72:2, pages 289–306.

William Harper's (1996) "Knowledge and Luck," *The Southern Journal of Philosophy*, Vol 34:3, pages 273–283.

These articles discuss other issues raised by the Gettier problems:

Alvin Plantinga's (1997) "Warrant and Accidentally True Beliefs," *Analysis*, 57:2, pages 140–145.

Stephen Hetherington's (1996) "Gettieristic Scepticism," *The Australasian Journal of Philosophy*, 74:1, pages 83–97.

For students interested in scepticism, a good place to start is Barry Stroud's (2000) *Understanding Human Knowledge*, or his (1984) *The Significance of Philosophical Scepticism*.

SECTION 3
NEW DEVELOPMENTS IN EPISTEMOLOGY

SECTION 3: NEW DEVELOPMENTS IN EPISTEMOLOGY

The readings in this section will introduce you to a variety of new develop-ments in epistemology. These developments are a consequence of new and different approaches to the study of knowledge and inquiry, and have been called naturalized epistemologies, feminist epistemologies, and social epistemologies. These readings are not so easily classified, as a number of the readings make contributions in two or more of these areas. Another feature that unifies these readings is the fact that they are more explicitly concerned with scientific knowledge and inquiry. Some of the articles are concerned with the relationship and relevance of science to epistemology, and others are concerned with developing an epistemology of scientific knowledge.

The first reading, by W.V. Quine, is a classic. In it, he lays out the foundations for a new approach to epistemology, which he calls naturalizing epistemology. Whereas traditional epistemologies have aimed to develop epistemic standards prior to our embarking on the project of knowing the world, Quine argues that such an approach is impossible. He suggests that once we realize this philosophers will also realize that they should draw on existing scientific theories about how the mind works in an effort to explain how it is that we come to develop our theories of the world. The principal task for epistemologists, Quine claims, is to explain how we get from our meagre sensory input to our torrential theoretical output.

The second reading, by Robert Almeder, raises concerns with Quine's proposal. Almeder critically examines a variety of arguments that have been advanced in support of Quine's approach to epistemology. Almeder also argues that epistemologists have concerns that extend beyond the scope of Quine's view of epistemology.

In the third reading, Hilary Putnam raises additional concerns against the project of naturalizing epistemology. Putnam takes issue with Alvin Gold-man's, Richard Rorty's, and Quine's approaches to naturalizing epistemology.

In the fourth reading, Elizabeth Anderson develops a feminist epistemol-ogy. Anderson conceives of feminist epistemology as a form of naturalized, social epistemology. She also discusses a variety of ways in which gender matters to epistemology.

In the fifth reading, Sandra Harding presents an alternative feminist epistemology. She argues that epistemology needs to be radically changed in order to eliminate distorting gender biases. Harding suggests that objectivity does not require the elimination of the influence of inquirers' values, as is traditionally thought. In fact, she suggests that political values can even be epistemic assets, leading us to develop more objective accounts of the world.

In the sixth reading, Helen Longino criticizes both traditional and feminist epistemologies for focussing on the relationship between the knowing subject and the object of knowledge. Longino argues that scientific inquiry is social in a more fundamental sense. In particular, she suggests that it is through interaction with other inquirers that scientists come to develop theories of the world that deserve to be called knowledge. The interaction that results from making public our views, and altering them in light of criticism raised by others, is an essential part of inquiry and it is what grounds our claims to objectivity.

In the seventh reading, John Hardwig examines the role of trust in inquiry. He argues that trust in the testimony of others is unavoidable, and that if we do not countenance trust as a basis of justification, then we will find that we know very little about the world. Further, he suggests that it is not feasible to try to calibrate the reliability of those whom we must trust. Consequently, he claims, trust in what others say, and in their character, is fundamental to knowledge.

In the eighth reading, Richard Rorty encourages us to give up on the goal of trying to represent the person-independent world, and measure our success in inquiry in terms of the breadth of the community to which we can justify ourselves. His approach to socializing epistemology is radical.

In the ninth and final reading, Philip Kitcher defends a rather conservative approach to socializing epistemology. Kitcher reviews a variety of arguments and claims made by various philosophers and sociologists of science who have defended more radical social epistemologies. According to Kitcher, more radical social epistemologies cannot adequately be supported. Kitcher's own approach to epistemology is similar to Goldman's reliabilism.

3.1

Epistemology Naturalized

W. V. Quine

Epistemology is concerned with the foundations of science. Conceived thus broadly, epistemology includes the study of the foundations of mathematics as one of its departments. Specialists at the turn of the century thought that their efforts in this particular department were achieving notable success: mathematics seemed to reduce altogether to logic. In a more recent perspective this reduction is seen to be better describable as a reduction to logic and set theory. This correction is a disappointment epistemologically, since the firmness and obviousness that we associate with logic cannot be claimed for set theory. But still the success achieved in the foundations of mathematics remains exemplary by comparative standards, and we can illuminate the rest of epistemology somewhat by drawing parallels to this department.

Studies in the foundations of mathematics divide symmetrically into two sorts, conceptual and doctrinal. The conceptual studies are concerned with meaning, the doctrinal with truth. The conceptual studies are concerned with clarifying concepts by defining them, some in terms of others. The doctrinal studies are concerned with establishing laws by proving them, some on the basis of others. Ideally the obscurer concepts would be defined in terms of the clearer ones so as to maximize clarity, and the less obvious laws would be proved from the more obvious ones so as to maximize certainty. Ideally the definitions would generate all the concepts from clear and distinct ideas, and the proofs would generate all the theorems from self-evident truths.

The two ideals are linked. For, if you define all the concepts by use of some favored subset of them, you thereby show how to translate all theorems into these favored terms. The clearer these terms are, the likelier it is that the truths couched in them will be obviously true, or derivable from obvious truths. If in particular the concepts of mathematics were all reducible to the clear terms of logic, then all the truths of mathematics would go over into truths of logic; and surely the truths of logic are all obvious or at least potentially obvious, i.e., derivable from obvious truths by individually obvious steps.

This particular outcome is in fact denied us, however, since mathematics reduces only to set theory and not to logic proper. Such reduction still enhances clarity, but only because of the interrelations that emerge and not because the end terms of the analysis are clearer than others. As for the end truths, the axioms of set theory, these have less obviousness and certainty to recommend them than do most of the mathematical theorems that we would derive from them. Moreover, we know from Gödel's work that no consistent axiom system can cover mathematics even when we renounce self-evidence. Reduction in the foundations of mathematics remains mathematically and philosophically fascinating, but it does not do what he epistemologist would like of it: it does not reveal the ground of mathematical knowledge, it does not show how mathematical certainty is possible.

Still there remains a helpful thought, regarding epistemology generally, in that duality of structure which was especially conspicuous in the foundations of mathematics. I refer to the bifurcation into a theory of concepts, or meaning, and a theory of doctrine, or truth; for this applies to the epistemology of natural knowledge no less than to the foundations of mathematics. The parallel is as follows. Just as mathematics is to be reduced to logic, or logic and set theory, so natural knowledge is to be based somehow on sense experience. This means explaining the notion of body in sensory terms; here is the conceptual side. And it means justifying our knowledge of truths of nature in sensory terms; here is the doctrinal side of the bifurcation.

Hume pondered the epistemology of natural knowledge on both sides of the bifurcation, the conceptual and the doctrinal. His handling of the conceptual side of the problem, the explanation of body in sensory terms, was bold and simple: he identified bodies outright with the sense impressions. If common sense distinguishes between the material apple and our sense impressions of it on the ground that the apple is one and enduring while the impressions are many and fleeting, then, Hume held, so much the worse for common sense; the notion of its being the same apple on one occasion and another is a vulgar confusion.

Nearly a century after Hume's *Treatise*, the same view of bodies was espoused by the early American philosopher Alexander Bryan Johnson.[1] "The word iron names an associated sight and feel," Johnson wrote.

What then of the doctrinal side, the justification of our knowledge of truths about nature? Here, Hume despaired. By his identification of bodies with impressions he did succeed in construing some singular statements about bodies as indubitable truths, yes; as truths about impressions, directly known. But general statements, also singular statements about the future, gained no increment of certainty by being construed as about impressions.

On the doctrinal side, I do not see that we are farther along today than where Hume left us. The Humean predicament is the human predicament. But on the conceptual side there has been progress. There the crucial step forward was made already before Alexander Bryan Johnson's day, although Johnson did not emulate it. It was made by Bentham in his theory of fictions. Bentham's step was the recognition of contextual definition, or what he called paraphrasis. He recognized that to explain a term we do not need to specify an object for it to refer to, nor even specify a synonymous word or phrase; we need only show, by whatever means, how to translate all the whole sentences in which the term is to be used. Hume's and Johnson's desperate measure of identifying bodies with impressions ceased to be the only conceivable way of making sense of talk of bodies, even granted that impressions were the only reality. One could undertake to explain talk of bodies in terms of talk of impressions by translating one's whole sentences about bodies into whole sentences about impressions, without equating the bodies themselves to anything at all.

This idea of contextual definition, or recognition of the sentence as the primary vehicle of meaning, was indispensable to the ensuing developments in the foundations of mathematics. It was explicit in Frege, and it attained its full flower in Russell's doctrine of singular descriptions as incomplete symbols.

Contextual definition was one of two resorts that could be expected to have a liberating effect upon the conceptual side of the epistemology of natural knowledge. The other is resort to the resources of set theory as auxiliary concepts. The epistemologist who is willing to eke out his austere ontology of sense impressions with these set-theoretic auxiliaries is suddenly rich: he has not just his impressions to play with, but sets of them, and set of sets, and so on up. Constructions in the foundations of mathematics have shown that such set-theoretic aids are a powerful addition; after all, the entire glossary of concepts of classical mathematics is constructible from them. Thus equipped, our epistemologist may not need either to identify bodies with impressions or to settle for contextual definition; he may hope to find in some subtle construction of sets upon sets of sense impressions a category of objects enjoying just the formula properties that he wants for bodies.

The two resorts are very unequal in epistemological status. Contextual definition is unassailable. Sentences that have been given meaning as wholes are undeniably meaningful, and the use they make of their component terms is therefore meaningful, regardless of whether any translations are offered for those terms in isolation. Surely Hume and A. B. Johnson would have used contextual definition with pleasure if they had thought of it. Recourse to sets, on the other hand, is a drastic ontological move, a retreat from the austere ontology of impressions. There are philosophers who would rather settle for bodies outright than accept all these sets, which amount, after all, to the whole abstract ontology of mathematics.

This issue has not always been clear, however, owing to deceptive hints of continuity between elementary logic and set theory. This is why mathematics was once believed to reduce to logic, that is, to an innocent and unquestionable logic, and to inherit these qualities. And this is probably why Russell was content to resort to sets as well as to contextual definition when in *Our Knowledge of the External World* and elsewhere he addressed himself to the epistemology of natural knowledge, on its conceptual side.

To account for the external world as a logical construct of sense data—such, in Russell's terms, was the program. It was Carnap, in his *Der logische Aufbau der Welt* of 1928, who came nearest to executing it.

This was the conceptual side of epistemology; what of the doctrinal? There the Humean predicament remained unaltered. Carnap's constructions, if carried successfully to completion, would have enabled us to translate all sentences about the world into terms of sense data, or observation, plus logic and set theory. But the mere fact that a sentence is *couched* in terms of observation, logic, and set theory does not mean that it can be *proved* from observation sentences by logic and set theory. The most modest of generalizations about observable traits will cover more cases than its utterer can have had occasion actually to observe. The hopelessness of grounding natural science upon immediate experience in a firmly logical way was acknowledged. The Cartesian quest for certainty had been the remote motivation of epistemology, both on its conceptual and its doctrinal side; but that quest was seen as a lost cause. To endow the truths of nature with the full authority of immediate experience was as forlorn a hope as hoping to endow the truths of mathematics with the potential obviousness of elementary logic.

What then could have motivated Carnap's heroic efforts on the conceptual side of epistemology, when hope of certainty on the doctrinal side was abandoned? There were two good reasons still. One was that such constructions could be expected to elicit and clarify the sensory evidence for science, even if the inferential steps between sensory evidence and scientific doctrine must fall short of certainty. The other reason was that such constructions would deepen our understanding of our discourse about the world, even apart from questions of evidence; it would make all cognitive discourse as clear as observation terms and logic and, I must regretfully add, set theory.

It was sad for epistemologists, Hume and others, to have to acquiesce in the impossibility of strictly deriving the science of the external world from sensory evidence. Two cardinal tenets of empiricism remained unassailable, however, and so remain to this day. One is that whatever evidence there *is* for science *is* sensory evidence. The other, to which I shall recur, is that all inculcation of meanings of words must rest ultimately on sensory evidence. Hence the continuing attractiveness of the idea of a *logischer Aufbau* in which the sensory content of discourse would stand forth explicitly.

If Carnap had successfully carried such a construction through, how could he have told whether it was the right one? The question would have had no point. He was seeking what he called a *rational reconstruction*. Any construction of physicalistic discourse in terms of sense experience, logic, and set theory would have been seen as satisfactory if it made the physicalistic discourse come out right. If there is one way there are many, but any would be a great achievement.

But why all this creative reconstruction, all this make-believe? The stimulation of his sensory receptors is all the evidence anybody has had to go on, ultimately, in arriving at his picture of the world. Why not just see how this construction really proceeds? Why not settle for psychology? Such a surrender of the epistemological burden to psychology is a move that was disallowed in earlier times as circular reasoning. If the epistemologists's goal is validation of the grounds of empirical science, he defeats his purpose by using psychology or other empirical science in the validation. However, such scruples against circularity have little point once we have stopped dreaming of deducing science from observations. If we are out simply to understand the link between observation and science, we are well advised to use any available information, including that provided by the very science whose link with observation we are seeking to understand.

But there remains a different reason, unconnected with fears of circularity, for still favoring creative reconstruction. We should like to be able to *translate* science into logic and observation terms and set theory. This would be a great epistemological achievement, for it would show all the rest of the concepts of science to be theoretically superfluous. It would legitimize them—to whatever degree the concepts of set theory, logic, and observation are themselves legitimate—by showing that everything done with the one apparatus could in principle be done with the other. If psychology itself could deliver a truly translational reduction of this kind, we should welcome it; but certainly it cannot, for certainly we did not grow up learning definitions of physicalistic language in terms of a prior language of set theory, logic, and observation. Here, then, would be good reason for persisting in a rational reconstruction: we want to establish the essential innocence of physical concepts, by showing them to be theoretically dispensable.

The fact is, though, that the construction which Carnap outlined in *Der logische Aufbau der Welt* does not give translational reduction either. It would not even if the outline were filled in. The crucial point comes where Carnap is explaining how to assign sense qualities to positions in physical space and time. These assignments are to be made in such a way as to fulfill, as well as possible, certain desiderata which he states, and with growth of experience the assignments are to be revised to suit. This plan, however illuminating, does not offer any key to *translating* the sentences of science into terms of observation, logic, and set theory.

We must despair of any such reduction. Carnap had despaired of it by 1936, when, in "Testability and meaning,"[2] he introduced so-called *reduction forms* of a type weaker than definition. Definitions had shown always how to translate sentences into equivalent sentences. Contextual definition of a term showed how to translate sentences containing the term into equivalent sentences lacking the term. Reduction forms of Carnap's liberalized kind, on the other hand, do not in general give equivalences; they give implications. They explain a new term, if only partially, by specifying some sentences which are implied by sentences containing the term, and other sentences which imply sentences containing the term.

It is tempting to suppose that the countenancing of reduction forms in this liberal sense is just one further step of liberalization comparable to the earlier one, taken by Bentham, of countenancing contextual definition. The former and sterner kind of rational reconstruction might have been represented as a fictitious history in which we imagined our ancestors introducing the terms of physicalistic discourse on a phenomenalistic and set-theoretic basis by a succession of contextual definitions. The new and more liberal kind of rational reconstruction is a fictitious history in which we imagine our ancestors introducing those terms by a succession rather of reduction forms of the weaker sort.

This, however, is a wrong comparison. The fact is rather that the former and sterner kind of rational reconstruction, where definition reigned, embodied no fictitious history at all. It was nothing more nor less than a set of directions—or would have been, if successful—for accomplishing everything in terms of phenomena and set theory that we now accomplish in terms of bodies. It would have been a true reduction by translation, a legitimation by elimination. *Definire est eliminare*. Rational reconstruction by Carnap's later and looser reduction forms does none of this.

To relax the demand for definition, and settle for a kind of reduction that does not eliminate, is to renounce the last remaining advantage that we supposed rational reconstruction to have over straight psychology; namely, the advantage of translational reduction. If all we hope for is a reconstruction that links science to experience in explicit ways short of translation, then it would seem more sensible to settle for psychology. Better to discover how science is in fact developed and learned than to fabricate a fictitious structure to a similar effect.

The empiricist made one major concession when he despaired of deducing the truths of nature from sensory evidence. In despairing now even of translating those truths into terms of observation and logico-mathematical auxiliaries, he makes another major concession. For suppose we hold, with the old empiricist Peirce, that the very meaning of a statement consists in the difference its truth would make to possible experience. Might we not formulate, in a chapter-length sentence in observational language, all the difference that the truth of a given statement might make to experience, and might we not then take all this as the translation? Even if the difference that the truth of the statement would make to experience ramifies indefinitely, we might still hope to embrace it all in the logical implications of our chapter-length formulation, just as we can axiomatize an infinity of theorems. In giving up hope of such translation, then, the empiricist is conceding that the empirical meanings of typical statements about the external world are inaccessible and ineffable.

How is this inaccessibility to be explained? Simply on the ground that the experiential implications of a typical statement about bodies are too complex for finite axiomatization, however lengthy? No; I have a different explanation. It is that the typical statement about bodies has no fund of experiential implications it can call its own. A substantial mass of theory, taken together, will commonly have experiential implications; this is how we make verifiable predictions. We may not be able to explain why we arrive at theories which make successful predictions, but we do arrive at such theories.

Sometimes also an experience implied by a theory fails to come off; and then, ideally, we declare the theory false. But the failure falsifies only a block of theory as a whole, a conjunction of many statements. The failure shows that one or more of those statements is false, but it does not show which. The predicted experiences, true and false, are not implied by any one of the component statements of the theory rather than another. The component statements simply do not have empirical meanings, by Peirce's standard; but a sufficiently inclusive portion of theory does. If we can aspire to a sort of *logischer Aufbau der Welt* at all, it must be to one in which the texts slated for translation into observational and logico-mathematical terms are mostly broad theories taken as wholes, rather than just terms or short sentences. The translation of a theory would be a ponderous axiomatization of all the experiential difference that the truth of the theory would make. It would be a queer translation, for it would translate the whole but none of the parts. We might better speak in such a case not of translation but simply of observational evidence for theories; and we may, following Peirce, still fairly call this the empirical meaning of the theories.

These considerations raise a philosophical question even about ordinary unphilosophical translation, such as from English into Arunta or Chinese. For, if the English sentences of a theory have their meaning only together as a body, then we can justify their translation into Arunta only together as a body. There will be no justification for pairing off the component English sentences with component Arunta sentences, except as these correlations make the translation of the theory as a whole come out right. Any translations of the English sentences into Arunta sentences will be as correct as any other, so long as the net empirical implications of the theory as a whole are preserved in translation. But it is to be expected that many different ways of translating the component sentences, essentially different individually, would deliver the same empirical implications for the theory as a whole; deviations in the translation of one component sentence could be compensated for in the translation of another component sentence. Insofar, there can be no ground for saying which of two glaringly unlike translations of individual sentences is right.

For an uncritical mentalist, no such indeterminacy threatens. Every term and every sentence is a label attached to an idea, simple or complex, which is stored in the mind. When on the other hand we take a verification theory of meaning seriously, the indeterminacy would appear to be inescapable. The Vienna Circle espoused a verification theory of meaning but did not take it seriously enough. If we recognize with Peirce that the meaning of a sentence turns purely on what would count as evidence for its truth, and if we recognize with Duhem that theoretical sentences have their evidence not as single sentences but only as larger blocks of theory, then the indeterminacy of translation of theoretical sentences is the natural conclusion. And most sentences, apart from observation sentences, are theoretical. This conclusion, conversely, once it is embraced, seals the fate of any general notion of propositional meaning or, for that matter, state of affairs.

Should the unwelcomeness of the conclusion persuade us to abandon the verification theory of meaning? Certainly not. The sort of meaning that is basic to translation, and to the learning of one's own language, is necessarily empirical meaning and nothing more. A child learns his first words and sentences by hearing and using them in the presence of appropriate stimuli. These must be external stimuli, for they must act both on the child and on the speaker from whom he is learning. Language is socially inculcated and controlled; the inculcation and control turn strictly on the keying of sentences to shared stimulation. Internal factors may vary *ad libitum* without prejudice to communication as long as the keying of language to external stimuli is undisturbed. Surely one has no choice but to be an empiricist so far as one's theory of linguistic meaning is concerned.

What I have said of infant learning applies equally to the linguist's learning of a new language in the field. If the linguist does not lean on related languages for which there are previously accepted translation practices, then obviously he has no data but the concomitances of native utterance and observable stimulus situation. No wonder there is indeterminacy of translation—for of course only a small fraction of our utterances report concurrent external stimulation. Granted, the linguist will end up with unequivocal translations of everything; but only by making many arbitrary choices—arbitrary even though unconscious—along the way. Arbitrary? By this I mean that different choices could still have made everything come out right that is susceptible in principle to any kind of check.

Let me link up, in a different order, some of the points I have made. The crucial consideration behind my argument for the indeterminacy of translation was that a statement about the world does not always or usually have a separable fund of empirical consequences that it can call its own. That consideration served also to account for the impossibility of an epistemological reduction of the sort where every sentence is equated to a sentence in observational and logico-mathematical terms. And the impossibility of that sort of epistemological reduction dissipated the last advantage that rational reconstruction seemed to have over psychology.

Philosophers have rightly despaired of translating everything into observational and logico-mathematical terms. They have despaired of this even when they have not recognized, as the reason for this irreducibility, that the statements largely do not have their private bundles of empirical consequences. And some philosophers have seen in this irreducibility the bankruptcy of epistemology. Carnap and the other logical positivists of the Vienna Circle had already pressed the term "metaphysics" into pejorative use, as connoting meaninglessness; and the term "epistemology" was next. Wittgenstein and his followers, mainly at Oxford, found a residual philosophical vocation in therapy: in curing philosophers of the delusion that there were epistemological problems.

But I think that at this point it may be more useful to say rather that epistemology still goes on, though in a new setting and a clarified status. Epistemology, or something like it, simply falls into place as a chapter of psychology and hence of natural science. It studies a natural phenomenon, viz., a physical human subject. This human subject is accorded a certain experimentally controlled input—certain patterns of irradiation in assorted frequencies, for instance—and in the fullness of time the subject delivers as output a description of the three-dimensional external world and its history. The relation between the meager input and the torrential output is a relation that we are prompted to study for somewhat the same reasons that always prompted epistemology; namely, in order to see how evidence relates to theory, and in what ways one's theory of nature transcends any available evidence.

Such a study could still include, even, something like the old rational reconstruction, to whatever degree such reconstruction is practicable; for imaginative constructions can afford hints of actual psychological processes, in much the way that mechanical simulations can. But a conspicuous difference between old epistemology and the epistemological enterprise in this new psychological setting is that we can now make free use of empirical psychology.

The old epistemology aspired to contain, in a sense, natural science; it would construct it somehow from sense data. Epistemology in its new setting, conversely, is contained in natural science, as a chapter of psychology. But the old containment remains valid, too, in its way. We are studying how the human subject of our study posits bodies and projects his physics from his data, and we appreciate that our position in the world is just like his. Our very epistemological enterprise, therefore, and the psychology wherein it is a component chapter, and the whole of natural science wherein psychology is a component book—all this is our own construction or projection from stimulations like those we were meting out to our epistemological subject. There is thus reciprocal containment, though containment in different senses: epistemology in natural science and natural science in epistemology.

This interplay is reminiscent again of the old threat of circularity, but it is all right now that we have stopped dreaming of deducing science from sense data. We are after an understanding of science as an institution or process in the world, and we do not intend that understanding to be any better than the science which is its object. This attitude is indeed one that Neurath was already urging in Vienna Circle days, with his parable of the mariner who has to rebuild his boat while staying afloat in it.

One effect of seeing epistemology in a psychological setting is that it resolves a stubborn old enigma of epistemological priority. Our retinas are irradiated in two dimensions, yet we see things as three-dimensional without conscious inference. Which is to count as observation—the unconscious two-dimensional reception or the conscious three-dimensional apprehension? In the old epistemological context the conscious form had priority, for we were out to justify our knowledge of the external world by rational reconstruction, and that demands awareness. Awareness ceased to be demanded when we gave up trying to justify our knowledge of the external world by rational reconstruction. What to count as observation now can be settled in terms of the stimulation of sensory receptors, let consciousness fall where it may.

The Gestalt psychologists' challenge to sensory atomism, which seemed so relevant to epistemology forty years ago, is likewise deactivated. Regardless of whether sensory atoms or Gestalten are what favor the forefront of our consciousness, it is simply the stimulations of our sensory receptors that are best looked upon as the input to our cognitive mechanism. Old paradoxes about unconscious data and inference, old problems about chains of inference that would have to be completed too quickly—these no longer matter.

In the old anti-psychologistic days the question of epistemological priority was moot. What is epistemologically prior to what? Are Gestalten prior to sensory atoms because they are noticed, or should we favor sensory atoms on some more subtle ground? Now that we are permitted to appeal to physical stimulation, the problem dissolves; A is epistemologically prior to B if A is causally nearer than B to the sensory receptors. Or, what is in some ways better, just talk explicitly in terms of causal proximity to sensory receptors and drop the talk of epistemological priority.

Around 1932 there was debate in the Vienna Circle over what to count as observation sentences, or *Protokollsätze*.[3] One position was that they had the form of reports of sense impressions. Another was that they were statements of an elementary sort about the external world, e.g., "A red cube is standing on the table." Another, Neurath's, was that they had the form of reports of relations between percipients and external things: "Otto now sees a red cube on the table." The worst of it was that there seemed to be no objective way of settling the matter: no way of making real sense of the question.

Let us now try to view the matter unreservedly in the context of the external world. Vaguely speaking, what we want of observation sentences is that they be the ones in closest causal proximity to the sensory receptors. But how is such proximity to be gauged? The idea may be rephrased this way: observation sentences are sentences which, as we learn language, are most strongly conditioned to concurrent sensory stimulation rather than to stored collateral information. Thus let us imagine a sentence queried for our verdict as to whether it is true or false; queried for our assent or dissent. Then the sentence is an observation sentence if our verdict depends only on the sensory stimulation present at the time.

But a verdict cannot depend on present stimulation to the exclusion of stored information. The very fact of our having learned the language evinces much storing of information, and of information without which we should be in no position to give verdicts on sentences however observational. Evidently then we must relax our definition of observation sentence to read thus: a sentence is an observation sentence if all verdicts on it depend on present sensory stimulation and on no stored information beyond what goes into understanding the sentence.

This formulation raises another problem: how are we to distinguish between information that goes into understanding a sentence and information that goes beyond? This is the problem of distinguishing between analytic truth, which issues from the mere meanings of words, and synthetic truth, which depends on more than meanings. Now I have long maintained that this distinction is illusory. There is one step toward such a distinction, however, which does make sense: a sentence that is true by mere meanings of words should be expected, at least if it is simple, to be subscribed to by all fluent speakers in the community. Perhaps the controversial notion of analyticity can be dispensed with, in our definition of observation sentence, in favor of this straightforward attribute of community-wide acceptance.

This attribute is of course no explication of analyticity. The community would agree that there have been black dogs, yet none who talk of analyticity would call this analytic. My rejection of the analyticity notion just means drawing no line between what goes into the mere understanding of the sentences of a language and what else the community sees eye-to-eye on. I doubt that an objective distinction can be made between meaning and such collateral information as is community-wide.

Turning back then to our task of defining observation sentences, we get this: an observation sentence is one on which all speakers of the language give the same verdict when given the same concurrent stimulation. To put the point negatively, an observation sentence is one that is not sensitive to differences in past experience within the speech community.

This formulation accords perfectly with the traditional role of the observation sentence as the court of appeal of scientific theories. For by our definition the observation sentences are the sentences on which all members of the community will agree under uniform stimulation. And what is the criterion of membership in the same community? Simply general fluency of dialogue. This criterion admits of degrees, and indeed we may usefully take the community more narrowly for some studies than for others. What count as observation sentences for a community of specialists would not always so count for a larger community.

There is generally no subjectivity in the phrasing of observation sentences, as we are now conceiving them; they will usually be about bodies. Since the distinguishing trait of an observation sentence is intersubjective agreement under agreeing stimulation, a corporeal subject matter is likelier than not.

The old tendency to associate observation sentences with a subjective sensory subject matter is rather an irony when we reflect that observation sentences are also meant to be the intersubjective tribunal of scientific hypotheses. The old tendency was due to the drive to base science on something firmer and prior in the subject's experience; but we dropped that project.

The dislodging of epistemology from its old status of first philosophy loosed a wave, we saw, of epistemological nihilism. This mood is reflected somewhat in the tendency of Polányi, Kuhn, and the late Russell Hanson to belittle the role of evidence and to accentuate cultural relativism. Hanson ventured even to discredit the idea of observation, arguing that so-called observations vary from observer to observer with the amount of knowledge that the observers bring with them. The veteran physicist looks at some apparatus and sees an x-ray tube. The neophyte, looking at the same place, observes rather "a glass and metal instrument replete with wires, reflectors, screws, lamps, and pushbuttons."[4] One man's observation is another man's closed book or flight of fancy. The notion of observation as the impartial and objective sources of evidence for science is bankrupt. Now my answer to the x-ray example was already hinted a little while back: what counts as an observation sentence varies with the width of community considered. But we can also always get an absolute standard by taking in all speakers of the language, or most.[5] It is ironical that philosophers, finding the old epistemology untenable as a whole, should react by repudiating a part which has only now moved into clear focus.

Clarification of the notion of observation sentence is a good thing, for the notion is fundamental in two connections. These two correspond to the duality that I remarked upon early in this lecture: the duality between concept and doctrine, between knowing what a sentence means and knowing whether it is true. The observation sentence is basic to both enterprises. Its relation to doctrine, to our knowledge of what is true, is very much the traditional one: observation sentences are the repository of evidence for scientific hypotheses. Its relation to meaning is fundamental too, since observation sentences are the ones we are in a position to learn to understand first, both as children and as field linguists. For observation sentences are precisely the ones that we can correlate with observable circumstances of the occasion of utterance or assent, independently of variations in the past histories of individual informants. They afford the only entry to a language.

The observation sentence is the cornerstone of semantics. For it is, as we just saw, fundamental to the learning of meaning. Also, it is where meaning is firmest. Sentences higher up in theories have no empirical consequences they can call their own; they confront the tribunal of sensory evidence only in more or less inclusive aggregates. The observation sentence, situated at the sensory periphery of the body scientific, is the minimal verifiable aggregate; it has an empirical content all its own and wears it on its sleeve.

The predicament of the indeterminacy of translation has little bearing on observation sentences. The equating of an observation sentence of our language to an observation sentence of another language is mostly a matter of empirical generalization; it is a matter of identity between the range of stimulations that would prompt assent to the one sentence and the range of stimulations that would prompt assent to the other.[6]

It is no shock to the preconceptions of old Vienna to say that epistemology now becomes semantics. For epistemology remains centered as always on evidence, and meaning remains centered as always on verification; and evidence is verification. What is likelier to shock preconceptions is that meaning, once we get beyond observation sentences, ceases in general to have any clear applicability to single sentences; also that epistemology merges with psychology, as well as with linguistics.

This rubbing out of boundaries could contribute to progress, it seems to me, in philosophically interesting inquiries of a scientific nature. One possible area is perceptual norms. Consider, to begin with, the linguistic phenomenon of phonemes. We form the habit, in hearing the myriad variations of spoken sounds, of treating each as an approximation to one or another of a limited number of norms—around thirty altogether—constituting so to speak a spoken alphabet. All speech in our language can be treated in practice as sequences of just those thirty elements, thus rectifying small deviations. Now outside the realm of language also there is probably only a rather limited alphabet of perceptual norms altogether, toward which we tend unconsciously to rectify all perceptions. These, if experimentally identified, could be taken as epistemological building blocks, the working elements of experience. They might prove in part to be culturally variable, as phonemes are, and in part universal.

Again there is the area that the psychologist Donald T. Campbell calls evolutionary epistemology.[7] In this area there is work by Hüseyin Yilmaz, who shows how some structural traits of color perception could have been predicted from survival value.[8] And a more emphatically epistemological topic that evolution helps to clarify is induction, now that we are allowing epistemology the resources of natural science.

NOTES

[1]   A. B. Johnson, *A Treatise on Language* (New York, 1836; Berkeley, 1947).

[2]   *Philosophy of Science* 3 (1936), 419–471; 4 (1937), 1–40.

[3]   Carnap and Neurath in *Erkenntnis* 3 (1932), 204–228.

[4]   N. R. Hanson, "Observation and interpretation," in S. Morgenbesser, ed., *Philosophy of Science Today* (New York: Basic Books, 1966).

[5]   This qualification allows for occasional deviants such as the insane or the blind. Alternatively, such cases might be excluded by adjusting the level of fluency of dialogue whereby we define sameness of language. (For prompting this note and influencing the development of this paper also in more substantial ways I am indebted to Burton Dreben.)

[6]   Cf. Quine, *Word and Object*, pp. 31–46, 68.

[7]   D. T. Campbell, "Methodological suggestions from a comparative psychology of knowledge processes," *Inquiry* 2 (1959), 152–182.

[8]   Hüseyin Yilmaz, "On color vision and a new approach to general perception," in E. E. Bernard and M. R. Kare, eds., *Biological Prototypes and Synthetic Systems* (New York: Plenum, 1962); "Perceptual invariance and the psychophysical law," *Perception and Psychophysics* 2 (1967), 533–538.

3.2

ON NATURALIZING EPISTEMOLOGY

Robert Almeder

I. Introduction

There are three distinct forms of naturalized epistemology. The first form asserts that the only legitimate questions about the nature of human knowledge are those we can answer in natural science. So described, naturalized epistemology is a branch of natural science wherein the questions asked about the nature of human knowledge make sense only because they admit of resolution under the methods of such natural sciences as biology and psychology. Characterized in this way, naturalised epistemology consists in empirically describing and scientifically explaining how our various beliefs originate, endure, deteriorate or grow. Unlike traditional epistemology, this form of naturalized epistemology does not seek to determine whether the claims of natural science are more or less justified. For this reason, it is not "normative" in the way traditional epistemology is normative. Not surprisingly, this first form of naturalized epistemology regards traditional "philosophical" questions about human knowledge, questions whose formulation and solution do not emerge solely from the practice of natural science, as pointless. Accordingly, this first form of naturalized epistemology seeks to *replace* traditional epistemology with the thesis that while we certainly have scientific knowledge, and whatever norms are appropriate for the successful conduct of natural science, we have no philosophical theory of knowledge sitting in judgment over the claims of natural science to determine whether they live up to a philosophically congenial analysis of justification or knowledge. As we shall see shortly, the classical defense of this first form of naturalized epistemology appears in Quine's *Naturalized Epistemology*.[1]

The second form of naturalized epistemology seeks less to *replace* traditional epistemology than it does to *transform* and supplement it by connecting it with the methods and insights of psychology, biology and cognitive science. In *Epistemology and Cognition*, for example, Alvin Goldman has argued for this second form which allows for traditionally normative elements but is "naturalized" for the reason that the practitioners of natural science, especially biology and psychology, will have the last word on whether anybody knows what they claim to know. For Goldman, although defining human knowledge and other epistemic concepts is legitimately philosophical and traditionally normative, whether anybody knows what they claim to know, and just what cognitive processes are involved, is ultimately a matter we must consign to psychologists or cognitive scientists. Unlike the first form of naturalized epistemology, this second form allows traditional epistemology to sit in judgment on the claims of natural science but the judgment must be made by the practitioners of natural science using the methods of natural science.

The third distinct form of naturalized epistemology simply insists that the method of the natural sciences is the only method for acquiring a proper understanding of the nature of the physical universe. On this view, natural science, and all that it implies, is the most epistemically privileged activity for understanding the nature of the physical world. Adopting this last form of naturalized epistemology is, however, quite consistent with rejecting both of the above forms of naturalized epistemology. This third form is quite compatible with traditional epistemology because it does not seek to *replace* traditional epistemology in the way that the Quine thesis does; nor does it seek to *transform* traditional epistemology by turning the question of who knows what over to psychologists and cognitive scientists in the way that the Goldman thesis does.

At any rate, the most currently pervasive and challenging form of naturalized epistemology is the radically anti-traditional, anti-philosophical thesis offered originally by Quine and recently defended by others. So, in the next few pages we shall focus *solely* on the Quinean thesis and five distinct arguments recently offered in defense of it. Along the way, we will discuss various objections to such a naturalized epistemology, objections proponents of the thesis have recently confronted. Unfortunately, because space is here limited, we will not examine the second and distinct form of naturalized epistemology offered by Alvin Goldman. To do so would involve a long discussion of the merits of the reliabilist theory of justification upon which Goldman's type of naturalism squarely rests.[2]

Finally, the modest conclusion of this paper is that there is no sound argument available for the Quinean form of naturalized epistemology. The immodest conclusion is that any argument proposed for the thesis will be incoherent, and that consequently there is no rational justification for anybody taking such a naturalistic turn.

II. Quine's Argument

In "Epistemology Naturalized," Quine begins his defense of naturalized epistemology by asserting that traditional epistemology is concerned with the foundations of science, broadly conceived. As such, it is supposed to show how the foundations of knowledge, whether it be the foundations of mathematics or natural science, reduce to certainty. In short, showing how certainty obtains is the core of traditional epistemology, and this implies that the primary purpose of traditional epistemology is to refute the Cartesian sceptic whose philosophical doubts over whether we can attain certainty has set the program for traditional epistemology.

But, for Quine, traditional epistemology has failed to refute the sceptic, and will never succeed in refuting the sceptic. Mathematics reduces only to set theory and not to logic; and even though this reduction enhances clarity it does nothing by way of establishing certainty because the axioms of set theory have less to recommend them by way of certainty than do most of the mathematical theorems we would derive from them. As he says:

> Reduction is the foundations of mathematics remains mathematically and philosophically fascinating, but it does not do what the epistemologist would like of it: it does not reveal the ground of mathematical knowledge, it does not show how mathematical certainty is possible. (p.71).

Moreover, mathematics aside, the attempt to reduce natural knowledge to a foundation in the certainty of statements of sense experience has also failed miserably. Common sense about sensory impressions provides no certainty. And, when it comes to justifying our knowledge about truths of nature, Hume taught us that general statements and singular statements about the future do not admit of justification by way of allowing us to ascribe certainty to our beliefs associated with such statements. For Quine, the problem of induction is still with us; "The Humean predicament is the human predicament." (p. 72). As Quine sees it, Hume showed us quite clearly that any attempt to refute the sceptic by uncovering some foundation of certainty associated with sense statements, whether about sense impressions or physical objects, is doomed equally to failure. (p.72)

This last consideration is crucial because as soon as we accept Quine's rejection of the analytic/synthetic distinction in favor of only synthetic propositions, Hume's argument casts a long despairing shadow over our ever being able to answer the sceptic because such propositions could never be certain anyway. The conclusion Quine draws from all this is that traditional epistemology is dead. There is no "first philosophy." There are no strictly philosophical truths validating the methods of the natural sciences. Nor can we validate in any non-circular way the methods of the natural sciences by appeal to psychology or the methods of the natural sciences. As he says, "If the epistemologist's goal is validation of the grounds of empirical science, he defeats his purpose by using psychology or other empirical science in the validation." (pp. 75–76). We may well have justified beliefs based upon induction, but we cannot have any justified belief that we can have justified beliefs based upon induction. Accordingly, if epistemology is to have any content whatever, it will seek to explain, *via* the methods of natural science, the origin and growth of beliefs we take to be human knowledge and natural science. Construed in this way, epistemology continues as a branch of natural science wherein the only meaningful questions are questions answerable in science by scientists using the methods of natural science. This reconstrual of the nature of epistemology consigns the enterprise to a descriptive psychology whose main function is to describe the origin of our beliefs and the conditions under which we take them to be justified. On this view, all questions and all doubts are scientific and can only be answered or resolved in science by the methods of science. Philosophical discussions on the nature and limits of scientific knowledge, questions that do not lend themselves to resolution via the methods of natural science are simply a part of traditional philosophy that cannot succeed. What can we say about all this?

III. Response to Quine's Argument

In "The Significance of Naturalized Epistemology," Barry Stroud criticizes Quine's defense of naturalized epistemology.[3] After a brief description of Quine's position, Stroud argues that Quine is inconsistent for arguing *both* that there is no appeal to scientific knowledge that could non-circularly establish the legitimacy of scientific knowledge in the presence of the traditional epistemological sceptic, *and* in *Roots of Reference* that we should take seriously the project of validating our knowledge of the external world.[4] For Stroud, it was in *Roots of Reference* that Quine came to believe in the coherent use of the resources of natural science to validate the deliverances of natural science. But that would be to countenance the basic question of traditional epistemology when in fact the thrust of Quine's thesis on naturalized epistemology is that such a question forms part of "first philosophy" which is impossible. Apart from such an inconsistency, Stroud also argues that Quine's attempt to validate scientific inference fails. (p. 81) Stroud's thesis here is that Quine attempts to offer a naturalized defense of science in "The Nature of Natural Knowledge,"[5] but the effort fails because, on Quine's reasoning, we can see how others acquire their beliefs but we are denied thereby any evidence of whether such beliefs are correct beliefs about the world. By implication, we have no reason for thinking our own beliefs are any better off. (p. 81) In commenting on Quine's defense, Stroud says:

> Therefore, if we follow Quine's instructions and try to see our own position as "just like" the position we can find another "positing" or "projecting" subject to be in, we will have to view ourselves as we view another subject when we can know nothing more than what is happening at his sensory surfaces and what he believes or is disposed to assert. (p. 81)

His point here is that when we examine how another's beliefs originate, we have no way to look beyond his positing to determine whether his beliefs are true or correct. In that position we never can understand how the subject's knowledge or even true belief is possible. Therefore, we never can understand how our own true beliefs are possible either. Stroud says:

> The possibility that our own view of the world is a *mere* projection is what had to be shown not to obtain in order to explain how our knowledge is possible. Unless that challenge has been met, or rejected, we will never understand how our knowledge is possible at all. (p. 83)

> ...if Quine's naturalized epistemology is taken as an answer to the philosophical question of our knowledge of the external world, then I think that for the reasons I have given, no satisfactory explanation is either forthcoming or possible. (p. 83)

He goes on to conclude that if naturalized epistemology is *not* taken as an answer to the philosophical question of our knowledge of the external world, and if the question is a legitimate question (and Quine has not shown that it is not) then naturalized epistemology cannot answer the question:

> I conclude that even if Quine is right in saying that sceptical doubts are scientific doubts, the scientific source of these doubts has no anti-sceptical force in itself. Nor does it establish the relevance and legitimacy of a scientific epistemology as an answer to the traditional epistemological question. If Quine is confident that a naturalized epistemology can answer the traditional question about knowledge, he must have some other reason for that confidence. He believes that sceptical doubts are scientific doubts and he believes that in resolving those doubts we may make free use of all the scientific knowledge we possess. But if, as he allows, it is possible for the skeptic to argue by *reductio* that science is not known, then it cannot be that the second of those beliefs (that a naturalized epistemology is all we need) follows from the first.

> Until the traditional philosophical question has been exposed as in some way illegitimate or incoherent, there will always appear to be an intelligible question about human knowledge in general which, as I have argued, a naturalised epistemology cannot answer. And Quine himself seems committed at least to the coherence of that traditional question by his very conception of knowledge. (pp. 85–86)

Stroud's closing remark is that the traditional question has not been demonstrated as illegitimate, and Quine's attempt to resolve skeptical doubts as scientific doubts within science has failed. Moreover, for Stroud, apart from the question of whether Quine succeeded, his effort is predicated on the legitimacy of the traditional question of whether science provides us with knowledge of the external world.

Some naturalized epistemologists will probably disagree with Stroud's analysis and urge that Quine's attempt to validate scientific knowledge is misunderstood when construed as an attempt to establish first philosophy. Better by far that we read Quine as asserting that there is simply no way to validate the deliverances of science as more or less warranted. Whether this last response is adequate, we cannot now discuss.

At any rate, Quine has responded to Stroud with the following remarks:

> What then does our overall scientific theory really claim regarding the world? Only that it is somehow structured as to assure the sequences of stimulation that our theory gives us to expect....

In what way then do I see the Humean predicament as persisting? Only in the fallibility of prediction: the fallibility of induction and the hypothetico-deductive method in anticipating experience.

I have depicted a barren scene. The furniture of our world, the people and sticks and stones along with the electrons and molecules, have dwindled to manners of speaking. And other purported objects would serve as well, and may as well be said already to be doing so.

So it would seem. Yet people, sticks, stones, electrons and molecules are real indeed, on my view, and it is these and no dim proxies that science is all about. Now, how is such robust realism to be reconciled with what we have just been through? The answer is naturalism: the recognition that it is within science itself, and not in some prior philosophy, that reality is properly to be identified and described.[6]

In reflecting on this response to Stroud, Ernest Sosa has been quick to note the incoherence involved in accepting science as the "reality-claims court coupled with the denial that it is anything but free and arbitrary creation."[7] Continuing his criticism of Quine, Sosa goes on to say:

The incoherence is not removed, moreover, if one now adds:

(Q1) What then does our overall scientific theory really claim regarding the world? Only that it is somehow so structured as to assure the sequence of stimulation that our theory gives us to expect.

(Q2) Yet people, sticks, stones, electrons and molecules are real indeed.

(Q3) [It]...is within science itself and not in some prior philosophy, that reality is properly to be identified and described.

If it is within science that we settle, to the extent possible for us, the contours of reality; and if science really claims regarding the world only that it is so structured as to assure certain sequences of stimulation; then how can we possibly think reality to assume the contours of people, sticks, stones and so on?

We cannot have it all three ways: (Q1), (Q2) and (Q3) form an incoherent triad. If we trust science as the measure of reality, and if we think there really are sticks and stones, then we can't have science accept only a world "somehow so structured as to assure" certain sequences of stimulations or the like. Our science must also claim that there really are sticks and stones.

What is more, if science really is the measure of reality it cannot undercut itself by saying that it really isn't, that it is only convenient "manners of speaking" to guide us reliably from stimulation to stimulation. (p. 69)

Sosa's criticism seems quite pointed. Moreover, even if the critique offered by both Stroud and Sosa should turn out to be a misconstrual of Quine's position, there are other plausible objections we might raise to Quine's argument for naturalized epistemology. For one thing, it is obvious that Quine's argument itself for naturalized epistemology is a philosophical argument, which, *ex hypothesi*, should not count by way of providing evidence for the thesis of naturalized epistemology. Further, the thesis of naturalized epistemology is arguably fundamentally incoherent. It argues against there being a "first philosophy" by appealing to two premises both of which are sound only if philosophical arguments about the limits of human knowledge are permissible and sound. The first premise consists in asserting that Hume's skepticism about factual knowledge is indeed established. Hume's thesis is certainly not empirically confirmable. The so-called "problem of induction" is a philosophical problem based upon a certain philosophical view about what is necessary for scientific knowledge. It is certainly not a problem in natural science or naturalised epistemology. The second premise is the denial of the analytic/synthetic distinction; and that is a thesis largely resting on a philosophical argument about the nature of meaning. Such premises only make sense within a commitment to the validity of some form of first philosophy and the legitimacy of traditional epistemology. Finally, there is the problematic premise that traditional epistemology has been exclusively concerned to establish the foundations of certainty in order to show that we have knowledge of the world. A close look at traditional epistemology, however, suggests that the primary concern is as much a matter of getting clear on, or (as Sosa has noted) understanding just what it *means* to know, and just what the concept of certainty relative to different senses of "knows" consists in, as it is a matter of validating knowledge claims or seeking the foundations of certainty (p. 50–51). Indeed, there is good reason to think that the primary concern of traditional epistemology is one of *defining* concepts of knowledge, certainty, justification and truth; and only then of determining whether anybody has the sort of certainty associated with the correct definition of knowledge. The history of epistemology is as apt to criticize the program of the Cartesian sceptic (and the definition of knowledge implied therein) as it is to accept it. Certainly, if the concept of knowledge and justification had been defined differently than Hume had defined them, Hume's predicament would never have occurred. Traditional epistemology is probably as concerned with what it means for a belief to be certain, as it is with determining whether scientific knowledge is certain. With these few considerations in mind, and realizing that much more can be said on the issue, it would appear that Quine's defense of naturalized epistemology admits of a number of solid objections. Let us turn to a more recent and quite distinct defense of the Quinean thesis.

IV. The "Philosophy is Science" Argument

Among recent arguments for the Quine thesis, the argument offered by William Lycan in *Judgement and Justification* is quite different from Quine's.[8] Unlike the Quinean argument, it does not rest on the alleged failure of the analytic/synthetic distinction and upon the subsequent classification of all propositions as synthetic. Nor does it feed upon Quine's Humean argument that synthetic propositions cannot be justified from the viewpoint of a first philosophy and so, if epistemology is to continue, it can only be in terms of the deliverances of a descriptive psychology. What is the argument?

Lycan begins by characterising classical philosophy in terms of the deductivist model. He calls it "deductivism" and under this model philosophy gets characterised in a certain way:

> Philosophers arrive at conclusions that are guaranteed to be as indisputably true as the original premises once the ingenious deductive arguments have been hit upon. This attitude has pervaded the rationalist tradition and survives among those who are commonly called "analytic philosophers" in a correctly narrow sense of that expression. Of course the quality of self-evidence that the deductivist premises are supposed to have and to transmit to his conclusion has been variously described (as for example, analyticity, a prioricity, clarity and distinctness, mere obviousness, or just the property of having been agreed upon by all concerned.)....

> In any case, the deductivist holds that philosophy and science differ in that deductive argument from self-evident premises pervades the former but not the latter. (Some deductivists have held a particularly strong version of this view, identifying the philosophy/science distinction with the a priori/empirical

distinction.) Now Quine (1960, 1963, 1970) has a rather special reason for rejecting the dichotomy between philosophy and science, or, to put the point more accurately, between philosophical method and scientific method. He rejects the analytic-synthetic distinction, and thus the proposal that there are two kinds of truths ("conceptual" or "a priori," and "empirical" or scientific.), one of which is the province of philosophy and the other the province of science....

I side with Smart and Quine against the deductivist, but for what I think is a more fundamental and compelling reason, one that does not depend on the rejection of the analytic/synthetic distinction. If my argument is sound, then one can countenance that distinction and still be forced to the conclusion that the Smart/Quine methodological view is correct.

Suppose we try to take a strict deductivist stance. Now, as is common knowledge, one cannot be committed (by an argument) to the conclusion of that argument unless one accepts the premises. Upon being presented with a valid argument, I always have the option of denying its conclusion, so long as I am prepared to accept the denial of at least one of the premises.

Thus, every deductive argument can be set up as an inconsistent set. (Let us, for simplicity, consider only arguments whose premises are internally consistent.) Given an argument P, Q ∴ R the cognitive cash value of which is that R follows deductively from the set of P and Q, we can exhaustively convey its content simply by asserting that the set (P, Q, not-R) is inconsistent, and all the original argument has told us, in fact, is that for purely logical reasons we must deny either P, Q, or not-R. The proponent of the original argument, of course, holds that P and Q are true; therefore, she says, we are committed to the denial of not-R, that is, to R. But how does she know that P and Q are true? Perhaps she has constructed deductive arguments with P and Q as conclusions. But, if we are to avoid regress, we must admit that she relies ultimately on putative knowledge gained nondeductively; so let us suppose that she has provided nondeductive arguments for P and Q. On what grounds then does she accept them? The only answer that can be given is that she finds each of P and Q more plausible than not-R, just as Moore found the statement "I had breakfast before I had lunch" more plausible than any of the metaphysical premises on which rested the fashionable arguments against the reality of time.

But these are just the sorts of considerations to which the theoretical scientist appeals. If what I have said here is (more or less) right, then we appear to have vindicated some version of the view that (1) philosophy, except for that relatively trivial part of it that consists in making sure that controversial arguments are formally valid, is just very high level science and that consequently (2) the proper philosophical method for acquiring interesting new knowledge cannot differ from proper scientific method. (pp. 116–118).

In defending this general argument, Lycan then responds to two basic objections which he offers against his own thesis. The first objection is that even if all philosophical arguments rest on plausibility arguments, the above argument has not established what is necessary, namely, that considerations that make for plausibility in science are the same considerations that make for plausibility in philosophy. The second objection is that even if we were to establish as much, it would not thereby obviously follow that philosophy is just very high-level science. Philosophy and science might have the same method but differ by way of subject matter. (pp. 116–118). The core of Lycan's defense of his general argument consists in responding to the first objection. So, let us see whether the response overcomes the objection.

In response to the first objection, Lycan constructs the following argument:

P1. The interesting principles of rational acceptance are not the deductive ones (even in philosophy).

P2. There are, roughly speaking, three kinds of ampliative, non-deductive principles of inference: principles of self-evidence (gnostic access, incorrigibility, a priori, clarity and distinctness, etc.), principles of what might be called "textbook induction" (enumerative induction, eliminative induction, statistical syllogism, Mill's Methods, etc.), and principles of sophisticated ampliative inference (such as PS principles and the other considerations of theoretical elegance and power mentioned earlier, which are usually construed as filling out the "best" in "inference to the best explanation").

P3. Principles of textbook induction are not the interesting principles of rational acceptance in philosophy.

P4. Principles of "self-evidence," though popular throughout the history of philosophy and hence considered interesting principles of rational acceptance, cannot be used to settle philosophical disputes.

Therefore: If there are any interesting and decisive principles of rational acceptance in philosophy, they are the elegance principles (p. 119).

Lycan adds that the elegance principles are to be extracted mainly from the history of science, and that we can obtain precise and useful statements of such principles only by looking to the history of science, philosophy, and logic in order to see exactly what considerations motivate the replacement of an old theory by a new theory. (pp. 119–120). So, the answer to the question "Why does it follow that the considerations that make for plausibility in philosophy are the same as those that make for plausibility in science?" is simply "there is nowhere else to turn" (p. 120). For a number of reasons, however, this response to the objection seems problematic.

To begin with, *P*1 is not true. It is common knowledge that one cannot be rationally justified in accepting the conclusion of an argument unless the argument is valid and consistent in addition to the premises being true. So, we cannot construe *P*1 to assert that validity and consistency are redundant or eliminable as a condition necessary for the rational acceptability of an argument. Lycan does not mean to argue that point. Rather *P*1 asserts that even though validity and consistency are necessary conditions for the soundness of an argument, validity and consistency provide no grounds for thinking that the conclusion deduced is plausible. In short, *P*1 asserts that it is not even a necessary condition for the *plausibility* of a proposed argument that it be both sound and consistent. The reasons offered for *P*1, however, seem particularly questionable and the reasons for thinking *P*1 false seem straightforwardly compelling. Let me explain.

Lycan claims that *P*1 is true because deductive rules are not controversial in their application (p. 119). But how exactly would that establish that such rules of inference are not interesting, meaning thereby not plausibility-conferring on the conclusion? Why not say instead that *because* such rules are noncontroversially applied they are interesting, that is, plausibility conferring? In other words, what does the fact that such rules are non-controversial in their application have to do with their not being plausibility-conferring on the conclusions that follow from them? Is it meant to be obvious that a deductive rule of inference is plausibility-conferring only when its application is controversial? Why should anyone accept such a definition of plausibility, especially because it seems to endorse saying such things as "Your argument is perfectly plausible even though it is both invalid and inconsistent." Why aren't deductive rules interesting (or plausibility-conferring) because they are more likely to guarantee truth from premises that are true? If "interest" is relative to purpose and, if one's purpose is to provide a system of inferential rules that is strongly truth-preserving, then such rules are quite interesting, even if their application is non-controversial. This in itself is sufficient to show *P*1 is involved in a questionable bit of semantic legislation.

Moreover, Lycan's second reason for *P*1 is that any deductive argument can be made valid in a perfectly trivial way by the addition of some inference-licensing premise (p. 119). But how exactly does it follow from the fact (if it be a fact) that any deductive argument can be made trivially valid that *no* deductive principle (including consistency) is interesting in the sense of conferring plausibility in any degree on what follows from the deductive principle? Here again, is it meant to be obvious that deductive principles are plausibility-conferring only if they function in arguments incapable of being rendered valid and consistent in non-trivial ways? Does not such a claim presuppose a definition of plausibility which, by stipulation, asserts that the plausibility of a deductive conclusion has nothing to do with the fact that the argument is valid and consistent? And is that not precisely what needs to be shown? Indeed, if any deductive argument could be rendered valid and consistent in wholly trivial ways and the conclusion still be plausible, why insist, as we do, on validity and consistency for soundness as a necessary condition for rational acceptance? Why insist on rules that are truth-preserving for soundness if one can get it in trivial ways and it has nothing to do with the plausibility of the conclusion?

Lycan's third reason for *P*1 is that deductive rules are not plausibility conferring because such rules are uninteresting. They are uninteresting precisely because deductive inferences obviously do not accomplish the expansion of our total store of explicit and implicit knowledge, since they succeed only in drawing out information already implicit in the premises (p. 119). Here again, however, even if deductive inference only renders explicit what is implicitly contained in the premises that would only show that deductive inference is not inductive inference, and, unless one *assumes* that the only plausibility considerations that will count are those relevant to expanding our factual knowledge base, rather than showing that one's inferences are the product of truth-preserving rules, why would the fact that deductive inference is not inductive inference be a sufficient reason for thinking that deductive inference is uninteresting as a way of enhancing the plausibility of one's conclusions deductively inferred? The reason Lycan offers here (like the two offered above) strongly implies that the plausibility of a person's beliefs has nothing to do with whether it is internally consistent, or follows logically from well-confirmed beliefs, or is consistent with a large body of well-confirmed beliefs, or is the product of truth-preserving rules of inference; and this just flies in the face of our epistemic practices.

Lycan's last reason for *P*1 is that any deductive argument can be turned upon its head (p. 120). Once again, what needs proving is assumed. Even if we can turn a valid deductive argument on its head, so to speak, does that mean that there are no valid arguments? If the answer is yes, why say that valid deductive inference is uninteresting rather than impossible? But if we are not arguing that valid deductive inference is impossible, why exactly would such inference be uninteresting if it is truth-preserving, and would guarantee consistency, coherence with well-confirmed beliefs, and the explicit addition of true verifiable sentences not formerly in the corpus of our beliefs? If such considerations do not count as plausibility-conferring, it could only be because "plausibility" is stipulatively defined to rule out such considerations as plausibility-conferring. Such a definition needs defending rather than pleading.

By way of general observation with regard to P1, it seems clear that plausibility considerations rest quite squarely on questions of consistency and derivability. One of the traditional tests for theory confirmation (and hence by implication for plausibility) is derivability from above. For example, the fact that Balmer's formula for the emission spectra for gases derives logically from Bohr's theory on the hydrogen atom, counts strongly in favor of Balmer's formula above and beyond the evidence Balmer gave for his formula. What is that to say except that considerations purely deductive in nature function to render theories more or less plausible? What about the rest of Lycan's argument against the first objection to his general argument?

Well, suppose, for the sake of discussion that *P*2 and *P*3 are true. Will *P*4 be true? In other words, will it be true that principles of self-evidence do not count for plausibility unless they can be used to settle some philosophical disputes? Here the argument seems to be suggesting that a common-sense principle will be plausibility-conferring only if it can be used to "settle" (in the sense of everybody agreeing henceforth to the answer) some philosophical dispute. But such a requirement seems arbitrarily too strong. Obviously, a conclusion can be plausible and worthy of rational acceptance even when others will disagree to some degree. Two mutually exclusive conclusions may both be rationally plausible without the principle that renders them plausible "settling" the dispute once and for all. Moreover, are we sure that appeals to common sense principles have failed to resolve or settle philosophical disputes? In a very strong sense of "settle," of course, nothing is settled in philosophy.

But that would be to impose an arbitrarily strong sense of "settle" on philosophy, a sense we certainly would not impose on science. In a suitably weak sense, "appeals to obviousness or self-evidence" often, but not always, settles disputes. Indeed, isn't the basic reason that the question of solipsism consistently fails to capture anybody's sustained attention is that it is so implausible by way of appeal to common sense? Who these days really takes the possibility of solipsism seriously? Isn't that a philosophical problem pretty much settled by appeal to common sense or self-evidence? Of course, not all appeals to common sense are so successful, and some are more successful than others as clean "conversation stoppers."

These reasons show that Lycan's reply to the first objection fails. Further, it would have been surprising if the reply had succeeded because it seems clear that in science, but not in philosophy, a necessary condition for any explanation being even remotely plausible is that it be in principle empirically testable. As a matter of fact, if we consult practicing scientists and not philosophers, unless one's scientific explanations are ultimately testable, and we know what empirical evidence would need to occur to falsify the hypothesis, we say that the explanation is not plausible. We may even go so far as to say that it is meaningless because it is not testable. Minimally, in science a hypothesis or a theory will be plausible only if it is empirically testable, and it will be testable only if what the hypothesis virtually predicts is in principle observable under clearly specifiable conditions, and would occur as expected if we were to accept the hypothesis as worthy. On the other hand, if we are not to beg the question against philosophy as distinct from science, and look at philosophical theses, we will find that a philosophical thesis can be more or less plausible quite independently of whether the thesis is empirically confirmable or testable. As a matter of fact, consider, for example, the dispute between classical scientific realists and classical anti-realists of an instrumental sort. What empirical test might one perform to establish or refute the view that the long-term predictive success of some scientific hypotheses is a function of the truth of claims implied or assumed by the hypotheses? Surely one of these theses must be correct, and yet neither the realist nor the anti-realist position here is testable by appeal to any known experimental or non-experimental test.[9] Does that mean that while one position must be correct *neither* is plausible? Paradox aside, if we say yes, how is that anything more than assuming what needs to be proven, namely that considerations that count for plausibility in science are the same as those that count for plausibility in philosophy?

Surely, however, there are also other philosophical arguments that in fact do depend for their plausibility on the verification and falsification of certain factual claims. For example, Aristotle once argued that humans are quite different from animals because they use tools, whereas animals do not. Aristotle's argument here is implausible because readily falsified by careful observations of the sort Jane Goodall and others continually make. So, in philosophy plausibility may sometimes root in considerations of testability just because one of the premises in the argument asserts that some factual claim about the world is true or false. But, as we just showed in the case of the dispute between the scientific realist and the scientific anti-realist, plausibility may have very little or nothing to do with the empirical testability of the hypothesis. It may simply be a matter of showing the internal inconsistency of a particular argument, or the dire consequences of adopting one position over the other, or the informal (or formal) fallacies attending the argumentation of one position over the other. In short, as practiced, philosophical reasoning often requires both deductive and inductive principles of rational acceptance for plausibility. But it certainly is not a necessary condition for philosophical plausibility that one's philosophical positions be testable or explainable in a way that accommodates empirical testability as a necessary condition for significance. Moreover, it should be apparent by now that to insist that plausibility in philosophy must accommodate the canons of empirical testability or the canons of explanation in the natural sciences is simply a blatant question-begging move against the objection offered against Lycan's main argument. As such, it would be a rationally unmotivated stipulation against philosophy as distinct from natural science.

In sum, Lycan's reply to the first objection to his general argument fails unless one wants to suppose that there is nothing at all plausible about any philosophical argument primarily because philosophical arguments are not straightforwardly verifiable or falsifiable in the way that empirical claims are. Besides, it seems that the dark shadow of Quine's "Epistemology Naturalized" is having an unrealized effect on the main argument Lycan offers. This is because if one excludes philosophical arguments from the realm of the analytic or a priori, (as Quine does), it would appear that if there is anything to them at all, they must fall into the realm of the synthetic; and hence it seems only too natural to suppose that synthetic claims are meaningful only if testable and confirmable in some basic way by the method of the natural sciences. But the very argument offered from this view supposes, once again, what needs defending, namely, that philosophical plausibility depends on plausibility considerations that are appropriate only to the methods of the natural sciences. When we look to the actual practice of philosophy that assumption seems quite false or the argument Lycan offers begs the question against the distinctness of philosophy. Let's turn to another recent argument for the Quine thesis.

V. The "Traditional Epistemology Will Become Irrelevant" Argument

In his recent book *Explaining Science: A Cognitive Approach,* Ron Giere argues that the justification for the naturalizing of philosophy will not come from explicitly refuting the old paradigm of traditional epistemology, by explicitly refuting on a philosophical basis the philosophical arguments favoring the traditional posture. Rather the argument for naturalizing epistemology will simply be a function of the empirical success of those practitioners in showing how to answer certain questions and, at the same time, showing the irrelevance of the questions asked under the old paradigm.[10] Comparing the naturalised epistemologist with the proponents of seventeenth century physics, he says:

> Proponents of the new physics of the seventeenth century won out not because they explicitly refuted the arguments of the scholastics but because the empirical success of their science rendered the scholastics' arguments irrelevant (p. 9).

This same sort of argument has been offered by philosophers such as Patricia Churchland and Paul Churchland, who have claimed that traditional epistemology or "first philosophy" will disappear as a consequence of the inevitable elimination of folk psychology in favor of some future successful neuroscientific account of cognitive functioning.[11]

While there are various reasons for thinking that the eliminative materialism implied by the above argument cannot occur,[12] what seems most obvious is that the assertion made by Giere and the Churchlands is simply not an *argument* for naturalized epistemology. Rather, it is a buoyantly optimistic prediction that, purely and simply because of the expected empirical success of the new model, we will naturally come to regard traditional epistemology (normative epistemology) as having led us nowhere. In short, we will come to view the questions of traditional epistemology as sterile and no longer worth asking. In spite of the optimism of this prediction, it is difficult to see what successes to date justify such a prediction. What central traditional epistemological problems or questions have been rendered trivial or meaningless by the advances in natural science or neuroscience? Unless one proves that a basic question in traditional epistemology is "How does the Brain Work?" the noncontroversial advances made in neuroscience will be quite irrelevant to answering the questions of traditional epistemology. While some people seem to have *assumed* as much,[13] it is by no means clear that knowing how one's beliefs originate is in any way relevant to their being justified or otherwise worthy of acceptance.[14] Without being able to point to such successes, the eliminative thesis amounts to an unjustified assertion that traditional philosophy is something of an unwholesome disease for which the doing of natural science or neuroscience is the sure cure. In the absence of such demonstrated success, however, no traditional epistemologist need feel compelled by the prediction to adopt the posture of naturalized epistemology.

As a program committed to understanding the mechanisms of belief-acquisition, naturalized epistemology may very well come to show that our traditional ways of understanding human knowledge is in important respects flawed and, as a result, we may indeed need to recast dramatically our understanding of the nature of human knowledge. It would be silly to think that this could not happen. After all, Aristotle's conception of human rationality, and the way in which it was allegedly distinct from animal rationality, was shown to be quite wrong when we all saw Jane Goodall's films showing Gorillas making and using tools. Thereafter, Aristotle's philosophical argument that humans think, whereas animals do not, because the former but not the latter use tools, disappeared from the philosophical landscape. So, it is quite possible that there are certain empirical assumptions about the nature of human knowledge that may well be strongly and empirically falsified in much the same way that Aristotle's position was falsified. But even that sort of progress is still quite consistent with construing epistemology in non-naturalized ways. Traditional epistemology should have no difficulty with accepting the view that some philosophical theses can be conclusively refuted by the occurrence of certain facts. That would be simply to acknowledge that philosophy, and philosophical arguments, are not purely a priori and hence immune from rejection by appeal to the way the world is. So, the traditional epistemologist will need to wait and see just what naturalized epistemology comes us with. Whether it lives up to the expectations of Giere and others who, like the Churchlands, offer the same basic argument is still an open question, at best. As things presently stand, there are good reasons, as we shall see, for thinking that no amount of naturalized epistemology will ever be able in principle to answer certain crucial questions about the nature of justification.

Otherwise Giere's defense of naturalized epistemology consists in responding to others who argue against naturalized epistemology. In responding to these objections, Giere seeks to show that there is certainly no compelling reason why one should not proceed on the new model. He considers the following three arguments.

A. *Putnam's Objection*

In his "Why Reasons Can't be Naturalized" (*Synthese*, vol. 52, 1982, pp. 3–23), Putnam says:

> A cognitive theory of science would require a definition of rationality of the form: A belief is rational if and only if it is acquired by employing some specified cognitive capacities. But any such formula is either obviously mistaken or vacuous, depending on how one restricts the range of beliefs to which the definition applies. If the definition is meant to cover *all* beliefs, then it is obviously mistaken because people do sometimes acquire irrational beliefs using the same cognitive capacities as everyone else. But restricting the definition to rational beliefs renders the definition vacuous. And so the program of constructing a naturalistic philosophy of science goes nowhere (*Synthese*, vol. 52, 1982, pp. 3–23).

In response to this particular argument, Giere says:

> The obvious reply is that a naturalistic theory of science need not require any such definition. A naturalist in epistemology, however, is free to deny that such a conception can be given any coherent content. For such a naturalist, there is only hypothetical rationality which many naturalists, including me, would prefer to describe simply as "effective goal-directed action," thereby dropping the word "rationality" altogether (p. 9).

In short, for Giere, Putnam is just begging the question by insisting that there must be a coherent concept of categorical rationality. In defense of Putnam's intuition, however, one can argue that Giere missed Putnam's point. Putnam's point is just as easily construed as asserting that if the naturalised epistemologist is not to abandon altogether the concept of rationality, (and thereby abandon any way of sorting justifiable or warranted beliefs from those that are not) the rationality of a belief will be purely and simply a function of the reliability of the mechanisms that cause the beliefs. But because a belief can be produced by a reliable belief-making mechanism and be rationally unjustified, such a definition will not work. Putnam's objection, when construed in this way, is compelling. Unfortunately, Giere's response seems to miss the point Putnam makes. Presumably, Putnam would respond that even if we were to stop talking about rationality, we would still need some way of determining which beliefs are more or less justified; and the naturalized epistemologist would need to define such concepts in terms of the mechanisms that produce certain beliefs. And Putnam's point is that that just will not work because unjustified beliefs can emerge just as easily from reliable mechanisms.

B. *Siegel's Objection*

In his "Justification, Discovery and the Naturalizing of Epistemology,"[15] Harvey Siegel challenges the naturalistic approach by arguing that rationality of means is not enough. There must be a rationality of goals as well because there is no such thing as rational action in pursuit of an irrational goal. In response to this objection, Giere notes:

> This sort of argument gains its plausibility mainly from the way philosophers use the vocabulary of "rationality." If one simply drops this vocabulary, the point vanishes. Obviously, there can be effective action in pursuit of any goal whatsoever—as illustrated by the proverbial case of the efficient Nazi....
>
> Nor does the restriction to instrumental rationality prevent the study of science from yielding normative claims about how science should be pursued. Indeed, it may be argued that the naturalistic study of science provides the only legitimate basis for sound science policy (Campbell, 1985). (p. 10.)

Along with Giere, we may find it difficult to take Siegel's objection seriously for two reasons. Firstly, it is not at all obvious that naturalized epistemology is committed to rationality of means only and not also to the rationality of goals. It is not even clear what that claim amounts to. Secondly, as Giere also points out, there certainly seems to be cases in which irrational ends can be pursued by rational action. Anyway, as we shall see later, there are much more persuasive objections to naturalized epistemology.

C. *The Objection from Vicious Circularity*

There is another common objection to eliminating traditional epistemological questions in favor of questions about effective means to desired goals. Giere characterises it in the following way:

> To show that some methods are effective, one must be able to show that they can result in reaching the goal. And this requires being able to say what it is like to reach the goal. But the goal in science is usually taken to be "true" or "correct" theories. And the traditional epistemological problem has always been to justify the claim that one has in fact found a correct theory. Any naturalistic theory of science that appeals only to effective means to the goal of discovering correct theories must beg this question. Thus a naturalistic philosophy of science can be supported only by a circular argument that assumes some means to the goal are in fact effective. (p. 11.)

Giere then proceeds to show that this sort of objection (which he does not cite anybody in fact offering) is based on some dubious items of Cartesian epistemology. A more direct response, however, is that this objection is unacceptable because it assumes rather than proves that the goal of scientific theories is to achieve truth rather than empirical adequacy. In other words, a proper response would consist in straightforwardly denying that the goal of science is to discover "true" or "correct" theories rather than ones that are instrumentally reliable as predictive devices. So, for other reasons, we need not take this objection very seriously. In the end, apart from Putnam's objection, these last two objections to naturalized epistemology do not have the necessary bite, and Giere seems quite justified in rejecting them. Later we shall see better objections. For now, however, we need only note that the above argument in favor of naturalized epistemology is not an argument, and that the author's response to the above three objections to naturalized epistemology selects only three and fails to deal effectively with Putnam's objection.

In the end, for Giere, evolutionary theory provides an alternative foundation for the study of science:

> It explains why the traditional projects of epistemology, whether in their Cartesian, Humean, or Kantian form, were misguided. And it shows why we should not fear the charge of circularity (p. 12).

But what exactly is it about traditional epistemology that made it misguided? That it sought to refute universal scepticism? Whoever said that that was *the goal* of traditional epistemology? As we noted earlier when we examined Quine's argument, to define the concept of knowledge and then to determine whether, and to what extent, human knowledge exists in the various ways we define it seems equally the major goal of traditional epistemology. And why, exactly, is that a misguided activity? Such an activity seems justified by the plausible goal that if we get very clear on just what we mean by basic epistemological concepts, we might just be in a better position to determine the snake-oil artist from those whose views are worthy of adoption. This goal is based on the noncontroversial point that knowledge just isn't a matter of accepting everything a passerby might say. At the root of most arguments for naturalized epistemology, as we shall see, is this peculiar claim to the effect that traditional epistemology somehow has failed or been misguided in its search for some cosmic skyhook. Certainly we saw as much when we examined Quine's argument. But when the arguments are laid on the table, some philosophers may come to think that what gets characterized as traditional epistemology is quite different from the real thing. Socrates, after all, began his discussion in *Theatetus* with the question "What is knowledge?" and not "Is Human knowledge possible?" or "How does the mind represent reality?" or (as one philosopher recently claimed) "How does the brain work?"[16] That anybody could seriously think that Socrates was really asking for an account of how the brain works is difficult to comprehend. And to say that that is what he *should* have been asking (because nobody has or can answer whatever other question he might have asked) presupposes that one can show that the questions he did ask are misguided or bad questions, and that is yet to be shown in any way that does not beg the question against philosophy. We may now turn to the fourth argument in favor of Quine's thesis.

VI. The Argument from Evolutionary Theory

Evolutionary epistemology is a form of naturalized epistemology which insists that the only valid questions about the nature of human knowledge are those that can be answered in biological science by appeal to evolutionary theory. For the evolutionary epistemologist, the Darwinian revolution underscored the point that human beings, as products of evolutionary development, are natural beings whose capacities for knowledge and belief can be understood by appeal to the basic laws of biology under evolutionary theory. As Michael Bradie has recently noted, evolutionary epistemologists often seem to be claiming that Darwin or, more generally, biological considerations are relevant in deciding in favor of a non-justificational or purely descriptive approach to the theory of knowledge.[17] When we examine the arguments proposed by specific evolutionary epistemologists, there seems to emerge two distinct arguments. The first argument, allegedly offered by philosophers such as Karl Popper, and reconstructed by Peter Munz is as follows:

P1. We do in fact have human knowledge.

P2. No justification is possible.

Therefore: P3. Human knowledge does not involve justification.

Therefore: P4. Every item of knowledge is a provisional proposal or hypothesis subject to revision.[18]

For this reason Popper held that the only problem in epistemology was the problem of the growth of human knowledge, or the biological question of how human knowledge originates and grows. Therefore, epistemology is not normative in the way that traditional epistemology is normative but rather purely descriptive. As Bradie has noted, Popper's argument for P2 is based on his acceptance of Hume's critique of induction and the corollary that no empirical universal statements are provable beyond doubt. (p. 10.) The second argument, inspired by Quine's reference to Darwin, is offered by Hilary Kornblith and reconstructed by Bradie as follows:

P1. Believing truths has survival value.

Therefore: P2. Natural selection guarantees that our innate intellectual endowment gives us a predisposition for believing truths.

Therefore: P3. Knowledge is a necessary by-product of natural selection.

In order to get the desired conclusion of a purely descriptive epistemology, Kornblith supplies the following premise

Therefore: P4. If nature has so constricted us that our belief-generating processes are inevitably biased in favor of true beliefs, then it must be that the processes by which we arrive at beliefs just are those by which we ought to arrive at them.

warranting the final conclusion:

Therefore: *P5*. The processes by which we arrive at our beliefs are just those by which we ought to arrive at them.[19]

What can we say about these two arguments?

With regard to the first argument, the one Peter Munz ascribes to Popper, the first thing to note is that there is nothing particularly "biological" or "evolutionary" about it at all. It is simply a philosophical argument based on a philosophical acceptance of Hume's philosophical scepticism to the effect that no factual claim about the world could be justified sufficiently for knowledge. So, the argument does not provide a justification deriving from evolutionary theory for taking the naturalistic turn. Secondly, as we saw when we discussed Quine's argument above, accepting a philosophical argument for a purely descriptive epistemology is radically incoherent. A philosophical argument to the effect that there is no first philosophy because Hume was correct in his defense of the problem of induction, is radically incoherent and self-defeating in a way apparently not yet appreciated by naturalized epistemologists.

The second argument has already been well-criticised by Michael Bradie who has noted (along with many others, including Stich, Leowontin, and Wilson) that *P2* is quite questionable. The fact that certain beliefs endure and have survival value by no means implies that they are the product of natural selection. There are many traits that evolve culturally which have no survival value (see Bradie, p. 16). Moreover, even if it were true that our cognitive capacities have evolved by natural selection, the important point is that that by itself is no reason for thinking that we are naturally disposed to believe truths rather than falsity. On the contrary, the evidence seems pretty strong that, given the history of scientific theorizing, the species is more disposed to accept empirically adequate rather than true hypotheses.

One interesting response to this last line of reasoning comes from Nicholas Rescher who has argued in *Methodological Pragmatism* that say what we will, the methods of the natural sciences have indeed been selected out by nature, otherwise they would not have endured as such reliable instruments for prediction and control. Rescher's basic point is that on any given occasion, an instrumentally reliable belief or thesis may well fail to be true. But that is no reason for thinking that nature has not selected out the methods of the natural sciences because in the long run the methods of the natural sciences provide truth.[20] Rescher's point is well taken, but it is certainly not an argument for the thesis that epistemology is purely descriptive. Rescher certainly is not a naturalized epistemologist in that sense. Rather it is an argument for regarding the deliverances of the methods of natural science as epistemically privileged. In offering the argument he does here, Rescher is merely showing how the usual arguments against Pragmatism hold for *thesis* pragmatism and not for *methodological* Pragmatism. Nor does his argument provide the evidence necessary for making sound Kornblith's reconstructed argument from evolution. This is because Kornblith's proposed argument still falters on *P2*. Rescher's argument by no means shows or supports the view that people by nature are innately disposed to believe only true propositions. If that were so, it would be difficult to see why we would ever need the methods of the natural sciences anyway. Nature selected out the methods of the natural sciences just *because* we are not natively disposed to believe only true propositions.

But, if the above two arguments are the best evolutionary biologists can offer in defense of the first form of naturalized epistemology, it would seem that biology itself, and especially evolutionary biology, is yet to offer a persuasive argument for naturalized epistemology. Along with Bradie, we can only conclude that there does not seem to be any persuasive argument from evolutionary theory in favor of the first form of naturalized epistemology.[21]

VII. The "Impossibility of Defining Justification" Argument

The last, and perhaps the most interesting, argument for the first form of naturalized epistemology appears in a forthcoming paper by Richard Ketchum entitled "The Paradox of Epistemology: A Defense of Naturalism." Ketchum's argument is the following: An adequate traditional epistemology will require, among other things, an acceptable definition, or explication of the concept of justification. But there is no non-question begging definition, or explication of the concept of justification. This latter claim rests on the reason that whatever definition one would offer for the concept of justification admits of the question "Are you justified in accepting or believing this definition of justification?" And, of course, if one were to answer yes and then defend the answer by saying it is an instance of the definition (which presumably one would need to say), the questioner would reply that the appeal is question-begging because what is at issue is whether *that* definition itself is justified. Appealing to the analysans of the definition to justify the definition is a patent bit of question-begging. So, no matter what one's definition might be, there would be no non-question begging way of answering the question of whether one is justified in accepting that definition. Thus, traditional epistemology is dead.[22] What about this argument?

One possible response is that while one may not be justified in believing one's definition of justification, one might certainly have good reasons for accepting one's definition of justification. But the problem with this response is that it arbitrarily prevents one from defining justification in terms of having good reasons. Besides, if having good reasons for accepting a definition of justification is sufficient for accepting it, then why is that not the definition of justification? Can one have sufficient reasons for accepting something and not be justified in accepting it?

Another possible response asserts that the problem with this argument is not in the assumption that we must be justified in believing our definition of justification. Rather it is in the assumption that justification in believing a definition has the same meaning as justification when the term applies to non-definitions. On this view, being justified in believing a definition is simply a matter of whether one has correctly generalised from the conditions of correct usage in natural or scientific discourse (or, if our definitions are stipulative, a matter of whether they lead us to conclusions that satisfy the purpose behind defining things the way we do); whereas being justified in believing a non-definition, or a proposition about the world, is a matter of whether one can give (if necessary) good reasons for thinking that the proposition is a reasonably adequate description of one's mental content or of the non-mental world. Is there anything wrong with this proposed solution?

Yes, and it is this: The original question returns in the form of the question "Are you justified in believing that the concept of justification differs for reportive definitions and non-definitions in the way indicated?" Here again, if one answers affirmatively, one could only defend the answer by making it an instance of the concept of justification appropriate for non-definitions, and that is what is at issue. In short, the question returns with a sting even when we try to distinguish various senses of justification.

By implication, suppose one were to say "I am justified in accepting my definition of justification because the definition conforms to the rules we require for generating acceptable definitions." Once again, the obvious response is "Are you justified in accepting the rules for generating acceptable definitions?"; if the answer is yes (as presumably it would be), then the answer is defensible only if it is an instance of one's definition of justification for non-definitions; but one's definition of justification for non-definitions is justifiable only if it is an instance of the definition of justification for non-definitions. But the latter is itself what is at issue, and so we come back to the original question and the impossibility of answering it in a non-question-begging way.

Yet another response consists in trying to rule against the meaningfulness of the question on the grounds that if we take it seriously, then it would lead to an infinite regress and that in itself is good evidence for the inappropriateness of the question. On this view, whatever answer one gives, the respondent could still ask "But are you justified in believing that?" Differently stated, to countenance the question in the first instance is to countenance more properly the assumption that one must be justified in all one's beliefs and, as we know from Aristotle's argument in the first book of *Prior Analytics*, that requirement guarantees scepticism, because the need for an infinite amount of justification prevents there ever being any demonstrative knowledge. Is this response acceptable?

It is not acceptable as a way of establishing non-traditional epistemology because the same question cuts equally strongly against the naturalized epistemologist. The naturalized epistemologist, like Quine, still says that one's beliefs about the world are more or less justified by appeal to the canons of scientific inference. Accordingly, suppose we grant that traditional epistemology is dead and that one could still be justified in one's beliefs about the world because we need only follow the canons of justification as practiced in science. But if the question "Are you justified in believing that your definition of justification is appropriate or correct?" is a legitimate question to ask of the classical epistemologist, it is also a legitimate question to ask of the naturalized epistemologist who asserts that "In natural science, being justified in one's beliefs is simply a matter of x." And if this is so, the nature of justification in science is as problematic as it would be in traditional epistemology. Why is it that for the naturalized epistemologist the natural scientist (but not the traditional epistemologist) can well ignore the philosopher's question "Are you justified in accepting x as the correct definition of justification in science?" Indeed, it would seem that the question cuts both ways, and is not any more devastating for the traditional epistemologist than it is for the practice of science in general or for the naturalized epistemologist. If the naturalized epistemologist feels justified in ignoring such questions because they are so obviously philosophical, why exactly is that an argument in favor of natural-ized epistemology rather than an unargued rejection of philosophy in general? Thus if the question is persuasive, it tends to show the truth of skepticism in general and not simply the failure of traditional epistemology. This is hardly a desirable result for anybody.

By way of confronting this pesky argument for the impossibility of traditional epistemology, another interesting response consists in asserting that we must begin by accepting the fact that we know something, and that just means that we must reject any and all questions about human knowledge that can only be answered with a question-begging response. So, the truth of the matter is that there is no non-question begging way to answer questions such as "Are you justified in believing your definition of justification?" But if we insist on answering such questions we make global skepticism certain. Presumably, even naturalized epistemologists do not want to go that far. Consequently, such questions are not permissible. What this means is that generalizing from the facts of ordinary usage and scientific practice to determine what we mean by certain epistemic concepts is simply where we start and what we do to get clear about what human knowledge is. To ask that we be justified in the conclusions we draw here is to demand that we begin somewhere else when there is in fact nowhere else to go, and if we do not stop here or somewhere else (which will certainly happen if we allow the skeptic's eternal question "But are you justified in believing that?") there could be no knowledge about anything at all.

Is this a compelling response, or is it merely a grand way of begging the question against global skepticism which, if the original question is permissi-ble, turns out to be forceful? Are we dismissing the question as meaningful because otherwise we would need to accept global skepticism? It is tempting to think not, but the skeptic will doubtless see things differently. It appears that we have no knock-down argument against the skeptic except to say that he begins with a view that we cannot accept, namely, that it is possible that nobody knows anything. But that is not an argument.

In the end, however, the best way to confront the claim that there is no non-question begging way to justify any definition or analysis of justification consists in arguing as follows: Whoever asks the question "Are you justified in accepting your definition of justification?" can be met with the response "What do you mean when you ask whether I am justified in accepting this definition?" When anyone asks the question "Are you justified in accepting or believing your definition of justification?" he must have in mind just what it means to be justified, otherwise it is not a meaningful question because if he did not have in mind just what it meant, he would not know what would count for a good answer if an answer were possible. So, if the question makes any sense at all, the questioner must be prepared to say just what he means when he asks the question "Are you justified in believing your definition of justification?" In fact, then, it is a necessary condition for this question being meaningful that the questioner be able to say what it would mean for someone to be justified in believing that a particular definition of justification is correct. If the questioner cannot answer the question "What do you mean?" then the question need not be taken seriously. If he can, then his question is easily answered. For example, if the questioner is asking for a good reason for accepting the definition, the response might well be that we have a good reason because the definition is a sound generalisation of the facts of ordinary usage (and that's a good reason because evolution selects out this way of determining the meaning of expressions).

In sum, if the question is an honest one, then the questioner is asking for a justification and if he cannot say what would count as an answer to his question (thereby saying what he means by "justification") then we need not, and will not, take his question seriously. On the other hand, as soon as he tells us just what he means by "justification" his question seems meaningful and answerable. But now comes the rub: we can still refuse to take his question seriously because *we* can now raise the question of whether his understanding of "justification" is justified, because if it is not, we do not need to answer his question; and if he says our question is meaningless, then so too was his initial question. But now the shoe is on the other foot, as it were. The person who questions the original definition of justification can make sense of his question only if he is willing to say just what justification consists in; but if the original question makes sense then it will make equal sense when the question is asked of him—meaning that *he* has no non-question begging way of answering a question necessary for his meaningfully asking "Are you justified in believing your definition of justification?" Thus it appears that we are justified in ignoring the question because the questioner cannot, ex hypothesi, satisfy a condition necessary for the meaningfulness of the proposition. He cannot, ex hypothesi, answer in any non-question begging way the question we can ask of him, namely, "Are you justified in accepting your definition of justification?"

VIII. Conclusion

Given the above considerations, it seems that, in spite of the popularity of the thesis, there is no sound argument presently available supporting the Quinean version of naturalized epistemology. Nor should we be tempted to suppose that because we have never achieved a consensus in traditional epistemology, it looks as though we have good inductive grounds that the program of traditional epistemology will never work. That sort of argument blatantly begs the question in favor of a concept of success that is appropriate to the methods of the natural sciences and so, by implication, begs the question in favor of the naturalized epistemology for which it is supposed to be an argument. The interesting question is whether there is something fundamentally incoherent about arguing philosophically for such a naturalized epistemology. As was suggested above in the discussion on Quine's argument, it certainly seems that offering a philosophical argument in favor of denying that philosophical arguments will count when it comes to answering questions about the nature of epistemology is incoherent when the point of it is to defend a particular view about the nature of human knowledge. But perhaps this is merely a philosophical point.[23]

NOTES

[1]   In *Ontological Relativity and Other Essays* (New York: Columbia University Press, 1969).

[2]   For a full discussion of Goldman's thesis as it occurs in *Epistemology and Cognition* (Cambridge, Mass: Harvard University Press, 1985) see R. Almeder and F. Hogg, "Reliabilism and Goldman's Theory of Justification," *Philosophia* (1989).

[3]   In Hilary Kornblith, ed., *Naturalizing Epistemology* (Cambridge: MIT Press, 1985), pp. 71–85.

[4]   *Roots of Reference* (LaSalle: Open Court, 1975).

[5]   In S. Guttenplan, ed., *Mind and Language* (Oxford: Clarendon Press, 1975).

[6]   See "Reply to Stroud" in *Midwest Studies in Philosophy* Vol. VI, P. French, E. Uehling, and H. Wettstein, (eds.) (Minneapolis: University of Minnesota Press, 1981), p. 474.

[7]   See "Nature Unmirrored, Epistemology Naturalized" in *Synthese* vol. 55 (1983), p. 69.

[8]   See *Judgement and Justification* (Cambridge: Cambridge University Press, 1988).

[9]   This same point is made by P. Skagestadt in "Hypothetical Realism" in Brewer and Collins (eds.) *Scientific Inquiry and the Social Sciences: A Volume in Honor of Donald T. Campbell* (San Francisco: Jossey-Bass, 1981), p. 92.

[10] Ron Giere, *Explaining Science: A Cognitive Approach* (Chicago: University of Chicago Press, 1988).

[11] See P.S. Churchland's *Neurophilosophy* (Cambridge: MIT Press, 1986); P.M. Churchland's "Eliminative Materialism and the Propositional Attitudes," *Journal of Philosophy* (1981), vol. 78, pp. 67–90 and "Some Reductive Strategies in Cognitive Neurobiology," *MIND* (1986), vol. 95, pp. 279–309. For a similar argument see S. Stich's, *From Folk Psychology to Cognitive Science* (Cambridge: MIT Press, 1983).

[12] For an interesting argument to the effect that folk psychology is not likely to be eliminated in the way the Churchland's assert that it will, see Robert McCauley's "Epistemology in an Age of Cognitive Science," *Philosophical Psychology*, vol. 1 (1988), pp. 147–149.

[13] See, for example, P.S. Churchland's "Epistemology in an Age of Neuroscience," *The Journal of Philosophy*, vol. LXXXIV, No. 10 (Oct. 1987), p. 546 where she asserts, without benefit of argument, that the basic question in epistemology is indeed the question "How does the brain work?" Also, as an interesting example of an argument seeking to show that traditional epistemological questions can be eliminated owing to advances in cognitive science (advances that presumably show how we can understand human knowledge on a non-propositional basis), see William Bechtel and Adel Abrahamson, "Beyond the Exclusively Propositional Era," *Synthese*, vol. 82 (1990).

[14] This same point is made by Ernest Sosa in "Nature Unmirrored: Epistemology Naturalised," *Synthese*, vol. 55 (1983), p. 70. Naturally, if one were able to defend a form of reliabilism similar to that offered by Alvin Goldman, the question "How does the brain work?" would turn out to be a most crucial question in epistemology; but at that point we would not be defending the sort of naturalised epistemology defended by Quine rather than the form offered and defended by Goldman.

[15] See Harvey Siegel, *Philosophy of Science* vol. 47 (1980), pp. 297–321.

[16] See P.S. Churchland, "Epistemology in the Age of Neuroscience," *Journal of Philosophy* (Oct. 1987), p. 546.

[17] See Michael Bradie, "Evolutionary Epistemology as Naturalised Epistemology," (forthcoming), p. 3.

[18] See Peter Munz, *Our Knowledge of the Growth of Knowledge: Popper or Wittgenstein?* (London: Routledge and Kegan Paul, 1987), p. 371. For a defense of a similar argument, see also Michael Ruse's *Taking Darwin Seriously: A Naturalistic Approach to Philosophy* (Oxford: Blackwell, 1986), and W.W. Bartley III, "Philosophy of Biology versus Philosophy of Physics," in G. Radnitzky and W.W. Bartley, III (eds.) *Evolutionary Epistemology, Theory of Rationality and the Sociology of Knowledge* (LaSalle: Open Court, 1987), p. 206.

[19] See Hilary Kornblith, *Naturalizing Epistemology* (Cambridge: MIT Press, 1985), p. 4.

[20] Nicholas Rescher, *Methodological Pragmatism* (Oxford: Basil Blackwell, 1977), Ch. 6.

[21] For further reasons why evolutionary epistemology has in fact failed to offer any compelling explanation of how what we take to be knowledge, especially scientific knowledge, has developed, see William Bechtel's "Toward Making Evolutionary Epistemology Into a Truly Naturalized Epistemology" in N. Rescher, *Evolution, Cognition and Realism* (Washington, D.C.:

University Press of America, 1990).

22   This is an informal reconstruction of the argument defended by Richard Ketchum in his forthcoming paper in *Philosophical Studies*.

23   I would like to thank the Center for the Philosophy of Science at the University of Pittsburgh for the Senior Fellowship and the stimulating environment that made the writing of this essay possible. For the same reason, I am grateful to the Hambridge Center. Also, Nicholas Rescher, David Blumfeld, Bill Bechtel, Milton Snoeyenbos, Douglas Winblad, and Richard Ketchum all provided valuable comments and criticisms.

3.3

WHY REASON CAN'T BE NATURALIZED

Hilary Putnam

In the present chapter I shall examine attempts to naturalize the fundamental notions of the theory of knowledge, for example the notion of a belief's being *justified* or *rationally acceptable*.

While the two sorts of attempts are alike in that they both seek to reduce "intentional" or mentalistic notions to materialistic ones, and thus are both manifestations of what Peter Strawson (1979) has described as a permanent tension in philosophy, in other ways they are quite different. The materialist metaphysician often uses such traditional metaphysical notions as *causal power*, and *nature* quite uncritically. (I have even read papers in which one finds the locution "realist truth," as if everyone understood this notion except a few fuzzy anti-realists.) The "physicalist" generally doesn't seek to *clarify* these traditional metaphysical notions, but just to show that science is progressively verifying the *true* metaphysics. That is why it seems just to describe *his* enterprise as "natural metaphysics," in strict analogy to the "natural theology" of the eighteenth and nineteenth centuries. Those who raise the slogan "epistemology naturalized," on the other hand, generally *disparage* the traditional enterprises of epistemology. In this respect, moreover, they do not differ from philosophers of a less reductionist kind; the criticism they voice of traditional epistemology—that it was in the grip of a "quest for certainty," that it was unrealistic in seeking a "foundation" for knowledge as a whole, that the "foundation" it claimed to provide was by no means indubitable in the way it claimed, that the whole "Cartesian enterprise" was a mistake, etc.,—are precisely the criticisms one hears from philosophers of all countries and types. Hegel already denounced the idea of an "Archimedean point" from which epistemology could judge all of our scientific, legal, moral, religious, etc. beliefs (and set up standards for all of the special subjects). It is true that Russell and Moore ignored these strictures of Hegel (as they ignored Kant), and revived "foundationalist epistemology"; but today that enterprise has few defenders. The fact that the naturalized epistemologist is trying to reconstruct what he can of an enterprise that few philosophers of any persuasion regard as unflawed is perhaps the explanation of the fact that the naturalistic tendency in epistemology expresses itself in so many incompatible and mutually divergent ways, while the naturalistic tendency in metaphysics appears to be, and regards itself as, a unified movement.

Evolutionary epistemology

The simplest approach to the problem of giving a naturalistic account of reason is to appeal to Darwinian evolution. In its crudest form, the story is familiar: reason is a capacity we have for discovering truths. Such a capacity has survival value; it evolved in just the way that any of our physical organs or capacities evolved. A belief is rational if it is arrived at by the exercise of this capacity.

This approach assumes, at bottom, a metaphysically "realist" notion of truth: truth as "correspondence to the facts" or something of that kind. And this notion, as I have argued in the papers in this volume, is incoherent. We don't have notions of the "existence" of things or of the "truth" of statements that are independent of the versions we construct and of the procedures and practices that give sense to talk of "existence" and "truth" within those versions. Do *fields* "exist" as physically real things? Yes, fields really exist: relative to one scheme for describing and explaining physical phenomena; relative to another there are particles, plus "virtual" particles, plus "ghost" particles, plus…Is it true that *brown* objects exist? Yes, relative to a common-sense version of the world: although one cannot give a necessary and sufficient condition for an object to be brown,[1] (one that applies to all objects, under all conditions) in the form of a finite closed formula in the language of physics. Do *dispositions* exist? Yes, in our ordinary way of talking (although disposition talk is just as recalcitrant to translation into physicalistic language as counterfactual talk, and for similar reasons). We have many irreducibly different but legitimate ways of talking, and true "existence" statements in all of them.

To postulate a set of "ultimate" objects, the furniture of the world, or what you will, whose "existence" is *absolute*, not relative to our discourse at all, and a notion of truth as "correspondence" to these ultimate objects is simply to revive the whole failed enterprise of traditional metaphysics.

Truth, in the only sense in which we have a vital and working notion of it, is rational acceptability (or, rather, rational acceptability under sufficiently good epistemic conditions; and which conditions are epistemically better or worse is relative to the type of discourse in just the way rational acceptability itself is). But to substitute this characterization of truth into the formula "reason is a capacity for discovering truths" is to see the emptiness of that formula at once: "reason is a capacity for discovering what is (or would be) rationally acceptable" is *not* the most informative statement a philosopher might utter. The evolutionary epistemologist must either presuppose a "realist" (i.e., a metaphysical) notion of truth or see his formula collapse into vacuity.

Roderick Firth[2] has argued that, in fact, it collapses into a kind of epistemic vacuity on *any* theory of rational acceptability (*or* truth). For, he points out, whatever we take the correct epistemology (or the correct theory of truth) to be, we have no way of *identifying* truths except to posit that the statements that are currently rationally acceptable (by our lights) are true. Even if these beliefs are false, even if our rational beliefs contribute to our survival for some reason *other* than truth, the way "truths" are identified *guarantees* that reason will seem to be a "capacity for discovering truths." This characterization of reason has thus no real empirical content.

The evolutionary epistemologist could, I suppose, try using some notion *other* than the notion of "discovering truths." For example, he might try saying that "reason is a capacity for arriving at beliefs which *promote our survival*" (or our "inclusive genetic fitness"). But this would be a loser! Science itself, and the methodology which we have developed since the seventeenth century for constructing and evaluating theories, has *mixed* effects on inclusive genetic fitness and all too uncertain effects on survival. If the human race perishes in a nuclear war, it may well be (although there will be no one alive to say it) that scientific beliefs did *not*, in a sufficiently long time scale, promote "survival." Yet that will not have been because the scientific theories were not rationally acceptable, but because our *use* of them was irrational. In fact, if rationality were measured by survival value, then the proto-beliefs of the cockroach, who has been around for tens of millions of years longer than we, would have a far higher claim to rationality than the sum total of human knowledge. But such a measure would be cockeyed; there is no contradiction in imagining a world in which people have utterly irrational beliefs which for some reason enable them to survive, or a world in which the most rational beliefs quickly lead to extinction.

If the notion of "truth" in the characterization of rationality as a "capacity for discovering truths" is problematic, so, almost equally, is the notion of a "capacity." In one sense of the term, *learning* is a "capacity" (even, a "capacity for discovering truths"), and *all* our beliefs are the product of *that* capacity. Yet, for better or worse, not all our beliefs are rational.

The problem here is that there are no sharp lines in the brain between one "capacity" and another (Chomskians to the contrary). Even seeing includes not just the visual organs, the eyes, but the whole brain; and what is true of seeing is certainly true of *thinking* and *inferring*. We draw lines between one "capacity" and another (or build them into the various versions we construct); but a sharp line at one level does not usually correspond to a sharp line at a lower level. The table at which I write, for example, is a natural unit at the level of everyday talk; I am aware that the little particle of food sticking to its surface (I must do something about that!) is not a "part" of the table; but at the physicist's level, the decision to consider that bit of food to be outside the boundary of the table is not natural at all. Similarly, "believing" and "seeing" are quite different at the level of ordinary language psychology (and usefully so); but the corresponding brain-processes interpenetrate in complex ways which can only be separated by looking outside the brain, at the environment and at the output behavior *as structured by our interests and saliencies*. "Reason is a capacity" is what Wittgenstein called a "grammatical remark"; by which he meant (I think) not an analytic truth, but simply the sort of remark that philosophers often *take* to be informative when in fact it tells us nothing useful.

None of this is intended to deny the obvious scientific facts: that we would not be able to reason if we did not have brains, and that those *brains* are the product of evolution by natural selection. What is wrong with evolutionary epistemology is not that the scientific facts are wrong, but that they don't answer any of the philosophical questions.

The reliability theory of rationality

A more sophisticated recent approach to these matters, proposed by Professor Alvin Goldman (1978), runs as follows: let us call a *method* (as opposed to a single belief) *reliable* if the method leads to a high frequency (say, 95%) of *true* beliefs in a long run series of representative applications (or *would* lead to such a high truth-frequency in such a series of applications). Then (the proposal goes) we can define a *rational* belief to be one which is *arrived at by using a reliable method.*

This proposal does not avoid the first objection we raised against evolutionary epistemology: it too presupposes a metaphysical notion of truth. Forgetting that rational acceptability does the lion's share of the work in fixing the notion of "truth," the reliability theorist only pretends to be giving an analysis of rationality in terms that do not presuppose it. The second objection we raised against evolutionary epistemology, namely that the notion of a "capacity" is hopelessly vague and general, is met, however, by replacing that notion with the notion of an arbitrary method for generating true or false statements, and then restricting the class to those methods (in this sense) whose reliability (as defined) is high. "Learning" may be a method for generating statements, but its *reliability* is not high enough for every statement we "learn" to count as rationally acceptable, on this theory. Finally, *no* hypothesis is made as to whether the reliable methods we employ are the result of biological evolution, cultural evolution, or what: this is regarded as no part of the theory of what rationality *is*, in this account.

This account is vulnerable to many counterexamples, however. *One* is the following: suppose that Tibetan Buddhism is, in fact, *true*, and that the Dalai Lama is, in fact, *infallible* on matters of faith and morals. Anyone who believes in the Dalai Lama, and who invariably believes any statement the Dalai Lama makes on a matter of faith or morals, follows a method which is 100% reliable; thus, if the reliability theory of rationality were correct, such a person's beliefs on faith and morals would all be rational *even if his argument for his belief that the Dalai Lama is never wrong is "the Dalai Lama says so."*

Cultural relativism

I have already said that, in my view, truth and rational acceptability—a claim's being right and someone's being in a position to make it—are relative to the sort of language we are using and the sort of context we are in. "That weighs one pound" may be true in a butcher shop, but the same sentence would be understood very differently (as demanding four decimal places of precision, perhaps) if the same object were being weighed in a laboratory. This does not mean that a claim is right *whenever* those who employ the language in question would accept it as right in its context, however. There are two points that must be *balanced*, both points that have been made by philosophers of many different kinds: (1) talk of what is "right" and "wrong" in any area only makes sense against the background of an *inherited tradition*; but (2) traditions themselves can be *criticized*. As Austin (1961) says, remarking on a special case of this, "superstition and error and fantasy of all kinds do become incorporated in ordinary language and even sometimes stand up to the survival test (only, when they do, why should we not detect it?)."

What I am saying is that the "standards" accepted by a culture or a subculture, either explicitly or implicitly, cannot *define* what reason is, even in context, because they *presuppose* reason (reasonableness) for their interpretation. On the one hand, there is no notion of reasonableness at all *without* cultures, practices, procedures; on the other hand, the cultures, practices, procedures we inherit are not an algorithm to be slavishly followed. As Mill said, commenting on his own inductive logic, there is no rule book which will not lead to terrible results "if supposed to be conjoined with universal idiocy." Reason is, in this sense, both immanent (not to be found outside of concrete language games and institutions) and transcendent (a regulative idea that we use to criticize the conduct of *all* activities and institutions).

Philosophers who lose sight of the immanence of reason, of the fact that reason is always relative to context and institution, become lost in characteristic philosophical fantasies. "The ideal language," "inductive logic," "the empiricist criterion of significance"—these are the fantasies of the positivist, who would replace the vast complexity of human reason with a kind of intellectual Walden II. "The absolute idea": this is the fantasy of Hegel, who, without ignoring that complexity, would have us (or, rather, "spirit") reach an endstage at which we (it) could comprehend it all. Philosophers who lose sight of the transcendence of reason become cultural (or historical) relativists.

I want to talk about cultural relativism, because it is one of the most influential—perhaps the most influential—forms of naturalized epistemology extant, although not usually recognized as such.

The situation is complicated, because cultural relativists usually *deny* that they are cultural relativists. I shall count a philosopher as a cultural relativist for our purposes if I have not been able to find anyone who can explain to me why he *isn't* a cultural relativist. Thus I count Richard Rorty as a cultural relativist, because his explicit formulations are relativist ones (he identifies truth with right assertibility by the standards of one's cultural peers, for example), and because his entire attack on traditional philosophy is mounted on the basis that the nature of reason and representation are non-problems, because the only kind of truth it makes sense to seek is to convince one's cultural peers. Yet he himself *tells* us that relativism is self-refuting (Rorty,

1980*b*). And I count Michel Foucault as a relativist because his insistence on the determination of beliefs by language is so overwhelming that it is an incoherence on his part not to apply his doctrine to his *own* language and thought. Whether Heidegger ultimately escaped something very much like cultural, or rather historical, relativism is an interesting question.

Cultural relativists are not, in their own eyes, scientistic or "physicalistic." They are likely to view materialism and scientism as just the hang-ups of one particular cultural epoch. If I count them as "naturalized epistemologists" it is because their doctrine is, none the less, a product of the same deference to the claims of nature, the same desire for harmony with the world version of some science, as physicalism. The difference in style and tone is thus explained: the physicalist's paradigm of science is a *hard* science, *physics* (as the term "physicalism" suggests); the cultural relativists's paradigm is a *soft* science: anthropology, or linguistics, or psychology, or history, as the case may be. That reason is whatever the norms of the local culture determine it to be is a naturalist view inspired by the *social* sciences, including history.

There is something which makes cultural relativism a far more dangerous cultural tendency than materialism. At bottom, there is a deep irrationalism to cultural relativism, a denial of the possibility of *thinking* (as opposed to making noises in counterpoint or in a chorus). An aspect of this which is of special concern to philosophy is the suggestion, already mentioned, that the deep questions of philosophy are not deep at all. A corollary to this suggestion is that philosophy, as traditionally understood, is a *silly* enterprise. But the questions *are* deep, and it is the easy answers that are silly. Even seeing that relativism is inconsistent is, if the knowledge is taken seriously, seeing something important about a deep question. Philosophers *are* beginning to talk about the great issues again, and to feel that something can be *said* about them, even if there are no grand or ultimate solutions. There is an excitement in the air. And if I react to Professor Rorty's book (1980*a*) with a certain sharpness, it is because one more "deflationary" book, one more book telling us that the deep questions aren't deep and the whole enterprise was a mistake, is just what we *don't* need right now. Yet I am grateful to Rorty all the same, for his work has the merit of addressing profound questions head-on.

So, although we all know that cultural relativism is inconsistent (or say we do) I want to take the time to say again that it is inconsistent. I want to point out one reason that it is: not one of the quick, logic-chopping refutations (although every refutation of relativism teaches us something about reason) but a somewhat messy, somewhat "intuitive," reason.

I shall develop my argument in analogy with a well-known argument against "methodological solipsism." The "methodological solipsist"—one thinks of Carnap's *Logische Aufbau* or of Mach's *Analyse der Empfindungen*—holds that *all* our talk can be reduced to talk about experiences and logical constructions out of experiences. More precisely, he holds that everything he can conceive of is identical (in the ultimate logical analyses of his language) with one or another complex of his *own* experiences. What makes him a *methodological* solipsist as opposed to a real solipsist is that he kindly adds that *you*, dear reader, are the "I" of this construction when *you* perform it: he says that *everybody* is a (methodological) solipsist.

The trouble, which should be obvious, is that his two stances are ludicrously incompatible. His solipsist stance implies an enormous asymmetry between two persons: my body is a construction out of my experiences, in the system, but *your* body isn't a construction out of *your* experiences. It's a construction out of *my* experiences. And your experiences—viewed from within the system—are a construction out of your bodily behavior, which, as just said, is a construction out of *my* experiences. My experiences are different from everyone else's (within the system) in that they are what *everything* is constructed from. But his transcendental stance is that it's all symmetrical: the "you" he addresses his higher-order remark to cannot be the *empirical* "you" of the system. But if it's really true that the "you" of the system is the only "you" he can *understand*, then the transcendental remark is *unintelligible*. Moral: don't be a methodological solipsist unless you are a *real* solipsist!

Consider now the position of the cultural relativist who says, "When I say something is *true*, I mean that it is correct according to the norms of *my* culture." If he adds, "When a member of a different culture says that something is true, what he means (whether he knows it or not) is that it is in conformity with the norms of *his* culture," then he is in exactly the same plight as the methodological solipsist.

To spell this out, suppose R.R., a cultural relativist, says

When Karl says "Schnee ist weiss," what Karl means (whether he knows it or not) is that snow is white *as determined by* the norms of Karl's culture

(which we take to be German culture).

Now the sentence "Snow is white as determined by the norms of German culture" is itself one which R.R. has to *use*, not just mention, to say what Karl says. On his own account, what R.R. means by *this* sentence is

"Snow is white as determined by the norms of German culture" is true by the norms of R.R.'s culture

(which we take to be American culture).

Substituting this back into the first displayed utterance, (and changing to indirect quotation) yields:

When Karl says "Schnee ist weiss," what he means (whether he knows it or not) is that it is true as determined by the norms of American culture that it is true as determined by the norms of German culture that snow is white.

In general, if R.R. understands every utterance *p* that *he* uses as meaning "it is true by the norms of American culture that *p*," then he must understand his own hermeneutical utterances, the utterances he uses to interpret others, the same way, no matter how many qualifiers of the "according to the norms of German culture" type or however many footnotes, glosses, commentaries on the cultural differences, or whatever, he accompanies them by. Other cultures become, so to speak, logical constructions out of the procedures and practices of American culture. If he now attempts to add "the situation is reversed from the point of view of the *other* culture" he lands in the predicament the methodological solipsist found himself in: the transcendental claim of a *symmetrical* situation cannot be *understood* if the relativist doctrine is right. And to say, as relativists often do, that the other culture has "incommensurable" concepts is no better. This is just the transcendental claim in a special jargon.

Stanley Cavell (1979, part IV) has written that skepticism about other minds can be a significant problem because we don't, in fact, always fully acknowledge the reality of others, their equal *validity* so to speak. One might say that the methodological solipsist is led to his transcendental observation that everyone is equally the "I" of the construction by his praiseworthy desire to *acknowledge* others in this sense. But you *can't* acknowledge others in this sense, which involves recognizing that the situation *really is* symmetrical, if you think they are really constructions out of *your* sense data. Nor can you acknowledge others in this sense if you think that the *only* notion of truth there is for *you* to understand is "truth-as-determined-by-the-norms-of-*this*-culture."

For simplicity, I have discussed relativism with respect to truth, but the same discussion applies to relativism about rational acceptability, justification, etc; indeed, a relativist is unlikely to be a relativist about one of these notions and not about the others.

Cultural imperialism

Just as the methodological solipsist can become a *real* solipsist, the cultural relativist can become a cultural imperialist. He can say, "Well then, truth—the only notion of truth I understand—is defined by the norms of *my* culture." ("After all," he can add, "which norms should I rely on? The norms of *somebody else's* culture?") Such a view is no longer relativist at all. It postulates an *objective* notion of truth, although one that is said to be a product of our culture, and to be defined by our culture's criteria (I assume the culture imperialist is one of *us*). In this sense, just as consistent solipsism becomes indistinguishable from realism (as Wittgenstein said in the *Tractatus*), consistent cultural relativism also becomes indistinguishable from realism. But cultural imperialist realism is a special *kind* of realism.

It is realist in that it accepts an objective difference between what is true and what is merely thought to be true. (Whether it can consistently *account for* this difference is another question.)

It is not a *metaphysical* or transcendental realism, in that truth cannot go beyond right assertibility, as it does in metaphysical realism. But the notion of right assertibility is fixed by "criteria," in a positivistic sense: something is rightly assertible only if the norms of the culture specify that it is; these norms are, as it were, an *operational definition* of right assertibility, in this view.

I don't know if any philosopher holds such a view, although several philosophers have let themselves fall into talking at certain times as if they did. (A philosopher in this mood is likely to say, "*X* is *our* notion," with a certain petulance, where *X* may be *reason, truth, justification, evidence,* or what have you.)

This view is, however, self-refuting, at least in our culture. I have discussed this elsewhere (Putnam, 1981); the argument turns on the fact that our culture, unlike totalitarian or theocratic cultures, does not have "norms" which decide *philosophical* questions. (Some philosophers have thought it does; but they had to postulate a "depth grammar" accessible only to *them*, and not describable by ordinary linguistic or anthropological investigation.) Thus the philosophical statement:

A statement is true (rightly assertible) only if it is assertible according to the norms of modern European and American culture

is itself neither assertible nor refutable in a way that requires assent by everyone who does not deviate from the norms of modern European and American culture. So, if this statement is true, it follows that it is not true (not rightly assertible). Hence it is not true QED. (I believe that all theories which identify truth or right assertibility with what people agree with, or with what they would agree with in the long run, or with what educated and intelligent people agree with, or with what educated and intelligent people would agree with in the long run, are contingently self-refuting in this same way.)

Cultural imperialism would not be contingently self-refuting in this way if, as a matter of contingent fact, our culture were a totalitarian culture which erected its own cultural imperialism into a required dogma, a culturally normative belief. But it would still be wrong. For every culture has norms which are vague, norms which are unreasonable, norms which dictate inconsistent beliefs. We have all become aware how many inconsistent beliefs about *women* were culturally normative until recently, and are still strongly operative, not only in subcultures, but in all of us to some extent; and examples of inconsistent but culturally normative beliefs could easily be multiplied. Our task is not to mechanically *apply* cultural norms, as if they were a computer program and we were the computer, but to interpret them, to criticize them, to bring them and the ideals which inform them into reflective equilibrium. Cavell has aptly described this as "confronting the culture with itself, along the lines in which it meets in me." And he adds (Cavell, 1979, p. 125), "This seems to me a task that warrants the name of Philosophy." In this sense, we are all called to be philosophers, to a greater or lesser extent.

The culturalist, relativist or imperialist, like the historicist, has been caught up in the fascination of something really fascinating; but caught up in a sophomorish way. Traditions, cultures, history, deserve to be emphasized, as they are not by those who seek Archimedian points in metaphysics or epistemology. It is true that we speak a public language, that we inherit versions, that talk of truth and falsity only make sense against the background of an "inherited tradition," as Wittgenstein says. But it is also true that we constantly remake our language, that we make new versions out of old ones, and that we have to use reason to do all this, and, for that matter, even to understand and apply the norms we do not alter or criticize. Consensus definitions of reason do not work, because consensus among grown-ups *presupposes* reason rather than defining it.

Quinian positivism

The slogan "epistemology naturalized" is the title of a famous paper by Quine (1969). If I have not discussed that paper up to now, it is because Quine's views are much more subtle and much more elaborate than the disastrously simple views we have just reviewed, and it seemed desirable to get the simpler views out of the way first.

Quine's philosophy is a large continent, with mountain ranges, deserts, and even a few Okefenokee Swamps. I do not know how all of the pieces of it can be reconciled, if they can be; what I shall do is discuss two different strains that are to be discerned in Quine's epistemology. In the present section I discuss the positivistic strain; the next section will discuss "epistemology naturalized."

The positivist strain, which occurs early and late, turns on the notion of an *observation sentence*. In his earliest writings, Quine gave this a phenomenalistic interpretation but, since the 1950s at least, he has preferred a definition in neurological and cultural terms. First, a preliminary notion: The *stimulus meaning* of a sentence is defined to be the set of stimulations (of "surface neurons") that would "prompt assent" to the sentence. It is thus supposed to be a *neurological* correlate of the sentence. A sentence may be called "stimulus-true" for a speaker if the speaker is actually experiencing a pattern of stimulation of his surface neurons that lie in its stimulus meaning; but one should be careful to remember that a stimulus-true sentence is not necessarily true *simpliciter*. If you show me a life-like replica of a duck, the sentence, "That's a duck," may be stimulus-true for me, but it isn't true. A sentence is defined to be an *observation* sentence for a community if it is an occasioned sentence (one whose truth value is regarded as varying with time and place, although this is not the Quinian definition) and it has the *same* stimulus meaning for all speakers. Thus "He is a bachelor" is not an observation sentence, since different stimulations will prompt you to assent to it than will prompt me (we know different people); but "That's a duck" is (nearly enough) an observation sentence. Observe that the criterion is supposed to be entirely physicalistic. The key idea is that observation sentences are distinguished among occasioned sentences by being keyed to the same stimulations *intersubjectively*.

Mach held that talk of unobservables, including (for him) material objects, is justified only for reasons of "economy of thought." The business of science is *predicting regularities in our sensations*; we introduce "objects" other than sensations only as needed to get theories which neatly predict such regularities. Quine (1975) comes close to a "physicalized" version of Mach's view. Discussing the question, whether there is more than one correct "system of the world," he gives his criteria for such a system: (1) it must predict a certain number of stimulus-true observation sentences;[3] (2) it must be finitely axiomatized; (3) it must contain nothing unnecessary to the purpose of predicting stimulus-true observation sentences and conditionals. In the terminology Quine introduces in this paper, the theory formulation must be a "tight fit"[4] over the relevant set of stimulus-true observation conditionals. (This is a formalized version of Mach's "economy of thought.")

If this were all of Quine's doctrine, there would be no problem. It is reconciling what Quine says here with what Quine says elsewhere that is difficult and confusing. I am *not* claiming that it is impossible however; a lot, if not all, of what Quine says *can* be reconciled. What I claim is that Quine's position is much more complicated than is generally realized.

For example, what is the *status* of Quine's ideal "systems of the world?" It is tempting to characterize the sentences in one of Quine's ideal "theory formulations" as *truths* (relative to that language and that choice of formulation from among the equivalent-but-incompatible-at-face-value formulations of what Quine would regard as the *same* theory) and as *all* the truths (relative to the same choice of language and formulation), but this would conflict with *bivalence*, the principle that *every* sentence, in the ideal scientific language Quine envisages, is true or false.

To spell this out: Quine's ideal systems of the world are *finitely axiomatizable theories*, and contain standard mathematics. Thus Gödel's celebrated result applies to them: there are sentences in them which are neither provable nor refutable on the basis of the system. If being *true* were just being a theorem in the system, such sentences would be neither true nor false, since neither they nor their negations are theorems. But Quine (1981) holds to bivalence.

If Quine were a metaphysical realist there would again be no problem: the ideal system would contain everything that could be *justified* (from a very idealized point of view, assuming knowledge of all observations that *could* be made, and logical omniscience); but, Quine could say, the undecidable sentences are still determinately true or false—only we can't tell which. But the rejection of metaphysical realism, of the whole picture of a determinate "copying" relation between words and a noumenal world, is at the heart of Quine's philosophy. And, as we shall see in the next section, "justification" is a notion Quine is leery of. So what *is* he up to?[5]

I hazard the following interpretation: bivalence has *two* meanings for Quine: a "first-order" meaning, a meaning as viewed *within* the system of science (including its Tarskian metalanguage) and a "second-order" meaning, a meaning as viewed by the philosopher. In effect, I am claiming that Quine too allows himself a "transcendental" standpoint which is different from the "naive" standpoint that we get by just taking the system at face value. (I am not claiming that this is *inconsistent* however; some philosophers feel that such a move is *always* an inconsistency, but taking this line would preclude using *any* notion in science which one would explain away as a useful fiction in one's commentary on one's first-order practice. There was an inconsistency in the case of the methodological solipsist, because he claimed his first-order system reconstructed the *only* way he could understand the notion of another mind; if he withdraws that claim, then his position becomes perfectly consistent; it merely loses all philosophical interest.)

From *within* the first-order system, "*p* is true or *p* is false" is simply true; a derivable consequence of the Tarskian truth definition, given standard propositional calculus. From *outside*, from the meta-metalinguistic point of view Quine occupies, there is no unique "world," no unique "intended model." Only *structure* matters; every model of the ideal system (I assume there is just one ideal theory, and we have fixed a formulation) is an intended model. Statements that are provable are true in *all* intended models; undecidable statements are true or false in each intended model, but not *stably* true or false. Their truth value varies from model to model.

If *this* is Quine's view, however, then there is still a problem. For Quine, what the philosopher says from the "transcendental" standpoint is subject to the same methodological rules that govern ordinary first-order scientific work. Even mathematics is subject to the same rules. Mathematical truths, too, are to be certified as such by showing they are theorems in a system which we need to predict sensations (or rather, stimulus-true observation conditionals), given the physics which we are constructing as we construct the mathematics. More precisely, the *whole system of knowledge* is justified *as a whole* by its utility in predicting observations. Quine emphasizes that there is no room in this view for a special status for philosophical utterances. There is no "first philosophy" above or apart from science, as he puts it.

Consider, now, the statement:

> A statement is *rightly assertible* (true in all models) just in case it is a theorem of the relevant "finite formulation," and that formulation is a "tight fit" over the appropriate set of stimulus-true observation conditionals.

This statement, like most philosophical statements, does not imply *any* observation conditionals, either by itself or in conjunction with physics, chemistry, biology, etc. Whether we say that some statements which are undecidable in the system are really rightly assertible or deny it does not have any effects (that one can foresee) on prediction. Thus, *this* statement *cannot* itself be rightly assertible. In short, *this* reconstruction of Quine's positivism makes it *self-refuting*.

The difficulty, which is faced by all versions of positivism, is that positivist exclusion principles are always self-referentially inconsistent. In short, *positivism produced a conception of rationality so narrow as to exclude the very activity of producing that conception.* (Of course, it also excluded a great many other kinds of rational activity.) The problem is especially sharp for Quine, because of his explicit rejection of the analytic/synthetic distinction, his rejection of a special status for philosophy, etc.

It may be, also, that I have just got Quine wrong. Quine would perhaps reject the notions of "right assertibility," "intended model," and so on. But then I just don't know *what* to make of this strain in Quine's thought.

"Epistemology naturalized"

Quine's paper "Epistemology naturalized" takes a very different tack. "Justification" has failed. (Quine considers the notion only in its strong "Cartesian" setting, which is one of the things that makes his paper puzzling.) Hume taught us that we *can't* justify our knowledge claims (in a foundational way). Conceptual reduction has also failed (Quine reviews the failure of phenomenalism as represented by Carnap's attempt in the *Logische Aufbau*.) So, Quine urges, let us give up epistemology and "settle for psychology."

Taken at face value, Quine's position is sheer epistemological eliminationism: we should just *abandon* the notions of justification, good reason, warranted assertion, etc., and *reconstrue* the notion of "evidence" (so that the "evidence" becomes the sensory stimulations that *cause us* to have the scientific beliefs we have). In conversation, however, Quine has repeatedly said that he didn't mean to "rule out the normative"; and this is consistent with his recent interest in such notions as the notion of a "tight fit" (an economical finitely axiomatized system for predicting observations).

Moreover, the expression "naturalized epistemology" is being used today by a number of philosophers who explicitly consider themselves to *be* doing normative epistemology, or at least methodology. But the paper "Epistemology naturalized" really does rule all that out. So it's all *extremely* puzzling.

One way to reconcile the conflicting impulses that one sees at work here might be to replace justification theory by reliability theory in the sense of Goldman; instead of saying that a belief is justified if it is arrived at by a reliable method, one might say that the notion of justification should be *replaced* by the notion of a verdict's being the product of a reliable method. This is an *eliminationist* line in that it does not try to reconstruct or analyze the traditional notion; that was an intuitive notion that we now perceive to have been defective from the start, such a philosopher might say. Instead, he proposes a *better* notion (by his lights).

While some philosophers would, perhaps, move in this direction, Quine would not for a reason already given: Quine rejects metaphysical realism, and the notion of reliability presupposes the notion of *truth*. Truth is, to be sure, an acceptable notion for Quine, if defined à la Tarski, but so defined, it cannot serve as the primitive notion of epistemology or of methodology. For Tarski simply defines "true" so that "*p* is true" will come out equivalent to "*p*"; so that, to cite the famous example, "*Snow is white*" *is true* will come out equivalent to "Snow is white." What the procedure does is to define "true" so that saying that a statement is true is equivalent to *assenting* to the statement; truth, as defined by Tarski, is not a *property* of statements at all, but a syncategoramatic notion which enables us to "ascend semantically," i.e., to talk about sentences instead of about objects.[6]

I will assent to "*p* is true" whenever I assent to *p*; therefore, I will accept a method as reliable whenever it *yields verdicts I would accept*. I believe that, in fact, this is what the "normative" becomes for Quine: the search for methods that yield verdicts that one oneself would accept.

Why we can't eliminate the normative

I shall have to leave Quine's views with these unsatisfactory remarks. But why not take a full blown eliminationist line? Why *not* eliminate the normative from our conceptual vocabulary? Could it be a superstition that there is such a thing as reason?

If one abandons the notions of justification, rational acceptability, warranted assertibility, right assertibility, and the like, completely, then "true" goes as well, except as a mere device for "semantic ascent," that is, a mere mechanism for switching from one level of language to another. The mere introduction of a Tarskian truth predicate cannot define for a language any notion of *rightness* that was not already defined. To reject the notions of justification and right assertibility while *keeping a metaphysical realist notion of truth* would, on the other hand, not only be peculiar (what ground could there be for regarding truth, in the "correspondence" sense, as *clearer* than right assertibility?), but incoherent; for the notions the naturalistic metaphysician uses to explain truth and reference, for example the notion of causality (explanation), and the notion of the *appropriate type* of causal chain depend on notions which presuppose the notion of reasonableness.

But if *all* notions of rightness, both epistemic and (metaphysically) realist are eliminated, then what are our statements but noise-makings? What are our thoughts but *mere* subvocalizations? The elimination of the normative is attempted mental suicide.

The notions, "verdict I accept" and "method that leads to verdicts I accept" are of little help. If the *only* kind of rightness any statement has that I can understand is "being arrived at by a method which yields verdicts *I* accept," then I am committed to a solipsism of the present moment. To solipsism, because this *is* a methodologically solipsist substitute for assertibility ("verdicts *I* accept"), and we saw before that the methodological solipsist is only consistent if he is a real solipsist. And to solipsism of the present moment because this is a *tensed* notion (a substitute for warranted assertibility at *a time*, not for assertibility in the best conditions); and if the *only* kind of rightness my present "subvocalizations" have is *present* assertibility (however defined); if there is no notion of a *limit* verdict, however fuzzy; then there is no sense in which my "subvocalizations" are *about* anything that goes beyond the present moment. (Even the thought "there is a future" is "right" only in the sense of being *assertible at the present moment*, in such a view.)

One could try to overcome this last defect by introducing the notion of "a verdict I would accept *in the long run*," but this would at once involve one with the use of counterfactuals, and with such notions as "similarity of possible worlds." But it is pointless to make further efforts in this direction. Why should we expend our mental energy in convincing ourselves that we aren't thinkers, that our thoughts aren't really *about* anything, noumenal *or* phenomenal, that there is *no* sense in which any thought is *right* or *wrong* (including the thought that no thought is right or wrong) beyond being the verdict of the moment, and so on? This is a self-refuting enterprise if there ever was one! Let us recognize that one of our fundamental self-conceptualizations, one of our fundamental "self-descriptions," in Rorty's phrase, is that we are *thinkers,* and that *as* thinkers we are committed to there being *some* kind of truth, some kind of correctness which is substantial and not merely "disquotational." That means that there is no eliminating the normative.

If there is no eliminating the normative, and no possibility of reducing the normative to our favorite science, be it biology, anthropology, neurology, physics, or whatever, then where are we? We might try for a grand theory of the normative in its *own* terms, a formal epistemology, but that project seems decidedly overambitious. In the meantime, there is a great deal of philosophical work to be done, and it will be done with fewer errors if we free ourselves of the reductionist and historicist hang-ups that have marred so much recent philosophy. If reason is both transcendent and immanent, then philosophy, as culture-bound reflection and argument about eternal questions, is both in time and eternity. We don't have an Archimedean point; we always speak the language of a time and place; but the rightness and wrongness of what we say is not *just* for a time and a place.

NOTES

[1]   I chose brown because brown is not a spectral color. But the point also applies to spectral colors: if being a color were purely a matter of reflecting light of a certain wavelength, then the objects we see would change color a number of times a day (and would all be black in total darkness). Color depends on background conditions, edge effects, reflectancy, relations to amount of light etc. Giving a description of all of these would only define *perceived* color; to define the "real" color of an object one also needs a notion of "standard conditions": traditional philosophers would have said that the color of a red object is a power (a disposition) to look red to normal observers under normal conditions. This, however, requires a counterfactual conditional (whenever the object is *not* in normal conditions) and we saw in the previous chapter that the attempt to define counterfactuals in "physical" terms has failed. What makes color terms

physically undefinable is not that color is subjective but that it is *subjunctive*. The common idea that there is some one molecular structure (or whatever) common to all objects which look red "under normal conditions" has no foundation: consider the difference between the physical structure of a red star and a red book (and the difference in what we count as "normal conditions" in the two cases).

[2] This argument appears in Firth's Presidential Address to the Eastern Division of the American Philosophical Association (29 December 1981), titled "Epistemic merit, intrinsic and instrumental." Firth does not specifically refer to evolutionary epistemology, but rather to "epistemic utilitarianism"; however, his argument applies as well to evolutionary epistemology of the kind I describe.

[3] Quine actually requires that a "system of the world" predict that certain "pegged observation sentences" be true. I have oversimplified in the text by writing "observation sentence" for "pegged observation sentence." Also the "stimulus meaning" of an observation sentence includes a specification of conditions under which the speaker *dissents*, as well as the conditions under which he assents. The details are in Quine (1975).

[4] A theory is a "tight fit" if it is interpretable in *every* axiomatizable theory which implies the observation conditionals (conditionals whose antecedent and consequent are pegged observation sentences) in question in a way that holds the pegged observation sentences fixed. To my knowledge, no proof exists that a "tight fit" even exists, apart from the trivial case in which the observation conditionals can be axiomatized *without* going outside of the observation vocabulary.

[5] Quine *rejected* the interpretation I offer below (discussion at Heidelberg in 1981), and opted for saying that our situation is "asymmetrical": he is a "realist" with respect to his *own* language but not with respect to other languages. See pp. xii–xiii above and pp. 278–9 below for my rejoinder.

[6] Quine himself puts this succinctly. "Whatever we affirm, after all, we affirm as a statement within our aggregate theory of nature as we now see it; and to call a statement true is just to reaffirm it." (Quine, 1975, p. 327)

3.4

FEMINIST EPISTEMOLOGY:
AN INTERPRETATION AND A DEFENSE

Elizabeth Anderson

Feminist epistemology has often been understood as the study of feminine "ways of knowing." But feminist epistemology is better understood as the branch of naturalized, social epistemology that studies the various influences of norms and conceptions of gender and gendered interests and experiences on the production of knowledge. This understanding avoids dubious claims about feminine cognitive differences and enables feminist research in various disciplines to pose deep internal critiques of mainstream research.

Feminist epistemology is about the ways gender influences what we take to be knowledge. Consider impersonal theoretical and scientific knowledge, the kind of knowledge privileged in the academy. Western societies have labeled this kind of knowledge "masculine" and prevented women from acquiring and producing it, often on the pretext that it would divert their vital energies from their "natural" reproductive labor (Hubbard 1990; Schiebinger 1989). Theoretical knowledge is also often tailored to the needs of mostly male managers, bureaucrats, and officials exercising power in their role-given capacities (H. Rose 1987; Smith 1974; Collins 1990). Feminist epistemologists claim that the ways gender categories have been used to understand the character and status of theoretical knowledge, whether men or women have produced and applied this knowledge, and whose interests it has served have often had a detrimental impact on its content. For instance, feminist epistemologists suggest that various kinds of practical know-how and personal knowledge (knowledge that bears the marks of the knower's biography and identity), such as the kinds of untheoretical knowledge that mothers have of children, are undervalued when they are labeled "feminine." Given the androcentric need to represent the "masculine" as independent of the "feminine," this labeling has led to a failure to use untheoretical knowledge effectively in theoretical reasoning (Smith 1974; H. Rose 1987).

Traditional epistemology finds these claims of feminist epistemology to be highly disturbing, if not plainly absurd. Some feminist epistemologists in turn have rejected empiricism (Harding 1986) or even traditional epistemology as a whole (Flax 1983) for its seeming inability to comprehend these claims. I argue, contrary to these views, that a naturalized empiricist epistemology offers excellent prospects for advancing a feminist epistemology of theoretical knowledge.

The project of feminist epistemology with respect to theoretical knowledge has two primary aims (Longino 1993a). First, it endeavors to explain the achievements of feminist criticism of science, which is devoted to revealing sexism and androcentrism in theoretical inquiry. An adequate feminist epistemology must explain what it is for a scientific theory or practice to be sexist and androcentric, how these features are expressed in theoretical inquiry and in the application of theoretical knowledge, and what bearing these features have on evaluating research. Second, the project of feminist epistemology aims to defend feminist scientific practices, which incorporate a commitment to the liberation of women and the social and political equality of all persons. An adequate feminist epistemology must explain how research projects with such moral and political commitments can produce knowledge that meets such epistemic standards as empirical adequacy and fruitfulness. I will argue that these aims can be satisfied by a branch of naturalized, social epistemology that retains commitments to a modest empiricism and to rational inquiry. Feminist naturalized epistemologists therefore demand no radical break from the fundamental internal commitments of empirical science. They may propose changes in our conceptions of what these commitments amount to, or changes in our methods of inquiry. But these can be derived from the core concept of reason, conjoined with perhaps surprising yet empirically supported hypotheses about social or psychological obstacles to achieving them, and the social and material arrangements required for enabling better research to be done. To see how such derivations are possible, modest conceptions of empiricism and reason must be explained before I outline a feminist epistemology that employs these notions.

A Modest Empiricism

[handwritten: Foundational but in the sense that it's empirical]

I shall call "empiricism" the view that experience ultimately provides all the evidence we have about the world (Nelson 1990), or more modestly, that observation provides the least defeasible evidence we have about the world (Longino 1993a). No thought process operating independently of empirical evidence can rule out any conceivable hypothesis about the world. I believe that empiricism, so understood, is congenial to the puzzling and seemingly bizarre hypotheses of feminist epistemology because it implies two things. First, for all we know, *anything* can cause *anything,* and *anything* might provide an illuminating fruitful model for *any other phenomenon.* There are no sound a priori restrictions on the concepts or vocabulary we use in describing and explaining the world, so long as these concepts "turn wheels" in theories that have empirical implications. Second, empiricism implies that the discovery of the best theories demands the fullest and freest development of our imaginations. There is no reason to think our presently cramped and stunted imaginations set the actual limits of the world, but they do set the limits of what we now take to be possible. We can never know what further stretch of the imagination might uncover and explain what further expanse of the world. Since feminist epistemology and feminist criticism of science contain many empirical claims about the influence of gender on science that appear at first glance to be unimaginable, it is important to note that nothing in empiricism justifies dismissing such claims out of hand.

[handwritten margin note: No restrictions on process]

Empiricism is commonly taken to mean something else: a doctrine that imposes a priori substantive restrictions on the kinds of entities and concepts that can ultimately figure in science. Various self-described empiricists have tried to eliminate from science reference to unobservables, and use of intentional, modal, and evaluative concepts, or to reduce these to concepts thought to be more "naturalistic". These substantive commitments are simply bets as to how empirical science will actually turn out. Transformed into restrictions on the permissible content of theories, they are attempts to win the bets by rigging the game in advance, preventing the exploration of hypotheses that might show them wrong. This contradicts what I take to be the fundamental commitments of modest empiricism. Since feminist epistemology and feminist criticism of science contain many empirical claims couched in unreduced social, intentional, and evaluative vocabularies, it is important to note that modest empiricism is not committed to eliminating such claims from scientific theories.

I take modest empiricism, then, to be a purely methodological doctrine, which rejects a priori commitments to what the content of our theories and models must be. Empiricism is promiscuous in its permissible ontology and opportunistic in its methods and models. Any hypothesis or method is permitted that advances the goals of discovering and explaining novel phenomena consistent with the constraint that the theories produced seek empirical adequacy.

Rationality as Reflective Endorsability

Reason is the power to change our attitudes, intentions, and practices in response to reflection on the merits of having them or engaging in them. Theoretical reason is the power to acquire, reject, and revise our cognitive attitudes (beliefs and theoretical commitments) and our practices of inquiry through reflection on our reasons for holding them and engaging in them—that is, through reflection on arguments and evidence for our beliefs and about the consequences of our practices. Reflective endorsement is the only test for whether a consideration counts as a reason for having any attitude or engaging in any practice of inquiry: we ask, on reflecting on the ways the consideration could or does influence our attitudes and practices and the implications of its influencing us, whether we can endorse its influencing us in other ways. If we can reflectively endorse its influence, we count the consideration as a reason for our attitudes or practices (Anderson 1993, 91–98).

This conception of reason as reflective self-government rejects the ideal of individualistic self-sufficiency, which some feminists have argued is andro-centric, or expressive of specifically male needs (Bordo 1987; Duran 1991). Rational inquiry is a social enterprise (Longino 1990; Nelson 1993). Anything that counts as evidence for a theory must be publicly accessible, and in experimental contexts, replicable by others. Individuals must use tools, methods, and conceptual frameworks developed by others in order to get their own inquiries under way. They must rely on the testimony of others to get evidence that is too costly or difficult for them to gather on their own, and even to interpret the evidence of their own senses (Coady 1992). Thus it is impossible for individuals to rely only on themselves, for the very reason and interpretations of their experience on which they rely and which seems most to be their own, is a social achievement, not an individual endowment (Nelson 1990; Scheman 1983).

The social character of rational inquiry suggests two things. First, the theories produced by our practices of inquiry may bear the marks of the social relations of the inquirers. To the extent that conceptions of gender inform these social relations, we might expect these conceptions to influence theoretical inquiry. Second, insofar as we reflectively reject certain ways that gender influences the practices and products of inquiry, we need not try to correct these problems by demanding that individual investigators somehow abstract from their gender or gender-related values and commitments. Each individual might be subject to perhaps ineradicable cognitive biases or partiality due to gender or other influences. But if the social relations of inquirers are well arranged, then each person's biases can check and correct the others'. In this way, theoretical rationality and objectivity can be expressed by the whole community of inquirers even when no individual's thought processes are perfectly impartial, objective, or sound (Longino 1990; Nelson 1990; Solomon 1994).

[handwritten margin note: This tches work. requires courage]

[handwritten note below paragraph: we must do this work, not just for women, but all marginalized groups, and by proxy all human kind]

Feminist Epistemology as a Branch of Naturalized, Social Epistemology

Many theorists have proposed that we think of feminist epistemology as a social branch of naturalized epistemology (Nelson 1990; Harding 1986; Potter 1993; Tuana 1992; Antony 1993; Duran 1991). Naturalized epistemologists consider knowledge production as an activity in which inquirers are subject to the same causal forces that affect their objects of study (Quine 1969). They ask of science that it provide an account of its own activity. This point of view enables us to investigate empirically how knowledge changes as we change factors concerning the inquirers. Social epistemology is the branch of naturalized epistemology that investigates the influence of specifically social factors on knowledge production: who gets to participate in theoretical inquiry, who listens to whom, the relative prestige of different styles and fields of research, the political and economic conditions in which inquirers conduct their investigations, the social settings in which they interact with the subjects of study, their ideological commitments, the availability of models and narrative forms in the culture that can be used to structure scientific observation and explain phenomena, and so forth. Feminist epistemology can be regarded as the branch of social epistemology that investigates the influence of *socially constructed conceptions and norms of gender and gender-specific interests and experiences* on the production of knowledge. It asks how the historical exclusion of women from theoretical inquiry has affected the direction and content of research in fields such as anthropology, philosophy, and psychology; how the use of gender metaphors in biology has made some phenomena more salient than others; how history, economics, and medicine would change if we viewed phenomena from the standpoint of women's rather than men's lives; how the feminist movement has changed our data, our ways of describing the data, and our theories about differences between men and women.

These are all empirical questions. By framing the questions of feminist epistemology as empirical ones, feminist theorists can challenge mainstream theorists, who are largely empiricists, in a way that they cannot responsibly ignore or dismiss. This way of framing feminist epistemology also enables feminists to make arguments for reforming theoretical practice in terms internal to the self-critical commitments of science itself. Feminist criticisms and remedies can be seen as particular, if surprising, instances of general types of criticism and remedy already acknowledged and accommodated by scientific practice. For naturalized epistemology, considered as a tool for improving scientific practices, is already incorporated into the self-critical and self-reforming institutions of science.

How can naturalized epistemology, which studies how knowledge claims are actually produced, support normative views about how we ought to produce knowledge claims? This gap between "is" and "ought" is bridged by the reflective self-endorsement test. Naturalized epistemology considers inquirers in their social relations as systems of belief-formation processes, and theoretical inquiry as a social practice that uses these processes to generate new beliefs. These beliefs in turn are related to one another through various explanatory theories, models, or narratives that aim to produce understanding of the phenomena being studied. This two-level representation of theoretical inquiry suggests two ways naturalize epistemology can get critical leverage on our knowledge practices. First, we can examine our belief-formation processes. Some of these processes are such that, once we reflect on how they work or what they do, we lose confidence in the beliefs to which they give rise, since they do not reliably lead to true beliefs (consider optical illusions). Other processes satisfy the reflective endorsement test: reflecting on how they work or what they do leads us to endorse them and the beliefs to which they give rise (consider deductive inference). A knowledge practice is rational to the extent that it promotes such critical self-reflections and responds to them by checking or canceling out the unreliable belief-formation mechanisms and enabling the reliable ones.

The institution of placebo-controlled, double-blind, multi-center trials as the standard for testing drugs represents an exemplary critical achievement of naturalized epistemology. Each feature of this experimental standard was instituted in response to the discovery of an unreliable belief-formation mechanism that had to be checked. The well-known placebo effect, in which subjects report symptom improvement when they receive *any* intervention they believe may help them, is checked by requiring that the therapeutic effects of drugs be measured against a control group which is administered a placebo, and by requiring that subjects not know whether they belong to the control or the experimental group. Wishful thinking on the part of experimenters, which leads to exaggerated reports of the therapeutic effectiveness of drugs on trial, is checked by making the tests double-blind, so that even the experimenter does not know which group subjects belong to. Multi-center trials ensure that experimental outcomes are not merely an artifact of the micro-culture of researchers at a single site. These are all reforms scientific institutions have made in the past few decades, in response to scientific studies of its own practice.

The normative implications of much feminist epistemology and feminist criticism of science can be modeled on the case of double-blind testing. If a gendered norm is found to influence the production of knowledge claims in ways that cannot be reflectively endorsed, then we have epistemic reasons to reform our knowledge practices so that this norm is changed or its effects are blocked. Feminist empiricist epistemology thus produces arguments of the same logical type as those already accepted by our knowledge practices.

Feminist empiricist epistemology can generate normative implications for theory in a second way. The model of double-blind testing works only at the level of weeding out false beliefs. But getting an adequate understanding of phenomena is not simply a matter of removing sexist or androcentric bias from factual claims so as to allow scientists to see unvarnished truth. For theoretical inquiry does not aim simply to generate true beliefs. One can add to the stock of true beliefs without the aid of systematic theorizing. Although empirical adequacy poses a fundamental constraint on theorizing, the point of theory is to organize beliefs and generate understanding through models that explain phenomena that people find significant, important, or fundamental, and that abstract from phenomena thought to be unimportant. But whether a phenomenon is considered important or fundamental depends on practical needs and interests, which may be gendered or staked in other socially constructed positions such as class (Tiles 1987). Theories or models offer us only partial maps of the world. Thus different people may find different models satisfactory, depending on which aspects of the world the models highlight (Longino 1993b, 114–16).

This relativity of the value of a model to the socially conditioned interests and experiences of the people to whom it is offered does not imply that theoretical explanations must be false, or that all are equally good, or that there is no common basis for comparing their merits. Empirical adequacy provides the fundamental and common standard for comparing all theories. But a theory can be empirically adequate without being interesting or useful.

Thus, feminist naturalized epistemology uses reason both to constrain and to expand the range of acceptable theories, given what we know about how theories are formed. By raising the standards for evaluating methods of data collection and interpretation in the light of the reflective endorsement test, feminist epistemologists limit the field of credible theories. By legitimizing the explicit introduction of feminist interests to justify the choice of different models, feminist epistemologists use reason in its permissive mode to open up space for alternative theories oriented toward liberatory ends and to contest theories that close off possibilities for social change by representing the subjects of study as if they had no room to maneuver (Longino 1989, 210–13).

Such moves to multiply available explanatory models, like the moves to reform scientific practices on the lines of the double-blind experiment, are internal to the practices of science. These two types of critical activity correspond to the two goals of the feminist epistemology of theoretical knowledge: to legitimate science oriented toward feminist ends and to underwrite feminist criticism of sexist and androcentric science. The fact that these activities can be situated inside science does not mean that the changes feminist epistemology recommends for science must be modest. The sorts of criticism that generate internal reform of scientific practices today focus on such matters as improving data-gathering instruments and technical features of experimental method. Feminist epistemology and feminist criticism of science focus on changing the background social conditions in which science is practiced. It is therefore an explicitly political enterprise, but one that is justified by epistemic values, such as reason and empirical adequacy, to which science already declares its allegiance.

The variety of claims made by feminist epistemologists and feminist critics of science is bewildering. Without attempting to account for or endorse all the conflicting claims made in the name of feminist epistemology, I shall follow the strategy of reading most of them as contributions to a research program in naturalized social epistemology. I propose that we can sort most of them into four categories, each specifying a particular type of gender influence on theoretical inquiry. Feminist epistemology has generally been better at identifying the ways gender is implicated in our knowledge practices than at explaining how these findings should affect our evaluations of the practices or the theories they produce (Longino 1993a). Naturalized epistemology provides a framework for developing such explanations. So I suggest some questions that probe the normative implications of each category of gender influence on theorizing.

First, studies that investigate *gender structures* focus on the ways gender norms structure the division of labor in society, including the divisions between intellectual and manual and service labor, and within the academy, among different disciplines and subfields, and among primary researchers, teachers, and assistants. These studies consider how the content of theories has been affected by historical discrimination against women entering the sciences, by the difficulties women scientists have getting their work recognized, and by the ways women have changed the orientation of fields of study once they have entered the elite ranks of significant numbers. These studies seek to answer the question, What difference does, or would, an equal representation and status of women researchers make to theoretical inquiry?

Second, some studies consider the uses of *gender symbolism*, which occurs when we represent nonhuman or inanimate phenomena as "masculine" or "feminine" and model them after gender ideals or stereotypes. Feminist epistemologists have found gender symbolism to be pervasive in theoretical inquiry. It is used to represent the relations of scientists to their subjects of study and the relations of different types of knowledge or of different disciplines and subfields to one another, to describe the character of scientific objectivity, and to model nonhuman and inanimate phenomena. These studies seek to answer the question, What difference does it make to our theories and our scientific practices that we conceive of theoretical inquiry itself and its subjects of study as gendered phenomena? How would our theories and practices of inquiry change if we altered our conceptions of the "masculine" and the "feminine," or ceased to employ gender symbolism in understanding our own theorizing or inanimate objects?

Third, some studies focus on *androcentrism* in biology, the social sciences, and cultural and literary studies. Androcentrism occurs when theories take males, men's lives, or "masculinity" to set the norm for humans or animals generally, with female differences either ignored or represented as deviant; when phenomena are viewed from the perspective of men's lives, without regard to how women see them differently; and when male activities or predicaments are represented as the primary causes or sites of important changes, without regard to the roles of females in initiating or facilitating changes or the ways the situation of females has been crucial to determining structural constraints and potentials for change. These studies ask, How would the content of theories be different if we viewed phenomena from the perspective of women's lives, or refused to accept either "masculinity" or "femininity" as setting the norm for humans or animals generally?

Fourth, some studies focus on *sexism* in theory, which can appear either in practices that apply the theory or in the content of the theory itself. Sexism is evident when theories are *applied* in ways that undermine women's interests or that reinforce their subordination to men. The *content* of a theory is sexist when it asserts that women are inferior to men, justly or inevitably subordinated to men, or properly confined to gender-stereotyped roles, or when it judges or describes women according to sexist ideals or double standards, or when it uses such claims as background assumptions to secure an evidential link between observations and theoretical claims. Feminist studies of sexism in theories explore the prospects for alternative scientific theories that meet criteria of empirical adequacy while seeking to serve women's interests and to promote universal equality.

The Gendered Division of Theoretical Labor

Feminist critics of science have carefully documented the history of women's exclusion from theoretical inquiry (Rossiter 1982; Schiebinger 1989). Although formal barriers to women's entry into various academic disciplines are now illegal in the United States, informal barriers at all levels remain. Girls are socialized by parents and peers to avoid studying or excelling in subject considered "masculine," such as mathematics and the natural sciences. Teachers and school counselors actively discourage girls from pursuing these subjects (Curran 1980, 30–32). The classroom climate in mixed-gender schools favors boys. Teachers pay more attention and offer more encouragement to white boys than to girls, solicit their participation more, and expect them to achieve more, especially in mathematics courses (Becker 1981; AAUW 1992). Boys marginalize girls in class by interruption and sexual harassment (AAUW 1992). These behaviors in mixed-gender schools have a detrimental impact on girls' academic ambitions and performance. Girls in all-girl schools express a wider diversity of academic interests and perform better academically than girls in mixed-gender schools (Curran 1980, 34). The disadvantage to women's academic performance and interests from attending mixed-gender schools extends to college. The predominantly male faculty in mixed-gender colleges support women students' academic ambitions less than male and female faculty at women's colleges. Women's colleges produce 50 percent more high-achieving women relative to the number of their female graduates than coeducational institutions (Tidball 1980). Graduate schools present women with informal barriers or costs to advancement, including sexual harassment and exclusion from networks of male mentors and colleagues often vital to the advancement of aspiring academics (Reskin 1979; S. Rose 1989).

Women who overcome these obstacles and obtain advanced degrees are not treated as equals once they enter academic positions. Women whose qualifications are comparable to their male colleagues get lower pay, less research support, jobs in less prestigious institutions, lower-ranking positions, and positions that assign more and lower-level teaching (Astin and Beyer 1973; Fox 1981). The prestige of the graduate institution, publications, and having one's work cited aid men's career advancement much more than women's (Rosenfeld 1981). Women in scientific and engineering professions with publication rates equal to those of their male peers have higher unemployment rates, lower starting salaries, and lower academic rank than men. These differences cannot be explained by the greater impact on women of marriage and children (Vetter 1981). The National Science Foundation (1984) found that after adjusting for factors such as women interrupting their careers to take care of children, half the salary differential between male and female scientists could be explained only by sex discrimination.

The gendered division of theoretical labor does not simply prevent women from doing research or getting published. It fits into a broader gendered structure of epistemic authority which assigns greater credibility, respect, and importance to men's than women's claims. Laboratory, field, and natural experiments alike show that the perceived gender of the author influences people's judgments of the quality of research, independent of its content. Psychologists M.A. Paludi and W.D. Bauer (1983) found that a group told that a paper's author was "John T. McKay" assigned it a much higher average ranking than a group told that the same paper's author was "Joan T. McKay." A group told that its author was "J.T. McKay" rated the paper between the other groups' evaluations, reflecting the suspicion that the author was a woman trying to conceal her gender identity. Academics are no less disposed than others to judge the quality of work higher simply because they believe a man has done it. L.S. Fidell (1970) sent vitae identical in all but name to heads of psychology departments that advertised open rank positions. The jobs the psychologists said they would offer to the purportedly male applicant were higher-ranking than those they were willing to offer to the purportedly female applicant. When the Modern Language Association reviewed papers submitted for their meetings with authors' names attached, men's submissions were accepted at significantly higher rates than women's. After the MLA instituted blind reviewing of papers, women's acceptance rates rose to equality with men's (Lefkowitz 1979).

The concerns raised by the influence of sexist norms on the division of theoretical labor and epistemic authority are not simply matters of justice. Feminist epistemology asks what impact these injustices toward women students and researchers have had on the content, shape, and progress of theoretical knowledge. In some cases, sex discrimination in the academy has demonstrably retarded the growth of knowledge. It took more than three decades for biologists to understand and recognize the revolutionary importance of Barbara McClintock's discovery of genetic transposition. Her attempts to communicate this discovery to the larger scientific community met with incomprehension and disdain. This failure can be partly explained by the fact that no biology department was willing to hire her for a permanent position despite her distinguished record of discoveries and publications. Lacking the opportunities such a position would have provided to recruit graduate students to her research program, McClintock had no one else doing research like hers who could replicate her results or help communicate them to a wider scientific community (Keller 1983).

Cases such as McClintock's demonstrate that the gendered structure of theoretical labor and cognitive authority sometimes slows the progress of knowledge. But does it change the content or shape of knowledge or the direction of knowledge growth? If the gender of the knower is irrelevant to the content of what is investigated, discovered, or invented, then the impact of removing sex discrimination would be to add to the pace of knowledge growth by adding more inquirers and by raising the average level of talent and dedication in the research community. Feminist epistemology would then recommend strictly "gender-blind" changes in the processes by which research jobs get assigned and epistemic authority distributed. The MLA's adoption of blind reviewing of papers to reduce cognitive bias due to sexism in the evaluation of research represents an exemplary application of this side of feminist epistemology. It is logically on a par with the institution of double-blind testing in drug research to reduce cognitive bias due to wishful thinking.

But if the gender of the inquirer makes a difference to the content of what is accepted as knowledge, then the exclusion and undervaluation of women's participation in theoretical inquiry does not merely set up randomly distributed roadblocks to the improvement of understanding. It imparts a systematic bias on what is taken to be knowledge. If the gender of the inquirer makes a difference to what is known, then feminist epistemology would not confine its recommendations to purely gender-blind reforms in our knowledge practices. It could recommend that these knowledge practices actively seek gender diversity and balance among inquirers and actively attend to the gender of the researchers in evaluating their products.

The gender of the researcher is known to make a difference to what is known in certain areas of social science. In survey research, subjects give different answers to questions depending on the perceived gender of the interviewer (Sherif 1987, 47–48). The perceived race of the interviewer also influences subjects' responses. It is a highly significant variable accounting for subjects' responses to questions about race relations (Schuman and Hatchett 1974). In anthropology, informants vary their responses depending on the gender of the anthropologist. In many societies, male anthropologists have less access to women's social worlds than female anthropologists do (Leacock 1982). The race of the research affects access to social worlds as well. Native Americans sometimes grant Asian anthropologists access to religious rituals from which they ban whites (Pai 1985).

Where the perceived gender and race of the researcher are variables influencing the phenomena being observed or influencing access to the phenomena, sound research design must pay attention to the gender and racial makeup of the researchers. In survey research, these effects can be analytically excised by ensuring a gender balanced and racially diverse research team and then statistically isolating the variations in responses due to factors other than subjects' responses to the characteristics of the interviewers. In anthropology, the method of reflexive sociology, instead of attempting to analyze away these effects, treats them as a subject of study in their own right. It advises researchers to interpret what informants tell them not as straightforward native observation reports on their own culture, but as reflections of a strategic interaction between informant and researcher and between the informant and other members of the community being studied (Bourdieu 1977). To obtain a complete representation of informants' report strategies with respect to gender, both male and female researchers must interact with both male and female informants and consider why informants varied their responses according to their own and the researcher's gender (see Bell, Caplan, and Karim [1993] for exemplary cases of feminist reflexive anthropology). Similar reasoning applies to factors such as race, class, nationality, and sexual orientation. So reflexive sociology, like survey research, requires a diversity of inquirers to obtain worthwhile results.

The phenomena just discussed concern the *causal* impact of the gender of the researcher on the *object* of knowledge. Many feminist epistemologists claim that the gender of the inquirer influences the *character* of knowledge itself by another route, which travels through the subjectivity of the researcher herself. The gender of the researcher influences what is known not just through her influence on the object of knowledge but by what are claimed to be gender-specific or gender-typical cognitive or affective dispositions, skills, knowledge, interests, or methods that she brings to the study of the object. The variety of claims of this type must be sorted through and investigated with great care. Some are local and modest. No one disputes that personal knowledge of what it is like to be pregnant, undergo childbirth, suffer menstrual cramps, and have other experiences of a female body is specific to women. Gynecology has certainly progressed since women have entered the field and have brought their personal knowledge to bear on misogynist medical practices. The claims get more controversial the more global they are in scope. Some people claim that women have gender-typical "ways of knowing," styles of thinking, methodologies, and ontologies that globally govern or characterize their cognitive activities across all subject matters. For instance, various feminist epistemologists have claimed that women think more intuitively and contextually, concern themselves more with particulars than abstractions, emotionally engage themselves more with individual subjects of study, and frame their thoughts in terms of a relational rather than an atomistic ontology (Belenky, Clinchy, Goldberger and Tarule 1986; Gilligan 1982; H. Rose 1987; Smith 1974; Collins 1990).

There is little persuasive evidence for such global claims (Tavris 1992, chap. 2). I believe the temptation to accept them is based partly on a confusion between gender symbolism—the fact that certain styles of thinking are *labeled* "feminine"—and the actual characteristics of women. It is also partly due to the lack of more complex and nuanced models of how women entering certain fields have changed the course of theorizing for reasons that seem connected to their gender or their feminist commitments. I will propose an alternative model toward the end of this essay, which does not suppose that women theorists bring some shared feminine difference to all subjects of knowledge. Controversies over supposed global differences in the ways men and women think have tended to overshadow other highly interesting work in feminist epistemology that does not depend on claims that men and women think in essentially different ways. The influence of gendered concepts and norms in our knowledge practices extends far beyond the ways male and female individuals are socialized and assigned to different roles in the division of labor. To see this, consider the role of *gender symbolism* in theoretical knowledge.

Gender Symbolism (1): The Hierarchy of Knowledge

It is a characteristic of human thought that our concepts do not stay put behind the neat logical fences philosophers like to erect for them. Like sly coyotes, they slip past these flimsy barriers to range far and wide, picking up consorts of all varieties, and, in astonishingly fecund acts of miscegenation shocking to conceptual purists, leave offspring who bear a disturbing resemblance to the wayward parent and inherit the impulse to roam the old territory. The philosophical guardians of these offspring, trying to shake off the taint of sexual scandal but feeling guilty about the effort, don't quite know whether to cover up a concept's pedigree or, by means of the dis-covery/justification distinction, deny that it matters. The latter strategy can work only if, like keepers of a zoo, the philosophers can keep their animals fenced in. Feminist epistemologists track these creatures sneaking past their fences while their keepers dream of tamed animals happy to remain confined.

The most cunning and promiscuous coyotes are our gender concepts. In a manner befitting their own links to sex, they will copulate with *anything*. Feminist epistemologists note that there is hardly any conceptual dichotomy that has not been modeled after and in turn used to model the mascu-line/feminine dichotomy: mind/body, culture/nature, reason/emotion, objec-tive/subjective, tough-minded/soft-hearted, and so forth. These scandalous metaphorical unions generate conceptions of knowledge, science, and rational inquiry, as well as conceptions of the objects of these inquiries, that are shaped in part by sexist views about the proper relations between men and women. Feminist epistemologists investigate how these conceptions are informed and distorted by sexist imagery. They also consider how alternative conceptions are suppressed by the limits imposed by sexism on the imagination, or by the sexist or androcentric interests served by their present symbolic links to gender (Rooney 1991).

Gender symbolism appears on at least two levels of our knowledge practices: in the construction of a hierarchy of prestige and authority among kinds and fields of knowledge and in the content of theoretical inquiry itself. Consider first the ways different kinds and fields of knowledge are gendered. At the most general level, impersonal theoretical knowledge is coded "masculine." Personal knowledge—the kind of knowledge that is inseparable from the knower's identity, biography, and emotional experiences—is coded "feminine." Theoretical knowledge is thought to be masculine in part because it lays claims to objectivity, which is thought to be achieved through the rigorous exclusion from thought of feminine subjectivity—of emotions, particularity, interests, and values. These uses of gender symbolism have *epistemic* import because they structure a hierarchy of prestige and cognitive authority among kinds of knowledge, and hence of knowers, that is homologous with the gender hierarchy. As men in sexist society express contempt for women and enjoy higher prestige than women, so do theoretical knowers express contempt for those with "merely" personal knowledge of the same subject matters, and enjoy higher prestige than they. Echoing the sexist norms that women must obey men but men need not listen to women, the gender-coded hierarchy of knowledge embodies the norm that personal knowledge must submit to the judgments of impersonal theoretical knowledge, while theoretical knowledge has nothing to learn from personal knowledge and may ignore its claims.

These epistemic norms cannot withstand reflective scrutiny. Successful theorizing deeply depends on personal knowledge, particularly embodied skills, and often depends on emotional engagement with the subjects of study (Polanyi 1958; Keller 1983, 1985). Cora Diamond's (1991) insightful discussion of Vicki Hearne's personal knowledge as an animal trainer provides a particularly fine illustration of this point. Hearne's writings (1982) expose the failures of knowledge that occur when theorists ignore the experiences, skills, and language of animal trainers. In her animal training classes, Hearne observed that people's success in training their pets was inversely related to their training in the behavioral sciences. The anthropomorphic and value-laden language of animal trainers enables them to understand what animals are doing in ways not readily accessible to the impersonal, behavioristic language favored by most behavioral scientists. And their skills and personal knowledge of the animals they work with empower trainers to elicit from animals considerably more complex and interesting behaviors than scientists elicit. These powers are not irrelevant to theorizing about animals. Reflecting on Hearne's story about the philosopher Ray Frey, Diamond writes:

> [Frey] attempted to set up a test for his dog's capacity to rank rational desires. When, in order to see how the dog would rank desires, he threw a stick for his dog…and at the same time put food before the dog, the dog stood looking at him. Frey could not see that the dog wanted to know what Frey wanted him to do; Frey's conception of the dog as part of an experimental set-up (taken to include two possible desired activities but not taken to include queer behavior by the dog's master), with Frey as the observer, block his understanding. Frey's past experience with his dog did not feed an understanding of how the dog saw him; he could not grasp his own failure, as the dog's master, to make coherent sense, so could not see the dog as responding to that failure to make sense. (Diamond 1991, 1014 n. 15)

Diamond diagnoses this epistemic failure as the product of Frey's attachment to a theory of knowledge that distrusts personal experience on the ground that it is distorted by the subject's emotional engagement with the object of knowledge. The theory supposes that we can't achieve objective knowledge of our object through such engagement because all it will offer is a reflection of the subject's own emotions. Subjectivity merely projects qualities onto the object and does not reveal qualities of the object. But the theory is mistaken. Love and respect for another being, animal or person, and trust in the personal experiences of engagement that are informed by such love and respect may be essential both for drawing out and for grasping that being's full potentialities. One of the reasons why behaviorists tend to elicit such boring behavior from animals and humans is that they don't give them the opportunities to exhibit a more impressive repertoire of behaviors that respect for them would require them to offer.

The gender-coded hierarchy of knowledge extends to specific subject matters and methods within theoretical knowledge. The natural sciences are "harder," more like the male body and hence more prestigious, than the social sciences or the "soft" humanities, supposed to be awash in feminine emotionality and subjectivity. Mathematics is coded masculine and is the language of physics, the most prestigious science. Through their closer association with physics, quantitative subfields of biology and the social sciences enjoy higher prestige than subfields of the same discipline or branch of science employing a qualitative, historical, or interpretive methodology. Experimentation asserts more control over subjects of study than observation does. So experimental subfields in biology and psychology are coded masculine and command more cognitive authority than observational subfields of the same disciplines. Values are designated feminine. So normative subfields in philosophy such as ethics and political philosophy enjoy less prestige than supposedly nonnormative fields such as philosophy of language and mind. Social interpretation is thought to be a feminine skill. So interpretive anthropology is designated less masculine, scientific, and rigorous than physical anthropology, which deals with "hard" facts like fossil bones. In each of these cases, the socially enforced norm for relations between fields of knowledge mirrors that of the relations between husband and wife in the ideal patriarchal family: the masculine science is autonomous from and exercises authority over the feminine science, which is supposedly dependent on the former's pronouncements to know what it should think next.

This gendered hierarchy of theoretical subfields produces serious cognitive distortions. Carolyn Sherif (1987) has investigated how the hierarchy of prestige generates cognitive biases in psychology. Forty years ago, experimental psychology dominated developmental and social psychology. The gendered character of this difference in cognitive authority is not difficult to read. Experimental psychologists, by imitating the methods of the "hard" sciences through manipulating quantified variables, claim some of the prestige of the natural sciences. Developmental and social psychologists engage in labor that looks more like the low-status labor conventionally assigned to women. Developmental psychologists work with children; social psychologists deal with human relationships, and forty years ago usually did so in settings not under the control of the researcher. Following the norm that "masculine" sciences need not pay attention to findings in "feminine" sciences, which it is assumed cannot possibly bear on their more "fundamental" research, experimental psychology has a history of constructing experiments that, like Ray Frey's, ignore the ways the social context of the experiment itself and the social relation between experimenter and subject influence outcomes. The result has been a history of findings that lack robustness because they are mere artifacts of the experimental situation. In experimental research on sex differences, this error has taken the form of ascribing observed differences in male and female behavior under experimental conditions to innate difference in male and female psychology rather than to the ways the experiment has socially structured the situation so as to elicit different responses from men and women.

The notorious claim in experimental psychology that women are more suggestible than men offers an instructive illustration of the perils of ignoring social psychology (Sherif 1987, 49–50). The original experiments that confirmed the hypothesis of greater suggestibility involved male researchers trying to persuade men and women to change their beliefs with respect to subject matters oriented to stereotypical male interests. Unaware of how their own gender-typical interests had imparted a bias in the selection of topics of persuasion, the predominantly male researchers confidently reported as a sex difference in suggestibility what was in fact a difference in suggestibility owing to the degree of interest the subjects had in the topics. Differences in the gender-typed cognitive authority of the researcher also affect subjects' responses. Men are more open to the suggestions of a female researcher when the topic is coded feminine, while women are more open to the suggestions of a male researcher when the topic is coded masculine.

Cognitive distortions due to the gender-coding of types and fields of knowledge are strictly separable from any claims about differences in the ways men and women think. Although it is true that the "feminine" sciences and subfields attract more women researchers than the "masculine" sciences do, the differences in cognitive authority between the various sciences and subfields were modeled on differences in social authority between men and women before women constituted a significant portion of the researchers in any field. Men still predominate even in fields of study that are designated feminine. And scientists' neglect of personal knowledge deprives many men who engage in stereotypically male activities of cognitive authority. For example, animal behaviorists ignore the personal knowledge male policemen have about their police dogs (Diamond 1991). For these reasons, Diamond and Sherif have questioned how gender figures into the cognitive distortions instituted by the hierarchy of knowledge and by scientistic conceptions of objectivity.[1] By shifting our focus from gender structure and supposed gender differences in ways of knowing to gender symbolism, we can see how ideas about gender can distort the relations between forms of knowledge independently of the gender of the knower. In the light of the cognitive distortions caused by the gender-coding of types and domains of knowledge, feminist naturalized epistemologists should recommend that we no longer model the relations between different kinds of knowledge on a sexist view of the authority relations between men and women.

Gender Symbolism (II): The Content of Theories

Gender symbolism figures in the *content* of theories as well as in their relations of cognitive authority whenever conceptions of human gender relations or gendered characteristics are used to model phenomena that are not gendered. Biology is particularly rich with gender symbolism—in models of gamete fertilization, nucleus-cell interaction, primatology, and evolutionary theory (Biology and Gender Study Group 1988; Haraway 1989; Keller 1985, 1992). Evelyn Fox Keller, a mathematical biologist and feminist philosopher of science, has explored gender symbolism in evolutionary theory most subtly (Keller 1992). Consider the fact that evolutionary theory tends to delineate the unit of natural selection, the entity accorded the status of an "individual," at the point where the theorist is willing to use complex and cooperative rather than competitive models of interaction. Among individuals, antagonistic competition predominates and mutualistic interactions are downplayed. The individual is considered "selfish" in relation to other individuals. Thus, theories that take the gene to be the unit of selection characterize the gene as a ruthless egoist ready to sacrifice the interests of its host organism for the sake of reproducing itself (Dawkins 1976). Where the organism is taken to be the unit of selection, it is represented as selfishly competitive with respect to other individual organisms. But within the individual, cooperation among constitutive parts prevails. Cooperation is modeled after the family, often a patriarchal family. The cells of an individual organism cooperate because of the bonds of kinship: they share the same genes. The constitutive parts of an individual cell cooperate because they are ruled by a wise and benevolent patriarch, the "master molecule" DNA, which autonomously tells all the other parts of the cell what to do, solely on the basis of information it contains within itself. Thus, evolutionary theory models the biological world after a sexist and androcentric conception of liberal society, in which the public sphere is governed by competition among presumably masculine selfish individuals and the private sphere of the family is governed by male heads of households enforcing cooperation among its members (Keller 1992, chap. 8). This model is not rigidly or consistently applied in evolutionary theory, but it does mark theoretical tendencies that can be traced back to the fact that Darwin modeled his theory of natural selection after Malthus's dismal model of capitalist society.

Taken by itself, that evolutionary theory employs a sexist ideology of liberal society to model biological phenomena does not have any straightforward normative implications. Defenders of the theory can appeal to the discovery/justification distinction here: just because a theory had its origins in politically objectionable ideas or social context does not mean that it is false or useless. Evolutionary theory is extraordinarily fruitful and empirically well confirmed. The model-theoretic view of theories, widely used by feminist empiricists and feminist postmodernists to analyze the roles of gender in the construction of theoretical knowledge, affirms the epistemic legitimacy of any coherent models, hence of any coherent sexist models, in science (Longino 1993b; Haraway 1986).

In the model-theoretic view, scientific theories propose elaborate metaphors or models of phenomena. Their virtues are empirical adequacy, simplicity, clarity, and fruitfulness. Theories are empirically adequate to the extent that the relations among entities in the model are homologous with the observed relations among entities in the world. Empirically adequate models offer a satisfactory explanation of phenomena to the extent that they model unfamiliar phenomena in ways that are simple, perspicuous and analytically tractable. They are fruitful to the extent that they organize inquirers' conceptions of their subjects in ways that suggest lines of investigation that uncover novel phenomena that can be accommodated by further refinements of the model. Empiricists place no a priori constraints on the things that may constitute useful models for phenomena. Anything might be an illuminating model for anything else. So, empiricists can offer no a priori epistemic objections to modeling nongendered phenomena after gendered ones, even if the models are overtly sexist or patriarchal. Such models may well illuminate and effectively organize important aspects of the objects being studied.

So the trouble with using sexist gender symbolism in theoretical models is not that the models are sexist. The trouble lies rather in the extraordinary political salience and rhetorical power of sexist gender ideology, which generates numerous cognitive distortions. Keller has carefully delineated several such distortions in evolutionary theory, especially with respect to its privileging of models of competitive over cooperative or mutualist interactions among organisms. First, to the extent that political ideology incorporates false conceptual identities and dichotomies, a scientific model borrowing its vocabulary and structure is likely to overlook the alternatives suppressed by that ideology or to elide distinctions between empirically distinct phenomena. The ideology of possessive individualism falsely identifies autonomy with selfishness and falsely contrasts self-interest with cooperation. When used to model phenomena in evolutionary biology, it leads to a false identification of

The tech. term falsly tries to deny the implications of the colloqual one. it hides it, embeds it.

peaceful, passive consumption activity with violent, competitive behavior, and to a neglect of mutualist interactions among organisms. Thus, the mathematical tools of population biology and mathematical ecology are rarely used to model cooperation among organisms although they could do so; in contrast with sociobiology, these mathematical subfields of biology have even neglected the impact of sexual intercourse and parenting behavior on the fitness of organisms (Keller 1992, 119–21). Although the technical definition of competition avoids false identities and dichotomies, biologists constantly turn to its colloquial meanings to explain their findings and frame research questions. In this way, "the use of a term with established colloquial meaning in a technical context permits the simultaneous transfer and denial of its colloquial connotations" (Keller 1992, 121). When the language used in a model has particularly strong ideological connotations, the cognitive biases it invites are particularly resistant to exposure and criticism.

The symbolic identification of the scientific with a masculine outlook generates further cognitive distortions. The ideology of masculinity, in representing emotion as feminine and as cognitively distorting, falsely assimilates emotion-laden thoughts—and even thoughts about emotions—to sentimentality. In identifying the scientific outlook with that of a man who has outgrown his tutelage, cut his dependence on his mother, and is prepared to meet the competitive demands of the public sphere with a clear eye, the ideology of masculinity tends to confuse seeing the natural world as indifferent in the sense of devoid of teleological laws with seeing the social world as hostile in the sense of full of agents who pursue their interests at others' expense (Keller 1992, 116–18). This confusion tempts biologists into thinking that the selfishness their models ascribe to genes and the ruthless strategic rationality their models ascribe to individual organisms (mere metaphors, however theoretically powerful) are more "real" than the actual care a dog expresses toward her pups. Such thoughts also reflect the rhetoric of unmasking base motivations behind policies that seem to be benevolent, a common if overused tactic in liberal politics and political theory. The power of this rhetoric depends on an appearance/reality distinction that has no place where the stakes are competing social *models* of biological phenomena, whose merits depend on their metaphorical rather than their referential powers. Thus, to the extent that the theoretical preference for competitive models in biology is underwritten by rhetoric borrowed from androcentric political ideologies, the preference reflects a confusion between models and reality as well as an unjustified intrusion of androcentric political loyalties into the scientific enterprise.

These are not concerns that can be relieved by deploying the discovery/justification distinction. To the extent that motivations tied to acquiring a masculine-coded prestige as a theorist induce mathematical ecologists to overlook the epistemic defects of models of natural selection that fail to consider the actual impact of sexual selection, parenting, and cooperative interactions, they distort the context of justification itself. Some of the criteria of justification, such as simplicity, are also distorted in the light of the androcentric distinction between public and private values. For example, simplicity in mathematical biology has been characterized so as to prefer explanations of apparently favorable patterns of group survival in terms of chance to explanations in terms of interspecific feedback loops, if straightforward individualistic mechanisms are not available to explain them (Keller 1992, 153). Finally, to the extent that gender ideologies inform the context of discovery by influencing the direction of inquiry and development of mathematical tools, they prevent the growth of alternative models and the tools that could make them tractable, and hence they bias our views of what is "simple" (Keller 1992, 160). The discovery/justification distinction, while useful when considering the epistemic relation of a theory to its confirming or disconfirming evidence, breaks down once we consider the relative merits of alternative theories. In the latter context, any influence that biases the development of the field of alternatives will bias the evaluation of theories. A theoretical approach may appear best justified not because it offers an adequate model of the world but because androcentric ideologies have caused more thought and resources to be invested in it than in alternatives.

So feminist naturalized epistemologists should offer a complex verdict on gender symbolism in the content of theories. They should leave open the possibility that gendered models of ungendered phenomena may be highly illuminating and successful, and hence legitimately used in the theoretical inquiry. The impressive explanatory successes of evolutionary theory demonstrate this. At the same time, the ideological power of gender symbolism sometimes gets the better of otherwise careful theorists. It can generate conceptual confusion in ways that are hard to detect, and obscure theoretical possibilities that may be worth pursuing. The most reliable way to tell when the use of gender symbolism is generating such cognitive distortions is to critically investigate the gender ideology it depends on and the role this ideology plays in society. In other words, theorists who use gendered models would do well to consider how feminist theory can help them avoid cognitive distortion. Feminist naturalized epistemologists therefore should recommend that theorists attracted to gendered models of ungendered phenomena proceed with caution, in consultation with feminist theorists. It recommends an important change in the cognitive authority of disciplines, through its demonstration that biologists have something to learn from feminist theory after all.

Androcentrism

A knowledge practice is androcentric if it reflects an orientation geared to specifically or typically male interests or male lives. Androcentrism can appear in a knowledge practice in at least two ways: in the content of theories or research programs and in the interests that lead inquirers to frame their research in certain terms or around certain problems. Feminists in the natural and social sciences have advanced feminist epistemology most fully and persuasively by exposing androcentrism in the content of social-scientific and biological theories.

The content of theories can be androcentric in several ways. A theory may reflect the view that males, male lives, or "masculinity" set the norm for humans or animals generally. From this point of view, females, their lives, or "feminine" characteristics are represented as problematic, deviations from the norm, and hence in need of a type of explanation not required for their male counterparts. Androcentrism of this sort often appears in the ways theoretical questions are framed. For decades, psychological and biological research about sex differences has been framed by the question, "Why are women different from men?" and the presumed sex difference has cast women in a deviant position. Researchers have been preoccupied with such questions as why girls are more suggestible, less ambitious, less analytically minded, and have lower self-esteem than boys. Let us leave aside the fact that all these questions are based on unfounded beliefs about sex differences (Maccoby and Jacklin 1974). Why haven't researchers asked why boys are less responsive to others, more pushy, less synthetically minded, and more conceited than girls? The framing of the problem to be investigated reflects not just a commitment to asymmetrical explanation of men's and women's characteristics, but to an evaluation of women's differences as dimensions of inferiority (Tavris 1992, chap. 1). It is thus sexist as well as androcentric.

Another way in which the content of theories can be androcentric is in describing or defining phenomena from the perspective of men or typically male lives, without paying attention to how they would be described differently if examined from the point of view of women's lives. Economists and political scientists have traditionally defined class and socioeconomic status from the point of view of men's lives: a man's class or socioeconomic status is defined in terms of his own occupation or earnings, whereas a women's status is defined in terms of her father's or husband's occupation or earnings. Such definitions obscure the differences in power, prestige, and opportunities between male managers and their homemaker wives, and between homemaker wives and female manager (Stiehm 1983). They also prevent an analysis of the distinctive economic roles and status of full-time homemakers and of adult independent unmarried women. The distinction between labor and leisure, central to standard economic analyses of the supply of wage labor, also reflects the perspective of male heads of households (Waring 1990). Classically, the distinction demarcates the public from the private spheres by contrasting their characteristic activities as having negative versus positive utility, or instrumental versus intrinsic value, or as controlled by others versus freely self-directed. From the standpoint of the lives of women with husbands or children, these demarcations make no sense. These women are not at leisure whenever they are not engaged in paid labor. Professional women often find much of their unpaid work to constitute a drudgery from which paid labor represents an escape with positive intrinsic value. Middle-class and working-class women who engage in paid labor and who cannot afford to hire others to perform their household tasks and child care are better represented as engaged in (sometimes involuntary) dual-career or double-shift labor than in trading off labor for leisure. Full-time mothers and homemakers often view what some consider to be their leisure activities as highly important work in its own right, even if it is unpaid.

The androcentrism implicit in the standard economic definition of productive labor has profound implications for national income account, the fundamental conceptual framework for defining and measuring what counts as economically relevant data for macroeconomic theory. It effectively excludes women's gender-typical unpaid domestic labor from gross national product (GNP) calculations, making women's work largely invisible in the economy. In the advanced industrialized nations, economists explain this omission by arguing that GNP figures properly measure only the economic value of production for market exchange. In developing nations, where only a modest proportion of productive activity shows up in market exchanges, economists have long recognized the uselessness of measures of national production that look only at the market; so they impute a market value to various unmarked domestic production activities associated with subsistence agriculture, home construction, and the like. But which of these household activities do economists choose to count as productive? In practice, they have defined the "production boundary" in such societies by imposing an obsolete Western androcentric conception of the household. They assume that households consist of a productive primary producer, the husband, who supports a wife engaged in "housework," which is assumed to be economically unimportant or unproductive. "Housework" has no clear definition in societies where most production takes place within the household. So economists apply the concept of "housework" to whatever productive activities a society conventionally assigns to women. Thus, women's unmarketed labor in these societies counts as productive only if men usually perform it too, whereas men's unmarketed labor is usually counted in the national income statistics regardless of its relation to women's labor (Waring 1990, 74–87). The result is that in Africa, where women do 70 percent of the hoeing and weeding of subsistence crops, 80 percent of crop transportation and storage, and 90 percent of water and fuel collecting and food processing, these vital activities rarely appear in the national income accounts (Waring 1990, 84). Here, androcentrism is built into the very data for economic theorizing, in such a way that women's gender-typical activities become invisible.

Even when a theory does not go so far as to define the phenomena in a way that excludes female activities, it may still be androcentric in assuming that male activities or predicaments are the sole or primary sources of important changes or events. Until recently, primatologists focused almost exclusively on the behavior of male primates. They assumed that male sexual and dominance behaviors determined the basic structure of primate social order, and that the crucial social relationships among troop-dwelling primates that determined the reproductive fitness of individuals and maintained troop organization were between the dominant male and other males. The assumption followed from a sociobiological argument that claimed to show that females of any species will typically be the "limiting resource" for reproduction; most females will realize an equal and maximum reproductive potential, while males will vary enormously in their reproductive fitness. Natural selection, the driving force of evolutionary change, would therefore operate primarily on male characteristics and behavior (Hrdy 1986).

These assumptions were not seriously challenged until women, some inspired by the feminist movement, started entering the field of primatology in substantial numbers in the mid-1970s. Many studied female-female and female-infant interactions, female dominance and cooperative behavior, and female sexual activity. By turning their focus from male to female behaviors and relationships, they found that infant survival varied enormously, depending on the behavior and social status of the mothers, that troop survival itself sometimes depended on the eldest female (who would teach others the location of distant water holes that had survived droughts), and that female-directed social and sexual behaviors play key roles in maintaining and changing primate social organizations (Hrdy 1981; Haraway 1989). Today the importance of female primates is widely recognized and studied by both male and female primatologists.

What normative implications should be drawn about the epistemic status of androcentric theories? Some feminist epistemologists propose that theory can proceed better by viewing the world through the eyes of female agents. Gynocentric theory can be fun. What could be a more amusing retort to a study that purports to explain why women lack self-esteem than a study that explains why men are conceited? It can also be instructive. Richard Wrangham (1979) has proposed a gynocentric model of primate social organization that has achieved widespread recognition in primatology. The model assumes the centrality of female competition for food resources, and predicts how females will space themselves (singly or in kin-related groups) according to the distribution of the foods they eat. Males then space themselves so as to gain optimum access to females. The model is gynocentric both in defining the core of primate social groups around female kin-relations rather than around relations to a dominant male and in taking the situation of females to constitute the primary variable that accounts for variations in male and general primate social organization. According to the feminist primatologist Sarah Hrdy (1981, 126), Wrangham's model offers the best available explanation of primate social organization.

The three androcentric theoretical constructs mentioned correspond to three different ways in which a theory could be "gender-centric": in taking one sex or gender to set the norm for both, in defining central concepts with respect to the sex-or gender-typical characteristics, behaviors, or perspectives of males or females alone, and in taking the behaviors, situation, or characteristics of one sex or gender to be causally central in determining particular outcomes. These logical differences in gender-centric theorizing have different epistemic implications. As Wrangham's theory shows, gynocentric causal models can sometimes be superior to androcentric models. Whether they are superior in any particular domain of interest is an empirical question. It can only be answered by comparing rival gender-centric models to one another and to models that do not privilege either male- or female-typical activities or situations in their causal accounts, but rather focus on activities and situations common to both males and females. An important contribution of feminist scholarship in the social sciences and biology has been to show that the activities and situations of females have been far more causally important in various domains than androcentric theories have recognized.

The other two types of gender-centrism are much more problematic than their causal type. A theory that takes one gender to set the norm for both must bear an explanatory burden not borne by theories that refuse to represent difference as deviance. It must explain why an asymmetrical explanation is required for male- and female-specific characteristics. Given the dominant background assumption of modern science that the cosmos does not have its own telos, it is hard to justify any claim that one gender naturally sets the norm for both. Claims about norms must be located in human value judgments, which is to say that the only justification for normative gender-centrism would have to lie in a substantive sexist moral or political theory. As we shall see below, empiricism does not rule out the use of value judgments as background assumptions in scientific theories. Nevertheless, this analysis of normative gender-centrism suggests why feminists should not be satisfied with a table-turning, "why men are so conceited" type of gynocentric theorizing. Posing such questions may expose the androcentrism of standard ways of framing research problems in sex-differences research to healthy ridicule. But because feminists are interested in upholding the equality of all persons, not the domination of women over men, they have no interest in claiming that women set the norm for humans generally.

Theories that tailor concepts to the activities or positions specific to or typical of one gender only and then apply them to everyone are straightforwardly empirically inadequate. As the case of androcentric definitions of class showed, they obscure actual empirical differences between men and women and between differently situated women. As the case of the labor/leisure distinction showed, they overgeneralize from the typical situation of one gender to that of both. When conceptually androcentric theories guide public policy, the resulting policies are usually sexist, since theories cannot respond to phenomena they make invisible. Thus, when GNP statistics fail to count women's labor as productive, and public policies aim to increase GNP, they may do so in ways that fail to improve the well-being of women and their families and may even reduce it. In Malawi and Lesotho, where women grow most of the food for domestic consumption, foreign aid projects have provided agricultural training to the men who have no use for it, and offered only home economics education to women (Waring 1990, 232, 234). In the Sahel, a USAID drought-relief project forced women into economic dependency on men by replacing only men's cattle herds, on the androcentric assumption that women did not engage in economically significant labor (Waring 1990, 176–77).

Feminist naturalized epistemologists therefore pass different judgments on different kinds of gender-centrism in the theoretical inquiry. Conceptual gender-centrism is plainly inadequate in any society with overlapping gender roles, because it leads to overgeneralization and obscures the differences between empirically distinct phenomena. It could work only in societies where men and women inhabit completely and rigidly segregated spheres, and only for concepts that apply exclusively to one or the other gender in such a society. Normative gender-centrism either depends on a problematic cosmic teleology or on sexist values. This does not automatically make it epistemically inadequate, but it does require the assumption of an explanatory burden (why men's and women's traits do not receive symmetrical explanatory treatment) that non-gender-centric theories need not assume. In addition, its dependence on sexist values give theorists who repudiate sexism sufficient reason to conduct inquiry that is not normatively gender-centric. Finally, causal gender-centrism may or may not be empirically justified. Some events do turn asymmetrically on what men or women do, or on how men or women are situated.

The chief trap in causal gender-centrism is the temptation to reify the domain of events that are said to turn asymmetrically on the actions or characteristics of one or the other gender. The selection of a domain of inquiry is always a function of the interests of the inquirer.[2] Failure to recognize this may lead androcentric theorists to construct their domain of study in ways that confine it to just those phenomena that turn asymmetrically on men's activities. They may therefore declare as an objective fact that, say, women have little causal impact on the "economy," when all that is going on is that they have not taken any interest in women's productive activities, and so have not categorized those activities as "economic." Feminist naturalized epistemologists caution against the view that domains of inquiry demarcate natural kinds. Following Quine, they question supposed conceptual barriers between natural and social science, analytic and synthetic knowledge, personal and impersonal knowledge, fact and value (Nelson 1990, chap. 3). Their empiricist commitments enable them to uncover surprising connections among apparently distant points in the web of belief. If naturalized epistemologists use space-age technology to explore the universe of knowledge, feminist naturalized epistemologists could be said to specialize in the discovery of wormholes in that universe. Gender and science are not light-years apart after all; subspace distortions in our cognitive apparatus permit surprisingly rapid transport from one of the other, but feminist navigators are needed to ensure that we know the route we are travelling and have reason to take it.

Sexism in Scientific Theories

One frequently traveled route between gender and science employs normative assumptions about the proper relations between men and women, or about the respective characteristics and interests of men and women, in the content or application of scientific theories. When a theory asserts that women are inferior to men, properly subordinated to men, or properly confined to gender-stereotyped roles, or when it judges or describes women according to sexist or double standards, the content of the theory is sexist. When people employ such assumptions in applying theories, the application of the theory is sexist. Naturalized feminist epistemology considers how our evaluations of theories should change once their sexism is brought to light.

The application of theories can be sexist in direct or indirect ways. Theories may be used to provide direct ideological justification for patriarchal structures. Steven Goldberg (1973) uses his theory of sex differences in aggression to justify a gendered division of labor that deliberately confines women to low-prestige occupations. More usually, the application of theories is indirectly sexist in taking certain sexist values for granted rather than trying to justify them. For example, research on oral contraceptives for men and women uses a double standard for evaluating the acceptability of side effects. Oral contraceptives for men are disqualified if they reduce libido, but oral contraceptives for women are not rejected for reducing women's sexual desire.

In a standard positivist analysis, neither form of sexism in the application of theories has any bearing on the epistemic value of the theories in question. That a theory is used to support unpopular political programs does not show that the theory is false. At most, it reflects a failure of the proponents of the program to respect the logical gap between fact and value. But opponents of the program fail to respect this gap in attacking a theory for the uses to which it is put. According to this view, theories supply facts that all persons must accept, regardless of their political commitments. That a theory is indirectly applied in sexist ways provides even less ground for attacking its content. The question of truth must be strictly separated from the uses to which such truths are put.

Naturalized epistemology does not support such a sanguine analysis of theories that are applied in sexist ways. "Successful" technological applications of theories are currently taken to provide evidence of their epistemic merits. If knowledge is power, then power is a criterion of adequate understanding. The prevailing interpretation of this criterion does not consider whose power is enhanced by the theory and whose interests are served by it. Feminists urge that these considerations be taken explicitly into account when one evaluates whether technological applications of theories supply evidence of an adequate understanding of the phenomena they control (Tiles 1987). It may be true that certain drugs would be effective in controlling the phenomena of women's hormonal cycles that are currently designated as pathologies constitutive of premenstrual syndrome. Such control may come at the expense of women's interests, not just because of undesirable side effects but also because the legitimation of drug treatment reinforces the medicalization of women's complaints, as if these complaints were symptoms to be medicated rather than as claims on others to change their behavior (Zita 1989). Doctors may be satisfied that such a "successful" drug treatment of PMS supplies evidence that the theory it applies provides them with an adequate understanding of women's menstrual cycles. But should women be satisfied with this under-standing? Suppose the phenomena associated with PMS could also be eliminated, or revalued, by widespread acceptance of feminist conceptions of women's bodies or by egalitarian changes that would make social arrangements less frustrating to women. (This would be possible if women's symptoms of distress in PMS were partly caused by misogynist social expectations that represent women's menstrual cycles as pathological.) Such a successful "technological" application of feminist theory would provide women with an understanding of their own menstrual cycles that would empower them. Where the sexist medical technology would enable women to adapt their bodies to the demands of a sexist society, the feminist technology would empower women to change society so that their bodies were no longer considered "diseased." Thus, applications of theories may influence the content of theories whenever "success" in application is taken to justify the theory in questions. Sexist or feminist values may inform criteria of success in application, which may in turn inform competing criteria of adequate understanding. The epistemic evaluation of theories therefore cannot be sharply separated from the interests their applications serve.

Feminist naturalized epistemology also rejects the positivist view that the epistemic merits of theories can be assessed independently of their direct ideological applications (Longino 1990; Antony 1993; Potter 1993). Although any acceptable ideology must make sure that it does not fly in the face of facts, theories do not merely state facts but organize them into systems that tell us what their significance is. Theories logically go beyond the facts; they are "underdetermined" by all the empirical evidence that is or ever could be adduced in their favor (Quine 1960, 22). The evidential link between an observed fact and a theoretical hypothesis can only be secured by background auxiliary hypotheses. This leaves open the logical possibility that ideological judgments may not be implications of an independently supported theory but figure in the justification of the theory itself, by supplying evidential links between empirical observations and hypotheses.

A particularly transparent example of this phenomenon may be found in theories about sex differences in intelligence. Girls scored significantly higher than boys on the first Standord-Binet IQ tests developed by Lewis Terman. To correct for this "embarrasment," Terman eliminated portions of the test where girls scored higher than boys and inserted questions on which boys scored higher than girls. The substitution was considered necessary to ensure the validity of the test against school grades, the only available independent measures of children's intelligence, which did not differ by gender. But Terman did not adjust his test to eliminate sex differences on subtests of the IQ, such as those about quantitative reasoning. These differences seemed unproblematic because they conformed to prevailing ideological assumptions about appropriate gender roles (Mensh and Mensh 1991, 68–69). Today, that IQ scores are good predicators of a child's school grades is still taken to provide key evidence for the claim that differences in IQ scores measure differences in children's innate intelligence. But the evidential link tying school grades of this theoretical claim depends on the background value judgments that schools provide fair educational opportunities to all children with respect to all fields of study. Those schools that discourage girls from pursuing math and science assume that girls have inferior quantitative reasoning ability; they do not recognize that lack of encouragement can cause relatively lower performance on math tests.

From a positivist point of view, this reasoning is defective on two counts. First, it is circular to claim that IQ tests demonstrate innate sex differences in quantitative reasoning ability when the assumption of innate sex differences is built into the background hypotheses needed to validate the tests. Second, no reasoning is scientifically sound that incorporates value judgments into the background assumptions that link observations to theory. The salience of positivist views of science as well as their usefulness to feminists in criticizing research about sex differences has tempted some feminists to use the positivist requirement that science be value-free to discredit all scientific projects that incorporate sexist values in the explicit or implicit content of their theories. But this appropriation of positivism puts at odds the two aims of feminist epistemology—to criticize sexist science and to promote feminist science. If incorporating sexist values into scientific theories is illegitimate on positivist grounds, then so is incorporating feminist values into scientific theories (Longino 1993a, 259).

Feminist naturalized epistemologists offer a more nuanced response to the presence of value judgments in scientific inference. Even "good science" can incorporate such value judgments. The logical gap between theory and observation ensures that one cannot in principle rule out the possibility that value judgments are implicit in the background assumptions used to argue that a given observation constitutes evidence for a given hypothesis (Longino 1990). From the perspective of an individual scientist, it is not unreasonable to use any of one's firm beliefs, including beliefs about values, to reason from an observation to a theory. Nor does the prospect of circularity threaten the scientific validity of one's reasoning, as long as the circle of reasoning is big enough. In a coherence web of belief, every belief offers some support for every other belief, and no belief is perfectly self-supporting. Theories that incorporate value judgments can be scientifically sound as long as they are empirically adequate.

This reasoning underwrites the legitimacy of feminist scientific research, which incorporates feminist value into its theories. Such values may be detected in the commitment of feminist researchers to regard women as intelligent agents, capable of reflecting on and changing the conditions that presently constrain their actions. This commitment tends to support a theoretical preference for causal models of female behavior that highlight feedback loops between their intentional states and their social and physical environments, and that resist purely structuralist accounts of female "nature" that leave no room for females to resist their circumstances or maneuver among alternate possibilities (Longino 1989, 210–13; Haraway 1989, Chap. 13). In contrast, most behaviorist and some sociobiological theories favor models that highlight linear causal chains from fixed physiological or physical conditions to determinate behaviors, and that emphasize the structural constraints on action. The epistemic values of simplicity, prediction, and control might seem to support linear, structural causal models. But we have seen that control at least is a contested value; the kinds of control taken to warrant claims of adequate understanding depend on substantive value judgments about the importance of particular human interests. Is adequate understanding achieved when a theory empowers scientists to control women's lives, or when it empowers women to control their own lives? Rival interpretations of the other epistemic values also depend on contested nonepistemic values. The kind of simplicity one favors depends on one's aesthetic values. In any event, other epistemic values, such as fruitfulness, appear to favor complex, nonlinear causal models of human behavior. Such models support experiments that generate novel behaviors disruptive of presumed structural constraints on action.

Naturalized feminist epistemology thus permits scientific projects that incorporate feminist values into the content and application of theories. It does not provide methodological arguments against the pursuit of sexist theories. It does claim, however, that it is irrational for theorists to pursue sexist research programs if they do not endorse sexist values. Moral and political arguments about the rationality of particular values may therefore have a bearing on the rationality of pursuing particular research programs. In addition, the objectivity of science demands that the background assumptions of research programs be exposed to criticism. A scientific community composed of inquirers who share the same background assumptions is unlikely to be aware of the roles these assumptions play in licensing inferences from observations to hypotheses, and even less likely to examine these assumptions critically. Naturalized epistemology therefore recommends that the scientific community include a diversity of inquirers who accept different background assumptions. A community of inquirers who largely accept sexist values and incorporate them into their background assumptions could enhance the objectivity of the community's practice by expanding its membership to include researchers with feminist commitments (Longion 1993a, 267–269).

The Local Character of Naturalized Feminist Epistemology

In reading the project of feminist epistemology along naturalized, empiricist lines, I have tried to show how its interest and critical power do not depend on the global, transcendental claims that all knowledge is gendered or that rationality as a regulatory epistemic ideal is masculine. Naturalized feminist epistemologists may travel to distant locations in the universe of belief, but they always remain inside that universe and travel from gender to science by way of discrete, empirically discovered paths. They have an interest in constructing new paths to empirically adequate, fruitful, and useful forms of feminist science and in breaking up other paths that lead to cognitively and socially unsatisfactory destinations. All the paths by which naturalized epistemologists find gender to influence theoretical knowledge are local, contingent, and empirically conditioned. All the paths by which they propose to change these influences accept rationality as a key epistemic ideal and empirical adequacy as a fundamental goal of acceptable theories. This ideal and this goal are in principle equally open to pursuit by male and female inquirers, but may be best realized by mixed-gender research communities. Naturalized epistemologists find no persuasive evidence that indicates that all women inquirers bring some shared global feminine difference in ways of thinking to all subjects of study nor that such a feminine difference gives us privileged access to the way the world is.

In rejecting global, transcendental claims about differences in the ways men and women think, naturalized feminist epistemologists do not imply that the entry and advancement of significant numbers of women into scientific communities makes no systematic difference to the knowledge these communities produce. But, following their view of inquiry as a social, not an individual, enterprise, they credit the improvements in knowledge such entry produces to the greater diversity and equality of membership in the scientific community rather than to any purportedly privileged subject position of women as knowers (Tuana 1992; Longino 1993a). Men and women do have *some* gender-specific experiences and personal knowledge due to their different socialization and social status. We have seen that such experiences and forms of knowledge can be fruitfully brought to bear upon theoretical inquiry. So it should not be surprising that women researchers have exposed and criticized androcentrism in theories much more than men have. The diversity and equality of inquirers help ensure that social models do not merely reflect or fit the circumstances of a narrow demographic segment of the population when they are meant to apply to everyone. They correct a cognitive bias commonly found among inquirers belonging to all demographic groups, located in the habit of assuming that the way the world appears to oneself is the way it appears to everyone.

This survey of some findings of naturalized feminist epistemology has also identified improvements in knowledge that have or would come about through the entry of *feminist* theorists into various fields, and through revisions in the system of cognitive authority among fields that would bring the findings of feminist theorists to bear upon apparently distant subjects.[3] We have seen that the use of gender symbolism to model nonhuman phenomena is fraught with cognitive traps. So it should not be surprising that feminist researchers, who make it their business to study the contradictions and incoherences in our conceptions of gender, can improve theories by exposing and clearing up the confusions they inherit from the gender ideologies they use as models. By pursuing feminist research in the humanities, social sciences, and biology, feminist researchers also pose challenges to prevailing theories. Here again, the kinds of changes we should expect in theoretical knowledge from the entry of feminist researchers into various fields do not typically consist in the production of specifically feminist ontologies, methodologies, standpoints, paradigms, or doctrines. Feminist contributions to theorizing are more usefully conceived as altering the field of theoretical possibilities (Haraway 1986, 81, 96). Research informed by feminist commitments makes new explanatory models available, reframes old questions, exposes facts that undermine the plausibility of previously dominant theories, improves data-gathering techniques, and shifts the relations of cognitive authority among fields and theories. In these and many other ways, it reconfigures our assessments of the prospects and virtues of various research programs. Without claiming that women, or feminists, have a globally different or privileged way of knowing, naturalized feminist epistemology explains how feminist theory can productively transform the field of theoretical knowledge.

NOTES

I wish to thank Ann Cuddy, Sally Haslanger, Don Herzog, David Hills, Peter Railton, Justin Schwartz, Miriam Solomon, and the faculties at the Law Schools of Columbia University, the University of Chicago, and Northwestern University for helpful comments and criticisms.

[1]   Diamond (1991, 1009) writes that the exclusion of animal trainers' knowledge from the realm of authoritative knowledge "cannot in any very simple way be connected to gender." Pointing out that the terms "hard" and "soft" as applied to forms of knowledge are used by "men trying to put down other men," Sherif argues that for this reason it is "particularly misleading" to infer that these terms symbolize "masculine" and "feminine" (1987, 46–47). I would have thought that her observation supports the gendered reading, since a standard way for men to put down other men is to insinuate that they are feminine.

[2]   The interests at stake need not be self-interests or even ideological interests of a broader sort. One might just be curious about how rainbows form, without seeking this knowledge for the sake of finding out how to get the proverbial pot of gold at the end. Curiosity is one kind of interest we can express in a phenomenon.

[3]   The question of the impact of feminist theorists on knowledge is distinct from but related to the question of the impact of women theorists on knowledge. Not all women theorists are feminists, and some feminist theorists are men. At the same time, there could be no genuine feminist theory that was conducted by men alone. Feminist theory is theory committed to the liberation and equality of women. These goals can only be achieved through the exercise of women's own agency, especially in defining and coming to know themselves. Feminist theory is one of the vehicles of women's agency in pursuit of these goals, and therefore cannot realize its aims if it is not conducted by women. So it should nor be surprising that most of the transformations of knowledge induced by feminist theory were brought about by women.

REFERENCES

Alcoff, Linda, and Elizabeth Potter, eds. 1993. *Feminist epistemologies*. New York: Routledge.

American Association of University Women. 1992. *The AAUW report: How schools shortchange girls*. Prepared by Wellesley College Center for Research on Women.

Anderson, Elizabeth. 1993. *Value in ethics and economics*. Cambridge: Harvard University Press.

Antony, Louise, 1993. Quine as feminist: The radical import of naturalized epistemology. In *A mind of one's own: Feminist essays on reason and objectivity*. See Antony and Witt 1993.

Antony, Louise, and Charlotte Witt. 1993. *A mind of one's own: Feminist essays on reason and objectivity*. Boulder, CO: Westview.

Astin, Helen S., and Alan E. Beyer. 1973. Sex discrimination in academe. In *Academic women on the move*, ed. Alice. S. Rossi and Ann Calderwood. New York: Russell Sage Foundation.

Becker, Joanne Rossi. 1981. Differential treatment of females and males in mathematics classes. *Journal for Research in Mathematics Education* 12 (1): 40–53.

Belenky, Mary, Blythe Clinchy, Nancy Goldberger, and Jill Tarule. 1986. *Women's ways of knowing*. New York: Basic Books.

Bell, Diane, Pat Caplan, and Wazir Karin, eds. 1993. *Gendered fields: Women, men and ethnography*. New York: Routledge.

Biology and Gender Study group. 1988. The importance of feminist critique for contemporary cell biology. *Hypatia* 3 (1): 61–76.

Bordo, Susan. 1987. *The flight to objectivity: Essays on cartesianism and culture.* Albany: State University of New York Press.

Bourdieu, Pierre. 1977. *Outline of a theory of practice.* Cambridge: Cambridge University Press.

Coady, C.A.J. 1992. *Testimony.* Oxford: Clarendon Press.

Collins, Patricia Hill. 1990. *Black feminist thought: Knowledge, consciousness, and the politics of empowerment.* Boston: Unwin Hyman.

Curran, Libby. 1980. Science education: Did she drop out or was she pushed? In *Alice through the microscope,* ed. Brighton Women and Science Group. London: Virago.

Dawkins, Richard. 1976. *The selfish gene.* New York: Oxford University Press.

Diamond, Cora. 1991. Knowing tornadoes and other things. *New Literary History* 22: 1001–15.

Duran, Jane. 1991. *Toward a feminist epistemology.* Totowa, JJ: Rowman and Littlefield.

Fidell, L.S. 1970. Empirical verification of sex discrimination in hiring practices in psychology. *American Psychologist* 25 (12): 1094–98.

Flax, Jane. 1983. Political philosophy and the patriarchal unconscious. In *Discovering reality.* See Harding and Hintikka 1983.

Fox, Mary Frank. 1981. Sex segregation and salary structure in academia. *Sociology of Work and Occupations* 8 (1): 39–60.

Gilligan, Carol. 1982. *In a different voice.* Cambridge: Harvard University Press.

Goldberg, Steven. 1973. *The inevitability of patriarchy.* New York: Morrow.

Haraway, Donna. 1986. Primatology is politics by other means. In *Feminist approaches to science,* ed. Ruth Bleier. New York: Pergamon.

____, 1989. *Primate visions.* New York: Routledge.

Harding, Sandra. 1986. *The science question in feminism.* Ithaca: Cornell University Press.

Harding, Sandra, and Merrill B. Hintikka, eds. 1983. *Discovering Reality.* Dodrecht, Holland: D. Reidel.

Hearne, Vicki. 1982. *Adam's task.* New York: Vintage.

Hrdy, Sarah. 1981. *The woman that never evolved.* Cambridge: Harvard University Press.

____, 1986. Empathy, polyandry, and the myth of the coy female. In *Feminist approaches to science,* ed. Ruth Bleier. New York: Pergamon.

Hubbard, Ruth. 1990. *The politics of women's biology.* New Brunswick, NJ: Rutgers University Press.

Keller, Evelyn Fox. 1983. *A feeling for the organism.* New York: Freeman.

____, 1985. The force of the pacemaker concept in theories of aggregation in cellular slime mold. In *Reflections on gender and science.* New Haven: Yale University Press.

____, 1992. *Secrets of life, secrets of death.* New York: Routledge.

Leacock, Eleanor. 1982. *Myths of male dominance.* New York: Monthly Review Press.

Lefkowitz, M.R. 1979. Education for women in a man's world. *Chronicle of Higher Education,* 6 August, p. 56.

Longino, Helen. 1989. Can there be a feminist science? In *Women, knowledge, and reality,* ed. Ann Garry and Marilyn Pearsall. Boston: Unwin Hyman.

____, 1990. *Science as social knowledge.* Princeton, NJ: Princeton University Press.

____, 1993a. Essential tensions—Phase two: Feminist, philosophical and social studies of science. In *A mind of one's own.* See Antony and Witt 1993.

____, 1993b. Subjects, power, and knowledge: Description and prescription in feminist philosophies of science. In *Feminist epistemologies.* See Alcoff and Potter 1993.

Maccoby, Eleanor, and Carol Jacklin. 1974. *The psychology of sex differences.* Stanford: Stanford University Press.

Mensh, Elaine, and Harry Mensh. 1991. *The IQ mythology.* Carbondale: Southern Illinois University Press.

National Science Foundation. 1984. *Women and minorities in science and engineering.*

Nelson, Lynn. 1990. *Who knows? From Quine to a feminist empiricism.* Philadelphia: Temple University Press.

____, 1993. Epistemological communities. In *Feminist epistemologies.* See Alcoff and Potter 1993.

Pai, Hyung Il. 1985. (Anthropologist, University of California, Santa Barbara). Personal communication.

Paludi, Michele Antoinette, and William D. Bauer. 1983. Goldberg revisited: What's in an author's name. *Sex Roles* 9(3): 287–390.

Polanyi, Michael. 1958. *Personal knowledge.* Chicago: University of Chicago Press.

Potter, Elizabeth. 1993. Gender and epistemic negotiation. In *Feminist epistemologies.* See Alcoff and Potter 1993.

Quine, W.V.O. 1960. *Word and object.* Cambridge: MIT Press.

____, 1969. Epistemology naturalized. In *Ontological relativity and other essays.* New York: Columbia University Press.

Reskin, Barbara. 1979. Academic sponsorship and scientists' careers. *Sociology of Education* 52(3): 129–46.

Rooney, Phyllis. 1991. Gendered reason: Sex metaphor and conceptions of reason. *Hypatia* 6(2): 77–103.

Rose, Hilary. 1987. Hand, brain, and heart: A feminist epistemology for the natural sciences. In *Sex and scientific inquiry,* ed. Sandra Harding and Jean O'Barr. Chicago: University of Chicago Press.

Rose, Suzanna. 1989. Women biologists and the "old boy" network. *Women's Studies International Forum* 12(3): 349–54.

Rosenfeld, Rachel. 1981. Academic career mobility for psychologists. In *Women in scientific and engineering professions,* ed. Violet Haas and Carolyn Perrucci. Ann Arbor: University of Michigan Press.

Rossiter, Margaret. 1982. *Women scientists in America: Struggles and strategies to 1940.* Baltimore: Johns Hopkins University Press.

Scheman, Naomi. 1983. Individualism and the objects of psychology. In D*iscovering reality.* See Harding and Hintikka 1983.

Schiebinger, Londa. 1989. *The mind has no sex?* Cambridge: Harvard University Press.

Schuman, Howard, and Shirley Hatchett. 1974. *Black racial attitudes: Trends and complexities.* Ann Arbor: University of Michigan Press.

Sherif, Carolyn. 1987. Bias in psychology. In *Feminism and methodology,* ed. Sandra Harding. Bloomington: Indiana University Press.

Smith, Dorothy. 1974. Women's perspective as a radical critique of sociology. *Sociological inquiry* 44(1): 7–13.

Solomon, Miriam. 1994. Social epistemology. *Nous* 28: 325–343.

Stiehm, Judith. 1983. Our aristotelian hangover. In *Discovering reality.* See Harding and Hintikka 1983.

Tavris, Carol. 1992. *The mismeasure of woman.* New York: Simon and Schuster.

Tidball, M. Elizabeth. 1980. Women's colleges and women achievers revisited. *Signs* 5(3): 504–17.

Tiles, Mary. 1987. A science of Mars or of Venus? *Philosophy* 62(July): 293–306.

Tuana, Nancy. 1992. The radical future of feminist empiricism. *Hypatia* 7(1): 100–14.

Vetter, Betty. 1981. Changing patterns of recruitment and employment. In *Women in scientific and engineering professions,* ed. Violet Haas and Carolyn Perrucci. Ann Arbor: University of Michigan Press.

Waring, Marilyn. 1990. *If women counted.* San Francisco: HarperCollins.

Wrangham, Richard. 1979. On the evolution of ape social systems. *Biology and Social Life: Social Sciences Information* 18: 335–68.

Zita, Jacquelyn. 1989. The premenstrual syndrome: "Dis-easing" the female cycle. In *Feminism and science,* ed. Nancy Tuana. Bloomington: Indiana University Press.

3.5

RETHINKING STANDPOINT EPISTEMOLOGY: WHAT IS "STRONG OBJECTIVITY"?

Sandra Harding

> *"Feminist objectivity means quite simply situated knowledges."*
> —Donna Haraway[1]

1. Both Ways

For almost two decades, feminists have engaged in a complex and charged conversation about objectivity. Its topics have included which kinds of knowledge projects have it, which don't, and why they don't; whether the many different feminisms need it, and if so why they do; and if it is possible to get it, how to do so.[2] This conversation has been informed by complex and charged prefeminist writings that tend to get stuck in debates between empiricists and intentionalists, objectivists and interpretationists, and realists and social constructionists (including poststructuralists).[3]

Most of these feminist discussions have *not* arisen from attempts to find new ways either to criticize or carry on the agendas of the disciplines. Frequently they do not take as their problematics the ones familiar within the disciplines. Instead, these conversations have emerged mainly from two different and related concerns. First, what are the causes of the immense proliferation of theoretically and empirically sound results of research in biology and the social sciences that have discovered what is not supposed to exist: a rampant sexist and androcentric bias—"politics"!—in the dominant scientific (and popular) descriptions and explanations of nature and social life? To put the point another way, how should one explain the surprising fact that politically guided research projects have been able to produce less partial and distorted results of research than those supposedly guided by the goal of value-neutrality? Second, how can feminists create research that is *for* women in the sense that it provides less partial and distorted answers to questions that arise from women's lives and are not only about those lives but also about the rest of nature and social relations? The two concerns are related because recommendations for future scientific practices should be informed by the best accounts of past successes. That is, how one answers the second question depends on what one thinks is the best answer to the first one.

Many feminists, like thinkers in the other new social liberation movements now hold that it is not only desirable but also possible to have that apparent contradiction in terms—socially situated knowledge. In conventional accounts, socially situated beliefs only get to count as opinions. In order to achieve the status of knowledge, beliefs are supposed to break free of—to transcend—their original ties to local, historical interests, values, and agendas. However, as Donna Haraway has put the point, it turns out to be possible "to have *simultaneously* an account of radical historical contingency for all knowledge claims and knowing subjects, a critical practice for recognizing our own 'semiotic technologies' for making meanings, and a no-nonsense commitment to faithful accounts of a 'real' world....."[4]

The standpoint epistemologists—and especially the feminists who have most fully articulated this kind of theory of knowledge—have claimed to provide a fundamental map or "logic" for how to do this: "start thought from marginalized lives" and "take everyday life as problematic."[5] However, these maps are easy to misread if one doesn't understand the principles used to construct them. Critics of standpoint writings have tended to refuse the invitation to "have it both ways" by accepting the idea of real knowledge that is socially situated. Instead they have assimilated standpoint claims either to objectivism or some kind of conventional foundationalism or to ethnocentrism, relativism, or phenomenological approaches in philosophy and the social sciences.

Here I shall try to make clear how it really is a misreading to assimilate standpoint epistemologies to those older ones and that such misreadings distort or make invisible the distinctive resources that they offer. I shall do so by contrasting the grounds for knowledge and the kinds of subjects/agent of knowledge recommended by standpoint theories with those favored by the older epistemologies. Then I shall show why it is reasonable to think that the socially situated grounds and subjects of standpoint epistemologies require and generate stronger standards for objectivity than do those that turn away from providing systematic methods for locating knowledge in history. The problem with the conventional conception of objectivity is not that it is too rigorous or too "objectifying," as some have argued, but that it is *not rigorous or objectifying enough*; it is too weak to accomplish even the goals for which it has been designed, let alone the more difficult projects called for by feminisms and other new social movements.[6]

2. Feminist Standpoint versus Spontaneous Feminist Empiricist Epistemologies

Not all feminists who try to explain the past and learn lessons for the future of feminist research in biology and the social sciences are standpoint theorists. The distinctiveness of feminist standpoint approaches can be emphasized by contrasting them with what I shall call "spontaneous feminist empiricist epistemology."[7]

By now, two forms of feminist empiricism have been articulated: the original "spontaneous" feminist empiricism and a recent philosophical version. Originally, feminist empiricism arose as the "spontaneous consciousness" of feminist researchers in biology and the social sciences who were trying to explain what was and what wasn't different about their research process in comparison with the standard procedures in their field.[8] They thought that they were just doing more carefully and rigorously what any good scientist should do; the problem they saw was one of "bad science." Hence they did not give a special name of their philosophy of science; I gave it the name "feminist empiricism" in *The Science Question in Feminism* to contrast feminist standpoint theory with the insistence of empiricism's proponents that sexism and androcentrism could be eliminated from the results of research if scientists would just follow more rigorously and carefully the existing methods and norms of research—which, for practicing scientists, are fundamentally empiricist ones.

Recently, philosophers Helen Longino and Lynn Hankinson Nelson have developed sophisticated and valuable feminist empiricist philosophies of science (Longino calls hers "contextual empiricism") that differ in significant respects from what most prefeminist empiricists and probably most spontaneous feminist empiricists would think of as empiricism.[9] This is no accident, because Longino and Nelson both intend to revise empiricism, as feminists in other fields have fruitfully revised other theoretical approaches—indeed, as feminist standpoint theorists revise the theory from which they begin. Longino and Nelson incorporate into their epistemologies elements that also appear in the standpoint accounts (many would say that they have been most forcefully articulated in such accounts)—such as the inescapable but also sometimes positive influence of social values and interests in the content of science—that would be anathema to even the spontaneous feminist empiricists of the late 1970s and early 1980s as well as to their many successors today. These philosophical feminist empiricisms are constructed in opposition partly to feminist standpoint theories, partly to radical feminist arguments that exalt the feminine and essentialize "woman's experience" (which they have sometimes attributed to standpoint theorists), and partly to the prefeminist empiricists.

It would be an interesting and valuable project to contrast in greater detail these important philosophical feminist empiricisms with both spontaneous feminist empiricism and with feminist standpoint theory. But I have a different goal in this essay: to show how strongly feminist reflections on scientific knowledge challenge the dominant prefeminist epistemology and philosophy of science that are held by all of those people inside and outside science who are still wondering just what are the insights about science and knowledge that feminists have to offer. In my view, this challenge is made most strongly by feminist standpoint epistemology.

One can understand spontaneous feminist empiricism and feminist standpoint theory to be making competing arguments on two topics —scientific method and history—in order to explain in their different ways the causes of sexist and androcentric results of scientific research.[10] As already indicated, spontaneous feminist empiricists think that insufficient care and rigor in following existing methods and norms is the cause of sexist androcentric results of research, and it is in these terms that they try to produce plausible accounts of the successes of empirically and theoretically more adequate results of research. Standpoint theorists think that this is only part of the problem. They point out that retroactively, and with the help of the insights of the women's movement, one can see these sexist or androcentric practices in the disciplines. However, the methods and norms in the disciplines are too weak to permit researchers *systematically* to identify and eliminate from the results of research those social values, interests, and agendas that are shared by the entire scientific community or virtually all of it. Objectivity has not been "operationalized" in such a way that scientific method can detect sexist and androcentric assumptions that are "the dominant beliefs of an age"—that is, that are collectively (versus only individually) held. As far as scientific method goes (and feminist empiricist defenses of it), it is entirely serendipitous when cultural beliefs that are assumed by most members of a scientific community are challenged by a piece of scientific research. Standpoint theory tries to address this problem by producing stronger standards for "good method," ones that can guide more competent efforts to maximize objectivity.[11]

With respect to history, spontaneous feminist empiricists argue that movements of social liberation such as the women's movement function much like the little boy who is the hero of the folk tale about the Emperor and his clothes. Such movements "make it possible for people to see the world in an enlarged perspective because they remove the covers and blinders that obscure knowledge and observation."[12] Feminist standpoint theorists agree with this assessment, but argue that researchers can do more than just wait around until social movements happen and then wait around some more until their effects happen to reach inside the processes of producing maximally objective, causal accounts of nature and social relations. Knowledge projects can find active ways incorporated into their principles of "good method" to use history as a resource by socially situating knowledge projects in the scientifically and epistemologically most favorable historical locations. History can become the systematic provider of scientific and epistemological resources rather than an obstacle to or the "accidental" benefactor of projects to generate knowledge.[13]

It is spontaneous feminist empiricism's great strength that it explains the production of sexist and nonsexist results of research with only a minimal challenge to the fundamental logic of research as this is understood in scientific fields and to the logic of explanation as this is understood in the dominant philosophies of science. Spontaneous feminist empiricists try to fit feminist projects into prevailing standards of "good science" and "good philosophy." This conservativism makes it possible for many people to grasp the importance of feminist research in biology and the social sciences without feeling disloyal to the methods and norms of their research traditions. Spontaneous feminist empiricism appears to call for even greater rigor in using these methods and following these norms. However, this conservatism is also this philosophy's weakness; this theory of knowledge refuses fully to address the limitations of the dominant conceptions of method and explanation and the ways the conceptions constrain and distort results of research and thought about this research even when these dominant conceptions are most rigorously respected. Nevertheless, its radical nature should not be underestimated. It argues persuasively that the sciences have been blind to their own sexist and androcentric research practices and results. And it thereby clears space for the next question: are the existing logics of research and explanation really so innocent in the commission of this "crime" as empiricism insists, or are they part of its cause?[14]

The intellectual history of feminist standpoint theory is conventionally traced to Hegel's reflections on what can be known about the master/slave relationship from the standpoint of the slave's life versus that of the master's life and to the way Marx, Engels, and Lukacs subsequently developed this insight into the "standpoint of the proletariat" from which have been produced marxist theories of how class society operates.[15] In the 1970s, several feminist thinkers independently began reflecting on how the marxist analysis could be transformed to explain how the structural relationship between women and men had consequences for the production of knowledge.[16] However, it should be noted that even though standpoint arguments are most fully articulated as such in feminist writings, they appear in the scientific projects of all of the new social movements.[17] A *social* history of standpoint theory would focus on what happens when marginalized peoples begin to gain public voice. In societies where scientific rationality and objectivity are claimed to be highly valued by dominant groups, marginalized peoples and those who listen attentively to them will point out that from the perspective of marginal lives, the dominant accounts are less than maximally objective. Knowledge claims are always socially situated, and the failure by dominant groups critically and systematically to interrogate their advantaged social situation and the effect of such advantages on their beliefs leaves their social situation a scientifically and epistemologically disadvantaged one for generating knowledge. Moreover, these accounts end up legitimating exploitative "practical politics" even when those who produce them have good intentions.

The starting point of standpoint theory—and its claim that is most often misread—is that in societies stratefied by race, ethnicity, class, gender, sexuality, or some other such politics shaping the very structure of a society, the *activities* of those at the top both organize and set limits on what persons who perform such activities can understand about themselves and the world around them. "There are some perspectives on society from which, however well-intentioned one may be, the real relations of humans with each other and with the natural world are not visible."[18] In contrast, the activities of those at the bottom of such social hierarchies can provide starting points for thought—for *everyone's* research and scholarship—from which humans' relations with each other and the natural world can become visible. This is because the experience and lives of marginalized peoples, as they understand them, provide particularly significant *problems to be explained* or research agendas. These experiences and lives have been devalued or ignored as a source of objectivity-maximizing questions—the answers to which are not necessarily to be found in those experiences or lives but elsewhere in the beliefs and activities of people at the center who make policies and engage in social practices that shape marginal lives.[19] So one's social situation enables and sets limits on what one can know; some social situations—critically unexamined dominant ones—are more limiting than others in this respect, and what makes these situations more limiting is their inability to generate the most critical questions about received belief.[20]

It is this sense in which Dorothy Smith argues that women's experience is the "grounds" of feminist knowledge and that such knowledge should change the discipline of sociology.[21] Women's lives (our many different lives and different experiences!) can provide the starting point for asking new, critical questions about not only those women's lives but also about men's lives and, most importantly, the causal relations between them.[22] For example, she points out that if we start thinking from women's lives, we (anyone) can see that women are assigned the work that men do not want to do for themselves, especially the care of everyone's bodies—the bodies of men, babies, children, old people, the sick, and their own bodies. And they are assigned responsibility for the local places where those bodies exist as they clean and care for their own and others' houses and work places.[23] This kind of "women's work" frees men in the ruling groups to immerse themselves in the world of abstract concepts. The more successful women are at this concrete work, the more invisible it becomes to men as distinctively social labor. Caring for bodies and the places bodies exist disappears into "nature," as, for example, in sociobiological claims about the naturalness of "altruistic" behavior for females and its unnaturalness for males or in the systematic reticence of many prefeminist marxists actually to analyze who does what in everyday sexual, emotional, and domestic work, and to integrate such analyses into their accounts of "working class labor." Smith argues that we should not be surprised that men have trouble seeing women's activities as part of distinctively human culture and history once we notice how invisible the social character of this work is from the perspective of their activities. She points out that if we start from women's lives, we can generate questions about why it is that it is primarily women who are assigned such activities and what the consequences are for the economy, the state, the family, the educational system, and other social institutions of assigning body and emotional work to one group and "head" work to another.[24] These questions lead to less partial and distorted understandings of women's worlds, men's worlds, and the causal relations between them than do the questions originating only in that part of human activity that men in the dominant groups reserve for themselves—the abstract mental work of managing and administrating.

Standpoint epistemology sets the relationship between knowledge and politics at the center of its account in the sense that it tries to provide causal accounts—to explain—the effects that different kinds of politics have on the production of knowledge. Of course, empiricism also is concerned with the effects politics has on the production of knowledge, but prefeminist empiricism conceptualizes politics as entirely bad. Empiricism tries to purify science of all such bad politics by adherence to what it takes to be rigorous methods for the testing of hypotheses. From the perspective of standpoint epistemology, this is *far too weak a strategy* to maximize the objectivity of the results of research that empiricists desire. Thought that begins from the lives of the oppressed has no chance to get its critical questions voiced or heard within such an empiricist conception of the way to produce knowledge. Prefeminist empiricists can only perceive such questions as the intrusion of politics into science, which therefore deteriorates the objectivity of the results of research. Spontaneous feminist empiricism, for all its considerable virtues, nevertheless contains distorting traces of these assumptions, and they block the ability of this theory of science to develop maximally strong criteria for systematic ways to maximize objectivity.

Thus the standpoint claims that all knowledge attempts are socially situated and that some of these objective social locations are better than others as starting points for knowledge projects challenge some of the most fundamental assumptions of the scientific world view and the Western thought that takes science as its model of how to produce knowledge. It sets out a rigorous "logic of discovery" intended to maximize the objectivity of the results of research and thereby to produce knowledge that can be *for* marginalized people (and those who would know what the marginalized can know) rather than *for* the use only of dominant groups in their projects of administering and managing the lives of marginalized people.

3. What Are the Grounds for Knowledge Claims?

Standpoint theories argue for "starting off thought" from the lives of marginalized peoples; beginning in those determinate, objective locations in any social order will generate illuminating critical questions that do not arise in thought that begins from dominant group lives. Starting off research from women's lives will generate less partial and distorted accounts not only of women's lives but also of men's lives and of the whole social order. Women's lives and experiences provide the "grounds" for this knowledge, though these clearly do not provide foundations for knowledge in the conventional philosophical sense. These grounds are the site, the activities, from which scientific questions arise. The epistemologically advantaged starting points for research do not guarantee that the researcher can maximize objectivity in her account; these grounds provide only a necessary—not a sufficient—starting point for maximizing objectivity. It is useful to contrast standpoint grounds for knowledge with four other kinds: the "God-trick," ethnocentrism, relativism, and the unique abilities of the oppressed to produce knowledge.

Standpoint Theories versus the "God-Trick"

First, for standpoint theories, the grounds for knowledge are fully saturated with history and social life rather than abstracted from it. Standpoint knowledge projects do not claim to originate in purportedly universal human problematics; they do not claim to perform the "God-trick."[25] However, the fact that feminist knowledge claims are socially situated does not in practice distinguish them from any other knowledge claims that have ever been made inside or outside the history of Western thought and the disciplines today; all bear the fingerprints of the communities that produce them. All thought by humans starts off from socially determinate lives. As Dorothy Smith puts the point, "women's perspective, as I have analyzed it here, discredits sociology's claim to constitute an objective knowledge independent of the sociologist's situation. Its conceptual procedures, methods, and relevances are seen to organize its subject matter from a determinate position in society."[26]

It is a delusion—and a historically identifiable one—to think that human thought could completely erase the fingerprints that reveal its production process. Conventional conceptions of scientific method enable scientists to be relatively good at eliminating those social interests and values from the results of research that differ *within* the scientific community, because whenever experiments are repeated by different observers, differences in the social values of individual observers (or groups of them from different research teams) that have shaped the results of their research will stand out from the sameness of the phenomena that other researchers (or teams of them) report.[27] But scientific method provides no rules, procedures, or techniques for even identifying, let alone eliminating, social concerns and interests that are shared by all (or virtually all) of the observers, nor does it encourage seeking out observers whose social beliefs vary in order to increase the effectiveness of scientific method. Thus culturewide assumptions *that have not been criticized within the scientific research process* are transported into the results of research, making visible the historicity of specific scientific claims to people at other times, other places, or in other groups in the very same social order. We could say that standpoint theories not only acknowledge the social situatedness that is the inescapable lot of all knowledge-seeking projects but also, more importantly, transform it into a systematically available scientific resource.

Standpoint Theories versus Ethnocentrism

Universalists have traditionally been able to imagine only ethno-centrism and relativism as possible alternatives to "the view from nowhere" that they assert grounds universal claims, so they think standpoint epistemologies must be supporting (or doomed to) one or the other of these positions. Is there any reasonable sense in which the ground for knowledge claimed by feminist standpoint theory is ethnocentric?

Ethnocentrism is the belief in the inherent superiority of one's own ethnic group or culture.[28] Do feminist standpoint theorists argue that the lives of *their own group or culture* is *superior* as a grounds for knowledge?[29] At first glance, one might think that this is the case if one notices that it is primarily women who have argued for starting thought from women's lives. However, there are several reasons why it would be a mistake to conclude from this fact that feminist standpoint theory is ethnocentric.

First, standpoint theorists themselves all explicitly argue that marginal lives that are not their own provide better grounds for certain kind of knowledge. Thus the claim by women that women's lives provide a better starting point for thought about gender systems is not the same as the claim that *their own* lives are the best such starting points. They are not denying that their own lives can provide important resources for such projects, but they are arguing that other, different (and sometimes oppositional) women's lives also provide such resources. For example, women who are not prostitutes and have not been raped have argued that startling thought from women's experiences and activities in such events reveals that the state is male because it looks at women's lives here just as men (but not women) do. Dorothy Smith writes of the value of starting to think about a certain social situation she describes from the perspective of Native Canadian lives.[30] Bettina Aptheker has argued that starting thought from the everyday lives of women who are holocaust survivors, Chicana cannery workers, older lesbians, African-American women in slavery, Japanese-American concentration camp survivors, and others who have had lives different from hers increases our ability to understand a great deal about the distorted way the dominant groups conceptualize politics, resistance, community, and other key history and social science notions.[31] Patricia Hill Collins, an African-American sociologist, has argued that starting thought from the lives of poor and in some cases illiterate African-American women reveals important truths about the lives of intellectuals, both African-American and European-American, as well as about those women.[32] Many theorists who are not mothers (as well as many who are) have argued that starting thought in mother-work generates important questions about the social order. Of course some women no doubt do argue that their own lives provide the one and only best starting point for all knowledge projects, but this is not what standpoint theory holds. Thus, although it is not an accident that so many women have argued for feminist standpoint approaches, neither is it evidence that standpoint claims are committed to ethnocentrism.

Second, and relatedly, thinkers with "center" identities have also argued that marginalized lives are better places from which to start asking causal and critical questions about the social order. After all, Hegel was not a slave, though he argued that the master/slave relationship could better be understood from the perspective of slaves' activities. Marx, Engels, and Lukacs were not engaged in the kind of labor that they argued provided the starting point for developing their theories about class society. There are men who have argued for the scientific and epistemic advantages of starting thought from women's lives, European-Americans who understand that much can be learned about their lives as well as African-American lives if they start their thought from the latter, and so on.[33]

Third, women's lives are shaped by the rules of femininity or womanliness; in this sense they "express feminine culture." Perhaps the critic of standpoint theories thinks feminists are defending femininity and thus "their own culture." But all feminist analyses, including feminist standpoint writings, are in principle ambivalent about the value of femininity and womanliness. Feminists criticize femininity on the grounds that it is fundamentally defined by and therefore part of the conceptual project of exalting masculinity; it is the "other" against which men define themselves as admirably and uniquely human. Feminist thought does not try to substitute loyalty to femininity for the loyalty to masculinity it criticizes in conventional thought. Instead, it criticizes all gender loyalties as capable of producing only partial and distorted results of research. However, it must do this while also arguing that women's lives have been inappropriately devalued. Feminist thought is forced to "speak as" and on behalf of the very notion it criticizes and tries to dismantle—women. In the contradictory nature of this project lies both its greatest challenge and a source of its great creativity. It is because the conditions of women's lives are worse than their brothers' in so many cases that women's lives provide better places from which to start asking questions about a social order that tolerates and in so many respects even values highly the bad conditions for women's lives (women's double-day of work, the epidemic of violence against women, women's cultural obligation to be "beautiful," and so on).[34] Thus research processes that problematize how gender practices shape behavior and belief—that interrogate and criticize both masculinity and femininity—stand a better chance of avoiding such biasing gender loyalties.

Fourth, there are many feminisms, and these can be understood to be starting off their analyses from the lives of different historical groups of women. Liberal feminism initially started off its analyses from the lives of women in the eighteenth- and nineteenth-century European and U.S. educated classes; Marxist feminism, from the lives of wage-working women in the nineteenth- and early twentieth-century industrializing or "modernizing" societies; Third World feminism, from the lives of late twentieth-century women of Third World descent—and these different Third World lives produce different feminisms. Standpoint theory argues that each of these groups of women's lives is a good place to start in order to explain certain aspects of the social order. There is no single, ideal woman's life from which standpoint theories recommend that thought start. Instead, one must turn to all of the lives that are marginalized in different ways by the operative systems of social stratification. The different feminisms inform each other; we can learn from all of them and change our patterns of belief.

Last, one can note that from the perspective of marginalized lives, it is the dominant claims that we should in fact regard as ethnocentric. It is relatively easy to see that overtly racist, sexist, classist, and heterosexist claims have the effect of insisting that the dominant culture is superior. But it is also the case that claims to have produced universally valid beliefs—principles of ethics, of human nature, epistemologies, and philosophies of science—are ethnocentric. Only members of the powerful groups in societies stratified by race, ethnicity, class, gender, and sexuality could imagine that their standards for knowledge and the claims resulting from adherence to such standards should be found preferable by all rational creatures, past, present, and future. This is what the work of Smith, Hartsock, and the others discussed earlier shows. Moreover, standpoint theory itself is a historical emergent. There are good reasons why it has not emerged at other times in history; no doubt it will be replaced by more useful epistemologies in the future—the fate of all human products.[35]

Standpoint Theory versus Relativism, Perspectivalism, and Pluralism

If there is no single, transcendental standard for deciding between competing knowledge claims, then it is said that there can be only local historical ones, each valid in its own lights but having no claims against others. The literature on cognitive relativism is by now huge, and here is not the place to review it.[36] However, standpoint theory does not advocate—not is it doomed to—relativism. It argues against the idea that all social situations provide equally useful resources for learning about the world and against the idea that they all set equally strong limits on knowledge. Contrary to what universalists think, standpoint theory is not committed to such a claim as a consequence of rejecting universalism. Standpoint theory provides arguments for the claim that some social situations are scientifically better than others as places from which to start off knowledge projects, and those arguments must be defeated if the charge of relativism is to gain plausibility.[37]

Judgmental (or epistemological) relativism is anathema to any scientific project, and feminist ones are no exception.[38] It is not equally true as its denial that women's uteruses wander around in their bodies when they take math courses, that only Man the Hunter made important contributions to distinctively human history, that women are biologically programmed to succeed at mothering and fail at equal participation in governing society, that women's preferred modes of moral reasoning are inferior to men's, that targets of rape and battering must bear the responsibility for what happens to them, that the sexual molestation and other physical abuses children report are only their fantasies, and so on—as various sexist and androcentric scientific theories have claimed. Feminist and prefeminist claims are usually not complementary but conflicting, just as the claim that the earth is flat conflicts with the claim that it is round. *Sociological* relativism permits us to acknowledge that different people hold different beliefs, but what is at issue in rethinking objectivity is the different matter of *judgmental* or epistemological relativism. Standpoint theories neither hold nor are doomed to it.

Both moral and cognitive forms of judgmental relativism have determinate histories; they appear as intellectual problems at certain times in history in only some cultures and only for certain groups of people. Relativism is not fundamentally a problem that emerges from feminist or any other thought that starts in marginalized lives; it is one that emerges from the thought of the dominant groups. Judgmental relativism is sometimes the most that dominant groups can stand to grant to their critics—"OK, your claims are valid for you, but mine are valid for me."[39] Recognizing the importance of thinking about who such a problem belongs to—identifying its social location—is one of the advantages of standpoint theory.

Standpoint Theory versus the Unique Abilities of the Oppressed to Produce Knowledge

This is another way of formulating the charge that standpoint theories, in contrast to conventional theories of knowledge, are ethnocentric. However, in this form the position has tempted many feminists, as it has members of other liberatory knowledge projects.[40] We can think of this claim as supporting "identity science" projects—the knowledge projects that support and are supported by "identity politics." In the words of the Combahee River Collective's critique of liberal and marxist thought (feminist as well as prefeminist) that failed to socially situate anti-oppression claims: "Focusing upon our own oppression is embodied in the concept of identity politics. We believe that the most profound and potentially the most radical politics come directly out of our own identity, as opposed to working to end somebody else's oppression."[41] (They were tired of hearing about how they should be concerned to improve others' lives and how others were going to improve theirs.)

To pursue the issue further, we will turn to examine just who is the "subject of knowledge" for standpoint theories. But we can prepare for that discussion by recollecting yet again that Hegel was not a slave, though he grasped the critical understanding of the relations between master and slave that became available only if he started off his thought from the slave's activities, and that Marx, Engels and Lukacs were not proletarians. Two questions are raised by these examples: What is the role for marginalized experience in the standpoint projects of members of dominant groups? And what are the special resources, but also limits, that the lives of people in dominant groups provide in generating the more objective knowledge claims standpoint theories call for? We shall begin to address these issues in the next section.

To conclude this one, marginalized lives provide the scientific problems and the research agendas—not the solutions—for standpoint theories. Starting off thought from these lives provides fresh and more critical questions about how the social order works than does starting off thought from the unexamined lives of members of dominant groups. Most natural and social scientists (and philosophers!) are themselves members of these dominant groups, whether by birth or through upward mobility into scientific and professional/managerial careers. Those who are paid to teach and conduct research receive a disproportionate share of the benefits of that very nature and social order that they are trying to explain. Thinking from marginal lives leads one to question the adequacy of the conceptual frameworks that the natural and social sciences have designed to explain (for themselves) themselves and the world around them. This is the sense in which marginal lives ground knowledge for standpoint approaches.

4. New Subjects of Knowledge

For empiricist epistemology, the subject or agent of knowledge—that which "knows" the "best beliefs" of the day—is supposed to have a number of distinctive characteristics. First, this subject of knowledge is culturally and historically disembodied or invisible because knowledge is by definition universal. "Science says…," we are told. Whose science, we can ask? The drug and cigarette companies? The Surgeon General's? The National Institute of Health's? The science of the critics of the NIH's racism and sexism? Empiricism insists that scientific knowledge has no particular historical subject. Second, in this respect, the subject of scientific knowledge is different in kind from the objects whose properties scientific knowledge describes and explains, because the latter are determinate in space and time. Third, though the subject of knowledge for empiricists is transhistorical, knowledge is initially produced ("discovered") by individuals and groups of individuals (reflected in the practice of scientific awards and honors), not by culturally specific societies or subgroups in a society such as a certain class or gender or race. Fourth, the subject is homogeneous and unitary, because knowledge must be consistent and coherent. If the subject of knowledge were permitted to be multiple and heterogeneous, then the knowledge produced by such subjects would be multiple and contradictory and thus inconsistent and incoherent.

The subjects of knowledge for standpoint theories contrast in all four respects. First, they are embodied and visible, because the lives from which thought has started are always present and visible in the results of that thought. This is true even though the way scientific method is operationalized usually succeeds in removing all personal or individual fingerprints from the results of research. But personal fingerprints are not the problem standpoint theory is intended to address. The thought of an age is *of an age*, and the delusion that one's thought can escape historical locatedness is just one of the thoughts that is typical of dominant groups in these and other ages. The "scientific world view" is, in fact, a view of (dominant groups in) modern, Western societies, as the histories of science proudly point out. Standpoint theories simply disagree with the further ahistorical and incoherent claim that the content of "modern and Western" scientific thought is also, paradoxically, not shaped by its historical location.

Second, the fact that subjects of knowledge are embodied and socially located has the consequence that they are not fundamentally different from objects of knowledge. We should assume causal symmetry in the sense that the same kinds of social forces that shape objects of knowledge also shape (but do not determine) knowers and their scientific projects.

This may appear to be true only for the objects of social science knowledge, not for the objects that the natural sciences study. After all, trees, rocks, planetary orbits, and electrons do not constitute themselves as historical actors. What they are does not depend on what they think they are; they do not think or carry on any of the other activities that distinguish human communities from other constituents of the world around us. However, this distinction turns out to be irrelevant to the point here because, in fact, scientists never can study the trees, rocks, planetary orbits, or electrons that are "out there" and untouched by human concerns. Instead, they are destined to study something different (but hopefully systematically related to what is "out there"); *nature as an object of knowledge*. Trees, rocks, planetary orbits, and electrons always appear to natural scientists only as they are already socially constituted in some of the ways that humans and their social groups are already socially constituted for the social scientist. Such objects are already effectively "removed from pure nature" into social life—they are social objects—by, first of all, the contemporary general cultural meanings that these objects have for everyone, including the entire scientific community.[42] They also become socially constituted objects of knowledge through the shapes and meanings these objects gain for scientists because of earlier generations of scientific discussion about them. Scientists never observe nature apart from such traditions; even when they criticize some aspects of them they must assume others in order to carry on the criticism. They could not do science if they did not both borrow from and also criticize these traditions. Their assumptions about what they see are always shaped by "conversations" they carry on with scientists of the past. Finally, their own interactions with such objects also culturally constitute them; to treat a piece of nature with respect, violence, degradation, curiosity, or indifference is to participate in culturally constituting such an object of knowledge. In these respects, nature as an object of knowledge simulates social life, and the processes of science themselves are a significant contributor to this phenomenon. Thus the subject and object of knowledge for the natural sciences are also not significantly different in kind. Whatever kinds of social forces shape the subjects are also thereby shaping their objects of knowledge.

Third, consequently, communities and not primarily individuals produce knowledge. For one thing, what I believe that I thought through all by myself (in my mind), which I know, only gets transformed from my personal belief to knowledge when it is socially legitimated. Just as importantly, my society ends up assuming all the claims I make that neither I nor my society critically interrogate. It assumes the eurocentric, androcentric, heterosexist, and bourgeois beliefs that I do not critically examine as part of my scientific research and that, consequently, shape my thought and appear as part of my knowledge claims. These are some of the kinds of features that subsequent ages (and Others today) will say make my thought characteristic of my age, or society, community, race, class, gender, or sexuality. The best scientific thought of today is no different in this respect from the thought of Galileo or Darwin; in all can be found not only brilliant thoughts first expressed by individuals and then legitimated by communities but also assumptions we now regard as false that were distinctive to a particular historical era and not identified as part of the "evidence" that scientists actually used to select the results of research.[43]

Fourth, the subjects/agents of knowledge for feminist standpoint theory are multiple, heterogeneous, and contradictory or incoherent, not unitary, homogeneous, and coherent as they are for empiricist epistemology.[44] Feminist knowledge has started off from women's lives, but it has started off from many different women's lives; there is no typical or essential woman's life from which feminisms start their thought. Moreover, these different women's lives are in important respects opposed to each other. Feminist knowledge has arisen from European and African women, from economically privileged and poor women, from lesbians and heterosexuals, from Protestant, Jewish, and Islamic women. Racism and imperialism, local and international structures of capitalist economies, institutionalized homophobia and compulsory heterosexuality, and the political conflicts between ethnic and religious cultures produce multiple, heterogeneous, and contradictory feminist accounts. Nevertheless, thought that starts off from each of these different kinds of lives can generate less partial and distorted accounts of nature and social life.

However, the subject/agent of feminist knowledge is multiple, heterogeneous, and frequently contradictory in a second way that mirrors the situation for women as a class. It is the thinker whose consciousness if bifurcated, the outsider within, the marginal person now located at the center,[45] the person who is committed to two agendas that are by their nature at least partially in conflict—the liberal feminist, socialist feminist, Sandinista feminist, Islamic feminist, or feminist scientist—who has generated feminist sciences and new knowledge. It is starting off thought from a contradictory social position that generates feminist knowledge. So the logic of the directive to "start thought from women's lives" requires that one start one's thought from multiple lives that are in many ways in conflict with each other, each of which itself has multiple and contradictory commitments. This may appear an overwhelming requirement—or even an impossible one—because Western thought has required the fiction that we have and thus think from unitary and coherent lives. But the challenge of learning to think from the perspective of more than one life when those lives are in conflict with each other is familiar to anthropologists, historians, conflict negotiators, domestic workers, wives, mothers—indeed, to most of us in many everyday contexts.

Both empiricist philosophy and marxism could maintain the fiction that unitary and coherent subjects of knowledge were to be preferred only by defining one socially distinctive group of people as the ideal knowers and arguing that all others lacked the characteristics that made this group ideal. Thus, the liberal philosophy associated with empiricism insisted that it was the possession of reason that enabled humans to know the world the way it is and then defined as not fully rational women, Africans, the working class, the Irish, Jews, other peoples from Mediterranean cultures, and so on. It was said that no individuals in these groups were capable of the dispassionate, disinterested exercise of individual moral and cognitive reason that was the necessary condition for becoming the ideal subject of knowledge. Similarly, traditional marxism argued that only the industrial proletariat possessed the characteristics for the ideal subject of marxist political economy. Peasants', slaves' and women's work, as well as bourgeois activities, made these people's lives inferior starting points for generating knowledge of the political economy.[46] In contrast, the logic of standpoint theory leads to the refusal to essentialize its subjects of knowledge.

This logic of multiple subjects leads to the recognition that the subject of liberatory feminist knowledge must also be, in an important if controversial sense, the subject of every other liberatory knowledge project. This is true in the collective sense of "subject of knowledge," because lesbian, poor, and racially marginalized women are all women, and therefore all feminists will have to grasp how gender, race, class, and sexuality are used to construct each other. It will have to do so if feminism is to be liberatory for marginalized women, but also if it is to avoid deluding dominant group women about their/our own situations. If this were not so, there would be no way to distinguish between feminism and the narrow self-interest of dominant group women—just as conventional androcentric thought permits no criterion for distinguishing between "best beliefs" and those that serve the self-interest of men as men. (Bourgeois thought permits no criterion for identifying specifically bourgeois self-interest; racist thought, for identifying racist self-interest; and so on.)

But the subject of every other liberatory movement must also learn how gender, race, class, and sexuality are used to construct each other in order to accomplish their goals. That is, analyses of class relations must look at their agendas from the perspective of women's lives, too. Women, too, hold class positions, and they are not identical to their brothers'. Moreover, as many critics have pointed out, agendas of the left need to deal with the fact that bosses regularly and all too successfully attempt to divide the working class against itself by manipulating gender hostilities. If women are forced to tolerate lower wages and double-days of work, employers can fire men and hire women to make more profit. Antiracist movements must look at their issues from the perspective of the lives of women of color, and so forth. Everything that feminist thought must know must also inform the thought of every other liberatory movement, and vice versa. It is not just the women in those other movements who must know the world from the perspective of women's lives. Everyone must do so if the movements are to succeed at their own goals. Most importantly, this requires that women be active directors of the agendas of these movements. But it also requires that men in those movements be able to generate original feminist knowledge from the perspective of women's lives as, for example, John Stuart Mill, Marx and Engels, Frederick Douglass, and later male feminists have done.[47]

However, if every other liberatory movement must generate feminist knowledge, it cannot be that women are the unique generators of feminist knowledge. Women can not claim this ability to be uniquely theirs, and men must not be permitted to claim that because they are not women, they are not obligated to produce fully feminist analyses. Men, too, must contribute distinctive forms of specifically feminist knowledge from their particular social situation. Men's thought, too, will begin first from women's lives in all the ways that feminist theory, with its rich and contradictory tendencies, has helped us all—women as well as men—to understand how to do. It will start there in order to gain the maximally objective theoretical frameworks within which men can begin to describe and explain their own and women's lives in less partial and distorted ways. This is necessary if men are to produce more than the male supremacist "folk belief" about themselves and the world they live in to which female feminists object. Women have had to learn how to substitute the generation of feminist thought for the "gender nativism" androcentric cultures encourage in them, too. Female feminists are made, not born. Men, too must learn to take historic responsibility for the social position from which they speak.

Patricia Hill Collins has stressed the importance to the development of Black feminist thought of genuine dialogue across differences, and of the importance of making coalitions with other groups if that dialogue is to happen.

> While Black feminist thought may originate with Black feminist intellectuals, it cannot flourish isolated from the experiences and ideas of other groups. The dilemma is that Black women intellectuals must place our own experiences and consciousness at the center of any serious efforts to develop Black feminist thought yet not have that thought become separatist and exclusionary....
>
> By advocating, refining, and disseminating Black feminist thought, other groups—such as Black men, white women, white men, and other people of color—further its development. Black women can produce an attenuated version of Black feminist thought separated from other groups. Other groups cannot produce Black feminist thought without African-American women. Such groups can, however, develop self-defined knowledge reflecting their own standpoints. But the full actualization of Black feminist thought requires a collaborative enterprise with Black women at the center of a community based on coalitions among autonomous groups.[48]

It seems to me that Collins has provided a powerful analysis of the social relations necessary for the development of less partial and distorted belief by any knowledge community.

Far from licensing European-Americans to appropriate African-American thought or men to appropriate women's thought, this approach challenges members of dominant groups to make themselves "fit" to engage in collaborative, democratic, community enterprises with marginal peoples. Such a project requires learning to listen attentively to marginalized people; it requires educating oneself about their histories, achievements, preferred social relations, and hopes for the future; it requires putting one's body on the line for "their" causes until they feel like "our" causes; it requires critical examination of the dominant institutional beliefs and practices that systematically disadvantage them; it requires critical self-examination to discover how one unwittingly participates in generating disadvantage to them...and more. Fortunately, there are plenty of models available to us not only today but also through an examination of the history of members of dominant groups who learned to think from the lives of marginalized people and to act on what they learned. We can choose which historical lineage to claim as our own.

To conclude this section, we could say that since standpoint analyses explain how and why the subject of knowledge always appears in scientific accounts of nature and social life as part of the object of knowledge of those accounts, standpoint approaches have had to learn to use the social situatedness of subjects of knowledge systematically as a resource for maximizing objectivity. They have made the move from declaiming as a problem or acknowledging as an inevitable fact to theorizing as a *systematically accessible* resource for maximizing objectivity the inescapable social situatedness of knowledge claims.

5. Standards for Maximizing Objectivity

We are now in a position to draw out of this discussion of the innovative grounds and subject of knowledge for feminist standpoint theories the stronger standards for maximizing objectivity that such theories both require and generate. Strong objectivity requires that the subject of knowledge be placed on the same critical, causal plane as the objects of knowledge. Thus, strong objectivity requires what we can think of as "strong reflexivity." This is because culturewide (or nearly culturewide) beliefs function as evidence at every stage in scientific inquiry: in the selection of problems, the formation of hypotheses, the design of research (including the organization of research communities), the collection of data, the interpretation and sorting of data, decisions about when to stop research, the way results of research are reported, and so on. The subject of knowledge—the individual and the historically located social community whose unexamined beliefs its members are likely to hold "unknowingly," so to speak—must be considered as part of the object of knowledge from the perspective of scientific method. All of the kinds of objectivity-maximizing procedures focused on the nature and/or social relations that are the direct object of observation and reflection must also be focused on the observers and reflectors—scientists and the larger society whose assumptions they share. But a maximally critical study of scientists and their communities can be done only from the perspective of those whose lives have been marginalized by such communities. Thus, strong objectivity requires that scientists and their communities be integrated into democracy-advancing projects for scientific and epistemological reasons as well as moral and political ones.

From the perspective of such standpoint arguments, empiricism's standards appear weak; empiricism advances only the "objectivism" that has been so widely criticized from many quarters.[49] Objectivism impoverishes its attempts at maximizing objectivity when it turns away from the task of critically identifying all of those broad, historical social desires, interests, and values that have shaped the agendas, contents, and results of the sciences much as they shape the rest of human affairs.

Consider, first, how objectivism too narrowly operationalizes the notion of maximizing objectivity.[50] The conception of value-free, impartial, dispassionate research is supposed to direct the identification of all social values and their elimination from the results of research, yet it has been operationalized to identify and eliminate only those social values and interests that differ among the researchers and critics who are regarded by the scientific community as competent to make such judgments. If the community of "qualified" researchers and critics systematically excludes, for example, all African-Americans and women of all races and if the larger culture is stratified by race and gender and lacks powerful critiques of this stratification, it is not plausible to imagine that racist and sexist interests and values would be identified within a community of scientists composed entirely of people who benefit—intentionally or not—from institutionalized racism and seism. This kind of blindness is advanced by the conventional belief that the truly scientific part of knowledge seeking—the part controlled by methods of research—occurs only in the context of justification. The context of discovery, in which problems are identified as appropriate for scientific investigation, hypotheses are formulated, key concepts are defined—this part of the scientific process is thought to be unexaminable within science by rational methods. Thus "real science" is restricted to those processes controllable by methodological rules. The methods of science—or rather, of the special sciences—are restricted to procedures for the testing of already formulated hypotheses. Untouched by these methods are those values and interests entrenched in the very statement of what problem is to be researched and in the concepts favored in the hypotheses that are to be tested. Recent histories of science are full of cases in which broad social assumptions stood little chance of identification or elimination through the very best research procedures of the day.[51] Thus objectivism operationalizes the notion of objectivity in much too narrow a way to permits the achievement of the value-free research that is supposed to be its outcome.

But objectivism also conceptualizes the desired value-neutrality of objectivity too broadly. Objectivists claim that objectivity requires the elimination of *all* social values and interests from the research process and the results of research. It is clear, however, that not all social values and interests have the same bad effects upon the results of research. Democracy-advancing values have systematically generated less partial and distorted beliefs than others.[52]

Objectivism's rather weak standards for maximizing objectivity make objectivity a mystifying notion, and its mystificatory character is largely responsible for its usefulness and its widespread appeal to dominant groups. It offers hope that scientists and science institutions, themselves admittedly historically located, can produce claims that will be regarded as objectively valid without having to examine critically their own historical commitments from which—intentionally or not—they actively construct their scientific research. It permits scientists and science institutions to be unconcerned with the origins or consequences of their problematics and practices or with the social values and interests that these problematics and practices support. It offers the false hope of enacting what Francis Bacon erroneously promised for the method of modern science: "The course I propose for the discovery of sciences is such as leaves but little to the acuteness and strength of wits, but places all wits and understandings nearly on a level." His "way" of discovering science goes far to level men's wits, and leaves but little to individual excellence, because it performs everything by surest rules and demonstrations."[53] In contrast, standpoint approaches requires the strong objectivity that can take the subject as well as the object of knowledge to be a necessary object of critical, causal—scientific!—social explanations. This program of strong reflexivity is a resource of objectivity, in contrast to the obstacle that de facto reflexivity has posed to weak objectivity.

Some feminists and thinkers from other liberatory knowledge projects have thought that the very notion of objectivity should be abandoned. They say that it is hopelessly tainted by its use in racist, imperialist, bourgeois, homophobic, and androcentric scientific projects. Moreover, it is tied to a theory of representation and concept of the self or subject that insists on a rigid barrier between subject and object of knowledge—between self and Other—which feminism and other new social movements label as distinctively androcentric or eurocentric. Finally, the conventional notion of objectivity institutionalizes a certain kind of lawlessness at the heart of science, we could say, by refusing to theorize any criteria internal to scientific goals for distinguishing between scientific method, on the one hand, and such morally repugnant acts as torture or ecological destruction, on the other. Scientists and scientific institutions disapprove of, engage in political activism against, and set up special committees to screen scientific projects for such bad consequences, but these remain ad hoc measures, extrinsic to the conventional "logic" of scientific research.

However, there is not just one legitimate way to conceptualize objectivity, any more than there is only one way to conceptualize freedom, democracy, or science. The notion of objectivity has valuable political and intellectual histories; as it is transformed into "strong objectivity" by the logic of standpoint epistemologies, it retains central features of the older conception. In particular, might should not make right in the realm of knowledge production any more than in matters of ethics. Understanding ourselves and the world around us requires understanding what others think of us and our beliefs and actions, not just what we think of ourselves and them.[54] Finally, the appeal to objectivity is an issue not only between feminist and prefeminist science and knowledge projects but also within each feminist and other emancipatory research agenda. There are many feminisms, some of which result in claims that distort the racial, class, sexuality, and gender relationships in society. Which ones generate less or more partial and distorted accounts of nature and social life? The notion of objectivity is useful in providing a way to think about the gap that should exist between how any individual or group wants the world to be and how in fact it is.[55]

6. An Objection Considered

"Why not just keep the old notion of objectivity as requiring value-neutrality and argue instead that the problem feminism raises is how to get it, not that the concept itself should be changed? Why not argue that it is the notion of scientific method that should be transformed, not objectivity?"

This alternative position is attractive for several reasons. For one thing, clearly feminist standpoint theorists no less than other feminists want to root out sexist and androcentric bias from the results of research. They want results of research that are not "loyal to gender"—feminine or masculine. In this sense, don't they want to maximize value-neutrality—that is, old-fashioned objectivity—in the results of research?

Moreover, in important respects an epistemology and a method for doing research in the broadest sense of the term have the same consequences or, at least, are deeply implicated in each other. What would be the point of a theory of knowledge that did not make prescriptions for how to go about getting knowledge or of a prescription for getting knowledge that did not arise from a theory about how knowledge can be and has been produced? So why not appropriate and transform what the sciences think of as scientific method, but leave the notion of objectivity intact? Why not argue that the standpoint theories have finally completed the quest for a "logic of discovery" begun and then abandoned by philosophers some decades ago? They are calling for an "operationalization" of scientific method that includes the context of discovery and the social practices of justification in the appropriate domain of its rules and recommended procedures.[56] Scientific method must be understood to begin back in the context of discovery, in which scientific "problems" are identified and bold hypotheses conjectured. Then "starting from marginalized lives" becomes part of the method of maximizing value-neutral objectivity. This possibility could gain support from the fact that some standpoint theorists consistently talk about their work interchangeably as an epistemology and a method for doing research.[57]

Attractive as this alternative is, I think it is not attractive enough to convince that only method and not also the concept of objectivity should be reconceptualized. For one thing, this strategy makes it look reasonable to think it possible to gain value-neutrality in the results of research. It implies that human ideas can somehow escape their location in human history. But this no longer appears plausible in the new social studies of science.

Second, and relatedly, this strategy leads away from the project of analyzing how our beliefs regarded as true as well as those regarded as false have social causes and thus, once gain, to the assumption of a crucial difference between subjects and objects of knowledge. It would leave those results of research that are judged by the scientific community to be maximally objective to appear to have no social causes, to be the result only of nature's impressions on our finally well-polished, glassy-mirror minds. Objects of knowledge then become, once again, dissimilar for the subjects of knowledge. Subjects of real knowledge, unlike subjects of mere opinion, are disembodied and socially invisible, whereas their natural and social objects of knowledge are firmly located in social history. Thus the "strong method" approach detached from "strong objectivity" leaves the opposition between subjects and objects firmly in place—an opposition that both distorts reality and has a long history of use in exploiting marginalized peoples. The "strong objectivity" approach locates this very assumed difference between subject and object of knowledge in social history; it calls for a scientific account of this assumption, too.

Third, this strategy leaves reflexivity merely a perpetual problem rather than also the resource into which standpoint theorists have transformed it. Observers do change the world that they observe, but refusing to strengthen the notion of objectivity leaves reflexivity always threatening objectivity rather than also as a resource for maximizing it.

Finally, it is at least paradoxical and most certainly likely to be confusing that the "strong method only" approach must activate in the process of producing knowledge those very values, interests, and politics that it regards as anathema in the results of research. It is at least odd to direct would-be knowers to go out and reorganize social life—as one must do to commit such forbidden (and difficult) acts as starting thought from marginal lives—in order to achieve value-neutrality in the results of research. Standpoint approaches want to eliminate dominant group interests and values from the results of research as well as the interests and values of *successfully colonized* minorities—loyalty to femininity as well as to masculinity is to be eliminated through feminist research. But that does not make the results of such research value-neutral. It will still be the thought of this era, making various distinctive assumptions that later generations and others today will point out to us.

On balance, these disadvantages outweigh the advantages of the "strong method only" approach.

Can the new social movements "have it both ways?" Can they have knowledge that is fully socially situated? We can conclude by putting the question another way: if they cannot, what hope is there for anyone else to maximize the objectivity of *their* beliefs?

NOTES

[1]   "Situated Knowledges: The Science Question in Feminism and the Privilege of Partial Perspective," *Feminist Studies* 14, 3 (1988): 581. Reprinted and revised in Donna J. Haraway, *Simians, Cyborgs, and Women* (New York: Routledge, 1991). I thank Linda Alcoff and Elizabeth Potter for helpful comments on an earlier draft.

[2]   Important works here include Susan Bordo, *The Flight of Objectivity: Essays on Cartesianism & Culture* (Albany: SUNY Press, 1987); Anne Fausto-Sterling, *Myths of Gender* (New York: Basic Books, 1985); Elizabeth Fee, "Women's Nature and Scientific Objectivity," in *Woman's Nature: Rationalizations of Inequality*, ed. Marion Lowe and Ruth Hubbard (New York: Pergamon Press, 1981); Donna Haraway, op. cit. and *Primate Visions: Gender, Race and Nature in the World of Modern Science* (New York: Routledge, 1989); Ruth Hubbard, *The Politics of Women's Biology* (New Brunswick: Rutgers University Press, 1990); Evelyn Keller, *Reflections on Gender and Science* (New Haven: Yale University Press, 1984); Helen Longino, *Science as Social Knowledge* (Princeton, N.J.: Princeton University Press, 1990); and Lynn Hankinson Nelson, *Who Knows: From Quine to a Feminist Empiricism* (Philadelphia: Temple University Press, 1990). These are just *some* of the important works on the topic; many other authors have made contributions to the discussion. I have addressed these issues in *The Science Question in Feminism* (Ithaca: Cornell University Press, 1986) and *Whose Science? Whose Knowledge? Thinking From Women's Lives* (Ithaca: Cornell University Press, 1991); see also the essays in Sandra Harding and Merrill Hintikka, ed., *Discovering Reality: Feminist Perspectives on Epistemology, Metaphysics, Methodology and the Philosophy of Science* (Dordrecht: Reidel 1983). An interesting parallel discussion occurs in the feminist jurisprudence literature in the course of critiques of conventional conceptions of what "the rational man" would do, "the objective observer" would see, and "the impartial judge" would reason; see, for example many of the essays in the special issue of the *Journal of Legal Education on Women in Legal Education—Pedagogy, Law, Theory, and Practice* 39, 1–2 (1988), ed. Carrie Menkel-Meadow, Martha Minow, and David Vernon; and Katharine T. Bartlett, "Feminist Legal Methods," *Harvard Law Review* 103, 4 (1990).

[3]   This literature is by now huge. For a sampling of its concerns, see Richard Bernstein, *Beyond Objectivism and Relativism* (Philadelphia: University of Pennsylvania Press, 1983): Martin Hollis and Steven Lukes, eds., *Rationality and Relativism* (Cambridge, Mass.: Harvard University Press, 1982); Michael Krausz and Jack Meiland, eds., *Relativism: Cognitive and Moral* (Notre Dame, Ind.: University of Notre Dame Press, 1982); and Stanley Aronowitz, *Science and Power: Discourse and Ideology in Modern Society* (Minneapolis: University of Minnesota Press, 1988).

[4]   Haraway, "Situated Knowledges," loc. cit., 579. In the phrase "a critical practice for recognizing our own 'semiotic technologies' for making meanings," she also raises here the troubling issue of reflexivity, to which I shall return.

[5]   Dorothy Smith, *The Everyday World as Problematic: A Feminist Sociology*, (Boston: Northeastern University Press, 1987) and *The Conceptual Practices of Power: A Feminist Sociology of Knowledge*, (Boston: Northeastern University Press, 1990); Nancy Hartsock, "The Feminist Standpoint: Developing the Ground for a Specifically Feminist Historical Materialism," in Harding and Hintikka, eds., *Discovering Reality*; Hilary Rose, "Hand, Brain and Heart: A Feminist Epistemology of the Natural Sciences," *Signs* 9, 1 (1983); and my discussion of these writings in chapter 6 of *The Science Question in Feminism*. Alison Jaggar also developed an influential account of standpoint epistemology in chapter 11 of *Feminist Politics and Human Nature* (Totowa, N.J.: Rowman & Allenheld, 1983). For more recent developments of standpoint theory see Patricia Hill Collins, chapters 10 and 11 of *Black Feminist thought: Knowledge, Consciousness and the Politics of Empowerment* (Boston: Unwin Hyman, 1990) and chapters 5, 6, 7, and 11 of my *Whose Science? Whose Knowledge?*

[6]   Chapter 6 of *Whose Science?*, " 'Strong Objectivity' and Socially Situated Knowledge," addresses some of the issues I raise here. However, here I develop further the differences between the "grounds" and the subject of knowledge for standpoint theory and for other epistemologies. This is partly an archeology of standpoint theory—bringing to full light the obscured aspects of its logic—and partly a reformulation of some of its claims.

[7]   Scientists sometimes confuse the philosophy of science called "empiricism" with the idea that it is a good thing to collect information about the empirical world. All philosophies of science recommend the latter. Empiricism is that account of such practices associated paradigmatically with Locke, Berkeley and Hume and claiming that sensory experience is the only or fundamental source of knowledge. It contrasts with theological accounts that were characteristic of European science of the Middle Ages, with rationalism, and with Marxist philosophy of science. However, from the perspective of standpoint theory, it also shares key features with one or another of these three philosophies. For example, it borrows the monologic voice that seems proper if one assumes the necessity of a unitary and coherent subject of knowledge, as do all three.

[8]   Roy Bhaskar writes that although positivism mystifies the processes of science, nevertheless it has a certain degree of necessity in that it reflects the spontaneous consciousness of the lab bench—the tenets of positivism reflect how it feels like science is done when one is actually gathering observations of nature. Similarly, from the perspective of standpoint approaches, the "spontaneous" feminist empiricism I discuss here mystifies the processes of feminist research, although it has a certain necessity in that it just felt to these feminist empirical workers like what it was that they were doing as their work overturned the results of supposedly value-free prefeminist research. See Roy Bhaskar, "Philosophies as Ideologies of Science: A Contribution to the Critique of Positivism," in *Reclaiming Reality* (New York: Verso, 1989). Not all forms of empiricism are reasonably thought of as positivist, of course, but the most prevalent contemporary forms are. The philosophical feminist empiricism noted below is not positivist.

[9]   Longino, *Science as Social Knowledge*; Nelson, *Who Knows*.

[10]   There are many standpoint theorists and many spontaneous feminist empiricists. I present here ideal types of these two theories of knowledge. I have contrasted these two theories in a number of earlier writings, most recently on p. 111–37 of *Whose Science: Whose Knowledge?* The following passage draws especially on pp. 111–20.

[11]   Dorothy Smith was right, I now think, to insist (in effect) that standpoint theory appropriates and transforms the notion of scientific method, not just of epistemology; see her comments on a paper of mine in *American Philosophical Association Newsletter on Feminism* 88, 3 (1989). It is interesting to note that by 1989, even the National Academy of Science—no rabble-rousing antiscience critic!—argues that the methods of science should be understood to include "the judgments scientists make about the interpretation or reliability of data..., the decisions scientists make about which problems to pursue or when to conclude an investigation," and even "the ways scientists work with each other and exchange information" [*On Being a Scientist* (Washington D.C.: National Academy Press, 1989), 5–6].

[12]   Marcia Millman and Rosabeth Moss Kanter, "Editor's Introduction" to *Another Voice: Feminist Perspectives on Social Life and Social Science* (New York: Anchor Books, 1975), vii. [Reprinted in S. Harding, ed., *Feminism and Methodology,* (Bloomington: Indiana University Press, 1987.)]

[13]   This description seems to imply that scientists are somehow outside of the history they are using—for example, capable of determining which are, in fact, the scientifically and epistemologically most favorable historical locations. This is not so, of course, and that is why the reflexivity project Haraway refers to is so important.

[14]   "Of course here and there will be found careless or poorly trained scientists, but no *real* scientist, no *good* scientist, would produce sexist or androcentric results of research." This line of argument has the consequence that there have been no real or good scientists except for feminists! See "What Is Feminist Science?," chapter 12 of *Whose Science? Whose Knowledge?,* for discussions of this and other attempts to resist the idea that feminist science is exactly good science but that refusing to acknowledge the feminist component in good science obscures what makes it good.

[15]   Frederic Jameson has argued that the feminist standpoint theorists are the only contemporary thinkers fully to appreciate the Marxist epistemology. See *"History and Class Consciousness* as an 'Unfinished Project,'" *Rethinking Marxism* 1 (1988): 49–72. It should be noted that empiricist explanations of Marxist accounts are common: "Marx had this puzzle....He made a bold conjecture and then attempted to falsify it....The facts supported his account and resolved the puzzle." These make the accounts plausible to empiricists but fail to engage both with Marx's own different epistemology and with the additional "puzzle" of the historical causes of the emergence of his account, to which Marxist epistemology draws attention.

[16]   See note 6.

[17]   Cf., for example, Edward Said, *Orientalism* (New York: Pantheon Books, 1978); Samir Amin, *Eurocentrism* (New York: Monthly Review Press, 1989); Monique Wittig, "The Straight Mind," *Feminist Issues* 1, 1 (1980); Marilyn Frye, *The Politics of Reality* (Trumansburg, N.Y.: The Crossing Press, 1983); and Charles Mills, "Alternative Epistemologies," *Social Theory and Practice* 14, 3 (1988).

[18]   Hartsock, "The Feminist Standpoint," 159. Hartsock's use of the term "real relations" may suggest to some readers that she and other standpoint theorists are hopelessly mired in an epistemology and metaphysics that have been discredited by social constructionists. This judgment fails to appreciate the way standpoint theories reject *both* pure realist and pure social

constructionist epistemologies and metaphysics. Donna Haraway is particularly good on this issue. (See her "Situated Knowledges," cited in note 1.)

[19] We shall return later to the point that, for standpoint theorists, reports of marginalized experience or lives or phenomenologies of the "lived world" of marginalized people are not the *answers* to questions arising either inside or outside those lives, though they are necessary to asking the best questions.

[20] For an exploration of a number of different ways in which marginal lives can generate more critical questions, see chapter 5, "What is Feminist Epistemology?" in *Whose Science? Whose Knowledge?*

[21] See, for example, *The Conceptual Practices of Power: A Feminist Sociology of Knowledge*, 54.

[22] The image of knowledge seeking as a journey—"starting off thought from women's lives"—is a useful corrective to misunderstandings that more easily arise from the visual metaphor—"thinking from the perspective of women's lives." The journey metaphor appears often in writings by Hartsock, Smith, and others.

[23] Some women are assigned more of this work than others, but even wealthy and aristocratic women with plenty of servants are left significantly responsible for such work in ways their brothers are not.

[24] Of course body work and emotional work also require head work—contrary to the long history of sexist, racist, and class-biased views. See, for example, Sara Ruddick, *Maternal Thinking* (New York: Beacon Press, 1989). And the kind of head work required in administrative and managerial work—what Smith means by "ruling"—also involves distinctive body and emotional work, though it is not acknowledged as such. Think of how much of early childhood education of middle-class children is really about internalizing a certain kind of (gender-specific) regulation of bodies and emotions.

[25] This is Donna Haraway's phrase in "Situated Knowledges" cited in note 1.

[26] Smith, "Women's Perspective as a Radical Critique of Sociology," in *Feminism and Methodology*, 91.

[27] I idealize the history of science here as is indicated by recent studies of fraud, carelessness, and unconscious bias that is not detected. See, for example, Stephen Jay Gould, *The Mismeasure of Man* (New York: W.W. Norton, 1981); L. Kamin, *The Science and Politics of IQ* (Potomac, Md.: Erlbaum, 1974); and William Broad and Nicholas Wade, *Betrayers of the Truth* (New York: Simon & Schuster, 1982). The issue here can appear to be one about the sins of individuals, which it is. But far more importantly, it is an issue about both the unwillingness and impotence of scientific institutions to police their own practices. They *must* do so, for any other alternative is less effective. But science institutions will not want to or be competent to do so until they are more integrated into democratic social projects.

[28] Richard Rorty is unusual in arguing that because social situatedness is indeed the lot of all human knowledge projects, we might as well embrace our ethnocentrism while pursuing the conversations of mankind. His defense of ethnocentrism is a defense of a kind of fatalism about the impossibility of people ever transcending their social situation; in a significant sense this comes down to and converges with the standard definition of ethnocentrism centered in my

argument here. (I thank Linda Alcoff for helping me to clarify this point.) He does not imagine that one can effectively change one's "social situation" by, for example, participating in a feminist political movement, reading and producing feminist analyses, and so on. From the perspective of his argument, it is mysterious how any woman (or man) ever becomes a feminist because our "social situation" is initially to be constrained by patriarchal institutions, ideologies, and the like. How *did* John Stuart Mill or Simone de Beauvoir ever come to think such thoughts as they did? See his *Objectivity, Relativism and Truth* (New York: Cambridge University Press, 1991).

29   Of course a gender is not an ethnicity. Yet historians and anthropologists write of women's cultures, so perhaps it does not stretch the meaning of ethnicity too far to think of women's cultures this way. Certainly some of the critics of standpoint theory have done so.

30   "Women's Perspective," cited in note 26.

31   Bettina Aptheker, *Tapestries of Life: Women's Work, Women's Consciousness, and the Meaning of Daily Life* (Amherst: University of Massachusetts Press, 1989).

32   *Black Feminist Thought,* cited in note 6.

33   The preceding citations contain many examples of such cases.

34   "So many," but not all. African-American and Latina writers have argued that in U.S. society, at least, a poor African-American and Latino man cannot be regarded as better off than his sister in many important respects.

35   What are the material limits of standpoint theories? Retroactively, we can see that they require the context of scientific culture; that is, they center claims about greater objectivity, the possibility and desirability of progress, the value of causal accounts for social projects, and so on. They also appear to require that the barriers between dominant and dominated be not absolutely rigid; there must be some degree of social mobility. Some marginal people must be able to observe what those at the center do, some marginal voices must be able to catch the attention of those at the center, and some people at the center must be intimate enough with the lives of the marginalized to be able to think how social life works from the perspective of their lives. A totalitarian system would be unlikely to breed standpoint theories. So a historical move to antiscientific or to totalitarian systems would make standpoint theories less useful. No doubt there are other historical changes that would limit the resources standpoint theories can provide.

36   See the citations in note 3.

37   All of the feminist standpoint theorists and science writers insist on distinguishing their positions from relativist ones. I have discussed the issue of relativism in several places, most recently in chapters 6 and 7 of *Whose Science? Whose Knowledge?*

38   See S.P. Mohanty, "Us and Them: On the Philosophical Bases of Political Criticism," *Yale Journal of Criticism,*2, 2(1989); and Donna Haraway's "Situated Knowledges" for especially illuminating discussions of why relativism can look attractive to many thinkers at this moment in history, but why it should nevertheless be resisted.

39   Mary G. Belenky and her colleagues point out that the phrase "It's my opinion . . ." has different meanings for the young men and women they have studied. For men this phrase means "I've got a right to my opinion," but for women it means "It's just my opinion." Mary G.

Belenky, B.M. Clincy, N.R. Goldeberger, and J.M. Tarule, *Women's Ways of Knowing: the Development of Self, Voice, and Mind* (New York: Basic Books, 1986).

[40] Critics of standpoint theories usually attribute this position to standpoint theorists. Within the array of feminist theoretical approaches, the claim that only women can produce knowledge is most often made by Radical Feminists.

[41] The Combahee River Collective, "A Black Feminist Statement," in *This Bridge Called My Back: Writings by Radical Women of Color,* ed. Cherrie Moraga and Gloria Anzaldua (Latham, N.Y.: Kitchen Table: Women of Color Press, 1983), 212.

[42] For example, mechanistic models of the universe had different meanings for Galileo's critics than they have had for modern astronomers or, later, for contemporary ecologists, as Carolyn Merchant and other historians of science point out. See Carolyn Merchant, *The Death of Nature: Women, Ecology and the Scientific Revolution* (New York: Harper & Row, 1980). To take another case, "wild animals" and more generally, "nature" are defined differently by Japanese, Indian, and Anglo-American primatologists, as Donna Haraway points out in *Primate Visions* (cited in note 2). The cultural character of nature as an object of knowledge has been a consistent theme in Haraway's work.

[43] Longino and Nelson's arguments are particularly telling against the individualism of empiricism. See Nelson's "Who Knows," chapter 6 in *Who Knows,* and Longino's discussion of how the underdetermination of theories by their evidence insures that "background beliefs" will function as if they were evidence in many chapters of *Science as Social Knowledge* (cited in note 2) but especially in chapters 8, 9, and 10.

[44] See Elizabeth Spelman, *Inessential Woman: Problems of Exclusion in Feminist Thought* (Boston: Beacon Press, 1988) for a particularly pointed critique of essentialist tendencies in feminist writings. Most of the rest of this section appears also in "Subjectivity, Experience and Knowledge: An Epistemology from/for Rainbow Coalition Politics," forthcoming in *Questions of Authority: The Politics of Discourse and Epistemology in Feminist Thought,* ed. Judith Roof and Robyn Weigman. I have also discussed these points in several other places.

[45] These ways of describing this kind of subject of knowledge appear in the writings of, respectively, Smith ("Women's Perspective"), Collins (*Black Feminist Thought*) and Bell Hooks, *Feminist Theory From Margin to Center* (Boston: South End Press, 1983).

[46] Consequently, a main strategy of the public agenda politics of the new social movements has been to insist that women, or peoples of African descent, or the poor, and so on do indeed possess the kinds of reason that qualify them as "rational men"; that women's, industrial, or peasant labor makes these groups also the "working men" from whose laboring lives can be generated less partial and distorted understandings of local and international economies.

[47] I do not say these thinkers are perfect feminists—they are not, and no one is. But here and there one can see them generating original feminist knowledge as they think from the perspective of women's lives as women have taught them to do.

[48] Collins, *Black Feminist Thought,* 35–36, Chapters 1, 2, 10 and 11 of this book offer a particular rich and stimulating development of standpoint theory.

[49]   See the citations in note 3. The term "objectivism" has been used to identify the objectionable notion by Bernstein, Keller, and Bordo (see earlier citations), among others.

[50]   The following arguments are excerpted from pp. 143–48 in my *Whose Science? Whose Knowledge?*

[51]   See note 27.

[52]   Many Americans—even (especially?) highly educated ones—hold fundamentally totalitarian notions of what democracy is, associating it with mob rule or some at least mildly irrelevant principle of representation but never with genuine community dialogue. (A physicist asked me if by democracy I really meant that national physics projects should be managed by, say, fifty-two people, one selected randomly from each state! This made me think of the wisdom of William Buckley, Jr.'s desire to be governed by the first 100 people in the Boston phone book rather than the governors we have.) A good starting point for thinking about how to advance democracy is John Dewey's proposal: those who will bear the consequence of a decision should have a proportionate share in making it.

[53]   Quoted in Werner Van den Daele, "The Social Construction of Science," in *The Social Production of Scientific Knowledge,* ed., E. Mendelsohn, P. Weingart, and R. Whitley (Dordrecht: Reider, 1977), 34.

[54]   David Mura puts the point this way in "Strangers in the Village," in *The Graywolf Annual Five: Multi-cultural Literacy,* ed. Rick Simonson and Scott Walker (St. Paul: Graywolf Press, 1988), 152.

[55]   These arguments for retaining the notion of objectivity draw on ones I have made several times before, most recently in *Whose Science? Whose Knowledge?* p. 157–61.

[56]   The National Academy of Sciences recommends such an explanation, as indicated earlier.

[57]   For example, Smith and Hartsock, cited in note 5.

3.6

SUBJECTS, POWER, AND KNOWLEDGE: DESCRIPTION AND PRESCRIPTION IN FEMINIST PHILOSOPHIES OF SCIENCE

Helen Longino

I. Prologue

Feminists, faced with traditions in philosophy and in science that are deeply hostile to women, have had practically to invent new and more appropriate ways of knowing the world. These new ways have been less invention out of whole cloth than the revival or reevaluation of alternative or suppressed traditions. They range from the celebration of insight into nature through identification with it to specific strategies of survey research in the social sciences. Natural scientists and laypersons anxious to see the sciences change have celebrated Barbara McClintock's loving identification with various aspects of the plants she studied, whether whole organism or its chromosomal structure revealed under the microscope. Social scientists from Dorothy Smith to Karen Sacks have stressed designing research *for* rather than merely about women, a goal that requires attending to the specificities of women's lives and consulting research subjects themselves about the process of gathering information about them. Such new ways of approaching natural and social phenomena can be seen as methods of discovery, ways of getting information about the natural and social worlds not available via more traditional experimental or investigative methods.

Feminists have rightly pointed out the blinders imposed by the philosophical distinction between discovery and justification; a theory of scientific inquiry that focuses solely on the logic of justification neglects the selection processes occurring in the context of discovery that limit what we get to know about. Methods of discovery, or heuristics, are in effect selection processes that present for our consideration certain sorts of hypotheses and not other sorts.

Feminists have identified heuristic biases—androcentrism, sexism, and gender ideology—that limit the hypotheses in play in specific areas of inquiry and have also pointed out that alternative heuristics put different hypotheses in play. However, a theory of scientific inquiry that focuses solely on methods of discovery presents its own difficulties. In particular, a given heuristic method that puts certain hitherto suppressed or invisible hypotheses into play is not ipso facto ratifiable as a producer of knowledge, as distinct from interesting or even plausible ideas. Something more is required before we can speak of knowledge (or even confirmation) as opposed to plausibility. One way to articulate the distinctions I am urging is to treat analysis of the context of discovery as a primarily descriptive analysis of how hypotheses are generated and to treat analysis in the context of justification as involving a normative or prescriptive analysis regarding the appropriate criteria for the acceptance of hypotheses. This is problematic because philosophers in the past who made this distinction sometimes concluded that only the context of justification is worthy of philosophical analysis. Nevertheless, ignoring the context of justification for the context of discovery is equally problematic. I wish in this essay to explore some of the tensions between descriptivism and normativism (or prescriptivism) in the theory of knowledge, arguing that although many of the most familiar feminist accounts of science have helped us to redescribe the process of knowledge (or belief) acquisition, they stop short of an adequate normative theory. However, these accounts do require a new approach in normative epistemology because of their redescription.

Although this essay focuses on issues in the epistemology of science, it bears on general issues in epistemology in two ways. First, to the extent that "science" simply means knowledge, an analysis of scientific knowledge is an analysis of knowledge. Second, philosophy of science to a large degree relies on general epistemological principles. Critical discussion of their adequacy for the philosophy of science is relevant to, although not conclusive regarding, their tenability in a general theory of knowledge. To the extent that human knowledge is not coextensive with scientific knowledge, however, remarks bearing on science are only partially relevant to knowledge in general.

The relevance relations from general epistemology to scientific knowledge are even less direct. In contemplating the problems of developing new and more appropriate knowledge, it is tempting to suppose that epistemology could provide the key that would unlock the right door—that if we could just get the epistemology right, we would get the science right, too. Surely one source of this belief is the close relationship between the science and the philosophy done at the beginning of the modern period. Does not the epistemology of Descartes and of Locke have something to do with the theories of nature that took hold during the Seventeenth Century? Another is reflection on the persistence of misogynist views in biological theories, from the various subfields of evolutionary theory to theories of development. If one hallmark of the modern period is the development of rule-based inquiry, something in the justification rules must account for this persistence. If getting the epistemology wrong accounts for harmful science, getting the epistemology right must be the key to better science. This is probably an oversimplification of the thinking that has underlain the attraction to epistemology for many feminist scholars outside of philosophy, but I do not think it is too far off the mark. And although I do think that new approaches in the theory of knowledge would alter some of our attitudes in and about science, I also think that the relationship between epistemology—the theory of what practices produce knowledge—and science—what counts as knowledge—in any given period is more complicated than the temptation allows. We cannot produce knowledge of the world on the strength of a general theory of knowledge.

Nor can we simply dismiss the accumulated knowledge of the natural world produced by the traditional methods of the natural sciences. These sciences have transformed conditions of life in industrialized portions of the world, both conceptually as models of knowledge and materially through science-based technologies. Why, then, do some of us feel so uneasy not only about the theories directly concerning females and gender but also about the very nature of scientific knowledge and the power it creates? After all, even feminists who wish to change the sciences are also, by that very ambition, expressing a hope for power. There are surely various sources for and locations of this uneasiness. Those of us who are feminists have been struck by the interlocking character of several aspects of knowledge and power in the sciences. Women have been excluded from the practice of science, even as scientific inquiry gets described both as a masculine activity and as demonstrating women's unsuitability to engage in it, whether because of our allegedly deficient mathematical abilities or our insufficient independence. Some of us notice the location of women in the production of the artifacts made possible by new knowledge: swift and nimble fingers on the microelectronics assembly line. Others notice the neglect of women's distinctive health issues by the biomedical sciences, even as new techniques for preserving the fetuses they carry are introduced into hospital delivery rooms. The sciences become even more suspect as analysis of their metaphors (for example, in cell biology and in microbiology) reveals an acceptance (and hence reinforcement) of the cultural identification of the male with activity and of the female with passivity. Finally, feminists have drawn a connection between the identification of nature as female and the scientific mind as male and the persistent privileging of explanatory models constructed around relations of unidirectional control over models constructed around relations of interdependence. Reflection on this connection has prompted feminist critics to question the very idea of a scientific method capable of adjudicating the truth or probability of theories in a value-neutral way.

Although the sciences have increased human power over natural processes, they have, according to this analysis, done so in a lop-sided way, systematically perpetuating women's cognitive and political disempowerment (as well as that of other groups marginalized in relation to the Euro-American drama). One obvious question, then, is whether this appropriation of power is an intrinsic feature of science or whether it is an incidental feature of the sciences as practiced in the modern period, a feature deriving from the social structures within which the sciences have developed. A second question is whether it is possible to seek and possess empowering knowledge without expropriating the power of others. Is seeking knowledge inevitably an attempt at domination? And are there criteria of knowledge other than the ability to control the phenomena about which one seeks knowledge? Feminists have answered these questions in a number of ways. I will review some of these before outlining my own answer.

II. Feminist Epistemological Strategies 1: Changing the Subject

Most traditional philosophy of science (with the problematic exception of Descartes's) has adopted some form of empiricism. Empiricism's silent partner has been a theory of the subject, that is, of the knower.[1] The paradigmatic knower in Western epistemology is an individual—an individual who, in several classic instances, has struggled to free himself from the distortions in understanding and perception that result from attachment. Plato, for example, maintained that knowledge of the good is possible only for those whose reason is capable of controlling their appetites and passions, some of which have their source in bodily needs and pleasures and others of which have their source in our relations with others. The struggle for epistemic autonomy is even starker for Descartes, who suspends belief in all but his own existence in order to recreate a body of knowledge cleansed of faults, impurities, and uncertainties.

For Descartes, only those grounds available to a single, unattached, disembodied mind are acceptable principles for the construction of a system of beliefs. Most subsequent epistemology has granted Descartes's conditions and disputed what those grounds are and whether any proposed grounds are sufficient grounds for knowledge. Descartes's creation of the radically and in principle isolated individual as the ideal epistemic agent has for the most part gone unremarked.[2] Locke, for example, adopts the Cartesian identification of the thinking subject with the disembodied soul without even remarking upon the individualism of the conception he inherits and then struggles with the problem of personal identify. Explicitly or implicitly in modern epistemology, whether rationalist or empiricist, the individual consciousness that is the subject of knowledge is transparent to itself, operates according to principles that are independent of embodied experience, and generates knowledge in a value-neutral way.

One set of feminist epistemological strategies, sometimes described as modifications or rejections of empiricism, can also, and perhaps better, be described as changing the subject. I will review three such strategies of replacement, arguing that although they enrich our understanding of how we come to have the beliefs we have and so are more descriptively adequate than the theories they challenge, they fall short of normative adequacy. The strategies identify the problems of contemporary science as resulting from male or masculinist bias. Each strategy understands both the bias and its remedy differently. One holds out the original ideal of uncontaminated or unconditioned subjectivity. A second identifies bias as a function of social location. A third identifies bias in the emotive substructure produced by the psychodynamics of individuation.

Feminist empiricism has by now taken a number of forms. That form discussed and criticized by Sandra Harding is most concerned with those fields of scientific research that have misdescribed or misanalyzed women's lives and bodies. It's not clear that any feminist scholars have totally conformed to the profile identified by Harding, but certain moments in the analyses offered by practicing scientists who are feminists do fit this model.[3] At any rate, feminist empiricism (*sub* Harding) identifies the problems in the scientific accounts of women and gender as the product of male bias. Typical examples of problematic views are the treatment of the male of the species as the locus of variation (and hence the basis of evolutionary change for a species), the persistent treatment of male difference as male superiority, the assumption of universal male dominance, and the treatment of sexual divisions of labor in the industrialized societies as the product of biological species evolution. Each of these involves neglecting contradictory empirical information. It should be no surprise that a focus on these sorts of problems suggests their solution in replacing the androcentric subject of knowledge with an unbiased subject—one that would not ignore the empirical data already or easily available. From this perspective, certain areas of science having to do with sex and gender are deformed by gender ideology, but the methods of science are not themselves masculinist and can be used to correct the errors produced by ideology. The ideal knower is still the purified mind, and epistemic or cognitive authority inheres in this purity. This strategy, as Harding has observed, is not effective against those research programs that feminists find troublesome but that cannot be faulted by reference to the standard methodological precepts of scientific inquiry. I have argued, for example, that a critique of research on the influence of prenatal gonadal hormones on behavioural sex differences that is limited to methodological critique of the data fails to bring out the role of the explanatory model that both generates the research and gives evidential relevance to that data.[4]

Another approach is, therefore, the standpoint approach. There is no one position from which value-free knowledge can be developed, but some positions are better than others. Standpoint epistemologies notice systematic distortions in description and analysis produced by those occupying social positions of power. Traditional Marxists identified the standpoint of the bourgeoisie as producing such distortions, whereas feminists have identified the standpoint of men (of the dominant class and race) as equally distorting. Nancy Hartsock and other feminist standpoint theorists have argued that the activities or ruling-class men produce a knowledge of the world characterized by abstractness and impersonality, that their own politically structured freedom from the requirements of re/producing the necessities of daily life is reflected in the kind of understanding they produce of the social and natural world.[5] Women's work, by contrast, is characterized by greater interaction with material substances, by constant change, and by its requirement of emotional investment in the form of caring. Not only does women's characteristic activity and relation to the means of production/reproduction produce its own unique form of understanding, but also women who become self-conscious agents in this work are able to incorporate men's perspectives as well as their own and hence to develop a more accurate, more objective, set of beliefs about the world.

By valorizing the perspectives uniquely available to those who are socially disadvantaged, standpoint theorists turn the table on traditional epistemology; the ideal epistemic agent is not an unconditioned subject but the subject conditioned by the social experiences of oppression. The powerless are those with epistemic legitimacy, even if they lack the power that could turn that legitimacy into authority. One of the difficulties of the standpoint approach comes into high relief, however, when it is a women's or a feminist standpoint that is in question. Women occupy many social locations in a racially and economically stratified society. If genuine or better knowledge depends on the correct or a more correct standpoint, social theory is needed to ascertain which of these locations is the epistemologically privileged one. But in a standpoint epistemology, a standpoint is needed to justify such a theory. What is that standpoint and how do we identify *it*? If no single standpoint is privileged, then either the standpoint theorist must embrace multiple and incompatible knowledge positions or offer some means of transforming or integrating multiple perspectives into one. Both of these moves require either the abandonment or the supplementation of standpoint as an epistemic criterion.

Standpoint theory faces another problem as well. It is by now commonplace to note that standpoint theory was developed by and for social scientists. It has been difficult to see what its implications for the natural sciences might be. But another strategy has seemed more promising. Most standpoint theorists locate the epistemic advantage in the productive/reproductive experience of the oppressed whose perspective they champion. A different change of subject is proposed by those identifying the problems with science as a function of the psychodynamics of individuation. Evelyn Fox Keller has been asking, among other things, why the scientific community privileges one kind of explanation or theory over others. In particular she has asked why, when both linear reductionist and interactionist perspectives are available, the scientific community has preferred the linear or "master molecule" theory that understands a natural process as controlled by a single dominant factor. This question was made vivid by her discussion of her own research on slime mold aggregation and the fate of Barbara McClintock's work on genetic transposition.[6]

Keller's original response, spelled out in *Reflections on Gender and Science*, involved an analysis of the traditional ideal of scientific objectivity, which she understood as the ideal of the scientist's detachment from the object of study.[7] In her view, epistemic and affective ideals are intermingled, and from the psychoanalytical perspective she adopted, distorted affective development—autonomy as exaggerated separateness—was expressed in a distorted epistemic ideal—objectivity as radical detachment. Drawing on and developing object relations theory, she attributed this "static autonomy" to the conditions under which boys develop psychologically: exaggerated separateness is a solution to the anxieties provoked by those conditions. Keller analyzed the consequent ideal of static objectivity as generating and satisfied by accounts of natural processes that foreground controlling relationships—for example, accounts of organismic development as determined by the individual's genetic program. She, therefore, proposed an alternative conceptualization of autonomy, contrasting static autonomy with what she called dynamic autonomy, an ability to move in and out of intimate connection with the world. Dynamic autonomy provides the emotional substructure for an alternative conception of objectivity: dynamic objectivity. The knower characterized by dynamic objectivity, in contrast to the knower characterized by static objectivity, does not seek power over phenomena but acknowledges instead the ways in which knower and phenomena are in relationship as well as the ways in which phenomena themselves are complexly interdependent. Barbara McClintock's work has offered one of the most striking examples of the effectiveness of such an approach, although interactionist approaches have also been applied in areas besides developmental biology. McClintock's work, long ignored, was finally vindicated by developments in molecular biology of the 1970s—the acknowledgment of genetic transposition in the prokaryotes that had been the model organisms for contemporary molecular genetics. Dynamic objectivity is not presented as a typically feminine epistemological orientation but as an alternative to an epistemological orientation associated with both masculine psychological development and masculinist gender ideology. But however much interactionist approaches might appeal to us, and however much dynamic objectivity might appeal to us, there isn't a general argument to the truth of interactionism or to the epistemological superiority of dynamic objectivity.

Both standpoint theory and the psychodynamic perspective suggest the inadequacy of an ideal of a pure transparent subjectivity that registers the world as it is in itself (or, for Kantians, as structured by universal conditions of apperception or categories of understanding). I find it most useful to read them as articulating special instances of more general descriptive claims that subjectivity is conditioned by social and historical location and that our cognitive efforts have an ineluctably affective dimension. Classical standpoint theory identifies relation to production/reproduction as the key, but there are multiple, potentially oppositional relations to production/reproduction in a complex society, and there are other kinds of social relation and location that condition subjectivity. For example, one of the structural features of a male-dominant society is asymmetry of sexual access. Men occupy a position of entitlement to women's bodies, whereas women, correspondingly, occupy the position of that to which men are entitled. Complications of the asymmetry arise in class- and race-stratified societies. There may be other structural features as well, such as those related to the institutions of heterosexuality, that condition subjectivity. Because each individual occupies a location in a multidimensional grid marked by numerous interacting structures of power asymmetry, the analytical task is not to determine which is epistemically most adequate. Rather, the task is to understand how these complexly conditioned subjectivities are express in action and belief. I would expect that comparable complexity can be introduced into the psychodynamic account.

Treating subjectivity as variably conditioned and cognition as affectively modulated opens both opportunities and problems. The opportunities are the possibilities of understanding phenomena in new ways; by recognizing that mainstream accounts of natural processes have been developed from particular locations and reflect particular affective orientations, we can entertain the possibility that quite different accounts might emerge from other locations with the benefit of different emotional orientations. Although either transferring or diffusing power, the strategies discussed so far have in common a focus on the individual epistemic agent, on the autonomous subject. (The subject in the second and third approaches comes to be in a social context and as a consequence of social interactions, but its knowledge is still a matter of some relation between it and the subject matter.) The standpoint and psychodynamically based theories recommend certain new positions and orientations as superior to others but fail to explain how we are to decide or to justify decisions between what seem to be conflicting claims about the character of some set of natural processes. On what grounds can one social location or affective orientation be judged epistemically superior to another? Normative epistemology arises in the context of conflicting knowledge claims. Naturalism, or descriptivism, in epistemology presupposes that we know what we think we know and asks how. But the existence of comparably persuasive incompatible claims calls into question whether we know at all, requires that we reexamine what we take to be adequate justification, and may even call into question our very concept of knowledge.

Feminist science critics have provided analyses of the context of discovery that enable us to see how social values, including gender ideology in various guises, could be introduced into science. Some theories that have done so go on to recommend an alternate subject position as epistemically superior. But arguments are missing—and it's not clear that any particular subject position could be adequate to generate knowledge. Can a particular subject position be supported by an a priori argument? It can, but only by an argument that claims a particular structure for the world and then identifies a particular subjectivity as uniquely capable of knowing that structure. The problem with such arguments is that they beg the question. The one subject position that could be advanced as epistemically superior to others without presupposing something about the structure of the world is the unconditioned position, the position of no position that provides a view from nowhere. Attractive as this ideal might seem, arguments in the philosophy of science suggest that this is a chimera. Let me turn to them.

III. Feminist Epistemological Strategies 2: Multiplying Subjects

The ideal of the unconditioned (or universally conditioned) subject is the traditional proposal for escaping the particularity of subjectivity. Granting the truth of the claim that individual subjectivities are conditioned, unconditioned subjectivity is treated as an achievement rather than a natural endowment. The methods of the natural sciences constitute means to that achievement. Some well-known arguments in the philosophy of science challenge this presumption. As they have received a great deal of attention in the philosophical literature, I shall only mention them here in order to bring out their relevance to the general point. The methods of the natural sciences, in particular, have been thought to constitute the escape route from conditioned subjectivity. The difficulty just outlined for the feminist epistemological strategy of changing the subject, however, has a parallel in developments in the philosophy of science. Both dilemmas suggest the individual knower is an inappropriate focus for the purpose of understanding (and changing) science.

In the traditional view, the natural sciences are characterized by a methodology that purifies scientific knowledge of distortions produced by scientists' social and personal allegiances. The essential features of this methodology—explored in great detail by positivist philosophers of science—are observation and logic. Much philosophy of science in the last twenty-five years has been preoccupied with two potential challenges to this picture of scientific methodology—the claim of Kuhn, Feyerabend, and Hanson that observation is theory laden and the claim of Pierre Duhem that theories are underdetermined by data. One claim challenges the stability of observations themselves, the other the stability of evidential relations. Both accounts have seemed (at least to their critics and to some of their proponents) to permit the unrestrained expression of scientists' subjective preferences in the content of science. If observation is theory laden, then observation cannot serve as an independent constraint on theories, thus permitting subjective elements to constrain theory choice. Similarly, if observations acquire evidential relevance only in the context of a set of assumptions, a relevance that changes with a suitable change in assumptions, then it's not clear what protects theory choice from subjective elements hidden in background assumptions. Although empirical adequacy serves as a constraint on theory acceptance, it is not sufficient to pick out one theory from all contenders as the true theory about a domain of the natural world. These analyses of the relation between observation, data, and theory are often thought to constitute arguments against empiricism, but, like the feminist epistemological strategies, they are more effective as arguments against empiricism's silent partner, the theory of the unconditioned subject. The conclusion to be drawn from them is that what has been labelled scientific method does not succeed as a means to the attainment of unconditioned subjectivity on the part of individual knowers. And as long as the scientific knower is conceived of as an individual, knowing best when freed from external influences and attachment (that is, when detached or free from her/his context), the puzzles introduced by the theory-laden nature of observation and the dependence of evidential relations on background assumptions will remain unsolved.

It need not follow from these considerations, however, that scientific knowledge is impossible of attainment. Applying what I take to be a feminist insight—that we are all in relations of interdependence—I have suggested that scientific knowledge is constructed not by individuals applying a method to the material to be known but by individuals in interaction with one another in ways that modify their observations, theories and hypotheses, and patterns of reasoning. Thus scientific method includes more than just the complex of activities that constitutes hypothesis testing through comparison of hypothesis statements with (report of) experiential data, in principle an activity of individuals. Hypothesis testing itself consists of more than the comparison of statements but involves equally centrally the subjection of putative data, of hypotheses, and of the background assumptions in light of which they seem to be supported by those data to varieties of conceptual and evidential scrutiny and criticism.[8] Conceptual criticism can include investigation into the internal and external consistency of a hypothesis and investigation of the factual, moral, and social implications of background assumptions; evidential criticism includes not only investigation of the quality of the data but of its organization, structuring, and so on. Because background assumptions can be and most frequently are invisible to the members of the scientific community for which they are background and because unreflective acceptance of such assumptions can come to define what it is to be a member of such a community (thus making criticism impossible), effective criticism of background assumptions requires the presence and expression of alternative points of view. This sort of account allows us to see how social values and interests can become enshrined in otherwise acceptable research programs (i.e., research programs that strive for empirical adequacy and engage in criticism). As long as representatives of alternative points of view are not included in the community, shared values will not be identified as shaping observation or reasoning.

Scientific knowledge, on this view, is an outcome of the critical dialogue in which individuals and groups holding different points of view engage with each other. It is constructed not by individuals but by an interactive dialogic community. A community's practice of inquiry is productive of knowledge to the extent that it facilitates transformative criticism. The constitution of the scientific community is crucial to this end as are the interrelations among its members. Community level criteria can, therefore, be invoked to discriminate among the products of scientific communities, even though context-independent standards of justification are not attainable. At least four criteria can be identified as necessary to achieve the transformative dimension of critical discourse.

1. There must be publicly recognized forums for the criticism of evidence, of methods, and of assumptions and reasoning.
2. The community must not merely tolerate dissent, but its beliefs and theories must change over time in response to the critical discourse taking place within it.
3. There must be publicly recognized standards by reference to which theories, hypotheses, and observational practices are evaluated and by appeal to which criticism is made relevant to the goals of the inquiring community. With the possible exception of empirical adequacy, there

needn't be (and probably isn't) a set of standards common to all communities. The general family of standards from which those locally adopted might be drawn would include such cognitive virtues as accuracy, coherence, and breadth of scope, and such social virtues as fulfilling technical or material needs or facilitating certain kinds of interactions between a society and its material environment or among the society's members.

4. Finally, communities must be characterized by equality of intellectual authority. What consensus exists must not be the result of the exercise of political or economic power or of the exclusion of dissenting perspectives; it must be the result of critical dialogue in which all relevant perspectives are represented.

Although requiring diversity in the community, this is not a relativist position. True relativism, as I understand it, holds that there are no legitimate constraints on what counts as reasonable to believe apart from the individual's own beliefs. Equality of intellectual authority does not mean that anything goes but that everyone is regarded as equally capable of providing arguments germane to the construction of scientific knowledge. The position outlined here holds that both nature and logic impose constraints. It fails, however, to narrow reasonable belief to a single one among all contenders, in part because it does not constrain belief in a wholly unmediated way. Nevertheless, communities are constrained by the standards operating within them, and individual members of communities are further constrained by the requirement of critical interaction relative to those standards. To say that there may be irreconcilable but coherent and empirically adequate systems for accounting for some portion of the world is not to endorse relativism but to acknowledge that cognitive needs can vary and that this variation generates cognitive diversity.

Unlike the view from nowhere achievable by unconditioned subjectivity or the view from that somewhere identified as maximizing knowledge, this notion of knowledge through interactive intersubjectivity idealizes the view from everywhere (perhaps better thought of as *views* from *many wheres*). These criteria for objective communities represent not a description of actual scientific communities but a set of prescriptions that are probably not anywhere satisfied. Nevertheless, they provide a measure against which actual communities and, indirectly, criteria for the comparison of theories can be evaluated. For example, theories accepted in different communities can be compared with respect to the conditions under which the critical dialogue concerning a given theory has occurred. Although there are any number of objections that advocates of such a notion must address, I will confine myself here to one major problem, the answer to which opens up some future directions for feminist analysis and scientific practice.

IV. Dilemmas of Pluralism

This sort of account is subject to the following dilemma.[9] What gets produced as knowledge depends on the consensus reached in the scientific community. For knowledge to count as genuine, the community must be adequately diverse. But the development of a theoretical idea or hypothesis into something elaborate enough to be called knowledge requires a consensus. The questions must stop somewhere, at some point, so that a given theory can be developed sufficiently to be applied to concrete problems. How is scientific knowledge possible while pursuing socially constituted objectivity? That is, if objectivity requires pluralism in the community, then scientific knowledge becomes elusive, but if consensus is pursued, it will be at the cost of quieting critical oppositional positions.

My strategy for avoiding this dilemma is to detach scientific knowledge from consensus, if consensus means agreement of the entire scientific community regarding the truth or acceptability of a given theory. This strategy also means detaching knowledge from an ideal of absolute and unitary truth. I suggest that we look at the aims of inquiry (at least some) as satisfied by embracing multiple and, in some cases, incompatible theories that satisfy local standards. This detachment of knowledge from universal consensus and absolute truth can be made more palatable than it might first appear by two moves. One of these is implicit in treating science as a practice or set of practices; the other involves taking up some version of a semantic or model-theoretic theory of theories.

Beginning with the second of these, let me sketch what I take to be the relevant aspects and implications of the semantic view.[10] This view is proposed as an alternative to the view of theories as sets of propositions (whether axiomatized or not). If we take the semantic view, we understand a theory as a specification of a set of relations among objects or processes characterized in a fairly abstract way. Another characterization would be that on the semantic view, a theory is the specification of a structure. The structure as specified is neither true nor false; it is just a structure. The theoretical claim is that the structure is realized in some actual system. As Mary Hesse has shown, models are proposed as models of some real world system on the basis of an analogy between the model and the system, that is, the supposition that the model and the system share some significant features in common.[11] Models often have their start as metaphors. Examples of such metaphoric models are typical philosophers' examples like the billiard ball model of particle interactions or the solar system model of the atom. What many feminists have pointed out (or can be understood as having pointed out) is the use of elements of gender ideology and social relations as metaphors for natural processes and relations. Varieties of heterosexual marriage have served as the metaphoric basis for models of the relation between nucleus and cytoplasm in the cell, for example.[12] The master molecule approach to gene action, characterized by unidirectional control exerted on organismal processes by the gene, reflects relations of authority in the patriarchal household. Evelyn Fox Keller has recently been investigating the basis of models in molecular biology in androcentric metaphors of sexuality and procreation.[13] When Donna Haraway says that during and after the Second World War the organism changed from a factory to a cybernetic system, she can be understood as saying that the metaphor generating models of organismic structure and function shifted from a productive system organized by a hierarchical division of labor to a system for generating and processing information.[14] Alternatively put, cells, gene action, and organisms have been modelled as marriage, families, and factories and cybernetic networks, respectively. Supporting such analysis of particular theories or models requires not merely noticing the analogies of structure but also tracing the seepage of language and meaning from one domain to another as well as studying the uses to which the models are put.[15]

The adequacy of a theory conceived as a model is determined by our being able to map some subset of the relations/structures posited in the model onto some portion of the experienced world. (Now the portions of the world stand in many relations to many other portions.) Any given model or schema will necessarily select among those relations. So its adequacy is not just a function of isomorphism of one of the interpretations of the theory with a portion of the world but of the fact that the relations it picks out are ones in which we are interested. A model guides our interactions with and interventions in the world. We want models that guide the interactions and interventions we seek. Given that different subcommunities within the larger scientific community may be interested in different relations or that they may be interested in objects under different descriptions, different models (that if taken as claims about an underlying reality would be incompatible) may well be equally adequate and provide knowledge, in the sense of an ability to direct our interactions and interventions, even in the absence of a general consensus as to what's important. Knowledge is not detached from knowers in a set of propositions but consists in our ability to understand the structural features of a model and to apply it to some particular portion of the world; it is knowledge of that portion of the world through its structuring by the model we use. The notion of theories as sets of propositions requires that we view the adequacy of a theory as a matter of correspondence of the objects, processes, and relations described in the propositions of the theory with the objects, processes, and relations in the domain of the natural world that the theory purports to explain; that is, it requires that adequacy be conceptualized as truth. The model-theoretic approach allows us to evaluate theories in relation to our aims as well as in relation to the model's isomorphism with elements of the modeled domain and permits the adequacy of different and incompatible models serving different and incompatible aims. Knowledge is not contemplative but active.

The second move to escape the dilemma develops some consequences of treating science as practice. There are two worth mentioning. If we understand science as practice, then we understand inquiry as ongoing, that is, we give up the idea that there is a terminus of inquiry that just is the set of truths about the world. (What LaPlace's demon knew, for example.) Scientific knowledge from this perspective is not the static end point of inquiry but a cognitive or intellectual expression of an ongoing interaction with our natural and social environments. Indeed, when we attempt to identify the goals of inquiry that organize scientific cognitive practices, it becomes clear that there are several, not all of which can be simultaneously pursued.[16] Scientific knowledge, then, is a body of diverse theories and their articulations onto the world that changes over time in response to the changing cognitive needs of those who develop and use the theories, in response to the new questions and anomalous empirical data revealed by applying theories, and in response to changes in associated theories. Both linear-reductionist and interactionist models reveal aspects of natural processes, some common to both and some uniquely describable with the terms proper to one but not both sorts of model. If we recognize the partiality of theories, as we can when we treat them as models, we can recognize pluralism in the community as one of the conditions for the continued development of scientific knowledge in this sense.

In particular, the models developed by feminists and others dissatisfied with the valuative and affective dimensions of models in use must at the very least (given that they meet the test of empirical adequacy) be recognized as both revealing the partiality of those models in use and as revealing some aspects of natural phenomena and processes that the latter conceal. These alternative models may have a variety of forms and a variety of motivations, and they need not repudiate the aim of control. We engage in scientific inquiry to direct our interactions with and interventions in the world. Barbara McClintock was not a feminist, but she was in part reacting against the gendered meanings in natural philosophy, meanings which shut her out of inquiry; Ruth Hubbard advocates interactionist perspectives out of more explicitly political commitments; feminists and others concerned with the environment reject the control orientation of technocrats effective in the short term for more complex models that can address long-term change and stasis in the ecosystem. If we aim for effective action in the natural world, something is to be controlled. The issue should be not whether but what and how. Rather than repudiate it, we can set the aim of control within the larger context of overall purposes and develop a more refined sense of the varieties of control made possible through scientific inquiry.

A second consequence for feminist and other oppositional scientists of adopting both the social knowledge thesis and a model-theoretic analysis of theories is that the constructive task does not consist in finding the one best or correct feminist model. Rather, the many models that can be generated from the different subject positions ought to be articulated and elaborated. Very few will be exclusively feminist if that means exclusively gender-based or developed only by feminists. Some will be more appropriate for some domains, others for others, and some for none. We can't know this unless models get sufficiently elaborated to be used as guides for interactions. Thus, this joint perspective implies the advocacy of subcommunities characterized by local standards. To the extend that they address a common domain and to the extent that they share some standards in common, these subcommunities must be in critical dialogue with each other as well as with those subcommunities identified with more mainstream science. The point of dialogue from this point of view is not to produce a general and universal consensus but to make possible the refinement, correction, rejection, and sharing of models. Alliances, mergers, and revisions of standards as well as of models are all possible consequences of this dialogic interaction.

V. Conclusions

Understanding scientific knowledge in this way supports at least two further reflections on knowledge and power. First of all, the need for models within which we can situate ourselves and the interactions we desire with the natural world will militate against the inclusiveness required for an adequate critical practice, if only because the elaboration of any model requires a substantial commitment of material and intellectual resources on the part of a community.[17] This means that, in a power-stratified society, the inclusion of the less powerful and hence of models that could serve as a resource for criticism of the received wisdom in the community of science will always be a matter of conflict. At the same time, the demand for inclusiveness should not be taken to mean that every alternative view is equally deserving of attention. Discussion must be conducted in reference to public standards, standards which, as noted above, do not provide timeless criteria, but which change in response to changes in cognitive and social needs. Nevertheless, by appeal to standards adopted and legitimated through processes of public scrutiny and criticism, it is possible to set aside as irrelevant positions such as New Age "crystalology" or creationism. To the extent that these satisfy none of the central standards operative in the scientific communities of their cultures, they indeed qualify as crackpot. Programs for low-tech science appropriate to settings and problems in developing nations may, by contrast, be equally irritating to or against the grain of some of the institutionalized aspects of science in the industrialized nations, but as long as they do satisfy some of the central standards of those communities, then the perspectives they embody must be included in the critical knowledge-constructive dialogue. Although there is always a danger that the politically marginal will be conflated with the crackpot, one function of public and common standards is to remind us of that distinction and to help us draw it in particular cases. I do not know of any simple or formulaic solution to this problem.

Second, those critiques of scientific epistemology that urge a change of subject preserve the structures of cognitive authority but propose replacing those currently wielding authority with others: a genuinely unbiased subject in one case, a differently located or a differently formed subject in the other. Either no assumptions or different assumptions will be engaged in the knowledge-constructive process. In the position I am advocating, which makes salient those features of knowledge construction made invisible by more traditional accounts, the structures of cognitive authority themselves must change. No segment of the community, whether powerful or powerless, can claim epistemic privilege. If we can see our way to the dissolution of those structures, then we need not understand the appropriation of power in the form of cognitive authority as intrinsic to science. Nevertheless, the creation of cognitive democracy, of democratic science, is as much a matter of conflict and hope as is the creation of political democracy.

Notes

I wish to thank the members of the Centre for Women's Research at the University of Oslo for their hospitality and for the stimulating discussions that shaped the final draft of this essay. I am grateful also for the editorial suggestions of Elizabeth Potter and Linda Alcoff. An earlier and much abbreviated version was prepared for the December 1991 meetings of the Eastern Division of the American Philosophical Association and published as "Multiplying Subjects and Diffusing Power" in the *Journal of Philosophy*, LXXXVIII, II (December, 1991).

[1]   Empiricist philosophers have found themselves in great difficulty when confronting the necessity to make their theory of the knower explicit, a difficulty most eloquently expressed in David Hume's Appendix to a *Treatise of Human Nature* ed. L.A. Selby-Bigge (Oxford, UK: Clarendon Press, 1960).

[2]   The later philosophy of Wittgenstein does challenge the individualist ideal. Until recently few commentators have developed the anti-individualist implications of his work. See Naomi Scheman, "Individualism and the Objects of Psychology" in *Discovering Reality*, ed. Sandra Harding and Merrill Hintikka (Boston: Reidel, 1983), 225–44.

[3]   Harding has treated Marcia Millman and Rosabeth Kantor's Introduction to their collection, *Another Voice* (New York: Doubleday, 1975) and my essay with Ruth Doell, "Body, Bias and Behavior," from *Signs* 9, 2 (Winter 1983) as exemplars of feminist empiricism. The latter is discussed extensively in Harding's *The Science Question in Feminism* (Ithaca: Cornell University Press, 1986). Because the article nowhere claims that masculinist bias can be corrected by application of current methodologies in the sciences, I have always found the discussion in *The Science Question* a puzzling perverse misreading.

[4]   Cf. Longino, "Can There Be A Feminist Science?" in *Hypatia* 2,3, (Fall 1987); and chapter 7 of Longino, *Science as Social Knowledge* (Princeton: Princeton University Press, 1990).

[5]   Cf. Nancy Hartsock, "The Feminist Standpoint: Developing the Ground for a Specifically Feminist Historical Materialism," in Harding and Hintikka, *Discovering Reality*, 283–310.

[6]   Cf. Evelyn F. Keller, "The Force of the Pacemaker Concept in Theories of Slime Mold Aggregation," in *Perspectives in Biology and Medicine* 26 (1983); 515–21; and *A Feeling for the Organism* (San Francisco: W.H. Freeman, 1983).

[7]   Evelyn F. Keller, *Reflections on Gender and Science* (New Haven: Yale University Press, 1984).

[8]   For argument for and exposition of these points, see Longino, *Science as Social Knowledge*, especially chapter 4.

[9]   Thanks to Sandra Mitchell for this formulation.

[10]   My understanding of the semantic view is shaped by its presentations in Bas van Fraassen, *The Scientific Image* (New York: Oxford University Press, 1980); and Ronald Giere, *Explaining Science* (Chicago: University of Chicago Press, 1988); as well as by conversations with Richard Grandy and Elisabeth Lloyd. Nancy Cartwright's views on explanation, as developed in *How the Laws of Physics Lie* (New York: Oxford University Press, 1983) have deeply influenced my thinking.

[11]   Mary Hesse, *Models and Analogies in Science* (Notre Dame: Notre Dame University Press, 1966).

[12]   The Gender and Biology Study Group, "The Importance of Feminist Critique for Contemporary Cell Biology," in *Hypatia* 3, 1 (1988).

[13]   Evelyn Fox Keller, "Making Gender Visible in the Pursuit of Nature's Secrets," in *Feminist Studies/Critical Studies,* Teresa de Lauretis, ed., (Bloomington: Indiana University Press, 1986), 67–77; and "Gender and Science," in *The Great Ideas Today* (Chicago: Encyclopedia Britannica, 1990).

[14]   Donna Haraway, "The Biological Enterprise: Sex, Mind, and Profit from Human Engineering to Sociobiology," in *Radical History Review* 20 (1979): 206–37

[15]   This is the strategy adopted in chapter 8 of *Science as Social Knowledge.*

[16]   This point is developed further in *Science as Social Knowledge,* chapter 2.

[17]   For a somewhat different approach to a similar question, see Philip Kitcher, "The Division of Cognitive Labor," in *Journal of Philosophy* LXXXVII, 1 (January 1990): 5–23.

3.7

THE ROLE OF TRUST IN KNOWLEDGE*

John Hardwig

> The whole fabric of knowledge is trust.
>
> Elizabeth Neufeld

> It seems paradoxical that scientific research, in many ways one of the most questioning, and skeptical of human activities, should be dependent on personal trust. But the fact is that without trust the research enterprise could not function....Research is a collegial activity that requires its practitioners to trust the integrity of their colleagues.
>
> Arnold S. Relman

We do not normally notice the air we breathe. Similarly, we epistemologists have not noticed the climate of trust that is required—or so I shall argue—to support much of our knowledge. Thus, the title of this paper may seen strange, for most epistemologists and philosophers of science see no role for trust in knowledge. Although epistemologists debate various theories of knowledge, almost all seem united in the supposition that knowledge rests on evidence, not trust. After all, trust, in order to be trust, must be at least partially blind. And how can knowledge be blind? Thus, for most epistemologists, it is not only that trust plays no role in knowing; trusting and knowing are deeply antithetical. We can not know by trusting in the opinions of others; we may have to trust those opinions when we do not know.

I shall argue that this is badly mistaken. Modern knowers cannot be independent and self-reliant, not even in their own fields of specialization. In most disciplines, those who do not trust cannot know; those who do not trust cannot have the best-evidence for their beliefs. In an important sense, then, trust is often epistemologically even more basic than empirical data or logical arguments: the data and the argument are available only through trust. If the metaphor of foundation is still useful, the trustworthiness of members of epistemic communities is the ultimate foundation for much of our knowledge.

I think my argument is applicable to many areas of knowledge. I shall take science and mathematics as my paradigms, however, for they have provided the primary models of knowing for Western epistemology for the last 350 years. I shall attempt to show how and why trust is essential to scientists and mathematicians, and assume that, if I can show this, most epistemologists will agree that we must make room in our epistemologies for trust.

The conclusion that much of our knowledge rests on trust will, I believe, have far-reaching implications. It may force basic changes in epistemology and the philosophy of science. But it is worth emphasizing that I am not here proposing a new epistemology nor endorsing a "nonstandard" analysis, such as that of Lorraine Code,[1] Michael Welbourne,[2] or the "strong programme" of the Science Studies Unit at Edinburgh. Quite the opposite: I wish to address my argument to as many philosophers as possible. I therefore aim to work within the standard analyses of knowledge and of science. My purpose here is to call attention to a feature of modern science and mathematics which has not received sufficient attention. I leave for another occasion the large question of whether accepting my conclusion would force basic changes in epistemology and the philosophy of science or whether the idea of knowledge based on trust could be assimilated by the received views.

1

In the early 1960s, Derek de Solla Price[3] observed that there was a rapid trend away from single-author papers in scientific journals. In fact, the trend is toward an ever-increasing number of authors per article.[4] Modern science is collegial not only in the sense that scientists build on the work of those who have preceded them, but also in the sense that research is increasingly done by teams and, indeed, by larger and larger teams. This is true for two reasons.

(1) The process of gathering and analyzing data sometimes just takes too long to be accomplished by one person. In an earlier paper, I discussed an experiment that measured the lifespan of charm particles.[5] The paper reporting the results of this experiment has 99 authors, in part because it took about 280 person/years to do the experiment. Moreover, even for experiments that require less than a lifetime to run, the pace of science is often far too rapid for a lone experimenter to make any contribution at all by doing them. One of the authors of this paper on charm particles, William Bugg, estimated at the time of publication that, within three years, some other team would come up with a technique that gives a considerably better measurement and that, within five

years, the paper would no longer be of interest. Five year later, his prediction has been borne out.

(2) Even more important for the purposes of epistemological analysis, research is increasingly done by teams because no one knows enough to be able to do the experiment by herself. Increasingly, no one could know enough—sheer limitations of intellect prohibit it. The cooperation of researchers from different specializations and the resulting division of cognitive labor are, consequently, often unavoidable if an experiment is to be done at all. No one particle physicist knows enough to measure the lifespan of charm particles. Indeed, Bugg reports that no one university or national laboratory could have done their experiment. None of the authors of such a paper is in a position to vouch for the entire content of the paper.

Teamwork is pretty standard fare within the empirical sciences. But it is not completely unknown in mathematics as well, due to the many areas of specialization required to complete some proofs. As just one example, consider J. Korevaar's[6] recounting of a critical stage in Louis de Branges's proof of Ludwig Bieberbach's conjecture (a conjecture in complex analysis which dates back to 1916, but which had resisted proof for almost 70 years):

> For relatively small n, de Branges could verify immediately that the sums...are positive on $(0, \infty)$. But what about larger values of n? At this stage de Branges went to his numerical colleague Gautschi at Purdue University for help. He told Gautschi that he had a way of proving the Bieberbach conjecture, but needed to establish certain inequalities involving hypergeometric functions. Would Gautschi be willing to check as many of these inequalities as possible on the computer? Gautschi wrote a suitable program with a feeling that he might soon hit a value of n for which the consistent positivity of expressions...would come to an end. Much to his surprise, however, he discovered that the crucial expressions were positive for all values of n which he tried: $2 \leq n \leq 30$. Thus at this time, assuming that the theoretical work was correct, de Branges and the computer had verified the Bierberbach conjecture for all n up to 30!
>
> How to continue? Gautschi had the idea to call Askey at the University of Wisconsin, the world's expert on special functions. At first Askey was incredulous that the supposed positivity of sums...would prove the Bieberbach conjecture. However, he realized very soon that those sums were essentially generalized hypergeometric functions of a very special kind which are known to be positive (*ibid.*, pp. 512–3).

Specialization and teamwork are thus inescapable features of much modern knowledge acquisition. This point is not merely a genetic point about "the context of discovery." Classical epistemology can admit—though usually not much is made of this fact—that trust plays a role in the origins of someone's knowledge. But specialization and teamwork apply in the "context of justification" as well. It is quite likely that no one mathematician has or will ever have the logical justification for each step in de Branges's proof. Those (like Askey) who know enough about hypergeometric functions probably do not know enough complex analysis to verify other parts of the proof; those (like de Branges) who know enough complex analysis have not mastered Askey's work. Possibly one mathematician could learn enough different mathematical specialties to grasp each step in de Branges's proof. But mathematicians do not think that would be a particularly useful thing to do, especially since no one can learn everything in mathematics. (Askey's work on special functions is apparently a small niche.) And clearly one particle physicist could never have sufficient justification for any claim at all about the lifespan of charm particles.

What are we epistemologists to say about de Branges's proof or the 99 physicists' measurement of the lifespan of charm particles? I think cases like these force us to make very basic choices: either we can modify our epistemological theories, or we can cling to them and deny that they could possibly be cases of knowing, since they fail to meet our requirements.

The latter option would be to say that experiments or "proofs" requiring teamwork could not possibly yield knowledge or even rational belief. Why not? Because knowing requires good reasons for believing, and none of the mathematicians or physicists has sufficient reasons (except in testimonial form—more on that later) to accept the conclusions of their papers.

Moreover, it will not do epistemologically to have many tiny shreds of the empirical evidence or fragments of the mathematical proof in many separate minds. For it is the interconnection, the structure of these bits of evidence into a unified whole, that enables them to add up to a justified conclusion about charm particles or the Bieberbach conjecture. Since no one has sufficient evidence to justify the conclusion, there is no one who knows. But there is no knowledge without a knower, so the lifespan of charm particles is not known and could not be known. At least, not by humans. And de Branges has produced nothing that could count as a proof.

If this conclusion is unpalatable—as I think it is—we need an epistemological analysis of research teams, for knowledge of many things is possible only through teamwork. Knowing, then, is often not a privileged psychological state. If it is a privileged state at all, it is a privileged social state. So, we need an epistemological analysis of the social structure that makes the members of some teams knowers while the members of others are not. An analysis of testimony and testimonial evidence will provide a start on this project and also the next step in the present argument about the role of trust in epistemology.

II

It is the testimony of one scientist or mathematician to another that connects the bits of evidence gathered by different researchers into a unified whole that can justify a conclusion. By accepting each others' testimony, individual researchers are united into a team that may have what no individual member of the team has: sufficient evidence to justify their mutual conclusion.

Elsewhere, I have developed an epistemological principle, "the principle of testimony" (*op. cit.*):[7]

(T)   If *A* has good reasons to believe that *B* has good reasons to believe *p*, then *A* has good reasons to believe *p*.

This principle is general enough to capture the epistemic structure of appeals by a layperson to the intellectual authority of experts. But we are speaking here, not of laypersons, but of research scientists, and of research scientists within the domains of their own specialties. So if such researchers are sometimes knowers, we must consider a stronger version of the principle of testimony:

(T[1])   If *A* knows that *B* knows *p*, then *A* knows *p*.

The problems epistemologists have seen in testimonial evidence are evident in both T and T[1]. Our epistemological training leads us to ask: How can *A* know that *B* knows *p* unless *A* herself first knows *p*? How can *A* even know that *B* has good reasons unless she herself has those reasons and knows that they are good reasons? Of course, *A* can learn from *B*, but how can *A* know through *B*?

These are good questions, important questions. But the epistemological requirement implicit in the rhetorical version of these questions would render testimony epistemically useless. In order to ground her knowledge that p, A appeals to B. Why? Clearly, the whole point of appealing to the testimony of others is that they know things we do not. If this were not the case, basing belief on testimony would be pointless at best, hence nonrational or irrational. The appeal to B must be able to strengthen A's reasons for believing p; A now knows p at least partly because she knows that B knows p.

To count as good testimony evidence for p, testimony must be working well (more on that below). But when testimony is working well, belief based on testimony is often not, as traditional epistemology would have it, a poor, second-best substitute for direct evidence. On the contrary, belief based on testimony is often epistemically superior to belief based entirely on direct, nontestimonial evidence. For B's reasons for believing p will often be epistemically better than any A would/could come up with on her own. If the best reasons for believing p are sometimes primarily testimonial reasons, if knowing requires having the best reasons for believing, and if p can be known, then knowledge will also sometimes rest on testimony.

Nor is this conclusion always dependent on A's limited competence in the domain of whether or not p: the only respectable beliefs anyone has or could ever have about charm particles must be based largely on the testimony of others. In fact, a belief based partly on second-hand evidence will be epistemically superior to any belief based completely on direct empirical evidence whenever the relevant evidence becomes too extensive or too complex for any one person to gather it all. For in all such cases, one can have sufficient evidence only through testimony. We are thus driven to accept the stronger principle of testimony: if A knows that B knows p, then A knows p. We must modify our epistemologies to make them compatible with this principle.

Testimonial evidence has potential problems as well as strengths, however, and they arise from the same feature: in order for testimony to be useful, A cannot already have B's reasons. So, if A accepts p on B's say-so, those reasons (B's reasons) which are necessary to justify A's belief are reasons which A does not have. Sometimes it is feasible for B to share with A all the evidence necessary to justify the claim that p. But usually not. Indeed, if A and B come from different disciplines or even different specialties within the same discipline, A often will not know what B's reasons are, much less why they are good reasons for believing p.

Thus, the blindness of A's knowledge that p: those reasons which are necessary to justify p (and A's belief that p) are reasons which A does not have. Obviously, since she lacks part of the evidence that justifies the claim that p,

A is limited in the extent to which she can effectively scrutinize or challenge *B*'s claim about *p*. And yet we are to say that *A* knows that *p*, despite this blindness, this lack of the evidence necessary to justify *p*, this inability to evaluate the case for *p*?

Strange as this may seem, this is what we must say, unless we wish to maintain (1) that there can no longer be knowledge in many scientific disciplines because there is now too much available evidence (!); (2) that one can know *p* only by ignoring most of the best evidence for *p* (!); or (3) that some knowledge is known by teams or communities, but not by any individual person. Although I believe this third option has more plausibility than is generally acknowledged (it may also be the view of C.S. Peirce and John Dewey), in this paper I shall continue to pursue the idea that *A* does know *p* and that we need to modify our accounts of knowledge and rational belief to account for *A*'s knowledge.

Now, given the fact that *A* does not/cannot have *B*'s reasons, *A*'s position is really this:

(1) *A* knows that *B* says that *p*.

(2) *A* believes (and has good reasons to believe?[8]) that *B* is speaking truthfully, i.e., that *B* is saying what she believes.

(3) *A* believes (and has good reasons to believe?) that *B* (unlike *A*) is in a position, first, to know what would be good reasons to believe *p* and, second, to have the needed reasons.

(4) *A* believes (and has good reasons to believe?) that *B* actually has good reasons for believing *p* when she thinks she does.

Although obvious, it is important to note two things about *B* and her contribution to *A*'s good reasons. First, unless *B* believes what she is saying, *B*'s knowledgeability about *p* will not give *A* good reasons to believe *p*. Thus, *A*'s good reasons depend on whether *B* is truthful, or at least being honest in this situation.

Second, even *B*'s truthfulness will not give *A* good reasons to believe *p* if *B* believes she has good reasons when she does not. So, in addition to being truthful, *B* must, first, be competent—she must be knowledgeable about what constitutes good reasons in the domain of her expertise, and she must have kept herself up to date with those reasons. Second, *B* must be conscientious—she must have done her own work carefully and thoroughly. And third, *B* must have "adequate epistemic self-assessment"—*B* must not have a tendency to deceive herself about the extent of her knowledge, its reliability, or its applicability to whether p.

Although the usefulness and the rationality of belief based on testimony stem from the fact that A does not, often even cannot, have B's reasons for believing p, this fact also reveals that A's reliance on B's testimony must include reliance on B. The reliability of A's belief depends on the reliability of B's character. B's truthfulness is part of her moral character. Competence, conscientious work, and epistemic self-assessment are aspects of B's "epistemic character." I shall return to this point frequently, and "character" will refer to these moral and epistemic qualities. (Although competence is not a character trait per se, it standardly depends on character: becoming knowledgeable and then remaining current almost always requires habits of self-discipline, focus, and persistence.)

In short, A must TRUST B, or A will not believe that B's testimony gives her good reasons to believe p. And B must be TRUSTWORTHY or B's testimony will not in fact give A good reasons to believe p, regardless of what she might believe about B. A team of scientific experimentalists, for example, must both trust each other and be worthy of that trust or their experiment will not give anyone enough good reasons to believe their conclusions.

We thus reach another epistemologically odd conclusion: the rationality of many of our beliefs depends not only on our own character but on the character of others as well; the rationality of many of our beliefs depends on what others do and hence is not within our individual control. This is perhaps not a strange conclusion when we think about the various ways in which we as laypersons depend on others to have the evidence that supports our beliefs. But it becomes much stranger when we realize that this dependence on the character of others applies even to some of the epistemically best beliefs, i.e., to those of the top experts within their own fields of expertise. The oddness stems, I contend, from the individualistic bias of most epistemology—with its penchant for epistemic self-reliance and self-sufficiency, and its flight from any form of epistemic vulnerability. But if our epistemic authorities are unreliable, we simply have no alternative but to hold less rational beliefs. Either we must then accept the testimony of unreliable authorities or we must rely on our own relatively inexpert and uninformed judgments.

Now, if B must be reliable in order for her testimony to be reliable, it seems that A must know B—at least to the extent of knowing that B is both morally and epistemically reliable—before A can have good reasons for believing p on the say-so of B. But scientists usually must rely on scientific testifiers who are not personally known to them. Clearly, this is often true for scientific testimony embodied in the literature. It is sometimes true even among members of a research team. (The team that measured charm particles was scattered over three continents, and Bugg reports that he knows only 10 or 12 of his 98 coauthors well enough to be able to form any judgment about the quality of their work.)

If B is not personally known to A, there are two strategies for attempting to ascertain the reliability of B and thus her testimony. The first is to check with someone who does know B and the quality of her work. This strategy can be expressed by extending the principle of testimony:

> A has good reasons for believing C (also, D, E,...) has good reasons for believing B has good reasons for believing p.

Normally, however, A will not be in a position to ascertain C's reliability as a testifier about B, and C will often rely on the testimony of still others in order to form her judgment about B. This is not merely a philosophical quibble: as we shall see, the difficulty of gathering dependable testimony about the reliability of B is a problem of considerable practical import in contemporary science. Still, by repeating this procedure, i.e., checking with several knowledgeable people in B's field, A will be able to ascertain B's reputation within B's discipline, and this surely will give A some evidence about the reliability of B and her testimony. But this process does not obviate the need for trust—it only redistributes and refines that trust.

There is a second strategy for attempting to ascertain the reliability of B when B is not personally known to A. That is to get a second opinion about the truth of what B has said. Often, A can find a C (also D, E...) who is independent of B and who is also knowledgeable about whether p. If C, D and E corroborate B's testimony, A will have better reason to believe it.

We shall return to these strategies below, for they have played a central role in explanations of the special reliability of scientific testimony and, consequently, of the scientific process itself. The second, under the rubric of "replication of experimental results," has been especially important.

III

I have claim that trust in the testimony of others is necessary to ground much of our knowledge, and that this trust involves trust in the character of the testifiers. But there is a basic objection to this thesis: that prudential consider-ations alone are sufficient to guarantee that the members of a scientific community will be truthful and also constantly vigilant against self-deception.

Michael Blais has developed this objection in his paper, "Epistemic Tit for Tat."[9] Blais argues that trustworthiness can be modeled as a strategy—indeed, the only prudent strategy—for a member of a scientific community. Blais acknowledges that trust is essential to science, because cooperation is essential, but he maintains that the type of cooperation at work does not require trust in the moral sense. "Only cooperation, as defined...in game theory and as illustrated in the Prisoner's dilemma, is necessary for the justification of vicarious knowledge" (*ibid.*, p. 370). In science, cooperation means not defecting in the knowledge game—in other words, not cheating by fudging, fabricating, or otherwise publishing unreliable results. "Defection means succumbing to the temptation of leaving the other players in the knowledge game with the sucker's pay-off, while attempting to maximize immediate gain" (*ibid.*, pp. 370–1).

Blais echoes the common faith of scientists and philosophers that peer review and replication of results will detect defectors. "What count are factual results that are reproducible. If results cannot be reproduced, they may simply be rejected" (*ibid.*, p. 371). "Peer review and blind refereeing ensure that, in the long run, defectors should be found out" (*ibid.*, p. 372). Since Blais maintains that, in the game of science, the punishment for defecting is permanent exclusion from the game, he concludes that defecting is very imprudent.

At least one scientific community, however, the biomedical research community, has had its faith in replication and peer review shattered by a number of spectacular and highly publicized examples of research fraud.[10] Within biomedical science, the names of the fraudulent researchers have become well-known—John Darsee, Robert Slutsky, John Long, Vijay Soman, William Summerlin, Mark Spector, Stephen Breuning, and now Thereza Imanishi-Kari. Although there are other sloppy, careless, or deceptive research practices that may be even more damaging to the reliability of scientific testimony, "scientific misconduct"—commonly defined as plagiarism or the fabrication, falsification, or deliberate misrepresentation of data—is the most blatant example of defection in the knowledge game. The phenomenon of scientific misconduct reveals that a more thorough-going trust than mere strategic trust is involved in science. The consensus within the biomedical sciences is that neither peer review nor replication is likely to detect careless, sloppy, or even fraudulent research.

The number of really well-qualified referees for peer reviews is often inadequate, given the quantity of articles submitted and the complexity and multiplicity of techniques involved in research. Furthermore, an internally consistent and plausible fabrication cannot be detected by referees, since they do not examine the original data or the gathering of that data. Slutsky's fraud, for example, was detected only because of his statistical naivete and also his very bad luck (two of his papers were read in quick succession by an astute reader). Those who investigated the Slutsky case maintain that his fraudulent papers could have been read independently for years without arousing any suspicion.

Nor will careless or fraudulent research normally be detected by replication, for the structure of modern science acts to prevent replication, not to ensure it. It is virtually impossible to obtain funding for attempts to replicate the work of others, and academic credit normally is given only for new findings.

When replication is attempted, it will not always detect fraudulent papers. In fact, replication paradoxically will support rather than unmask those fraudulent papers which happen to have correct conclusions. Thus, fraudulent papers announcing results that are predictable extensions of basic work done by others are quite likely to pass the test of replication. Even when attempted replication fails to produce similar results, there are often other explanations. Thus, when a group of Swiss researchers failed to replicate some of Darsee's work, they considered various explanations for their inability to confirm his findings, but they did not consider the possibility of fraud. And both Darsee and Spector argued that their experiments were too delicate to work unless the experimenter had extremely subtle skills. For these reasons, Relman,[11] a respected observer, has concluded that "fraudulent data may be rapidly identified in an area of great importance where research activity is intense, but that is probably not true in most fields" (*ibid.*, p. 1416).

We can see why Blais's argument must fail. Game-theoretic arguments such as Blais's rest on two assumptions. The first, which Blais acknowledges, is that the relationship be durable: "a cooperative strategy…has little chance in the short or medium term; only long-term relationships permit it to hold its own" (*op. cit.,* p. 368). The second assumption is, obviously, that the other players will recognize when they have received the sucker's pay-off.

These assumptions are the Achilles' heel of Blais's application of game theory to the issues of scientific testimony. Usually, the cooperative relationship is precisely the short- or medium-term relationship. By the standards of game theory, 20 or 30 trials is not a very long run, but a researcher can substantially enhance her career if she can successfully publish several fraudulent articles. Also, as we have seen, it is often very difficult for others to detect defectors. Indeed, there is a class of lapses from acceptable scientific practice which are not discoverable by anyone else, since only the researchers have the actual empirical data upon which their paper is, presumably, based. Even if lab logbooks are kept in a form that allows inspection by others, one would need to have been present during the experiment to know that the logbooks are not themselves fraudulent.

Reliance upon inside informants—co-investigators or others in the lab—is widely recognized to be crucial to the detection of scientific misconduct. But this reliance is also problematic, for many reasons. Detection is often very difficult for those not in the defector's field of specialization, which compounds the problem in multidisciplinary work. Moreover, co-investigators are often not the ones who will be damaged by the defection, since the prevailing ethos within science is that joint authors are not responsible and should not be penalized for the fraudulent or sloppy work of one member of their team. (Consequently, there is a temptation to collaborate with someone you personally know to be a defector—to leave, for example, the collection of data to someone you know to be "sloppy.") Finally, there is a whole range of deterrents to informing on one's colleagues in the lab, ranging from loyalty, to reluctance to meddle in others' affairs, to the absence of adequate protection for scientific whistle blowers. Virtually all observers agree that the confidentiality of an informant cannot be successfully protected. Some informants have paid dearly for their work in uncovering scientific fraud.

Thus, contrary to what Blais suggests, detection is often quite difficult. And, contrary to what Blais maintains, the punishment for proven defection is also often not severe. Although fraudulent researchers whose cases attract wide publicity may well forfeit their reputations and careers, others do not. Some quietly relocate to other institutions; others do not even lose their jobs. A recent survey suggests that scientists themselves do not believe that even temporary exclusion from research would result from proven fraud.[12]

There are reasons, of course, for less than Draconian punishment of research fraud. These include fear of liability, of unfairly tainting the reputations of co-authors, of shaking public confidence in science, or of jeopardizing the reputation and the funding of the laboratory and university in which a fraudulent researcher worked. Since a fraudulent researcher's institution can achieve the penalty of permanent exclusion from the scientific community only at the cost of a great deal of effort and unfavorable publicity, institutions have a strong incentive to settle for less severe and more private punishments.

Clearly, a researcher's prudential concerns are often insufficient to ensure her trustworthiness and thus the reliability of her testimony. General recognition of this fact naturally leads to two responses: (1) deterrents to defection should be strengthened, even if they may be insufficient; (2) if prudential reasons are not sufficient to assure trustworthy testifiers, ethical researchers are required. The need for "research ethics" is now widely acknowledged. The Institute of Medicine—sister to the National Academy of Sciences—has, for example, recently called for universities to provide formal instruction in research ethics for all science students at both the undergraduate and graduate level.

Scientists working in some other fields maintain that attempts to replicate experimental findings are still common in their sciences and thus that "it can't happen here." Perhaps there really is more replication in some sciences than in others, but it seems reasonable to conjecture that there will be less replication (1) of long, costly, or very time-consuming experiments; (2) of experiments that require exotic equipment, substances, or specimens; (3) in those fields in which senior scientists can train their graduate students (and post-docs, residents, fellows) by having them gather new data rather than replicate existing results; (4) of experiments requiring the cooperation of multidisciplinary teams. It also seems likely that (5) considerations of the ethical use of research subjects will ensure that there will be no routine or even widespread replication of experiments involving human—or, increasingly, even animal—research subjects. These conditions apply to many sciences—and they apply increasingly as scientific research becomes more sophisticated, complex, and costly.

Peer review and attempted replication may once have been effective deterrents to fraudulent or deceptive publication. They are now much weaker deterrents. In any case, they can never have been completely effective detectors of fraudulent or misleading testimony, for, as we have seen, both have in-principle weaknesses.

IV

Often, then, a scientific community has no alternative to trust, including trust in the character of its members. The modern pursuit of scientific knowledge is increasingly and unavoidably a very cooperative enterprise. Cooperation, not intellectual self-reliance, is the key virtue in any scientific community. But epistemic cooperation is possible only on the basis of reliance on the testimony of others. Scientific propositions often must be accepted on the basis of evidence that only others have. Consequently, much scientific knowledge rests on the moral and epistemic character of scientists. Unavoidably so. Not because "hard data" and logical arguments are not necessary, but because the relevant data and arguments are too extensive and too difficult to be had by any means other than testimony.

Indeed, a scientific community is often forced to rely on the testimony of one testifier. Replication of experiments is not standard. Moreover, peer review can never detect plausible and internally consistent fabrications, and attempted replication will support rather than unmask fraudulent reports that happen to have true conclusions. So, there sometimes simply are no C, D, and E who can corroborate or effectively challenge the testimony of B. And the testimony of C, D, and E about the professional reputation of B may well be seriously misleading: before their frauds were detected, some fraudulent biomedical researchers were widely regarded within their disciplines as outstanding exemplars of scientific productivity, even as scientific geniuses.

Institutional reforms of science may diminish but cannot obviate the need for reliance upon the character of testifiers. There are no "people-proof" institutions. And even if it were possible fully to police scientific research, it would still be necessary to rely on the integrity of the newly-created "science cops" and the reliability of their testimony. (There has, for example, been Congressional concern over the lack of independence of those now being assigned the responsibility of investigating research fraud.)

Science, then, is not completely different from other cooperative enterprises: the reliability of scientific testimony, like the reliability of most other testimony, ultimately depends on the reliability of the testifier, or on the reliability of those charged with ensuring the reliability of the testifier. Obviously, none of this means that deterrents to scientific misconduct are unimportant. Since knowledge of right and wrong will not deter the unscrupulous, deterrents remain important, even if insufficient. Still, the main point here is that scientific knowledge rests on trust, and not only on trust in deterrents, but also on trust in the character of scientists.

The view of Blais (and many, many others) thus becomes part of the problem: one reason the problem of fraudulent research looms so large is that for decades scientists have insisted that science is virtually fraud-proof. Philosophers have too often joined in the chorus. Inability to see the role of trust in science effectively destroys our ability to combat unreliable scientific testimony. It undermines any attempt to formulate and teach research ethics and it stifles any attempt to introduce new deterrents to fraud. A fraud-proof institution has no need for additional protection against fraud.

We must, however, guard against jumping to the conclusions that we should try to redesign our epistemic institutions so as to minimize the role of trust in knowledge. For the alternative to trust is, often, ignorance. An untrusting, suspicious attitude would impede the growth of knowledge, perhaps without even substantially reducing the risk of unreliable testimony. Trust in one's epistemic colleagues is not, then, a necessary evil. It is a positive value for any community of finite minds, provided only that this trust is not too often abused. For finite minds can know many things only through epistemic cooperation. There is, then, a very delicate balance between places for trust within epistemic communities and places for insisting on better safeguards against untrustworthy testifiers.

Philosophers of science, epistemologists, logicians, and ethicists all should be helping concerned members of scientific communities both to formulate an ethics of scientific research and testimony, and also to design structural reforms that will strengthen the deterrents to scientific misconduct without destroying collegiality and creativity. But we may not be able to help until we get our own conceptual houses in better order. The conclusion that knowledge often is based on certain kinds of relationships between people, on trust, and consequently on the character of other people is an epistemologically odd conclusion. It is odd even for pragmatists, though pragmatists have generally had more room for epistemic community in their theories. To my mind, this oddness is symptomatic of what will be needed to assimilate an acknowledgement of the role of trust into our epistemologies. We have a lot of work to do.

Clearly, the implications of the role of trust in knowledge will reach beyond epistemology and the philosophy of science into ethics and social philosophy. I close with just one example. The prevailing tenor of twentieth-century Anglo-American philosophy has been that epistemology is more basic than ethics. On this view, ethics must meet epistemological standards on pains of bankruptcy. And the prevailing suspicion in our culture—a suspicion nurtured by philosophy—is that ethics cannot pass the epistemological test, and that there is thus no ethical knowledge. Science, in contrast, is commonly believed to be too "hard" and "objective" to require anything as mushy and subjective as ethics.

But scientific realism—indeed any theory that grants objectivity to scientific judgments—turns out to be incoherent when combined with subjectivism or skepticism in ethics. It remains true, of course, that ethical claims must meet epistemological standards. But if much of our knowledge rests on trust in the moral character of testifiers, then knowledge depends on morality and epistemology also requires ethics. In order to qualify as knowledge (or even as rational belief), many epistemic claims must meet ethical standards. If they cannot pass the ethical muster, they fail epistemologically.

NOTES

*   I wish to thank James O. Bennett, Kathleen Bohstedt, George Brenkert, E. Roger Jones, John Nolt, Dan Turner, and especially Mary Read English and the members of the Philosophy Department at East Tennessee State for helpful comments. Research for this paper has been supported by the National Endowment for the Humanities and by East Tennessee State University.

1   *Epistemic Responsibility* (Hanover: New England UP, 1987)

2   *The Community of Knowledge* (Aberdeen, Scotland: University Press, 1986).

3   *Little Science, Big Science* (New York: Columbia, 1963), pp. 87–8.

4   Limitations of space prevent giving references for statements I make about the current state of science or about the opinions of the scientific community. Readers interested in my sources should write me for a documented version of this paper.

5   "Epistemic Dependence," this JOURNAL, LXXXII, 7 (1985): 335–49.

6   "Ludwig Bieberbach's Conjecture and Its Proof by Louis de Branges," *The American Mathematical Monthly*, XCIII (1986): 505–14. I owe this reference to Carl Wagner, who also informs me that there is now a much simpler proof of the Bieberbach conjecture which avoids reliance upon Askey's work.

7   Cf. also "Evidence, Testimony, and the Problem of Individualism—A Response to Schmitt," *Social Epistemology*, II (1988): 309–21. I owe the name, "principle of testimony," to Frederick Schmitt.

[8]   The reason for the parenthetical question in this statement and the next two is that I am undecided about what to say about implicit trust. If *A* trusts *B* implicitly, she will often not have or even feel the need to have good reasons to believe what *B* says. I think epistemic communities in which the climate of implicit trust prevails have real advantages over those in which good reasons for trusting are felt to be needed and are then supplied.

[9]   This JOURNAL LXXXIV, 7 (1987): 363–75. Blais has reaffirmed this view in a more recent article, "Misunderstanding Epistemic Tit for Tat: Reply to John Woods," this JOURNAL, LXXXVII, 7 (1990): 369–74.

[10]   No one knows how widespread fraud in science is. But a survey mailed to more than 2,100 scientists in six fields—physics, chemistry, biology, economics, psychology, and sociology—revealed that nearly one-quarter of the respondents personally knew someone who had falsified data and 2/5 believed that some of their own work had been plagiarized (M. Davis, *The Perceived Seriousness and Incidence of Ethical Misconduct in Academic Science*. Unpublished Ph.D. Thesis. The Ohio State University, 1989).

[11]   "Lessons from the Darsee Affair," *New England Journal of Medicine*, CCCVIII, 23 (1983): 1415–7.

[12]   J.P. Tangney, "Fraud Will Out—Or Will It?" *New Scientist*, CXV (August 6, 1987), pp. 62–3.

3.8

Solidarity or Objectivity?

Richard Rorty

There are two principal ways in which reflective human beings try, by placing their lives in a larger context, to give sense to those lives. The first is by telling the story of their contribution to a community. This community may be the actual historical one in which they live, or another actual one, distant in time or place, or a quite imaginary one, consisting perhaps of a dozen heroes and heroines selected from history or fiction or both. The second way is to describe themselves as standing in immediate relation to a nonhuman reality. This relation is immediate in the sense that it does not derive from a relation between such a reality and their tribe, or their nation, or their imagined band of comrades. I shall say that stories of the former kind exemplify the desire for solidarity, and that stories of the latter kind exemplify the desire for objectivity. Insofar as a person is seeking solidarity, she does not ask about the relation between the practices of the chosen community and something outside that community. Insofar as she seeks objectivity, she distances herself from the actual persons around her not by thinking of herself as a member of some other real or imaginary group, but rather by attaching herself to something which can be described without reference to any particular human beings.

The tradition in Western culture which centers around the notion of the search for Truth, a tradition which runs from the Greek philosophers through the Enlightenment, is the clearest example of the attempt to find a sense in one's existence by turning away from solidarity to objectivity. The idea of Truth as something to be pursued for its own sake, not because it will be good for oneself, or for one's real or imaginary community, is the central theme of this tradition. It was perhaps the growing awareness by the Greeks of the sheer diversity of human communities which stimulated the emergence of this ideal. A fear of parochialism, of being confined within the horizons of the group into which one happens to be born, a need to see it with the eyes of a stranger, helps produce the skeptical and ironic tone characteristic of Euripides and

Socrates. Herodotus' willingness to take the barbarians seriously enough to describe their customs in detail may have been a necessary prelude to Plato's claim that the way to transcend skepticism is to envisage a common goal of humanity—a goal set by human nature rather than by Greek culture. The combination of Socratic alienation and Platonic hope gives rise to the idea of the intellectual as someone who is in touch with the nature of things, not by way of the opinions of his community, but in a more immediate way.

Plato developed the idea of such an intellectual by means of distinctions between knowledge and opinion, and between appearance and reality. Such distinctions conspire to produce the idea that rational inquiry should make visible a realm to which non-intellectuals have little access, and of whose very existence they may be doubtful. In the Enlightenment, this notion became concrete in the adoption of the Newtonian physical scientist as a model of the intellectual. To most thinkers of the eighteenth century, it seemed clear that the access to Nature which physical science had provided should now be followed by the establishment of social, political, and economic institutions which were in accordance with Nature. Ever since, liberal social thought has centered around social reform as made possible by objective knowledge of what human beings are like—not knowledge of what Greeks or Frenchmen or Chinese are like, but of humanity as such. We are the heirs of this objectivist tradition, which centers around the assumption that we must step outside our community long enough to examine it in the light of something which transcends it, namely, that which it has in common with every other actual and possible human community. This tradition dreams of an ultimate community which will have transcended the distinction between the natural and the social, which will exhibit a solidarity which is not parochial because it is the expression of an ahistorical human nature. Much of the rhetoric of contemporary intellectual life takes for granted that the goal of scientific inquiry into man is to understand "underlying structures," or "culturally invariant factors," or "biologically determined patterns."

Those who wish to ground solidarity in objectivity—call them "realists"—have to construe truth as correspondence to reality. So they must construct a metaphysics which has room for a special relation between beliefs and objects which will differentiate true from false beliefs. They also must argue that there are procedures of justification of belief which are natural and not merely local. So they must construct an epistemology which has room for a kind of justification which is not merely social but natural, springing from human nature itself, and made possible by a link between that part of nature and the rest of nature. On their view, the various procedures which are thought of as providing rational justification by one or another culture may or may not really *be* rational. For to be truly rational, procedures of justification *must* lead to the truth, to correspondence to reality, to the intrinsic nature of things.

By contrast, those who wish to reduce objectivity to solidarity—call them "pragmatists"—do not require either a metaphysics or an epistemology. They view truth as, in William James' phrase, what is good for *us* to believe. So they do not need an account of a relation between beliefs and objects called "correspondence," nor an account of human cognitive abilities which ensures that our species is capable of entering into that relation. They see the gap between truth and justification not as something to be bridged by isolating a natural and transcultural sort of rationality which can be used to criticize certain cultures and praise others, but simply as the gap between the actual good and the possible better. From a pragmatist point of view, to say that what is rational for us now to believe may not be *true*, is simply to say that somebody may come up with a better idea. It is to say that there is always room for improved belief, since new evidence, or new hypotheses, or a whole new vocabulary, may come along.[1] For pragmatists, the desire for objectivity is not the desire to escape the limitations of one's community, but simply the desire for as much intersubjective agreement as possible, the desire to extend the reference of "us" as far as we can. Insofar as pragmatists make a distinction between knowledge and opinion, it is simply the distinction between topics on which such agreement is relatively easy to get and topics on which agreement is relatively hard to get.

"Relativism" is the traditional epithet applied to pragmatism by realists. Three different views are commonly referred to by this name. The first is the view that every belief is as good as every other. The second is the view that "true" is an equivocal term, having as many meanings as there are procedures of justification. The third is the view that there is nothing to be said about either truth or rationality apart from descriptions of the familiar procedures of justification which a given society—*ours*—uses in one or another area of inquiry. The pragmatist holds the ethnocentric third view. But he does not hold the self-refuting first view, nor the eccentric second view. He thinks that his views are better than the realists', but he does not think that his views correspond to the nature of things. He thinks that the very flexibility of the word "true"—the fact that it is merely an expression of commenda- tion—insures its univocity. The term "true," on his account, means the same in all cultures, just as equally flexible terms like "here," "there," "good," "bad," "you," and "me" means the same in all cultures. But the identify of meaning is, of course, compatible with diversity of reference, and with diversity of procedures for assigning the terms. So he feels free to use the term "true" as a general term of commendation in the same way as his realist opponent does—and in particular to use it to commend his own view.

However, it is not clear why "relativist" should be thought an appropriate term for the ethnocentric their view, the one which the pragmatist *does* hold. For the pragmatist is not holding a positive theory which says that something is relative to something else. He is, instead, making the purely *negative* point that we should drop the traditional distinction between knowledge and opinion, construed as the distinction between truth as correspondence to reality and truth as a commendatory term for well-justified beliefs. The reason that the realist calls this negative claim "relativistic" is that he cannot believe that anybody would seriously deny that truth has an intrinsic nature. So when the pragmatist says that there is nothing to be said about truth save that each of us will commend as true those beliefs which he or she finds good to believe, the realist is inclined to interpret this as one more positive theory about the nature of truth: a theory according to which truth is simply the contemporary opinion of a chosen individual or group. Such a theory would, of course, be self-refuting. But the pragmatist does not have a theory of truth, much less a relativistic one. As a partisan of solidarity, his account of the value of cooperative human inquiry has only an ethical base, not an epistemological or metaphysical one. Not having *any* epistemology, *a fortiori* he does not have a relativistic one.

The question of whether truth or rationality has an intrinsic nature, of whether we ought to have a positive theory about either topic, is just the question of whether our self-description ought to be constructed around a relation to human nature or around a relation to a particular collection of human beings, whether we should desire objectivity or solidarity. It is hard to see how one could choose between these alternatives by looking more deeply into the nature of knowledge, or of man, or of nature. Indeed, the proposal that this issue might be so settled begs the question in favor of the realist, for it presupposes that knowledge, man, and nature *have* real essences which are relevant to the problem at hand. For the pragmatist, by contrast, "knowledge" is, like "truth," simply a compliment paid to the beliefs which we think so well justified that, for the moment, further justification is not needed. An inquiry into the nature of knowledge can, on his view, only be a sociohistorical account of how various people have tried to reach agreement on what to believe.

The view which I am calling "pragmatism" is almost, but not quite, the same as what Hilary Putnam, in his recent *Reason, Truth, and History,* calls "the internalist conception of philosophy."[2] Putnam defines such a conception as one which gives up the attempt at a God's-eye view of things, the attempt at contact with the nonhuman which I have been calling "the desire for objectivity." Unfortunately, he accompanies his defense of the antirealist views I am recommending with a polemic against a lot of the other people who hold these views—e.g., Kuhn, Feyerabend, Foucault, and myself. We are criticized as "relativists." Putnam presents "internalism" as a happy *via media* between realism and relativism. He speaks of "the plethora of relativistic doctrines being marketed today"[3] and in particular of "the French philosophers" as holding "some fancy mixture of cultural relativism and 'structuralism.'"[4] But when it comes to criticizing these doctrines all that Putnam finds to attack is the so-called "incommensurability thesis": vis., "terms used in another culture cannot be equated in meaning or reference with any terms or expressions *we* possess."[5] He sensibly agrees with Donald Davidson in remarking that this thesis is self-refuting. Criticism of this thesis, however, is destructive of, at most, some incautious passages in some early writings by Feyerabend. Once this thesis is brushed aside, it is hard to see how Putnam himself differs from most of those he criticizes.

Putnam accepts the Davidsonian point that, as he puts it, "the whole justification of an interpretative scheme…is that it renders the behavior of others at least minimally reasonable by *our* lights."[6] It would seem natural to go on from this to say that we cannot get outside the range of those lights, that we cannot stand on neutral ground illuminated only by the natural light of reason. But Putnam draws back from this conclusion. He does so because he construes the claim that we cannot do so as the claim that the range of our thought is restricted by what he calls "institutionalized norms," publicly available criteria for settling all arguments, including philosophical arguments. He rightly says that there are no such criteria, arguing that the suggestion that there are is as self-refuting as the "incommensurability thesis." He is, I think, entirely right in saying that the notion that philosophy is or should become such an application of explicit criteria contradicts the very idea of philosophy.[7] One can gloss Putnam's point by saying that "philosophy" is precisely what a culture becomes capable of when it ceases to define itself in terms of explicit rules, and becomes sufficiently leisured and civilized to rely on inarticulate know-how, to substitute *phronesis* for codification, and conversation with foreigners for conquest of them.

But to say that we cannot refer every question to explicit criteria institutionalized by our society does not speak to the point which the people whom Putnam calls "relativists" are making. One reason these people are pragmatists is precisely that they share Putnam's distrust of the positivistic idea that rationality is a matter of applying criteria.

Such a distrust is common, for example, to Kuhn, Mary Hesse, Wittgenstein, Michael Polanyi, and Michael Oakeshott. Only someone who did think of rationality in this way would dream of suggesting that "true" means something different in different societies. For only such a person could imagine that there was anything to pick out to which one might make "true" relative. Only if one shares the logical positivists' idea that we all carry around things called "rules of language" which regulate what we say when, will one suggest that there is no way to break out of one's culture.

In the most original and powerful section of his book, Putnam argues that the notion that "rationality...is defined by the local cultural norms" is merely the demonic counterpart of positivism. It is, as he says, "a scientistic theory inspired by anthropology as positivism was a scientistic theory inspired by the exact sciences." By "scientism" Putnam means the notion that rationality consists in the application of criteria.[8] Suppose we drop this notion, and accept Putnam's own Quinean picture of inquiry as the continual reweaving of a web of beliefs rather than as the application of criteria to cases. Then the notion of "local cultural norms" will lose its offensively parochial overtones. For now to say that we must work by our own lights, that we must be ethnocentric, is merely to say that beliefs suggested by another culture must be tested by trying to weave them together with beliefs we already have. It is a consequence of this holistic view of knowledge, a view *shared* by Putnam and those he criticizes as "relativists," that alternative cultures are not to be thought of on the model of alternative geometries. Alternative geometries are irreconcilable because they have axiomatic structures, and contradictory axioms. They are *designed* to be irreconcilable. Cultures are not so designed, and do not have axiomatic structures. To say that they have "institutionalized norms" is only to say, with Foucault, that knowledge is never separable from power—that one is likely to suffer if one does not hold certain beliefs at certain times and places. But such institutional backups for beliefs take the form of bureaucrats and policemen, not of "rules of language" and "criteria of rationality." To think otherwise is the Cartesian fallacy of seeing axioms where there are only shared habits, of viewing statements which summarize such practices as if they reported constraints enforcing such practices. Part of the force of Quine's and Davidson's attack on the distinction between the conceptual and the empirical is that the distinction between different cultures does not differ in kind from the distinction between different theories held by members of a single culture. The Tasmanian aborigines and the British colonists had trouble communicating, but this trouble was different only in extent from the difficulties in communication experienced by Gladstone and Disraeli. The trouble in all such cases is just the difficulty of explaining why other people disagree with us, of reweaving our beliefs so as to fit the fact of disagreement together with the other beliefs we hold. The same Quinean arguments which dispose of the positivists' distinction between analytic and synthetic truth dispose of the anthropologists' distinction between the intercultural and the intracultural.

On the holistic account of cultural norms, however, we do not need the notion of a universal transcultural rationality which Putnam invokes against those whom he calls "relativists." Just before the end of his book, Putnam says that once we drop the notion of a God's-eye point of view we realize that:

> we can only hope to produce a more rational *conception* of rationality or a better *conception* of morality if we operate from *within* our tradition (with its echoes of the Greek agora, of Newton, and so on, in the case of rationality, and with its echoes of scripture, of the philosophers, of the democratic revolutions, and so on…in the case of morality.) We are invited to engage in a truly human dialogue.[9]

With this I entirely agree, and so, I take it, would Kuhn, Hesse, and most of the other so-called "relativists"—perhaps even Foucault. But Putnam then goes on to pose a further question:

> Does this dialogue have an ideal terminus? Is there a *true* conception of rationality, an ideal morality, even if all we ever have are our conceptions of these?

I do not see the point of this question. Putnam suggests that a negative answer—the view that "there is only the dialogue"—is just another form of self-refuting relativism. But, once again, I do not see how a claim that something does not exist can be construed as a claim that something is relative to something else. In the final sentence of his book, Putnam says that "The very fact that we speak of our different conceptions as different conceptions of *rationality* posits a *Grenzbegriff,* a limit-concept of ideal truth." But what is such a posit supposed to do, except to say that from God's point of view the human race is heading in the right direction? Surely Putnam's "internalism" should forbid him to say anything like that. To say that *we* think we're heading in the right direction is just to say, with Kuhn, that we can, by hindsight, tell the story of the past as a story of progress. To say that we still have a long way to go, that our present views should not be cast in bronze, is too platitudinous to require support by positing limit-concepts. So it is hard to see what difference is made by the difference between saying "there is only the dialogue" and saying "there is also that to which the dialogue converges."

I would suggest that Putnam here, at the end of the day, slides back into the scientism he rightly condemns in others. For the root of scientism, defined as the view that rationality is a matter of applying criteria, is the desire for objectivity, the hope that what Putnam calls "human flourishing" has a transhistorical nature. I think that Feyerabend is right in suggesting that until we discard the metaphor of inquiry, and human activity generally, as converging rather than proliferating, as becoming more unified rather than more diverse, we shall never be free of the motives which once led us to posit gods. Positing *Grenzbegriffe* seems merely a way of telling ourselves that a nonexistent God would, if he did exist, be pleased with us. If we could ever be moved solely by the desire for solidarity, setting aside the desire for objectivity altogether, then we should think of human progress as making it possible for human being to do more interesting things and be more interesting people, not as heading towards a place which has somehow been prepared for humanity in advance. Our self-image would employ images of making rather than finding, the images used by the Romantics to praise poets rather than the images used by the Greeks to praise mathematicians. Feyerabend seems to me right in trying to develop such self-image for us, but his project seems misdescribed, by himself as well as by his critics, as "relativism."[10]

Those who follow Feyerabend in this direction are often thought of as necessarily enemies of the Enlightenment, as joining in the chorus which claims that the traditional self-descriptions of the Western democracies are bankrupt, that they somehow have been shown to be "inadequate" or "self-deceptive." Part of the instinctive resistance to attempts by Marxists, Sartreans, Oakeshottians, Gadamerians and Foucauldians to reduce objectivity to solidarity is the fear that our traditional liberal habits and hopes will not survive the reduction. Such feelings are evident, for example, in Habermas' criticism of Gadamer's position as relativistic and potentially repressive, in the suspicion that Heidegger's attacks on realism are somehow linked to his Nazism, in the hunch that Marxist attempts to interpret values as class interests are usually just apologies for Leninist takeovers, and in the suggestion that Oakeshott's skepticism about rationalism in politics is merely an apology for the status quo.

I think that putting the issue in such moral and political terms, rather than in epistemological or metaphilosophical terms, makes clearer what is at stake. For now the question is not about how to define words like "truth" or "rationality" or "knowledge" or "philosophy," but about what self-image our society should have of itself. The ritual invocation of the "need to avoid relativism" is most comprehensible as an expression of the need to preserve certain habits of contemporary European life. These are the habits nurtured by the Enlightenment, and justified by it in terms of an appeal of Reason, conceived as a transcultural human ability to correspond to reality, a faculty whose possession and use is demonstrated by obedience to explicit criteria. So the real question about relativism is whether these same habits of intellectual, social, and political life can be justified by a conception of rationality as criterionless muddling through, and by a pragmatist conception of truth.

I think that the answer to this question is that the pragmatist cannot justify these habits without circularity, but then neither can the realist. The pragmatists' justification to toleration, free inquiry, and the quest for undistorted communication can only take the form of a comparison between societies which exemplify these habits and those which do not, leading up to the suggestion that nobody who has experienced both would prefer the latter. It is exemplified by Winston Churchill's defense of democracy as the worst form of government imaginable, except for all the others which have been tried so far. Such justification is not by reference to a criterion, but by reference to various detailed practical advantages. It is circular only in that the terms of praise used to describe liberal societies will be drawn from the vocabulary of the liberal societies themselves. Such praise has to be in *some* vocabulary, after all, and the terms of praise current in primitive or theocratic or totalitarian societies will not produce the desired result. So the pragmatist admits that he has no ahistorical standpoint from which to endorse the habits of modern democracies he wishes to praise. These consequences are just what partisans of solidarity expect. But among partisans of objectivity they give rise, once again, to fears of the dilemma formed by ethnocentrism on the one hand and relativism on the other. Either we attach a special privilege to our own community, or we pretend an impossible tolerance for every other group.

I have been arguing that we pragmatists should grasp the ethnocentric horn of this dilemma. We should say that we must, in practice, privilege our own group, even though there can be no noncircular justification for doing so. We must insist that the fact that nothing is immune from criticism does not mean that we have a duty to justify everything. We Western liberal intellectuals should accept the fact that we have to start from where we are, and that this means that there are lots of views which we simply cannot take seriously. To use Neurath's familiar analogy, we can *understand* the revolutionary's suggestion that a sailable boat can't be made out of the planks which make up ours, and that we must simply abandon ship. But we cannot take his suggestion seriously. We cannot take it as a rule for action, so it is not a live option. For some people, to be sure, the option *is* live. These are the people who have always hoped to become a New Being, who have hoped to be converted rather than persuaded. But we—the liberal Rawlsian searchers for consensus, the heirs of Socrates, the people who wish to link their days dialectically each to each—cannot do so. Our community—the community of the liberal intellectuals of the secular modern West—wants to be able to give a *post factum* account of any change of view. We want to be able, so to speak, to justify ourselves to our earlier selves. This preference is not built into us by human nature. It is just he way *we* live now.[11]

This lonely provincialism, this admission that we are just the historical moment that we are, not the representatives of something ahistorical, is what makes traditional Kantian liberals like Rawls draw back from pragmatism.[12] "Relativism," by contrast, is merely a red herring. The realist is, once gain, projecting his own habits of thought upon the pragmatist when he charges him with relativism. For the realist thinks that the whole point of philosophical thought is to detach oneself from any particular community and look down at it from a more universal standpoint. When he hears the pragmatist repudiating the desire for such a standpoint he cannot quite believe it. He thinks that everyone, deep down inside, *must* want such detachment. So he attributes to the pragmatist a perverse form of his own attempted detachment, and sees him as an ironic, sneering aesthete who refuses to take the choice between communities seriously, a mere "relativist." But the pragmatist, dominated by the desire for solidarity, can only be criticized for taking his own community *too* seriously. He can only be criticized for ethnocentrism, not for relativism. To be ethnocentric is to divide the human race into the people to whom one must justify one's beliefs and the others. The first group—one's *ethnos*—comprises those who share enough of one's beliefs to make fruitful conversation possible. In this sense, everybody is ethnocentric when engaged in actual debate, no matter how much realist rhetoric about objectivity he produces in his study.[13]

What is disturbing about the pragmatist's picture is not that it is relativistic but that it takes away two sorts of metaphysical comfort to which our intellectual tradition has become accustomed. One is the thought that membership in our biological species carries with it certain "rights," a notion which does not seem to make sense unless the biological similarities entail the possession of something nonbiological, something which links our species to a nonhuman reality and thus gives the species moral dignity. This picture of rights as biologically transmitted is so basic to the political discourse of the Western democracies that we are troubled by any suggestion that "human nature" is not a useful moral concept. The second comfort is provided by the thought that our community cannot wholly die. The picture of a common human nature oriented towards correspondence to reality as it is in itself comforts us with the thought that even if our civilization is destroyed, even if all memory of our political or intellectual or artistic community is erased, the race is fated to recapture the virtues and the insights and the achievements which were the glory of that community. The notion of human nature as an inner structure which leads all members of the species to converge to the same point, to recognize the same theories, virtues, and works of art as worthy of honor, assures us that even if the Persians had won, the arts and sciences of the Greeks would sooner or later have appeared elsewhere. It assures us that even if the Orwellian bureaucrats of terror rule for a thousand years the achievements of the Western democracies will someday be duplicated by our remote descendants. It assures us that "man will prevail," that something reasonably like *our* world-view, *our* virtues, *our* art, will bob up again whenever human beings are left alone to cultivate their inner natures. The comfort of the realist picture is the comfort of saying not simply that there is a place prepared for our race in our advance, but also that we now know quite a bit about what that place looks like. The inevitable ethnocentrism to which we are all condemned is thus as much a part of the realist's comfortable view as of the pragmatist's uncomfortable one.

The pragmatist gives up the first sort of comfort because he thinks that to say that certain people have certain rights is merely to say that we should treat them in certain ways. It is not to give a *reason* for treating them in those ways.

As to the second sort of comfort, he suspects that the hope that something resembling *us* will inherit the earth is impossible to eradicate, as impossible as eradicating the hope of surviving our individual deaths through some satisfying transfiguration. But he does not want to turn this hope into a theory of the nature of man. He wants solidarity to be our *only* comfort, and to be seen not to require metaphysical support.

My suggestion that the desire for objectivity is in part a disguised form of the fear of the death of our community echoes Nietzsche's charge that the philosophical tradition which stems from Plato is an attempt to avoid facing up to contingency, to escape from time and chance. Nietzsche thought that realism was to be condemned not only by arguments from its theoretical incoherence, the sort of argument we find in Putnam and Davidson, but also on practical, pragmatic, grounds. Nietzsche thought that the test of human character was the ability to live with the thought that there was no convergence. He wanted us to be able to think of truth as:

> a mobile army of metaphors, metonyms, and anthromorphisms—in short a sum of human relations, which have been enhanced, transposed, and embellished poetically and rhetorically and which after long use seem firm, canonical, and obligatory to a people.[14]

Nietzsche hoped that eventually there might be human beings who could and did think of truth in this way, but who still liked themselves, who saw themselves as *good* people for whom solidarity was *enough*.[15]

I think that pragmatism's attack on the various structure-content distinctions which butress the realist's notion of objectivity can best be seen as an attempt to let us think of truth in this Nietzschean way, as entirely a matter of solidarity. That is why I think we need to say, despite Putnam, that "there is only the dialogue," only *us*, and to throw out the last residues of the notion of "trans-cultural rationality." But this should not lead us to repudiate, as Nietzsche sometimes did, the elements in our movable host which embody the ideas of Socratic conversation, Christian fellowship, and Enlightenment science. Nietzsche ran together his diagnosis of philosophical realism as an expression of fear and resentment with his own resentful idiosyncratic idealizations of silence, solitude, and violence. Post-Nietzschean thinkers like Adorno and Heidegger and Foucault have run together Nietzsche's criticisms of the metaphysical tradition on the one hand with his criticisms of bourgeois civility, of Christian love, and of the nineteenth century's hope that science would make the world a better place to live, on the other. I do not think that there is any interesting connection between these two sets of criticisms. Pragmatism seems to me, as I have said, a philosophy of solidarity rather than of despair. From this point of view, Socrates' turn away from the gods, Christianity's turn from an Omnipotent Creator to the man who suffered on the Cross, and the Baconian turn from science as contemplation of eternal truth to science as instrument of social progress, can be seen as so many preparations for the act of social faith which is suggested by a Nietzschean view of truth.[16]

The best argument we partisans of solidarity have against the realistic partisans of objectivity is Nietzsche's argument that the traditional Western metaphysico-epistemological way of firming up our habits simply isn't working anymore. It isn't doing its job. It has become as transparent a device as the postulation of deities who turn out, by a happy coincidence, to have chosen us as their people. So the pragmatist suggestion that we substitute a "merely" ethical foundation for our sense of community—or, better, that we think of our sense of community as having no foundation except shared hope and the trust created by such sharing—is put forward on practical grounds. It is *not* put forward as a corollary of a metaphysical claim that the objects in the world contain no intrinsically action-guiding properties, nor of an epistemological claim that we lack a faculty of moral sense, nor of a semantic claim that truth is reducible to justification. It is a suggestion about how we might think of ourselves in order to avoid the kind of resentful belated-ness—characteristic of the bad side of Nietzsche—which now characterizes much of high culture. This resentment arises from the realization, which I referred to at the beginning of this chapter, that the Enlightenment's search for objectivity has often gone sour.

The rhetoric of scientific objectivity, pressed too hard and taken too seriously, has led us to people like B.F. Skinner on the one hand and people like Althusser on the other—two equally pointless fantasies, both produced by the attempt to be "scientific" about our moral and political lives. Reaction against scientism led to attacks on natural science as a sort of false god. But there is nothing wrong with science, there is only something wrong with the attempt to divinize it, the attempt characteristic of realistic philosophy. This reaction has also led to attacks on liberal social thought of the type common to Mill and Dewey and Rawls as a mere ideological superstructure, one which obscures the realities of our situation and represses attempts to change that situation. But there is nothing wrong with liberal democracy, nor with the philosophers who have tried to enlarge its scope. There is only something wrong with the attempt to see their efforts as failures to achieve something which they were not trying to achieve—a demonstration of the "objective" superiority of our way of life over all other alternatives. There is, in short, nothing wrong with the hopes of the Enlightenment, the hopes which created the Western democracies. The value of the ideals of the Enlightenment is, for us pragmatists, just the value of some of the institutions and practices which they have created. In this essay I have sought to distinguish these institutions and practices from the philosophical justifications for them provided by partisans of objectivity, and to suggest an alternative justification.

NOTES

[1]   This attitude toward truth, in which the consensus of a community rather than a relation to a nonhuman reality is taken as central, is associated not only with the American pragmatic tradition but with the work of Popper and Habermas. Habermas' criticisms of lingering positivist elements in Popper parallel those made by Deweyan holists of the early logical empiricists. It is important to see, however, that the pragmatist notion of truth common to James and Dewey is not dependent upon either Peirce's notion of an "ideal end of inquiry" nor on Habermas' notion of an "ideally free community." For criticism of these notions, which in my view are insufficiently ethnocentric, see my "Pragmatism, Davidson and Truth" and "Habermas and Lyotard on Postmodernity."

[2]   Hilary Putnam, *Reason, Truth and History* (Cambridge: Cambridge University Press, 1981), pp. 49–50.

[3]   Ibid., p. 119.

[4]   Ibid., p. x.

[5]   Ibid., p. 114.

[6]   Ibid., p. 119. See Davidson's "On the very idea of a conceptual scheme," in his *Inquiries into Truth and Interpretation* (Oxford: Oxford University Press, 1984) for a more complete and systematic presentation of this point.

[7]   Putnam, p. 113.

[8]   Ibid., p. 126.

[9]   Ibid., p. 216.

[10]   See, e.g., Paul Feyerabend, *Science in a Free Society* (London: New Left Books, 1978), p. 9, where Feyerabend identifies his own view with "relativism (in the old and simple sense of Protagoras)." This identification is accompanied by the claim that "'Objectively' there is not much to choose between anti-semitism and humanitarianism." I think Feyerabend would have served himself better by saying that the scare-quoted word "objectively" should simply be dropped from use, together with the traditional philosophical distinctions which buttress the

subjective-objective distinction, than by saying that we may keep the word and use it to say the sort of thing Protagoras said. What Feyerabend is really against is the correspondence theory of truth, not the idea that some views cohere better than others.

[11]   This quest for consensus is opposed to the sort of quest for authenticity which wishes to free itself from the opinion of our community. See, for example, Vincent Descombes' account of Deleuze in *Modern French Philosophy* (Cambridge: Cambridge University Press, 1980), p. 153: "Even if philosophy is essentially demystificatory, philosophers often fail to produce authentic critiques; they defend order, authority, institutions. 'decency,' everything in which the ordinary person believes." On the pragmatist or ethnocentric view I am suggesting, all that critique can or should do is play off elements in "what the ordinary person believes" against other elements. To attempt to do more than this is to fantasize rather than to converse. Fantasy may, to be sure, be an incentive to more fruitful conversation, but when it no longer fulfills this function it does not deserve the name of "critique."

[12]   In *A Theory of Justice* Rawls seemed to be trying to retain the authority of Kantian "practical reason" by imagining a social contract devised by choosers "behind a veil of ignorance"—using the "rational self-interest" of such choosers as a touchstone for the ahistorical validity of certain social institutions. Much of the criticism to which that book was subjected, e.g., by Michael Sandel in his *Liberalism and the Limits of Justice* (Cambridge: Cambridge University Press, 1982), has centered on the claim that one cannot escape history in this way. In the meantime, however, Rawls has put forward a meta-ethical view which drops the claim to ahistorical validity. Concurrently, T.M. Scanlon has urged that the essence of a "contractualist" account of moral motivation is better understood as the desire to justify one's action to others than in terms of "rational self-interest." See Scanlon, "Contractualism and Utilitarianism," in A. Sen and B. Williams, eds., *Utilitarianism and Beyond* (Cambridge: Cambridge University Press, 1982). Scanlon's emendation of Rawls leads in the same direction as Rawls' later work, since Scanlon's use of the notion of "justification to others on grounds they could not reasonably reject" chimes with the "constructivist" view that what counts for social philosophy is what can be justified to a particular historical community, not to "humanity in general." On my view, the frequent remark that Rawls' rational choosers look remarkably like twentieth-century American liberals is perfectly just, but not a criticism of Rawls. It is merely a frank recognition of the ethnocentrism which is essential to serious, nonfantastical, thought. I defend this view in "The Priority of Democracy to Philosophy" and "Postmodernist Bourgeois Liberalism."

[13]   In an important paper called "The Truth in Relativism," included in his *Moral Luck* (Cambridge: Cambridge University Press, 1981), Bernard Williams makes a similar point in terms of a distinction between "genuine confrontation" and "notional confrontation." The latter is the sort of confrontation which occurs, asymmetrically, between us and primitive tribespeople. The belief-systems of such people do not present, as Williams puts it, "real options" for us, for we cannot imagine going over to their view without "self-deception or paranoia." These are the people whose beliefs on certain topics overlap so little with ours that their inability to agree with us raises no doubt in our minds about the correctness of our own beliefs. Williams' use of "real option" and "notional confrontation" seems to me very enlightening, but I think he turns these notions to purposes they will not serve. Williams wants to defend ethical relativism, defined as the claim that when ethical confrontations are merely notional "questions of appraisal do not genuinely arise." He thinks they *do* arise in connection with notional confrontations between,

e.g., Einsteinian and Amazonian cosmologies. (See Williams, p. 142.) This distinction between ethics and physics seems to me an awkward result to which Williams is driven by his unfortunate attempt to find *something* true in relativism, an attempt which is a corollary of his attempt to be "realistic" about physics. On my (Davidsonian) view, there is no point in distinguishing between true sentences which are "made true by reality" and true sentences which are "made by us," because the whole idea of "truth-makers" needs to be dropped. So I would hold that there is *no* truth in relativism, but this much truth in ethnocentrism: we cannot justify our beliefs (in physics, ethics, or any other area) to everybody, but only to those whose beliefs overlap ours to some appropriate extent. (This is not a theoretical problem about "untranslatability," but simply a practical problem about the limitations of argument; it is not that we live in different worlds than the Nazis or the Amazonians, but that conversion from or to their point of view, though possible, will not be a matter of inference from previously shared premises.)

[14] Nietzsche, "On Truth and Lie in an Extra-Moral Sense," in *The Viking Portable Nietzsche*, Walter Kaufmann, ed. and trans., pp. 46–47.

[15] See Sabina Lovibond, *Realism and Imagination in Ethics* (Minneapolis: University of Minnesota Press, 1983), p. 158: "An adherent of Wittgenstein's view of language should equate that goal with the establishment of a language-game in which we could participate ingenuously, while retaining our awareness of it as a specific historical formation. A community in which such a language-game was played would be one...whose members understood their own form of life and yet were not embarrassed by it."

[16] See Hans Blumenberg, *The Ligitimation of Modernity* (Cambridge, Mass.: MIT Press, 1982), for a story about the history of European thought which, unlike the stories told by Nietzsche and Heidegger, sees the Enlightenment as a definitive step forward. For Blumenberg, the attitude of "self-assertion," the kind of attitude which stems from a Baconian view of the nature and purpose of science, needs to be distinguished from "self-foundation," the Cartesian project of grounding such inquiry upon ahistorical criteria of rationality. Blumenberg remarks, pregnantly, that the "historicist" criticism of the optimism of the enlightenment, criticism which began with the Romantics' turn back to the Middle Ages, undermines self-foundation but not self-assertion.

3.9

Contrasting Conceptions of Social Epistemology

Philip Kitcher

I

The history of epistemology has been dominated by an individualistic perspective on human knowledge, most dramatically displayed in Descartes's scenario for the aspiring knower who was resolutely contemplating the dubitability of beliefs in the privacy of a stove-heated room.[1] Like other epistemologists before and after him, Descartes did not overlook the obvious fact that all of us learn from others. Individualists have believed, however, that this epistemic dependence could be transcended, holding that we have available to us individualistic grounds for accepting some propositions and that this set of propositions can be used to assess information we receive from others. Proceeding in this fashion, we can ultimately calibrate informants, much as we calibrate instruments, so that all that we claim to know comes to be based upon the exercise of our individual judgment.[2]

Neglect of social epistemology thus results, I believe, from (typically tacit) acceptance of a reductionist program. It is assumed that there is a set of propositions—the individualistic basis—that we can know without reliance on others. Given this individualistic basis, we are supposed to be able to assess the reliability of potential sources by checking their deliverances against propositions in the basis. Once a source's reliability has been evaluated in this way, simple inductive inferences can lead us to employ that source in instances in which individualistic checking is impossible. So it is assumed that all that we take ourselves to know can be obtained by relying only on sources whose credentials have been individualistically checked.

To the best of my knowledge, nobody has ever carried out this reductionist program in any detail. There are plainly two sources of problems: one arising from the possibility that we employ sources for whom comparisons with the individualistic basis are far too slender to support the extensive use we make of them (think, for example, of the paucity of ways in which we can check directly the deliverances of national news media); the other stemming from the worry that there may be no propositions that we can know without being epistemically dependent on others. These points are analogous in obvious ways to objections encountered by logical empiricist programs for the reduction of "theoretical" knowledge; and just as the issue of the theory-ladenness of perception was crucial to that debate, so too, it seems to me, the second concern, which stresses the social dependence of all our knowledge, is fundamental to the prospects of individualistic reduction.[3]

Both in our abstract thinking and in our perceptual experience, the conclusions we draw depend on the conceptual repertoire that we deploy and on the habits for reaching or inhibiting belief in which we have been trained. Early absorption of the lore of our societies affects us even at those points at which we appear most able to take our epistemic lives into our own hands. These points can probably best be appreciated by considering the differences between our formation of belief, both in perception and in reasoning, and the analogous processes that occur in others whose initial socialization is different.[4] Unless we hold, as Descartes did, that there is some presuppositionless point from which we can begin inquiry, we must abandon the individualistic reduction as a failure. But, since my primary purpose in what follows is to contrast different styles of social epistemology, I shall not try to present the argument in detail, leaving would-be individualists the challenge of showing that prospects for reduction are brighter than I have taken them to be.

Social epistemology begins at the point of rejecting the individualistic reduction. One may go on in a number of different ways. I shall start with an approach that remains relatively close to the individualistic tradition.

II

According to a venerable conception of knowledge, the primary subjects of knowledge are individual human beings. To talk about the knowledge current in a community is to say something, possibly quite complex, about what the members of that community know. Ascription of knowledge to individuals turns on recognizing that they have beliefs with special properties: beliefs that are true and that are "properly grounded," "justified," or "warranted." So one comes to the traditional formula, "X knows that p just in case p and X believes that p and X is justified in believing that p" or its more sophisticated modern equivalents (for example, "X knows that p just in case p and X believes that p and X's belief that p was formed by a process that is reliable (in the appropriate sense)").[5] Theories of knowledge that begin from this familiar type of account may venture into social epistemology solely because they are persuaded of the breakdown of the individualistic reduction canvassed above. In consequence, the exact point at which epistemology becomes social is in the appreciation of the possibility that whether or not a subject is justified (or whether or not a belief-forming process counts as reliable in the pertinent sense) turns on the properties of other people or of the group to which the subject belongs.

For purposes of convenience in what follows, I shall assume a (bland and undeveloped) version of a reliabilist account of knowledge—although I believe that the distinctions I shall draw and the questions I shall raise would emerge in strictly parallel fashion, given any of the main alternatives to reliabilism. We can thus present the elements of a *minimal social epistemology* as follows:

(1)   Individuals are the primary subjects of knowledge. To ascribe knowledge to a community is to make an assertion about the epistemic states of members of the community.

(2) X knows that p if and only if (a) X believes that p and (b) p and (c) X's belief that p was formed by a reliable process.

(3)   The reliability of the process that produces X's belief that p depends on the properties and actions of agents other than X.

My designation of this position as *minimal* is intended to prepare the way for recognition of far more radical versions of social epistemology. As we shall see, these may reject the individualistic assumption (1), modify conditions (2b) and/or (2c), and make corresponding alterations—in (3). However, before considering these possibilities, I want to explore the epistemological agenda for a position based on (1)–(3).

One primary task for a theory of knowledge of this form consists in understanding the reliability of various types of belief-generating processes. Part of this task consists in recognizing the standards of reliability that should be invoked in particular contexts—the law courts, the laboratory, the everyday transmission of information, for examples—and aspects of identification of such standards surely involve questions of social epistemology.[6] However, the main social epistemological project consists in the investigation of the reliability of various types of social processes. Once we have recognized that individuals form beliefs by relying on information supplied by others, there are serious issues about the conditions that should be met if the community is to form a consensus on a particular issue—questions about the division of opinion and of cognitive effort within the community, and issues about the proper attribution of authority. I shall refer to the field of problems just outlined as *the study of the organization of cognitive labor.*[7]

Just as individualistic epistemology concerns itself with those processes that promote an individual's attainment of true belief, so too social epistemology should be concerned with the organization of communities of knowers and with the processes that occur among knowers within such communities that promote both the collective and the individual acquisition of true belief. Consider, for instance, the problem of consensus formation. Communities that set lenient standards for the adoption of a proposal made by some subset of their members as part of community lore are evidently more likely to pass on false beliefs than those that are more exacting. By the same token, communities that demand exacting independent checks of such proposals will be inclined to waste valuable cognitive efforts. How should the balance be struck?

We have here a well-defined optimization problem that can be treated precisely by making assumptions about the cognitive capacities of individuals and about the positions that they hold within the society. To the extent that we can make realistic presuppositions about human cognitive capacities and about the social relations found in actual communities of inquirers, we can explain, appraise, and *in principle* improve our collective epistemic performance. In similar fashion, the standard institutions of inquiry can submit to precise critical analyses.

The considerations of the last paragraph suggest a way of thinking about the requirements on knowledge that enables us to defuse an important objection.[8] Reliabilist analyses of knowledge and justification (as well as other approaches to the problem of analysing "X knows that p") often seem to take as their target the precise reconstruction of our everyday intuitions about what would count as instances of human knowledge. But why should these ordinary intuitions be privileged? Why should we want to exhibit the structure of the concept of knowledge we currently possess? The obvious answer is that an explicit account of the everyday concept might enable us to improve it or to replace it with a more adequate concept. However, skeptics may legitimately demand to know what criterion of adequacy is alluded to here. What turns on whether we define "knowledge" in one way rather than another, or on whether we set this or that standard of reliability?

Recognizing the role that classifying propositions as items of knowledge plays in the achievement of consensus, and thus in both the transmission of belief and the shaping of further inquiry, enables us to reply to this skeptical query. Assume that the ultimate standard for appraising the processes that guide our investigations is their propensity to lead to the community-wide acceptance of truth (or, better, of significant truth).[9] Proposals for classifying beliefs as justified or as known under conditions that vary with respect to the type of reliability that is understood can be evaluated according to the social roles that such classifications would play in the genesis of community-wide true belief. Some standards for justification, for example, might be too liberal in that they would allow too easily for the introduction and dissemination of error. Hence the problem of deciding how consensus should properly be formed is deeply relevant to the issue of the standards that analyses of knowledge and justification should satisfy. Analytic epistemology thus presupposes answers to questions in social epistemology.

III

The enterprise of the preceding section is attractive: it offers a plethora of precise, challenging problems, all connected with the central issues of the theory of knowledge, and all virtually unexplored. Nonetheless, for all its charms, this project is not what most of those who take the social turn in epistemology find exciting and liberating.[10] In the rest of this essay, I want to explore various ways in which one can try to reject some of the traditional epistemological assumptions that are taken over in (1)–(3), and thus make a more radical break with the epistemological past. My own bias in favor of the more limited conception of social epistemology outlined in section II will be evident in what follows. Nonetheless, because the issues are complex, I cannot hope to offer detailed, knockdown arguments in favor of that conception. Instead, I intend to identify the major issues that divide various conceptions and to see what notions must be clarified if the debate among them is to be more fruitfully pursued.

A relatively minor deviation from the project of section II consists in retaining the overall conception offered in (1)–(3) but retracting a part of the individualism maintained in (1) by allowing that there may be properties relevant to collective inquiry that cannot be reduced to properties of and relations among individual inquirers. The optimality analyses envisaged in section II—and those articulated in preliminary attempts to work out the enterprise envisaged there—adopt as their preferred framework the language of rational decision theory, microeconomics, and other parts of social science that are resolutely committed to methodological individualism. In principle, one might want to allow for an expansion of this framework to incorporate references to irreducible collectivities (or collective properties). While I hold no brief for reductionism in general (recognizing the limitations of particular types of reductionist programs in biology and psychology),[11] there seems to be no reason to be committed to an expansion of this framework in advance of detailed arguments that show why specific social facets of inquiry are affected by irreducible social factors. Casual gestures in the direction of Durkheim are not sufficient. For it is not only a matter of controversy whether Durkheim's alleged social facts are needed to explain the phenomena that concerned him,[12] but also quite possible that there should be irreducible social causes in some areas of human life (for example, suicide, forms of religious life) and not in others (for example, the growth of human knowledge).

As I have already remarked, this is a minor deviation, and one that could quite easily be accommodated. A more consistent methodological holist would, I suspect, be far more inclined to question the principles (1) and (2) than to try to tack some social causes onto a fundamentally individualist project. One important criticism of the version of social epistemology developed in section II is that it slights the social by making the most individualistic parts of social science—psychology, microeconomics—central to the development of social epistemology. If we were to start, instead, with sociology, political theory, or cultural anthropology as our paradigms of social science, we might develop a far more *social* social epistemology.

Consider many of the slogans that are currently fashionable in discussions of social epistemology: "knowledge is power"; "knowledge circulates in communities"; "knowledge is institutionalized belief."[13] These slogans invite us to invert the traditional picture of knowledge as produced by individuals, who may be dependent upon the epistemic efforts of *other* individuals, and as becoming community-wide knowledge through recognition of the characteristics of what has been individually produced. Instead, we should regard the community-wide knowledge as primary, identifying individual knowledge with belief that accords (in some sense to be explained) with the knowledge current in the community. As it stands, this thesis is vague.[14] I suggest the following more precise version of it: starting with an account of community knowledge, the social epistemologist proposes that items of individual belief count as knowledge just in case, first, the propositions believed are members of the set known in the community and, second, the processes that underlie the formation of the beliefs are of types approved as knowledge-generating within the community. Social epistemologies of this form thus reject (1), and they may also diverge from (2b) and (2c).

One source of the repudiation of (1) lies in appreciation of the multiplicity of ways in which contemporary scientific knowledge is embodied—in printed texts, in pictures, in instruments, in experimental systems, in artifacts, in social institutions.[15] Faced with this diversity of forms of knowledge, philosophical focus on the beliefs of an individual may seem a peculiar obsession. Moreover, when we examine the different embodiments of knowledge, it may appear that what they have in common is not any propositional content with a distinctive status, but rather an ability to be employed in various ways, to direct the activities of people and other things. The experimental apparatus enables us to control certain phenomena. The diagram serves to display what we ought to perceive. These, like other embodiments of knowledge, are devices for intervening in nature and for regulating our social conduct. To count something as knowledge is to recognize it as having a certain power.

Despite the suggestiveness of these ideas, the account of knowledge they "embody" seems to me intolerably vague. What sorts of entities can count as items of knowledge? What differentiates those entities of these types which are pieces of knowledge from those which are not? *One* route that social epistemology can take at this juncture is to adopt a full-blooded relativism, averring that the types of entities that can count as items of knowledge are as diverse as the "forms of life" in which they are embedded, and that the standards of knowledge are simply those of social acceptance. It is enough that an instrument, diagram, or text is "reproduced and circulated," or that it forms "part of an enduring network" within a society—under such conditions it counts as an item of knowledge *within that society*. There are apparent losses in settling for relativism—most obviously, the possibility of drawing a distinction between what is current in a society and what is genuine knowledge—and I shall explore these later. For the moment, I want to step back and ask if the phenomena that inspire the "multiple embodiments" approach to knowledge really demand a break with the traditional conception of knowledge as something that is located in (or possessed by) an individual subject.

In recent years, philosophers (as well as historians and sociologists of science) have become, quite rightly, impressed with the "craft knowledge" of scientists (and others).[16] Part of the story is no news: epistemology has always recognized that subjects have both skill knowledge (knowing how) and propositional knowledge (knowing that).[17] Many interesting debates have raged around the possibility of showing that an apparently irreducible piece of skill knowledge is really underlain by propositional knowledge.[18] Whether or not the champions of deep propositional representations are right about our ability to learn a language or to perceive three-dimensional objects, it seems initially that our most striking abilities to control natural phenomena are dependent on instances of human propositional knowledge. We would not be able to synthesize compounds or to design organisms with specifiable properties unless some person(s) had come to know propositions about molecules in the one instance or about genes in the other.

Detailed studies of the replication of apparatus and of experiments have made it plain that scientists sometimes have skills that cannot be articulated as propositional recipes: field geologists know what unconformities look like, molecular biologists know how to run gels, and so forth.[19] I shall suppose that there is no reduction of these skills to items of tacit propositional knowledge that the adept fail to articulate. Nevertheless, these pieces of knowledge are still localized in individuals: particular subjects have (or lack) the skills. Moreover, a plausible individualistic analysis of skill knowledge suggests itself. Associated with each skill is a set of manifestation conditions, under which the subject should display a particular type of performance. X knows how to Z if and only if, when conditions $M(Z)$ are realized, X Zs (where $M(Z)$ are, of course, the manifestation conditions associated with Zing). Let us now ask if the point about the diverse embodiments of knowledge can be accommodated by showing how the various entities acclaimed as pieces of knowledge obtain that status as the result of the skill knowledge and propositional knowledge of individuals.

Consider the double helical model of the structure of DNA, copies of which can be found in innumerable laboratories around the world. Why does this count as an item (or embodiment) of knowledge? We have already looked briefly at the suggestion that this status accrues because of the ways in which the copies are treated and the ways in which they function in social interaction. An alternative (traditional) proposal is that the DNA model is an embodiment of knowledge because there are people who know that DNA molecules correspond to the arrangement of wires, plastic, and metal in certain specifiable respects. In saying that the model is an item (embodiment) of *community* knowledge, we recognize that, first, there is a class of people within the community who know the propositions that record the correspondence and, second, (almost) everyone else in the community believes that this class includes all the people who are reliable with respect to matters of that kind.[20] In similar fashion, a picture of the stages of meiotic division counts as an item (embodiment) of knowledge because there are people who know that the processes of cell division correspond to the picture in certain specifiable respects. (And again, we can account for the community knowledge in terms of the recognition that the people in question are those who are reliable about such matters.) The air pump counts as an embodiment of knowledge because the pump can be used to achieve certain interventions in nature; that is, the pump serves as a prop in manifestations of certain types of skill knowledge. (It is also true that people know that when the air pump is employed under specifiable conditions certain effects will be produced, but the skill knowledge outruns the propositional knowledge.)

I claim that the prospects for giving an individualist account of the phenomena of craft and community knowledge are quite bright. We thus encounter an obvious asymmetry. While the sociologizing program based on the rejection of (1) seems headed either for relativism or for vagueness, the approach sketched in section II seems to have resources for coping with the phenomena that its rival takes as principal sources of motivation. Let us now turn to consider the possibility that relativism may have independent attractions.

IV

Much of the point of classical epistemology and philosophy of science arises from distinguishing between what people think (even when they are in entire agreement) and what is correct. Truth, and its relatives, enter discussions of knowledge in two places: first, and most obviously, in the claim that what is known must be true (2b);[21] and second, in the understanding of reliability as grounded in the propensity for generating true belief. Traditionalists presuppose that the notion of truth is epistemically independent, that we are not to reduce the notion of truth in terms of what people know, or believe, or what the members of a society accept. Precisely this epistemic independence of the concept of truth inspires the radical versions of social epistemology to break with tradition.

On what grounds? What is wrong with the traditional invocation of an epistemically independent notion of truth? Three main arguments figure in the recent literature.[22] The first campaigns for relativism by appealing to the fundamental tenets of the Strong Programme in the sociology of knowledge (most notably, the Symmetry Principle). The second invokes a venerable anti-realist attack on the correspondence theory of truth. The third rests on a thesis about the underdetermination of our claims about reality by our encounters with reality. I shall consider these arguments in turn.

The Strong Programme in the sociology of knowledge is based upon the attractive ideas that *all* beliefs should submit to causal explanation, and that this causal explanation will involve social causes.[23] In effect, the arguments of sections I and II have already acknowledged this basic point, although they have resisted the idea that the social causes to which we must appeal violate the principle of methodological individualism. (The minor deviation envisaged in section III would introduce Durkheimian entities into the explanatory apparatus.) Thus, in a certain sense, all the conceptions of social epistemology so far envisaged—even the most traditional—honor the Symmetry Principle. All suppose that "the same types of causes" must be invoked to explain both true and false beliefs. For, if we are out to explain X's belief that p, we shall surely do so by identifying X's cognitive capacities, X's interactions with reality, and X's social background. Even in cases of perception, X's socialization will be relevant, if only to help us understand why X forms a belief under the conditions that obtain and why X's belief employs the categories that it does. Hence, *at a very general level*, the same types of causes will be invoked to understand any belief, irrespective of its truth value.

To make the Symmetry Principle imply more exciting, relativistic conclusions, it is necessary to interpret it in a much stronger—and quite controversial—way. "Type" is, of course, highly ambiguous, and the ecumenical conclusions of the last paragraph depended on individuating types very broadly. If, however, we individuate types narrowly then, *so long as we make traditional assumptions about truth*, the Symmetry Principle yields highly counterintuitive consequences. To see this, suppose that we think of processes like the following: (a) perceiving macroscopic objects in good light; (b) forming conclusions about probabilities through the use of careful sampling and the use of Bayes's Theorem; (c) forming beliefs by listing the first thirty-eight propositions that come into one's head, assigning them numbers 00, 0, 1–36, spinning a roulette wheel, and believing the propositions that correspond to the first six numbers that come up; (d) ingesting large quantities of alcohol, going outside in the twilight, and forming beliefs about the numbers of objects of various kinds that are present; and (e) forming beliefs about probabilities by using small, biased samples or using the gambler's fallacy. The processes that I have described are far more narrowly individuated than my earlier references to causal factors involving social background, cognitive capacities, and interactions between the subject and nature. If we suppose that the Symmetry Principle applies to the more specific processes (a)–(e), then it will follow that each of these processes should be invoked to explain the presence of both true and false beliefs *and indeed that each should be invoked equally often in this enterprise.* For otherwise there would be an asymmetry: as we listed the true beliefs and false beliefs that were explained, we should find that some processes turn up more frequently in the explanation of true beliefs while others occur more frequently in the explanation of false beliefs.[24]

Now the symmetry required here is intuitively absurd, and one's first thought is that only a fetishistic devotion to symmetry at all costs could inspire one to think that processes of types (c)–(e) are equally likely to generate true beliefs as processes (a) and (b). This thought is perfectly correct so long as we are taking for granted a nonepistemic notion of truth, and assuming that some of the most stable claims that are widely shared across different cultures are true. However, if one has *already* adopted the view that the only notions of truth that are coherent are those that identify truth with some type of institutional or community-wide belief, then the impression of absurdity can be dispelled. For in that case it is possible to hold that different types of processes can equally be made part of a community's standards for truth, so that, while the symmetry may be broken *locally*, the breach of symmetry can and must be explained in terms of the particular choices that the community has made. While we live in a culture that has institutionalized processes like (a) as truth promoting, others might just as well (and perhaps even do) take processes like (d) as truth promoting.

If the line of argument that I have constructed is correct, then appeal to the Symmetry Principle alone should not force us to adopt a version of social epistemology more radical than that discussed in section II (possibly with the deviation alluded to in section III). For there is no compelling motivation for adopting the Symmetry Principle in the strong sense in which types of processes are individuated narrowly.[25] Defenders of nonepistemic approaches to truth will view such adoption as leading quickly to absurdity. However, for those who already believe that traditional, nonepistemic notions of truth must be abandoned, the absurd consequences are artifacts of a misbegotten approach to truth, and the Symmetry Principle can be given a far stronger interpretation. The popular belief that acceptance of the Symmetry Principle thus leads to relativism seems to me to be quite mistaken. Only in the context of independent arguments against nonepistemic notions of truth does the principle obtain that kind of force. At best, the first line of argument can only reinforce conclusions that have already been reached on different grounds.

On, then, to the second line of argument. This begins with the suggestion that traditionalists are committed to a particular type of nonepistemic notion of truth, to wit, the correspondence theory. It then suggests that the notion of correspondence is incoherent (some versions) or idle (others), so that the only useable notion of truth is one that identifies truth with some type of acceptance.[26] Both parts of the argument can be (and have been) questioned. A currently fashionable approach to the treatment of truth proposes that no elaborate theory of truth is required. We can avoid identifying truth with any type of acceptance without embracing the correspondence theory of truth, simply by adopting a minimal (or deflationary) conception of truth.[27] I shall not examine the credentials of this inviting line of escape, since I believe that it ultimately fails.[28] Instead, I shall try to meet the challenge to correspondence truth head-on.

Correspondence theorists claim that there are linguistic/conceptual items that correspond (or fail to correspond) to parts of nature. Their opponents typically inquire how this correspondence is *set up* or how it is *checked*.[29] Allegedly, to establish or to scrutinize the correspondence between thought/language and reality would require the attainment of some perspective from which both sides of the dichotomy could be viewed and the connections between them identified. Since there is no such out-of-theory position, no sense can be given to correspondence or failure to correspond, and the notion of correspondence is senseless/incoherent/useless.

I shall call this argument the "Inaccessibility of Reality Argument"—or the IRA, for short. The IRA is a terrorist weapon which anti-realists employ with enormous confidence. I believe that the confidence is misplaced.

As I have already noted, many of our interventions in reality are guided by our representations of objects that we manipulate. Some of these representations are public (for example, maps, diagrams, descriptions), some are internal states. Realists believe that there are referential relations between elements of representations and entities that are typically independent of the subject who has/uses the representation. These referential relations, together with the state of reality, jointly determine the truth values of statements and the accuracy values of other forms of representations (such as maps, diagrams). Such, at least in roughest outline, is the correspondence theory of truth—or, more generally, of accuracy—to which real realists are committed.

Now why should anyone accept this idea of correspondence, and how can the correspondence ever be checked? To answer such questions, we do best to start from a situation in which ordinary people occupy a position analogous to that transcendent perspective denied by the IRA. Imagine that you are observing the behavior of another person and that you know not only what that person desires and intends but also how she represents the objects with which she interacts. Your explanation of the success of that person's behavior will appeal to the accuracy of her representations: she gets what she wants, to the extent that she does, because she represents the objects whose properties she controls, modifies, or compensates for in her own actions in ways that correspond to their actual dispositions. Reflection on such cases should bring home to us the importance of explaining the behavior of *others* by recognizing their representations, the correspondence of elements of those representations to objects that are independent of the individuals under study, and the connection between accurate (true) representations and success in dealing with those objects.[30]

None of this presupposes any problematic perspective because we, the observers, are part of the story. If you like, the entities that are independent of the subjects whose behavior is explained are "internal" to the worldview of the observer(s). But real realists think that this point about the presence of an analyst is trivial. Why should the relations between the subject, the subject's representations, and the independent objects depend on the presence of another to note them?[31] Why should the presence of an observer affect the connection between accurate representation and success? Why should the case of any of us—or of all of us—be any different?

Real realism is the position that makes an analogical move from the everyday situation in which we observe and explain the behavior and the behavioral success of another to the predicament of all of us. Just as I recognize objects that are independent of those I observe, referential relations between elements of others' representations and those objects, and a connection between accurate representation and successful behavior, so too I suppose that there are objects independent of me (and indeed of all of us) that there are referential relations between elements of my representations and those objects, and that the success of my interventions in nature correlates with, and so signals, the accuracy of my representations. Not to take this view of myself would be to grant myself a peculiar status, perhaps privileged, perhaps underprivileged—and would indeed involve an *unmotivated* asymmetry.

The line of thought that I have sketched represents what I take to be the central tendency of realism (hence my label "real realism"). There are many complications that need to be addressed if it is to be made completely clear and persuasive;[32] but, since the forms of the IRA that emerge in discussions of social epistemology are typically *very* quick and straightforward, I shall not take up the subtleties here. Suffice it to note that, given the approach I have adopted, there is no reason to claim that acceptance of the correspondence theory of truth requires some transcendent perspective, or that it presupposes some privileged position for the epistemic subject in which reality directly manifests itself.[33] The story I have told frankly admits that all of our representations are partially produced by causal processes that extend back into our societies and their historical progenitors.

Some approaches in contemporary epistemology proceed far too swiftly from appreciation of the socio-historical situatedness of the knower to dismissal of the independence of what is known. Feminist epistemology offers important insights in its recognition that each of us occupies a standpoint, and that standpoints make epistemic differences. But, in light of my response to the IRA, I propose that the way to extend this insight is not to dismiss the ideal of objectivity, nor to reject the correspondence theory of truth, which supplies its most obvious underpinnings, but rather to probe systematically the ways in which different standpoints make available more or less epistemically apt dispositions, more or less reliable ways of generating true beliefs. There are differences between subjects, or between temporal stages of the same subject, according to their dispositions to acquire true beliefs or to be moved by reliable belief-forming processes. Some of these differences are surely traceable to the distortions introduced by social biases or personal prejudices. We can recognize the differences without supposing that there is some perfect state in which the world is inevitably made manifest to us.

Reliabilists should thus insist that some standpoints are better or worse than others with respect to particular types of propositions: given that the issue is to determine whether *p*, the chances of doing so may be greater if one's circumstances are one way rather than another. I doubt that issues about the character of the ultimate constituents of matter will be resolved on the top of a kitchen table (even in Utah) or that those who know nothing of population genetics will be able to settle controversies about sexual selection. More interesting instances of the foibles and virtues of particular standpoints are familiar from the history of science. Membership of a particular ethnic group within a particular society may interfere with one's ability to acquire true beliefs about the distribution of characteristics that are believed to be important to human worth (witness the history of nineteenth-century craniometry).[34] By the same token, gender-associated biases can render invisible some of the most important features of the phenomena under study—a point dramatically demonstrated by the changes that have been wrought in primatology since the entry of many women into primatology in the 1970s.[35]

The claim that a particular standpoint is preferable to others can thus be recast in terms of the relative reliability of the processes that standpoints make available. We should assess any such claim by drawing on what we think we know about the deliverances of the contending standpoints. Yet it seems initially unlikely that any single standpoint will be preferable across the board. There will surely be occasions on which the critique of the outsider is needed to stimulate a community that has fallen into complacency, and other circumstances in which the comments of the marginalized are useless because they are ignorant.

At this point, we can fruitfully return to the project of social epistemology envisaged in section II. Instead of thinking of the merits of rival standpoints that individuals might adopt, each of which might influence their chances of obtaining true beliefs, we should consider what *distribution* of standpoints might serve the community best, facilitating the goal of reaching consensus on the truth.[36]

I conclude that the IRA does not force us to relativism or any other position that abandons the correspondence theory of truth. Nor does the rebuttal of the IRA presuppose that there is some privileged epistemic position in which access to REALITY is achieved, or even that there is a unique best epistemic standpoint. So far we seem to have combined realism with social epistemology in a way that avoids those deficiencies that motivate more radical departures.

V

However, another argument remains to be confronted, and the picture here is far more blurred. As noted in my outline reply to the IRA, an important part of the story is the connection between success (construed as getting what one wants) and accuracy of representation. Any such connection can be undermined if one can argue that there are rival schemes of representation that are equally successful. Appropriate instances of such schemes of representation can be sought either in cross-cultural variation or in history. I shall not try to discriminate the two forms of argument.[37]

Much work in the sociology of scientific knowledge, and, derivatively, in social epistemology, starts with the topic of variation in belief.[38] Different groups of people—culturally distinct contemporaries as well as temporally separated societies—may hold radically different views about all sorts of things. There is no challenge to the traditionalist's invocation of truth and the demand that propositions known to be true so long as these differences can be explained in terms of differences in success: for in such instances we can appeal to the correlation between success and accuracy to distinguish genuine knowledge. Trouble arises, however, if the practices of both groups are successful, that is, if neither has problems in coping with reality. Under those circumstances, the idea of explaining success by appeal to accuracy of representation founders—since not both of the representations can be accurate—and it is tempting to claim that we can simply make do by noting the success of the practice itself. "It works because it's true" can no longer be sustained as more informative than the bare recognition that "it works."[39] Invocation of nonepistemic truth becomes idle.

There are popular, rather casual, ways of making the general argument. One is to appeal to the "Duhem-Quine thesis." Now there should be no doubt that the writings of Duhem, Quine, and others contain important, challenging arguments about the underdetermination of something by something else. But it is important to be quite exact about the somethings. In the most obvious versions, Duhem and Quine are concerned with the possibility that incompatible sets of statements might prove observationally equivalent, either in the sense of yielding the same set of observational consequences or in the sense of accommodating the same set of stimulations of nerve endings. (There are intricate problems in explicating "observational consequence" and "accommodating" that need not concern us here.)[40] It is important to separate versions of the thesis and to assess their plausibility and equally important to connect those versions with the prima facie quite different situations envisaged in the rebuttal of the IRA, which involve recognition of *local* successes. The argument from the Duhem-Quine thesis needs considerable development if it is to show that there are alternatives to commonsense ideas about the nutritive value of different substances *that would abandon or reverse our most basic ideas on this subject*, and that would be equally successful in keeping us alive.

When we consider commonly cited examples of cultural variation, it is quite clear that the situations studied by Duhem and Quine are very different from those relevant to the assessment of the connection between practical success and representational accuracy. Consider the differences between the claims of Western biology about plants and animals, and those advanced in non-Western cultures and eagerly pounced on by aspiring relativists. The non-Westerners, we are told, are equally successful, even though their practice employs different representations. But there is no sense of empirical equivalence, or even of "accommodation of the same sensory stimulations," behind this notion of "equal success." The successes are of quite different types, since the biologists want to engage in activities with respect to plants and animals that diverge from those favored by the non-Westerners. If there is an issue raised by the citation of this kind of example, it is the question, "Are there different types of success that should be accommodated by different sets of representations?"—not, "Are there different sets of representations that will generate exactly the same practical successes?"

Now the issue of the potential relativity of success, to which we have been led, may itself look threatening. To understand the extent of possible trouble, let us consider the example of those non-Western societies that hold what we regard as radically false beliefs about the properties of certain taboo animals. It is quite possible that we should find, after detailed analysis, that these false beliefs play an important part in the way in which members of the society cope with reality. Suppose, specifically, that the false beliefs are invoked to defuse various types of social friction, and that, in consequence, these beliefs are partially responsible for the social order that members of the culture value. Thus we have an example of two societies in which incompatible claims are made about certain kinds of animals, both of which facilitate successful practices.

I believe that we should question the terms in which I have described the example, specifically by breaking up the blockish notion of "successful practice." My hypothetical non-Western culture is successful in certain types of social intervention; and if we pursued the example in more realistic detail, we would find that this success can be traced to tacit understanding of how to manage certain types of interchange among people who are potentially in conflict. Perhaps the same type of understanding is also found in Western societies, and is hidden only because those societies do not regularly confront the kinds of situations in which it would be applicable. But the important point is that what we view as the faulty beliefs about animals are not implicated in any way in the generation of successful interventions (whether predictive or manipulative) with respect to those animals. Hence it would appear possible to achieve a broader set of representations that would incorporate the Western biological views and the non-Western social understanding in a system that would preserve both sets of successes. Because there would be no internal inconsistency, there would be no challenge to the link between success and accuracy.

The discussion of the preceding paragraph indicates the lines along which we should seek resolution of cases in which incompatible beliefs apparently figure in distinct successes. A full resolution of the issues concerning underdetermination must await the outcome of attempts to show that the recipe will work for the examples which have been most frequently cited in the cause of relativism. But our preliminary verdict should be that the case against realism is so far not proven.

VI

I save until the end what has increasingly come, it seems to me, to be a major source of motivation—if not of argument—for a radical version of social epistemology founded in relativism. For those whose voices have traditionally been silenced, or ignored, an epistemology that seeks objective standards may appear inevitably oppressive, so that resistance to it is based more on concern than on the construction of detailed arguments. Thus some contemporary scholars might view the dialectic that I have sketched in earlier sections as itself something that needs to be transcended.[41] For those sections envisage truth as emerging from the clash of ideas and knowledge as obtainable by finding and occupying better (though imperfect) epistemological positions. Mindful of the harm that has been done by treating some standards as objective, some conclusions as established, and some positions as superior, radical critics of traditional epistemology propose that we rethink our reigning metaphors. They envisage different ends for inquiry—not the control of nature grounded in the apprehension of the truth, but the enhancement of human life through the sympathetic exploration of rival viewpoints and the development of attitudes of care and concern.[42]

While I believe that these considerations are powerful and significant, and that they call for detailed exploration of the ways in which the growth of human knowledge has affected human well-being,[43] the fault may lie not with the epistemological notions of objectivity, truth, and epistemically superior position but with the ways in which those notions have been too hastily applied to support the prejudices and further the interests of a dominant group. Fallibilism is a commonplace of twentieth-century epistemology, but it by no means follows that our sense of our own fallibility is represented in our epistemic practice. Concern for objectivity seems to me potentially liberating and, by the same token, ignorance is confining; but the history of inquiry (most vividly, the history of studies of human behavior) shows clearly how ignoring our own fallibility may have profoundly damaging consequences. The challenge for the more conservative versions of social epistemology is to respond to genuine concerns about the oppressive force of standards without abandoning the benefits that the search for such standards makes possible.

Two different errors thus seem to me to hinder fruitful cooperation in social epistemology. One is the frequent tendency of radical social epistemologists to assume that certain kinds of conclusions have been definitively established and that they can dismiss any enterprise that retains connections with the objectivist notions of traditional epistemology. I do not pretend that the arguments of the preceding two sections have been worked out in detail: as my notes below indicate, there are numerous thorny issues that need to be explored. But those arguments do reveal that the passage from traditional epistemology to the "social construction of reality" or to the "study of knowledge as a form of power" is far more bumpy than is usually appreciated.

The countervailing error results from appreciation of the fact that many radical proposals are based on swallowing lines of arguments that appear dubious. Hence epistemologists feel entitled to neglect the considerations from history, sociology, and anthropology that motivate those radical departures. If the disease of radical social epistemology is premature theorizing (specifically, the jump to quick dismissal of important epistemological concepts), its counterpart in more traditional programs is neglect of the phenomena and insensitivity to the human consequences of epistemological overconfidence. I hope that even an outline account of some rival possibilities may point the way towards a more constructive dialogue.

NOTES

[1] This paper grew out of my commentary on the presentations given by Helen Longino and Joseph Rouse at an American Philosophical Association symposium on social epistemology in December 1991. I have tried to place the contrast between their approaches and my own in a more general setting, concentrating less on the details of their proposals than on the kinds of positions advanced not only in their work but in the writings of David Bloor, Harry Collins, Steve Fuller, Donna Haraway, Sandra Harding, Bruno Latour, Steven Shapin, and others. In the text I am primarily concerned to identify the logical relations among various controversial theses. Attributions of these theses to individual authors and texts are confined to footnotes. I am grateful to Longino and Rouse for the stimulus provided by their papers and discussions. I would also like to thank Fred Schmitt for his penetrating and constructive comments on an earlier draft.

[2] For this conception of calibrating potential informants, see Kitcher (1992, 1993, ch. 8).

[3] Classic attempts to formulate the reductionist project are Carnap (1967) and Goodman (1955). For a more liberal version, see Carnap (1958). Concise presentation of the position and its foibles are given by Quine (1969a). The *locus classicus* for the attack on the reductionist position is Sellars (1963a).

[4] For a somewhat more extensive formulation of this argument, see Kitcher (forthcoming a).

[5] See the extensive literature that followed Gettier (1963). The developments are reviewed in Shope (1983). For reliabilism, the classic source is Goldman (1986).

[6] See Goldman (1991a).

[7] For formulation of this project, see Goldman (1987b), Hull (1988), Kitcher (1993, especially ch. 8). Implementation is begun in Goldman and Shaked (1991) and in Kitcher (1990, 1991, 1993, ch. 8).

[8] Launched forcefully by Stich (1990, pp. 89–98) against the project of the first part of Goldman (1986).

[9] For this conception of the goals of inquiry, see Kitcher (1993, ch. 4).

[10] I suspect that the project I have sketched seems almost indistinguishable from classical epistemology ("positivism") to those like Bruno Latour, Donna Haraway, Andrew Pickering, Sharon Traweek, and the many others in sociology, anthropology, and history of science who want to develop a more radical critique. I hope that the first sections of this chapter reveal that there are significant differences among philosophical proposals that are often lumped together under what is taken to be an insulting label. (There is some irony in the fact that while outsiders view the charge of positivism as especially damning, philosophical research on the work of the Vienna Circle and its affiliates is revealing how subtle and insightful were the ideas of the logical positivists.) The goal of the remaining sections is to show how large is the gulf that more radical thinkers urge us to cross—and how some of the motivating forces they take for granted are, in fact, far from compelling.

[11] Fodor (1974); Kitcher (1984).

[12] See, for example, Papineau (1979, ch. 1).

[13] See Rouse (1987), Latour (1987), and Bloor (1976 [2nd edn, 1991]).

[14] For discussions of this thesis, I am indebted to Fred Schmitt.

[15] These points are forcefully made by Rouse (1987), and Latour (1987), Latour and Woolgar (1979). For cogent arguments against the bias of thinking solely about scientific knowledge in propositional terms, see Hacking (1983).

[16] See Polanyi (1958), Hacking (1983), and Collins (1985).

[17] For an admirably clear presentation of these points, see Ryle (1948).

[18] See, for example, Marr (1982) and Chomsky (1980).

[19] The *locus classicus* is Collins (1985).

[20] Equally, some embodied knowledge might be founded in individual *skills*, rather than in individual propositional knowledge. As Fred Schmitt pointed out to me, there is no reason to suppose that all embodied knowledge reduces to individual *propositional* knowledge. The embodiment of knowledge is, I suggest, best understood as grounded in individual items of knowledge, together with the public recognition of the achievements of the knowers.

[21] This is a standard way of formulating (2b), but friends of deflationary approaches to truth are likely to protest that invocation of truth is quite unnecessary here.

[22] Main sources of the arguments I discuss are the writings of defenders of the Strong Programme in the sociology of knowledge (see, particularly, Bloor 1976 [2nd edn, 1991]; Barnes 1974; Shapin 1982; Shapin and Schaffer 1985), defenders of empirical relativism in the study of scientific knowledge (Collins 1985), and a variety of other approaches to the history, sociology, and anthropology of science (Pickering 1984; Latour 1987; Haraway 1990; Keller 1985; Traweek 1988). The arguments are often presented in very abbreviated form in these sources. More extensive, and subtle, versions can be found within recent philosophy. See, for example, Putnam (1981), Rorty (1980), and Fine (1986). I outline responses to some of the more subtle lines of argument in Kitcher (1993, forthcoming a, and especially forthcoming b).

[23] See Bloor (1991).

[24] Moreover, as Fred Schmitt pointed out to me, since the Symmetry Principle is an *empirical* principle, similar belief-forming processes should be found in the genesis of roughly equal numbers of *actual* true beliefs and *actual* false beliefs. In approaching situations of scientific decision-making symmetrically, sociologists of science do not of course make a priori assumptions about the correctness of various scientific claims. But it seems to me that they often presuppose that particular, quite specific types of processes will yield true and false beliefs with roughly equal frequency. One should ask whether this is a different a priori assumption, and, if not, what its empirical basis is.

[25] A fortiori there is no motivation for the slavish devotion to symmetry confessed in Latour (1991).

[26] Sophisticated approaches along these lines can be found in Rorty (1980) and Putnam (1981). Much simpler versions appear in the writings of Bloor, Barnes, and many other writers cited in note 20 above. Helen Longino (1990) attempts to show how objectivity is possible within a framework that identifies truth with consensus belief in societies that follow certain types of procedures, but I do not see how her approach avoids collapse into relativism.

[27] See Horwich (1990). Both Fine (1986) and Rouse (1987) develop their accounts of scientific knowledge on the basis of this type of account of truth.

[28] This is argued in outline fashion in Kitcher (forthcoming a), and at greater length in Kitcher (forthcoming b).

[29] The argument thus comes in two slightly different forms: one that inquires into how the correspondence between word and world is set up; and the other that asks how it is checked. Sophisticated versions of the former line of argument culminate in Putnam's intricate considerations about reference (e.g., Putnam 1981). The latter form of argument leads to debates about the connections between truth and the explanation of success.

[30] The issues here are extremely complex, as Putnam (1978, 1981, 1983), Horwich (1990), and Field (1986) make clear.

[31] As Rorty (1980, p. xxvi) insightfully notes, part of the motivation for strong versions of realism stems from the recognition that "our beliefs have very limited causal efficacy." As the text indicates, I draw far more from this point than Rorty would expect.

[32] Most importantly, there is a compelling need to respond to the arguments of the first two chapters of Putnam's (1981). I try to discharge this duty in Kitcher (forthcoming b).

[33] See Longino (1991) and Harding (1993).

[34] See Gould (1981).

[35] See Haraway (1990) for thorough documentation of the point. While the more radical claims made in some parts of this book (and, even more, in Haraway's subsequent writings) strike me as based upon fallacious arguments, her indictment of the male-dominated practice of mid-twentieth-century primatology is both powerful and moving. For further brief discussion of a range of issues raised by Haraway and others (which may correspond more closely to their aims), see section VI.

[36] See Kitcher (1990).

[37] For separate treatment, see Kitcher (forthcoming a).

[38] See the early pages of Bloor (1976 [2nd edn, 1991]).

[39] This is a central theme of the introduction to Rorty (1980).

[40] For an extremely insightful discussion of some of these issues, see Laudan and Leplin (1991).

[41] I suspect that this would be the attitude of Donna Haraway, Sharon Traweek, and Evelyn Fox Keller.

[42] Although these themes are touched on in various philosophical, anthropological, and sociological works, I find them most lucidly expressed in Belensky, Clinchy, Goldberger, and Tarule (1986).

43   See the closing paragraphs of Kitcher (1993). I should note that similar points were made long ago by Paul Feyerabend (1978).

BIBLIOGRAPHY

Alcoff, L. and Potter, E., eds (1993) *Feminist Epistemologies*, London: Routledge.

Barnes, B. (1974) *Scientific Knowledge and Sociological Theory*, London: Routledge.

Belensky, M. F., Clinchy, B. M., Goldberger, N. R., and Tarule, J. M., eds (1986) *Women's Ways of Knowing*, New York: Basic Books.

Bloor, D. (1976) *Knowledge and Social Imagery*, London: Routledge; (1991) 2nd edn, Chicago: University of Chicago Press.

Carnap, R. (1958) "The methodological character of theoretical concepts," in *Minnesota Studies in the Philosophy of Science*, vol. 1, Minneapolis: University of Minnesota Press.

—— (1967) *The Logical Structure of the World*, trans. R. A. George, Berkeley: University of California Press.

Chomsky, N. (1980) *Rules and Representations*, New York: Columbia University Press.

Collins, H. (1985) *Changing Order*, London: Sage.

Feyerabend, P. (1978) *Science in a Free Society*, London: New Left Books.

Field, H. (1986) "The deflationary conception of truth," in MacDonald and Wright (1986).

Fine, A. (1986) *The Shaky Game*, Chicago: University of Chicago Press.

Fodor, J. (1974) "Special sciences, or the disunity of science as a working hypothesis," *Synthese* 28: 77–115.

Gettier, E. (1963) "Is justified true belief knowledge?" *Analysis* 23: 121–123.

Goldman, A. I. (1986) *Epistemology and Cognition*, Cambridge, Mass.: Harvard University Press.

—— (1987) "Foundations of social epistemics," *Synthese* 73: 109–144.

—— (1991) "Epistemic paternalism: Communication control in law and society," *Journal of Philosophy* 88: 113–131.

Goldman, A. I. and Shaked, M. (1991) "An economic model of scientific activity and truth acquisition," *Philosophical Studies* 63: 31–55.

Goodman, N. (1955) *Fact, Fiction and Forecast*, Cambridge, Mass.: Harvard University Press.

Gould, S. J. (1981) *The Mismeasure of Man*, New York: Norton.

Hacking, I. (1983) *Representing and Intervening*, Cambridge: Cambridge University Press.

Haraway, D. (1990) *Primate Visions*, London: Routledge.

Harding, S. (1993) "Rethinking standpoint epistemology: What is 'strong objectivity'?" in Alcoff and Potter (1993).

Horwich, P. (1990) *Truth*, Oxford: Basil Blackwell.

Hull, D. (1988) *Science as a Process*, Chicago: University of Chicago Press.

Keller, E. F. (1985) *Reflections on Gender and Science*, New Haven: Yale University Press.

Kitcher, P. (1984) "1953 and all that: A tale of two sciences," *Philosophical Review* 93: 335–373.

—— (1990) "The division of cognitive labor," *Journal of Philosophy* 87: 5–22.

—— (1992) "Authority, deference, and the role of individual reasoning in science," in McMullin (1992).

—— (1993) *The Advancement of Science*, Oxford: Oxford University Press.

—— (forthcoming a) "Knowledge, society, and history," *Canadian Journal of Philosophy*.

———— (forthcoming b) "Real realism."

Latour, B. (1987) *Science in Action*, Cambridge, Mass.: Harvard University Press.

———— (1992) "One more turn after the social turn," in McMullin (1992b).

Latour, B. and Woolgar, S. (1979) *Laboratory Life*, London: Sage.

Laudan, L. and Leplin, J. (1991) "Empirical equivalence and underdetermination," *Journal of Philosophy* 88: 449–472.

Longino, H. (1990) *Science as Social Knowledge: Values and Objectivity in Scientific Inquiry*, Princeton: Princeton University Press.

Marr, D. (1982) *Vision*, San Francisco, Freeman.

McMullin, E. (1992) *The Social Dimensions of Science*, South Bend, Ind.: Notre Dame University Press.

Papineau, D. (1979) *For Science in the Social Sciences*, New York: St. Martin's Press.

Pickering, A. (1984) *Constructing Quarks*, Chicago: University of Chicago Press.

Polanyi, M. (1958) *Personal Knowledge*, Chicago: University of Chicago Press.

Putnam, H. (1978) *Meaning and the Moral Sciences*, London: Routledge.

———— (1981) *Reason, Truth, and History*, Cambridge: Cambridge University Press.

———— (1983) *Realism and Reason*, Cambridge: Cambridge University Press.

Quine, W. V. (1969a) "Epistemology naturalized," in Quine (1969b).

———— (1969b) *Ontological Relativity and Other Essays*, New York: Columbia University Press.

Rorty, R. (1980) *Consequences of Pragmatism*, Minneapolis: University of Minnesota Press.

Rouse, J. (1987) *Knowledge and Power: Toward a Political Philosophy of Science*, Ithaca: Cornell University Press.

Ryle, G. (1948) *The Concept of Mind*, London: Hutchinson.

Sellars, W. (1963a) "Empiricism and the philosophy of mind," in (Sellars 1963b).

———— (1963b) *Science, Perception, and Reality*, London: Routledge.

Shapin, S. (1982) "History of science and its social reconstructions," *History of Science* 20: 157–211.

Shapin, S. and Schaffer, S. (1985) *Leviathan and the Air-pump*, Princeton: Princeton University Press.

Shope, R. (1983) *The Analysis of Knowing*, Princeton: Princeton University Press.

Traweek, S. (1988) *Beamtimes and Lifetimes*, Cambridge, Mass.: Harvard University Press.

Section 3: Study Questions

1. According to Quine, what is it that makes an epistemology naturalized?

2. In what sense did traditional epistemologies try to contain natural science?

3. Why is circularity a problem for traditional epistemologies but not for Quine's naturalized epistemology?

4. Explain why Quine's observation sentences are not equivalent to the foundationalist's basic beliefs.

5. In what sense is Goldman's approach to epistemology aptly described as a naturalized epistemology?

6. Critically evaluate Almeder's criticism of Quine's naturalized epistemology.

7. What is the relationship between epistemology and science? Distinguish between the various theses discussed in Almeder's article.

8. Why does Almeder insist that epistemology should be more than descriptive? What is wrong with a purely descriptive epistemology?

9. Explain and evaluate Putnam's criticisms of Goldman's reliabilism.

10. Explain and evaluate Putnam's criticisms of Quine's approach to naturalizing epistemology.

11. Why does Putnam believe that cultural relativism is a form of naturalism? Is he correct?

12. Explain what Putnam means when he says that reason is both immanent and transcendent.

13. Explain the difference between sexism and androcentrism. Give examples of each.

14. Explain Anderson's claim, that even empirically adequate theories may be sexist or androcentric. Should this make us sceptical about the possibility of having knowledge? Provide a justification for your answer.

15. Why is Anderson reluctant to claim that women and men approach inquiry differently?

16. Explain why Anderson claims that gendered models can sometimes play a constructive role in scientific theorizing. Can you think of an example where a gendered model was fruitful for scientific inquiry? Explain why Anderson thinks gendered models are often detrimental.

17. Why does Harding object to feminist empiricist epistemologies? Would she regard Anderson's feminist epistemology as a feminist empiricist epistemology?

18. Why does Harding believe that we should examine the social causes of both our false beliefs and our true beliefs?

19. Why does Harding claim that feminist standpoint epistemologies give us a stronger conception of objectivity? In what respects is it stronger than traditional conceptions of objectivity?

20. Explain and evaluate Longino's criticism of Harding's standpoint theory. How might Harding respond to such criticism?

21. Why does Longino think that the various feminist strategies of "changing the subject" are descriptively superior to the traditional conception of the knowing subject? Why does she object to these strategies? What is her own preferred alternative?

22. Longino argues that scientific inquiry is interest driven. Are inquirer's interests apt to lead them to develop distorted theories of the world? How might Longino address this concern?

23. Why does Hardwig think that in our efforts to come to terms with the problem of trust it is not feasible to aim to gauge the reliability of those we have to trust?

24. Can Hardwig's insights about our epistemic dependence be reconciled with traditional theories of justification (coherentism, foundationalism, and reliabilism)? Provide a justification for your answer.

25. Do Hardwig's insights about our epistemic dependence support scepticism? Provide a justification for your answer.

26. Explain the difference between what Rorty calls "stories of objectivity" and "stories of solidarity." Why does Rorty prefer the latter?

27. Recall that Putnam accuses Rorty of relativism. Is this an apt criticism? Explain and evaluate Rorty's response to this criticism.

28. Are stories of solidarity adequate to account for our successful interactions in the non-social world?

29. Is Kitcher's minimal social epistemology social enough?

30. Can Kitcher's approach to social epistemology accommodate the insights of (a) Harding, (b) Longino, (c) Hardwig, and (d) Rorty? Does Kitcher provide grounds for resisting the changes recommended by these other authors?

31. Explain the IRA. Explain and evaluate Kitcher's response to the inaccessibility of reality argument.

Additional Readings

Hilary Kornblith's (ed.) *Naturalized Epistemology* is a very useful source. In it are a variety of readings on naturalizing epistemology.

In addition to Goldman's *Epistemology and Cognition* (mentioned in the list of additional readings in Section 1), Stephen Stich's *The Fragmentation of Reason* is a very engaging book on naturalized epistemology.

Robert Almeder develops his criticisms of naturalized epistemologies in greater detail in his *Harmless Naturalism*.

There are a number of very good anthologies in feminist epistemology, including Linda Alcoff's and Elizabeth Potter's (eds.) *Feminist Epistemologies*.

Sandra Harding's standpoint theory is discussed in greater detail in her *Whose Science? Whose Knowledge?*

Helen Longino's *Science as Social Knowledge* addresses issues in both feminist epistemology and social epistemology.

Richard Rorty's pragmatism is developed in a variety of his books. The essays in his *Objectivity, Relativism, and Truth* are focussed on issues in epistemology.

Fred Schmitt's (ed.) *Socializing Epistemology* is a useful anthology of readings on social epistemology.

Philip Kitcher's social epistemology of scientific knowledge is developed in detail in his *The Advancement of Science*.

In *Knowledge in a Social World,* Alvin Goldman extends his reliabilist theory of justification to issues in social epistemology.

You may also find a number of my own publications in social epistemology useful. In my (1999) "The Role of Solidarity in a Pragmatic Epistemology" I discuss Richard Rorty's views. This article is published in *Philosophia.* In my (1999) "A Defense of Longino's Social Epistemology" I discuss Longino's view, and in my (2001) "Science, Biases, and the Threat of Global Pessimism" I critically discuss Philip Kitcher's views. My (2000) "Invisible Hands and the Success of Science" and (2002) "The Epistemic Significance of Collaborative Research" also address issues in social epistemology. These last four articles are published in *Philosophy of Science.*